T0318154

ECONOMIC FOUNDATIONS OF SYMMETRIC PROGRAMMING

The search for symmetry is part of the fundamental scientific paradigm in mathematics and physics. Can this be valid also for economics? This textbook represents an attempt to explore this possibility. The behavior of price-taking producers, monopolists, monopsonists, sectoral market equilibria, behavior under risk and uncertainty, and two-person zero- and non-zero-sum games are analyzed and discussed under the unifying structure called the linear complementarity problem. Furthermore, the equilibrium problem allows for the relaxation of often-stated but unnecessary assumptions. This unifying approach offers the advantage of a better understanding of the structure of economic models. It also introduces the simplest and most elegant algorithm for solving a wide class of problems.

Quirino Paris is Professor of Agricultural and Resource Economics at the University of California, Davis, where he has taught since 1969. He received his Ph.D. from the University of California, Berkeley, in 1966 and then served on the university staff of the Advanced Training Center for Economic Research at the University of Naples, Italy.

Professor Paris's research has concentrated on investigations of producer and consumer behavior, of which the present text is the most recent example. He is the author of more than 100 journal articles in economics and research methodology and of the textbook *An Economic Interpretation of Linear Programming* (1991). Professor Paris is also a Fellow of the European Association of Agricultural Economists. He has served as a visiting professor at universities around the world.

Economic Foundations of Symmetric Programming

QUIRINO PARIS

University of California, Davis

CAMBRIDGE
UNIVERSITY PRESS

Shaftesbury Road, Cambridge CB2 8EA, United Kingdom

One Liberty Plaza, 20th Floor, New York, NY 10006, USA

477 Williamstown Road, Port Melbourne, VIC 3207, Australia

314–321, 3rd Floor, Plot 3, Splendor Forum, Jasola District Centre, New Delhi – 110025, India

103 Penang Road, #05–06/07, Visioncrest Commercial, Singapore 238467

Cambridge University Press is part of Cambridge University Press & Assessment,
a department of the University of Cambridge.

We share the University's mission to contribute to society through the pursuit of
education, learning and research at the highest international levels of excellence.

www.cambridge.org
Information on this title: www.cambridge.org/9780521123020

First published 2011

A catalogue record for this publication is available from the British Library

Library of Congress Cataloging-in-Publication data
Paris, Quirino.
Economic foundations of symmetric programming / Quirino Paris.
p. cm.
Includes index.
ISBN 978-0-521-19472-3 (hardback)
1. Microeconomics – Mathematical models. I. Title.
HB172.P225 2010
338.501′519703–dc22 2010020690

ISBN 978-0-521-19472-3 Hardback
ISBN 978-0-521-12302-0 Paperback

TO FRANCESCA PATANÈ

for her professional integrity
in the pursuit of truth
with wit and beauty
in a symmetric way

Contents

Foreword

Since moving from UC Davis in 2003, I have come to appreciate even more what Quirino has to offer colleagues and students. Take, for example, the symmetry paradigm he expounds in the opening chapter. Quirino effectively demonstrates how the application of the symmetry principle, when combined with the implementation of well-known mathematical programming theory, can be used not only to numerically solve various microeconomic models, but also to gain deeper economic understanding of them. Although this is exciting to those of us who work in this field, it might come off as a bit abstract and technical to students. No problem, as Quirino motivated the symmetry principle quite differently to the students by bringing a symmetric vegetable to class! As I recall, it was broccoli Romanesco, whose symmetry was with respect to scale, that is, it is a fractal veggie. Neither faculty nor students of that era will forget that day, or more generally, the passion and unique point of view that Quirino brought to every conversation, lecture, and seminar. This book embodies all of that fervor and zeal, and more, as it is the culmination of his lifelong research in the application of mathematical programming to economics. What's more, Quirino's guiding concept of symmetry is peppered all throughout the text, and this fact alone separates it from the multitude of books on mathematical programming and applications. It really does not get much better than this for a user of these methods.

Professor Michael R. Caputo
Department of Economics
University of Central Florida

Preface

This book formulates and discusses models of producers' economic behavior using the framework of mathematical programming. Furthermore, it introduces the Symmetry Principle in economics and demonstrates its analytical power in dealing with problems hitherto considered either difficult or intractable. It assumes that its readers have a beginner's knowledge of calculus and linear algebra and that, at least, they have taken an intermediate course in microeconomics.

The treatment of economic behavior expounded in this book acquires an operational character that, in general, is not present in a theory course. In a microeconomics course, for example – even at the graduate level – the treatment of a monopolist's behavior considers only one commodity. Often, however, a monopolist owns demand functions for three or more commodities (think of Microsoft) and her firm's equilibrium requires a careful analysis, especially in the case of perfectly discriminating behavior. Another example regards the analysis of risk and uncertainty in the presence of nonzero covariances between risky output market prices and input supplies. These and many other "realistic" economic scenarios require the introduction of a structure called the Equilibrium Problem. Although this specification is the logical representation of quantity and price equilibrium conditions for any commodity, economic theory courses privilege statements of economic models that involve a dual pair of maximizing and minimizing objective functions. This book makes it clear that these optimizing structures are only special cases of the class of Equilibrium Problems and that, often, they impose unnecessary restrictions on the specification of economic models.

The computational structure that is the twin of the Equilibrium Problem is called the Linear Complementarity Problem (LCP). Every model presented in this book is ultimately cast in the form of an LCP. Lemke and

Howson have provided the most elegant algorithm for the solution of a large class of LC problems. This unifying structure contributes to a deeper understanding of all the economic problems discussed in this book and provides the researcher with a powerful framework for analyzing many other problems that have not been dealt with here.

The economic behavior of a price-taking entrepreneur is analyzed in the framework of linear programming assuming a constant coefficient technology. Monopolistic and monopsonistic behavior requires the framework of quadratic programming and of the equilibrium problem. Behavior under risky market prices, input supplies, and technical coefficients is presented in a nested series of models that culminate, once again, in the structure of an Equilibrium Problem. The chapter on general market equilibrium deals with models of increasing complexity, from a final commodity model to a model of intermediate and final goods, to a model of endogenous income. It also deals with the specification and discussion of spatial models of trade. Special attention is given to the problem of multiple optimal solutions in linear and quadratic programming. Empirical mathematical programming models often exhibit the conditions for alternative optimal solutions. And, more often than not, commercially available computer applications and researchers ignore them. Computationally, the enumeration of all multiple optimal solutions in linear and quadratic programming presents a challenge to writers of solvers. This admission, however, cannot constitute a justification for neglecting such an important aspect. The information about multiple optimal solutions is already present – implicitly – in the model. It is just a matter of making it explicit. A chapter on positive mathematical programming presents a series of calibrating models that are capable of reproducing a solution that is close to the corresponding levels of commodities in a given base year. Chapters 16 and 17 present a Fortran 77 computer program that solves the Linear Complementarity Problem in its generality. It solves quadratic programming problems, Equilibrium Problems, and two-person non-zero-sum games.

This book is the result of teaching graduate courses in microeconomics for more than 40 years using mathematical programming as the scaffolding of the various subjects. Hence, it has been widely tested in a classroom environment. Its gradual develpment has benefited immensely from students criticism and their interaction. It is aimed at first-year graduate students' in either a master's or Ph.D. program in economics and agricultural economics.

Introduction

The notion of symmetric programming grew out of a gradual realization that symmetric structures – as defined in this book – provide the means for a wide ranging unification of economic problems. A conjecture immediately and naturally followed: symmetric structures are more general than asymmetric ones as long as the right approach to symmetry is embraced. There are, in fact, two ways to symmetrize asymmetric problems: a reductionist and an embedding approach. The reductionist strategy eliminates, by assumption, those elements that make the original problem asymmetric. This is the least interesting of the two approaches but one that is followed by the majority of researchers. The alternative strategy seeks to embed the original asymmetric problem into a larger symmetric structure. The way to execute this research program is never obvious but is always rewarding. This book is entirely devoted to the illustration of this second approach.

With the unification of problems there comes also the unification of methodologies. Rather than associating different algorithms to different problems, symmetric programming allows for the application of the same algorithm to a large family of problems.

Unification has always been one of the principal objectives of science. When different problems are unified under a new encompassing theory, a better understanding of those problems and of the theory itself is achieved. Paradoxically, unification leads to simplicity, albeit a kind of rarefied simplicity whose understanding requires long years of schooling. The astonishing aspect of this scientific process is that unification is often achieved through a conscious effort of seeking symmetric structures. On further thought, this fact should not surprise, because symmetry means harmony of the various parts, and it is indeed harmony that is sought in a scientific endeavor. The explicit quest for unification, simplicity, harmony, and symmetry has often induced scientists to speak in the language of art. Many of them have eloquently written about this preeminent aesthetic concern of the scientific process. These visionaries openly state that beauty, not truth, is (or should be) the direct goal of a scientist. When beauty is in sight, surprisingly, truth is not far behind. These famous pronouncements are likely to be known and subscribed more often among mathematicians and physicists than among economists, especially students. But the fervor and the clarity expressed on the subject by eminent scientists leave no doubt as to their motivation in pursuing scientific research. One of the earliest and more extensive discussions of the aesthetic principle in science is due to the French mathematician Henri Poincaré (1854–1912), who wrote:

The scientist does not study nature because it is useful; he studies it because he delights in it, and he delights in it because it is beautiful. If nature were not beautiful, it would not be worth knowing, and if nature were not worth knowing, life would not be worth living. Of course I do not here speak of the beauty that strikes the senses, the beauty of qualities and of appearances; not that I undervalue such beauty, far from it, but it has nothing to do with science; I mean that profounder beauty which comes from the harmonious order of the parts and which a pure intelligence can grasp. This it is which gives body, a structure so to speak, to the iridescent appearances which flatter our senses, and without this support the beauty of these fugitive dreams would be only imperfect, because it would be vague and always fleeting. On the contrary, intellectual beauty is sufficient unto itself, and it is for its sake, more perhaps than for the future good of humanity, that the scientist devotes himself to long and difficult labors.

It is, therefore, the quest of this especial beauty, the sense of the harmony of the cosmos, which make us choose the facts most fitting to contribute to this harmony, just as the artist chooses among the features of his model those which perfect the picture and give it character and life. And we need not fear that this instinctive and unavowed prepossession will turn the scientist aside from the search for the true. One may dream an harmonious world, but how far the real world will leave it behind! The greatest artists that ever lived, the Greeks, made their heavens; how shabby it is beside the true heavens, ours!

And it is because simplicity, because grandeur, is beautiful, that we preferably seek simple facts, sublime facts, that we delight now to follow the majestic course of the stars, now to examine with the microscope that prodigious littleness which is also a grandeur, now to seek in geologic time the traces of a past which attracts because it is far away.

We see too that the longing for the beautiful leads us to the same choice as the longing for the useful. And so it is that this economy of thought, this economy of effort, which is, according to Mach, the constant tendency of science, is at the same time a source of beauty and a practical advantage. (*Science and Method*, p. 366)

Mathematicians attach great importance to the elegance of their methods and their results. This is not pure dilettantism. What is it indeed that gives us the feeling of elegance in a solution, in a demonstration? It is the harmony of the diverse parts, their symmetry, their happy balance; in a word it is all that introduces order, all that gives unity, that permits us to see clearly and to comprehend at once both the *ensemble* and the details. But this is exactly what yields great results; in fact the more we see this aggregate clearly and at a single glance, the better we perceive its analogies with other neighboring objects, consequently the more chances we have of divining the possible generalizations. Elegance may produce the feeling of the unforeseen by the unexpected meeting of objects we are not accustomed to bring together; there again it is fruitful, since it thus unveils for us kinships before unrecognized. It is fruitful even when it results only from the contrast between the simplicity of the means and the complexity of the problem set; it makes us then think of the reason for this contrast and very often makes us see that chance is not the reason; that it is to be found in some unexpected law. In a word, the feeling of mathematical elegance is only the satisfaction due to any adaptation of the solution to the needs of our mind, and it is because of this very adaptation that this solution can be for us an instrument. Consequently this aesthetic satisfaction is bound up with the economy of thought. (*Science and Method,* p. 372)

Poincaré's research program was taken seriously by his followers, notably by the mathematical physicist Hermann Weyl (as reported by Freeman Dyson in his obituary of the scientist), who said:

My work always tried to unite the true with the beautiful; but when I had to choose one or the other, I usually chose the beautiful.

These quotations represent only two among the many instances when the scientist has adopted the perspective and the language of the artist. Beauty above truth as a scientific criterion constitutes a paradigm that disconcerts the student as well as the scientist who has not experienced it. Paradoxically, it was left to an artist to restore the balance between beauty and truth, that balance that must have been secretly present also in the mind of Hermann Weyl. The relevant "theorem," then, was stated by John Keats who wrote (*Ode on a Grecian Urn*)

> Beauty is truth, truth beauty, – that is all
> Ye know on earth, and all ye need to know.

This research program has worked astonishingly well for mathematicians and physicists. Can it work also for economists? Many people are skeptical about this possibility, but, personally, I am unable to recognize any other strategy capable of directing and sustaining the development of economics. This book is a modest attempt to apply the research program based on beauty using symmetry as the fundamental criterion for stating and analyzing economic problems. As illustrated throughout the book, symmetry can interpret and solve many asymmetric problems and gives further insights into their structure. As Hermann Weyl again said:

Symmetry, as wide or narrow as you may define its meaning, is one idea by which man through the ages has tried to comprehend and create order, beauty, and perfection.

Symmetric programming provides a clear example of Poincaré's economy of thought. The elegance of the approach is indeed accompanied by an extraordinary efficiency of representation: all the asymmetric problems analyzed in this book can be restated in a symmetric specification with a smaller number of constraints and of variables.

Symmetry further refines the reciprocal relations of duality. The two notions are intimately associated, and neither can be fully comprehended and appreciated in isolation. Symmetric duality is, therefore, the main focus of this book. There is a special sense of beauty in assembling and contemplating a symmetric dual pair of problems. An interesting aspect of this analysis is that symmetric duality imposes economic interpretations that are never obvious. Nowhere is this fact more evident than in the interpretation of monopsonist's behavior in Chapter 9.

Duality, Symmetry, and the Euler-Legendre Transformation

During the past 30 years, economists have come to fully appreciate duality in the articulation and analysis of economic theory. What they have not done, however, is to take advantage of the notion of symmetry. This fact is somewhat surprising, because duality embodies a great deal of symmetry. Actually, the most general specification of duality is symmetric, as is shown further on.

The foregoing statement unilaterally resolves the following uncommon question: Is the most general specification of reality symmetric or asymmetric? Many people would assert and have asserted that reality, as we see it, is asymmetric and, thus, an asymmetric specification best describes it. Modern scientists, however, have learned to discount our sensory perception of reality. Some of them have actually concluded that reality, if it exists, can best be analyzed and understood by means of a symmetric specification. This point of view has led to astonishing discoveries, and it is difficult to argue against success.

A stylized representation of the scientific process as embodied in modern science, therefore, can be illustrated by the following scheme:

As the diagram indicates, scientific symmetry is achieved by increasing the dimensions of an asymmetric problem. A reduction of the dimensions trivializes the problem. Unfortunately, this strategy is often chosen by many economists to deal with their problems.

Reality is perceived through our senses (and their extensions) and gives rise to an asymmetric specification that is, in general, difficult to analyze. What we call science works through scientific symmetry that can be achieved by the introduction of new parameters. Symmetry works because it imposes "simplifying" restrictions that are easily understood, and it allows the formulation of interesting scientific statements.

Economic theory, like any other scientific discipline attempts to uncover stable (invariant) laws. As Emmy Noether showed at the beginning of the last century, every invariance corresponds to a symmetry and vice versa. Since then, the search for symmetry has become a veritable obsession for modern scientists, an obsession that has been gradually transformed into the foremost scientific criterion. Hence, if the notion of symmetry is fundamental for science in general, there remains little room for doubting its importance also for economics.

There are many types of symmetries (mirror, rotational, gauge, etc.). The goal of this book is to introduce the notion of symmetry by means of its relation to duality. The framework is a static one, although the extension to a dynamic specification is possible and rich in applications to economic analysis.

The notion of duality is introduced via the Euler-Legendre transformation. In this book, we called the Euler-Legendre transformation what in the scientific literature is referred to as the Legendre transformation. Stäckel, in fact, found that the "Legendre transformation" appeared in writings of Euler published several years before those of Legendre. Hence, we intend to contribute to the historical origin of the famous transformation by naming it after both its inventor and its popularizer.

The Euler-Legendre transformation applies directly to specifications of problems that do not involve constraints of any sort. The structure of such problems' duality is symmetric. The duality of problems with constraints (equations and inequalities) requires the introduction of the Lagrangean function. At first, it appears that this type of duality, associated with constrained optimization problems, is asymmetric. That is, the introduction of constraints destroys the symmetry of the Euler-Legendre transformation. This result, however, constitutes only a temporary setback because it is possible to reformulate the problem by applying the Euler-Legendre transformation to the Lagrangean function, as suggested by Dantzig, Eisenberg, and Cottle. This operation preserves duality and restores symmetry. An alternative but less general way to restore symmetry to problems with constraints is to redefine the primal problem by inserting into it a function of the Lagrange multipliers. This procedure will work only if the function is linearly homogeneous.

In this introductory discourse, we have been talking about primal problems, Lagrangean function, and Euler-Legendre transformation without introducing their definitions. In the next few sections, therefore, we proceed to give a precise statement of these mathematical relations.

Duality without Constraints

The first notion of duality was introduced by Euler (and, soon after, was elaborated by Legendre) around 1750 as a means for solving differential equations. It involves a change of variables from point coordinates to plane coordinates. In Figure 1.1, a concave differentiable function $q = f(x)$ can be expressed in a dual way as the locus of points with (x, q) coordinates and as a family of supports defined by the tangent lines (planes, hyperplanes) to the function $f(x)$ at each (x, q) point. The q-intercept, $g(t_1)$, of the tangent line at x_1 depends on the line's slope t_1. Thus, in general, the slope of the tangent line at x is defined as

$$t \stackrel{def}{=} \frac{f(x) - g(t)}{x} = \frac{\partial f}{\partial x} \tag{1.1}$$

and, therefore, the family of intercepts is characterized by the following relation:

$$g(t) \stackrel{def}{=} f(x) - xt = f(x) - x\frac{\partial f}{\partial x}. \tag{1.2}$$

Equation (1.2) represents the Euler-Legendre transformation from point to plane (lines, in this case) coordinates. A sufficient condition for the existence of the Euler-Legendre transformation is that the function $f(x)$ be strictly concave (convex). The function $g(t)$ is said to be dual to the function $f(x)$

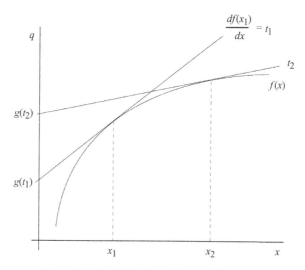

Figure 1.1. The Euler-Legendre transformation.

with the symmetric property

$$\frac{\partial g}{\partial t} = -x \tag{1.3}$$

which is easily derived from the total differential of $g(t)$, that is,

$$dg(t) = \frac{\partial f}{\partial x}dx - tdx - xdt = -xdt. \tag{1.4}$$

Mathematicians call relation (1.3) the contact (or the envelope) transformation, while economists, within the context of profit maximization, refer to it as the "Hotelling lemma." The symbol for partial derivatives was used in relations (1.1) and (1.3) to indicate that the notion of Euler-Legendre transformation and the same formula are valid also for a strictly concave function of $\mathbf{x}$, where $\mathbf{x}$ is a vector of arbitrary, finite dimensions.

The symmetry and the duality of the Euler-Legendre transformation is exhibited by relations (1.1) and (1.3). We must acknowledge, however, that the transformation introduced by (1.1) leads to an asymmetry with respect to the sign of the derivatives. To eliminate even this minor asymmetry, many authors define the Euler-Legendre transformation as $g(t) + f(x) = xt$.

The recovery of the primal function $f(x)$ is obtained from relations (1.1), (1.2), and (1.3) as

$$f(x) = g(t) - t\frac{\partial g}{\partial t}. \tag{1.5}$$

For applications of the Euler-Legendre transformation, the reader can consult the appendix at the end of this chapter.

A classical example of symmetric duality in economics using the Euler-Legendre transformation is given by the production function and the normalized profit function. With p and $\mathbf{r}$ as the price of a single output q and the vector of input prices, respectively, and the input quantity vector $\mathbf{x}$, the strictly concave production function $q = f(\mathbf{x})$ is dual to the normalized profit function $\pi(\mathbf{r}/p)$ by means of the Euler-Legendre transformation

$$\pi\left(\frac{\mathbf{r}}{p}\right) = f(\mathbf{x}) - \mathbf{x}'\left(\frac{\mathbf{r}}{p}\right) \tag{1.6}$$

where $\partial f/\partial \mathbf{x} = \mathbf{r}/p$ is the necessary condition for profit maximization with the vector $(\mathbf{r}/p)$ forming a supporting hyperplane to the production possibility set. The derivative of $\pi(\mathbf{r}/p)$ with respect to the normalized input prices $(\mathbf{r}/p)$ is the envelope transformation corresponding to relation (1.3):

$$\frac{\partial \pi}{\partial(\mathbf{r}/p)} = -\mathbf{x}(\mathbf{r}/p) \tag{1.7}$$

which expresses the (negative) input-derived demand functions. In economic circles, relation (1.7) is known as the "Hotelling lemma," although one can be rather confident that Hotelling knew he was dealing with an Euler-Legendre transformation. The output supply function is easily obtained from relations (1.6) and (1.7) as

$$q(\mathbf{r}/p) = \pi(\mathbf{r}/p) - \frac{\partial \pi}{\partial(\mathbf{r}/p)}\left(\frac{\mathbf{r}}{p}\right). \tag{1.8}$$

A second important way to introduce the notion of duality is illustrated in Figure 1.2. Given a set $\mathbf{S}$ and an exterior point P, the dual relation between P and $\mathbf{S}$ can be specified either as the minimum among all the distances between P and $\mathbf{S}$ (dashed line) or as the maximum among all the distances between P and the supporting hyperplanes that are tangent to $\mathbf{S}$.

The notion of duality presented in Figure 1.2 requires neither convexity nor differentiability. When the set $\mathbf{S}$ is not convex, the distance measures are taken with respect to the convex hull of $\mathbf{S}$. The supporting hyperplanes to $\mathbf{S}$ are well defined even when the boundary of $\mathbf{S}$ is not differentiable.

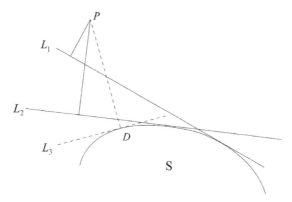

Figure 1.2. Duality without convexity and differentiability.

Asymmetric Duality with Constraints

When either equality or inequality constraints are introduced into the problem, the elegant simplicity of the Euler-Legendre transformation is temporarily lost. With it, the structural symmetry of duality uncovered in the previous section also disappears. Suppose now that the primal problem is specified as

$$\max_{\mathbf{x}} \; f(\mathbf{x}) \tag{1.9}$$

$$\text{subject to} \qquad \mathbf{g}(\mathbf{x}) \leq \mathbf{0},$$

where $\mathbf{x}$ is an n-dimensional vector, $f(\mathbf{x})$ is a differentiable concave function, and $\mathbf{g}(\mathbf{x})$ is a vector of m differentiable convex functions. This type of problem is handled through the classical Lagrangean function as modified by Karush (1939) and Kuhn and Tucker (1951), and explained in more detail in the next two chapters. Hence, the dual problem corresponding to problem (1.9) can be stated as

$$\min_{\mathbf{x}, \mathbf{y}} \; L(\mathbf{x}, \mathbf{y}) = f(\mathbf{x}) - \mathbf{y}' \mathbf{g}(\mathbf{x}) \tag{1.10}$$

$$\text{subject to} \qquad \frac{\partial L}{\partial \mathbf{x}} = \frac{\partial f}{\partial \mathbf{x}} - \left(\frac{\partial \mathbf{g}}{\partial \mathbf{x}} \right) \mathbf{y} \leq \mathbf{0}$$

where $L(\mathbf{x}, \mathbf{y})$ is the Lagrangean function and $\mathbf{y}$ is an m-dimensional vector of Lagrange multipliers (or dual variables). This specification of the dual pair of nonlinear problems corresponds to the duality discussion presented by Wolfe (1961) and Huard (1962). It is clear that, as specified in (1.9) and (1.10), the two problems are not symmetric: the primal problem contains only primal variables, **x**, whereas the dual problem exhibits both primal and dual variables, **x** and **y**. Furthermore, the structure of the objective function and of the constraints in the primal problem is different, in general, from that of the dual specification.

Examples of this asymmetry are presented in Chapter 5 with the discussion of asymmetric quadratic programming and in Chapters 8 and 9 with the discussion of monopolistic and monopsonistic behavior, respectively.

Is it possible to symmetrize the foregoing nonlinear problem, and what are the advantages of such an operation?

Symmetric Dual Nonlinear Programs

Dantzig, Eisenberg, and Cottle (1965) conceived an application of the Euler-Legendre transformation that encompasses the Lagrangean function as a special case. En route to symmetrize a rather general model, they formulated the following symmetric pair of dual problems. Let $F(\mathbf{x}, \mathbf{y})$ be a twice differentiable function, concave in **x** for each **y** and convex in **y** for each **x**, where **x** and **y** are vectors of n and m dimensions, respectively. Then,

$$\textit{Primal} \qquad \text{Find } \mathbf{x} \geq \mathbf{0}, \ \mathbf{y} \geq \mathbf{0} \quad \text{such that} \qquad (1.11)$$

$$\max_{\mathbf{x}, \mathbf{y}} P(\mathbf{x}, \mathbf{y}) = F(\mathbf{x}, \mathbf{y}) - \mathbf{y}'\left(\frac{\partial F}{\partial \mathbf{y}}\right)$$

$$\text{subject to} \quad \frac{\partial F}{\partial \mathbf{y}} \geq \mathbf{0}$$

$$\textit{Dual} \qquad \text{Find } \mathbf{x} \geq \mathbf{0}, \ \mathbf{y} \geq \mathbf{0} \quad \text{such that} \qquad (1.12)$$

$$\min_{\mathbf{x}, \mathbf{y}} D(\mathbf{x}, \mathbf{y}) = F(\mathbf{x}, \mathbf{y}) - \mathbf{x}'\left(\frac{\partial F}{\partial \mathbf{x}}\right)$$

$$\text{subject to} \quad \frac{\partial F}{\partial \mathbf{x}} \leq \mathbf{0}.$$

The treatment of inequality constraints is discussed in detail in Chapter 3. Problems (1.11) and (1.12) are symmetric and accommodate as a special case the specification of problems (1.9) and (1.10). The symmetry of the dual pair of nonlinear problems (1.11) and (1.12) is verified by the fact that both primal and dual specifications contain the vectors of **x** and **y** variables. Furthermore, the dual constraints are specified as a vector of first derivatives of the function $F(\mathbf{x}, \mathbf{y})$ and, similarly, the primal constraints are stated as a vector of first derivatives of the same function.

From the definition of the Lagrangean function given in equation (1.10), $L(\mathbf{x}, \mathbf{y}) = f(\mathbf{x}) - \mathbf{y}'\mathbf{g}(\mathbf{x})$ (and anticipating the use of Karush-Kuhn-Tucker conditions discussed in Chapter 3), we can restate problems (1.9) and (1.10) in the form of the symmetric problems (1.11) and (1.12) as the dual pair of problems

Primal   Find $\mathbf{x} \geq \mathbf{0},\ \mathbf{y} \geq \mathbf{0}$ such that   (1.13)

$$\max_{\mathbf{x},\mathbf{y}} P(\mathbf{x}, \mathbf{y}) = L(\mathbf{x}, \mathbf{y}) - \mathbf{y}'\left(\frac{\partial L}{\partial \mathbf{y}}\right)$$

$$= f(\mathbf{x}) - \mathbf{y}'\mathbf{g}(\mathbf{x}) - \mathbf{y}'[-\mathbf{g}(\mathbf{x})]$$

$$= f(\mathbf{x})$$

subject to $-\mathbf{g}(\mathbf{x}) \geq \mathbf{0}$

Dual   Find $\mathbf{x} \geq \mathbf{0},\ \mathbf{y} \geq \mathbf{0}$ such that   (1.14)

$$\min_{\mathbf{x},\mathbf{y}} D(\mathbf{x}, \mathbf{y}) = L(\mathbf{x}, \mathbf{y}) - \mathbf{x}'\left(\frac{\partial L}{\partial \mathbf{x}}\right)$$

$$= f(\mathbf{x}) - \mathbf{y}'\mathbf{g}(\mathbf{x}) - \mathbf{x}'\left[\frac{\partial f}{\partial \mathbf{x}} - \left(\frac{\partial \mathbf{g}}{\partial \mathbf{x}}\right)\mathbf{y}\right]$$

$$= f(\mathbf{x}) - \mathbf{y}'\mathbf{g}(\mathbf{x}) = L(\mathbf{x}, \mathbf{y})$$

subject to $\dfrac{\partial f}{\partial \mathbf{x}} - \left(\dfrac{\partial \mathbf{g}}{\partial \mathbf{x}}\right)\mathbf{y} \leq \mathbf{0}.$

Karush-Kuhn-Tucker conditions, as discussed in Chapter 3, require that $\mathbf{x}'[\frac{\partial f}{\partial \mathbf{x}} - (\frac{\partial \mathbf{g}}{\partial \mathbf{x}})\mathbf{y}] = 0$.

The formalism of the preceding discussion about symmetry and duality has been presented without reference to either physical or economic problems in order to induce the reader to contemplate the various components of the two specifications and gradually assimilate the notion of symmetry that includes the similarity of the primal and dual structures and the presence of all the variables in both primal and dual problems.

Balinsky and Baumol have utilized this dual specification to discuss the economic problem of the competitive firm. This interpretation is elaborated extensively in Chapter 3, after the presentation of the Karush-Kuhn-Tucker theory.

APPENDIX 1.1 – THE EULER-LEGENDRE TRANSFORMATION

In this appendix we illustrate the use of the Euler-Legendre transformation.

Example 1: Let the function

$$f(x_1, x_2) = 4x_1 + 10x_2 - 15x_1^2 + 20x_1x_2 - 9x_2^2 \qquad (A1.1.1)$$

be the original function. The tangent lines corresponding to equation (1.1) are

$$t_1 = \frac{\partial f}{\partial x_1} = 4 - 30x_1 + 20x_2 \qquad (A1.1.2)$$

$$t_2 = \frac{\partial f}{\partial x_2} = 10 + 20x_1 - 18x_2. \qquad (A1.1.3)$$

The Euler-Legendre transformation is defined as in equation (1.2),

$$g(t_1, t_2) = f(x_1, x_2) - x_1\frac{\partial f}{\partial x_1} - x_2\frac{\partial f}{\partial x_2} \qquad (A1.1.4)$$

$$= 4x_1 + 10x_2 - 15x_1^2 + 20x_1x_2 - 9x_2^2$$

$$- x_1[4 - 30x_1 + 20x_2] - x_2[10 + 20x_1 - 18x_2]$$

$$= 15x_1^2 - 20x_1x_2 + 9x_2^2.$$

In order to recover the original function $f(x_1, x_2)$, we use relations (1.3) and (1.5) as follows:

$$f(x_1, x_2) = g(t_1, t_2) - t_1\frac{\partial g}{\partial t_1} - t_2\frac{\partial g}{\partial t_2} \qquad (A1.1.5)$$

$$= 15x_1^2 - 20x_1x_2 + 9x_2^2$$

$$+ x_1[4 - 30x_1 + 20x_2] + x_2[10 + 20x_1 - 18x_2]$$

$$= 4x_1 + 10x_2 - 15x_1^2 + 20x_1x_2 - 9x_2^2$$

that is precisely the function stated in (A1.1.1).

Example 2: Given the tangent lines

$$t_1 = \frac{\partial f}{\partial x_1} = \frac{a_1}{x_1} \qquad (A1.1.6)$$

$$t_2 = \frac{\partial f}{\partial x_2} = \frac{a_2}{x_2} \qquad (A1.1.7)$$

for $a_i > 0$ and $0 < x_i < +\infty$, $i = 1, 2$, and the Euler-Legendre transformation

$$g(t_1, t_2) = -a_1 - a_2 + a_1 \log x_1 + a_2 \log x_2, \qquad (A1.1.8)$$

recover the original function $f(x_1, x_2)$.

Following equations (1.3) and (1.5), the original function is defined as

$$f(x_1, x_2) = g(t_1, t_2) - t_1 \frac{\partial g}{\partial t_1} - t_2 \frac{\partial g}{\partial t_2} \qquad (A1.1.9)$$

$$= -a_1 - a_2 + a_1 \log x_1 + a_2 \log x_2 + x_1 \left(\frac{a_1}{x_1}\right) + x_2 \left(\frac{a_2}{x_2}\right)$$

$$= a_1 \log x_1 + a_2 \log x_2.$$

Example 3: Given the tangent lines

$$t_1 = \frac{\partial f}{\partial x_1} = \frac{a_1}{x_1} + \beta_{11} \frac{\log x_1}{x_1} + \beta_{12} \frac{\log x_2}{x_1} \qquad (A1.1.10)$$

$$t_2 = \frac{\partial f}{\partial x_2} = \frac{a_2}{x_2} + \beta_{12} \frac{\log x_1}{x_2} + \beta_{22} \frac{\log x_2}{x_2} \qquad (A1.1.11)$$

for $a_i > 0$ and $0 < x_i < +\infty$, $i = 1, 2$, and the Euler-Legendre transformation

$$g(t_1, t_2) = -a_1 - a_2 + a_1 \log x_1 + a_2 \log x_2, \qquad (A1.1.12)$$

$$- \beta_{11} \log x_1 - \beta_{12} \log x_2 - \beta_{12} \log x_1 - \beta_{22} \log x_2$$

$$+ \beta_{11} (\log x_1)^2 / 2 + \beta_{12} \log x_1 \log x_2 + \beta_{22} (\log x_2)^2 / 2$$

recover the original function $f(x_1, x_2)$.

Following equations (1.3) and (1.5), the original function is defined as

$$f(x_1, x_2) = g(t_1, t_2) - t_1 \frac{\partial g}{\partial t_1} - t_2 \frac{\partial g}{\partial t_2} \qquad (A1.1.13)$$

$$= -a_1 - a_2 + a_1 \log x_1 + a_2 \log x_2,$$

$$- \beta_{11} \log x_1 - \beta_{12} \log x_2 - \beta_{12} \log x_1 - \beta_{22} \log x_2$$

$$+ \beta_{11} (\log x_1)^2 / 2 + \beta_{12} \log x_1 \log x_2 + \beta_{22} (\log x_2)^2 / 2$$

$$+ x_1 \left[\frac{a_1}{x_1} + \beta_{11} \frac{\log x_1}{x_1} + \beta_{12} \frac{\log x_2}{x_1} \right]$$

$$+ x_2 \left[\frac{a_2}{x_2} + \beta_{12} \frac{\log x_1}{x_2} + \beta_{22} \frac{\log x_2}{x_2} \right]$$

$$= a_1 \log x_1 + a_2 \log x_2$$

$$+ \beta_{11} (\log x_1)^2 / 2 + \beta_{12} \log x_1 \log x_2 + \beta_{22} (\log x_2)^2 / 2.$$

References

Balinsky, M. L., and Baumol, W. J. (1968). "The Dual in Nonlinear Programming and Its Economic Interpretation," *Review of Economic Studies*, 35, 237–56.

Chandrasekhar, S. (1987). *Truth and Beauty, Aesthetics and Motivations in Science* (Chicago and London: University of Chicago Press).

Dantzig, G. B., Eisenberg, E., and Cottle, R. W. (1965). "Symmetric Dual Nonlinear Programs," *Pacific Journal of Mathematics*, 15, 809–12.

Dyson, F. J. (1956). "Obituaries: Prof. Hermann Weyl, For.Mem.R.S," *Nature*, 177, 457–8.

Hotelling, H. (1932). "Edgeworth Taxation Paradox and the Nature of Demand and Supply Functions." *Journal of Political Economy*, 40, 577–616.

Huard, P. (1962). "Dual Programs," *Journal of Research and Development*, 6, 137–9.

Karush, W. (1939). "Minima of Functions of Several Variables with Inequalities as Side Constraints," Master's Thesis, University of Chicago.

Keats, J. (1884). *Poetical Works* (London: Macmillan).

Kuhn, H. W., and Tucker, A. W. (1951). "Nonlinear Programming," *Proceedings of the 2nd Berkeley Symposium on Mathematical Statistics and Probability* (Berkeley: University of California Press), pp. 481–92.

Poincaré, H. (1908). *Science et Méthod* (Paris: Flammarion). Translated in 1914 as *Science and Method*.

Stäckel, P. (1900). "Antwort auf die Anfrage 84 über die Legendre'sche Transformation," *Bibliotheca Mathematica*, Series 3, 1, 517.

Wolfe, P. (1961). "A Duality Theorem for Non-linear Programming," *Quarterly of Applied Mathematics*, 19, 239–44.

2

Lagrangean Theory

The purpose of this chapter is to outline an overview of the basic criteria for characterizing the solution of static optimization problems. Its intent is neither rigor nor generality but a sufficient understanding for the logic leading to the conditions of optimization and a sufficient degree of practicality. An immediate issue is whether we are satisfied with relative optima or require global optima as the solution of our problems. Any further elaboration necessitates a definition of these two notions.

Definition: A point $\mathbf{x}^* \in R^n$ is a relative (or local) maximum point of a function f defined over R^n if there exists an $\epsilon > 0$ such that $f(\mathbf{x}^*) \geq f(\mathbf{x})$ for all $\mathbf{x} \in R^n$ and $|\mathbf{x} - \mathbf{x}^*| < \epsilon$.

A point $\mathbf{x}^* \in R^n$ is a strict relative (or local) maximum point of a function f defined over R^n if there exists an $\epsilon > 0$ such that $f(\mathbf{x}^*) > f(\mathbf{x})$ for all $\mathbf{x} \in R^n$ and $|\mathbf{x} - \mathbf{x}^*| < \epsilon$.

In general, we would like to deal with solution points that correspond to global optima.

Definition: A point $\mathbf{x}^* \in R^n$ is a global maximum point of a function f defined over R^n if $f(\mathbf{x}^*) \geq f(\mathbf{x})$ for all $\mathbf{x} \in R^n$.

A point $\mathbf{x}^* \in R^n$ is a strict global maximum point of a function f defined over R^n if $f(\mathbf{x}^*) > f(\mathbf{x})$ for all $\mathbf{x} \in R^n$.

We initiate the discussion with an entirely unconstrained maximization problem and follow with a problem to be maximized subject to equality constraints.

Unconstrained Maximization

Consider the optimization problem of the form

$$\text{maximize } f(\mathbf{x}) \tag{2.1}$$

where f is a real-valued function and $\mathbf{x} \in R^n$. Further assume that $f \in C^2$, that is, it possesses continuous first and second derivatives.

An unconstrained (local or global) maximum point $\mathbf{x}^*$ is characterized by the following first-order necessary conditions:

$$\nabla f(\mathbf{x}^*) = \mathbf{0} \tag{2.2}$$

where ∇f is the gradient (or vector of first partial derivatives) of the function f defined as

$$\nabla f = \left(\frac{\partial f}{\partial x_1}, \frac{\partial f}{\partial x_2}, \ldots, \frac{\partial f}{\partial x_n} \right).$$

The optimum point $\mathbf{x}^*$ is the solution of the system of n equations (2.2). The geometric meaning of those conditions is that the maximum point of the hill to be climbed is reached when the tangent plane to the hill has a zero slope.

Second-order sufficient conditions for an unconstrained local maximum point are

$$\nabla f(\mathbf{x}^*) = \mathbf{0} \tag{2.3}$$

$$H(\mathbf{x}^*) \quad \text{is negative definite} \tag{2.4}$$

where H is the matrix of second partial derivatives of the f function, called also the Hessian matrix. The proof of these conditions can be developed using a Taylor expansion of $f(\mathbf{x})$ around the assumed maximum point $\mathbf{x}^*$

$$f(\mathbf{x}) = f(\mathbf{x}^*) + \nabla f(\mathbf{x}^*)'\mathbf{h} + \tfrac{1}{2}\mathbf{h}' H(\mathbf{x}^*)\mathbf{h} + o(|\mathbf{h}|^2) \tag{2.5}$$

where $\mathbf{h} = \mathbf{x} - \mathbf{x}^*$ and $o(|\mathbf{h}|^2)$ is a term that goes to zero faster than $|\mathbf{h}|^2$. For small $\mathbf{h}$ (a condition that permits us to neglect the term in $o(|\mathbf{h}|^2)$), the application of conditions (2.3) and (2.4) to equation (2.5) produces

$$f(\mathbf{x}^*) - f(\mathbf{x}) = -\tfrac{1}{2}\mathbf{h}' H(\mathbf{x}^*)\mathbf{h} > 0 \tag{2.6}$$

indicating that $\mathbf{x}^*$ is a local maximum relative to all the points $\mathbf{x} \in R^n$ that lie within a distance $\mathbf{h}$ of $\mathbf{x}^*$.

Concave and Convex Functions

To guarantee the attainment of a global maximum (minimum) point of the function f we introduce the notion of a concave (convex) function.

Definition: A function f defined on R^n is said to be concave if, for every pair of points $(x_1, x_2) \in R^n$ and for every scalar α such that $0 \le \alpha \le 1$, the following relation holds:

$$\alpha f(x_1) + (1 - \alpha) f(x_2) \le f(\alpha x_1 + (1 - \alpha)x_2). \qquad (2.7)$$

A function f defined on R^n is said to be strictly concave if, for every pair of points $(x_1, x_2) \in R^n$ and for every scalar α such that $0 < \alpha < 1$, the following relation holds:

$$\alpha f(x_1) + (1 - \alpha) f(x_2) < f(\alpha x_1 + (1 - \alpha)x_2). \qquad (2.8)$$

The geometric meaning of this definition is that a function is concave if the chord joining the points $f(x_1)$ and $f(x_2)$ does not lie above the point $f(\alpha x_1 + (1 - \alpha)x_2)$.

Definition: A function g is said to be (strictly) convex if $g = -f$, where f is (strictly) concave.

Concave and convex functions enjoy several important properties.

Property 1: The multiplication of a concave function by a nonnegative scalar, $c \ge 0$, is a concave function. If f is a concave function over R^n, then, for any two points $(x_1, x_2) \in R^n$, and for every scalar α such that $0 \le \alpha \le 1$,

$$\alpha c f(x_1) + (1 - \alpha)c f(x_2) \le cf[\alpha x_1 + (1 - \alpha)x_2].$$

Property 2: The sum of any two concave functions f_1 and f_2 is another concave function f, $f_1 + f_2 = f$.

For any two points $(x_1, x_2) \in R^n$, and for every scalar α such that $0 \le \alpha \le 1$, let $x_\alpha = \alpha x_1 + (1 - \alpha)x_2$. Then, the following relations are true by the definition of a concave function:

$$\alpha f_1(x_1) + (1 - \alpha) f_1(x_2) \le f_1[\alpha x_1 + (1 - \alpha)x_2]$$

$$\alpha f_2(x_1) + (1 - \alpha) f_2(x_2) \le f_2[\alpha x_1 + (1 - \alpha)x_2]$$

$$\alpha[f_1(x_1) + f_2(x_1)] + (1 - \alpha)[f_1(x_2) + f_2(x_2)] \le f_1(x_\alpha) + f_2(x_\alpha)$$

$$\alpha f(x_1) + (1 - \alpha) f(x_2) \le f[\alpha x_1 + (1 - \alpha)x_2].$$

Property 3: The intersection of m sets defined on m concave functions is a convex set.

In order to explain this property it is convenient to demonstrate an intermediate result: the set $X_c = \{x \mid x \in R^n, \; f(x) \geq c\}$ is convex for every real scalar c. In fact, if $x_1, x_2 \in X_c$, then $f(x_1) \geq c$ and $f(x_2) \geq c$. Hence, for any α such that $0 < \alpha < 1$,

$$c \leq \alpha f(x_1) + (1 - \alpha) f(x_2) \leq f(\alpha x_1 + (1 - \alpha) x_2).$$

Therefore, $\alpha x_1 + (1 - \alpha) x_2 \in X_c$. This relation holds for any set X_{c_i} defined on a concave function f_i. Hence, the intersection of the m convex sets is a convex set.

The same result holds for sets defined on convex functions, that is, for a set $X_c = \{x \mid x \in R^n, \; f(x) \leq c\}$, where the f function is convex. In mathematical programming problems, the constraint functions are often concave (convex) functions.

Constrained Maximization

The characterization of the solution of a maximization (minimization) problem defined by a differentiable objective function subject to equality constraints and unrestricted variables has been known for at least 200 years since Lagrange introduced his renowned "Lagrangean function" approach.

Consider the optimization problem

$$\text{maximize} \quad f(x) \tag{2.9}$$

$$\text{subject to } g(x) = b \tag{2.10}$$

where $f, g \in C^2$ and $x \in R^n$. Lagrange's intuition was to transform the constrained problem into an unconstrained specification, whose characterization of the associated solution is known, as in problem (2.1), by embedding the constraint (2.10) into a new objective function. The effect of this transformation is to enlarge the given problem by one additional variable for every equality constraint. The challenge, therefore, is to derive a characterization of the new problem that is equivalent to that of the original specification.

The first step, therefore, is to define the Lagrangean function as the sum of the original objective function and of the product of the constraint and the new variable, y, called a Lagrange multiplier for obvious reasons:

$$\text{maximize } L(x, y) = f(x) + y[b - g(x)]. \tag{2.11}$$

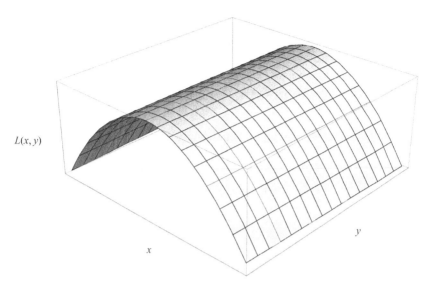

$L(x, y)$

x

y

Figure 2.1. The asymmetric Lagrangean function. The corresponding Lagrangean function is $L(x, y) = 10x - 0.5x^2 + y(0.3 - 0.1x)$.

The function L in $n + 1$ variables is now similar to the function f of problem (2.1), and its maximization is subject to analogous first-order and second-order necessary conditions such as

$$L_{\mathbf{x}} = f_{\mathbf{x}} - yg_{\mathbf{x}} = \mathbf{0} \qquad (2.12)$$

$$L_y = b - g(\mathbf{x}) = 0 \qquad (2.13)$$

and

$$H(\boldsymbol{\alpha}) \equiv \begin{bmatrix} L_{\mathbf{xx'}} & L_{\mathbf{xy}} \\ L_{y\mathbf{x'}} & L_{yy} \end{bmatrix} = \begin{bmatrix} (f_{\mathbf{xx'}} - yg_{\mathbf{xx'}}) & -g_{\mathbf{x}} \\ -g_{\mathbf{x'}} & 0 \end{bmatrix} \qquad (2.14)$$

where $\boldsymbol{\alpha} \equiv (\mathbf{x}, y)$. The matrix $H(\boldsymbol{\alpha})$ is symmetric negative semidefinite.

The Lagrangean function (2.11) is not a symmetric specification. Notice that the Lagrange multiplier y enters the Lagrangean function (2.11) in a linear way, by construction. As a consequence, the second derivative of $L(\mathbf{x}, y)$ with respect to y is identically equal to zero, that is, $L_{yy} = 0$. The Lagrangean function, when simplified in the appropriate dimensions, gives rise to a picture as illustrated in Figure 2.1.

The function $L(x, y)$ has a maximum in the direction of x for every value of y. The half-barreled picture signifies that, for any value of x, the function $L(x, y)$ grows linearly as y increases. This half-barreled representation is a general property of the Lagrangean function as stated in (2.11).

The Lagrange multiplier has the meaning of a marginal response of the objective function to an infinitesimal change in the constraint, evaluated at the optimal solution. This result can be established by inserting the solution $\mathbf{x}^* = \mathbf{x}(b)$ and $y^* = y(b)$ into the Lagrangean function (2.11) and by differentiating it with respect to the constraint b. The Lagrangean function is first restated as

$$L[\mathbf{x}(b), y(b)] = f[\mathbf{x}(b)] + y(b)\{b - g[\mathbf{x}(b)]\}.$$

The relevant derivative is then computed as

$$L_b = f_\mathbf{x}'\frac{\partial \mathbf{x}}{\partial b} + \frac{\partial y}{\partial b}\{b - g[\mathbf{x}(b)]\} - y(b)g_\mathbf{x}'\frac{\partial \mathbf{x}}{\partial b} + y^*$$

$$= \underbrace{(f_\mathbf{x}' - yg_\mathbf{x}')}_{=\,0\text{ from}(2.12)}\frac{\partial \mathbf{x}}{\partial b} + \frac{\partial y}{\partial b}\underbrace{\{b - g[\mathbf{x}(b)]\}}_{=\,0\text{ from }(2.13)} + y^*$$

$$= y^*.$$

Finally, from the assumption of an optimal solution, $L(\mathbf{x}^*, y^*) = f(\mathbf{x}^*)$ and, therefore,

$$\frac{\partial L(\mathbf{x}^*, y^*)}{\partial b} = \frac{\partial f(\mathbf{x}^*)}{\partial b} = y^*.$$

The Lagrangean function satisfies the saddle point property of a properly specified saddle problem. From Figure 2.1, however, we extract the idea that the "saddle" feature of the Lagrangean function is rather stylized in the sense that the "saddle" is flat in the direction of the Lagrange multiplier y. For this reason, the Lagrangean function stated in (2.11) rapresents a degenerate saddle point problem.

Saddle Point Problem

A function $F(\mathbf{x}, \mathbf{y})$ is said to have a saddle point $(\mathbf{x}, \mathbf{y})$ if there exists an ϵ such that for all $\mathbf{x}$, $|\mathbf{x} - \mathbf{x}^*| < \epsilon$, and all $\mathbf{y}$, $|\mathbf{y} - \mathbf{y}^*| < \epsilon$,

$$F(\mathbf{x}, \mathbf{y}^*) \leq F(\mathbf{x}^*, \mathbf{y}^*) \leq F(\mathbf{x}^*, \mathbf{y}). \qquad (2.15)$$

The Lagrangean function (2.11) fits the saddle point problem, as we show now. Assuming that an optimal point $\mathbf{x}^*$ exists, satisfying the constraint (2.10) $g(\mathbf{x}) = b$, we can write the following two relations:

$$\max_\mathbf{x} L(\mathbf{x}, y) = \max_\mathbf{x} f(\mathbf{x}) = f(\mathbf{x}^*) \qquad (2.16)$$

$$\max_\mathbf{x} L(\mathbf{x}, y) = L(\mathbf{x}^*, y) = h(y). \qquad (2.17)$$

The existence of an optimal solution $\mathbf{x}^*$ implies (by the first-order necessary conditions (2.12) and (2.13)) the existence of a Lagrange multiplier y^* such that

$$f(\mathbf{x}^*) = L(\mathbf{x}^*, y^*) = h(y^*). \tag{2.18}$$

Hence, from (2.17) and (2.18), we can write

$$L(\mathbf{x}, y^*) \leq L(\mathbf{x}^*, y^*) = h(y^*). \tag{2.19}$$

Finally, for any fixed y, a solution vector $\mathbf{x}^*$, satisfying the constraint (2.10) $g(\mathbf{x}) = b$, produces

$$L(\mathbf{x}^*, y^*) = f(\mathbf{x}^*) \tag{2.20}$$

and, therefore,

$$L(\mathbf{x}, y^*) \leq L(\mathbf{x}^*, y^*) = L(\mathbf{x}^*, y). \tag{2.21}$$

The right-hand-side equality of relation (2.21) expresses the degenerate character of the saddle point property of the Lagrangean function (2.11) that is also illustrated by Figure 2.1. Given the relation $L(\mathbf{x}, y^*) \leq L(\mathbf{x}^*, y)$ from (2.21) that is valid for all $\mathbf{x}$, $|\mathbf{x} - \mathbf{x}^*| < \epsilon$, and all y, $|y - y^*| < \epsilon$, it follows that we can write

$$\max_{\mathbf{x}} L(\mathbf{x}, y^*) = L(\mathbf{x}^*, y^*) = \min_{y} L(\mathbf{x}^*, y). \tag{2.22}$$

This means that the Lagrange multipliers can be interpreted as dual variables with the minimization of the Lagrangean function with respect to the Lagrange multipliers representing the dual problem of the primal problem (2.9) and (2.10).

Homogeneous Functions

Homogeneous functions play a prominent role in economics. Here we give the definition of a homogeneous function and state two important theorems associated with it. The proof of these theorems can be found in any elementary calculus textbook.

Definition: A function $f(x_1, x_2)$ is homogeneous of degree β if for every positive number τ

$$f(\tau x_1, \tau x_2) = \tau^\beta f(x_1, x_2)$$

for all values of $(x_1, x_2) \in R^2$. The assumption of a positive number τ guarantees the validity of the following theorems jointly considered.

Euler's Theorem: Let the function $f(x_1, x_2)$ be continuous with continuous first derivatives. If $f(x_1, x_2)$ is homogeneous of degree β,

$$\frac{\partial f}{\partial x_1}x_1 + \frac{\partial f}{\partial x_2}x_2 = \beta f(x_1, x_2).$$

Converse Euler's Theorem. Let the function $f(x_1, x_2)$ be continuous with continuous first derivatives. If $f_{x_1}x_1 + f_{x_2}x_2 = \beta f(x_1, x_2)$ for all values of $(x_1, x_2) \in R^2$, then $f(x_1, x_2)$ is homogeneous of degree β.

A function that is homogeneous of degree one is also said to be linearly homogeneous.

A Symmetric Lagrangean Function

In this section we give an example of a symmetric Lagrangean function, that is, a function that satisfies a saddle point problem strictly. This example will generate a picture of a Lagrangean function that, in contrast to Figure 2.1, is strictly convex in the direction of the Lagrange multiplier. This specification is an example of a symmetric nonlinear program according to the work of Dantzig, Eisenberg, and Cottle briefly presented in Chapter 1.

Consider the problem

$$\max_{\mathbf{x}, y} \{ f(\mathbf{x}) - yq(y)\} \qquad (2.23)$$

$$\text{subject to} \qquad g(\mathbf{x}) - 2q(y) = b \qquad (2.24)$$

where $f, g \in C^2$, $\mathbf{x} \in R^n$, and $q(y)$ is a linearly homogeneous function with respect to y. We demonstrate that the Lagrangean function corresponding to problem [(2.23), (2.24)] can be stated using the same variable y as the Lagrange multiplier associated with constraint (2.24). For the moment, let us assume that this is indeed the case and that the relevant Lagrangean function associated with problem [(2.23), (2.24)] is

$$\max_{\mathbf{x}, y} L(\mathbf{x}, y) = f(\mathbf{x}) - yq(y) + y[b - g(\mathbf{x}) + 2q(y)]. \qquad (2.25)$$

The first-order necessary conditions of the Lagrangean function (2.25) are

$$L_{\mathbf{x}} = f_{\mathbf{x}}(\mathbf{x}) - yg_{\mathbf{x}}(\mathbf{x}) = 0 \qquad (2.26)$$

$$L_y = -q(y) - yq_y(y) + b - g(\mathbf{x}) + 2q(y) + 2yq_y(y) = 0 \qquad (2.27)$$

$$= b - g(\mathbf{x}) + 2q(y) = 0.$$

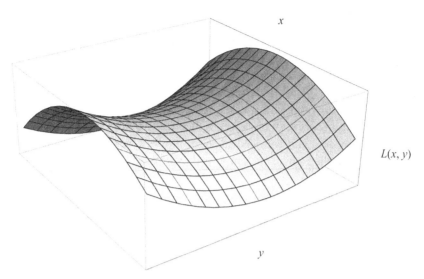

$L(x, y)$

Figure 2.2. The symmetric Lagrangean function. The corresponding Lagrangean function is $L(x, y) = 10x - 0.5x^2 - 0.4y^2 + y(0.3 - 0.1x + 0.8y)$. In this example, the function $q(y) = 0.4y$.

The notation q_y represents the derivative of the function $q(y)$ with respect to y. Relation (2.27) reduces to the constraint (2.24) because the function $q(y)$ is homogeneous of degree 1. Furthermore, Lagrange's idea, as embedded in his theory, has accustomed us to expect that the derivative of the Lagrangean function with respect to the Lagrange multiplier recovers the constraint.

The second-order derivatives of the Lagrangean function (2.25) are

$$H(\boldsymbol{\alpha}) \equiv \begin{bmatrix} L_{\mathbf{xx'}} & L_{\mathbf{x}y} \\ L_{y\mathbf{x'}} & L_{yy} \end{bmatrix} = \begin{bmatrix} (f_{\mathbf{xx'}} - yg_{\mathbf{xx'}}) & -g_{\mathbf{x}} \\ -g_{\mathbf{x'}} & 2q_y(y) \end{bmatrix} \quad (2.28)$$

where $\boldsymbol{\alpha} \equiv (\mathbf{x}, y)$. Contrary to the Hessian matrix (2.14), the Hessian matrix (2.28) is an indefinite matrix that is a property characterizing a strict saddle point problem.

A numerical example illustrating the structure of problem [(2.23), (2.24)] is given in Figure 2.2, which exhibits the picture of a classic (English) saddle. For any fixed value of the Lagrange multiplier y, the function $L(x, y)$ has a maximum in the direction of x. Similarly, for any fixed value of x, the function $L(x, y)$ has a minimum in the direction of y.

The peculiar feature of this symmetric Lagrangean problem is that the Lagrange multiplier enters the primal problem [(2.23), (2.24)], thus assuming the simultaneous role of a primal and a dual variable. This is, in fact, one important aspect of the meaning of symmetry in mathematical programming.

To complete the discussion, we need to demonstrate that the variable y can indeed be regarded as a Lagrange multiplier according to the traditional Lagrangean setup. In order to achieve this goal, let us regard problem [(2.23), (2.24)] as an ordinary maximization problem and apply to it the traditional Lagrangean framework. In this case, both $\mathbf{x}$ and y are regarded exclusively as primal variables and we need to select another variable, say μ, as the Lagrange multiplier. Thus, the temporarily relevant Lagrangean function is now

$$\max_{\mathbf{x}, y, \mu} L(\mathbf{x}, y, \mu) = f(\mathbf{x}) - yq(y) + \mu[b - g(\mathbf{x}) + 2q(y)] \quad (2.29)$$

to which there correspond the following first-order necessary conditions:

$$L_{\mathbf{x}} = f_{\mathbf{x}} - \mu g_{\mathbf{x}} = \mathbf{0} \quad (2.30)$$

$$L_y = -q(y) - yq_y + 2\mu q_y = 0 \quad (2.31)$$

$$L_\mu = b - g(\mathbf{x}) + 2q(y) = 0. \quad (2.32)$$

Multiplying the second relation (2.31) by y and using the fact that the function $q(y)$ is linearly homogeneous along with $q(y) \neq 0$ for $y \neq 0$, one obtains that $y \equiv \mu$, as desired. In fact,

$$-yq(y) - y^2 q_y + 2\mu y q_y = 0$$

$$-2yq(y) + 2\mu q(y) = 0$$

$$2q(y)(\mu - y) = 0.$$

Hence, the symmetric Lagrangean function (2.25) is equivalent to the asymmetric Lagrangean function (2.29). The symmetric Lagrangean function is more economical than its asymmetric counterpart in terms of the number of first-order conditions required for finding the solution of the optimization problem. This symmetric feature of the Lagrangean function will be at the heart of this book.

The specification of symmetric nonlinear problems extends to models that include a vector of constraints. In this case, one additional condition must be verified. Consider the following model (the symbol $\mathbf{y}$ now is a vector conformable with the $\mathbf{q}$ vector)

$$\max_{\mathbf{x}, y} \{ f(\mathbf{x}) - \mathbf{y}'\mathbf{q}(\mathbf{y}) \} \quad (2.33)$$

$$\text{subject to} \quad \mathbf{g}(\mathbf{x}) - 2\mathbf{q}(\mathbf{y}) = \mathbf{b} \quad (2.34)$$

where $f \in C^2$, $\mathbf{x} \in R^n$, $\mathbf{b} \in R^m$, $\mathbf{y} \in R^m$, $\mathbf{g}$ and $\mathbf{q}$ are vector-valued functions of dimension m, and $\mathbf{g} \in C^2$, $\mathbf{q} \in C^2$. Finally, $\mathbf{q}(\mathbf{y})$ is a linearly homogeneous vector-valued function with symmetric Jacobian matrix. Under these assumptions, the matrix $\frac{\partial \mathbf{q}}{\partial \mathbf{y}}$ is symmetric and $\mathbf{q}(\mathbf{y}) = \frac{\partial \mathbf{q}}{\partial \mathbf{y}}\mathbf{y}$. This condition is sufficient for establishing that the vector $\mathbf{y}$ appearing in the primal problem [(2.33), (2.34)] is also the vector of Lagrange multipliers of the set of constraints (2.34). The development of this more general problem follows very closely the development presented earlier in the case of a single constraint.

Exercises

2.1 Analyze the behavior of a competitive firm that faces the following production technology: $q = 10x_1 + 4x_2 - 2x_1^2 - x_2^2 + x_1 x_2$ (where q is output and x_1, x_2 are inputs), output price $p = 5$, and input prices $w_1 = 2$, $w_2 = 3$. The entrepreneur wishes to maximize his profit.
  (a) Set up the problem in the format of equations (2.9) and (2.10).
  (b) Using the Lagrangean approach, derive the optimal combination of inputs and output that will maximize profit. Explain your work.
  (c) What is the value of the Lagrange multiplier?

2.2 Analyze the behavior of a competitive firm that faces the following production technology: $q = a_1 x_1 + a_2 x_2 - b_{11} x_1^2 - b_{22} x_2^2 + b_{12} x_1 x_2$ (where q is output and x_1, x_2 are inputs), output price $p > 0$, and input prices $w_1 > 0$, $w_2 > 0$. Coefficients are $(a_1 > 0, a_2 > 0, b_{11} > 0, b_{22} > 0, b_{12} > 0)$. The entrepreneur wishes to maximize his profit.
  (a) Set up the problem in the format of equations (2.9) and (2.10).
  (b) Using the Lagrangean approach, derive the demand functions for inputs 1 and 2.
  (c) Verify that the input demand functions slope downward with respect to their own prices.

2.3 Analyze the behavior of a competitive firm that faces the following production technology: $q = A x_1^{\alpha_1} x_2^{\alpha_2}$ (where q is output and x_1, x_2 are inputs), output price $p > 0$, and input prices $w_1 > 0$, $w_2 > 0$. Coefficients are $(A > 0, \alpha_1 > 0, \alpha_2 > 0, (\alpha_1 + \alpha_2 < 1))$. The entrepreneur wishes to maximize his profit.
  (a) Set up the problem in the format of equations (2.9) and (2.10).
  (b) Using the Lagrangean approach, derive the demand functions for inputs 1 and 2 and the output supply function.

(c) Verify that the supply function slopes upward with respect to its own price and the input demand functions slope downward with respect to their own prices.

2.4 Derive the cost function of a firm that faces technology $q = Ax_1^{\alpha_1} x_2^{\alpha_2}$ (where q is output and x_1, x_2 are inputs), and input prices $w_1 > 0$, $w_2 > 0$. Coefficients are $(A > 0, \alpha_1 > 0, \alpha_2 > 0, (\alpha_1 + \alpha_2 < 1))$. The entrepreneur wishes to minimize total costs.
  (a) Set up the problem in the format of equations (2.9) and (2.10), except for the minimization operator.
  (b) Derive the demand functions for inputs 1 and 2.
  (c) Derive the cost function.
  (d) Derive the value function of the Lagrange multiplier and show that it is equal to the marginal cost function.

2.5 A consumer has a utility function $U(x_1, x_2) = x_1 x_2 + x_1 + x_2$. Her income is $30, while prices of goods 1 and 2 are $8 and $2, respectively.
  (a) Find the optimal combination of goods 1 and 2 that will maximize the consumer's utility.
  (b) What is the maximum level of utility, given the budget constraint?
  (c) What is the value of the marginal utility of money income?

2.6 A consumer has a utility function $U(x_1, x_2) = x_1 x_2 + x_1 + x_2$. Her income is m dollars, while prices of goods 1 and 2 are p_1 and p_2, respectively.
  (a) Find the demand functions for goods 1 and 2.
  (b) Find the indirect utility function, that is, find the maximum level of utility in terms of prices and income.
  (c) Find the function that expresses the marginal utility of money income as a function of prices and income. Show that this function is equal to the Lagrange multiplier.

2.7 Given the utility function $U(x_1, x_2) = x_1^c x_2^d$, prices $p_1 > 0$, $p_2 > 0$ of goods 1 and 2, respectively, and income m,
  (a) Derive the demand functions for commodities x_1 and x_2.
  (b) Find the value of the marginal utility of income.
  (c) Find the proportion of income spent on good 1 and good 2.
  (d) Find the indirect utility function, that is the function expressed in terms of prices and income.

2.8 A consumer has a utility function $U(z, r) = z + 80r - r^2$, where r stands for the number of roses and z is the number of zinnias. She has 400 square feet to allocate to roses and zinnias. Each rose takes up

4 square feet of land and each zinnia takes up 1 square foot of land. She gets the plants for free from a generous friend. If she were to expand her garden for flowers by another 100 square feet of land, she will
(a) Plant 100 more zinnias and no more roses.
(b) Plant 25 more roses and no more zinnias.
(c) Plant 96 zinnias and 1 rose.

2.9 Consider the following nonlinear programming problem:

$$\max\ f(x_1, x_2)$$

subject to $\qquad g(x_1, x_2) = 0.$

Second-order sufficiency conditions for this problem can be stated in terms of the principal minors of the bordered Hessian, H_b, derived from the Lagrangean function $L(x_1, x_2, \lambda) = f + \lambda g$. For this example, these conditions are

$$|H_b| = \begin{vmatrix} L_{11} & L_{12} & g_{x_1} \\ L_{21} & L_{22} & g_{x_2} \\ g_{x_1} & g_{x_2} & 0 \end{vmatrix} = \begin{vmatrix} H_2 & g_x \\ g_x & 0 \end{vmatrix} > 0$$

where L_{ij}, $i, j = 1, 2$ is the second derivative of the Lagrangean function with respect to x_i and x_j, whereas g_{x_i} is the derivative of the constraint with respect to x_i.

In many textbooks, this second-order sufficiency condition is stated in the following way:

$$\mathbf{z}' H_2 \mathbf{z} < 0 \text{ for all } \mathbf{z}' = (z_1, z_2) \text{ such that } \mathbf{g}'_x \mathbf{z} = 0.$$

In words, the given nonlinear problem has a local maximum if the quadratic form defined by the Hessian matrix H_2 of the Lagrangean function is negative definite subject to the constraint $\mathbf{g}'_x \mathbf{z} = 0$.

Show that the two ways of stating the sufficient conditions are equivalent. These two conditions are equivalent also for functions involving more than two variables.

Reference

Dantzig, G. B., Eisenberg, E., and Cottle, R. W. (1965). "Symmetric Dual Nonlinear Programs," *Pacific Journal of Mathematics*, 15, 809–12.

3

Karush-Kuhn-Tucker Theory

In the introduction chapter it was shown that the Euler-Legendre transformation defines duality relations for differentiable concave/convex problems without constraints. When constraints of any kind are introduced into the specification, the Lagrangean function represents the link between primal and dual problems.

At first, it would appear that the duality established by the new function has little to do with that of the Euler-Legendre transformation. As illustrated in Chapter 1, however, this is not the case. It is in fact possible to reestablish the connection by applying the Euler-Legendre transformation to the Lagrangean function and obtain a symmetric specification of dual nonlinear programs. The relationship among the various specifications of duality is illustrated in the flow chart of Figure 3.1.

Starting with unconstrained problems, we have seen in Chapter 1 that these models can, under certain conditions such as concavity and convexity, be analyzed by means of the Euler-Legendre transformation that exhibits a symmetry between the components of the original and the transformation functions. There follow problems subject to equality constraints that must be analyzed by means of the traditional Lagrange approach that presents an asymmetric structure as illustrated in Figure 2.1 of Chapter 2. When problems are constrained by inequality relations, the Karush-Kuhn-Tucker theory must be invoked. This theory uses the Lagrangean function, which is usually an asymmetric structure. However, we have already seen in Chapter 1 that the Lagrangean function can be subject to the Euler-Legendre transformation that provides a symmetrization of the original structure.

The most relevant economic models exhibit either equality or inequality constraints and, therefore, it is imperative to thoroughly understand the

Problems

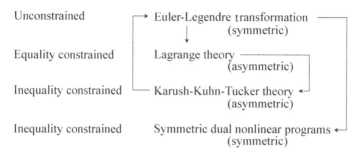

Figure 3.1. The hierarchy of duality in mathematical programming.

fundamental role of the Lagrangean function in the analysis of mathematical programming problems.

It is assumed that the reader is familiar with the necessary and sufficient conditions for maximizing a concave function $f(\mathbf{x})$, where $\mathbf{x}$ is a n-dimensional vector of decision variables. In particular, the necessary conditions are given by the vanishing gradient of $f(\mathbf{x})$ in an ϵ-neighborhood of the optimal point, $\mathbf{x}^*$:

$$\nabla_x f \equiv \frac{\partial f(\mathbf{x}^*)}{\partial \mathbf{x}} = 0. \tag{3.1}$$

Sufficient conditions require (3.1) as well as the negative semidefiniteness of $f(\mathbf{x})$ around the optimal point $\mathbf{x}^*$ and expressed as

$$\mathbf{z}' \nabla_{xx} f(\mathbf{x}^*) \mathbf{z} \leq 0 \tag{3.2}$$

for all $\mathbf{z}$ vectors in an ϵ-neighborhood of $\mathbf{x}^*$, where $\nabla_{xx} f$ is the Hessian matrix of $f(\mathbf{x})$.

The Lagrangean function, then, was introduced by Lagrange in order to transform an optimization problem subject to constraints into an equivalent unconstrained problem in such a way that the vanishing gradient criterion could be applied to it. Let us suppose that Lagrange analyzed the following problem:

$$\text{maximize } f(\mathbf{x}) \tag{3.3}$$

$$\text{subject to} \qquad g_i(\mathbf{x}) = b_i \qquad i = 1, \ldots, m$$

where $f(\mathbf{x})$ is a concave function, all the constraints $g_i(\mathbf{x})$ are convex functions, and $\mathbf{x}$ is an n-dimensional vector of decision variables. This problem is characterized by the exclusive presence of equality constraints and the absence of any restriction on the decision variables. We call (3.3) a classical

Lagrangean problem. A Lagrangean function associated with (3.3), then, is defined as

$$L(\mathbf{x}, \mathbf{y}) = f(\mathbf{x}) + \mathbf{y}'[\mathbf{b} - \mathbf{g}(\mathbf{x})] \tag{3.4}$$

where $\mathbf{y}$ is an m-dimensional vector of new variables called Lagrange multipliers. The constraint vector $\mathbf{b}$ is also m-dimensional. The reason for introducing these new vector of variables $\mathbf{y}$ is at least twofold: to transform the units of the constraint vector $\mathbf{b}$ into those of the objective function $f(\mathbf{x})$ and to provide an index of constraint tightness.

In order to find an optimal solution of (3.4), first-order necessary conditions (FONC) similar to conditions (2.2) can be applied to it:

$$\nabla_x L \equiv \frac{\partial L}{\partial \mathbf{x}} = \frac{\partial f}{\partial \mathbf{x}} - \left(\frac{\partial \mathbf{g}}{\partial \mathbf{x}}\right)\mathbf{y} = 0 \tag{3.5}$$

$$\nabla_y L \equiv \frac{\partial L}{\partial \mathbf{y}} = \mathbf{b} - \mathbf{g}(\mathbf{x}) = 0. \tag{3.6}$$

The solution of the system of equations (3.5) and (3.6), if it exists, provides a representation of the variables $\mathbf{x}$ and $\mathbf{y}$ in terms of the parameter $\mathbf{b}$, $\mathbf{x}^* = \mathbf{x}(\mathbf{b})$, $\mathbf{y}^* = \mathbf{y}(\mathbf{b})$.

Sufficient conditions for the existence of an optimal solution for problem (3.3) are given by (3.5), (3.6), and the negative semidefiniteness of the Hessian matrix $\nabla_{zz} L$, where $\mathbf{z}' = [\mathbf{x}, \mathbf{y}]'$, that is,

$$\mathbf{z}' \nabla_{zz} L \mathbf{z} = [\mathbf{z}_1, \mathbf{z}_2]' \begin{bmatrix} \nabla_{xx} L & \nabla_{xy} L \\ \nabla_{yx} L & \nabla_{yy} L \end{bmatrix} \begin{bmatrix} \mathbf{z}_1 \\ \mathbf{z}_2 \end{bmatrix} \leq 0 \tag{3.7}$$

$$= [\mathbf{z}_1, \mathbf{z}_2]' \begin{bmatrix} \nabla_{xx} L & -\nabla_x \mathbf{g} \\ -\nabla_x \mathbf{g}' & 0 \end{bmatrix} \begin{bmatrix} \mathbf{z}_1 \\ \mathbf{z}_2 \end{bmatrix} \leq 0$$

The Hessian submatrix $\nabla_{yy} L$ is identically a null matrix because the Lagrangean function (3.4) is linear in $\mathbf{y}$. The matrix $\nabla_{zz} L$ is called the bordered Hessian of L because the submatrix $\nabla_{xx} L$ is "bordered" by the negative gradient matrix of the constraint functions $\nabla_x \mathbf{g}$.

An alternative and more geometrical statement of the necessary and sufficient second-order conditions is in terms of the negative semidefiniteness of the Hessian matrix of the Lagrangean function L for all those directions $\mathbf{z}_1$ that are orthogonal to the gradient of the constraint function, that is,

$$\mathbf{z}_1' \nabla_{xx} L \mathbf{z}_1 \leq 0 \text{ for all } \mathbf{z}_1 \text{ such that } \mathbf{z}_1' \nabla_x \mathbf{g} = 0.$$

The Lagrangean function $L(\mathbf{x}, \mathbf{y})$ is concave in $\mathbf{x}$ for any $\mathbf{y}$, and it is convex in $\mathbf{y}$ for any $\mathbf{x}$, although the convexity in $\mathbf{y}$ of $L(\mathbf{x}, \mathbf{y})$ is a degenerate one because $L(\mathbf{x}, \mathbf{y})$ is a linear function of $\mathbf{y}$. This property of $L(\mathbf{x}, \mathbf{y})$ was illustrated in Figure 2.1 in the previous chapter.

This observation notwithstanding, it can be shown that the Lagrangean function $L(\mathbf{x}, \mathbf{y})$ is a saddle function to be maximized with respect to $\mathbf{x}$ and minimized with respect to $\mathbf{y}$. In order to show the saddle point property of the Lagrangean function, notice that

$$\text{maximize}_x \; L(\mathbf{x}, \mathbf{y}) = L(\mathbf{x}^*, \mathbf{y}) = f(\mathbf{x}^*) \tag{3.8}$$

since the FONC (3.6) require that $[\mathbf{b} - \mathbf{g}(\mathbf{x}^*)] = 0$. We can also write

$$\text{maximize}_x \; L(\mathbf{x}, \mathbf{y}) = L(\mathbf{x}^*, \mathbf{y}) = h(\mathbf{y}). \tag{3.9}$$

For (3.8) and (3.9) to hold, there must be Lagrange multipliers $\mathbf{y}$, say $\mathbf{y}^*$, such that

$$h(\mathbf{y}^*) = L(\mathbf{x}^*, \mathbf{y}^*) = f(\mathbf{x}^*). \tag{3.10}$$

The question of interest is: does the function $h(\mathbf{y}^*)$ possess a minimum or a maximum at $\mathbf{y}^*$? From (3.9)

$$L(\mathbf{x}, \mathbf{y}) \leq L(\mathbf{x}^*, \mathbf{y}) = h(\mathbf{y}). \tag{3.11}$$

For $\mathbf{y} = \mathbf{y}^*$, we have

$$L(\mathbf{x}, \mathbf{y}^*) \leq L(\mathbf{x}^*, \mathbf{y}^*) = h(\mathbf{y}^*). \tag{3.12}$$

On the other hand, we know that for any fixed $\mathbf{y}$, a vector $\mathbf{x}^*$ satisfying the constraints produces

$$L(\mathbf{x}^*, \mathbf{y}) = f(\mathbf{x}^*). \tag{3.13}$$

Consider now the two relations from (3.11) and (3.12):

$$L(\mathbf{x}, \mathbf{y}) - h(\mathbf{y}) \leq 0 \tag{3.14}$$

$$L(\mathbf{x}, \mathbf{y}^*) - h(\mathbf{y}^*) \leq 0. \tag{3.15}$$

Adding (3.14) and (3.15) and selecting $\mathbf{x}^*$ satisfying the constraints, we can deduce that

$$L(\mathbf{x}^*, \mathbf{y}) + \underbrace{L(\mathbf{x}^*, \mathbf{y}^*) - h(\mathbf{y}^*)}_{= 0 \text{ from } (3.10)} \leq h(\mathbf{y}) \tag{3.16}$$

$$f(\mathbf{x}^*) \qquad\qquad \leq h(\mathbf{y}) \qquad \text{from (3.13)}$$

$$h(\mathbf{y}^*) \qquad\qquad \leq h(\mathbf{y}) \qquad \text{from (3.10).}$$

We conclude that the function $h(\mathbf{y})$ has a minimum at $\mathbf{y}^*$. Therefore, the saddle point relation

$$L(\mathbf{x}, \mathbf{y}^*) \leq L(\mathbf{x}^*, \mathbf{y}^*) \leq L(\mathbf{x}^*, \mathbf{y}) \qquad (3.17)$$

characterizes the Lagrangean function.

Concave Nonlinear Programming

The discussion of the Lagrangean function presented in the previous section will provide the basis for the derivation of the Karush-Kuhn-Tucker conditions associated with optimization problems subject to inequality and nonnegativity constraints. These conditions are more commonly known as Kuhn-Tucker conditions, from the authors of a celebrated paper published in 1951. In 1939, however, Karush had already written a monograph (his master's degree dissertation) exploring several aspects of the problem. It seems appropriate, therefore, to honor his achievement by associating his name to those of the two more famous mathematicians.

The development of the Karush-Kuhn-Tucker (KKT) theory presented in this section is based solely upon the knowledge of the classical Lagrange problem, that is, an optimization problem subject only to equality constraints and without any restriction on the decision variables.

Consider now a general concave programming problem

$$\text{maximize}_x \ f(\mathbf{x}) \qquad (3.18)$$

$$\text{subject to} \qquad g_i(\mathbf{x}) \leq b_i \qquad i = 1, \ldots, m$$

$$x_j \geq b_{m+j} \equiv 0 \qquad j = 1, \ldots, n.$$

We assume that the f and g_i functions are twice differentiable, concave and convex, respectively, and, furthermore, that the feasible region defined by the contraints has a strictly interior point.

In order to apply the Lagrangean method outlined in the preceding section, it is necessary to restate problem (3.18) in the formal structure of problem (3.3) where all the constraints are equalities and no restrictions on the decision variables are admitted. This task can be achieved by exploiting a suggestion of Fritz John and by introducing appropriate slack variables as follows:

$$\text{maximize}_x \ f(\mathbf{x}) \qquad (3.19)$$

$$\text{subject to} \qquad g_i(\mathbf{x}) + s_i^2 = b_i \qquad i = 1, \ldots, m$$

$$x_j - s_j^2 = b_{m+j} \equiv 0 \qquad j = 1, \ldots, n.$$

The role of the squared terms s_i^2 and s_j^2 is to remove any restriction from the problem and to behave as slack variables because s_i and s_j can, in principle, take on any value on the real line. Now, the Lagrangean function of problem (3.19) can be stated as

$$\mathcal{L}(\mathbf{x}, \mathbf{s}, \mathbf{y}) = f(\mathbf{x}) + \sum_{i=1}^{m} y_i [b_i - s_i^2 - g_i(\mathbf{x})] + \sum_{j=1}^{n} y_{m+j} [b_{m+j} + s_j^2 - x_j]. \tag{3.20}$$

The first-order necessary conditions associated with (3.20) are

$$\frac{\partial \mathcal{L}}{\partial x_j} = \frac{\partial f}{\partial x_j} - \sum_{i=1}^{m} y_i \frac{\partial g_i}{\partial x_j} - y_{m+j} = 0 \quad j = 1, \ldots, n \tag{3.21}$$

$$\frac{\partial \mathcal{L}}{\partial s_i} = -2y_i s_i = 0 \qquad\qquad i = 1, \ldots, m \tag{3.22}$$

$$\frac{\partial \mathcal{L}}{\partial y_i} = b_i - s_i^2 - g_i(\mathbf{x}) = 0 \qquad\qquad i = 1, \ldots, m \tag{3.23}$$

$$\frac{\partial \mathcal{L}}{\partial y_{m+j}} = b_{m+j} + s_j^2 - x_j = 0 \qquad\qquad j = 1, \ldots, n \tag{3.24}$$

$$\frac{\partial \mathcal{L}}{\partial s_j} = 2y_{m+j} s_j = 0 \qquad\qquad j = 1, \ldots, n. \tag{3.25}$$

Equations (3.21) through (3.25) constitute the Karush-Kuhn-Tucker conditions of mathematical programming. Traditionally, however, they are presented in a different and more symmetric form. Hence, it remains to convert (3.21) through (3.25) into the usual KKT formulation. This can be done by means of simple algebraic manipulations.

At the optimal point, the variables $(x_j^*, s_j^*, s_i^*, y_i^*, y_{m+j}^*)$ are functions of the constraint coefficients (b_i, b_{m+j}), that is,

$$\mathcal{L}(\mathbf{x}^*, \mathbf{s}^*, \mathbf{y}^*) = f(\mathbf{x}(\mathbf{b})) + \sum_{i=1}^{m} y_i(\mathbf{b}) \big[b_i - s_i^2(\mathbf{b}) - g_i(\mathbf{x}(\mathbf{b})) \big]$$

$$+ \sum_{j=1}^{n} y_{m+j}(\mathbf{b}) \big[b_{m+j} + s_j^2(\mathbf{b}) - x_j(\mathbf{b}) \big] \tag{3.26}$$

where $\mathbf{b}' = [b_1, \ldots, b_m, b_{m+1}, \ldots, b_{m+n}]$.

To better understand the meaning of a Lagrange multiplier y_i, we differentiate the Lagrangean function with respect to the ith parameter b_i as

$$
\frac{\partial \mathcal{L}}{\partial b_i} = \sum_{j=1}^{n} \frac{\partial f}{\partial x_j} \frac{\partial x_j}{\partial b_i} - \sum_{j=1}^{n} \sum_{k=1}^{m} y_k \frac{\partial g_k}{\partial x_j} \frac{\partial x_j}{\partial b_i} + \sum_{k=1}^{m} \frac{\partial y_k}{\partial b_i} \underbrace{\left[b_k - s_k^2 - g_k(\mathbf{x}) \right]}_{= 0, \text{ from FONC}} + y_i
$$

$$
- 2 \sum_{k=1}^{m} \underbrace{y_k s_k}_{= 0} \frac{\partial s_k}{\partial b_i} + \sum_{j=1}^{n} \frac{\partial y_{m+j}}{\partial b_i} \underbrace{\left[b_{m+j} + s_j^2 - x_j \right]}_{= 0, \text{ from FONC}}
$$

$$
- y_{m+j} \frac{\partial x_j}{\partial b_i} + 2 \sum_{j=1}^{n} \underbrace{y_{m+j} s_j}_{= 0} \frac{\partial s_j}{\partial b_i}
$$

$$
= \sum_{j=1}^{n} \underbrace{\left[\frac{\partial f}{\partial x_j} - \sum_{k=1}^{m} y_k \frac{\partial g_k}{\partial x_j} - y_{m+j} \right]}_{= 0, \text{ from FONC}} \frac{\partial x_j}{\partial b_i} + y_i = y_i. \tag{3.27}
$$

In the neighborhood of the optimal solution, therefore, the rate of change of the Lagrangean function with respect to a change of a constraint parameter is equal to the Lagrange multiplier. Furthermore, at the same point, the objective function is equal to the Lagrangean function, as stated in (3.10), and we conclude that

$$
\frac{\partial \mathcal{L}(\mathbf{x}^*, \mathbf{y}^*)}{\partial b_i} = \frac{\partial f(\mathbf{x}^*)}{\partial b_i} = y_i \tag{3.28}
$$

$$
\frac{\partial \mathcal{L}(\mathbf{x}^*, \mathbf{y}^*)}{\partial b_{m+j}} = \frac{\partial f(\mathbf{x}^*)}{\partial b_{m+j}} = y_{m+j}.
$$

The next step is to determine the sign of the Lagrange multipliers (or dual variables). Let us first consider y_{m+j}. Its sign can be easily decided with the help of the two diagrams in Figure 3.2.

There are two possible cases: the constraint b_{m+j} can fall either to the left or to the right of the objective function's maximum point as illustrated by the two diagrams (A) and (B) of Figure 3.2. (It can also fall exactly at the maximum point. This event causes a degeneracy of the dual solution, as discussed later on. It does not require, however, a third diagram.)

In the case of the (A) diagram of Figure 3.2, the optimal value of x_j occurs at a point far away from b_{m+j}, $x_j > b_{m+j} \equiv 0$; that is, the constraint is not

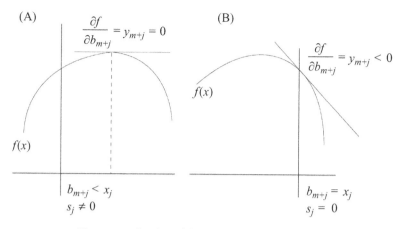

Figure 3.2. The sign of the Lagrange multiplier y_{m+j}.

binding and the corresponding slack variable s_j^2 is positive or, equivalently, $s_j \neq 0$. Perturbing the constraint b_{m+j} infinitesimally, as is done in a differentiation process, will have no effect on the optimal value of the objective function, and therefore, we conclude that when $s_j \neq 0$, $y_{m+j} = 0$.

In the case of the (B) diagram of Figure 3.2, the optimal value of x_j coincides with the value of the constraint parameter $b_{m+j} \equiv 0$ and the corresponding slack variable s_j^2 is equal to zero or, equivalently, $s_j = 0$. In this case, a perturbation of the constraint coefficient b_{m+j} has a direct effect on the optimal value of the objective function, and we conclude that $y_{m+j} < 0$.

The combination of the two events allows to state that when the decision variables are required to be nonnegative, the corresponding Lagrange multiplier is nonpositive, or $y_{m+j} \leq 0$. A second result of the analysis is that when $x_j > 0$, then $y_{m+j} = 0$ and when $y_{m+j} < 0$, then $x_j = 0$. Therefore, $x_j y_{m+j} = 0$, always.

A similar analysis can be articulated for determining the sign of the Lagrange multiplier y_i. This result is illustrated in Figure 3.3, where the behavior of the constraint $g_i(\mathbf{x}) \leq b_i$ is analyzed. As in the previous case, the conclusion is that in the presence of less-than-or-equal inequality constraints, the corresponding Lagrange multiplier (dual variable) is always nonnegative, that is, $y_i \geq 0$. A second result is that the product of the slack variable s_i^2 and the dual variable y_i is always equal to zero, that is, $s_i y_i = 0$.

Armed with these results, we return to evaluate the FONC relations (3.21) through (3.25) and turn them into the conventional form of the KKT

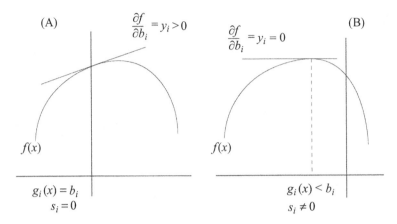

Figure 3.3. The sign of the Lagrange multiplier y_i.

conditions. From the nonpositive sign of y_{m+j} and (3.21), we obtain

$$\frac{\partial \mathcal{L}}{\partial x_j} = \frac{\partial f}{\partial x_j} - \sum_{i=1}^{m} y_i \frac{\partial g_i}{\partial x_j} \leq 0 \qquad j = 1, \ldots, n \qquad (3.29)$$

because the quantity $(-y_{m+j})$ is nonnegative and behaves as a dual slack variable. Furthermore, multiplying (3.21) by x_j

$$x_j \frac{\partial \mathcal{L}}{\partial x_j} = x_j \frac{\partial f}{\partial x_j} - x_j \sum_{i=1}^{m} y_i \frac{\partial g_i}{\partial x_j} - x_j y_{m+j} = 0 \qquad j = 1, \ldots, n$$

$$= x_j \left[\frac{\partial f}{\partial x_j} - \sum_{i=1}^{m} y_i \frac{\partial g_i}{\partial x_j} \right] = 0 \qquad (3.30)$$

since $x_j y_{m+j} = 0$, as demonstrated above. This result is called the complementary slackness condition involving the primal variables: slackness refers to the dual slack variable $(-y_{m+j})$, whereas the complementarity property is given by the null product of the primal variable x_j and the dual slack variable y_{m+j}. Also, from (3.24) it is clear that all the decision variables must be nonnegative because $x_j \geq b_{m+j} \equiv 0$.

The KKT conditions involving the dual variables are obtained from the remaining FONC relations. From (3.23), after erasing the slack variable s_i^2, we can write

$$\frac{\partial \mathcal{L}}{\partial y_i} = b_i - g_i(\mathbf{x}) \geq 0 \qquad i = 1, \ldots, m \qquad (3.31)$$

and multiplying (3.23) by y_i, we obtain

$$y_i \frac{\partial \mathcal{L}}{\partial y_i} = y_i b_i - y_i s_i^2 - y_i g_i(\mathbf{x}) = 0 \qquad i = 1, \ldots, m \qquad (3.32)$$

$$= y_i [b_i - g_i(\mathbf{x})] = 0$$

because $y_i s_i^2 = 0$ as a consequence of (3.22). Finally, the nonnegativity of the dual variables y_i was demonstrated earlier. All the information contained in the FONC (3.21) through (3.25) was utilized. It is convenient to summarize the six KKT conditions associated with problem (3.18) in order to exhibit their symmetry as follows: for all i's and j's

Dual		Primal	
(3.18.i)	$\dfrac{\partial \mathcal{L}}{\partial x_j} \leq 0$	(3.18.iv)	$\dfrac{\partial \mathcal{L}}{\partial y_i} \geq 0$
(3.18.ii)	$x_j \dfrac{\partial \mathcal{L}}{\partial x_j} = 0$	(3.18.v)	$y_i \dfrac{\partial \mathcal{L}}{\partial y_i} = 0$
(3.18.iii)	$x_j \geq 0$	(3.18.vi)	$y_i \geq 0.$

The importance of the KKT conditions stems from the fact that to solve problem (3.18), one needs to solve the auxiliary system of relations specified in (3.18.i) through (3.18.vi).

In a concave mathematical programming problem, KKT conditions are both necessary and sufficient for characterizing an optimal solution because the second-order conditions, represented by the negative definiteness of the Hessian matrix of $\mathcal{L}(\mathbf{x}, \mathbf{y})$, are guaranteed by the concavity assumption.

The foregoing development suggests that the dual pair of nonlinear programming problems associated with (3.18) can be written in a symmetric way using the notation of the Lagrangean function:

Primal	Dual
maximize$_\mathbf{x}$ $\mathcal{L}(\mathbf{x}, \mathbf{y})$	minimize$_\mathbf{y}$ $\mathcal{L}(\mathbf{x}, \mathbf{y})$
subject to $\dfrac{\partial \mathcal{L}}{\partial \mathbf{y}} \geq 0,\ \mathbf{x} \geq 0$	subject to $\dfrac{\partial \mathcal{L}}{\partial \mathbf{x}} \leq 0,\ \mathbf{y} \geq 0.$

The formulation of the primal problem in the form just exhibited is guaranteed to be equivalent to the original version (3.18) by means of the KKT conditions.

We must mention an important aspect of nonlinear programming. KKT conditions are valid only under a *Constraint Qualification* assumption. In the appendix of this chapter, we discuss the *Constraint Qualification* in more detail.

Alternative Specifications of Nonlinear Problems

Nonlinear programming problems may appear in slightly different versions than (3.18). In particular, they may exhibit equality constraints and the absence of nonnegativity restrictions on the decision variables. We are interested in examining the structure of the KKT conditions corresponding to either case.

A concave problem subject to equality constraints and nonnegativity restrictions on the decision variables can be stated as

$$\text{maximize}_{\mathbf{x}} \ f(\mathbf{x}) \tag{3.33}$$

$$\text{subject to} \ g_i(\mathbf{x}) = b_i \qquad i = 1, \ldots, m$$

$$x_j \geq 0 \qquad\qquad j = 1, \ldots, n.$$

In this case, the corresponding KKT conditions can be easily deduced by observing that the primal slack variable is identically equal to zero, $s_i^2 \equiv 0$, and therefore there is no opportunity to articulate the discussion about the sign of the Lagrange multiplier y_i as was done in Figure 3.3. Thus, this Lagrange multiplier is unrestricted (also called a free variable) because, in principle, it can take on any value on the real line, as in the classical Lagrangean problem. Furthermore, the complementary slackness conditions involving the primal equality constraints are trivially satisfied and need not be stated explicitly. All the other KKT conditions regarding the primal decision variables are not affected by the equality constraint. A summary of the KKT conditions corresponding to problem (3.33) is as follows:

(3.33.i)	$\dfrac{\partial L}{\partial x_j} \leq 0$	(3.33.iv)	$\dfrac{\partial L}{\partial y_i} = 0$
(3.33.ii)	$x_j \dfrac{\partial L}{\partial x_j} = 0$	(3.33.v)	$y_i \dfrac{\partial L}{\partial y_i} = 0$, trivially
(3.33.iii)	$x_j \geq 0$	(3.33.vi)	y_i, free variable.

When a mathematical programming problem exhibits inequality constraints and the absence of nonnegativity restrictions on the decision variables, it takes on the following specification:

$$\text{maximize}_{\mathbf{x}} \ f(\mathbf{x}) \tag{3.34}$$

$$\text{subject to} \ g_i(\mathbf{x}) \leq b_i \qquad i = 1, \ldots, m.$$

In this second case, the dual slack variable y_{m+j} vanishes identically and, therefore, the corresponding dual constraint is an equality. This fact can be verified from FONC (3.21). As a consequence, the complementarity slackness conditions corresponding to the dual equality constraints are trivially satisfied and need not be stated explicitly. A summary of the KKT conditions for problem (3.34) is:

$(3.34.i)$	$\dfrac{\partial L}{\partial x_j} = 0$	$(3.34.iv)$	$\dfrac{\partial L}{\partial y_i} \geq 0$
$(3.34.ii)$	$x_j \dfrac{\partial L}{\partial x_j} = 0$, trivially	$(3.34.v)$	$y_i \dfrac{\partial L}{\partial y_i} = 0$
$(3.34.iii)$	x_j, free variable	$(3.34.vi)$	$y_i \geq 0$.

Of course, nonlinear programming problems exhibit structures that combine the elements of problems (3.33) and (3.34). The discussion just presented is sufficient for stating the correct specification of the corresponding KKT conditions. Consider, in fact, the following nonlinear programming problem where the vector of decision variables has been partitioned in two subvectors, $\mathbf{x}_1$ and $\mathbf{x}_2$:

$$\text{maximize}_{\mathbf{x}_1, \mathbf{x}_2} \ f(\mathbf{x}_1, \mathbf{x}_2) \tag{3.35}$$

$$\text{subject to } g_1(\mathbf{x}_1, \mathbf{x}_2) = b_1$$

$$g_2(\mathbf{x}_1, \mathbf{x}_2) \leq b_2$$

$$\mathbf{x}_1 \geq 0$$

$$\mathbf{x}_2 \text{ free.}$$

Using the two schemes developed previously for problems (3.33) and (3.34), the KKT conditions for problem (3.35) can be stated as

$(2.35.i)_1$	$\dfrac{\partial L}{\partial \mathbf{x}_1} \leq 0$	$(3.35.iv)_1$	$\dfrac{\partial L}{\partial y_1} = 0$
$(3.35.ii)_1$	$\mathbf{x}_1' \dfrac{\partial L}{\partial \mathbf{x}_1} = 0$		
$(3.35.iii)_1$	$\mathbf{x}_1 \geq 0$		
$(3.35.i)_2$	$\dfrac{\partial L}{\partial \mathbf{x}_2} = 0$	$(3.35.iv)_2$	$\dfrac{\partial L}{\partial y_2} \geq 0$
		$(3.35.v)_2$	$y_2 \dfrac{\partial L}{\partial y_2} = 0$
		$(3.35.vi)_2$	$y_2 \geq 0$

where the subscript refers to either the first or the second constraint of problem (3.35).

Other combinations of equality and inequality constraints as well as restrictions on the decision variables are possible, but are left to the reader.

Interpretation of Karush-Kuhn-Tucker Conditions

In concave programming, KKT conditions are necessary and sufficient for identifying an optimal solution, if it exists. The large majority of algorithms for finding that solution is designed to solve the system of relations constituted by the associated KKT conditions.

The relations represented by the primal and dual inequality constraints are important because they define the corresponding feasible regions. The associated complementary slackness conditions are equally important, although their interpretation is less obvious. We use the theory of the firm as an empirical framework. The objective function $f(\mathbf{x})$ is then interpretable as total revenue, or some other meaningful index of economic performance. The set of constraints $g_i(\mathbf{x})$ define the technology of transforming commodity inputs into commodity outputs, while the parameter b_i signifies an initial level of the ith limiting input. Within this context, the six KKT conditions stated as relations (3.18) can be developed and interpreted as follows:

Marginal revenue $\leq$ marginal cost		Economic equilibrium
(3.18.i) $\dfrac{\partial f}{\partial x_j} \leq \displaystyle\sum_{i=1}^{m} y_i \dfrac{\partial g_i}{\partial x_j}$		Dual feasibility, part 1
jth good's total MR $=$ jth good's total MC		Break-even condition
(3.18.ii) $x_j \dfrac{\partial f}{\partial x_j} = x_j \displaystyle\sum_{i=1}^{m} y_i \dfrac{\partial g_i}{\partial x_j}$		Dual complementary slackness
Activities cannot be operated at negative levels		
(3.18.iii) $x_j \geq 0$		Primal feasibility, part 2
ith input demand $\leq$ ith input supply		Physical quantity equilibrium
(3.18.iv) $g_i(\mathbf{x}) \leq b_i$		Primal feasibility, part 1
ith input cost $=$ ith input value		Break-even condition
(3.18.v) $y_i g_i(\mathbf{x}) = y_i b_i$		Primal complementary slackness
Input shadow prices are nonnegative		
(3.18.vi) $y_i \geq 0$		Dual feasibility, part 2.

Complementary slackness conditions require a supplemental interpretation. Consider the dual complementary slackness conditions (3.18.*ii*) written as follows:

$$x_j \left[\frac{\partial f}{\partial x_j} - \sum_{i=1}^{m} y_i \frac{\partial g_i}{\partial x_j} \right] = 0. \tag{3.36}$$

Relation (3.36) contains at least two propositions: if the jth activity is operated at a positive level, the associated marginal cost and marginal revenue must be equal; or, if the marginal cost of the jth activity is strictly greater than the corresponding marginal revenue, the jth activity must be operated at zero level. The two propositions can be formally stated as

$$\text{if } x_j > 0 \quad \Longrightarrow \quad \frac{\partial f}{\partial x_j} = \sum_{i=1}^{m} y_i \frac{\partial g_i}{\partial x_j}$$

$$\text{if } \sum_{i=1}^{m} y_i \frac{\partial g_i}{\partial x_j} > \frac{\partial f}{\partial x_j} \quad \Longrightarrow \quad x_j = 0.$$

It is also possible to have the case of zero production ($x_j = 0$) together with the economic equilibrium condition $\left(\frac{\partial f}{\partial x_j} = \sum_{i=1}^{m} y_i \frac{\partial g_i}{\partial x_j} \right)$. This is a case of dual degeneracy, often encountered in mathematical programming models. The economic significance of dual degeneracy can be illustrated with reference to the formulation of an optimal production plan. For some jth activity not incorporated in such a plan, ($x_j = 0$), it is possible to have the same index of profitability as that of those activities included in the production plan (marginal cost = marginal revenue). The jth activity is not included in the optimal mix because of the exhaustion of the available resources among those activities already in the plan. The inclusion of the excluded jth activity is possible only if some resources are made available by reducing the levels of those activities already in the plan. This suggests the possibility of obtaining an alternative production plan that exhibits the same level of profit as the original one. Degeneracy, therefore, introduces the subject of multiple optimal solutions.

Consider the primal complementary slackness condition stated as

$$y_i [g_i(\mathbf{x}) - b_i] = 0. \tag{3.37}$$

Also, relation (3.37) contains at least two propositions: if the imputed (shadow) price of the ith input is positive, the demand and the supply of that input must be equal; if the supply of the ith input is strictly greater than its demand, the corresponding shadow price must be equal to zero.

This is a case of a free good. Formally, the two propositions result in

$$\text{if } y_i > 0 \quad \Longrightarrow \quad g_i(\mathbf{x}) = b_i$$

$$\text{if } b_i > g_i(\mathbf{x}) \quad \Longrightarrow \quad y_i = 0.$$

It is also possible to have the case of zero shadow price ($y_i = 0$) together with the physical quantity equilibrium condition, or demand for the input being equal to the corresponding supply, $g_i(\mathbf{x}) = b_i$. This is a case of primal degeneracy, also encountered rather often in mathematical programming models. The economic interpretation of this occurrence can be illustrated with reference to the optimal use of the available inputs. For the reason analogous to that underlying the existence of multiple optimal production plans, there is the possibility of multiple (shadow) input price systems. This event occurs when three or more resource constraints cross at the same point corresponding to the optimal production plan. Degeneracy and multiple optimal solutions will form the subject of a separate discussion.

Equilibrium Problem

There are relevant economic problems that cannot be formulated as a dual pair of optimization problems. In other words, there are problems whose primal specification cannot be stated as a maximization (or minimization) objective because the application of KKT theory does not lead to a dual problem that is consistent with the original information. For example, in Chapter 8 we show that the problem of a perfectly discriminating monopolist producing three or more outputs and facing a system of demand functions whose matrix of slopes is not symmetric cannot be stated as a pair of dual programming problems.

In this case, the specification of the corresponding problem takes on the more general structure of an *equilibrium problem*. An equilibrium problem is based on two sets of general economic and complementary conditions that are associated with any commodity, whether an input or an output:

QUANTITY side
  Demand/Supply $(S - D)P = 0$ (3.40)

PRICE side
  Marginal Cost/Marginal Revenue $(MC - MR)Q = 0$ (3.41)

where $S \equiv$ Supply, $D \equiv$ Demand, $P \equiv$ Price, $MC \equiv$ Marginal Cost, $MR \equiv$ Marginal Revenue, and $Q \equiv$ Quantity. Relations (3.40) and (3.41) do not involve, necessarily, any optimization. For the sake of clarity, we repeat here the interpretation of the three relations implied by each statement in (3.40) and (3.41). Beginning with (3.40):

$$(S - D)P = 0 \text{ means } \begin{cases} \text{if } S > D, & \text{then } P = 0 \\ \text{if } P > 0, & \text{then } S - D = 0 \\ \text{but also} & S - D = 0 \text{ and } P = 0. \end{cases} \qquad (3.42)$$

In words, if supply (of any commodity) is strictly greater than the demand (of that commodity), its price will be equal to zero; if the price (of any commodity) is strictly greater than zero, its supply must be equal to its demand. However, it is also possible that the price is equal to zero when the demand is equal to the supply. This is the case of primal degeneracy. From the three statements implied in (3.42), we conclude that $S \geq D$ and $P \geq 0$.

Continuing with (3.41):

$$(MC - MR)Q = 0 \text{ means } \begin{cases} \text{if } MC > MR, & \text{then } Q = 0 \\ \text{if } Q > 0, & \text{then } MC - MR = 0 \\ \text{but also} & MC - MR = 0 \text{ and } Q = 0. \end{cases}$$

$$(3.43)$$

In words, if marginal cost of a commodity is strictly greater than the marginal revenue of that commodity, the quantity of output produced will be equal to zero; if output is produced at positive quantities, the marginal cost of that commodity must be equal to its marginal revenue. However, it is also possible that the quantity is equal to zero when the marginal cost is equal to marginal revenue. This is a case of dual degeneracy. From the three statements implied in (3.43), we conclude that $MC \geq MR$ and $Q \geq 0$.

Hence, the analysis of the complementary relations (3.42) and (3.43) allows for the definition of the Equilibrium Problem:

The quantity component has three parts:

$$\begin{array}{ll} S \geq D & \textit{Supply} \geq \textit{Demand} \\ P \geq 0 & \textit{Nonnegative Price} \\ (S - D)P = 0 & \textit{Complementary Slackness.} \end{array}$$

The "price" component also has three parts:

$$\begin{array}{ll} MC \geq MR & \textit{Marginal Cost} \geq \textit{Marginal Revenue} \\ Q \geq 0 & \textit{Nonnegative Quantity} \\ (MC - MR)Q = 0 & \textit{Complementary Slackness.} \end{array}$$

It must be emphasized that the Equilibrium Problem is the most general framework for analyzing economic scenarios. It is more general than the dual pair of optimization problems. In fact, the Equilibrium Problem does not necessarily imply either a maximizing or a minimizing objective function.

The application of the Equilibrium Problem's structure is exemplified in the chapters ahead. In each of the chapters regarding the monopolistic and monopsonistic behavior, risk, and general equilibrium, we encounter economic scenarios whose analysis requires the specification of a corresponding equilibrium problem.

How to Solve Nonlinear Programming Problems

The discussion of previous sections has made abundantly clear that, for solving nonlinear programming problems that can be expressed as a dual pair of optimization models, it is necessary to solve the system of linear and nonlinear relations traditionally called KKT conditions. It has also brought to the fore the not-so-traditional notion of Equilibrium Problem as a class of models that are not necessarily associated with specifications admitting the optimization of an explicit objective function.

By now, there are many commercially available computer applications that can handle the solution of sophisticated and complex monlinear programming problems. In this book, however, we make use of two computer applications, one that is commercially available and the other that was expressly written for handling the Linear Complementarity Problem of Chapter 6 in its generality, including the two-person non-zero-sum games of Chapter 13.

The commercially available computer application is called GAMS (Generalized Algebraic Modeling System) and was written by a sizable group of programmers over a long period of years. The current edition, however, bears the responsibility of Brooke, Kendrick, and Meeraus. It is a very efficient program, powerful and at the same time easy to grasp by a beginner who can progress on his own to higher levels of this high-level programming language. A useful tutorial can be found online at www.gams/docs/document.html.

To facilitate the understanding of the GAMS language and to render operational the material discussed in this book, several numerical exercises are accompanied by the corresponding command file that was used to solve those problems.

The second computer application used in this book is a novel computer package that was written expressly for solving symmetric quadratic programming problems and two-person non-zero-sum games. It had a long gestation period. It began in 1968 as a Share Library program written by

Ravindran, who used the Fortran language for a code that could solve only asymmetric quadratic programming problems. It was extended in 1977 by the author to solve symmetric quadratic programming problems and was further extended in 2007 to solve two-person non-zero-sum games. This application is very easy to use. A user's manual and the entire Fortran 77 source code are provided in Chapters 16 and 17.

Exercises

3.1 Given the differentiable objective function $f(x_1, x_2)$ to be maximized subject to differentiable constraints $g_1(x_1, x_2) = b_1$ and $g_2(x_1, x_2) \leq b_2$ with $x_1 \geq 0$ and x_2 unrestricted, derive the dual constraints, that is, state the KKT conditions involving dual constraints and dual variables. Hint: Primal

$$\max\ f(x_1, x_2)$$

$$\text{subject to} \quad g_1(x_1, x_2) = b_1$$

$$g_2(x_1, x_2) \leq b_2$$

$$x_1 \geq 0$$

$$x_2 \text{ a free variable.}$$

3.2 Show that the following nonlinear programming problem:

$$\max x_1$$

$$\text{subject to} \quad x_2 - (1 - x_1)^3 \leq 0$$

$$x_1 + x_2 = 1$$

$$x_1 \geq 0,\ x_2 \geq 0$$

satisfies the KKT conditions and, therefore, has a solution. Find the solution. Compare and contrast this problem with the problem discussed in Appendix 3.1.

3.3 A monopolistic firm enters a contract to produce minimum quantities m_1 and m_2 of outputs q_1 and q_2. Therefore, the firm's problem is to maximize profits:

$$\max \pi = p_1(q_1)q_1 + p_2(q_2)q_2 - c(q_1, q_2)$$

$$\text{subject to} \quad q_1 \geq m_1 > 0$$

$$q_2 \geq m_2 > 0$$

where $p_1(q_1)$ and $p_2(q_2)$ are inverse demand functions and $c(q_1, q_2)$ is the firm's cost function. Show that, if the demand for q_1 is inelastic, the firm will maximize profits by producing as small a quantity q_1 as the contract permits (Boumol).

3.4 Write down and explain the dual of the following linear programming problem:

$$\max R = \mathbf{c}_1' \mathbf{x}_1 + \mathbf{c}_2' \mathbf{x}_2$$

subject to $\qquad A_{11}\mathbf{x}_1 + A_{12}\mathbf{x}_2 \leq \mathbf{b}_1$

$$A_{21}\mathbf{x}_1 + A_{22}\mathbf{x}_2 = \mathbf{b}_2$$

$$\mathbf{x}_1 \quad \text{a free variable}$$

$$\mathbf{x}_2 \geq \mathbf{0}.$$

3.5 Show that the following specification is a symmetric nonlinear programming model:

$$\max Z = f(x_1, x_2) - \tfrac{1}{2} y_1 h_1(y_1) - \tfrac{1}{2} y_2 h_2(y_2)$$

subject to $\qquad g_1(x_1, x_2) - h_1(y_1) \leq b_1$

$$g_2(x_1, x_2) - h_2(y_2) \leq b_2$$

with $x_j \geq 0$, $j = 1, 2$; $y_i \geq 0$, $i = 1, 2$, and where the functions $h_i(y_i)$, $i = 1, 2$ are linearly homogeneous. Derive all the KKT conditions of this problem and state the dual specification.

APPENDIX 3.1: CONSTRAINT QUALIFICATION

The reason for relegating the discussion of the *Constraint Qualification* to an appendix is partially justified by the nature of the nonlinear programming problems discussed in this book. For the great majority of economic scenarios presented in the next chapters, the corresponding models assume the specification of either a convex or a concave programming problem. In these cases, the *Constraint Qualification* condition is satisfied implicitly.

For more general specifications of nonlinear programming problems, however, KKT conditions are meaningful and necessary only if certain "irregularities" on the boundary of the feasible region are ruled out. These

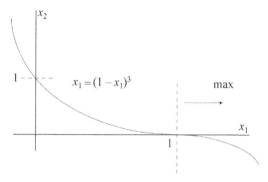

Figure 3.4. Violation of KKT conditions.

"irregularities" often assume the shape of a "cusp," as illustrated in Figure 3.4, which corresponds to a famous nonlinear programming problem:

$$\max x_1 \qquad (A3.1.1)$$

$$\text{subject to} \qquad x_2 - (1 - x_1)^3 \le 0 \qquad (A3.1.2)$$

$$x_1 \ge 0, \ x_2 \ge 0.$$

This problem fails to satisfy the associated KKT conditions. To verify this assertion, we specify the Lagrangean function

$$L = x_1 + \lambda[(1 - x_1)^3 - x_2] \qquad (A3.1.3)$$

with KKT condition for x_1 resulting in

$$\frac{\partial L}{\partial x_1} = 1 - 3\lambda(1 - x_1)^2 \le 0 \qquad (A3.1.4)$$

$$x_1 \frac{\partial L}{\partial x_1} = x_1[1 - 3\lambda(1 - x_1)^2] = 0. \qquad (A3.1.5)$$

Looking at Figure 3.4, the objective function in $(A3.1.1)$ is maximized at $x_1^* = 1$. But, at this optimal value, KKT condition $(A3.1.4)$ results in a contradiction because $1 \le 0$. KKT condition $(A3.1.5)$ also results in a contradiction because $1 = 0$. The presence of a cusp, however, is neither necessary nor sufficient for a violation of KKT conditions. It is sufficient to add suitable constraints to the numerical example to satisfy KKT conditions. In the next chapters, we assume that all the problems discussed there will satisfy the *Constraint Qualification*.

References

Baumol, W. J. (1972). *Economic Theory and Operations Analysis* (Third edition) (London: Prentice-Hall International).

Brooke, A., Kendrick, D., and Meeraus, A. (1988). *GAMS: A User's Guide* (Danvers, MA: Boyd & Fraser).

Karush, W. (1939), "Minima of Functions of Several Variables with Inequalities as Side Constraints," Master of Science Dissertation, Department of Mathematics, University of Chicago.

Kuhn, H. W., and Tucker, A. W. (1951). "Nonlinear Programming," *Proceedings of the 2nd Berkeley Symposium on Mathematical Statistics and Probability* (Berkeley: University of California Press), pp. 481–92.

4

Solving Systems of Linear Equations

The solution of linear and nonlinear programming problems involves the solution of a sequence of linear equation systems. In preparation for understanding the nature and the structure of algorithms for solving linear and nonlinear programming problems, we discuss in this chapter the fundamentals of a particular method of solving systems of linear equations that is known as the pivot method. We choose this algorithm because it articulates in great detail all the steps necessary to solve a system of equations with the opportunity of showing very clearly the structure of the linear system and of the steps leading to a solution, if it exists.

In the analysis and solution of a linear system of equations, the most important notion is that of a **basis**. A formal definition of a basis is given later. Here we discuss, in an informal way and borrowing from everyday life, the meaning of a basis. A basis is a system of measurement units. To measure temperature, we often use two systems of measurement units, the Fahrenheit and the Celsius systems. Equivalently, we could name them the Fahrenheit and the Celsius bases. Analogously, the decimal metric and the American systems are two different bases (systems of measurement units) for measuring length, surface, and volume. The essential role of a basis, therefore, is that of measuring objects. In an entirely similar way, the role of a basis in a given mathematical space is that of measuring objects (points, vectors) in that space. Furthermore, there are in general many bases (systems of measurement units) for measuring objects in a given space, just as there is more than one system of measurement units for measuring temperature, length, surface, and volume. Hence, the solution of a system of linear equations can be likened to finding the measurements of a mathematical object in terms of an appropriate system of measurement units or basis. We now tackle the formal discussion.

Suppose we are given a real matrix A of dimensions $(m \times n)$, $m < n$, of rank $r(A) = m$, and an m-vector $\mathbf{b}$, defining the following linear system:

$$A\mathbf{x} = \mathbf{b}. \tag{4.1}$$

System (4.1) has more variables than equations and, therefore, it can be rewritten as

$$B\mathbf{x}_B + A_{NB}\mathbf{x}_{NB} = \mathbf{b} \tag{4.2}$$

where B is a square matrix of order m and A_{NB} is a matrix of dimensions $[m \times (n - m)]$, whereas $\mathbf{x}_B$ and $\mathbf{x}_{NB}$ are vectors conformable to the associated matrices. The subscript $(\ldots)_B$ indicates basic vectors and the subscript $(\ldots)_{NB}$ stands for nonbasic vectors. If the matrix B has certain properties discussed later, it will be a **basis**.

Definition 1: *Linear Dependence.* A set of vectors $\mathbf{v}_1, \ldots, \mathbf{v}_m$ from R^m is said to be linearly dependent if there exist scalars α_i, $i = 1, \ldots, m$, not all zero, such that

$$\alpha_1\mathbf{v}_1 + \alpha_2\mathbf{v}_2 \cdots + \alpha_m\mathbf{v}_m = 0. \tag{4.3}$$

If all the scalars $\alpha_i = 0$, $i = 1, \ldots, m$, then the vectors are said to be linearly independent.

The geometric meaning of Definition 1 is that vectors that are linearly independent are not parallel to each other. The mathematical meaning is that the determinant of the matrix composed by the given vectors is not equal to zero. The notion of determinant is briefly reviewed in Appendix 4.1.

Definition 2: *Spanning Set.* A set of vectors $\mathbf{v}_1, \ldots, \mathbf{v}_r$ from the space of m dimensions R^m is said to span (or generate) R^m if every vector in R^m can be written as a linear combination of vectors $\mathbf{v}_1, \ldots, \mathbf{v}_r$.

Remark. We are looking for the smallest number of vectors that span the space.

Definition 3: *Basis.* In a space of m dimensions, R^m, a basis is a set of linearly independent vectors from R^m that span the entire space.

Assume that B is a basis for system (4.2). Then $\mathbf{x}_B$ is a vector of components of the solution for (4.2) associated with *basic vectors*, and $\mathbf{x}_{NB}$ is a vector of components of the solution for system (4.2) associated with *nonbasic vectors.* There are probably many bases in system (4.2). The mathematical object to be measured by means of the basis B is the right-hand-side vector $\mathbf{b}$.

Definition 4: *Basic Solution.* Given a system of equations such as (4.2), a *basic solution* is a vector $\mathbf{x}' \equiv (\mathbf{x}'_B, \mathbf{x}'_{NB})$ such that $\mathbf{x}'_{NB} = \mathbf{0}'$ and $\mathbf{x}'_B \neq \mathbf{0}'$.

Remark. There are <u>at most</u> m nonzero components of a basic solution to (4.1) [or (4.2)]. The vector $\mathbf{x}_B$ contains variables called *basic variables,* whereas the components of the vector $\mathbf{x}_{NB}$ are called *nonbasic variables.*

Consider now the linear system of equations

$$Ax = b, \qquad x \geq 0, \tag{4.4}$$

where the matrix A has dimensions $(m \times n)$, $m < n$, and $rank(A) = m$. The system (4.4) can always be rewritten as

$$B\mathbf{x}_B + A_{NB}\mathbf{x}_{NB} = \mathbf{b}, \quad \mathbf{x}_B \geq \mathbf{0}, \quad \mathbf{x}_{NB} \geq \mathbf{0}, \tag{4.5}$$

where B is a basis for (4.4) [or (4.5)] of dimension $(m \times m)$.

Definition 5: *Basic Feasible Solution and Feasible Basis.* A solution $\mathbf{x}' \equiv (\mathbf{x}'_B, \mathbf{x}'_{NB})$ is said to be a *basic feasible solution* for (4.4) [or (4.5)] if $\mathbf{x}_{NB} = \mathbf{0}$, $\mathbf{x}_B \geq \mathbf{0}$ and $\mathbf{x}_B$ satisfies the system of equations $B\mathbf{x}_B = \mathbf{b}$. The matrix B is said to be a *feasible basis.*

Definition 6: *Simplex.* In a space of m dimensions, a *simplex* is a set of $(m + 1)$ points not all lying on the same hyperplane.

Remark. In a 2-dimensional space, a triangle is a simplex. In a 3-dimensional space, a tetrahedron is a simplex, and so on.

System (4.4) has possibly many basic feasible solutions associated with many feasible bases. This means that the right-hand-side (RHS) vector $\mathbf{b}$ can be expressed (measured) with different feasible bases. Our interest is to develop a procedure that allows us to go from the current basic feasible solution to another basic feasible solution while changing only one component of the feasible basis. In other words, we must execute an operation called a *change of basis* while maintaining the feasibility of the basic solution. Assume, therefore, that the current basic feasible solution is $\mathbf{x}' \equiv (\mathbf{x}'_B, \mathbf{0}')$. This means that $\mathbf{x}_B \geq \mathbf{0}$, $B\mathbf{x}_B = \mathbf{b}$, and $\mathbf{x}'_{NB} = \mathbf{0}'$. Let us choose vector $\mathbf{a}_{NBj}$ from the matrix of nonbasic vectors A_{NB}. We wish to replace one vector of the basis B with the selected vector $\mathbf{a}_{NBj}$ and obtain a new basic feasible solution. This is achieved by using the property of a basis that is the ability to express (measure) any vector in R^m as a linear combination of the basic vectors. Hence,

$$B\mathbf{w}_j = \mathbf{a}_{NBj} \tag{4.6}$$

where the vector $\mathbf{w}_j$ is the basic solution of system (4.6).

We then multiply (4.6) by a nonnegative scalar θ (which is currently unknown) and subtract the result from $B\mathbf{x}_B = \mathbf{b}$ to obtain

$$B(\mathbf{x}_B - \theta\mathbf{w}_j) + \theta\mathbf{a}_{NBj} = \mathbf{b}. \tag{4.7}$$

The left-hand side of (4.7) contains $(m + 1)$ linearly dependent vectors, $(B, \mathbf{a}_{NBj})$. These $(m + 1)$ vectors constitute a *simplex*. We wish to eliminate one vector from the current basis B in order to replace it with the new vector $\mathbf{a}_{NBj}$. This objective must be achieved while guaranteeing that the new basic solution will also be feasible, that is, $\theta \geq 0$ and

$$\mathbf{x}_B - \theta\mathbf{w}_j \geq \mathbf{0}. \tag{4.8}$$

Therefore, we are searching for a value of the unknown parameter θ such that $\theta \geq 0$ and satisfies (4.8). Recall that $\mathbf{x}_B \geq \mathbf{0}$ by assumption. System (4.8) contains m inequalities and only one unknown, θ. We can, therefore, compute m values (*at most*) of θ and select the one that satisfies all the feasibility conditions. Such a critical value, θ_c, is computed as

$$\theta_c = \min_i \left\{ \frac{x_{Bi}}{w_{ji}} \;\middle|\; w_{ji} > 0 \right\}. \tag{4.9}$$

Condition (4.9) is called the *minimum-ratio criterion*, and its execution preserves the feasibility of the next basic solution. The choice of any other value of θ_c would violate the feasibility of the next basic solution.

Product Form of the Inverse

The pivot algorithm for solving systems of linear equations involves the computation of the inverse of the current basis in the form of the product of several transformation matrices.

Suppose we are given a nonsingular matrix B of dimension $(m \times m)$, $B = [\mathbf{b}_1, \mathbf{b}_2, \cdots, \mathbf{b}_m]$ and an m-vector $\mathbf{a}$. We take B to be a basis for R^m. Then,

$$\mathbf{a} = B\mathbf{y} \tag{4.10}$$

$$= y_1\mathbf{b}_1 + y_2\mathbf{b}_2 + \cdots + y_r\mathbf{b}_r + \cdots + y_m\mathbf{b}_m,$$

where **a** is any vector in R^m.

Suppose, now, that $y_r \neq 0$. It is thus possible to express the vector $\mathbf{b}_r$ in terms of the other vectors:

$$\mathbf{b}_r = -\frac{y_1}{y_r}\mathbf{b}_1 - \frac{y_2}{y_r}\mathbf{b}_2 - \cdots + \frac{1}{y_r}\mathbf{a} - \cdots - \frac{y_m}{y_r}\mathbf{b}_m. \qquad (4.11)$$

Let

$$\mathbf{t}_r = \left[-\frac{y_1}{y_r}, \ -\frac{y_2}{y_r}, \ \ldots, \ \frac{1}{y_r}, \ \ldots, \ -\frac{y_m}{y_r} \right] \qquad (4.12)$$

$$B_\mathbf{a} = \left[\mathbf{b}_1, \ \mathbf{b}_2, \ \ldots, \mathbf{a}, \ \ldots, \mathbf{b}_m \right]. \qquad (4.13)$$

The $B_\mathbf{a}$ matrix, therefore is the old B matrix with the vector **a** inserted in the rth position in place of the $\mathbf{b}_r$ vector. The vector $\mathbf{t}_r$ is called a *transformation vector*. Then (4.11) can be written as

$$\mathbf{b}_r = B_\mathbf{a}\mathbf{t}_r. \qquad (4.14)$$

Let the matrix T_r be a transformation matrix constructed by inserting the transformation vector $\mathbf{t}_r$ in the rth column of an identity matrix

$$T_r = \left[\mathbf{e}_1, \ \mathbf{e}_2, \ \ldots, \ \mathbf{t}_r, \ \ldots, \ \mathbf{e}_m \right] \qquad (4.15)$$

where $\mathbf{e}_j$, $j = 1, \ldots, m$, is a unit vector with a unit element in the jth position and zero everywhere else. Equation (4.14) can now be restated in a more general form as

$$B = B_\mathbf{a} T_r. \qquad (4.16)$$

Taking the inverse of (4.16) on both sides,

$$B_\mathbf{a}^{-1} = T_r B^{-1}. \qquad (4.17)$$

The inverse matrix $B_\mathbf{a}^{-1}$ exists because B^{-1} exists by assumption. The preceding discussion leads to the computation of the inverse of the matrix B. Suppose we begin with the identity matrix I, that is, $B_0 = I$, and $r = 1$. In the notation of (4.16),

$$B_0 = I = B_1 T_1, \qquad (4.18)$$

which means that B_1 is an identity matrix with the vector $\mathbf{b}_1$ inserted in the first column. The inverse of this matrix is

$$B_1^{-1} = T_1 I = T_1 B_0^{-1}. \qquad (4.19)$$

By inserting the second column vector of B, $\mathbf{b}_2$, into the previous matrix B_1, we obtain

$$B_2^{-1} = T_2 B_1^{-1} = T_2 T_1 I. \tag{4.20}$$

Repeating the process for $i = 1, \ldots, m$, we arrive at the computation of the inverse of the B matrix as a series of matrix multiplications that justifies the name of *product form of the inverse*:

$$B^{-1} = T_m B_{m-1}^{-1} = T_m T_{m-1} T_{m-2} \cdots T_3 T_2 T_1 I. \tag{4.21}$$

Summary of the Pivot Method's Rules

1. Define a square transformation matrix T_r, $r = 1, \ldots, m$. A transformation matrix is an identity matrix with one column being replaced by a transformation vector, as in equation (4.15).
2. Define a transformation vector $\mathbf{t}_r$, that is a vector that contains the rules for eliminating a variable from $(m - 1)$ equations in a given column and for normalizing the remaining coefficient in that column according to (4.12). Choose the first pivot in an arbitrary way, as long as it is not equal to zero.
   2.1 The reciprocal of the pivot is placed in the same row of the transformation vector as that of the pivot column.
   2.2 All the other coefficients of the pivot column are divided by the pivot and placed in the transformation vector with a changed sign.
3. Place the transformation vector in that **column** of the transformation matrix whose index corresponds to the **row** containing the pivot, according to equation (4.15).
4. Rule for choosing the pivot: successive pivots, different from zero, must be chosen in a different row and a different column from previous pivots.

A Numerical Example of the Pivot Method

Consider the following system of linear equations that requires a nonnegative solution:

$$A\mathbf{x} = \mathbf{b}, \qquad \mathbf{x} \geq \mathbf{0}, \tag{4.22}$$

where

$$A = [\mathbf{a}_1, \mathbf{a}_2, \mathbf{a}_3] = \begin{bmatrix} 1 & 2 & 3 \\ 6 & 5 & 4 \end{bmatrix}, \qquad \mathbf{b} = \begin{bmatrix} 7 \\ 28 \end{bmatrix}.$$

First, we choose the basis B and matrix A_{NB} as

$$B = [\mathbf{a}_1, \mathbf{a}_2] = \begin{bmatrix} 1 & 2 \\ 6 & 5 \end{bmatrix}, \quad A_{NB} = [\mathbf{a}_3] = \begin{bmatrix} 3 \\ 4 \end{bmatrix}.$$

Hence, for a basic feasible solution, we expect that $\mathbf{x}'_B = (x_1, x_2) \geq \mathbf{0}'$ and $\mathbf{x}'_{NB} = x_3 = 0$.

The arrangement of the given information is carried out in the form of a tableau as indicated later. Aside from the coefficients of the matrix A and vector $\mathbf{b}$, the tableau includes an identity matrix for the purpose of starting with an easy-to-find feasible basis and storing the inverse of the current basis. The unit vectors $\mathbf{e}_1$, $\mathbf{e}_2$ constitute the current auxiliary feasible basis and the associated auxiliary variables z_1, z_2 the current auxiliary basic feasible solution. The *BI* heading on the right of the tableau stands for *Basic Indexes* and indicates the *basic* indexes of the current feasible basis. In the first tableau, when we do not know what values the variables x_1, x_2, x_3 ought to take, we attribute to them a zero value and begin the computations using the auxiliary basic variables z_1, z_2 and the corresponding vectors $[\mathbf{e}_1, \mathbf{e}_2]$ as the current (auxiliary, easy-to-find) feasible basis. The heading "sol" stands for solution.

Initial tableau:

$$\begin{array}{cccccc} x_1 & x_2 & x_3 & z_1 & z_2 & \text{sol} \quad BI \\ \begin{bmatrix} 1 & 2 & 3 & 1 & 0 & 7 \\ 6 & 5 & 4 & 0 & 1 & 28 \end{bmatrix} \begin{array}{c} z_1 \\ z_2 \end{array} \end{array} \qquad (4.23)$$

To summarize, in the current tableau, the values of all the variables involved are $x_1 = 0$, $x_2 = 0$, $x_3 = 0$, $z_1 = 7$, $z_2 = 28$. Hence, the current feasible basis is

$$B = [\mathbf{e}_1, \mathbf{e}_2] = \begin{bmatrix} 1 & 0 \\ 0 & 1 \end{bmatrix}.$$

The pivot algorithm now is used to work toward the measurement of the vector $\mathbf{b}$ using the feasible basis B indicated previously. This will be done gradually, one step at the time, beginning with the (arbitrary) selection of the pivot element in the first column and the first row of the initial tableau.

With such a choice of the pivot (to be circled, for clarity, in the tableau later), the transformation vector will be defined as in equation (4.12) and placed in the transformation matrix in the column whose *column index* corresponds to the *row index* of the pivot. In equation (4.12), the symbol y_r is the pivot. Thus, the transformation vector is defined by the reciprocal of the pivot and by all the other coefficients in the pivot column being divided by the pivot and placed in the transformation vector with a changed sign. Then, the usual premultiplication of the matrix will be carried out for every column of the current tableau.

$$
T_1 \quad
\begin{array}{ccccccc}
x_1 & x_2 & x_3 & z_1 & z_2 & \text{sol} & BI
\end{array}
\quad (4.24)
$$

$$
\begin{bmatrix} 1 & 0 \\ -6 & 1 \end{bmatrix}
\begin{bmatrix} \boxed{1} & 2 & 3 & 1 & 0 & 7 \\ 6 & 5 & 4 & 0 & 1 & 28 \end{bmatrix}
\begin{matrix} z_1 \\ z_2 \end{matrix}
$$

$$
\begin{bmatrix} 1 & 2 & 3 & 1 & 0 & 7 \\ 0 & -7 & -14 & -6 & 1 & -14 \end{bmatrix}
\begin{matrix} x_1 \\ z_2 \end{matrix}
$$

The variable x_1 has taken the place of the auxiliary variable z_1 in the BI column, and the current basic solution corresponding to the last tableau of (4.24) is indicated as $x_1 = 7$, $x_2 = 0$, $x_3 = 0$, $z_1 = 0$, $z_2 = -14$. The current solution is not yet feasible because the auxiliary coordinate $z_2 = -14$. Variables that do not appear in the BI column have a value that is identically equal to zero, by construction (and by the definition of *basic feasible solution*). Hence, the current basis is

$$
B = [\mathbf{a}_1, \mathbf{e}_2] = \begin{bmatrix} 1 & 0 \\ 6 & 1 \end{bmatrix}.
$$

When the z_2 variable is also eliminated from the BI column, the basic solution will become feasible. The next step involves a repetition of the pivot algorithm using the coefficient (-7) of the second tableau in (4.24) as the next pivot element. This selection is dictated by the desire to utilize the basis B as indicated in (4.22). Hence, the new tableaux are:

$$
T_2 \quad
\begin{array}{ccccccc}
x_1 & x_2 & x_3 & z_1 & z_2 & \text{sol} & BI
\end{array}
\quad (4.25)
$$

$$
\begin{bmatrix} 1 & \frac{2}{7} \\ 0 & -\frac{1}{7} \end{bmatrix}
\begin{bmatrix} 1 & 2 & 3 & 1 & 0 & 7 \\ 0 & \boxed{-7} & -14 & -6 & 1 & -14 \end{bmatrix}
\begin{matrix} x_1 \\ z_2 \end{matrix}
$$

$$
\begin{bmatrix} 1 & 0 & -1 & \frac{-5}{7} & \frac{2}{7} & 3 \\ 0 & 1 & 2 & \frac{6}{7} & \frac{-1}{7} & 2 \end{bmatrix}
\begin{matrix} x_1 \\ x_2 \end{matrix}
$$

At this stage, the current basic feasible solution is $\mathbf{x}'^* = (x_1^* = 3, x_2^* = 2, x_3^* = 0, z_1^* = 0, z_2^* = 0)$. The feasible basis is constituted by those vectors of the original matrix A, or equivalently of the given matrix B in (4.22), that is, $B = [\mathbf{a}_1, \mathbf{a}_2]$, that are associated with the x_1 and x_2 basic variables. Therefore, notice that we have achieved the desired goal, that of expressing the RHS vector $\mathbf{b}$ in (4.22) in terms of the feasible basis B (equivalently, we have measured $\mathbf{b}$ with the feasible basis B), that is, we have solved the desired system of linear equations:

$$B\mathbf{x}_B^* = \mathbf{b} = \begin{bmatrix} 1 & 2 \\ 6 & 5 \end{bmatrix} \begin{bmatrix} 3 \\ 2 \end{bmatrix} = \begin{bmatrix} 7 \\ 28 \end{bmatrix}. \tag{4.26}$$

An important realization of what we obtained in the final tableau of (4.25) is the inverse of the current basis B, that is, B^{-1}, which corresponds to the matrix under the initial identity matrix in (4.24). To verify the correctness of the computation, then, we check whether $BB^{-1} = I$ or

$$\begin{bmatrix} 1 & 2 \\ 6 & 5 \end{bmatrix} \begin{bmatrix} \frac{-5}{7} & \frac{2}{7} \\ \frac{6}{7} & \frac{-1}{7} \end{bmatrix} = \begin{bmatrix} 1 & 0 \\ 0 & 1 \end{bmatrix}. \tag{4.27}$$

A further check of the computations' correctness, then, can be realized by the following verification:

$$\mathbf{x}_B^* = B^{-1}\mathbf{b} = \begin{bmatrix} x_1^* \\ x_2^* \end{bmatrix} = \begin{bmatrix} \frac{-5}{7} & \frac{2}{7} \\ \frac{6}{7} & \frac{-1}{7} \end{bmatrix} \begin{bmatrix} 7 \\ 28 \end{bmatrix} = \begin{bmatrix} 3 \\ 2 \end{bmatrix}. \tag{4.28}$$

A final realization is the *product form of the inverse*, which is represented by the multiplications of all the transformation matrices computed previously, that is,

$$B^{-1} = T^2 T^1 = \begin{bmatrix} 1 & \frac{2}{7} \\ 0 & \frac{-1}{7} \end{bmatrix} \begin{bmatrix} 1 & 0 \\ -6 & 1 \end{bmatrix} = \begin{bmatrix} \frac{-5}{7} & \frac{2}{7} \\ \frac{6}{7} & \frac{-1}{7} \end{bmatrix}. \tag{4.29}$$

We recall that the current basis for measuring the $\mathbf{b}$ vector is $B = [\mathbf{a}_1, \mathbf{a}_2]$. Now we want to show that the RHS vector $\mathbf{b}$ of problem (4.22) can also be expressed (measured) in terms of another basis belonging to the A matrix in (4.22). In particular, we wish to measure the RHS vector $\mathbf{b}$ with the following new basis:

$$B_{\text{new}} = [\mathbf{a}_1, \mathbf{a}_3] = \begin{bmatrix} 1 & 3 \\ 6 & 4 \end{bmatrix}. \tag{4.30}$$

Hence, starting from the second tableau of (4.25), we must perform a *change of basis* (as described in relations [(4.6)–(4.9)]), that is, eliminating in an appropriate fashion vector $\mathbf{a}_2$ from the current basis B and replacing it with vector $\mathbf{a}_3$ in the new basis B_{new}. The *appropriate fashion* characterization refers to the fact that the new basic solution must also be feasible.

First, we consider the expression (measurement) of vector $\mathbf{a}_3$ by means of the current basis B. This expression is similar to equation (4.6):

$$B\mathbf{w}_3 = \mathbf{a}_3 = \begin{bmatrix} 1 & 3 \\ 6 & 4 \end{bmatrix} \begin{bmatrix} w_{31} \\ w_{32} \end{bmatrix} = \begin{bmatrix} 3 \\ 4 \end{bmatrix}. \tag{4.31}$$

Therefore, the vector $\mathbf{w}_3$ can be computed as

$$\mathbf{w}_3^* = B^{-1}\mathbf{a}_3 = \begin{bmatrix} w_{31}^* \\ w_{32}^* \end{bmatrix} = \begin{bmatrix} \frac{-5}{7} & \frac{2}{7} \\ \frac{6}{7} & \frac{-1}{7} \end{bmatrix} \begin{bmatrix} 3 \\ 4 \end{bmatrix} = \begin{bmatrix} -1 \\ 2 \end{bmatrix}. \quad (4.32)$$

Notice that this $\mathbf{w}_3^*$ vector is precisely the vector that appears in the second tableau of (4.25) under the heading of x_3, as it should be, given the computations we performed at that stage.

Finally, we are ready to execute the *minimum ratio criterion* dictated by rule (4.9) in order to guarantee that the next basic solution will be feasible, as required by problem (4.22). Notice that in vector $\mathbf{w}_3^*$, there is only one positive component. Thus,

$$\theta_c = \min_i \left\{ \frac{x_{Bi}}{w_{ji}} \,\middle|\, w_{ji} > 0 \right\} = \min_i \left\{ \frac{2}{2} \right\} = 1. \quad (4.33)$$

Hence, starting from the second tableau of (4.25), the pivot element will be the only positive component of the vector under the x_3 heading. Then, with one other iteration of the pivot algorithm, we will obtain the desired result of expressing the RHS vector $\mathbf{b}$ in terms of the new basis.

$$
\begin{array}{ccccccccc}
T & x_1 & x_2 & x_3 & z_1 & z_2 & \text{sol} & BI & (4.34)
\end{array}
$$

$$
\begin{bmatrix} 1 & \frac{1}{2} \\ 0 & \frac{1}{2} \end{bmatrix}
\begin{bmatrix} 1 & 0 & -1 & \frac{-5}{7} & \frac{2}{7} & 3 \\ 0 & 1 & \boxed{2} & \frac{6}{7} & \frac{-1}{7} & 2 \end{bmatrix}
\begin{matrix} x_1 \\ x_2 \end{matrix}
$$

$$
\begin{bmatrix} 1 & \frac{1}{2} & 0 & \frac{-2}{7} & \frac{3}{14} & 4 \\ 0 & \frac{1}{2} & 1 & \frac{3}{7} & \frac{-1}{14} & 1 \end{bmatrix}
\begin{matrix} x_1 \\ x_3 \end{matrix}
$$

As indicated by the BI column of (4.34), the new basis is composed of the vectors associated with x_1, x_3, as desired. The new basic solution is feasible, as desired. Hence we have fulfilled the objective of expressing (measuring) the RHS vector $\mathbf{b}$ with two different bases, B and B_{new}. Therefore, we can write explicitly

$$B\mathbf{x}_B^* = \mathbf{b} \quad (4.35)$$

$$B_{\text{new}}\mathbf{x}_{B\text{new}}^* = \mathbf{b},$$

that is,

$$\begin{bmatrix} 1 & 2 \\ 6 & 5 \end{bmatrix} \begin{bmatrix} 3 \\ 2 \end{bmatrix} = \begin{bmatrix} 7 \\ 28 \end{bmatrix}$$

$$\begin{bmatrix} 1 & 3 \\ 6 & 4 \end{bmatrix} \begin{bmatrix} 4 \\ 1 \end{bmatrix} = \begin{bmatrix} 7 \\ 28 \end{bmatrix}.$$

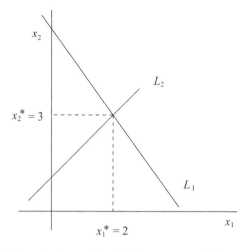

Figure 4.1. The primal meaning of solving a system of linear equations.

This example illustrates the meaning of measuring a mathematical object such as vector **b** with different bases (systems of measurement units) and how to go from one basis to the next.

The Geometric Meaning of a Solution

A system of linear equations can be read by rows and by columns. Let us consider the following (2×2) system of linear equations:

$$
\begin{aligned}
3x_1 + 2x_2 &= 12 \qquad (\text{row } 1 \equiv L_1) \\
-1x_1 + 1x_2 &= 1 \qquad (\text{row } 2 \equiv L_2).
\end{aligned}
\tag{4.36}
$$

A reading by rows gives rise to the traditional space where the coordinate axes are labeled with the symbols of the unknown variables, as in Figure 4.1. In system (4.36), each row represents the equation of a line reproduced in Figure 4.1. Hence, this first (primal) geometric meaning of solving a system of equations corresponds to the familiar notion of finding the point of intersection between two lines (planes, hyperplanes).

System (4.36) can also be read by columns. In this case, the information is arranged in vector form as follows:

$$
\begin{bmatrix} 3 \\ -1 \end{bmatrix} x_1 + \begin{bmatrix} 2 \\ 1 \end{bmatrix} x_2 = \begin{bmatrix} 12 \\ 1 \end{bmatrix}
\tag{4.37}
$$

$$
\mathbf{a}_1 x_1 \quad + \quad \mathbf{a}_2 x_2 = \quad \mathbf{b},
$$

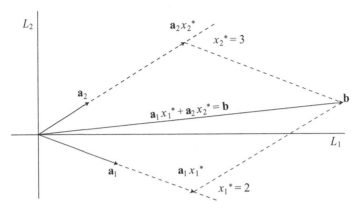

Figure 4.2. The dual meaning of solving a system of linear equations.

where vectors $\mathbf{a}_1$ and $\mathbf{a}_2$ constitute the **basis** of system (4.37) and vector $\mathbf{b}$ represents the object to be measured using this basis. The pair of values (x_1^*, x_2^*) constitutes the measurement, using the given basis. The solution of the given linear system in the form of equation (4.37) is illustrated in Figure 4.2.

In this case, the labels of the Cartesian axes are the lines (L_1 and L_2). We can thus state that a solution of a linear system from the dual viewpoint corresponds to the construction of the parallelogram, using the basis vectors $\mathbf{a}_1$ and $\mathbf{a}_2$, whose main diagonal is equal to the RHS vector $\mathbf{b}$. The construction of the parallelogram begins from the basis vectors $\mathbf{a}_1$ and $\mathbf{a}_2$ that are extended in the same direction up to a suitable length. Geometrically, vectors $\mathbf{a}_1$ and $\mathbf{a}_2$ form a cone that includes the right-hand-side vector $\mathbf{b}$. This condition is necessary for the feasibility of the solution, that is, for obtaining that $x_1^* \geq 0$, $x_2^* \geq 0$. Then, starting from the tip of vector $\mathbf{b}$, a parallel line is drawn to each of the basis vectors (and their dotted extensions) to form the required parallelogram. The points of intersection $\mathbf{a}_1 x_1^*$ and $\mathbf{a}_2 x_2^*$ establish the length of the vectors from which the solution will be measured.

The value of scalars x_1^* and x_2^* can be read from the diagram of Figure 4.2. In this case, the vector $\mathbf{a}_1 x_1^*$ is twice as long as the vector $\mathbf{a}_1$. Hence, the value of the associated scalar must be $x_1^* = 2$. Similarly, the vector $\mathbf{a}_2 x_2^*$ is three times as long as the vector $\mathbf{a}_2$. Hence, the value of the associated scalar must be $x_2^* = 3$. The necessary and sufficient condition for constructing the reference parallelogram is that the basis vectors $\mathbf{a}_1$ and $\mathbf{a}_2$ not be parallel. This dual geometrical way of solving a system of linear equations illustrates the importance of knowing the notion of a **basis**. Furthermore, we note that a feasible solution (in the sense that $x_1 \geq 0$ and $x_2 \geq 0$) is obtained only when the **basis** forms a cone that includes the vector **b** (which can also be considered as "included" in the cone when it is coincident with one or the other vectors of the basis).

We wish to emphasize the fact that knowledge of the pivot method is essential for understanding and computing the solution of linear programming problems as well as for the solution of problems that fall under the class of Linear Complementarity problems, to be discussed in Chapter 6. The famous and durable Simplex method for linear programming, devised by Dantzig in 1947, relies on the pivot approach. A concise discussion of the Simplex algorithm is given in Chapter 7.

Exercises

4.1 Verify whether the following vectors are linearly independent:

$$\begin{bmatrix} 2 \\ 9 \\ 5 \end{bmatrix}, \quad \begin{bmatrix} -4 \\ 1 \\ 3 \end{bmatrix}, \quad \begin{bmatrix} -1 \\ 5 \\ 4 \end{bmatrix}.$$

State clearly the criteria you may use for testing linear independence.

4.2 Show that the addition (subtraction) of two vectors, $(\mathbf{v}_1, \mathbf{v}_2) \in R^2$, corresponds to a parallelogram whose main diagonal is the sum (subtraction) of the two given vectors.

4.3 Show that the multiplication of a vector $\mathbf{v} \in R^2$ by a scalar k corresponds to the extension $(k > 1)$, shrinkage $(0 < k < 1)$, or reversal of direction $(k < 0)$, along the same line defined by the given vector.

4.4 Solve the following system of equations graphically using the primal and the dual geometric approaches:

$$A\mathbf{x} = \mathbf{b}$$

$$\begin{bmatrix} 1 & 1 \\ 2 & -2 \end{bmatrix} \begin{bmatrix} x_1 \\ x_2 \end{bmatrix} = \begin{bmatrix} 5 \\ 2 \end{bmatrix}.$$

Hint: First, read the system by row and plot the corresponding lines. Second, read the system by column and plot the corresponding vectors. Verify that the solution is the same in the two diagrams.

4.5 Given the following **bases** in R^2,

$$I = \begin{bmatrix} 1 & 0 \\ 0 & 1 \end{bmatrix}, \quad B_1 = \begin{bmatrix} 1 & 2 \\ 2 & -1 \end{bmatrix}, \quad B_2 = \begin{bmatrix} 3 & -1 \\ 1 & 3 \end{bmatrix},$$

and the vector $\mathbf{b}' = [5, 5]$, find the "measurements" of the vector $\mathbf{b}$ according to each basis. Hint: Graph the dual space.

4.6 The origin of a space is represented by the intersection of the Cartesian axes. In turn, the Cartesian **basis** spanning the space is given by the identity matrix, I:

$$I\mathbf{x} = \mathbf{b}$$

$$\begin{bmatrix} 1 & 0 \\ 0 & 1 \end{bmatrix} \begin{bmatrix} x_1 \\ x_2 \end{bmatrix} = \begin{bmatrix} 3 \\ 2 \end{bmatrix}.$$

Using the foregoing numerical example, verify that the primal and dual geometric representations of the preceding system give rise to the same diagram. Furthermore, verify that the nonnegative solution of the system occurs because the RHS vector $\mathbf{b}$ is included in the cone formed by the Cartesian basic vectors. Hint: Find the solution by constructing the parallelogram whose main diagonal is equal to the RHS vector $\mathbf{b}$.

4.7 Show that two ($n \times 1$) vectors, $\mathbf{c}, \mathbf{x}$, are othogonal if and only if their inner product is equal to zero.

4.8 Show that in a linear function $z = \mathbf{c}'\mathbf{x}$, the $\mathbf{c}$ vector is always orthogonal to the space where the vector $\mathbf{x}$ lies. This means that a vector $\mathbf{c}$ defines (up to a scalar multiplier) a unique hyperplane. Illustrate this notion with a diagram in R^2.

4.9 Using the pivot method, solve the following system of linear equations:

$$A\mathbf{x} = \mathbf{b}$$

$$\begin{bmatrix} 1 & 1 & -1 \\ -2 & -2 & 1 \\ 1 & -1 & 0 \end{bmatrix} \begin{bmatrix} x_1 \\ x_2 \\ x_3 \end{bmatrix} = \begin{bmatrix} 4 \\ 6 \\ 12 \end{bmatrix}.$$

Show all the iterations. Exhibit and verify the inverse matrix.
Select a different path in choosing the pivot elements and recompute the solution. Verify that the two solutions are identical.

4.10 State and explain the criterion for maintaining the feasibility of a basis.

4.11 Using the pivot method, solve the following system of linear equations:

$$Ax = b$$

$$\begin{bmatrix} 0 & 2 & 3 \\ 1 & 0 & 3 \\ 1 & 2 & 0 \end{bmatrix} \begin{bmatrix} x_1 \\ x_2 \\ x_3 \end{bmatrix} = \begin{bmatrix} 5 \\ 4 \\ 3 \end{bmatrix}.$$

Show all the iterations. Exhibit and verify the inverse matrix. Recompute the inverse matrix by multiplying all the transformation matrices in the right order.

4.12 Using the pivot method, solve the following system of linear equations:

$$Ax = b$$

$$\begin{bmatrix} 1 & 2 & 3 \\ 1 & 2 & 2 \\ 1 & 1 & 1 \end{bmatrix} \begin{bmatrix} x_1 \\ x_2 \\ x_3 \end{bmatrix} = \begin{bmatrix} 6 \\ 5 \\ 3 \end{bmatrix}.$$

Show all the iterations. Exhibit and verify the inverse matrix. Recompute the inverse matrix by multiplying all the transformation matrices in the right order.

APPENDIX 4.1: DETERMINANTS AND MINORS

We will recall a few elementary notions of determinants and minors. Given a square matrix

$$A = \begin{bmatrix} a_{11} & a_{12} \\ a_{21} & a_{22} \end{bmatrix},$$

the determinant of A, det A, is a number computed as

$$\det A = |A| = a_{11}a_{22} - a_{12}a_{21}.$$

For a (3×3) matrix A,

$$A = \begin{bmatrix} a_{11} & a_{12} & a_{13} \\ a_{21} & a_{22} & a_{23} \\ a_{31} & a_{32} & a_{33} \end{bmatrix},$$

the determinant must be computed by creating an array where the elements along all the left-to-right diagonals are associated with a positive $(+)$ sign, whereas the elements along the right-to-left diagonals are associated with a negative $(-)$ sign. The array is created by copying the first $(n - 1)$ columns of the A matrix to the right of the nth column.

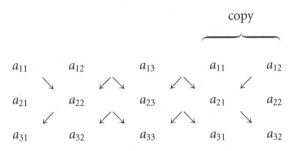

In the preceding array, there are three left-to-right diagonals, each of three elements, and three right-to-left diagonals. Beginning with the elements on the first left-to-right diagonal, multiply the three elements on it and write the resulting product with a positive sign. Then proceed to the second and third left-to-right diagonals. This operation is followed by the product of the elements on the first right-to-left diagonal that will be written with a negative sign. Complete the same operation for the three elements of the second and third right-to-left diagonals in the array. Thus, the determinant of A is computed as

$$\det A = |A| = a_{11}a_{22}a_{33} + a_{12}a_{23}a_{31} + a_{13}a_{21}a_{32}$$

$$- a_{13}a_{22}a_{31} - a_{11}a_{23}a_{32} - a_{12}a_{21}a_{33}.$$

The same procedure can be applied, in principle, to compute the determinant of square matrices of higher order.

A minor of the A matrix is a determinant of the same matrix when k rows and k columns have been eliminated. We distinguish between **principal** minors and **nonprincipal** minors.

Consider the matrix

$$A = \begin{bmatrix} a_{11} & a_{12} & a_{13} \\ a_{21} & a_{22} & a_{23} \\ a_{31} & a_{32} & a_{33} \end{bmatrix}.$$

Principal minors of order 1 are the determinants of all the elements on the main diagonal or $|a_{11}|$, $|a_{22}|$, $|a_{33}|$. **Principal** minors of order 2 are all the determinants of size (2×2) that can be arranged using two elements on the main diagonal of the matrix A, or

$$\begin{vmatrix} a_{11} & a_{12} \\ a_{21} & a_{22} \end{vmatrix}, \begin{vmatrix} a_{11} & a_{13} \\ a_{31} & a_{33} \end{vmatrix}, \begin{vmatrix} a_{22} & a_{23} \\ a_{32} & a_{33} \end{vmatrix}.$$

In this (3×3) case, the only **principal** minor of order 3 is the determinant of the matrix A. A **nonprincipal** minor is, for example, the determinant

$$\begin{vmatrix} a_{12} & a_{13} \\ a_{22} & a_{23} \end{vmatrix}$$

that lies off center from the main diagonal of the A matrix.

APPENDIX 4.2: SOLUTION OF A LINEAR SYSTEM OF EQUATIONS

We return to consider the meaning of a solution of a system of linear equations in order to emphasize that this notion is an essential pillar for understanding the material of this book. A system such as

$$B\mathbf{x} = \mathbf{b}$$

$$13x_1 + 2x_2 = 33$$

$$7x_1 - 5x_2 = 4,$$

for example, **measures** the vector $\mathbf{b}' = (33, \ 4)$ by means of the basis

$$B = \begin{bmatrix} 13 & 2 \\ 7 & -5 \end{bmatrix}.$$

The **measure** is the vector $\mathbf{x}^{*\prime} = (x_1^*, \ x_2^*)$, except that by looking even at the simple (2×2) system just shown it is difficult to discern what the values of the **measures**, (x_1^*, x_2^*), should be. Therefore, the main idea of solving a system of linear equations amounts to **transforming** the original system into a system that is easy to read, such as

$$x_1 \qquad = \bar{x}_1$$

$$x_2 = \bar{x}_2,$$

where $\bar{x}_1, \bar{x}_2$ constitute an appropriate transformation of the RHS coefficients $(33, 4)$. The pivot algorithm discussed in a previous section is an efficient procedure to achieve precisely the desired goal, with elimination of all the variables except one from each column of the original system. The remaining variable appears associated to a normalized (unit) coefficient.

5

Asymmetric and Symmetric
Quadratic Programming

This chapter introduces two important mathematical programming structures: asymmetric quadratic programming and symmetric quadratic programming. Asymmetric quadratic programming is the traditional model,
more generally known and utilized in research. Symmetric quadratic programming is a very interesting model, presented by Cottle, that allows a
better description and articulation of the behavior of economic agents.
In this chapter, however, we introduce both models for a first encounter
with these two important mathematical structures, without reference to
any economic context.

Preliminaries

In order to facilitate the understanding of quadratic programming we state
in this section the definition of quadratic forms and some of their properties.
This section borrows from Theil, Chapter 1.

Definition: *Quadratic Form.* If Q is a matrix of dimensions $(n \times n)$, the
scalar $q = \mathbf{x}' Q \mathbf{x}$ is called a *quadratic form.* More explicitly,

$$q = \mathbf{x}' Q \mathbf{x} = \sum_{i=1}^{n} \sum_{j=1}^{n} q_{ij} x_i x_j. \tag{5.1}$$

Without loss of generality, the matrix Q can be regarded as a symmetric
matrix because the value q of the quadratic form $\mathbf{x}' Q \mathbf{x}$ is invariant when
the matrix Q is replaced by the matrix $\frac{1}{2}(Q + Q')$ because

$$\tfrac{1}{2}\mathbf{x}'(Q + Q')\mathbf{x} = \tfrac{1}{2}\mathbf{x}' Q \mathbf{x} + \tfrac{1}{2}\mathbf{x}' Q'\mathbf{x} = \mathbf{x}' Q \mathbf{x}$$

given the fact that the quantity $\mathbf{x}' Q' \mathbf{x}$ is a scalar and, therefore, it is equal to its transpose $\mathbf{x}' Q\mathbf{x}$.

We now state, without proof, a series of important properties of quadratic forms.

1. A quadratic form $\mathbf{x}' Q\mathbf{x}$, with symmetric matrix Q, is said to be *positive definite* if $\mathbf{x}' Q\mathbf{x} > 0$ for any vector $\mathbf{x} \neq \mathbf{0}$.
2. A quadratic form $\mathbf{x}' Q\mathbf{x}$, with symmetric matrix Q, is said to be *positive semidefinite* if $\mathbf{x}' Q\mathbf{x} \geq 0$ for any vector $\mathbf{x}$.
3. A quadratic form $\mathbf{x}' Q\mathbf{x}$, with symmetric matrix Q, is said to be *negative definite* if $\mathbf{x}' Q\mathbf{x} < 0$ for any vector $\mathbf{x} \neq \mathbf{0}$.
4. A quadratic form $\mathbf{x}' Q\mathbf{x}$, with symmetric matrix Q, is said to be *negative semidefinite* if $\mathbf{x}' Q\mathbf{x} \leq 0$ for any vector $\mathbf{x}$.
5. A quadratic form $\mathbf{x}' Q\mathbf{x}$, with symmetric matrix Q, that is neither positive semidefinite nor negative semidefinite is said to be *indefinite*.
6. If Q is a positive definite matrix, then it is nonsingular. The inverse of Q is also positive definite.
7. A necessary and sufficient condition for the $(n \times n)$ symmetric matrix Q to be *positive definite* is that the **successive** principal minors of the matrix Q be all positive, that is,

$$q_{11} > 0, \quad \begin{vmatrix} q_{11} & q_{12} \\ q_{21} & q_{22} \end{vmatrix} > 0, \ldots \begin{vmatrix} q_{11} & q_{12} & \cdots & q_{1n} \\ q_{21} & q_{22} & \cdots & q_{2n} \\ \cdots & \cdots & \cdots & \cdots \\ q_{n1} & q_{n2} & \cdots & q_{nn} \end{vmatrix} > 0.$$

8. A necessary and sufficient condition for the $(n \times n)$ symmetric matrix Q to be *positive semidefinite* is that **all** the principal minors of any order be nonnegative, that is,

$$q_{11} \geq 0, q_{22} \geq 0, \ldots q_{nn} \geq 0$$

$$\begin{vmatrix} q_{11} & q_{12} \\ q_{21} & q_{22} \end{vmatrix} \geq 0, \begin{vmatrix} q_{11} & q_{13} \\ q_{31} & q_{33} \end{vmatrix} \geq 0, \begin{vmatrix} q_{22} & q_{23} \\ q_{32} & q_{33} \end{vmatrix} \geq 0, \ldots \begin{vmatrix} q_{n-1,n-1} & q_{n-1,n} \\ q_{n,n-1} & q_{nn} \end{vmatrix} \geq 0$$

$$\cdots \quad \cdots \quad \cdots \quad \cdots \quad \cdots \quad \cdots \quad \cdots \quad \cdots \quad \cdots \quad \cdots \quad \cdots \quad \cdots \quad \cdots \quad \cdots$$

$$\begin{vmatrix} q_{11} & q_{12} & \cdots & q_{1n} \\ q_{21} & q_{22} & \cdots & q_{2n} \\ \cdots & \cdots & \cdots & \cdots \\ q_{n1} & q_{n2} & \cdots & q_{nn} \end{vmatrix} \geq 0.$$

9. A necessary and sufficient condition for the $(n \times n)$ symmetric matrix Q to be *negative definite* is that the **successive** principal minors of the matrix Q alternate in sign, that is,

$$q_{11} < 0, \begin{vmatrix} q_{11} & q_{12} \\ q_{21} & q_{22} \end{vmatrix} > 0, \ldots (-1)^n \begin{vmatrix} q_{11} & q_{12} & \cdots & q_{1n} \\ q_{21} & q_{22} & \cdots & q_{2n} \\ \cdots & \cdots & \cdots & \cdots \\ q_{n1} & q_{n2} & \cdots & q_{n,n} \end{vmatrix} > 0.$$

10. A necessary and sufficient condition for the $(n \times n)$ symmetric matrix Q to be *negative semidefinite* is that **all** the principal minors of any order alternate in sign, that is,

$$q_{11} \leq 0, q_{22} \leq 0, \ldots q_{nn} \leq 0$$

$$\begin{vmatrix} q_{11} & q_{12} \\ q_{21} & q_{22} \end{vmatrix} \geq 0, \begin{vmatrix} q_{11} & q_{13} \\ q_{31} & q_{33} \end{vmatrix} \geq 0, \begin{vmatrix} q_{22} & q_{23} \\ q_{32} & q_{33} \end{vmatrix} \geq 0, \ldots \begin{vmatrix} q_{n-1,n-1} & q_{n-1,n} \\ q_{n,n-1} & q_{nn} \end{vmatrix} \geq 0$$

$$\cdots \quad \cdots \quad \cdots \quad \cdots \quad \cdots \quad \cdots \quad \cdots \quad \cdots \quad \cdots \quad \cdots \quad \cdots \quad \cdots \quad \cdots \quad \cdots \quad \cdots$$

$$(-1)^n \begin{vmatrix} q_{11} & q_{12} & \cdots & q_{1n} \\ q_{21} & q_{22} & \cdots & q_{2n} \\ \cdots & \cdots & \cdots & \cdots \\ q_{n1} & q_{n2} & \cdots & q_{nn} \end{vmatrix} \geq 0.$$

11. If a matrix Q is of dimensions $(m \times n)$ and of rank $m < n$, then the matrix QQ' is positive definite.
12. If a matrix Q is of dimensions $(m \times n)$ and of rank r and $r < m < n$, then the matrix QQ' is positive semidefinite.

An alternative criterion for establishing the definiteness of a real symmetric matrix is discussed in Appendix 5.2, based on the notion of characteristic roots.

Asymmetric Quadratic Programming

The traditional (asymmetric) quadratic programming model assumes the following specification:

$$\text{Primal} \qquad \max_{\mathbf{x}} Z = \mathbf{c}'\mathbf{x} - \mathbf{x}'D\mathbf{x} \qquad (5.2)$$

$$\text{subject to} \qquad A\mathbf{x} \leq \mathbf{b}$$

$$\mathbf{x} \geq 0$$

where the real matrix A is of dimensions $(m \times n)$, $m < n$, and the matrix D is a symmetric real square matrix of order n and, furthermore, is positive semidefinite. All the other elements of problem (5.2) are conformable to the two matrices A and D. Problem (5.2) is a nonlinear concave structure because the objective function is a quadratic relation with a quadratic form $\mathbf{x}' D \mathbf{x}$ that is positive semidefinite.

We are interested in deriving the dual specification corresponding to problem (5.2). As discussed in Chapter 3, the dual problem of any nonlinear maximization program is defined as the minimization of the Lagrangean function subject to constraints that are the derivatives of the Lagrangean function with respect to the primal variables.

In the case of problem (5.2), the Lagrangean function is stated as

$$L(\mathbf{x}, \mathbf{y}) = \mathbf{c}'\mathbf{x} - \mathbf{x}' D \mathbf{x} + \mathbf{y}'[\mathbf{b} - A\mathbf{x}] \tag{5.3}$$

where the vector $\mathbf{y}$ is an m-vector of Lagrange multipliers or dual variables. The Karush-Kuhn-Tucker conditions, as discussed in Chapter 3, are necessary and sufficient for this concave problem and can be stated as (the differentiation rules of a quadratic form are discussed in Appendix 5.1)

$$\frac{\partial L}{\partial \mathbf{x}} = \mathbf{c} - 2 D \mathbf{x} - A'\mathbf{y} \leq \mathbf{0} \tag{5.4}$$

$$\mathbf{x}' \frac{\partial L}{\partial \mathbf{x}} = \mathbf{x}'[\mathbf{c} - 2 D \mathbf{x} - A'\mathbf{y}] = 0 \tag{5.5}$$

$$\frac{\partial L}{\partial \mathbf{y}} = \mathbf{b} - A\mathbf{x} \geq \mathbf{0} \tag{5.6}$$

$$\mathbf{y}' \frac{\partial L}{\partial \mathbf{y}} = \mathbf{y}'[\mathbf{b} - A\mathbf{x}] = 0 \tag{5.7}$$

together with the nonnegativity of vectors $\mathbf{x} \geq \mathbf{0}$ and $\mathbf{y} \geq \mathbf{0}$.

Because relations (5.6) represent the primal constraints, KKT conditions (5.4) constitute the constraints of the dual problem. We can use KKT condition (5.5) to simplify the objective function of the dual problem (that is, the Lagrangean function) by recognizing that $\mathbf{x}'\mathbf{c} = 2\mathbf{x}' D \mathbf{x} + \mathbf{x}' A'\mathbf{y}$. Hence,

$$L(\mathbf{x}, \mathbf{y}) = \mathbf{c}'\mathbf{x} - \mathbf{x}' D \mathbf{x} + \mathbf{y}'\mathbf{b} - \mathbf{y}' A\mathbf{x} \tag{5.8}$$

$$= 2\mathbf{x}' D \mathbf{x} + \mathbf{x}' A'\mathbf{y} - \mathbf{x}' D \mathbf{x} + \mathbf{y}'\mathbf{b} - \mathbf{y}' A\mathbf{x}$$

$$= \mathbf{y}'\mathbf{b} + \mathbf{x}' D \mathbf{x}. \tag{5.9}$$

Therefore, the final form of the dual problem corresponding to the primal of the asymmetric quadratic programming problem (5.2) can be stated as

Dual $\min_{x,y} L(x, y) = y'b + x'Dx$ (5.10)

subject to $A'y + 2Dx \geq c$

$$y \geq 0, \quad x \geq 0.$$

The reason why the quadratic programming model (5.2) is called *asymmetric* can now be made clear by comparing the structure of the primal and dual constraints in problems (5.2) and (5.10). First, the primal specification contains only primal variables **x**. This seems to be a truism, but we anticipate here that this statement will acquire its full meaning during the discussion of the symmetric quadratic programming model. Second, the dual problem (5.10) contains both primal and dual variables, **x, y**. Third, the dual constraints of (5.10) contain the matrix of a quadratic form. Primal constraints of (5.2) do not contain a matrix corresponding to a quadratic form.

The Dual of the Least-Squares Problem

A famous quadratic programming problem was presented and discussed by Johann Carl Friedrich Gauss who, in 1801, used a "least-squares" methodology to predict the orbit of Ceres, the then recently discovered asteroid. Ever since, the least-squares (LS) approach has become a popular methodology in statistics, econometrics and any other science. The LS model is a typical quadratic programming problem of the asymmetric kind. Curiously, however, its dual specification has rarely appeared in the literature (Paris).

Borrowing the notation from statistics, the primal specification of the least-squares problem can be stated as

Primal $\min_{\beta,u} SSR(\beta, u) = \frac{1}{2}u'u$ (5.11)

subject to $X\beta + u = y$

where the vector **y** is an N-vector of sample information, typically called observations; the matrix X is a $(N \times K)$ matrix containing given values of "explanatory" variables; the vector β is a $(K \times 1)$ vector of unknown parameters to be estimated; and the vector **u** is a $(N \times 1)$ vector of unknown residuals. We wish to emphasize that, in this section, the meaning of the vector **y** is completely different from the meaning attributed to it throughout this book. In other words, the vector **y** in this section is not a vector of dual variables but a vector of given sample observations. We also wish to point out that vectors β and $\mathbf{u}$ should be regarded as vectors of primal variables. The LS model (5.11) is a convex quadratic programming problem with a quadratic form matrix $Q \equiv I$, the identity matrix.

Using terminology from information theory, the LS problem corresponds to minimizing a function of the sample "noise," as represented by the vector of residuals $\mathbf{u}$, subject to the linear statistical model. The sample information, $\mathbf{y}$, is divided into a "signal," $X\beta$, and a component called "noise," $\mathbf{u}$. The meaning of the function SSR is that of sum of squared residuals.

We are interested in deriving the dual specification of the LS problem (5.11) and in inquiring why statisticians may have no interest in knowing this other "side of the coin." We choose vector $\mathbf{e}$ as a vector of dual variables for the costraints in (5.11). Then, the Lagrangean function of the LS problem (5.11) can be stated as

$$L(\beta, \mathbf{u}, \mathbf{e}) = \tfrac{1}{2}\mathbf{u}'\mathbf{u} + \mathbf{e}'[\mathbf{y} - X\beta - \mathbf{u}]. \tag{5.12}$$

Necessary and sufficient conditions for the LS problem can be stated as

$$\frac{\partial L}{\partial \beta} = -X'\mathbf{e} = 0 \tag{5.13}$$

$$\frac{\partial L}{\partial \mathbf{u}} = \mathbf{u} - \mathbf{e} = 0 \tag{5.14}$$

$$\frac{\partial L}{\partial \mathbf{e}} = \mathbf{y} - X\beta - \mathbf{u} = 0. \tag{5.15}$$

From condition (5.14) it is immediately clear that the dual variables $\mathbf{e}$ of the LS primal constraints are identically equal to the primal variables $\mathbf{u}$ that are regarded as residuals of the LS problem. Using this fact, the dual constraints (5.13) can be stated as $X'\mathbf{u} = 0$, which corresponds to the orthogonality requirement between the estimated residuals and the matrix of "explanatory" variables. Hence, using the information of condition (5.13) and (5.14) in the Lagrangean function (5.12), we can state the dual specification of the LS problem (5.11) as

Dual $$\max_{\mathbf{u}} VSI = \mathbf{y}'\mathbf{u} - \tfrac{1}{2}\mathbf{u}'\mathbf{u} \tag{5.16}$$

subject to $$X'\mathbf{u} = 0.$$

The objective function of the dual LS model, VSI, can be interpreted as the maximization of the value of sample information. Because the vector $\mathbf{u}$ can be given two meanings, that of a vector of residuals and that of a vector of dual variables, the quantity $y'u$ appearing in the objective function (5.16) is interpreted as the gross value of sample information. This gross quantity is netted out of the "cost" of noise, which is given by the quantity $\frac{1}{2}u'u$. The dual variables of the dual constraints in (5.16) are represented by the vector of parameters β. The solution of the dual problem (5.16) guarantees the same values of the vector of parameters β and of the residuals u that are obtained by solving the traditional primal specification (5.11) of the LS problem.

Symmetric Quadratic Programming

The quadratic programming problem (5.2) was characterized as *asymmetric* because the dual constraints contained a positive semidefinite matrix that was absent in the primal constraints. Furthermore, the dual problem contained primal and dual variables x and y, whereas the primal problem contained only primal variables.

A symmetric quadratic programming (SQP) structure, therefore, will require primal and dual variables to appear in the primal problem and primal constraints to contain a positive semidefinite matrix. Such a structure can be stated as

$$\textbf{Primal} \quad \max_{x,y} Z = c'x - x'Dx - y'Ey \qquad (5.17)$$

Dual

Variables

$$\text{subject to} \quad Ax - 2Ey \le b \qquad y \qquad (5.18)$$

$$x \ge 0, \quad y \ge 0$$

where the matrix A is of dimensions $(m \times n)$, $m < n$, the matrix D is symmetric positive semidefinite of order n, the matrix E is symmetric positive semidefinite of order m, and all the other vectors are conformable to matrices A, D, and E. The peculiarity of this SQP problem is that variables y have to be regarded as both primal and dual variables. They are primal variables because they enter the primal constraints. They are dual variables because they assume the role of Lagrange multipliers, as will be demonstrated later. This uncommon assertion should not surprise because vector x, which is regarded as a primal variable in problem (5.2), also assumes a dual variable role in the dual problem (5.10).

The dual specification of the SQP problem [(5.17),(5.18)] is stated as follows:

$$\textbf{Dual} \quad \min_{x,y} R = \mathbf{b'y} + \mathbf{y'} E \mathbf{y} + \mathbf{x'} D \mathbf{x} \tag{5.19}$$

Dual

Variables

$$\text{subject to} \quad A'\mathbf{y} + 2 D \mathbf{x} \geq \mathbf{c} \qquad \mathbf{x} \tag{5.20}$$

$$\mathbf{x} \geq \mathbf{0}, \quad \mathbf{y} \geq \mathbf{0}.$$

In Chapter 3 it was demonstrated that the relation between primal and dual problems is established by means of the Lagrangean function. In other words, the Lagrangean function links the dual pair of programming problems as given in [(5.17), (5.18)] and [(5.19), (5.20)]. To verify this assertion, once again, we will state the Lagrangean function corresponding to problem [(5.17), (5.18)] and, by means of the associated KKT conditions, we derive the dual specification [(5.19), (5.20)].

The relevant Lagrangean function uses the vector variable $\mathbf{y}$ as a vector of Lagrange multipliers associated with the primal constraints (5.18). It is well known that one role of the Lagrange multipliers is to return the primal constraints in the KKT necessary conditions. This is, in fact, what happens. Then, let the Lagrangean function of the SQP problem be specified as

$$L(\mathbf{x}, \mathbf{y}) = \mathbf{c'x} - \mathbf{x'} D \mathbf{x} - \mathbf{y'} E \mathbf{y} + \mathbf{y'} [\mathbf{b} - A\mathbf{x} + 2 E \mathbf{y}]. \tag{5.21}$$

The KKT conditions can be stated as

$$\frac{\partial L}{\partial \mathbf{x}} = \mathbf{c} - 2 D \mathbf{x} - A'\mathbf{y} \leq \mathbf{0} \tag{5.22}$$

$$\mathbf{x'} \frac{\partial L}{\partial \mathbf{x}} = \mathbf{x'} [\mathbf{c} - 2 D \mathbf{x} - A'\mathbf{y}] = 0 \tag{5.23}$$

$$\frac{\partial L}{\partial \mathbf{y}} = -2 E \mathbf{y} + \mathbf{b} - A\mathbf{x} + 4 E \mathbf{y} \geq \mathbf{0}$$

$$= \mathbf{b} - A\mathbf{x} + 2 E \mathbf{y} \geq \mathbf{0} \tag{5.24}$$

$$\mathbf{y'} \frac{\partial L}{\partial \mathbf{y}} = \mathbf{y'} [\mathbf{b} - A\mathbf{x} + 2 E \mathbf{y}] = 0 \tag{5.25}$$

together with the nonnegativity of the $\mathbf{x}$ and $\mathbf{y}$ vectors. KKT condition (5.24) verifies the proper use of the vector $\mathbf{y}$ as a vector of Lagrange multipliers, because the result of the first derivative of the Lagrangean function with respect to $\mathbf{y}$ is indeed the set of primal constraints, as expected. Furthermore, by using the information of KKT condition (5.23) in the Lagrangean function (5.21), the objective function of the dual SQP specification is obtained as stated in the dual problem (5.19).

A Special Case of Self-Duality

On several occasions it was noted that the structure of problems discussed in this chapter is asymmetric. The dual constraints of problem (5.10), for example, contain both dual and primal variables, whereas the primal constraints exhibit only primal variables. In order to acquire an appreciation for symmetric structures, it is of interest to study the following special problem. Let D be a symmetric positive definite matrix. Given the primal

$$\max Z = \mathbf{c}'\mathbf{x} - \mathbf{x}'D\mathbf{x}, \quad \mathbf{x} \geq \mathbf{0} \tag{5.26}$$

the dual problem can be stated as

$$\min R = \mathbf{x}'D\mathbf{x} \tag{5.27}$$

$$\text{subject to} \qquad 2D\mathbf{x} \geq \mathbf{c}$$

$$\mathbf{x} \geq \mathbf{0}.$$

The dual of the dual problem (5.27) can be derived via KKT theory. For this purpose, the Lagrangean function of (5.27) is

$$L(\mathbf{x}, \mathbf{y}) = \mathbf{x}'D\mathbf{x} + \mathbf{y}'(\mathbf{c} - 2D\mathbf{x}) \tag{5.28}$$

where $\mathbf{y}$ is the vector of Lagrange multipliers. The goal of the subsequent analysis is to show that $\mathbf{y} = \mathbf{x}$ and, therefore, that the vector of dual variables is identically equal to a vector of primal variables. This conclusion establishes an important component of a symmetric structure. In this problem, the proof that $\mathbf{y} = \mathbf{x}$ relies crucially on the assumption of positive definiteness of the matrix D.

The relevant KKT conditions corresponding to (5.28) are

$$\frac{\partial L}{\partial \mathbf{x}} = 2D\mathbf{x} - 2D\mathbf{y} \geq \mathbf{0} \tag{5.29}$$

$$\mathbf{x}'\frac{\partial L}{\partial \mathbf{x}} = 2\mathbf{x}'D\mathbf{x} - 2\mathbf{x}'D\mathbf{y} = 0. \tag{5.30}$$

Rearranging (5.30) results in $\mathbf{x}'D(\mathbf{x} - \mathbf{y}) = 0$, and we can conclude that, for $\mathbf{x} \neq \mathbf{0}, \mathbf{y} = \mathbf{x}$ because the D matrix is positive definite. The identity between primal and dual variables characterizes the symmetry of the model. With this knowledge, the KKT condition (5.29) vanishes and the Lagrangean function in (5.28) can be restated as

$$\max L(\mathbf{x}) = \mathbf{x}'D\mathbf{x} + \mathbf{x}'(\mathbf{c} - 2D\mathbf{x}) = \mathbf{c}'\mathbf{x} - \mathbf{x}'D\mathbf{x} \qquad (5.31)$$

establishing the result that, in this case, the dual of the dual is the primal.

Numerical Example: The Dual of the Least-Squares Problem

The statistical estimation of a linear model by the method of least squares is a well-known procedure when the specification is formulated as in problem (5.11). The dual specification of the least-squares method as given in problem (5.16) is virtually unknown. The estimated values of the parameters are given by the Lagrange multipliers of the orthogonal constraints. We present, therefore, a numerical example of the least-squares estimation of a linear model using problem (5.16), which is reproduced here for convenience:

Dual $\qquad\qquad \max_{\mathbf{u}} VSI = \mathbf{y}'\mathbf{u} - \frac{1}{2}\mathbf{u}'\mathbf{u} \qquad (5.16)$

subject to $\qquad\qquad X'\mathbf{u} = \mathbf{0}.$

The relevant data are generated as follows:

$X_{i1} = 1$, a column representing the intercept

$X_{i2} = Uniform(2, 6)$, a column generated by a uniform distribution

$X_{i3} = Normal(10, 0.6)$, a column generated by a normal distribution

$X_{i4} = Uniform(5, 10)$, a column generated by a uniform distribution

$u_i = Normal(0, 1.1)$, a column of errors from a normal distribution

Then, the linear statistical model is assembled as

$$y_i = 2X_{i1} + 0.4X_{i2} - 0.7X_{i3} + 0.9X_{i4} + u_i.$$

A sample of 20 observations is presented in Table 5.1.

The solution of problem (5.16) produces an estimate of the residual vector of errors $\mathbf{u}$ and of the vector of parameters $\boldsymbol{\beta}$ of the linear model in (5.11) as the Lagrange multipliers of the orthogonality constraints in (5.16). The estimates of the true $\boldsymbol{\beta}$ coefficients used to generate the

Table 5.1. *The Sample Information for Model (5.16)*

Obs	y_i	X_{i1}	X_{i2}	X_{i3}	X_{i4}
1	4.03831	1.00	2.68699	9.22060	6.69275
2	5.03214	1.00	5.37307	9.17472	5.91050
3	2.57907	1.00	4.20150	10.19181	8.22864
4	1.05324	1.00	3.20455	10.71221	7.80373
5	3.82307	1.00	3.16885	9.30807	8.84981
6	0.81853	1.00	2.89621	10.42601	6.48903
7	2.80965	1.00	3.39932	10.61039	8.30553
8	6.78639	1.00	5.42508	9.56556	8.77911
9	3.23158	1.00	2.26845	9.40036	8.13724
10	1.59029	1.00	4.00084	10.00367	6.41932
11	2.78166	1.00	5.99247	9.40324	5.43212
12	1.93314	1.00	4.31493	9.45584	5.51257
13	2.55654	1.00	5.96453	10.39764	8.20626
14	3.31243	1.00	5.04900	10.94259	7.72655
15	−0.62552	1.00	2.52277	11.32800	5.15762
16	4.82745	1.00	4.55888	9.62513	8.96180
17	−0.27154	1.00	2.63807	9.86910	5.36384
18	0.54783	1.00	3.00032	9.42273	5.87831
19	3.71888	1.00	4.67571	9.93544	7.62816
20	4.64433	1.00	3.74143	9.84244	8.75104

vector of observations **y** are given next for an increasing number of observations:

N. Obs	$\beta_1 = 2$	$\beta_2 = 0.4$	$\beta_3 = -0.7$	$\beta_4 = 0.9$
20	8.1609	0.6042	−1.3769	0.8178
500	2.7234	0.4074	−0.7254	0.8286
1000	2.4550	0.4080	−0.7350	0.8892
10000	2.0238	0.3904	−0.6978	0.8991

The values of the estimated coefficients reported here illustrate the tendency toward consistency of the estimator represented by the dual model (5.16) of the traditional least-squares model (5.11).

GAMS Command File: Least-Squares Example

The following command GAMS file solves the numerical problem presented in the least-squares example. Asterisks in column 1 relate to comments. A useful tutorial and a user's manual can be found at www.gams.com.

```
$title the dual of the least-squares method
*
$offsymlist offsymxref
    option iterlim = 100000
    option reslim = 200000
    option nlp = conopt3
    option decimals = 7 ;
*
    sets i observations / 1*10000 /
    k parameters / 1*4 /
*
* declaration of parameters for the montecarlo
* experiment
*
    parameter x(i,k), y(i), e(i) ;
    x(i,"1") = 1 ;
    x(i,"2") = uniform(2,6) ;
    x(i,"3") = normal(10,0.6) ;
    x(i,"4") = uniform(5,10) ;
    e(i) = normal(0, 1.1) ;
    y(i) = 2*x(i,"1") + 0.4*x(i,"2") -0.7*x(i,"3") +
      0.9*x(i,"4") + e(i) ;
*
    display y, x, e ;
*
* specification of the dual of the least-squares
* problem
*
    variables
    vsi  value of sample information
    u(i)    residuals ;
*
    equations
    objeq   objective function
    orthoeq(k)    orthogonality constraints ;
*
    objeq..   vsi =e= sum(i,y(i)*u(i)) -
      sum(i,sqr(u(i)) )/2 ;
    orthoeq(k)..    sum(i, x(i,k)*u(i)) =e= 0 ;
*
* name and definition of the least-squares model
*
    model leastsquares / objeq, orthoeq / ;
```

```
      solve leastsquares using nlp maximizing vsi ;
*
      display vsi.l, u.l, orthoeq.m ;
```

Exercises

5.1 Discuss criteria based on successive and all principal minors for determining whether a $(n \times n)$ symmetric matrix A is
   (a) positive definite
   (b) positive semidefinite
   (c) negative definite
   (d) negative semidefinite.

5.2 By completing the square on x_2, justify your assertions in question (5.1) using the following quadratic form:

$$A(x_1, x_2) = ax_1^2 + 2bx_1x_2 + cx_2^2 = [x_1 \ x_2] \begin{bmatrix} a & b \\ b & c \end{bmatrix} \begin{bmatrix} x_1 \\ x_2 \end{bmatrix} = x'Ax.$$

5.3 Verify the definiteness of the following two matrices:

$$Q = \begin{bmatrix} 13 & -4 & 3 \\ -4 & 5 & -2 \\ 3 & -2 & 1 \end{bmatrix}, \qquad R = \begin{bmatrix} 13 & -5 & 1 \\ -3 & 5 & -3 \\ 5 & -1 & 1 \end{bmatrix}.$$

5.4 The matrix

$$Q = \begin{bmatrix} a & h \\ k & b \end{bmatrix}$$

with $h \neq k$ is clearly asymmetric. Show that the conditions for its definiteness are
   (a) positive definite: $a > 0$, $4ab - (h+k)^2 > 0$
   (b) negative definite: $a < 0$, $4ab - (h+k)^2 > 0$
   (c) positive semidefinite: $a \geq 0$, $b \geq 0$, $4ab - (h+k)^2 \geq 0$
   (d) negative semidefinite: $a \leq 0$, $b \leq 0$, $4ab - (h+k)^2 \geq 0$.

5.5 Let Q be an asymmetric matrix. Show that

$$\frac{x'[Q + Q']x}{2} = x'Qx \qquad \text{for all vectors x.}$$

Hence, it is possible to determine the definiteness of an asymmetric quadratic form by testing the definiteness of the matrix

$$\frac{[Q + Q']}{2}$$

which is symmetric.

5.6 Using the characteristic root criterion, verify the definiteness of the following symmetric matrix:

$$A = \begin{bmatrix} 4 & -1 \\ -1 & -1 \end{bmatrix}.$$

Hint: Use the quadratic formula in Appendix 5.2.

5.7 Using the GAMS command file presented in Appendix 5.2, determine the definiteness of the following symmetric matrix:

$$A = \begin{bmatrix} 13 & -4 & 3 & 6 \\ -4 & 5 & -2 & -4 \\ 3 & -2 & 1 & 2 \\ 6 & -4 & 2 & 4 \end{bmatrix}.$$

5.8 You are in a remote location and need to solve an ordinary least-squares problem with a large number of explanatory variables. You have access only to a computer program for solving linear programming problems. Would you be able to solve your least-squares problem? Explain. (Your problem is to estimate the vector of parameters $\boldsymbol{\beta}$ and the vector of residuals $\mathbf{u}$ in the following statistical linear model:

$$\mathbf{y} = X\boldsymbol{\beta} + \mathbf{u}$$

where X is a $(N \times K)$ matrix of predetermined regressors, $\boldsymbol{\beta}$ is a $(K \times 1)$ vector of unknown coefficients, $\mathbf{y}$ is a $(N \times 1)$ vector of realizations of the random variable Y, and $\mathbf{u}$ is a vector of random errors with zero mean and fixed variance.

5.9 Show that the following structure, which looks like a symmetric programming model, is not, in fact, a viable structure:

$$\max Z = \mathbf{c}'\mathbf{x} - \mathbf{x}'D\mathbf{x} - \mathbf{y}'E\mathbf{y}$$

subject to $\qquad\qquad A\mathbf{x} - E\mathbf{y} \leq \mathbf{b}$

with $\mathbf{x} \geq \mathbf{0}$, $\mathbf{y} \geq \mathbf{0}$. In other words, show that the foregoing specification is not a symmetric quadratic programming model. Hint: Define the corresponding Lagrangean function using the vector $\mathbf{y}$ as a vector of Lagrange multipliers; derive and comment on the implied KKT conditions. Explain the reason why the foregoing structure is not what it looks like. What is the requirement for turning it into a proper SQP model?

5.10 Given the following primal problem:

$$\min R = \mathbf{b}'\mathbf{y} + \mathbf{y}'E\mathbf{y}/2$$

subject to $\qquad\qquad A'\mathbf{y} \geq \mathbf{c}, \quad \mathbf{y} \geq \mathbf{0}$

where E is a symmetric positive semidefinite matrix, derive the dual problem (using the vector variable **x** as a vector of dual variables).

5.11 Given the following primal problem

$$\min R = \mathbf{b}_1'\mathbf{y}_1 + \mathbf{y}_1'E_1\mathbf{y}_1/2 + \mathbf{b}_2'\mathbf{y}_2$$

subject to
$$A_1'\mathbf{y}_1 \geq \mathbf{c}_1, \quad \mathbf{y}_1 \geq 0$$

$$A_2'\mathbf{y}_2 = \mathbf{c}_2, \quad \mathbf{y}_2 \geq 0$$

where E_1 is a symmetric positive semidefinite matrix, derive the dual problem.

APPENDIX 5.1: DIFFERENTIATION OF LINEAR AND QUADRATIC FORMS

Linear function: $z = c_1 x_1 + c_2 x_2 + \cdots + c_n x_n = \mathbf{c}'\mathbf{x}$, where **c** is a vector of fixed coefficients and **x** is a vector of variables.

Derivation of a linear function:

$$\frac{\partial z}{\partial x_1} = c_1$$
$$\frac{\partial z}{\partial x_2} = c_2 \quad \rightarrow \quad \begin{bmatrix} \dfrac{\partial z}{\partial x_1} \\[1mm] \dfrac{\partial z}{\partial x_2} \\[1mm] \vdots \\[1mm] \dfrac{\partial z}{\partial x_n} \end{bmatrix} = \begin{bmatrix} c_1 \\ c_2 \\ \vdots \\ c_n \end{bmatrix} \quad \rightarrow \quad \frac{\partial z}{\partial \mathbf{x}} = \mathbf{c}.$$
$$\vdots$$
$$\frac{\partial z}{\partial x_n} = c_n$$

Hence, the derivation of a linear function, written as $z = \mathbf{c}'\mathbf{x}$, with respect to vector **x**, produces the transposition of the vector **c**. The rules of vector differentiation must obtain conformable expressions.

Quadratic form: $z = c_1 x_1 + c_2 x_2 + b_{11} x_1^2 + b_{12} x_1 x_2 + b_{21} x_1 x_2 + b_{22} x_2^2$ can be written in matrix notation as

$$z = (c_1 \ c_2) \begin{pmatrix} x_1 \\ x_2 \end{pmatrix} + (x_1 \ x_2) \begin{bmatrix} b_{11} & b_{12} \\ b_{21} & b_{22} \end{bmatrix} \begin{pmatrix} x_1 \\ x_2 \end{pmatrix}$$

or

$$z = \mathbf{c}'\mathbf{x} + \mathbf{x}'Q\mathbf{x}$$

with obvious correspondence between components of the two specifications.

Derivation of a quadratic form:

$$\frac{\partial z}{\partial x_1} = c_1 + (b_{11} + b_{11})x_1 + b_{12}x_2 + b_{21}x_2$$

$$\frac{\partial z}{\partial x_2} = c_2 + b_{12}x_1 + b_{21}x_1 + (b_{22} + b_{22})x_2.$$

These equations can be rearranged as

$$\begin{bmatrix} \dfrac{\partial z}{\partial x_1} \\ \dfrac{\partial z}{\partial x_2} \end{bmatrix} = \begin{bmatrix} c_1 \\ c_2 \end{bmatrix} + \begin{bmatrix} b_{11} & b_{12} \\ b_{21} & b_{22} \end{bmatrix} \begin{bmatrix} x_1 \\ x_2 \end{bmatrix} + \begin{bmatrix} b_{11} & b_{21} \\ b_{12} & b_{22} \end{bmatrix} \begin{bmatrix} x_1 \\ x_2 \end{bmatrix}$$

or

$$\frac{\partial z}{\partial \mathbf{x}} = \mathbf{c} + Q\mathbf{x} + Q'\mathbf{x} = \mathbf{c} + (Q + Q')\mathbf{x}.$$

When the matrix Q is symmetric, $Q = Q'$, that is, the Q matrix is equal to its transpose Q', and the derivative of the quadratic form simplifies to

$$\frac{\partial z}{\partial \mathbf{x}} = \mathbf{c} + 2Q\mathbf{x}.$$

APPENDIX 5.2: EIGENVALUES AND EIGENVECTORS

A way to characterize the definiteness of a quadratic form that is an alternative criterion to the test based on minors, as discussed in a previous section, consists in specifying and studying the characteristic equation of a matrix. Consider a symmetric ($n \times n$) matrix A and the relation

$$A\mathbf{x} = \lambda\mathbf{x} \qquad \text{with } \mathbf{x}'\mathbf{x} = 1$$

where λ is a scalar symbol for the "roots" of the foregoing system, which implies unit-length vectors $\mathbf{x}$ by virtue of the constraint $\mathbf{x}'\mathbf{x} = 1$. We can write

$$(A - \lambda I)\mathbf{x} = \mathbf{0},$$

which means that the columns of the matrix $(A - \lambda I)$ are linearly dependent because $\mathbf{x} \neq \mathbf{0}$, as it must be for $\mathbf{x}'\mathbf{x} = 1$. Therefore, the determinant of the matrix $(A - \lambda I)$ is equal to zero, that is,

$$|A - \lambda I| = 0.$$

The determinant relation is called the characteristic equation of the matrix A, λ is a latent root (characteristic root, eigenvalue), and $\mathbf{x}$ is a characteristic vector (eigenvector, latent vector) of the matrix A.

For a (2×2) example, we write:

$$\left| \begin{bmatrix} a_{11} & a_{12} \\ a_{21} & a_{22} \end{bmatrix} - \lambda \begin{bmatrix} 1 & 0 \\ 0 & 1 \end{bmatrix} \right| = \begin{vmatrix} (a_{11} - \lambda) & a_{12} \\ a_{21} & (a_{22} - \lambda) \end{vmatrix} = 0$$

$$(a_{11} - \lambda)(a_{22} - \lambda) - a_{12}a_{21} = \lambda^2 - (a_{11} + a_{22})\lambda + a_{11}a_{22} - a_{12}a_{21} = 0$$

which represents a quadratic equation in λ with two solutions, λ_1, λ_2.

Recall that for a generic quadratic equation such as $ax^2 + bx + c = 0$, the solution formula is stated as

$$x = \frac{-b \pm \sqrt{b^2 - 4ac}}{2a}.$$

Hence, by letting $a = 1$, $b = -(a_{11} + a_{22})$ and $c = a_{11}a_{22} - a_{12}a_{21}$,

$$\lambda_1, \lambda_2 = \frac{(a_{11} + a_{22}) \pm \sqrt{(a_{11} + a_{22})^2 - 4(a_{11}a_{22} - a_{12}a_{21})}}{2}$$

$$= \tfrac{1}{2}(a_{11} + a_{22}) \pm \tfrac{1}{2}\sqrt{a_{11}^2 + a_{22}^2 + 2a_{11}a_{22} - 4a_{11}a_{22} + 4a_{12}a_{21}}$$

$$= \tfrac{1}{2}(a_{11} + a_{22}) \pm \tfrac{1}{2}\sqrt{(a_{11} - a_{22})^2 + 4a_{12}a_{21}}.$$

We now state criteria based on characteristic roots for testing the definiteness of a symmetric matrix A.

(a) Given a symmetric $(n \times n)$ matrix A, the quadratic form $\mathbf{x}'A\mathbf{x}$ is positive definite if and only if all the n characteristic roots (eigenvalues, latent roots) are positive and distinct.

(b) Given a symmetric $(n \times n)$ matrix A, the quadratic form $\mathbf{x}'A\mathbf{x}$ is positive semidefinite if and only if all the n characteristic roots (eigenvalues, latent roots) are nonnegative.

(c) Given a symmetric $(n \times n)$ matrix A, the quadratic form $\mathbf{x}'A\mathbf{x}$ is negative definite if and only if all the n characteristic roots (eigenvalues, latent roots) are negative and distinct.

(d) Given a symmetric $(n \times n)$ matrix A, the quadratic form $\mathbf{x}'A\mathbf{x}$ is negative semidefinite if and only if all the n characteristic roots (eigenvalues, latent roots) are nonpositive.

(e) Given a symmetric $(n \times n)$ matrix A, if some characteristic roots are positive and some are negative, the quadratic form $\mathbf{x}'A\mathbf{x}$ is indefinite.

The characteristic roots of a real $(n \times n)$ matrix A may not be real numbers, as they may be complex numbers. However, the characteristic roots of a real symmetric matrix are real numbers.

The number of nonzero roots of a symmetric matrix A is equal to the rank of A.

The computation of the eigenvalues for an $(n \times n)$ symmetric matrix A takes advantage of the fact that a symmetric matrix can be decomposed by means of an orthonormal matrix P in the following way:

$$A = P \Lambda P'$$

where P is an orthonormal matrix by virtue of the fact that $P P' = I$. The matrix Λ is a diagonal matrix of eigenvalues. The matrix P is nonsingular because $P P' = I$ and, therefore, the matrix A can be diagonalized by pre- and postmultiplying it by the inverse of P, that is,

$$P^{-1} A (P')^{-1} = \Lambda.$$

The following GAMS command file suggests an easy way to compute the eigenvalues of a symmetric matrix of any order.

GAMS Command File for Computing the Eigenvalues of an $(n \times n)$ Symmetric Matrix

```
$title general algorithm for eigenvalue problems of
* symmetric matrices
*
$offsymlist offsymxref
    option limrow = 0
    option limcol = 0
    option iterlim = 15000
    option reslim = 10000
    option nlp = conopt3
    option decimals = 7 ;
*
    sets j rows-columns / 1,2,3,4 /
    alias(j,k,kk,jj,n)
*
    parameter flag(j) ;
    flag(j) = ord(j) ;
*
```

```
    table a(j,k)

            1      2      3      4
      1     5     -2     -4     -4
      2    -2      4      2      3
      3    -4      2      7      6
      4    -4      3      6      1
*
    parameter ident(j,k)   identity matrix ;
    ident(j,k) = 0. ;
    ident(j,k)$(ord(j) eq ord(k) ) = 1. ;
*
* setup of the eigenvalue algorithm
*
    variables
    eigenobj   auxiliary objective function
    p(j,k)    orthonormal matrix
    el(j,k)    eigenvalue matrix ;
*
* if one knows a priori that the matrix a(j,k) is at
* least positive semidefinite
* it is convenient to declare (eliminate asterisk)
* positive variable el ;
*
    equations
    eigobjeq   objective function equation
    ae(j,k)    matrix equation
    ortho(j,k)   orthonormal conditions;
*
    ae(j,k)..    a(j,k) =e= sum(jj, p(j,jj)*sum(kk,
               el(jj,kk)* p(k,kk))) ;
    ortho(j,k)..    sum(jj, p(j,jj)*p(k,jj) )
                  =e= ident(j,k) ;
    eigobjeq..    eigenobj =e= sum((j,k),
                  sqr (el(j,k) ) );
*
* name and definition of the problem
*
    model eigen /ae, eigobjeq, ortho /;
*
* initial values
*
    el.l(j,k)$(flag(j) eq flag(k) ) = 1. ;
```

```
    el.fx(j,k)$(flag(j) ne flag(k) ) = 0. ;
    p.l(j,k) = 1. ;
*
    solve eigen using nlp minimizing eigenobj ;
*
    parameter condnumb   condition number of the a(j,k)
      matrix
    maxeigen   maximum eigenvalue
    mineigen   minimum eigenvalue ;
    maxeigen = smax(j, el.l(j,j) ) ;
    mineigen = smin(j, el.l(j,j) ) ;
*
  condnumb$mineigen = sqrt( abs( maxeigen / mineigen) );
*
    display el.l, p.l , condnumb ;
```

The solution of the eigenvalue problem defined in the foregoing GAMS command file has produced the following eigenvalues:
(15.4244047, 3.0000000, 1.8444827, −3.2688873). Hence, the matrix
shown in the GAMS command file is indefinite because three characteristic roots are positive and one is negative.

APPENDIX 5.3: INTEGRABILITY CONDITIONS

Many programming problems discussed in this book exhibit an objective
function that is nonlinear and differentiable and whose derivatives constitute a component of the KKT conditions. Systems of demand and supply
functions are often implied by these KKT conditions. Therefore, empirical
applications leading to the specification of a programming model require
the integration of a system of differential equations (often representing
either demand or supply relations) in order to define the desired objective
function. This reverse problem is called the "integrability problem" whose
solution requires "integrability conditions." In economics, this problem
was first discussed by Antonelli, in 1886, and has received attention by a
long list of distinguished economists. Silberberg (page 378) and Mas-Collel,
Winston and Green (page 79) provide a clear discussion of the integrability
problem.

For the purpose of this book, we summarize here the main result of the
integrability conditions for a system of at least three differential equations
regarded either as a system of demand or supply functions: the matrix of

quantity (price) slopes must be symmetric. To motivate this result, it is sufficient to start with an objective function that is twice differentiable. The Hessian matrix of such a function is symmetric. Hence, the reverse problem of integrating a system of at least three differential equations starting from relations that contain a matrix of second derivatives of the overall function requires that such a matrix be symmetric.

If that matrix is not symmetric, the desired integral does not exist and, therefore, it will not be possible to define an objective function that is consistent with the problem's information and data. Yet, the empirical problem at hand may make perfect sense, as in the case of a system of Marshallian demand functions whose quantity (price) slopes are not required to be symmetric by any theoretical consideration. This is the main reason for defining and using the structure of the equilibrium problem that does not require the specification of an objective function to be either maximized or minimized.

To exemplify, let us reconsider the asymmetric quadratic programming problem (5.2), which is reproduced here for convenience:

$$\textbf{Primal} \qquad\qquad \max_{\textbf{x}} Z = \textbf{c}'\textbf{x} - \textbf{x}'D\textbf{x} \qquad\qquad (5.2)$$

$$\text{subject to} \qquad\qquad A\textbf{x} \le \textbf{b}$$

$$\textbf{x} \ge \textbf{0}.$$

Assuming, now, that the matrix D is asymmetric, the first derivative of the objective function will result in a system of differential equations such as

$$\frac{\partial Z}{\partial \textbf{x}} = \textbf{c} - (D + D')\textbf{x}$$

where the matrix $(D + D')$ is symmetric and, in fact, it is the Hessian of the Z function.

We are now interested in the reciprocal problem that consists in starting with the system of first derivatives of the Z function and recovering the original function itself. For notational convenience, let the $(D + D')$ matrix be replaced with a matrix $2Q = (D + D')$, where Q is symmetric. Thus, the integral of the system of differential equations has the following solution:

$$\int_0^{\textbf{x}^*} (\textbf{c} - 2Q\textbf{x})' d\textbf{x} = \textbf{c}'\textbf{x}^* - \textbf{x}^{*'}Q\textbf{x}^* = \textbf{c}'\textbf{x}^* - \textbf{x}^{*'}\left[\frac{(D+D')}{2}\right]\textbf{x}^*$$

and using the equivalence of the quadratic forms

$$\textbf{x}'D\textbf{x} = \textbf{x}'\left[\frac{(D+D')}{2}\right]\textbf{x}$$

we can finally write

$$\int_0^{\mathbf{x}^*} (\mathbf{c} - (D + D')\mathbf{x})' d\mathbf{x} = \mathbf{c}'\mathbf{x}^* - \mathbf{x}^{*'} D\mathbf{x}^*$$

thus recovering the original Z function. Notice, therefore, that the integral was defined and its solution was possible only because we used a symmetric matrix as part of the integrand.

Hence, if we were given an empirical system of at least three relations (estimated by an econometrician, for example) such as

$$\mathbf{p} = \mathbf{c} - D\mathbf{x}$$

where the matrix D is asymmetric, and we were to regard it as a system of differential functions, it would be impossible to state a consistent integral because the matrix D is asymmetric. The integral simply does not exist. In conclusion, it is possible to start from an objective function that contains an asymmetric quadratic form matrix, but it is not possible to start from a system of relations that contains an asymmetric matrix and recover a consistent and meaningful objective function.

References

Antonelli, G. B. (1886). *Sulla teoria matematica della economia politica, On the Mathematical Theory of Political Economy*, translated by Chipman, J. S., and Kitman, A. P., in Chipman, J. S., Hurwicz, L., Richter, M. K., and Sonnenschein, H. F. (eds.), *Preferences, Utility, and Demand: A Minnesota Symposium* (New York: Harcourt Brace Jovanovich), Chapter 16, pp. 332–64.

Cottle, R. W. (1963). "Symmetric Dual Quadratic Programs," *Quarterly of Applied Mathematics*, 21, 237–43.

Mas-Colell, A., Winston, M., and Green, J. R. (1995). *Microeconomic Theory* (New York: Oxford University Press).

Paris, Q. (1980). "Il metodo dei minimi quadrati e il suo problema duale," *Statistica*, 40, 117–21.

Silberberg, E. (1990). *The Structure of Economics, A Mathematical Analysis* (New York: MacGraw-Hill).

Theil, H. (1971). *Principles of Econometrics* (New York: Wiley).

6

Linear Complementarity Problem

The discussion of all the programming models presented in previous chapters has indicated that the solution of such models can be found by solving a system of linear and nonlinear equations that are generated by the first-order necessary conditions of a Lagrangean function. In other words, to solve a large class of mathematical programming problems, it is necessary to solve the corresponding KKT conditions.

It turns out that the KKT conditions for all linear and quadratic programming models can be regarded as special cases of a general class of mathematical programming structures called the Linear Complementarity Problem (LCP). This unifying approach offers the advantage of a better understanding of the structure of mathematical programming models. Furthermore, it introduces the simplest and most elegant algorithm for solving a wide class of problems. Finally, the LC specification admits problems that cannot be specified as a dual pair of optimization problems, that is, they cannot be specified with an explicit objective function that ought to be either maximized or minimized. These problems are called *equilibrium* problems. Hence, the Linear Complementarity Problem is a mathematical programming structure of considerable generality. It encompasses as special cases a large number of economic problems. A nonexhaustive list of these problems will be given further on.

The LC problem is defined as follows: given a square matrix M of order K and a vector $\mathbf{q}$, find a vector $\mathbf{z} \geq \mathbf{0}$ such that

$$M\mathbf{z} + \mathbf{q} \geq \mathbf{0} \qquad \text{linearity} \qquad (6.1)$$

$$\mathbf{z}' M\mathbf{z} + \mathbf{z}'\mathbf{q} = 0 \qquad \text{complementarity.} \qquad (6.2)$$

The same LC problem is equivalently stated as: find vectors $\mathbf{z} \geq \mathbf{0}$ and $\mathbf{w} \geq \mathbf{0}$ such that

$$Mz + q = w \qquad \text{linearity} \qquad (6.3)$$

$$\mathbf{w}'\mathbf{z} = 0 \qquad \text{complementarity.} \qquad (6.4)$$

The vector $\mathbf{w}$ is interpreted as a vector of slack variables. The first system of equations in both (6.1) and (6.3) characterizes the linearity of the LC problem, whereas the second equation [either (6.2) or (6.4)] specifies its complementarity property: because the vectors of unknown variables must be nonnegative, $\mathbf{z} \geq \mathbf{0}$ and $\mathbf{w} \geq \mathbf{0}$, either the variable w_k or its complement z_k must be equal to zero, for $k = 1, \ldots, K$, according to relation (6.4). This is the meaning of complementarity.

In order to justify the proposition about the generality of the LCP structure, it is sufficient to anticipate that it represents the equilibrium specification of all the economic problems that can be stated in terms of linear demand and supply functions. This class includes models that can be specified as a dual pair of (max/min) primal and dual formulations as well as problems that cannot be decoupled into a pair of optimization structures. Two examples of such models are the perfectly discriminating monopolist facing output demand functions with asymmetric price/quantity slopes and the risk-averse entrepreneur operating in an economic environment with stochastic prices and limiting inputs admitting a nonzero covariance between prices and input quantities. Furthermore, the LCP includes the two-person non-zero-sum game and other interesting bilinear problems.

The importance of the LC problem for interpreting economic theory cannot be overemphasized. Although many economic problems are introduced and explained to students as if they were to require the maximization or minimization of an objective function subject to constraints, in reality economic analysis rests its foundation on the specification of quantity and price equilibrium conditions. The presence of explicit objective functions is not strictly necessary for justifying the price and quantity equilibrium conditions on economic grounds. To be specific, the quantity equilibrium conditions can be stated for any commodity as

$$\text{demand} \leq \text{supply}$$

whereas the "price" equilibrium conditions are the familiar

$$\text{marginal cost} \geq \text{marginal revenue.}$$

In the short run, the marginal cost is a function of the output supply, whereas marginal revenue is a function of the market demand for goods. In a competitive environment, the "price" equilibrium conditions are stated in terms of price functions rather than marginal revenues, but their structure and meaning remain unchanged.

Associated with these equilibrium relations there exist the corresponding "value" conditions stated as

total cost of input demand = total value of supply + producer surplus

and

total input cost + consumer surplus = total revenue.

A large body of economic theory is contained in these four sets of relations. In some problems, therefore, we can dispense with an explicit objective function, as in the cases mentioned earlier. However, using the primal and dual solutions obtained by solving the four sets of equilibrium and complementary relations discussed previously, it is possible to reconstruct the implied level of total revenue plus profit and total cost. The conclusion is that when the technology and the demand and supply functions are linear, the LC problem constitutes the most encompassing economic structure. Learning how to solve an LC problem, therefore, is equivalent to know how to solve all the economic problems that are special cases of it.

The Complementary Pivot Algorithm

The procedure for solving an LC problem discussed in this chapter is called the *complementary pivot* algorithm and was developed by Lemke and Howson in 1964. It is the simplest and most elegant of all solution methods, a sufficient reason for studying it.

The complementary pivot algorithm can solve a large class of LC problems. In this chapter, however, we assume that the M matrix is positive semidefinite. All the programming structures discussed in previous chapters lead to such a matrix. For the class of positive semidefinite M-matrices, Lemke's complementary pivot algorithm is guaranteed to find a solution, if one exists.

The ideas underlying the complementary pivot algorithm will be introduced using a numerical example. Suppose we are given the following asymmetric quadratic programming problem:

$$\text{maximize } Z = c'x - x'Dx \tag{6.5}$$

$$\text{subject to} \qquad Ax \leq b, \qquad x \geq 0$$

where A is a matrix of dimensions $(m \times n)$, the matrix D is a symmetric positive semidefinite matrix of order n, and all the other vectors are conformable to the given matrices. In this numerical example, the given parameter values are $\mathbf{c}' = [4, 3]$, $A = [1, 2]$, $\mathbf{b} = 4$ and $D = \begin{bmatrix} 2 & 1 \\ 1 & 0 \end{bmatrix}$.

The KKT conditions corresponding to problem (6.5) are

$$A\mathbf{x} \leq \mathbf{b} \tag{6.6}$$

$$A'\mathbf{y} + 2D\mathbf{x} \geq \mathbf{c} \tag{6.7}$$

$$\mathbf{y}' A\mathbf{x} = \mathbf{y}'\mathbf{b} \tag{6.8}$$

$$\mathbf{x}' A'\mathbf{y} + 2\mathbf{x}' D\mathbf{x} = \mathbf{x}'\mathbf{c}. \tag{6.9}$$

Notice that, by introducing nonnegative slack vectors $\mathbf{u}$ and $\mathbf{v}$ into the systems of inequality constraints (6.6) and (6.7), the KKT conditions can be equivalently stated as

$$\mathbf{u} = \mathbf{b} - A\mathbf{x} \tag{6.10}$$

$$\mathbf{v} = -\mathbf{c} + A'\mathbf{y} + 2D\mathbf{x} \tag{6.11}$$

$$\mathbf{y}'\mathbf{u} = 0 \tag{6.12}$$

$$\mathbf{x}'\mathbf{v} = 0. \tag{6.13}$$

Hence, the M matrix and the vectors $\mathbf{q}$, $\mathbf{z}$, and $\mathbf{w}$ of the LC problem corresponding to the KKT conditions of the asymmetric quadratic programming (6.5) can be stated as

$$M = \begin{bmatrix} 2D & A' \\ -A & 0 \end{bmatrix} = \begin{bmatrix} 4 & 2 & 1 \\ 2 & 0 & 2 \\ -1 & -2 & 0 \end{bmatrix}, \quad \mathbf{q} = \begin{bmatrix} -\mathbf{c} \\ \mathbf{b} \end{bmatrix} = \begin{bmatrix} -4 \\ -3 \\ 4 \end{bmatrix},$$

$$\mathbf{z} = \begin{bmatrix} \mathbf{x} \\ \mathbf{y} \end{bmatrix}, \quad \mathbf{w} = \begin{bmatrix} \mathbf{v} \\ \mathbf{u} \end{bmatrix}.$$

Let us closely examine the structure and the requirements of the LC problem. We begin by noticing that the complementarity condition of (6.4) can be spelled out more explicitly as

$$\mathbf{w}'\mathbf{z} = w_1 z_1 + w_2 z_2 + \cdots + w_{n+m} z_{n+m} = 0$$

where n and m are the numbers of primal and dual variables in the quadratic program, respectively. Because the w and z variables are required to be nonnegative, the complementarity condition implies that each product $w_k z_k = 0$ for all $k = 1, \ldots, K$, where $K = n + m$. Hence, either w_k or z_k must be equal to zero in any solution of the LC problem.

The second observation is related to the nonnegativity requirement of the solution. If vector $\mathbf{q} \geq \mathbf{0}$, a trivial solution of the LC problem is readily available as $\mathbf{w} = \mathbf{q}$ and $\mathbf{z} = \mathbf{0}$. It is obvious, therefore, that any meaningful LC problem must exhibit a $\mathbf{q}$ vector with at least one negative component. These two facts suggest the following strategy: embed the LC problem of interest into an *artificial* LC structure (introducing an *artificial* variable) that exhibits a vector $\mathbf{q}_a \geq \mathbf{0}$ (the subscript a stands for "artificial") and attempt to eliminate the artificial variable from the solution while

(a) maintaining the feasibility and
(b) maintaining the (almost) complementarity

of the current solution. In other words, because it is rather difficult to solve the true LC problem directly, we construct an artificial LC problem (that includes the true LC problem) of the following form:

$$\mathbf{w} - M\mathbf{z} - \mathbf{s}z_0 = \mathbf{q} \qquad (6.14)$$

where $\mathbf{s}' = [1, 1, \ldots, 1]$ and z_0 is an artificial variable whose role is to make all the components of the $\mathbf{q}$ vector nonnegative, as illustrated by a numerical example. The following tableau presents the quadratic programming information according to the form of the artificial LC problem (6.14):

$$
\begin{array}{ccccccc|cc}
w_1 & w_2 & w_3 & z_1 & z_2 & z_3 & z_0 & \mathbf{q} & BI \qquad (6.15) \\
\hline
1 & & & -4 & -2 & -1 & -1 & -4 & w_1 \\
 & 1 & & -2 & 0 & -2 & -1 & -3 & w_2 \\
 & & 1 & 1 & 2 & 0 & -1 & 4 & w_3
\end{array}
$$

In tableau (6.15), some of the elements of the vector $\mathbf{q}$ are negative. The *BI* heading of the rightmost column stands for "basic indexes," which identify the column vectors of the current basis. In solving linear systems of equations, the easiest strategy is to begin at the origin of the given space (corresponding to an identity matrix as a basis). The choice of the w_1, w_2, and w_3 basic indexes, therefore, signifies that the current basis is the identity matrix. The corresponding current basic solution is given by $\bar{\mathbf{w}} = \bar{\mathbf{q}}$, $\bar{\mathbf{z}} = \mathbf{0}$, and $\bar{z}_0 = 0$. At this initial stage, therefore, the vector associated with the artificial variable z_0 is not included in the basis.

The current solution $(\bar{\mathbf{w}}, \bar{\mathbf{z}})$, although complementary, is not a feasible solution because $\bar{\mathbf{w}} \not\geq \mathbf{0}$. Notice, however, that the basic indexes (in the *BI* column of (6.15)) represent an *uninterrupted* series from 1 to $(n + m)$. This is indeed the meaning of the complementary condition that requires $w_k z_k = 0$ for $k = 1, \ldots, n + m$. At least one of the two variables (w_k, z_k)

must be equal to zero. The other variable, therefore (even if degenerate or, equivalently, assuming a zero value), can be taken as a basic variable. From the beginning of the computations, therefore, we can easily establish the complementarity of the LC solution but not its feasibility. The artificial LC problem (6.14), as exemplified in (6.15), is instrumental for achieving this second objective.

It was previously stated that the role of the artificial variable z_0 (and the associated artificial vector $\mathbf{s}$) is exclusively that of achieving the feasibility of the solution, albeit an artificial one. This goal is easily achieved by identifying the minimum negative element of the $\mathbf{q}$ vector and adding an equivalent positive amount to every element. This operation is performed by pivoting on the element of the $\mathbf{s}$ vector corresponding to the minimum element of $\mathbf{q}$, as in the following display:

T_0			w_1	w_2	w_3	z_1	z_2	z_3	z_0	q	BI
-1			1			-4	-2	-1	$\boxed{-1}$	-4	$w_1 \rightarrow$
-1	1			1		-2	0	-2	-1	-3	w_2
-1		1			1	1	2	0	-1	4	w_3

second tableau:

						z_1	z_2	z_3	z_0	q	
-1						4	2	1	1	4	z_0
-1	1					2	2	-1	0	1	w_2
-1		1				5	4	1	0	8	w_3

$$(6.16)$$

The horizontal arrow identifies the most negative element of the $\mathbf{q}$ vector and the index of the column vector that must leave the current basis. The circle around the element of the $(-\mathbf{s})$ vector in the first tableau identifies the current *pivot* element. The T_0 matrix on the left-hand side of the display is the *transformation* matrix defined for achieving the nonnegativity of the $\mathbf{q}$ vector. This matrix is constructed according to the rules for changing a basis, as discussed in Chapter 4. The second tableau is the result of the premultiplication of the first tableau by the T_0 matrix.

At this stage, the $\bar{\mathbf{q}}$ vector is nonnegative, but it contains an element associated with the artificial vector $\mathbf{s}$, namely, the level of the artificial variable z_0. For this reason we may wish to refer to this vector using a subscript a (for *artificial*) as $\bar{\mathbf{q}}_a$. We can make a series of observations. First of all, the current solution is an artificial solution because $z_0 = 4$, $w_2 = 1$, $w_3 = 8$ and all the other variables are equal to zero. Secondly, the series of basic indexes is interrupted because in the BI column the indexes are (0, 2, 3). This fact indicates that $w_1 = z_1 = 0$ and the vectors associated with these variables are out of the current basis. For this reason, the solution corresponding to the second tableau of (6.16) is called an *almost complementary* solution. If it were possible to reduce the z_0 variable to a zero level (corresponding to the elimination of the artificial vector **s** from the current basis), while satisfying the feasibility and the complementarity criteria, the resulting solution would be both feasible and complementary and the true LC problem would be solved.

Notice that to satisfy the complementarity criterion, there is no choice but to select the column associated with the variable z_1 as the vector to enter the next basis. This conclusion is dictated by the fact that the vector associated with the variable w_1 was just eliminated from the basis. Any other selection would violate the complementarity condition.

In order to identify the vector to be eliminated from the current basis (and to be replaced by the vector associated with z_1), it is necessary to satisfy the *feasibility criterion* according to which all the elements of the $\bar{\mathbf{q}}_a$ vector must remain nonnegative. It should be clear that if it were possible to eliminate the artificial vector **s** from the current basis while mantaining feasibility, we would have reduced the $\bar{\mathbf{q}}_a \geq \mathbf{0}$ vector to a $\bar{\mathbf{q}} \geq \mathbf{0}$ vector and the solution of the true LC problem would be at hand. The feasibility criterion corresponding to the second tableau of (6.16) can be stated as follows:

$$\frac{\bar{q}_r}{\bar{m}_{1r}} = \min_k \left\{ \frac{\bar{q}_k}{\bar{m}_{1k}} \ \middle| \ \bar{m}_{1k} > 0 \right\} \qquad k = 1, \ldots, 3. \qquad (6.17)$$

This general criterion (a minimum ratio criterion) for feasibility of the solution can be illustrated by using the current solution of (6.16) and the selected vector $\bar{\mathbf{m}}_1$ associated with the z_1 variable.

The relevant relations corresponding to the second tableau of (6.16) are stated as follows:

$$z_0 - 4z_1 = 4 - 4z_1 \geq 0 \qquad (6.18)$$

new basic solution :
$$w_2 - 2z_1 = 1 - 2z_1 \geq 0$$

$$w_3 - 5z_1 = 8 - 5z_1 \geq 0.$$

In other words, if we wish to raise the nonbasic variable z_1 to a positive level, we must reduce some of the current basic variables to zero while guaranteeing that the new solution will also be feasible. Clearly, the nonnegativity of the new basic solution can be maintained only if the value of the z_1 variable is chosen as the minimum of all possible nonnegative ratios computable from the three relations of (6.18). In this numerical example, such a minimum is

$$z_1 = \frac{1}{2} = \min\left\{\frac{4}{4}, \frac{1}{2}, \frac{8}{5}\right\} = \frac{\bar{q}_2}{\bar{m}_{12} > 0}.$$

Therefore, the vector to leave the current basis is identified as the one that is associated with the w_2 variable (the index of the numerator) that is reduced to a zero level. The pivot element for the next change of basis is the number in the denominator of the minimum ratio. Any other choice of pivot would not satisfy the feasibility criterion for the next basic solution.

In summary, at each iteration the two steps of the complementary pivot algorithm identify the incoming (into the next basis) vector and the exiting (from the current basis) vector, in that order. The incoming vector is associated with the variable whose complement was eliminated from the basic solution in the previous iteration. The exiting vector is identified with the index of the solution element in the numerator of the minimum ratio. If, at any iteration, this index is the zero index, the artificial variable is reduced to a zero level and the next tableau will exhibit a solution of the true LC problem. When this occurs, the series of basic indexes in the BI column becomes again an uninterrupted series, and the cycle is completed.

The complementary pivot algorithm could terminate without the possibility of eliminating the artificial vector associated with the z_0 variable from the basis. This event can happen when the incoming column exhibits either negative or zero elements. In this case a pivot cannot be found and we must abandon the search for a solution because the series of equations that constitute the true LC problem is inconsistent.

With these rules in mind, we complete the computation of the solution for the numerical example initiated earlier.

mandatory initial step $\downarrow$

T_0			w_1	w_2	w_3	z_1	z_2	z_3	z_0	$\mathbf{q}$	BI
-1			1			-4	-2	-1	$\boxed{-1}$	-4	$w_1 \to$ most neg
-1	1			1		-2	0	-2	-1	-3	w_2
-1		1			1	1	2	0	-1	4	w_3

T_1 $\downarrow$ complement of w_1

T_1											
1	-2		-1			4	2	1	1	4	z_0
	$\frac{1}{2}$		-1	1		$\boxed{2}$	2	-1	0	1	$w_2 \to$ min ratio
	$-\frac{5}{2}$	1	-1		1	5	4	1	0	8	w_3

↓ complement of w_2

T_2 — left transformation matrix $\begin{bmatrix} 1 & 2 & \\ & 1 & \\ & 1 & 1 \end{bmatrix}$

w_1	w_2	w_3	z_1	z_2	z_3	z_0	q	BI
1	-2			-2	3	1	2	z_0
$-\frac12$	$\frac12$		1	$\boxed{1}$	$-\frac12$	0	$\frac12$	z_1 →min ratio
$\frac32$	$-\frac52$	1		-1	$\frac72$	0	$\frac{11}{2}$	w_3

T_3 — left transformation matrix $\begin{bmatrix} 1 & & \\ & \frac12 & \\ & 1 & 1 \end{bmatrix}$ ↓ complement of z_1

w_1	w_2	w_3	z_1	z_2	z_3	z_0	q	BI
0	-1		2		2	1	3	z_0
$-\frac12$	$\frac12$		1	1	$-\frac12$	0	$\frac12$	z_2
$\boxed{1}$	-2	1	1		3	0	6	w_3 →min ratio

T_4 — left transformation matrix $\begin{bmatrix} \frac12 & & \\ -\frac12 & 1 & \\ -\frac32 & & 1 \end{bmatrix}$ ↓ complement of w_3

w_1	w_2	w_3	z_1	z_2	z_3	z_0	q	BI
	-1		2		$\boxed{2}$	1	3	z_0 →min ratio
$-\frac12$	$\frac12$	$\frac32$	1	1		0	$\frac72$	z_2
1	-2	1	1		3	0	6	w_1

final tableau:

w_1	w_2	w_3	z_1	z_2	z_3	z_0	q	BI
$-\frac12$		1			1	$\frac12$	$\frac32$	z_3
0	$\frac12$	$\frac12$		1		$-\frac12$	2	z_2
1	$-\frac12$	1	-2			$-\frac32$	$\frac32$	w_1

(6.19)

The last tableau of (6.19) exhibits the solution of the original LC problem because the variable z_0 was eliminated from the list of basic variables while maintaining the feasibility and the complementarity of the solution. As anticipated earlier, the BI column presents an uninterrupted list of basic indexes, an indication of success in solving the LC problem. Four iterations (discounting the required initial transformation) were necessary for solving this numerical example. The vector associated with the variable z_1 entered at the first iteration and was eliminated from the basis in the next iteration, indicating that the path toward a solution can be a tortuous one. The explicit solution for the original quadratic programming problem is

$$z_1 = x_1 = 0 \qquad\qquad w_1 = v_1 = \tfrac32$$
$$z_2 = x_2 = 2 \qquad\qquad w_2 = v_2 = 0$$
$$z_3 = y_1 = \tfrac32 \qquad\qquad w_3 = u_1 = 0.$$

This solution is clearly complementary and nonnegative. Its feasibility is checked by verifying that it satisfies the linearity condition of the LC problem $Mz + q = w$:

$$\begin{bmatrix} 4 & 2 & 1 \\ 2 & 0 & 2 \\ -1 & -2 & 0 \end{bmatrix}\begin{bmatrix} 0 \\ 2 \\ \tfrac32 \end{bmatrix} + \begin{bmatrix} -4 \\ -3 \\ 4 \end{bmatrix} \overset{?}{=} \begin{bmatrix} \tfrac32 \\ 0 \\ 0 \end{bmatrix} : \text{yes.}$$

A final piece of information to be extracted from the final tableau of (6.19) and serving as the ultimate computational check is the final basis and its inverse:

$$
\begin{array}{cc}
\text{final basis} & \text{inverse} \\
\begin{bmatrix} -1 & -2 & 1 \\ -2 & 0 & 0 \\ 0 & 2 & 0 \end{bmatrix}
\begin{bmatrix} 0 & -\frac{1}{2} & 0 \\ 0 & 0 & \frac{1}{2} \\ 1 & -\frac{1}{2} & 1 \end{bmatrix}
\overset{?}{=}
\begin{bmatrix} 1 & 0 & 0 \\ 0 & 1 & 0 \\ 0 & 0 & 1 \end{bmatrix} : \text{yes.}
\end{array}
$$

$$
\begin{array}{ccc}
z_3 & z_2 & w_1
\end{array}
$$

The vectors of the final basis are identified by the indexes in the final *BI* column. The corresponding basis vectors are lifted from the initial tableau and, for computational convenience, should be arranged in the order indicated by the *BI* indexes. The inverse matrix of the final basis can be read in the columns of the final tableau corresponding to the identity matrix in the initial tableau. The reader can thus check that the inverse matrix so identified is the result of the product of all the transformation matrices defined during the various iterations. Hence, if B is the final basis and B^{-1} its inverse, $B^{-1} = T_4 T_3 T_2 T_1 T_0$ in product form.

Example of Symmetric Quadratic Programming as an LC Problem

Consider the symmetric quadratic programming problem

$$\text{maximize } Z = c'x - \tfrac{1}{2}x'Dx - \tfrac{1}{2}y'Ey \tag{6.20}$$

$$\text{subject to} \quad Ax - Ey \leq b, \quad x \geq 0, \ y \geq 0$$

where the matrices D and E are assumed to be symmetric positive semidefinite. Let the various parameters take on the following values:

$$
A = \begin{bmatrix} 1 & 0 & -2 \\ 3 & 1 & 0 \end{bmatrix}, \quad
b = \begin{bmatrix} 3 \\ -2 \end{bmatrix}, \quad
E = \begin{bmatrix} 2 & 1 \\ 1 & 2 \end{bmatrix},
$$

$$
c = \begin{bmatrix} 0 \\ 1 \\ 2 \end{bmatrix}, \quad
D = \begin{bmatrix} 13 & -4 & 3 \\ -4 & 5 & -2 \\ 3 & -2 & 1 \end{bmatrix}.
$$

The dual specification of the foregoing primal problem is

$$\text{minimize } R = b'y + \tfrac{1}{2}y'Ey + \tfrac{1}{2}x'Dx \tag{6.21}$$

$$\text{subject to} \quad A'y + Dx \geq c, \quad x \geq 0, \ y \geq 0.$$

Using the corresponding KKT conditions, the preceding dual pair of symmetric quadratic programming problems can be reformulated as an LC problem as follows: $\mathbf{z}' = \begin{bmatrix} \mathbf{x}', \mathbf{y}' \end{bmatrix} \geq [\mathbf{0}', \mathbf{0}']$ and

$$
M = \begin{bmatrix} D & A' \\ -A & E \end{bmatrix} = \begin{bmatrix} 13 & -4 & 3 & 1 & 3 \\ -4 & 5 & -2 & 0 & 1 \\ 3 & -2 & 1 & -2 & 0 \\ -1 & 0 & 2 & 2 & 1 \\ -3 & -1 & 0 & 1 & 2 \end{bmatrix}, \quad \mathbf{q} = \begin{bmatrix} -\mathbf{c} \\ \mathbf{b} \end{bmatrix} = \begin{bmatrix} 0 \\ -1 \\ -2 \\ 3 \\ -2 \end{bmatrix}.
$$

The solution of this numerical example is obtained using Lemke's complementary pivot algorithm in the sequence of iterations (only the transformation vector, rather than the entire transformation matrix, is reported on the left-hand side of each tableau) represented by the five tableaux of the LC problem that follow.

The successful termination of the complementary pivot algorithm is indicated by the event corresponding to the exit of the artificial vector from the basis and the associated restoration of an uninterrupted series of indexes from 1 to 5. The solution of the LC problem is exhibited in the $\mathbf{q}$ column of the final tableau. This solution is feasible and complementary. The feasibility is verified by the nonnegativity of all the components of the $\mathbf{z}$ vector and the fact that (in the absence of computational errors) this solution satisfies the linear inequalities expressed by $M\mathbf{z} + \mathbf{q} \geq \mathbf{0}$. A rigorous check of the computations' accuracy is performed by verifying that the product of the basis expressed by the final tableau and its inverse produces an identity matrix. The final basis is identified by the indexes of the variables appearing in the BI column, that is, w_1, z_5, z_2, w_4, z_3, to be taken in that order.

mandatory initial step ↓

T_0	w_1	w_2	w_3	w_4	w_5	z_1	z_2	z_3	z_4	z_5	z_0	q	BI
-1	1					-13	4	-3	-1	-3	-1	0	w_1
-1		1				4	-5	2	0	-1	-1	-1	w_2
-1			1			-3	2	-1	2	0	(-1)	-2	$w_3 \rightarrow$
-1				1		1	0	-2	-2	-1	-1	3	w_4
-1					1	3	1	0	-1	-2	-1	-2	w_5

↓ complement of w_3

T_1		w_1	w_2	w_3	w_4	w_5	z_1	z_2	z_3	z_4	z_5	z_0	q	BI
2		1		-1			-10	2	-2	-3	-3	0	2	w_1
-3			1	-1			7	-7	3	-2	-1	0	1	w_2
-1				-1			3	-2	1	-2	0	1	2	z_0
1				-1	1		4	-2	-1	-4	-1	0	5	w_4
1				-1		1	6	-1	(1)	-3	-2	0	0	$w_5 \rightarrow$

T_2 ↓ complement of w_5

		w_1	w_2	w_3	w_4	w_5	z_1	z_2	z_3	z_4	z_5	z_0	q	BI
$\frac{7}{5}$		1		-3		2	2	0	0	-9	-7	0	2	w_1
$\frac{1}{5}$			1	2		-3	-11	-4	0	7	(5)	0	1	$w_2 \rightarrow$
$-\frac{2}{5}$				0		-1	-3	-1	0	1	2	1	2	z_0
$\frac{3}{5}$				-2	1	1	10	-3	0	-7	-3	0	5	w_4
$\frac{2}{5}$				-1		1	6	-1	1	-3	-2	0	0	z_3

T_3 ↓ complement of w_2

		w_1	w_2	w_3	w_4	w_5	z_1	z_2	z_3	z_4	z_5	z_0	q	BI
$\frac{28}{3}$		1	$\frac{7}{5}$	$-\frac{1}{5}$		$-\frac{11}{5}$	$-\frac{67}{5}$	$-\frac{28}{5}$	0	$\frac{4}{5}$	0	0	$\frac{17}{5}$	w_1
$\frac{4}{3}$			$\frac{1}{5}$	$\frac{2}{5}$		$-\frac{3}{5}$	$-\frac{11}{5}$	$-\frac{4}{5}$	0	$\frac{7}{5}$	1	0	$\frac{1}{5}$	z_5
$\frac{5}{3}$			$-\frac{2}{5}$	$-\frac{4}{5}$		$\frac{1}{5}$	$\frac{7}{5}$	$(\frac{3}{5})$	0	$-\frac{9}{5}$	0	1	$\frac{8}{5}$	$z_0 \rightarrow$
9			$\frac{3}{5}$	$-\frac{4}{5}$	1	$-\frac{4}{5}$	$\frac{17}{5}$	$-\frac{27}{5}$	0	$-\frac{14}{5}$	0	0	$\frac{28}{5}$	w_4
$\frac{13}{3}$			$\frac{2}{5}$	$-\frac{1}{5}$		$-\frac{1}{5}$	$\frac{8}{5}$	$-\frac{13}{5}$	1	$-\frac{1}{5}$	0	0	$\frac{2}{5}$	z_3

	w_1	w_2	w_3	w_4	w_5	z_1	z_2	z_3	z_4	z_5	z_0	q	BI
	1	$-\frac{7}{3}$	$-\frac{23}{3}$		$-\frac{1}{3}$	$-\frac{1}{3}$	0	0	-16		$\frac{28}{3}$	$\frac{55}{3}$	w_1
		$-\frac{1}{3}$	$-\frac{2}{3}$		$-\frac{1}{3}$	$-\frac{1}{3}$	0	0	-1	1	$\frac{4}{3}$	$\frac{7}{3}$	z_5
		$-\frac{2}{3}$	$-\frac{4}{3}$		$\frac{1}{3}$	$\frac{7}{3}$	1	0	-3		$\frac{5}{3}$	$\frac{8}{3}$	z_2
		-3	-8	1	1	16	0	0	-19		9	20	w_4
		$-\frac{4}{3}$	$-\frac{11}{3}$		$\frac{2}{3}$	$\frac{23}{3}$	0	1	-8		$\frac{13}{3}$	$\frac{22}{3}$	z_3

The inverse matrix is read from the final tableau in the columns corresponding to the identity matrix in the initial tableau.

Hence, the product of the final basis times its corresponding inverse is equal to the identity matrix:

$$
\begin{array}{ccccc}
w_1 & z_5 & z_2 & w_4 & z_3
\end{array}
$$

$$
\begin{bmatrix}
1 & -3 & 4 & 0 & -3 \\
0 & -1 & -5 & 0 & 2 \\
0 & 0 & 2 & 0 & -1 \\
0 & -1 & 0 & 1 & -2 \\
0 & -2 & 1 & 0 & 0
\end{bmatrix}
\begin{bmatrix}
1 & -\frac{7}{3} & -\frac{23}{3} & 0 & -\frac{1}{3} \\
0 & -\frac{1}{3} & -\frac{2}{3} & 0 & -\frac{1}{3} \\
0 & -\frac{2}{3} & -\frac{4}{3} & 0 & \frac{1}{3} \\
0 & -3 & -8 & 1 & 1 \\
0 & -\frac{4}{3} & -\frac{11}{3} & 0 & \frac{2}{3}
\end{bmatrix}
=
\begin{bmatrix}
1 & & & & \\
 & 1 & & & \\
 & & 1 & & \\
 & & & 1 & \\
 & & & & 1
\end{bmatrix}.
$$

The solution of the original symmetric quadratic programming problem (6.20) is

$$
\begin{array}{ll}
z_1 = x_1 = 0 & w_1 = y_{s1} = \frac{55}{3} \\
z_2 = x_2 = \frac{8}{3} & w_2 = y_{s2} = 0 \\
z_3 = x_3 = \frac{22}{3} & w_3 = y_{s3} = 0 \\
z_4 = y_1 = 0 & w_4 = x_{s1} = 20 \\
z_5 = y_2 = \frac{7}{3} & w_5 = x_{s2} = 0
\end{array}
$$

Using this solution, it is a simple computation to evaluate the objective function of problem (6.20).

An easy-to-use code of the complementary pivot algorithm, written in Fortran 77 language, is given in Chapter 17 with the accompanying user's manual presented in Chapter 16. The application solves the LCP in considerable generality including the two-person non-zero-sum game. We reproduce next the input and output files of this computer program corresponding to the (5×5) LCP example just solved. The application was named after the autor of the complementary pivot algorithm who discovered one of the most elegant and efficient methods for solving an LCP. Once the Fortran 77 code is compiled and the command "runlemke7" is typed at the prompt, the program asks for the name of the input data file.

Input Data File for the Lemke Computer Program

INPUT DATA

The input lines in the $\langle datafile.dat \rangle$ file can be typed as shown below (here, the option IPACK = 0 was used) following the instructions of the user's manual in Chapter 16:

Line No.	Typed Data										
1	AN EXAMPLE OF A SQP PROBLEM – Title										
2	3 2 1 1 .5 .5 0 1 1 1										Parameter Indicators
3	13.	−4.	3.								
4	−4.	5.	−2.								D Matrix
5	3.	−2.	1.								
6	2.	1.									E Matrix
7	1.	2.									
8	1.	3.									
9	0.	1.									A' Matrix
10	−2.	0.									
11	0.	1.	2.								COST vector $\mathbf{c}'$
12	3.	−2.									RHS vector $\mathbf{b}'$

Output file from the Lemke Computer Program

OUTPUT (obtained in a ⟨*datafile.lis*⟩ file)

```
AN EXAMPLE OF A SQP PROBLEM
This is a Symmetric QP Problem (D and E Matrices)

This is a MAXIMIZATION problem
D is a positive semidefinite matrix
E is a positive definite matrix

LEMKE's algorithm is guaranteed to find
an optimal solution, if one exists, and
the M matrix is positive semidefinite

Input Parameters
   Full matrix input specified
   kD parameter = 0.50
   kE parameter = 0.50
   NCHKD parameter for D matrix = 1
   NCHKE parameter for E matrix = 1

D Matrix:

        13.0000   -4.0000    3.0000
        -4.0000    5.0000   -2.0000
         3.0000   -2.0000    1.0000

E Matrix:

         2.0000  1.0000
         1.0000  2.0000

A Matrix:

         1.0000  0.0000  -2.0000
         3.0000  1.0000   0.0000

Cost vector:

         0.0000  1.0000  2.0000

RHS vector:

         3.0000  -2.0000
```

Primal solution -- ITERATION NO. 4

$$X(1) = 0.000000$$
$$X(2) = 2.666667$$
$$X(3) = 7.333333$$

Primal Slacks

$$WP(1) = 20.000002$$
$$WP(2) = 0.000000$$

Dual solution

$$Y(1) = 0.000000$$
$$Y(2) = 2.333333$$

Dual Slacks

$$WD(1) = 18.333334$$
$$WD(2) = -0.000002$$
$$WD(3) = 0.000000$$

The primal value of the objective function at the optimal point is: 6.333334
The dual value of the objective function at the optimal point is: 6.333333

AX vector:

$$-15.666667 \quad 2.666667$$

ATY vector:

$$7.000000 \quad 2.333333 \quad 0.000000$$

YTAX =   6.222222
(KD)ATDX =   5.555555
C - (KD)DX vector:

$$-5.666667 \quad 1.666667 \quad 1.000000$$

C - (KD)(D + DT)X vector:

$$-11.333333 \quad 2.333333 \quad -0.000000$$

[C - (KD)DX]TX =   11.777778

```
[C - (KD)(D+DT)X]TX =     6.222223
(KE)YTEY =     5.444444
B + (KE)EY vector:
```

```
         4.166667   0.333333
```

```
B + (KE)(E + ET)Y vector:
```

```
         5.333333   2.666667
```

```
[B + (KE)EY]TY =     0.777778
[B + (KE)(E+ET)Y]TY =     6.222222
```

The solution obtained from the Lemke program is identical to the solution computed manually in the previous section. The computer program has given the solution according to the SQP structure of example (6.20).

Solving the LCP by Quadratic Programming

The result of the self-dual quadratic programming problem in Chapter 5 suggests the possibility of solving certain linear complementarity problems by quadratic programming. The LCP corresponds to finding a vector $z \geq 0$ such that

$$Mz + q \geq 0 \tag{6.22}$$

$$z'Mz + z'q = 0. \tag{6.23}$$

Can the linear complementarity problem as stated in (6.22) and (6.23) be reformulated as a quadratic programming problem and solved by procedures suitable for QP models? The answer is positive for a wide class of LC problems including those LC models characterized by a matrix M that is positive definite. Consider, therefore, the following QP specification:

$$\min \{z'q + z'Mz\} \tag{6.24}$$

$$\text{subject to} \quad Mz \geq -q$$

$$z \geq 0$$

where the matrix M is positive definite and the vector q is arbitrary. In general, the matrix M is asymmetric. It should be clear that in (6.24) we have taken the complementarity condition (6.23) of the LC problem and turned it into the objective function of a quadratic programming problem. Hence, we would expect that: $\min \{z'q + z'Mz\} = 0$.

The structure of (6.24) is similar to the symmetric dual specification of problem (5.27), in Chapter 5, where it was found that the vector of dual variables associated with the primal constraint is identically equal to the vector of primal variables.

To demonstrate that problem (6.24) is equivalent to a linear complementarity problem such as (6.22) and (6.23), it is necessary to show that the optimal value of the objective function in (6.24) is equal to zero. The Lagrangean function of problem (6.24) can be stated as

$$L = \mathbf{z}'\mathbf{q} + \mathbf{z}'M\mathbf{z} + \mathbf{h}'\big(-\mathbf{q} - M\mathbf{z}\big) \tag{6.25}$$

where $\mathbf{h}$ is a vector of Lagrange multipliers associated with the constraints in (6.24). A goal of the analysis that follows is to show that, at the optimal solution, $\mathbf{z} = \mathbf{h}$. The KKT conditions of (6.25) are

$$\frac{\partial L}{\partial \mathbf{z}} = \mathbf{q} + M\mathbf{z} + M'\mathbf{z} - M'\mathbf{h} \geq \mathbf{0} \tag{6.26}$$

$$\mathbf{z}'\frac{\partial L}{\partial \mathbf{z}} = \mathbf{z}'\mathbf{q} + \mathbf{z}'M\mathbf{z} + \mathbf{z}'M'\mathbf{z} - \mathbf{z}'M'\mathbf{h} = 0 \tag{6.27}$$

$$\frac{\partial L}{\partial \mathbf{h}} = -\mathbf{q} - M\mathbf{z} \leq \mathbf{0} \tag{6.28}$$

$$\mathbf{h}'\frac{\partial L}{\partial \mathbf{h}} = -\mathbf{h}'\mathbf{q} - \mathbf{h}'M\mathbf{z} = 0. \tag{6.29}$$

Adding KKT condition (6.27) to (6.29), we obtain

$$\mathbf{q}'(\mathbf{z} - \mathbf{h}) + 2(\mathbf{z} - \mathbf{h})'M\mathbf{z} = 0. \tag{6.30}$$

Furthermore, using (6.30), the Lagrangean function (6.25) can be rearranged as

$$L = \mathbf{q}'(\mathbf{z} - \mathbf{h}) + (\mathbf{z} - \mathbf{h})'M\mathbf{z} \tag{6.31}$$

$$= -(\mathbf{z} - \mathbf{h})'M\mathbf{z}. \tag{6.32}$$

Finally, because the Lagrangean function constitutes the dual objective function associated with a given primal problem, we want to maximize the Lagrangean function (6.32) and write

$$\max L = \max \left[-(\mathbf{z} - \mathbf{h})'M\mathbf{z} \right]. \tag{6.33}$$

Because the M matrix is positive definite, the dual objective function (6.33) achieves a maximum value at 0 when $\mathbf{z} = \mathbf{h}$. Therefore, by replacing the symbol $\mathbf{h}$ in KKT condition (6.29), we obtain the result that the primal objective function in (6.24) also attains a minimum value at 0, that is, $\min \{\mathbf{z}'\mathbf{q} + \mathbf{z}'M\mathbf{z}\} = 0$, as intended and stated previously.

In quadratic programming models, the M matrix is the sum of a positive semidefinite matrix Q and a skew (or antisymmetric) matrix S such that $M = Q + S$, where $Q = \begin{bmatrix} D & 0 \\ 0 & E \end{bmatrix}$ and $S = \begin{bmatrix} 0 & A' \\ -A & 0 \end{bmatrix}$. A skew symmetric (or antisymmetric) matrix S is a matrix for which $S = -S'$.

Example of Solution of LCP by Quadratic Programming

The SQP problem solved in a previous section by Lemke's complementary pivot algorithm will be solved here, again, using a quadratic programming specification and the GAMS computer application.

GAMS command file for solving an LCP by QP:

```
$title solution of an lcp by qp
*
$offsymlist offsymxref
    option limrow = 0
    option limcol = 0
    option iterlim =100000
    option reslim = 200000
    option nlp = conopt3
    option decimals = 7 ;
*
    sets j    z-lcp variables / x1, x2, x3, y1, y2 /
    n(j)  inputs / y1, y2 /
*
    alias(k,j)
    alias(n,nn) ;
*
    parameter q(j)    lemke rhs
    /  x1     0
       x2    -1
       x3    -2
       y1     3
       y2    -2  /
*
    table skewa(k,j)    technical coefficients
            x1    x2    x3    y1    y2
       x1                      1     3
       x2                      0     1
       x3                     -2     0
       y1    -1     0     2
       y2    -3    -1     0
```

```
*
    table qf(k,j)   quadratic form: slopes of demand and
    input supply
            x1    x2    x3    y1    y2
       x1   13    -4    3
       x2   -4    5    -2
       x3    3    -2    1
       y1                     2    1
       y2                     1    2
*
    parameter m(k,j)  matrix of the lc problem;
    m(k,j) = skewa(k,j) + qf(k,j) ;
    display m ;
*
* definition of the quadratic programming model
*
    variables
    pdobj    primal-dual objective function
    z(j)     z variables of the lcp ;
*
    positive variable z ;
*
    equations
    lcpeq    lcp objective function
    lcprhs(k)    rhs of the lc problem ;
    lcpeq..   pdobj =e= sum(j, z(j)*q(j)) + (sum((k,j),
    z(k)*qf(k,j)*z(j))) ;
    lcprhs(k)..    sum(j, m(k,j)*z(j)) =g= - q(k);
*
* name and definition of the quadratic programming
* model
*
    model lcpbyqp /all/ ;
    solve lcpbyqp using nlp minimizing pdobj ;
    display z.l, lcprhs.m ;
*
    parameter sqpobjf   objective function of the sqp
    problem
    inputsup(n)    input supply ;
*
    sqpobjf = sum(j, -z.l(j)*q(j)) - (1/2)*(sum((k,j),
    z.l(k)*qf(k,j)*z.l(j))) ;
    inputsup(n) = q(n) + sum(nn, m(n,nn)*z.l(nn) ) ;
    display sqpobjf, inputsup ;
```

The solution of the foregoing QP problem, solved using the GAMS application, is identical to the solution obtained previously with the complementary pivot algorithm, as expected. The vector of "primal" variables z is identical to the vector of "dual" variables h, as asserted earlier.

Solving Bimatrix Games

The Linear Complementarity Problem received special attention in the 1960s in relation to the solution of the two-person non-zero-sum game. This game theory problem was analyzed in the 1950s by John Nash, 1994 Nobel Prize winner for economics. It took, however, until 1964 before an algorithm for the solution of this mathematical structure was discovered by Lemke and Howson. The algorithm for solving a two-person non-zero-sum game, cast in the form of an LC problem, is slightly different from the algorithm presented in this chapter. Game theory is discussed in Chapter 13, where the required variant of the complementary pivot algorithm is presented.

Exercises

6.1 Given the LC problem (M, q) where the matrix M, vector q and vector z are partitioned as follows:

$$M = \begin{bmatrix} 0 & A' \\ -A & E \end{bmatrix}, \quad q = \begin{bmatrix} -c \\ b \end{bmatrix}, \quad z = \begin{bmatrix} x \\ y \end{bmatrix},$$

and where the matrix E is symmetric positive semidefinite, write down the primal of the implied quadratic programming model. Derive its dual specification. Compare and contrast your results with the asymmetric QP model such as problem (5.2).

6.2 Given the following programming problem:

$$Z = c'x - x'Dx - y_2' E_2 y_2$$

$$\text{subject to} \qquad A_1 x \qquad \leq b_1$$

$$A_2 x - 2 E_2 y_2 \leq b_2$$

where all the vector variables are nonnegative and the matrix E_2 is symmetric positive semidefinite, derive the dual specification and assemble the corresponding KKT conditions into an LC problem.

6.3 Consider the LC problem $(M, \mathbf{q})$ with the specification

$$M = \begin{bmatrix} (D_1 + D_1') & 0 & A_1' \\ 0 & 0 & A_2' \\ -A_1 & -A_2 & 0 \end{bmatrix}, \quad \mathbf{q} = \begin{bmatrix} -\mathbf{c}_1 \\ -\mathbf{c}_2 \\ \mathbf{b} \end{bmatrix}, \quad \mathbf{z} = \begin{bmatrix} \mathbf{x}_1 \\ \mathbf{x}_2 \\ \mathbf{y} \end{bmatrix},$$

with all nonnegative variables; the matrix D_1 is asymmetric positive semidefinite. State the primal of the implied QP problem and derive its dual specification. Confirm that the derived KKT conditions match the relations of the given LC problem.

6.4 Use the complementary pivot algorithm to solve the following LC problem:

$$M = \begin{bmatrix} 2 & 1 & 3 \\ 1 & 0 & 1 \\ -3 & -1 & 0 \end{bmatrix}, \quad \mathbf{q} = \begin{bmatrix} -4 \\ -6 \\ 12 \end{bmatrix}, \quad \mathbf{z} = \begin{bmatrix} z_1 \\ z_2 \\ z_3 \end{bmatrix}.$$

What kind of mathematical programming model is implied by the given numerical example? Define each component of such a model.

6.5 Consider the following LC problem $(M, \mathbf{q})$:

$$M = \begin{bmatrix} 5 & 7 & 33 \\ 1 & 4 & 12 \\ -33 & -12 & 0 \end{bmatrix}, \quad \mathbf{q} = \begin{bmatrix} -40 \\ -60 \\ 12 \end{bmatrix}, \quad \mathbf{z} = \begin{bmatrix} z_1 \\ z_2 \\ z_3 \end{bmatrix}.$$

What kind of programming model is implied by the given numerical example? Hint: Is it possible to define a dual pair of problems that requires optimization? State the complete and correct problem.

6.6 Given the LC problem $(M, \mathbf{q})$ where the matrix M, vector $\mathbf{q}$, and vector $\mathbf{z}$ are partitioned as follows:

$$M = \begin{bmatrix} (D + D') & A' \\ -A & E \end{bmatrix}, \quad \mathbf{q} = \begin{bmatrix} -\mathbf{c} \\ \mathbf{b} \end{bmatrix}, \quad \mathbf{z} = \begin{bmatrix} \mathbf{x} \\ \mathbf{y} \end{bmatrix},$$

and where the matrix D is asymmetric positive semidefinite and the matrix E is symmetric positive semidefinite, write down the primal of the implied quadratic programming model. Derive its dual specification.

6.7 Given the LC problem $(M, \mathbf{q})$ where the matrix M, vector $\mathbf{q}$, and vector $\mathbf{z}$ are partitioned as follows:

$$M = \begin{bmatrix} D & A' \\ -A & E \end{bmatrix}, \quad \mathbf{q} = \begin{bmatrix} -\mathbf{c} \\ \mathbf{b} \end{bmatrix}, \quad \mathbf{z} = \begin{bmatrix} \mathbf{x} \\ \mathbf{y} \end{bmatrix},$$

and where the D and E matrices are asymmetric positive semidefinite, write down the implied programming model.

References

Lemke, C. E., and Howson, J. T., Jr. (1964). "Equilibrium Points of Bimatrix Games," *Journal of the Society for Industrial Applied Mathematics*, 12, 413–23.

Nash, J. (1951). "Non-cooperative Games," *Annals of Mathematics*, 54, 286–95.

7

The Price Taker

The discussion of economic agents' behavior begins with this chapter. The analytical structures employed for this analysis will be mathematical programming models of the kind that were introduced in previous chapters. Before reexamining the duality relations that characterize each of these models, we wish to recall the fundamental duality relation that applies to a large class of economic models of producers. Hence, regardless of the mathematical programming structure adopted for the given agent, the general duality relation underlying the behavior of rational producers can be stated as follows:

$$
\begin{array}{ccc}
& \textbf{Primal} & \textbf{Dual} \\
& \max_{\mathbf{x}} TNR & \min_{\mathbf{y}} TC & (7.1) \\
\text{subject to} & & \\
& Demand \leq Supply & MC \geq MR
\end{array}
$$

where TNR and TC stand for total net revenue and total cost, respectively; $Demand$ and $Supply$ stand for demand and supply of any commodity, respectively; and MC and MR stand for marginal cost and marginal revenue, respectively, of any commodity.

The dual pair of economic problems stated in (7.1) signifies that the constraints of a primal problem involve, always, the physical quantity equilibrium conditions of commodities, whether inputs or outputs. The case of demand being greater than supply is not admissible as an equilibrium condition because entrepreneurs would be always available to fulfill that demand. Conversely, the dual constraints involve, always, the economic equilibrium condition according to which the marginal cost of a commodity must be greater than or equal to its marginal revenue. Again, the case of a marginal revenue being greater than marginal cost is not admissible as an equilibrium condition because it would not be rational to produce at a level where $MR > MC$ and losing the positive difference between MR and MC.

A competitive entrepreneur is an economic agent who makes decisions regarding the optimal output and input mix for his firm assuming that prices of all commodities produced are fixed (by the market). For this reason, this decision maker is said to be a price taker. Linear programming has been used extensively for representing the economic behavior of such an agent. The issue of short-run versus long-run behavior of the competitive entrepreneur, however, is not resolved by a linear programming model. In the short run, positive (or negative) profits are admissible for a competitive entrepreneur. In contrast, the structure of linear programming, which is a short-run specification, given the presence of limiting (fixed) inputs, distributes all the revenue among the primal constraints and leaves a zero level of profit for the firm. It is well known that zero profits characterize the long-run behavior of entrepreneurs operating in a competitive industry under the condition of free entry and exit.

Suppose that the technology for transforming limiting (sometime called fixed) inputs into outputs is represented by the fixed coefficient matrix A of dimensions $(m \times n)$, availability of resources and other commodity restrictions are given by the vector $\mathbf{b}$, and net revenue coefficients are included in the vector $\mathbf{c}$. A further specification of the problem is that the competitive entrepreneur wishes to maximize profits defined as the difference between total net revenue (TNR) and total cost (TC). This elementary formulation is represented exhaustively by the following dual pair of linear programming problems:

Primal	**Dual**	
$\max\limits_{\mathbf{x}} TNR = \mathbf{c}'\mathbf{x}$	$\min\limits_{\mathbf{y}} TC = \mathbf{b}'\mathbf{y}$	(7.2)
subject to $A\mathbf{x} \leq \mathbf{b}$	subject to $\mathbf{y} \geq \mathbf{0}$	
$\mathbf{x} \geq \mathbf{0}$	$A'\mathbf{y} \geq \mathbf{c}.$	

Close inspection of the Primal and Dual specifications of (7.2) reveals a *transposition rule* that involves all the information contained in the two problems. Hence, the $\mathbf{c}$ vector in the primal objective function appears as a transposed vector in the dual constraints. Similarly, the $\mathbf{b}$ vector in the primal constraints appears as a transposed vector in the dual objective function.

Finally, the matrix A of the primal problem appears as its transpose in the dual problem.

A general economic interpretation of the dual pair of LP problems stated in (7.2) brings into evidence the familiar components of a decision problem for the price-taking entrepreneur. The relation $A\mathbf{x} \leq \mathbf{b}$ is the specification of the technology available to the price taker with the vector $\mathbf{b}$ representing the supply of commodities necessary to produce (meet) the demand $A\mathbf{x}$ of the same commodities. The dual problem specifies the objective to minimize the total cost of the commodities supplied in the production process, $\mathbf{b}'\mathbf{y}$, subject to the equilibrium condition that the marginal cost (MC) of producing the vector of commodities, $\mathbf{x}$, be greater than or equal to their marginal revenue (MR), $\mathbf{c}$.

The vector of limiting factors of production and commodity restrictions $\mathbf{b}$ includes coefficients that may be either positive or negative, or equal to zero. In other words, $\mathbf{b}$ is not required to be a vector with all nonnegative components. A possible example of a negative coefficient is given by the requirement that the jth activity be operated at a minimum level. This condition arises every time the entrepreneur enters into a contract to deliver a certain level of a given product. In this case, the relevant specification of the contract is $x_j \geq \bar{x}_j$, which is transformed into the relation $(-x_j \leq -\bar{x}_j)$ for the purpose of maintaining the same direction of all inequalities. The right-hand-side element $(\bar{x}_j)$ represents the known level of the contract and becomes a negative component of the vector $\mathbf{b}$. It is possible to conclude that the primal constraints $A\mathbf{x} \leq \mathbf{b}$ represent the technological and institutional relations that define the production environment of the price-taking entrepreneur. In the general economic framework adopted for this discussion, they represent the physical equilibrium conditions of production according to which the demand (D) of commodities must always be less than or equal to the supply (S) of the same commodities, $D \leq S$. Analogously to what was said about $\mathbf{b}$, the vector $\mathbf{c}$ admits either positive or zero, or negative coefficients. A positive unit net revenue refers to a commodity intended as an output by the price taker. A negative coefficient is interpreted as a unit cost of a given limiting input. The terminology of "net revenue coefficients" is employed here to signify that, in linear programming, only the limiting (fixed) inputs should enter the technological relations expressed by the primal constraints. Variable inputs, in other words, are all those factors of production for which there are no plausible supply restrictions from the point of view of the price-taking entrepreneur. To exemplify, consider a farm operation defined by a given amount of land, machinery, and

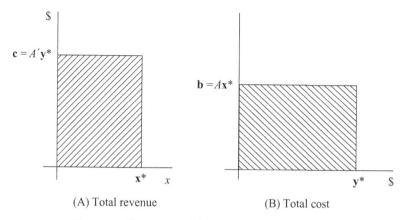

Figure 7.1. Illustration of the price taker's equilibrium.

family labor on the input side and field crops on the output side. Clearly, the successful cultivation of field crops requires the use of fertilizers, but it is highly improbable that the market supply of fertilizers would constitute a constraint for the demand of fertilizers coming from the decisions taken by this single farm operator. Because the components of the problems are linear functions of the unknown choices, the cost of fertilizers per unit of output of those commodities requiring fertilizers can be subtracted directly (before solving the LP problem) from the market price of those commodities in order to obtain the "net revenue coefficients" of the vector **c**. In symbolic terms, suppose that the market price of the jth commodity is p_j; whereas the prices of three variable inputs are p_{v1}, p_{v2}, p_{v3}, respectively. Furthermore, suppose that the technological requirements of the jth activity in terms of the three fertilizers are a_{v1j}, a_{v2j}, a_{v3j}. The "net revenue coefficient" of the jth activity that is relevant for the linear program is, therefore, $c_j = p_j - \sum_{i=1}^{3} a_{vij} p_{vi}$. A general exemplification of this approach is illustrated later with the discussion of a general model of production.

The diagrammatic interpretation of the price taker's specification outlined in (7.2) results in two diagrams each of which contains information of both the primal and the dual LP problems.

Figure 7.1.a represents the revenue side of the problem, with optimal output levels **x*** corresponding to the equilibrium condition where the unit net revenues **c** equal the output marginal costs $A'\mathbf{y}^*$ of the commodity vector **x***. Figure 7.1.b represents the input cost side of the problem where the vector of optimal input shadow prices, $\mathbf{y}^*$, is determined by the equality between the demand $A\mathbf{x}^*$ and the supply $\mathbf{b}$ of the production factors. The rectangles in the two diagrams have the same area establishing the zero-profit condition for the competitive entrepreneur.

Derivation of the Dual LP Problem

The specification of the dual pair of linear programming problems stated in (7.2) can be justified in more than one way but, here, it is of interest to apply the Karush-Kuhn-Tucker framework developed in Chapter 3. Toward this goal, the Lagrangean function of the primal problem in (7.2) is

$$L(\mathbf{x}, \mathbf{y}) = \mathbf{c}'\mathbf{x} + \mathbf{y}'[\mathbf{b} - A\mathbf{x}]. \qquad (7.3)$$

The question often arises as to the proper specification of the Lagrangean function, which often can be seen stated as

$$L(\mathbf{x}, \mathbf{y}) = \mathbf{c}'\mathbf{x} + \mathbf{y}'[A\mathbf{x} - \mathbf{b}].$$

The verdict should go in favor of the formulation given in (7.3) because it follows the scheme discussed in Chapter 3. Recall that the analysis of the KKT conditions carried out there was associated with a maximization problem subject to less-than-or-equal constraints. The general Lagrangean function specified within that context resulted in the conclusion that the Lagrange multipliers were nonnegative. The specification in (7.3) follows scrupulously the framework of Chapter 3. The consequence of stating the Lagrangean function as in the alternative formulation given earlier is that the Lagrange multipliers are nonpositive, an event that should be conveniently avoided for a meaningful economic interpretation of Lagrange multipliers as shadow prices.

The general procedure for deriving the dual specification corresponding to a given primal problem was discussed at great length in Chapter 3. Briefly stated, the dual problem optimizes the Lagrangean function subject to its derivatives with respect to the primal variables. The optimization is carried out in the direction opposite to that specified by the primal problem. The first step, therefore, consists in formulating the Lagrangean function associated to the primal problem. Then comes the derivation of the KKT conditions. Third and when possible (in linear and quadratic programming it is always possible), the complementary slackness conditions can be used to simplify the structure of the Lagrangean function.

The KKT conditions corresponding to the Lagrangean function specification given in (7.3) are as follows:

$$\frac{\partial L}{\partial \mathbf{x}} = \mathbf{c} - A'\mathbf{y} \leq \mathbf{0} \tag{7.4}$$

$$\mathbf{x}'\frac{\partial L}{\partial \mathbf{x}} = \mathbf{x}'[\mathbf{c} - A'\mathbf{y}] = 0 \tag{7.5}$$

$$\frac{\partial L}{\partial \mathbf{y}} = \mathbf{b} - A\mathbf{x} \geq \mathbf{0} \tag{7.6}$$

$$\mathbf{y}'\frac{\partial L}{\partial \mathbf{y}} = \mathbf{y}'[\mathbf{b} - A\mathbf{x}] = 0 \tag{7.7}$$

plus the nonnegativity restrictions $\mathbf{x} \geq \mathbf{0}$ and $\mathbf{y} \geq \mathbf{0}$. Finally, the specific dual problem is obtained by implementing the general definition of the dual stated in Chapter 3:

$$\min_{\mathbf{y}} L(\mathbf{x}, \mathbf{y})$$

$$\text{subject to} \quad \frac{\partial L}{\partial \mathbf{x}} \leq \mathbf{0}, \qquad \mathbf{y} \geq \mathbf{0}.$$

The linear character of our problem admits a drastic simplification of the dual objective function represented, in general, by the Lagrangean function. Using the information of the complementary slackness condition (7.5), it is possible to replace the term $\mathbf{c}'\mathbf{x}$ by its equivalent $\mathbf{x}'A'\mathbf{y}$ to obtain

$$\text{minimize}_{\mathbf{y}} \; L(\mathbf{x}, \mathbf{y}) = \mathbf{c}'\mathbf{x} + \mathbf{y}'\mathbf{b} - \mathbf{y}'A\mathbf{x} \tag{7.8}$$

$$= \mathbf{x}'A'\mathbf{y} + \mathbf{y}'\mathbf{b} - \mathbf{y}'A\mathbf{x}$$

$$= \mathbf{y}'\mathbf{b}.$$

To obtain the proper formulation, only the information contained in the complementary slackness conditions of the dual constraints was used. This simplifying procedure is admissible any time a portion of the dual objective function is linear in the primal variables. The foregoing objective function and the KKT condition (7.4) constitute the structure of the dual LP problem as stated in (7.2).

The pair of dual problems stated in (7.2) represents the complete specification of the rational behavior of a competitive (price-taking) entrepreneur who wishes to maximize total profit subject to the available technology. The primal problem states the maximization of total net revenue subject to the demand for inputs being less than or equal to their supply, whereas the dual problem indicates the minimization of the total cost of inputs subject to the condition that the marginal cost of any output be greater than or equal to its marginal revenue.

The KKT conditions [(7.4)–(7.7)] can be stated in the form of a linear complementarity problem $(M, \mathbf{q})$ with the following definition of the matrix M and vectors $\mathbf{q}$ and $\mathbf{z}$:

$$
M = \begin{bmatrix} 0 & A' \\ -A & 0 \end{bmatrix}, \quad \mathbf{q} = \begin{bmatrix} -\mathbf{c} \\ \mathbf{b} \end{bmatrix}, \quad \mathbf{z} = \begin{bmatrix} \mathbf{x} \\ \mathbf{y} \end{bmatrix}.
$$

It remains to show that, indeed, the profit-maximization objective of the competitive entrepreneur is achieved with the specification stated in (7.2). Toward this goal, let us recall that $\min_{\mathbf{y}} \mathbf{b}'\mathbf{y} = -\max_{\mathbf{y}} (-\mathbf{b}'\mathbf{y})$. Then, assuming that the LP problem has a solution, the two objective functions in (7.2) can be assembled as

$$
\max_{\mathbf{x}} \mathbf{c}'\mathbf{x} - \min_{\mathbf{y}} \mathbf{b}'\mathbf{y} = 0 \tag{7.9}
$$

$$
\max_{\mathbf{x}} \mathbf{c}'\mathbf{x} + \max_{\mathbf{y}} (-\mathbf{b})'\mathbf{y} = 0
$$

$$
\max_{\mathbf{x}, \mathbf{y}} (\mathbf{c}'\mathbf{x} - \mathbf{b}'\mathbf{y}) = 0.
$$

With the quantity $\mathbf{c}'\mathbf{x}$ representing total net revenue and $\mathbf{b}'\mathbf{y}$ representing total input cost, the bottom line of (7.9) must be interpreted as the maximization of profits that, for a competitive entrepreneur, should equal zero. An equivalent specification of the pair of dual problems stated in (7.2) can, therefore, be formulated as the following LP problem:

$$
\max_{\mathbf{x}, \mathbf{y}} (\mathbf{c}'\mathbf{x} - \mathbf{b}'\mathbf{y}) \tag{7.10}
$$

$$
\text{subject to} \quad A\mathbf{x} \leq \mathbf{b}
$$

$$
A'\mathbf{y} \geq \mathbf{c}
$$

$$
\mathbf{x} \geq 0, \ \mathbf{y} \geq 0.
$$

The objective function indicates the maximization of profit, whereas the constraints specify the familiar equilibrium conditions according to which the demand for input $(A\mathbf{x})$ must be less than or equal to the supply of the same inputs $\mathbf{b}$ and marginal cost of all production activities $(A'\mathbf{y})$ must be greater than or equal to marginal net revenue $\mathbf{c}$.

The dual specification of the LP problem in (7.10) can be stated as

$$\min_{\lambda, \gamma} (\mathbf{b}'\lambda - \mathbf{c}'\gamma) \qquad (7.11)$$

$$\text{subject to} \qquad A'\lambda \geq \mathbf{c}$$

$$A\gamma \leq \mathbf{b}$$

$$\lambda \geq 0, \ \gamma \geq 0.$$

Aside from the different names of the variables, problem (7.11) has exactly the same structure as problem (7.10) and, therefore, the two problems are equivalent. In particular, if problem (7.10) has a unique solution, problem (7.11) also has a unique solution, and the two solutions must be identical. Let $(\mathbf{x}^*, \mathbf{y}^*)$ and (γ^*, λ^*) be the unique solutions of problems (7.10) and (7.11), respectively. This means that $A\gamma^* \leq \mathbf{b}$, $A\mathbf{x}^* \leq \mathbf{b}$, $A'\lambda^* \geq \mathbf{c}$, and $A'\mathbf{y}^* \geq \mathbf{c}$. By adding together the first two sets of constraints as well as the last two, we obtain $A(\gamma^* + \mathbf{x}^*)/2 \leq \mathbf{b}$ and $A'(\mathbf{y}^* + \lambda^*)/2 \geq \mathbf{c}$. But by assumption, the two systems have a unique solution, thus requiring that $\lambda^* \equiv \mathbf{y}^*$ and $\mathbf{x}^* \equiv \gamma^*$. Furthermore, because the two sets of constraints in problem (7.10) are independent and the objective function is linear, the two subsystems of constraints in (7.10) can be decoupled without loss of information to form a pair of dual problems as stated in (7.2). The equivalency of specifications (7.2) and (7.10) is, therefore demonstrated and with it the interpretation that the pair of dual problems (7.2) corresponds to the profit maximization of a competitive entrepreneur.

A price-taker's LP problem is usually stated as {max *TNR* subject to $D \leq S$}. But we do not solve this problem directly. We solve the first-order necessary conditions derived from the associated Lagrangean function and corresponding to KKT conditions (7.4) through (7.7), including the nonnegativity conditions of vectors $\mathbf{x}$ and $\mathbf{y}$.

We, thus, can say that the structure of an LP problem corresponds to the structure of an Equilibrium Problem, as follows:

Quantity side

$$A\mathbf{x} \leq \mathbf{b} \quad \left\{ \begin{array}{c} \textit{Demand of Limiting} \\ \textit{Commodities} \end{array} \right\} \leq \left\{ \begin{array}{c} \textit{Supply of Limiting} \\ \textit{Commodities} \end{array} \right\}$$

$\mathbf{y} \geq 0$ *Nonnegative Limiting Commodity Price Vector*

$(\mathbf{b} - A\mathbf{x})'\mathbf{y} = 0$ *Complementary Slackness of Limiting*

                Commodities

Price side

$$A'y \geq c \quad \left\{ \begin{array}{c} \textit{Marginal Cost} \\ \textit{of Nonlimiting} \\ \textit{Commodities} \end{array} \right\} \geq \left\{ \begin{array}{c} \textit{Marginal Revenue} \\ \textit{of Nonlimiting} \\ \textit{Commodities} \end{array} \right\}$$

$$x \geq 0 \quad \textit{Nonnegative Nonlimiting Commodity Vector}$$

$$(A'y - c)'x = 0 \left\{ \begin{array}{c} \textit{Complementary Slackness} \\ \textit{of Nonlimiting Commodities} \end{array} \right\}$$

By inspecting the equilibrium problem, we conclude that the objective function of both primal and dual LP problems has been replaced by the appropriate complementary slackness condition. When stated in these terms, an LP problem is clearly a special case of the Equilibrium Problem.

General Linear Model of Joint Production

The following example illustrates the flexibility of linear programming to represent a rather complex scenario of production. This example is a reelaboration of a model of production from lecture notes by McFadden (1964). The development of this section illustrates in great detail the role of variable and limiting inputs in determining the specification of a dual pair of linear programming problems.

There exist commodities and productive activities that generate such commodities. Let:

(a) Commodities: $i = 1, \ldots, m$.
(b) Activities: $j = 1, \ldots, n$.
(c) Technical coefficients: $a_{ij} \equiv$ net output of commodity i obtained from activity j. If a_{ij} is negative, the commodity is considered an input; if a_{ij} is positive, the commodity is a product.
(d) Level of intensity at which the jth activity is operated: x_j.
(e) Net quantity of the ith commodity produced using all the n activities: $q_i = \sum_{j=1}^{n} a_{ij} x_j$, ($q_i$ can be either positive or negative depending on the sign and magnitude of the a_{ij} coefficients).
(f) Price of the ith commodity: p_i.

The firm faces a fixed price structure and possesses some bundle of resources employable in the productive activities. Furthermore, the firm engages in some contractual agreements that, when signed, become constraints enforceable by penalty. Finally, the firm is confronted by some institutional constraints. For example, tobacco growers and dairy farmers are constrained by quotas imposed on their output levels. The objective is to maximize profits, π, defined in the traditional specification of revenue minus costs:

$$\pi = \sum_{i=1}^{m} p_i q_i = \sum_{i=1}^{m} p_i \left(\sum_{j=1}^{n} a_{ij} x_j \right) = \sum_{j=1}^{n} \underbrace{\left(\sum_{i=1}^{m} p_i a_{ij} \right)}_{\substack{\text{unit profit} \\ \text{of the } j\text{th} \\ \text{activity}}} x_j. \quad (7.12)$$

In the conventional notation of linear programming, the unit profit coefficient of the jth activity is indicated as $c_j = \sum_{i=1}^{m} p_i a_{ij}$. The constraints under which profits must be maximized can be classified into the three following groups:

C1 $b_i^{\max} \equiv$ maximum amount of the ith commodity available or purchasable by the firm:

$$-\sum_{j=1}^{n} a_{ij} x_j \leq b_i^{\max}$$

C2 $b_i^{\min} \equiv$ minimum amount of the ith commodity that the firm must either purchase or produce:

$$\sum_{j=1}^{n} a_{ij} x_j \leq -b_i^{\min}$$

C3 $\bar{x}_j \equiv$ upper limit on the level of intensity at which the jth activity may be operated, due, for example, to institutional constraints.

The primal specification of the problem is summarized as

$$\max_{\mathbf{x}} \pi = \sum_{j=1}^{n} \left(\sum_{i=1}^{m} p_i a_{ij} \right) x_j \quad (7.13)$$

subject to $\qquad\qquad\qquad\qquad\qquad\qquad$ Dual Variables

$$-\sum_{j=1}^{n} a_{ij} x_j \leq b_i^{\max} \qquad\qquad y_i$$

$$\sum_{j=1}^{n} a_{ij} x_j \leq -b_i^{\min} \qquad\qquad z_i$$

$$x_j \leq \bar{x}_j \qquad\qquad r_j$$

$$x_j \geq 0,$$

$$i = 1, \ldots, m, \quad j = 1, \ldots, n.$$

Notice that if all the technical coefficients for the ith commodity are negative ($a_{ij} < 0$, $j = 1, \ldots, n$), the constraints become

$$\sum_{j=1}^{n} a_{ij}x_j \leq b_i^{\max}$$

and

$$\sum_{j=1}^{n} a_{ij}x_j \geq b_i^{\min}$$

and, therefore, the constraints are imposed on a commodity input (factor of production). If $a_{ij} > 0$, $j = 1, \ldots, n$, the sign of the inequalities in the original formulation of (7.13) does not change and the constraints are imposed on a commodity output (product). Hence, positive levels of $b_i^{\max}$ and $b_i^{\min}$ are bounds on inputs,

$$b_i^{\min} \leq \text{ inputs } \leq b_i^{\max}$$

whereas negative levels of $-b_i^{\max}$ and $-b_i^{\min}$ are bounds on outputs,

$$-b_i^{\max} \leq \text{ output } \leq -b_i^{\min}.$$

Let us consider now the profit function of the competitive entrepreneur. In a conventional framework of the theory, a necessary condition for profit maximization is that the value marginal product of the ith input be equal to its price:

$$\frac{\partial \pi}{\partial b_i} = \frac{\partial (\text{Revenue})}{\partial b_i} - p_i = 0 \tag{7.14}$$

where b_i is a factor of production, p_i is its price, and $\frac{\partial (\text{Revenue})}{\partial b_i}$ is the value marginal product of the ith input, (VMP_i). Furthermore, from Lagrangean theory, the derivative of the Lagrangean function with respect to a constraint is equal to its corresponding Lagrange multiplier. The Lagrangean function of the primal problem (7.13) is

$$L(\mathbf{x}, \mathbf{y}, \mathbf{z}, \mathbf{r}) = \sum_{j=1}^{n}\left(\sum_{i=1}^{m} p_i a_{ij}\right) x_j + \sum_{i=1}^{m} y_i \left[b_i^{\max} + \sum_{j=1}^{n} a_{ij}x_j \right] \tag{7.15}$$

$$+ \sum_{i=1}^{m} z_i \left[-\sum_{j=1}^{n} a_{ij}x_j - b_i^{\min} \right] + \sum_{j=1}^{n} r_j [\bar{x}_j - x_j].$$

Now suppose that the ith constraint of the max-type is binding. This means that $b_i^{max} = -\sum_{j=1}^{n} a_{ij} x_j$. Hence, the Lagrangean function (7.15) can be rewritten as

$$L(\cdot) = \sum_{i=1}^{m} p_i\left(-b_i^{max}\right) + \sum_{i=1}^{m} y_i \left[b_i^{max} + \sum_{j=1}^{n} a_{ij} x_j\right] + \text{etc.} \quad (7.16)$$

Differentiating (7.16) with respect to b_i^{max} gives the envelope condition

$$\frac{\partial L(\cdot)}{\partial b_i^{max}} = y_i - \frac{\partial \pi}{\partial b_i^{max}} = 0 \quad (7.17)$$

and applying the condition for profit maximization derived in (7.14),

$$\frac{\partial L(\cdot)}{\partial b_i^{max}} = y_i + p_i - VMP_i = 0 \quad (7.18)$$

or, equivalently $VMP_i = p_i + y_i$. The economic meaning of (7.18) is that rationing of some resource makes it convenient to expand production to the point where the value marginal product of that input is equal to its market price plus the economic value of the constraint. In the conventional theory of production without limits on resources, the competitive entrepreneur would expand production up to the point where $VMP_i = p_i$. This result is in line with the theorem on complementary slackness, which says that when a constraint is not binding, the corresponding dual variable is equal to zero.

An analogous development may be outlined for resources that have a lower limit and assuming that the ith constraint of the *min*-type is binding, $b_i^{min} = -\sum_{j=1}^{n} a_{ij} x_j$. Hence, the Lagrangean function (7.15) can be rewritten as

$$L(\cdot) = \sum_{i=1}^{m} p_i\left(-b_i^{min}\right) + \sum_{i=1}^{m} z_i \left[-\sum_{j=1}^{n} a_{ij} x_j - b_i^{min}\right] + \text{etc.} \quad (7.19)$$

Differentiating (7.19) with respect to b_i^{min} gives the envelope condition

$$\frac{\partial L(\cdot)}{\partial b_i^{min}} = -\frac{\partial \pi}{\partial b_i^{min}} - z_i = 0 \quad (7.20)$$

and applying the condition for profit maximization derived in (7.14),

$$\frac{\partial L(\cdot)}{\partial b_i^{min}} = -VMP_i + p_i - z_i = 0 \quad (7.21)$$

or, equivalently $VMP_i = p_i - z_i$. The dual variable z_i represents the marginal value of changing the minimum requirement of the ith resource. In economic terms, relation (7.21) means that, when $z_i > 0$, the entrepreneur would prefer to reduce her production because $VMP_i < p_i$ but she is forced to produce at the level that makes $z_i > 0$ because of the contract stipulated in advance.

The meaning of the dual variable r_j is the rent (or quasi-rent) of increasing (or decreasing) the plant capacity by one unit of the jth activity. Finally, the upper and lower bounds on the ith commodity may shrink to a point, that is, $b_i^{\min} \leq$ commodity $i \leq b_i^{\max}$ such that $b_i^{\min} = b_i^{\max}$. This case corresponds to a constraint in the form of an equation rather than an inequality.

The dual problem corresponding to the primal specification (7.13) can be stated as

$$\min\ TC = \underbrace{\sum_{i=1}^{m} y_i b_i^{\min}}_{\substack{\text{cost of} \\ \text{buying} \\ \text{the firm's} \\ \text{plant}}} - \underbrace{\sum_{i=1}^{m} y_i b_i^{\max}}_{\substack{\text{cost of} \\ \text{buying} \\ \text{the firm's} \\ \text{contracts}}} + \underbrace{\sum_{j=1}^{n} \hat{x}_j r_j}_{\substack{\text{cost of} \\ \text{buying} \\ \text{the firm's} \\ \text{licenses}}} \qquad (7.22)$$

subject to

$$\sum_{i=1}^{m} (-a_{ij}) y_i + \sum_{i=1}^{m} a_{ij} z_i + r_j \geq \sum_{i=1}^{m} p_i a_{ij}$$

$$y_i \geq 0\ z_i \geq 0\ r_j \geq 0.$$

The economic interpretation of the dual problem can be stated as follows. A second entrepreneur enters a bid to buy the firm of the original price taker as represented by the primal problem (7.13). Naturally, he wishes to minimize the total cost of acquiring the available resources (plant, options, contracts, production licenses, etc.). His bid, however, must satisfy lower limits set by the seller on the value of the various resources. Such limits are represented by the dual constraints

$$\underbrace{\sum_{i=1}^{m} (z_i - y_i) a_{ij} + r_j}_{\substack{\text{marginal activity} \\ \text{cost of the } j\text{th} \\ \text{commodity}}} \geq \underbrace{\sum_{i=1}^{m} p_i a_{ij.}}_{\substack{\text{unit profit} \\ \text{of the } j\text{th} \\ \text{activity}}} \qquad (7.23)$$

The marginal cost has two components: the marginal cost of all the resources involved in production, $\sum_{i=1}^{m}(z_i - y_i)a_{ij}$, and the rent on the jth activity, r_j.

Numerical Example 1: Linear Joint Production

The firm in question deals with five commodities: crude oil, equipment, labor, kerosene, and gasoline. There are several techniques for producing gasoline and kerosene. The first activity requires one unit of crude oil, one unit of equipment, and one unit of labor to produce two units of kerosene. The second activity employs one unit of crude oil, two units of equipment, and one unit of labor for producing a joint output of one unit of kerosene and one unit of gasoline. The third activity is a conversion of kerosene into gasoline. It does not require crude oil but needs a unit of equipment, labor, and kerosene to produce one unit of gasoline. The fourth activity produces nothing but requires a unit of plant (equipment). The detailed information regarding commodity prices and upper and lower limits imposed on the commodities is stated in the following table

	Commodity	Price	b_i^{max}	b_i^{min}
$i = 1$	Crude oil	1	4	0
$i = 2$	Equipment	2	3	3
$i = 3$	Labor	1	$+\infty$	0
$i = 4$	Kerosene	2	1	–
$i = 5$	Gasoline	6	–	–

The production technology can also be summarized in a convenient array of information:

	Activity	$a_{1.}$	$a_{2.}$	$a_{3.}$	$a_{4.}$	$a_{5.}$	$\bar{x}$
$j = 1$	Kerosene from crude oil	−1	−1	−1	2	0	1
$j = 2$	Kerosene and gasoline from crude oil	−1	−2	−1	1	1	1
$j = 3$	Gasoline from kerosene conversion	0	−1	−1	−1	1	2
$j = 4$	Idle plant	0	−1	0	0	0	–

Using the information of these two arrays, it is possible to calculate the unit profit of each activity. For example, the unit profit of activity 1, say c_1, is

$$c_1 \equiv \sum_{i=1}^{5} p_i a_{i1} = -1 + (-2) + (-1) + 4 + 0 = 0.$$

Similarly, the unit profit of the other activities is

$$c_2 \equiv \sum_{i=1}^{5} p_i a_{i2} = 2$$
$$c_3 \equiv \sum_{i=1}^{5} p_i a_{i3} = 1$$
$$c_4 \equiv \sum_{i=1}^{5} p_i a_{i4} = -2.$$

Finally, the primal specification of the joint production problem reads as follows:

$$\max_{\mathbf{x}} \pi = 0x_1 + 2x_2 + x_3 - 2x_4 \tag{7.24}$$

subject to				Dual Variables
Crude oil	$x_1 + x_2$	$\leq$	4	y_1
Equipment	$x_1 + 2x_2 + x_3 + x_4$	$\leq$	3	y_2
Kerosene	$-2x_1 - x_2 + x_3$	$\leq$	1	y_4
Equipment	$-x_1 - 2x_2 - x_3 - x_4$	$\leq$	-3	z_2
Kerosene	x_1	$\leq$	1	r_1
Kerosene and gasoline	x_2	$\leq$	1	r_2
Gasoline from kerosene	x_3	$\leq$	2	r_3

and all the variables x_1, x_2, x_3, x_4 are nonnegative. The constraint for equipment was specified as a complementary set of inequalities that are equivalent to an equation in order to exemplify the use of lower and upper limits on the level of resources.

Using the transposition rule, the specification of the dual problem takes on the following expression:

$$\min TC = 4y_1 + 3(y_2 - z_2) + y_4 + r_1 + r_2 + 2r_3 \tag{7.25}$$

subject to

$$
\begin{aligned}
y_1 + (y_2 - z_2) - 2y_4 + r_1 && \geq && 0 \\
y_1 + 2(y_2 - z_2) - y_4 + r_2 && \geq && 2 \\
(y_2 - z_2) + y_4 + r_3 && \geq && 1 \\
(y_2 - z_2) && \geq && -2
\end{aligned}
$$

with all nonnegative variables.

An optimal primal solution of the linear programming problem is $x_2 = x_3 = 1$ with all the other primal components at the zero level. Total profit is, therefore, equal to 3. The corresponding dual solution is $(y_2 - z_2) = 1$ with all the other dual components at the zero level. Total cost is, therefore, equal to 3.

The relevant conclusion derived from the discussion developed in this example is that the dual variables have an alternative structure and interpretation that depends on the treatment of market prices of limiting resources. If the market price of a resource is known, it can be included into the LP framework as in the unit profit coefficients of the joint production example. In this case, the dual variable has the structure of either (7.18) or (7.21) where $y_i = VMP_i - p_i$ and $z_i = p_i - VMP_i$, respectively. The interpretation is that, for a *max*-type constraint, the dual variable y_i is the nonnegative difference between the value marginal product and the market price. In the case of a *min*-type constraint, the dual variable z_i is the nonnegative difference between the market price and the value marginal product of the ith resource.

If prices of limiting resources are unknown, as is often the case with some inputs used in agriculture (land, family labor, service flow of building and machinery capital, underground water, etc.), the dual variable has the structure of value marginal product. From (7.18), and in the case of a max-type constraint, the dual variable, say w_i^{max}, is $w_i^{max} = p_i + y_i = VMP_i$. Analogously, and from (7.21), the dual variable corresponding to a min-type constraint is $w_i^{min} = p_i - z_i = VMP_i$.

Numerical Example 2: Two Plants, One Market

In the following example, a price-taking entrepreneur owns two physical plants that produce final commodities for the same market. The specification of the primal problem is as follows:

Primal

$$\max TR = \mathbf{c'x}$$

subject to

$$A_1\mathbf{x}_1 \leq \mathbf{b}_1 \qquad \text{technology at plant 1}$$

$$A_2\mathbf{x}_2 \leq \mathbf{b}_2 \qquad \text{technology at plant 2}$$

$$\mathbf{x}_1 + \mathbf{x}_2 \geq \mathbf{x} \qquad \text{market clearing}$$

$$\mathbf{x}_1 \geq 0, \ \mathbf{x}_2 \geq 0, \ \mathbf{x} \geq 0$$

The relevant data are given as follows:

$$\text{Plant 1:} \quad \mathbf{b}_1 = \begin{bmatrix} 7 \\ 24 \\ 8 \end{bmatrix}, \quad A_1 = \begin{bmatrix} 0.25 & 0.2 & 0.5 & 1.0 \\ 1.00 & 1.0 & 0.2 & 0.3 \\ 0.20 & 1.0 & 0.5 & 0.8 \end{bmatrix}$$

$$\text{Plant 2:} \quad \mathbf{b}_2 = \begin{bmatrix} 8 \\ 4 \\ 5 \end{bmatrix}, \quad A_2 = \begin{bmatrix} 0.7 & 1.0 & 0.5 & 0.3 \\ 1.0 & 0.2 & 0.2 & 0.3 \\ 0.5 & 1.0 & 0.1 & 0.9 \end{bmatrix}$$

$$\text{Net revenues:} \quad \mathbf{c} = \begin{bmatrix} 28 \\ 36 \\ 22 \\ 15 \end{bmatrix}$$

The GAMS solution of the foregoing problem gives the following results:

$$\text{Total Revenue} = 1092.86$$

$$\text{Total Cost at Plant 1} = 733.57$$

$$\text{Total Cost at Plant 2} = 359.29$$

$$\text{Total Cost} = 1092.86$$

$$\mathbf{x}_1 = \begin{bmatrix} x_{11} = 20.9399 \\ x_{21} = 2.5587 \\ x_{31} = 2.5065 \\ x_{41} = 0.0000 \end{bmatrix}, \mathbf{x}_2 = \begin{bmatrix} x_{12} = 0.0000 \\ x_{22} = 0.0000 \\ x_{32} = 13.5714 \\ x_{42} = 4.0476 \end{bmatrix}, \mathbf{x} = \begin{bmatrix} x_1 = 20.9399 \\ x_2 = 2.5587 \\ x_3 = 16.0780 \\ x_4 = 4.0476 \end{bmatrix}$$

$$\mathbf{y}_1 = \begin{bmatrix} y_{11} = 24.6475 \\ y_{21} = 19.5300 \\ y_{31} = 11.5404 \end{bmatrix}, \mathbf{y}_2 = \begin{bmatrix} y_{12} = 43.5714 \\ y_{22} = 0.0000 \\ y_{32} = 2.1428 \end{bmatrix}.$$

GAMS Command File: Numerical Example 2

We list a command file for the nonlinear package GAMS that solves the numerical problem presented in Example 2. Asterisks in column 1 relate to comments.

```
$title price taker, two plants and one market
*
$offsymlist offsymxref
```

```
   option limrow = 0
   option limcol = 0
   option iterlim = 100000
   option reslim = 200000
   option nlp = conopt3
   option decimals = 7 ;
*
   sets j   output variables / x1, x2, x3, x4 /
        i   inputs / y1, y2, y3 /
*
   alias(i,k,kk);
   alias(j,jj) ;
*
   parameter c(j)      intercept of demand functions

   /   x1    28
       x2    36
       x3    22
       x4    15   /
*
   parameter b1(i)     intercept of input supply for
     plant1

   /   y1    7
       y2    24
       y3    8   /
*
   parameter b2(i)     intercept of input supply for
     plant 2

   /   y1    8
       y2    4
       y3    5   /
*
   table a1(i,j)    technical coefficient matrix for
     plant 1

           x1      x2    x3      x4
       y1  0.25    0.2   0.5     1.0
       y2  1.00    1.0   0.2     0.3
       y3  0.20    1.0   0.5     0.8
*
   table a2(i,j)    technical coefficient matrix for
     plant 2
```

```
        x1      x2    x3      x4
  y1    0.7    1.0    0.5    0.3
  y2    1.0    0.2    0.2    0.3
  y3    0.5    1.0    0.1    0.9
*
* price taker's lp problem
*
   variables
   pritak    objective function
   x(j)      quantity demands
   x1(j)     quantities supplied from plant 1
   x2(j)     quantities supplied from plant 2 ;
*
   positive variables x, x1, x2 ;
*
   equations
   objeq    name of objective function's equation
   techeq1(i)    name of technical constraints of
                 plant 1
   techeq2(i)    name of technical constraints of
                 plant 2
   mktequil(j)   physical market equilibrium
                 conditions ;
*
   objeq..     pritak =e= sum(j, c(j)*x(j) );
   techeq1(i)..      sum(j, a1(i,j)*x1(j)) =l= b1(i) ;
   techeq2(i)..      sum(j, a2(i,j)*x2(j)) =l= b2(i) ;
   mktequil(j)..     x1(j) + x2(j) =g= x(j) ;
*
* name and define the lp model
*
   model pricetake / objeq, techeq1, techeq2,
     mktequil / ;
*
   solve pricetake using lp maximizing pritak ;
*
   parameter totplc1, totplc2, totcost, totrev ;
*
   totrev = sum(j, c(j)*x.l(j) ) ;
   totplc1 = sum(i,b1(i)*techeq1.m(i)) ;
   totplc2 = sum(i,b2(i)*techeq2.m(i)) ;
   totcost = totplc1 + totplc2 ;
```

*

```
display pritak.l, totrev, totplc1, totplc2,
   totcost, x1.l, x2.l, x.l, techeq1.m, techeq2.m ;
```

The Primal Simplex Algorithm

Although an LP problem is a special case of the linear complementarity structure, as shown in a previous section, the special features of the M matrix allow for a clear separation of the primal and dual specifications. Hence, the most efficient algorithm for solving LP problems has been the Simplex method discovered by Dantzig and other mathematicians as early as 1947. This algorithm has proven to be very robust and fast in spite of some theoretical issues of complexity that will not be discussed here. So far, it has beaten back the challenges of many attempts to improve the speed of solving LP problems. Furthermore, and for the scope of this book, the Simplex method is of special interest because each of its steps and iterations can be interpreted in economic terms.

The simplex algorithm is closely related to the pivot method for solving a system of linear equations that was discussed in Chapter 4. The only difference consists in the choice of the pivot that, in the Simplex method, is dictated by optimization and feasibility criteria that correspond to economic and technological considerations guiding the behavior of a price-taking entrepreneur. The name *Simplex* derives from the fact that, at each iteration, a simplex (as defined in Chapter 4) is constructed prior to changing the current feasible basis.

Using the structure of the Primal LP problem stated in (7.2), the first thing to do is to introduce surplus (slack) variables, x_s, into the constraints and to bring all the unknown variables, including those of the objective function, on one side of the equality sign:

$$A\mathbf{x} + \mathbf{x}_s = \mathbf{b} \tag{7.26}$$

$$TNR - \mathbf{c}'\mathbf{x} - \mathbf{0}'\mathbf{x}_s = 0. \tag{7.27}$$

For exposition reasons, we assume that $\mathbf{b} \geq \mathbf{0}$ and $\mathbf{c} \geq \mathbf{0}$. Furthermore, notice that the dual constraints of (7.2) define the condition of an optimal production plan when the vector of opportunity marginal costs is written as $OC \equiv A'\mathbf{y} - \mathbf{c} \geq \mathbf{0}$. In other words, when the opportunity cost of all the activities contemplated by the entrepreneur as feasible candidates for his production plan are nonnegative, that plan is also optimal. Thus, using both economic and mathematical languages, we list, side by side, the ideas that guide the development of the primal simplex algorithm.

Economic Language	Mathematical Language
1. Find the "do nothing" production plan.	1. Find an initial and easy basic feasible solution (BFS).
2. Check whether this producible production plan is optimal: if yes, stop. if no, continue;	2. Check whether this BFS is an optimal solution: if yes, stop. if no, continue;
3. Select another producible production plan that increases the *TNR* objective function and go to 2.	3. Select another adjacent BFS that improves the value of the objective function and go to 2.

The "do nothing" production plan consists of keeping idle all the limiting inputs with all their supplies going into storage as surplus activities, that is, $x = 0$, $x_s = b \geq 0$. This production plan is always producible, and it is chosen at the start of the simplex algorithm because it is easily identified in an explicit way. The "do nothing" production plan corresponds to the origin of the output space that is generated by the identity basis. Hence, the initial feasible basis is the identity matrix.

From a geometric viewpoint, a basic feasible solution of an LP problem corresponds to an extreme point of the feasible region defined by the intersection of all the linear constraints. The primal simplex algorithm chooses successively adjacent extreme points to reach an optimal BFS.

The next step is to set up the initial primal tableau using the information of equations (7.26) and (7.27), which is interpreted as follows:

$$
\begin{array}{cccc}
TNR & x' & x'_s & sol
\end{array}
$$

$$
\begin{bmatrix}
0 & \vdots & A & I & \vdots & b \\
1 & \vdots & -c' & 0' & \vdots & 0
\end{bmatrix}
\equiv
\begin{bmatrix}
0 & \vdots & \text{Technology} & \vdots & \text{Production Plan} \\
1 & \vdots & OC \equiv MC - MR & \vdots & TNR
\end{bmatrix}
$$

The opportunity costs of all the commodities, including the limiting inputs, are given in the bottom row of the tableau. At the start of the primal simplex algorithm, the "do nothing" production plan corresponds to $x = 0$, as we have seen. Hence, the marginal cost of these activities is equal to zero. This is the reason why, in the algebraic representation of the first tableau, the opportunity cost of these commodities is given by $OC \equiv -c' \leq 0'$. At this stage, therefore, the production plan is producible but, obviously, it is not an optimal plan because almost all the opportunity costs violate the optimality condition discussed earlier, $OC \equiv A'\mathbf{y} - \mathbf{c} \geq \mathbf{0}$. It remains, thus, to choose an activity among those ones whose opportunity cost is negative and compute the highest level of production that is compatible with the availability of limiting resources. This means liberating some inputs taken up by the current production plan to make them available to the selected activity or, in other words, replacing one activity of the current and nonoptimal production plan with the selected activity. In the literature, it has been customary to represent the opportunity cost of the jth activity by the symbol $(z_j - c_j)$, where z_j is the marginal cost and c_j is the marginal net revenue of the jth activity.

We summarize, now, the rules of the primal simplex algorithm assuming that there are J activities and I limiting inputs:

0. Assume a maximization problem and find a primal basic feasible solution (PBFS) (usually the "do nothing" production plan). Without a PBFS at hand, it is not possible to apply the primal simplex algorithm. A PBFS implies that all $x_{Bi} \geq 0$, $i = 1, \ldots, I$, $x_{NBj} = 0$, $j = 1, \ldots, J$, where the subscript $(\ldots)_B$ stands for basic variables and the subscript $(\ldots)_{NB}$ for nonbasic variables, as explained in Chapter 4.
1. Verify whether the current PBFS is optimal. That is:
   1.1 If **all** the opportunity costs are nonnegative, the current PBFS is optimal. In symbols: If **all** $(z_j - c_j) \geq 0$, stop.
   1.2 If **some** opportunity cost is negative, choose the activity associated with the most negative OC. In symbols: If **some** $(z_j - c_j) < 0$, choose the incoming activity as the rth column of the technology such that

$$z_r - c_r = \min_j\{z_j - c_j < 0\}$$

   for all the indices j for which the corresponding opportunity cost is negative. This rule is called the entry criterion because the rth activity will enter the next primal feasible basis.
2. In order to maintain the feasibility of the next PBFS (the producibility of the next production plan), compute the minimum ratio (as discussed for the pivot algorithm in Chapter 4) between the components of the current PBFS and the **positive** coefficients of the incoming activity. In symbols: To exit the current PBFS, choose the kth activity such that

$$\frac{x_{Bk}}{a^*_{kr}} = \min_i\left\{\frac{x_{Bi}}{a^*_{ir}} \,\middle|\, a^*_{ir} > 0\right\}$$

for all indices i for which $a^*_{ir} > 0$. This rule is called the exit criterion because the kth activity will be replaced by the rth activity in the next PBFS.

3. Identify the pivot (it is convenient to circle it) as the (kr)th element of the technology matrix and change the current basis using the pivot method as discussed in Chapter 4. Go to step 1.

Numerical Example 3: The Primal Simplex Algorithm

Let us solve the following LP problem using the primal simplex algorithm:

$$\max TNR = 3x_1 + 5x_2$$
$$\text{subject to} \qquad 2x_1 + 4x_2 \le 16 \qquad (7.28)$$
$$6x_1 + 3x_2 \le 18$$

with $x_1 \ge 0$, $x_2 \ge 0$. The following tableaux are computed according to the instructions and rules of the primal simplex algorithm discussed in the previous section. The example exhibits two inputs and two outputs.

Initial Tableau

	T_1			TNR		x_1	x_2	x_{s1}	x_{s2}		P sol	BI	ratios
$\frac{1}{4}$	0	:	0	0	:	2	$\boxed{4}$	1	0	:	16	x_{s1}	$\frac{16}{4} \rightarrow$ exit
$-\frac{3}{4}$	1	:	0	0	:	6	3	0	1	:	18	x_{s2}	$\frac{18}{3}$
$\frac{5}{4}$	0	:	1	1	:	-3	-5	0	0	:	0	TNR	

$\uparrow$ entry

Intermediate Tableau

	T_2			TNR		x_1	x_2	x_{s1}	x_{s2}		P sol	BI	ratios
1	$-\frac{1}{9}$	:	0	0	:	$\frac{1}{2}$	1	$\frac{1}{4}$	0	:	4	x_2	$\frac{4}{1/2}$
0	$\frac{2}{9}$	:	0	0	:	$\boxed{\frac{9}{2}}$	0	$-\frac{3}{4}$	1	:	6	x_{s2}	$\frac{6}{9/2} \rightarrow$ exit
0	$\frac{1}{9}$	:	1	1	:	$-\frac{1}{2}$	0	$\frac{5}{4}$	0	:	20	TNR	

$\uparrow$ entry

Final (Optimal) Tableau

TNR		x_1	x_2	x_{s1}	x_{s2}		P sol	BI
0	:	0	1	$\frac{1}{3}$	$-\frac{1}{9}$	:	$\frac{10}{3}$	x_2
0	:	1	0	$-\frac{1}{6}$	$\frac{2}{9}$	:	$\frac{4}{3}$	x_1
1	:	0	0	$\frac{7}{6}$	$\frac{1}{9}$	:	$\frac{62}{3}$	TNR
D sol		y_{s1}	y_{s2}	y_1	y_2		TC	

"P sol" stands for primal solution and "D sol" for dual solution. Variables y_{s1}, y_{s2} are the slack variables of the dual constraints. Their economic meaning is that of *marginal loss* because they are defined as the difference between marginal cost and marginal revenue of the given activity. The variables y_1, y_2, instead, are the shadow prices of the limiting inputs appearing in the dual problem. In fact, to clarify also this last aspect of the numerical example, we state the dual problem corresponding to the LP primal problem (7.28):

$$\min TC = 16y_1 + 18y_2 \tag{7.29}$$
$$\text{subject to} \quad 2y_1 + 6y_2 \geq 3$$
$$4y_1 + 3y_2 \geq 5$$

with $y_1 \geq 0$, $y_2 \geq 0$. The reader is invited to use the values of the dual solution exhibited in the final tableau to verify that they satisfy the dual constraints and give a value of the dual objective function that is equal to the value of the primal objective function. Notice that the pairing of the appropriate components of the primal and dual solutions satisfies the complementary slackness relation required by the KKT conditions discussed in Chapter 3.

The arsenal of algorithms for solving LP problems and based on the notion of a simplex includes the dual simplex algorithm, the artificial variable algorithm, and the artificial constraint algorithm. These algorithms are discussed in the original work of Dantzig.

The Dual Simplex Algorithm

By comparing the primal and the dual examples illustrated in problems (7.28) and (7.29), it should be clear that all the information appearing in the primal problem appears also in the dual specification, although in different locations. In technical terms, it is said that the information of the primal problem has been transposed in the dual problem, and vice versa. This fact is reinforced by the realization that, in solving the primal problem, using the primal simplex algorithm, we also obtained the optimal dual solution. This "discovery" suggests the reciprocal approach: it should be possible to solve a linear programming problem seeking directly a dual solution and obtaining the corresponding primal solution as a "bonus." This goal requires a mirror methodology called the dual simplex algorithm that was developed by Lemke in 1954. Hence, in spite of the clear symmetry of the LP structure, the development of the dual simplex algorithm took at least seven years from the discovery of the primal simplex algorithm.

To simplify the presentation of the dual simplex algorithm, we build on what we know about the primal simplex method, in a way suggested by Paris. Let us recall that the rules of the primal simplex algorithm presented earlier were developed keeping in mind an LP problem in the (max, $\leq$) format, where "max" stands for maximization and " $\leq$" for less-than-or-equal type of contraints. The corresponding initial primal tableau was set up according to this specification. We apply the same format to the dual problem (7.29) and write down the initial dual tableau in symbolic terms. Hence, the primal and the dual tableaux of a (max, $\leq$) LP problem will exhibit the following layout:

Primal Tableau   Dual Tableau

$$\begin{bmatrix} 0 & \vdots & a_{ij}^* & \vdots & x_{Bi} \\ \cdots & \vdots & \cdots & \vdots & \cdots \\ 1 & \vdots & (z_j - c_j) & \vdots & Z \end{bmatrix} \qquad \begin{bmatrix} 0 & \vdots & -a_{ji}^* & \vdots & (z_j - c_j) \\ \cdots & \vdots & \cdots & \vdots & \cdots \\ 1 & \vdots & x_{Bi} & \vdots & R \end{bmatrix}$$

Because we already know the rules of the primal simplex algorithm as applied to the primal tableau (and given in a previous section), we will write down the rules of the dual simplex algorithm as applied to the dual tableau by following, step by step, the rules of the primal simplex algorithm in a metamathematical operation.

Primal Simplex	Dual Simplex
Step 0: A PBFS must be known $x_{Bi} \geq 0, x_{NBj} = 0$ all i, j.	Step 0: A DBFS must be known $(z_j - c_j) \geq 0$ all j.
Step 1: Select $\min_j\{(z_j - c_j) < 0\}$, say $(z_k - c_k)$.	Step 1: Select $\min_i\{x_{Bi} < 0\}$, say x_{Br}.
Step 2: Select $\min_i\left\{\dfrac{x_{Bi}}{a_{ik}^*} \,\middle|\, a_{ik}^* > 0\right\}$	Step 2: Select $\min_j\left\{\left\|\dfrac{(z_j - c_j)}{-a_{jr}^*}\right\| - a_{jr}^* > 0\right\}$

The acronym PBFS stands for primal basic feasible solution and DBFS means dual basic feasible solution.

Numerical Example 4: The Dual Simplex Algorithm

Let us solve the following LP problem using the dual simplex algorithm:

$$\min Z = 2x_1 + x_2$$
$$\text{subject to} \quad x_1 + x_2 \geq 3$$
$$2x_1 + \tfrac{1}{2}x_2 \geq 2$$

with $x_1 \geq 0$, $x_2 \geq 0$.

As stated earlier, it is necessary to reformulate the given numerical problem in the (max, $\leq$) format and to set up the corresponding initial primal tableau. It must be emphasized, in fact, that both primal and dual simplex algorithms can be applied, and should be applied, only to the primal tableau, because it contains all the LP information.

Initial Primal Tableau

T_1			$-Z$	x_1	x_2	x_{s1}	x_{s2}	sol	BI	
-1	0	0	0	-1	(-1)	1	0	-3	x_{s1}	$\rightarrow$ exit
$-\tfrac{1}{2}$	1	0	0	-2	$-\tfrac{1}{2}$	0	1	-2	x_{s2}	criterion
1	0	1	1	2	1	0	0	0	$-Z$	

$$\text{entry criterion}: \min\left\{\frac{2}{-(-1)}, \frac{1}{-(-1)}\right\} = \frac{1}{1} = 1$$

Intermediate Primal Tableau

T_2			$-Z$	x_1	x_2	x_{s1}	x_{s2}	sol	BI	
1	$\tfrac{2}{3}$	0	0	1	1	-1	0	3	x_2	
0	$-\tfrac{2}{3}$	0	0	$(-\tfrac{3}{2})$	0	$-\tfrac{1}{2}$	1	$-\tfrac{1}{2}$	x_{s2}	$\rightarrow$ exit
0	$\tfrac{2}{3}$	1	1	1	0	1	0	-3	$-Z$	criterion

$$\text{entry criterion}: \min\left\{\frac{1}{-(-\tfrac{3}{2})}, \frac{1}{-(-\tfrac{1}{2})}\right\} = \frac{2}{3}$$

Optimal Primal Tableau

$-Z$	x_1	x_2	x_{s1}	x_{s2}	P sol	BI
0	0	1	$-\frac{4}{3}$	$\frac{2}{3}$	$\frac{8}{3}$	x_2
0	1	0	$\frac{1}{3}$	$-\frac{2}{3}$	$\frac{1}{3}$	x_1
1	0	0	$\frac{2}{3}$	$\frac{2}{3}$	$-\frac{10}{3}$	$-Z$
D sol	y_{s1}	y_{s2}	y_1	y_2		

The exit criterion corresponds to step 1, whereas the entry criterion is step 2. The use of the dual simplex algorithm is a crucial operation in any computer solver because, more often than not, the error accumulation during computations may result in infeasible solutions. At that stage, a few iterations of the dual simplex algorithm may, usually, restore feasibility.

Guidelines to Set Up LP Problems

The process of setting up correct and consistent primal and dual structures constitutes a most difficult challenge for anyone wishing to formulate linear programming problems. The difficulty consists in taking information scattered around in pieces (newspapers, accounting books, statistical databases) and in organizing it into a coherent LP structure. By following the guidelines recommended here, the task of setting up LP problems in a correct and complete form is greatly simplified.

Four stages should be scrupulously followed:

1. **Identify the activities** (production processes, outputs, etc.) of the problem. Activities will turn out to be organized as columns of information in the technology matrix A of the primal LP specification. In order to facilitate this identification, the reader should apply the following criterion: If the information can be associated in a meaningful way to an **action verb**, then that information should be classified among the activities. At this stage of the setup process it is sufficient to list the names of the activities in an explicit and shorthand fashion to be utilizied in the formal writing of the primal LP problem.
2. **Identify the constraints.** Constraints will turn out to be rows of the primal LP specification. It is not possible to associate an action verb

to the information leading to constraints. Again, at this stage it is sufficient to write down an appropriate name for a constraint together with its shorthand (symbolic) representation.

3. Associate each constraint with those activities that enter the given constraint according to the general economic specification $D \leq S$, that is, *Demand* $\leq$ *Supply* for any commodity.

4. We are ready to write down the dual pair of LP problems. There are four steps: two of them are of an economic nature and two of a purely mathematical nature.

Economic Step

(a) Use the constraint and activity classification and the $D \leq S$ relation to organize the given information according to the economic principle that, indeed, *Demand* $\leq$ *Supply* for any commodity. Notice that, in this step, no negative sign shows up in any of the $D \leq S$ relations.

Mathematical Step

(b) Rewrite the primal LP problem in algebraic form by regrouping all the variables (unknowns) on one side of the "$\leq$" relation and all constant parameters on the other side. A proper and convenient way to state primal and dual problems is to organize the information according to the formalism: [max *and* $\leq$] to which there corresponds the dual formalism [min *and* $\geq$].

Mathematical Step

(c) Use the transposition rule to write down the corresponding dual problem. Remember that, if the primal problem is specified as [max *and* $\leq$], then the dual must take the form [min *and* $\geq$]. Analogously, if the primal problem is specified as [min *and* $\geq$], then the associated dual problem takes the form of [max *and* $\leq$].

Economic Step

(d) Eliminate any negative sign in the constraints of the dual problem (by transferring the appropriate terms on either the left or the right side of the inequality, as necessary) and interpret each constraint as the $MC \geq MR$ for the given commodity.

These guidelines for setting up LP problems are valid also for nonlinear models of the type discussed in subsequent chapters.

Exercises

7.1 A price taker owns an initial endowment of factors of production represented by the vector $\mathbf{b}$. He intends to produce a vector of commodity outputs $\mathbf{x}_1$ to be sold on the market and purchases a vector of commodity inputs $\mathbf{x}_2$ to augment the initial endowment of resources. The technology to produce the output vector is given by the matrix A_1. The output price vector is $\mathbf{c}_1$ and the input price vector is $\mathbf{c}_2$. The price taker wishes to maximize profits. Set up the appropriate primal model and state its dual specification. Give an appropriate economic interpretation to each component of the dual problem.

7.2 A capital budgeting problem. Somebody receives an inheritance of $300,000 and wants to invest it for five years with the goal of ending up with the maximum amount of money. Each year she want to take out $20,000 for personal consumption. She can invest in five projects, or she may buy a five-year bond yielding a yearly dividend of 6 percent, or she may, each year, put her money into annual certificates of deposit and draw 5 percent interest on them. The investment projects are as follows: for one unit of participation in project 1, $1 should be disbursed at the beginning of year 1, $1 at the beginning of year 2 and, again, $1 at the beginning of year 3. After 3 years, the project starts to yield returns: $0.50 per unit of participation becomes available at the beginning of the fourth year and $0.60 at the beginning of year 5. The final return per unit of participation, which becomes available at the end of year 5, is quoted to be $2. The stream of outlays and returns (measured in $) for each of the five projects are reported below.

	Projects				
	1	2	3	4	5
Year 1	1	1	1	1	1
Year 2	1	2	0.5	2	2
Year 3	1	3	0.5	1	2
Year 4	−0.5	2	0.5	−1	0
Year 5	−0.6	−1	0.5	−1	−2
Final payoff	2	11	3	4	5

(a) Set up the appropriate primal linear programming problem.
(b) Derive the associated dual problem and give a meaningful economic interpretation to each of its components (objective function, constraints, dual variables).

7.3 Consider the following LP problem:

$$\max TNR = 3x_1 + 5x_2 + 2x_3$$
$$\text{subject to} \quad 2x_1 + 4x_2 - x_3 \le 24$$
$$3x_1 - 3x_2 + 2x_3 \le 30$$
$$-x_1 + 2x_2 + 2x_3 \ge 2$$

with all nonnegative primal variables. Write down the correct dual problem and explain your procedure.

7.4 Consider the following LP problem:

$$\max TNR = 3x_1 + 5x_2 + 2x_3$$
$$\text{subject to} \quad 2x_1 + 4x_2 - x_3 \le 24$$
$$3x_1 - 3x_2 + 2x_3 \le 30$$
$$-x_1 + 2x_2 + 2x_3 \le 12$$

with all nonnegative primal variables.
(a) Write down the correct dual problem and explain your procedure.
(b) Solve it by using the primal simplex algorithm discussed in a previous section. Exhibit all the relevant information about the primal and dual solutions.

7.5 A price taker is operating two plants and facing one market. Given the following primal problem, write down the corresponding dual problem and provide a meaningful economic interpretation of it.

$$\max TR = \mathbf{c'x}$$

subject to		
	$A_1\mathbf{x}_1 \le \mathbf{b}_1$	technology at plant 1
	$A_2\mathbf{x}_2 \le \mathbf{b}_2$	technology at plant 2
	$\mathbf{x}_1 + \mathbf{x}_2 \ge \mathbf{x}$	market clearing

$$\mathbf{x}_1 \ge 0, \ \mathbf{x}_2 \ge 0, \ \mathbf{x} \ge 0$$

You are requested to give a meaningful economic interpretation to each component of the dual problem.

7.6 A transportation problem involves I origins and J destinations. In its simplest formulation, the problem consists in transporting a homogeneous commodity from the origins to the destinations at the total minimum cost. Origins are equivalently called "warehouses" and destinations "markets." Markets place an order (demand) for the commodity and warehouses supply it. The information deals with knowledge of the routes connecting warehouses to markets, with the available supply and the requested demand, and with the unit cost of transportation on each route, c_{ij}. Hence, the primal of a transportation problem assumes the following structure:

$$\min TCT = \sum_{ij} c_{ij} x_{ij}$$

$$\text{subject to} \qquad \sum_{j} x_{ij} \leq S_i$$

$$\sum_{i} x_{ij} \geq D_j$$

where TCT stands for "total cost of transportation," S_i for "supply" of the commodity available at the ith warehouse, D_j for "demand" of the commodity at the retail markets, and c_{ij} for the unit cost of transportation from the ith warehouse to the jth market. The transported quantities, x_{ij} must be nonnegative.

Write down the dual of the transportation problem and provide a meaningful economic interpretation.

7.7 One plant and two markets. A price taker owns one plant and must supply two markets with the same commodities. The technology matrix is A, the resource vector is $\mathbf{b}$, and the price vectors at the two markets are $\mathbf{c}_1$ and $\mathbf{c}_2$, respectively. Write down the primal problem and its dual specification providing a meaningful economic interpretation.

References

Dantzig, G. B. (1963). *Linear Programming and Extensions* (Princeton: Princeton University Press).

Lemke, C. E. (1954). "The Dual Method for Solving the Linear Programming Problem," *Naval Research Logistic Quarterly*, 1, 36–47.

Murty, K. (1976). *Linear and Combinatorial Programming* (New York: Wiley).

Paris, Q. (1991). *An Economic Interpretation of Linear Programming* (Ames: Iowa State University Press).

8

The Monopolist

Many economic agents display monopolistic behavior. In particular, we will discuss two variants of monopolistic behavior as represented by a pure monopolist and by a perfectly dicriminating monopolist. We will assume that the monopolist will produce and sell a vector of outputs, as final commodities.

The essential characteristic of a monopolist is that he "owns" the set of demand functions that are related to his outputs. The meaning of "owning" the demand functions must be understood in the sense that a monopolist "develops" the markets for his products and, in this sense, he is aware of the demand functions for such products that can be satisfied only by his outputs.

Pure Monopolist

A pure monopolist is a monopolist who charges the same price for all the units of his products sold on the market. We assume that he faces inverse demand functions for his products defined as $\mathbf{p} = \mathbf{c} - D\mathbf{x}$, where D is a $(n \times n)$ symmetric positive semidefinite matrix representing the slopes of the demand functions, $\mathbf{p}$ is a $(n \times 1)$ vector of output prices, $\mathbf{c}$ is a $(n \times 1)$ vector of intercepts of the demand functions, and $\mathbf{x}$ is a $(n \times 1)$ vector of output quantities sold on the market by the pure monopolist.

A second assumption is that the monopolist uses a linear technology for producing his outputs. Such a technology is represented by the matrix A of dimensions $(m \times n)$, $m < n$. The supply of limiting (fixed) inputs is given by vector $\mathbf{b}$. Typically, a monopolist wishes to maximize profit. With these specifications we can state the primal problem of a pure monopolist:

Primal $\max\limits_{\mathbf{x}} TR = \mathbf{p'x} = \mathbf{c'x} - \mathbf{x'}D\mathbf{x}$ (8.1)

subject to $A\mathbf{x} \le \mathbf{b}$ (8.2)

$$\mathbf{x} \ge \mathbf{0}.$$

Problem [(8.1), (8.2)] can be interpreted as the maximization of total revenue subject to the linear technology represented by the demand for inputs, $A\mathbf{x}$, which must always be less than or equal to the supply of inputs, $\mathbf{b}$. The vector of limiting inputs, $\mathbf{b}$, may be regarded as describing the "physical plant" of the monopolist as it contains all the quantities of available "fixed" inputs.

We are interested in deriving the dual specification corresponding to the primal problem of the pure monopolist as stated in [(8.1), (8.2)]. This will require an application of KKT theory, as developed in Chapter 3. Hence, the Lagrangean function of problem [(8.1), (8.2)] is stated as

$$L(\mathbf{x}, \mathbf{y}) = \mathbf{c'x} - \mathbf{x'}D\mathbf{x} + \mathbf{y'}[\mathbf{b} - A\mathbf{x}]$$ (8.3)

where the vector $\mathbf{y}$ is a vector of Lagrange multipliers associated with the linear constraints (8.2). Equivalently, this vector $\mathbf{y}$ is to be regarded as the vector of shadow prices of the limiting inputs. The KKT conditions derived from (8.3) can be expressed as

$$\frac{\partial L}{\partial \mathbf{x}} = \mathbf{c} - 2D\mathbf{x} - A'\mathbf{y} \le \mathbf{0}$$ (8.4)

$$\mathbf{x'}\frac{\partial L}{\partial \mathbf{x}} = \mathbf{x'}[\mathbf{c} - 2D\mathbf{x} - A'\mathbf{y}] = 0$$ (8.5)

$$\frac{\partial L}{\partial \mathbf{y}} = \mathbf{b} - A\mathbf{x} \ge \mathbf{0}$$ (8.6)

$$\mathbf{y'}\frac{\partial L}{\partial \mathbf{y}} = \mathbf{y'}[\mathbf{b} - A\mathbf{x}] = 0$$ (8.7)

together with the nonnegativity of vectors $\mathbf{x} \ge \mathbf{0}$ and $\mathbf{y} \ge \mathbf{0}$.

Relations (8.6) are the primal constraints of the pure monopolist's problem, and relation (8.7) is the associated complementary slackness condition. Hence, the dual constraints of the pure monopolist must be given by relations (8.4), with relation (8.5) representing the associated complementary slackness condition.

Now we need to define the dual objective function. We recall that, in general, the dual objective function of a maximization problem is the minimization of the Lagrangean function with respect to the dual variables (or Lagrange multipliers). More explicitly, a dual problem is defined as

$$\min_{x,y} L(\mathbf{x}, \mathbf{y})$$

subject to $\qquad \dfrac{\partial L}{\partial \mathbf{x}} \leq \mathbf{0}, \qquad \mathbf{x} \geq \mathbf{0}.$

But notice that, in quadratic programming, it is possible to simplify the Lagrangean function by using the information contained in KKT (8.5), where we can write $\mathbf{c}'\mathbf{x} = 2\mathbf{x}'D\mathbf{x} + \mathbf{x}'A'\mathbf{y}$. Hence, using this result in the Lagrangean function (8.3) we can write

$$
\begin{aligned}
L(\mathbf{x}, \mathbf{y}) &= \mathbf{c}'\mathbf{x} - \mathbf{x}'D\mathbf{x} + \mathbf{y}'[\mathbf{b} - A\mathbf{x}] \\
&= 2\mathbf{x}'D\mathbf{x} + \mathbf{x}'A'\mathbf{y} - \mathbf{x}'D\mathbf{x} + \mathbf{y}'\mathbf{b} - \mathbf{y}'A\mathbf{x} \\
&= \mathbf{b}'\mathbf{y} + \mathbf{x}'D\mathbf{x}.
\end{aligned}
\tag{8.8}
$$

Therefore, the dual specification of the pure monopolist's model is given as

Dual $\qquad \min_{x,y} TC = \mathbf{b}'\mathbf{y} + \mathbf{x}'D\mathbf{x}$ $\qquad\qquad$ (8.9)

subject to $\qquad\qquad\qquad A'\mathbf{y} \geq \mathbf{c} - 2D\mathbf{x}$ $\qquad$ (8.10)

$$\mathbf{x} \geq \mathbf{0}, \qquad \mathbf{y} \geq \mathbf{0}.$$

The dual constraints (8.10) are interpreted as the economic equilibrium conditions according to which the marginal costs of the commodities produced by the pure monopolist, $A'\mathbf{y}$, must always be greater than or equal to their marginal revenues, $\mathbf{c} - 2D\mathbf{x}$.

To interpret the dual objective function (8.9) in a meaningful way it is convenient to introduce a second entrepreneur who wishes to take over the pure monopolist's firm. Toward this goal he will want to minimize the total cost of purchasing the physical plant, $\mathbf{b}'\mathbf{y}$, and he also will want to minimize the cost of purchasing the market options of the pure monopolist, $\mathbf{x}'D\mathbf{x}$. The market options (related to the market demand functions) constitute the market power of the (primal) pure monopolist from which he can derive his profit. It seems reasonable, therefore, that he will never give up such market options unless he will be compensated appropriately in the amount of $\mathbf{x}'D\mathbf{x}$.

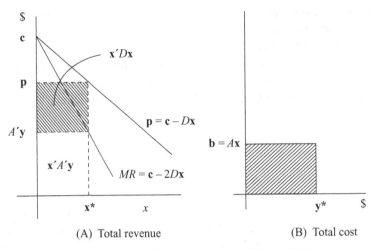

(A) Total revenue   (B) Total cost

Figure 8.1. Illustration of the pure monopolist's equilibrium.

This amount corresponds precisely to the pure monopolist's profit because, given the total revenue and total cost of the physical plant as expressed previously,

$$\text{Profit} = TR - (TC \text{ of physical plant}) \tag{8.11}$$

$$= [\mathbf{c}'\mathbf{x} - \mathbf{x}'D\mathbf{x}] - \mathbf{b}'\mathbf{y} = \mathbf{x}'D\mathbf{x}.$$

Equation (8.11) is justified by the two complementary slackness KKT conditions (8.5) and (8.7), which can be combined to produce the result given in (8.11).

The diagrammatic illustration of the dual pair of quadratic programming problems stated in (8.2) and (8.9) is reproduced in Figure 8.1, which illustrates the equilibrium on the output market: the pure monopolist's output is determined by the intersection of marginal activity cost, $A'\mathbf{y}$, and marginal revenue, $\mathbf{c} - 2D\mathbf{x}$. The pure monopolist's profit is represented by the shaded area, $\mathbf{x}'D\mathbf{x}$, whereas the area under the profit is interpretable as total cost of the physical plant, $\mathbf{x}'A'\mathbf{y}$. Following the KKT condition (8.5), total revenue can thus be restated as $\mathbf{p}'\mathbf{x} = \mathbf{c}'\mathbf{x} - \mathbf{x}'D\mathbf{x} = \mathbf{y}'A\mathbf{x} + \mathbf{x}'D\mathbf{x}$ or, equivalently, total revenue minus total cost (of the plant) equals profit, $\mathbf{p}'\mathbf{x} - \mathbf{y}'A\mathbf{x} = \mathbf{x}'D\mathbf{x}$. Figure 8.1B represents the equilibrium on the input side where the demand for inputs, $A\mathbf{x}$, equals their supply, $\mathbf{b}$, at the shadow price $\mathbf{y}^*$.

The pair of diagrams in Figure 8.1 reveals the structural asymmetry of the traditional pure monopolist's problem as represented by a quadratic programming problem. This asymmetric configuration is a direct consequence of the asymmetry inherent in the primal constraints of problem (8.2) and the dual constraints of problem (8.10). The distinctive features of the dual constraints in (8.10) are that both primal and dual variables enter those relations. Furthermore, the matrix D defining the quadratic form $x'Dx$ enters the dual constraints in an essential way. In contrast, no matrix associated with a quadratic form enters the primal constraints in (8.2), which are defined solely in terms of primal variables.

The KKT conditions [(8.4)–(8.7)] can be stated in the form of a linear complementarity problem $(M, \mathbf{q})$ with the following definition of the matrix M and vectors $\mathbf{q}$ and $\mathbf{z}$:

$$
M = \begin{bmatrix} 2D & A' \\ -A & \mathbf{0} \end{bmatrix}, \quad \mathbf{q} = \begin{bmatrix} -\mathbf{c} \\ \mathbf{b} \end{bmatrix}, \quad \mathbf{z} = \begin{bmatrix} \mathbf{x} \\ \mathbf{y} \end{bmatrix}.
$$

This reformulation of the KKT conditions in terms of an LC problem leads to the use of the complementary pivot algorithm discussed in Chapter 6.

Perfectly Discriminating Monopolist

An entrepreneur acting as a perfectly discriminating monopolist attempts to extract all the consumers' surplus available on his output markets. In other words, a perfectly discriminating monopolist considers the vector of market demand functions, $\mathbf{p} = \mathbf{c} - D\mathbf{x}$, as if it were his "marginal revenue" function and measures his total revenue as the integral under it, that is,

$$
TR = \int_0^{\mathbf{x}^*} (\mathbf{c} - D\mathbf{x})' \, d\mathbf{x} = \mathbf{c}'\mathbf{x}^* - \frac{1}{2}\mathbf{x}^{*'} D\mathbf{x}^*. \tag{8.12}
$$

In this discussion, the matrix D is assumed to be symmetric positive semidefinite. For three or more outputs, the integral (8.12) exists only under the condition that the matrix D is symmetric.

The quadratic programming specification of the perfectly discriminating monopolist's behavior is similar to that of the pure monopolist stated in (8.1) except for the quadratic form $\mathbf{x}'D\mathbf{x}$ that now is multiplied by the scalar $\frac{1}{2}$ as shown in (8.12).

	Primal		**Dual**	(8.13)
$\displaystyle\max_{\mathbf{x}} TR = \mathbf{c}'\mathbf{x} - \tfrac{1}{2}\mathbf{x}'D\mathbf{x}$			$\displaystyle\min_{\mathbf{x},\mathbf{y}} TC = \mathbf{b}'\mathbf{y} + \tfrac{1}{2}\mathbf{x}'D\mathbf{x}$	
subject to	$A\mathbf{x} \le \mathbf{b}$		subject to	$A'\mathbf{y} \ge \mathbf{c} - D\mathbf{x}$
	$\mathbf{x} \ge \mathbf{0}$			$\mathbf{y} \ge \mathbf{0}, \ \mathbf{x} \ge \mathbf{0}.$

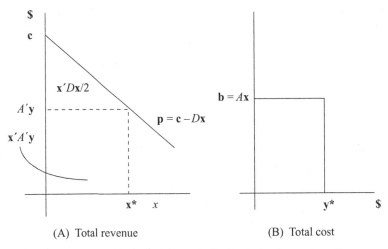

Figure 8.2. Equilibrium of the perfectly discriminating monopolist.

The quantity $\frac{1}{2}x'Dx$ is interpreted as the profit of the perfectly discriminating monopolist or, equivalently, as the value of his market options.

The dual constraints specify the equilibrium conditions according to which the marginal activity cost of this entrepreneur, $A'y$, must be greater than or equal to the market price, $p = c - Dx$. An illustration of the perfectly discriminating monopolist's problem is presented in Figure 8.2. The solution of the dual pair of problems stated in (8.13) is characterized by the equality of the two objective functions. The dual pair of problems (8.13) taken together, therefore, is equivalent to the profit maximization of the perfectly discriminating monopolist, which can be stated as

$$\max \pi = \max \left[c'x - \tfrac{1}{2}x'Dx - b'y \right] = \min \tfrac{1}{2}x'Dx.$$

If the system of inverse demand functions, $p = c - Dx$, exhibits a matrix D of price-quantity slopes that is asymmetric, it is no longer possible to express the problem of the perfectly discriminating monopolist as a dual pair of optimization models. This fact is a consequence of the nonintegrability of the system of demand functions (due to the asymmetry of the D matrix), which precludes the specification of a primal objective function consistent with the dual constraints, as discussed in Chapter 5. Symmetrizing the D matrix is not admissible because such an operation changes the structure of the demand functions and the meaning of the problem.

In order to clarify this point once again, we introduce a proof by contradiction of the impossibility to formulate meaningful maximization and minimization problems for the perfectly discriminating monopolist facing a system of (three or more) demand functions with an asymmetric D matrix. Let us recall first that, for any positive semidefinite quadratic form, $\mathbf{x}'D\mathbf{x} = \frac{1}{2}\mathbf{x}'(D + D')\mathbf{x}$, where D is asymmetric. Suppose, therefore, that the revenue function to be maximized by the perfectly discriminating monopolist is $TR = \mathbf{c}'\mathbf{x} - \frac{1}{2}\mathbf{x}'D\mathbf{x}$. It follows that the use of KKT theory generates a set of dual constraints of the following form: $A'\mathbf{y} \geq \mathbf{c} - \frac{1}{2}(D + D')\mathbf{x}$. The right-hand side of the inequality does not correspond to the required condition that the marginal cost be greater than or equal to the commodity price $\mathbf{p} = \mathbf{c} - D\mathbf{x}$ when the matrix D is asymmetric. Hence, the maximization of $(\mathbf{c}'\mathbf{x} - \frac{1}{2}\mathbf{x}'D\mathbf{x})$ is invalid because the use of KKT theory does not lead to the equilibrium conditions for the perfectly discriminating monopolist.

The absence of a dual pair of quadratic programming problems for representing the case of a perfectly discriminating monopolist (when the matrix D is asymmetric) does not preclude the possibility of specifying the behavior of this entrepreneur as an equilibrium problem. As stated in Chapter 3, an equilibrium problem is defined by a set of relations involving the demand and supply of commodities, their marginal costs and "marginal revenues." In this case, we put quotation marks around "marginal revenue" because the total revenue function does not exist and, therefore, neither does its derivative with respect to the vector $\mathbf{x}$. However, the demand function $\mathbf{p} = \mathbf{c} - D\mathbf{x}$ that acts as "marginal revenue" for the perfectly discriminating monopsonist does exist. More specifically, the physical quantities of commodities involved are related by the familiar conditions of demand less-than-or-equal to supply, $D \leq S$, the economic equilibrium conditions according to which marginal cost must be greater-than-or-equal to price, $MC \geq \mathbf{p}$, and the associated complementary conditions. Using the available information, the equilibrium problem of the perfectly discriminating monopolist (with an asymmetric D matrix) is that of finding nonnegative vectors $\mathbf{x}$ and $\mathbf{y}$ such that

$$
\begin{array}{lll}
\text{Demand/Supply} & A\mathbf{x} \leq \mathbf{b} & (8.14) \\
\text{Quantity Complementary Slackness} & \mathbf{y}'(\mathbf{b} - A\mathbf{x}) = 0 & \\
\text{Economic Equilibrium} & A'\mathbf{y} \geq \mathbf{c} - D\mathbf{x} & \\
\text{Economic Complementary Slackness} & \mathbf{x}'(A'\mathbf{y} - \mathbf{c} + D\mathbf{x}) = 0. &
\end{array}
$$

The equilibrium problem (8.14) can be easily reformulated as a linear complementarity problem (M, $\mathbf{q}$) where

$$M = \begin{bmatrix} D & A' \\ -A & 0 \end{bmatrix}, \quad \mathbf{q} = \begin{bmatrix} -\mathbf{c} \\ \mathbf{b} \end{bmatrix}, \quad \mathbf{z} = \begin{bmatrix} \mathbf{x} \\ \mathbf{y} \end{bmatrix}.$$

The solution of the equilibrium problem (8.14) is, thus, obtainable by solving a linear complementarity problem. With the solution, say $\mathbf{x}^*$ and $\mathbf{y}^*$, it is possible to recover the total cost of the limiting inputs, $\mathbf{b}'\mathbf{y}^*$, but it is not possible to recover the total revenue and total profit, separately, of the perfectly discriminating monopolist. Only the quantity $\mathbf{c}'\mathbf{x}^* - \mathbf{x}^{*\prime} D\mathbf{x}^*$, which combines total revenue and profit, can be computed without the possibility of separating the two quantities.

Discriminating Monopolist

Between the pure monopolist and the perfectly discriminating monopolist lies the problem of the discriminating monopolist. This framework arises any time the entrepreneur can segment his output market in separate areas of influence, each of which is characterized by a specific set of demand functions. Let us assume that an entrepreneur can operate as a pure monopolist in two separate and distinct markets identified by the following sets of inverse demand functions: $\mathbf{p}_1 = \mathbf{c}_1 - D_1\mathbf{x}_1$ and $\mathbf{p}_2 = \mathbf{c}_2 - D_2\mathbf{x}_2$. Furthermore, the matrices D_1 and D_2 are symmetric positive semidefinite. Finally, the discriminating monopolist produces all the necessary amounts of products at a single plant characterized by a linear technology A and input supply $\mathbf{b}$. The primal problem of such an entrepreneur is that of maximizing the total revenue from the two markets subject to the technological constraints involving inputs as well as the market clearing conditions involving outputs:

Primal

$$\max \ TR = \mathbf{c}_1'\mathbf{x}_1 - \mathbf{x}_1' D_1\mathbf{x}_1 + \mathbf{c}_2'\mathbf{x}_2 - \mathbf{x}_2' D_2\mathbf{x}_2 \qquad (8.15)$$

subject to $\qquad\qquad\qquad A\mathbf{x} \le \mathbf{b} \qquad\qquad$ technology

$$\mathbf{x}_1 + \mathbf{x}_2 \le \mathbf{x} \qquad\qquad \text{market clearing}$$

$$\mathbf{x}_1 \ge 0, \ \mathbf{x}_2 \ge 0, \ \mathbf{x} \ge 0.$$

The dual problem corresponding to (8.15) is derived via KKT theory beginning with the specification of an appropriate Lagrangean function

$$L = \mathbf{c}_1'\mathbf{x}_1 - \mathbf{x}_1' D_1\mathbf{x}_1 + \mathbf{c}_2'\mathbf{x}_2 - \mathbf{x}_2' D_2\mathbf{x}_2 + \mathbf{y}'(\mathbf{b} - A\mathbf{x}) + \mathbf{f}'(\mathbf{x} - \mathbf{x}_1 - \mathbf{x}_2)$$

$$(8.16)$$

where $\mathbf{y}$ and $\mathbf{f}$ are the Lagrange multipliers of the two sets of primal constraints, respectively. The KKT conditions of the foregoing problem are

$$\frac{\partial L}{\partial \mathbf{x}_1} = \mathbf{c}_1 - 2D_1\mathbf{x}_1 - \mathbf{f} \le \mathbf{0} \tag{8.17}$$

$$\mathbf{x}_1'\frac{\partial L}{\partial \mathbf{x}_1} = \mathbf{x}_1'(\mathbf{c}_1 - 2D_1\mathbf{x}_1 - \mathbf{f}) = 0 \tag{8.18}$$

$$\frac{\partial L}{\partial \mathbf{x}_2} = \mathbf{c}_2 - 2D_2\mathbf{x}_2 - \mathbf{f} \le \mathbf{0} \tag{8.19}$$

$$\mathbf{x}_2'\frac{\partial L}{\partial \mathbf{x}_2} = \mathbf{x}_2'(\mathbf{c}_2 - 2D_2\mathbf{x}_2 - \mathbf{f}) = 0 \tag{8.20}$$

$$\frac{\partial L}{\partial \mathbf{x}} = \mathbf{f} - A'\mathbf{y} \le \mathbf{0} \tag{8.21}$$

$$\mathbf{x}'\frac{\partial L}{\partial \mathbf{x}} = \mathbf{x}'(\mathbf{f} - A'\mathbf{y}) = 0 \tag{8.22}$$

$$\frac{\partial L}{\partial \mathbf{f}} = \mathbf{x} - \mathbf{x}_1 - \mathbf{x}_2 \ge \mathbf{0} \tag{8.23}$$

$$\mathbf{f}'\frac{\partial L}{\partial \mathbf{f}} = \mathbf{f}'(\mathbf{x} - \mathbf{x}_1 - \mathbf{x}_2) = 0 \tag{8.24}$$

$$\frac{\partial L}{\partial \mathbf{y}} = \mathbf{b} - A\mathbf{x} \ge \mathbf{0} \tag{8.25}$$

$$\mathbf{y}'\frac{\partial L}{\partial \mathbf{y}} = \mathbf{y}'(\mathbf{b} - A\mathbf{x}) = 0 \tag{8.26}$$

Karush-Kuhn-Tucker conditions (8.17), (8.19), and (8.21) constitute the dual constraints. Furthermore, using the information contained in the complementary slackness conditions (8.18), (8.20), and (8.22) in the simplification of the Lagrangean function (8.16), the dual problem can be stated in its final form as

Dual

$$\min TC = \mathbf{b}'\mathbf{y} + \mathbf{x}_1'D_1\mathbf{x}_1 + \mathbf{x}_2'D_2\mathbf{x}_2 \tag{8.27}$$

subject to
$$A'\mathbf{y} \ge \mathbf{f} \qquad \text{economic equilibrium}$$
$$\mathbf{f} \ge \mathbf{c}_1 - 2D_1\mathbf{x}_1 \qquad \text{economic efficiency}$$
$$\mathbf{f} \ge \mathbf{c}_2 - 2D_2\mathbf{x}_2 \qquad \text{economic efficiency}$$
$$\mathbf{x}_1 \ge \mathbf{0}, \ \mathbf{x}_2 \ge \mathbf{0}, \ \mathbf{y} \ge \mathbf{0}, \ \mathbf{f} \ge \mathbf{0}.$$

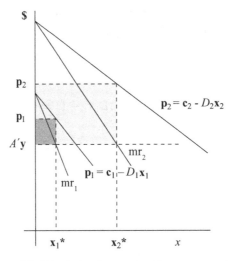

Figure 8.3. Discriminating monopolist on two markets.

The objective function of the dual problem states that an economic agent wishing to take over the discriminating monopolist's firm would like to minimize the total cost of the firm's resources, $\mathbf{b}'\mathbf{y}$, and the total cost of reimbursing the primal monopolist owner for his market options on the two distinct markets.

The expression $\mathbf{x}_1' D_1 \mathbf{x}_1 + \mathbf{x}_2' D_2 \mathbf{x}_2$ corresponds also to the total profit of the discriminating monopolist accruable on the two markets. From the point of view of the dual monopolist who wishes to bid for taking over the firm, this quantity should be minimized because it represents the cost of acquiring the monopolistic market power held currently by the primal monopolist. The first constraint of the dual problem states the conditions that the marginal cost $\mathbf{f}$ of producing the output vector $\mathbf{x}$ should be greater than or equal to marginal revenue. The two remaining dual constraints state that marginal revenue on both markets should be equalized. Output prices on the two separate markets may, and in general will, be different because nothing in the model requires their equality. Suppose that $D_1 \mathbf{x}_1 < D_2 \mathbf{x}_2$. Then, from the equality between marginal revenues, $\mathbf{p}_1 < \mathbf{p}_2$, as illustrated in Figure 8.3. In other words, if the demand functions on market 1 are more elastic than those on market 2, $\mathbf{p}_1 < \mathbf{p}_2$. This condition is often suggested in order to explain the practice of "dumping." A domestic monopolist may view the international market as more elastic than the domestic market. When these two markets are sufficiently insulated from each other, rational economic behavior suggests that marginal revenue should attain the same level on both markets, which, in turn, implies that the price on the international market should be lower than on the domestic market.

The linear complementarity problem $(M, \mathbf{q})$ corresponding to the discriminating monopolist model discussed in this section is defined by the following M matrix and vectors $\mathbf{q}$ and $\mathbf{z}$:

$$
M = \begin{bmatrix} 2D_1 & 0 & 0 & I & 0 \\ 0 & 2D_2 & 0 & I & 0 \\ 0 & 0 & 0 & -I & A' \\ -I & -I & I & 0 & 0 \\ 0 & 0 & -A & 0 & 0 \end{bmatrix}, \quad \mathbf{q} = \begin{bmatrix} -\mathbf{c}_1 \\ -\mathbf{c}_2 \\ 0 \\ 0 \\ \mathbf{b} \end{bmatrix}, \quad \mathbf{z} = \begin{bmatrix} \mathbf{x}_1 \\ \mathbf{x}_2 \\ \mathbf{x} \\ \mathbf{f} \\ \mathbf{y} \end{bmatrix}.
$$

Perfectly Discriminating Monopolist with Multiple Plants

In this section, an entrepreneur acts as a perfectly discriminating monopolist on each of two distinct and separate markets and owns two different plants where he produces the necessary output to meet the market demand. The objective of this entrepreneur is to maximize the overall profit accruable on the two markets. The demand functions on the two markets are $\mathbf{p}_i = \mathbf{c}_i - D_i\mathbf{x}_i$, $i = 1, 2$, where D_i is a symmetric positive semidefinite matrix. Accordingly, the primal problem is specified as

Primal

$$
\max TR = \mathbf{c}_1'\mathbf{x}_1 - \tfrac{1}{2}\mathbf{x}_1' D_1\mathbf{x}_1 + \mathbf{c}_2'\mathbf{x}_2 - \tfrac{1}{2}\mathbf{x}_2' D_2\mathbf{x}_2 \tag{8.28}
$$

subject to	$A_1\mathbf{v}_1 \leq \mathbf{b}_1$	technology at plant 1
	$A_2\mathbf{v}_2 \leq \mathbf{b}_2$	technology at plant 2
	$\mathbf{x}_1 + \mathbf{x}_2 \leq \mathbf{v}_1 + \mathbf{v}_2$	market clearing

$$
\mathbf{x}_1 \geq \mathbf{0}, \ \mathbf{x}_2 \geq \mathbf{0}, \ \mathbf{v}_1 \geq \mathbf{0}, \ \mathbf{v}_1 \geq \mathbf{0}
$$

where $\mathbf{v}_i$, $i = 1, 2$ are the output vectors supplied by the firm's plants and $\mathbf{x}_i$, $i = 1, 2$, are the vectors of commodities demanded by the two output markets.

The corresponding dual problem is obtained, as usual, by developing the appropriate KKT conditions and by defining the Lagrangean function to read

Dual

$$\min TC = \mathbf{b}_1'\mathbf{y}_1 + \mathbf{b}_2'\mathbf{y}_2 + \frac{1}{2}\mathbf{x}_1' D_1\mathbf{x}_1 + \frac{1}{2}\mathbf{x}_2' D_2\mathbf{x}_2 \tag{8.29}$$

subject to $\quad A_1'\mathbf{y}_1 \geq \mathbf{p}$ $\qquad\qquad$ economic equilibrium

$\qquad\qquad\qquad A_2'\mathbf{y}_2 \geq \mathbf{p}$ $\qquad\qquad$ economic equilibrium

$$\mathbf{p} \geq \mathbf{c}_1 - D_1\mathbf{x}_1$$

$$\mathbf{p} \geq \mathbf{c}_2 - D_2\mathbf{x}_2$$

$$\mathbf{x}_1 \geq \mathbf{0}, \ \mathbf{x}_2 \geq \mathbf{0}, \ \mathbf{y}_1 \geq \mathbf{0}, \ \mathbf{y}_2 \geq \mathbf{0}, \ \mathbf{p} \geq \mathbf{0}.$$

The specification of the dual problem provides an explicit illustration of the economic conditions required for the solution of the given problem. Let us assume that $\mathbf{x}_1 > \mathbf{0}, \ \mathbf{x}_2 > \mathbf{0}, \ \mathbf{y}_1 > \mathbf{0}, \ \mathbf{y}_2 > \mathbf{0}$. Then, the marginal output cost at the two plants must be the same. Second, the marginal revenue derived from each of the two commodity markets must also be the same. In this case, dealing with a perfectly discriminating monopolist, the marginal revenue is equal to the commodity price on each of the two markets. This is the reason for using the symbol $\mathbf{p}$ as a dual variable of the market clearing constraint in the primal specification. Finally, the marginal output cost at each of the two plants must be equal to the market price.

Pure Monopolist with Asymmetric D Matrix

In previous sections, the vector of demand functions facing the pure monopolist was stated as $\mathbf{p} = \mathbf{c} - D\mathbf{x}$, where the matrix D was assumed to be symmetric and positive semidefinite. This assumption is not a realistic hypothesis because there is no theoretical requirement for the symmetry of the price-quantity slopes of a system of Marshallian demand functions. Therefore, we now assume that the D matrix is asymmetric positive semidefinite, and we are interested to see how the dual pair of programming problems describing the pure monopolist's behavior will be affected by this assumption. The total revenue of the pure monopolist is always $TR = \mathbf{p}'\mathbf{x} = \mathbf{c}'\mathbf{x} - \mathbf{x}'D\mathbf{x}$, regardless of whether the D matrix is either symmetric or asymmetric, because this entrepreneur charges the same price for all the output units sold on the market. Hence, his total revenue is simply price times quantity. The primal problem, therefore, remains as in specification [(8.1), (8.2)], which we reproduce here for convenience:

Primal
$$\max_{\mathbf{x}} TR = \mathbf{p}'\mathbf{x} = \mathbf{c}'\mathbf{x} - \mathbf{x}'D\mathbf{x} \qquad (8.30)$$

subject to
$$A\mathbf{x} \leq \mathbf{b} \qquad (8.31)$$

$$\mathbf{x} \geq \mathbf{0}.$$

The dual problem will be obtained, as usual, via KKT theory. Hence, the Lagrangean function corresponding to problem [(8.30), (8.31)] is stated as

$$L(\mathbf{x}, \mathbf{y}) = \mathbf{c}'\mathbf{x} - \mathbf{x}'D\mathbf{x} + \mathbf{y}'[\mathbf{b} - A\mathbf{x}] \qquad (8.32)$$

with KKT conditions expressed as

$$\frac{\partial L}{\partial \mathbf{x}} = \mathbf{c} - (D + D')\mathbf{x} - A'\mathbf{y} \leq \mathbf{0} \qquad (8.33)$$

$$\mathbf{x}'\frac{\partial L}{\partial \mathbf{x}} = \mathbf{x}'[\mathbf{c} - (D + D')\mathbf{x} - A'\mathbf{y}] = 0 \qquad (8.34)$$

$$\frac{\partial L}{\partial \mathbf{y}} = \mathbf{b} - A\mathbf{x} \geq \mathbf{0} \qquad (8.35)$$

$$\mathbf{y}'\frac{\partial L}{\partial \mathbf{y}} = \mathbf{y}'[\mathbf{b} - A\mathbf{x}] = 0 \qquad (8.36)$$

together with the nonnegativity of vectors $\mathbf{x} \geq \mathbf{0}$ and $\mathbf{y} \geq \mathbf{0}$. The consequence of an asymmetric D matrix is reflected in the marginal revenue function that now assumes the following structure

$$MR = \mathbf{c} - (D + D')\mathbf{x}. \qquad (8.37)$$

This is the only effect on the specification of the dual constraints and the solution of the KKT conditions as given in [(8.32) through (8.36)] will correspond to the solution of the pure monopolist's problem. The verification that total revenue remains $TR = \mathbf{p}'\mathbf{x} = \mathbf{c}'\mathbf{x} - \mathbf{x}'D\mathbf{x}$ is done by integrating under the marginal revenue function as discussed in Appendix 5.3 of Chapter 5:

$$TR = \int_0^{\mathbf{x}^*} \left[\mathbf{c} - (D' + D)\mathbf{x} \right]' d\mathbf{x} = \mathbf{c}'\mathbf{x}^* - \tfrac{1}{2}\mathbf{x}^{*'}(D' + D)\mathbf{x}^*$$

$$= \mathbf{c}'\mathbf{x}^* - \mathbf{x}^{*'}D\mathbf{x}^*,$$

which corresponds to the objective function in (8.30). The equivalence between the two quadratic forms $\frac{1}{2}\mathbf{x}'(D' + D)\mathbf{x} = \mathbf{x}'D\mathbf{x}$ is easily established with the recognition that $\mathbf{x}'D'\mathbf{x} = \mathbf{x}'D\mathbf{x}$, because the two quantities are both scalars. Therefore, the dual specification of this scenario with asymmetric D matrix becomes

$$\textbf{Dual} \qquad \min_{\mathbf{x,y}} TC = \mathbf{b'y} + \mathbf{x}'D\mathbf{x} \qquad (8.38)$$

$$\text{subject to} \qquad A'\mathbf{y} \geq \mathbf{c} - (D + D')\mathbf{x} \qquad (8.39)$$

$$\mathbf{x} \geq \mathbf{0}, \quad \mathbf{y} \geq \mathbf{0}.$$

The discussion of different scenarios with and without a symmetric D matrix is not simply a mental exercise. Systems of demand functions for final commodities are estimated econometrically, and it is very unlikely that the matrix of slopes of those demand functions will be symmetric. Hence, we must know how to deal with this empirical fact.

Numerical Example 1: Pure Monopolist with Asymmetric D Matrix

A pure monopolist, with asymmetric matrix D of price/quantity slopes, solves the problem discussed in (8.30) and (8.31), which is reproduced here for convenience:

$$\textbf{Primal} \qquad \max_{\mathbf{x}} TR = \mathbf{p'x} = \mathbf{c'x} - \mathbf{x}'D\mathbf{x} \qquad (8.30)$$

$$\text{subject to} \qquad A\mathbf{x} \leq \mathbf{b} \qquad (8.31)$$

$$\mathbf{x} \geq \mathbf{0}.$$

The required data are given as

$$\mathbf{c} = \begin{bmatrix} 15 \\ 17 \\ 13 \\ 16 \end{bmatrix}, \quad \mathbf{b} = \begin{bmatrix} 1 \\ 3 \\ 2 \end{bmatrix}, \quad A = \begin{bmatrix} 2 & -2 & 0.5 & 1.0 \\ 1 & 3 & -2.1 & 3.0 \\ -2 & 1 & 0.5 & 0.9 \end{bmatrix},$$

$$D = \begin{bmatrix} 8 & -4 & 2 & -1 \\ -2 & 6 & 5 & 3 \\ 4 & 1 & 4 & -2 \\ -2 & 1 & -2 & 1 \end{bmatrix}.$$

The numerical solution of this problem was obtained using the GAMS application with the following results:

$$\text{AQP Pure Monopolist Profit} = 16.7778$$
$$\text{AQP Total Revenue} = 37.7351$$
$$\text{AQP Plant Total Cost} = 20.9573$$

$$\mathbf{x} = \begin{bmatrix} x_1 = 0.2680 \\ x_2 = 0.7306 \\ x_3 = 1.4542 \\ x_4 = 1.1981 \end{bmatrix}, \quad \mathbf{y} = \begin{bmatrix} y_1 = 7.1037 \\ y_2 = 2.4028 \\ y_3 = 3.3227 \end{bmatrix}, \quad \mathbf{p} = \begin{bmatrix} p_1 = 14.0681 \\ p_2 = 2.2873 \\ p_3 = 7.7769 \\ p_4 = 17.5157 \end{bmatrix}$$

where $\mathbf{p}$ is the vector of final commodity prices. To guide the reader in the formulation of the proper GAMS code, we provide the command file used to solve this numerical example. A useful tutorial and a user's manual can be found at www.gams.com.

GAMS Command File: Numerical Example 1

Asterisks denote either blank line or comments. The remarkable flexibility of the GAMS program rests with the declaration of variables, parameters and equations, which are represented in algebraic form, as they are written in the theoretical models.

```
$title an aqp model of pure monopolist with asymmetric
* d matrix
*
$offsymlist offsymxref
    option limrow = 0
    option limcol = 0
    option iterlim = 100000
    option reslim = 200000
    option nlp = conopt3
    option decimals = 7 ;
*
    sets  j  output variables / x1, x2, x3, x4 /
          i  inputs / y1, y2, y3 /
*
    alias(i,k,kk);
    alias(j,jj) ;
*
    parameter c(j)   intercept of demand functions
```

```
    /   x1      15
        x2      17
        x3      13
        x4      16    /
*
    parameter b(i)    intercept of input supply

    /   y1      1
        y2      3
        y3      2   /
*
    table a(i,j)   technical coefficient matrix

            x1     x2     x3        x4
        y1    2     -2     0.5      1.0
        y2    1      3    -2.1      3.0
        y3   -2      1     0.5      0.9          ;
*
    table d(j,jj)    asymmetric slopes of demand
      functions

            x1     x2     x3     x4
        x1    8     -4      2    -1
        x2   -2      6      5     3
        x3    4      1      4    -2
        x4   -2      1     -2     1
*
    scalar scale parameter to define economic agents/
      1.0 /;
*
* asymmetric qp for the pure monopolist problem
*
    variables
    monopol  objective function
    aqpx(j)  primal variables ;
*
    positive variables aqpx ;
*
    equations
    aqpobjeq  equation of the objective function
    techeq(i)  equations of primal constraints ;
*
    aqpobjeq..  monopol =e= sum(j, c(j)*aqpx(j) )
              - sum((j,jj), aqpx(j)*d(j,jj)*aqpx(jj) ) ;
    techeq(i)..   sum(j, a(i,j)*aqpx(j)) =l= b(i) ;
```

```
*
* name and definition of the monopolist problem
*
    model aqpmonop / aqpobjeq, techeq / ;
    solve aqpmonop using nlp maximizing monopol ;
*
    parameter
    monopolprof  monopolist profit,
    totplC    total cost of the monopolist's plant,
    p(j)   output prices ;
*
    monopolprof = sum((j,jj), aqpx.l(j)*d(j,jj)*
      aqpx.l(jj) ) ;
    totplC = sum(i,b(i)*techeq.m(i)) ;
    p(j) = c(j) - sum(jj, d(j,jj)*aqpx.l(jj) ) ;
*
    display monopol.l, monopolprof , totplC, p, aqpx.l,
      techeq.m ;
```

Numerical Example 2: Perfectly Discriminating Monopolist with Symmetric D Matrix

This type of monopolist's behavior is specified by problem (8.13), which is reproduced here for convenience:

Primal	**Dual**	(8.13)

$$\max_{\mathbf{x}} TR = \mathbf{c}'\mathbf{x} - \tfrac{1}{2}\mathbf{x}'D\mathbf{x} \qquad \min_{\mathbf{x},\mathbf{y}} TC = \mathbf{b}'\mathbf{y} + \tfrac{1}{2}\mathbf{x}'D\mathbf{x}$$

$$\text{subject to} \quad A\mathbf{x} \le \mathbf{b} \qquad\qquad \text{subject to} \quad A'\mathbf{y} \ge \mathbf{c} - D\mathbf{x}$$

$$\mathbf{x} \ge \mathbf{0} \qquad\qquad\qquad \mathbf{y} \ge \mathbf{0}, \ \mathbf{x} \ge \mathbf{0}.$$

The required data are specified as

$$\mathbf{c} = \begin{bmatrix} 15 \\ 19 \\ 20 \\ 16 \end{bmatrix}, \quad \mathbf{b} = \begin{bmatrix} 1 \\ 3 \\ 2 \end{bmatrix}, \quad A = \begin{bmatrix} 2 & -2 & 0.5 & 1.0 \\ 1 & 3 & -2.1 & 3.0 \\ -2 & 1 & 0.5 & 0.9 \end{bmatrix},$$

$$D = \begin{bmatrix} 8.0 & -3 & 3 & -1.5 \\ -3.0 & 6 & 3 & 2.0 \\ 3.0 & 3 & 4 & -2.0 \\ -1.5 & 2 & -2 & 1.0 \end{bmatrix}.$$

The GAMS solution of this problem results in

$$\text{AQP Perfectly Discriminating Monopolist Profit} = 50.9166$$
$$\text{AQP Total Revenue} = 76.4000$$
$$\text{AQP Plant Total Cost} = 25.4834$$

$$\mathbf{x} = \begin{bmatrix} x_1 = 1.1003 \\ x_2 = 1.8316 \\ x_3 = 3.0508 \\ x_4 = 0.9372 \end{bmatrix}, \quad \mathbf{y} = \begin{bmatrix} y_1 = 6.4810 \\ y_2 = 2.4967 \\ y_3 = 5.7562 \end{bmatrix}, \quad \mathbf{p} = \begin{bmatrix} p_1 = 3.9461 \\ p_2 = 0.2843 \\ p_3 = 0.8756 \\ p_4 = 19.1516 \end{bmatrix}$$

where $\mathbf{p}$ is the vector of final commodity prices.

Numerical Example 3: Perfectly Discriminating Monopolist with Asymmetric D Matrix: An Equilibrium Problem

This numerical example differs from example 2 only in the matrix D that is now asymmetric. We recall that when the D matrix is asymmetric, the system of demand functions cannot be integrated and, thus, a proper objective function expressing the total revenue of the perfectly discriminating monopolist cannot be established. Still, the problem of finding equilibrium values of the primal and dual variables that satisfy feasibility and complementarity relations can be solved by considering the associated equilibrium problem such as specified in (8.14), and reproduced here for convenience:

Demand/Supply	$\mathbf{v} = \mathbf{b} - A\mathbf{x}$	(8.14)
Quantity Complementary Slackness	$\mathbf{y}'(\mathbf{b} - A\mathbf{x}) = \mathbf{y}'\mathbf{v} = 0$	
Economic Equilibrium	$A'\mathbf{y} - \mathbf{c} + D\mathbf{x} = \mathbf{u}$	
Economic Complementary Slackness	$\mathbf{x}'(A'\mathbf{y} - \mathbf{c} + D\mathbf{x}) = \mathbf{x}'\mathbf{u} = 0$	

where $\mathbf{v}$ and $\mathbf{u}$ are nonnegative slack vectors. Vectors $\mathbf{x}$ and $\mathbf{y}$ are also nonnegative. This equilibrium problem can be solved by Lemke's complementary pivot algorithm discussed in Chapter 6. It can also be solved by a typical nonlinear programming package such as GAMS. In this case, it is necessary to specify an objective function to be optimized in the form of

$$\min_{\mathbf{v},\mathbf{u},\mathbf{y},\mathbf{x}} \{\mathbf{v}'\mathbf{y} + \mathbf{u}'\mathbf{x}\} = 0$$

subject to the linear equilibrium constraints. The relevant data for this numerical example are

$$c = \begin{bmatrix} 15 \\ 33 \\ 22 \\ 16 \end{bmatrix}, \quad b = \begin{bmatrix} 1 \\ 3 \\ 2 \end{bmatrix}, \quad A = \begin{bmatrix} 2 & -2 & 0.5 & 1.0 \\ 1 & 3 & -2.1 & 3.0 \\ -2 & 1 & 0.5 & 0.9 \end{bmatrix},$$

$$D = \begin{bmatrix} 8 & -4 & 2 & -1 \\ -2 & 6 & 5 & 3 \\ 4 & 1 & 4 & -2 \\ -2 & 1 & -2 & 1 \end{bmatrix}.$$

The GAMS solution of this equilibrium problem results in

$$\mathbf{x} = \begin{bmatrix} x_1 = 1.4752 \\ x_2 = 2.3276 \\ x_3 = 3.7701 \\ x_4 = 0.8197 \end{bmatrix}, \quad \mathbf{y} = \begin{bmatrix} y_1 = 7.7727 \\ y_2 = 3.2405 \\ y_3 = 0.8197 \end{bmatrix}, \quad \mathbf{p} = \begin{bmatrix} x_1 = 5.7883 \\ x_2 = 0.6750 \\ x_3 = 0.3306 \\ x_4 = 23.3432 \end{bmatrix}.$$

The different solutions between numerical examples 2 and 3 is due to the asymmetry of the D matrix and also to the different intercepts of commodities 2 and 3 to avoid negative prices.

GAMS Command File: Numerical Example 3

We list a command file for the nonlinear package GAMS that solves the numerical problem presented in numerical Example 3. Asterisks in column 1 relate to comments.

```
$title an equilibrium model of perfectly discriminating
* monopolist with
* asymmetric d matrix
*
$offsymlist offsymxref
    option limrow = 0
    option limcol = 0
    option iterlim = 100000
    option reslim = 200000
    option nlp = conopt3
    option decimals = 7 ;
*
    sets  j output variables / x1, x2, x3, x4 /
          i inputs / y1, y2, y3 /
```

```
*
    alias(i,k,kk);
    alias(j,jj) ;
*
    parameter c(j)  intercept of demand functions

        /   x1    15
            x2    33
            x3    22
            x4    16   /
*
   parameter b(i)   intercept of input supply

        /   y1    1
            y2    3
            y3    2  /
*
    table a(i,j)   technical coefficient matrix

              x1    x2     x3     x4
       y1    2.0    -2    0.5    1.0
       y2    1.0     3   -2.1    3.0
       y3   -2.0     1    0.5    0.9
*
    table d(j,jj)   asymmetric slopes of demand
       functions

            x1    x2    x3    x4
      x1     8    -4     2    -1
      x2    -2     6     5     3
      x3     4     1     4    -2
      x4    -2     1    -2     1
*
    scalar scale parameter to define economic agents /
       1.0 /;
*
* equilibrium problem for the perfectly discriminating
* monopolist
* with asymmetric d matrix
*
    variables
    equil equilibrium objective function -
       complementary slackness
    equix(j)   equilibrium primal variables x
```

```
    equiy(i)   equilibrium dual variables y
    v(i)    equilibrium primal slack variables
    u(j)    equilibrium dual slack variables  ;
*
    positive variables equix, equiy, v, u ;
*
    equations
    slackobjeq   equation of the auxiliary equilibrium
                 problem
    techeq(i)  equations of the equilibrium primal
                 constraints
    marcost(j)   equations of the equilibrium dual
                 constraints ;
    slackobjeq.. equil =e= sum(j, ( equix(j)*u(j) ))
                 + sum(i, ( equiy(i)*v(i)) ) ;
    techeq(i).. b(i)- sum(j, a(i,j)*equix(j))=e= v(i) ;
    marcost(j).. sum(i,a(i,j)*equiy(i)) + sum(jj,
                 d(j,jj)* equix(jj) )- c(j) =e= u(j) ;
*
    model equilib / slackobjeq, techeq, marcost / ;
*
* initial values
    u.l(j) = 1 ;
    v.l(i) = 1 ;
    equix.l(j) = .5 ;
    equiy.l(i) = .5 ;
*
    solve equilib using nlp minimizing equil ;
*
  parameter p(j) ;
  p(j) = c(j) - sum(jj, d(j,jj)*equix.l(jj) ) ;
*
  display equil.l, p, equix.l ,u.l , equiy.l, v.l,
    techeq.m , compltech.m, marcost.m, complmc.m ;
```

Numerical Example 4: Discriminating Monopolist with One Physical Plant and Two Markets

The next numerical example deals with a monopolist who operates in two different and isolated markets and, therefore, can establish different prices according to his goal of maximizing the overall profit. This scenario was discussed in problem (8.15), which is reproduced here, for convenience:

Primal

$$\max TR = \mathbf{c}_1' \mathbf{x}_1 - \mathbf{x}_1' D_1 \mathbf{x}_1 + \mathbf{c}_2' \mathbf{x}_2 - \mathbf{x}_2' D_2 \mathbf{x}_2 \tag{8.15}$$

subject to $\qquad\qquad A\mathbf{x} \leq \mathbf{b}$ $\qquad\qquad$ technology

$$\mathbf{x}_1 + \mathbf{x}_2 \leq \mathbf{x} \qquad\qquad \text{market clearing}$$

$$\mathbf{x}_1 \geq \mathbf{0}, \ \mathbf{x}_2 \geq \mathbf{0}, \ \mathbf{x} \geq \mathbf{0}.$$

The required data are given as:

The Plant: $\quad \mathbf{b} = \begin{bmatrix} 10 \\ 30 \\ 20 \end{bmatrix}, \quad A = \begin{bmatrix} 2 & -2 & 0.5 & 1.0 \\ 1 & 3 & -2.1 & 3.0 \\ -2 & 1 & 0.5 & 0.9 \end{bmatrix}$

Market 1: $\quad \mathbf{c}_1 = \begin{bmatrix} 24 \\ 36 \\ 20 \\ 15 \end{bmatrix}, \quad D_1 = \begin{bmatrix} 5.0 & 1 & 3 & -1.5 \\ 1.0 & 4 & 1 & 1.0 \\ 3.0 & 1 & 4 & -2.0 \\ -1.5 & 1 & -2 & 1.0 \end{bmatrix}$

Market 2: $\quad \mathbf{c}_2 = \begin{bmatrix} 23 \\ 31 \\ 29 \\ 26 \end{bmatrix}, \quad D_2 = \begin{bmatrix} 8 & -5 & 4 & -3 \\ -5 & 7 & 3 & 3 \\ 4 & 3 & 5 & -2 \\ -3 & 3 & -2 & 4 \end{bmatrix}.$

The GAMS solution of this problem is given for each market and the overall monopolistic firm:

$$\text{Monopolist Profit on Market 1} = 24.0389$$
$$\text{Total Revenue on Market 1} = 294.9855$$
$$\text{Monopolist Profit on Market 2} = 51.9986$$
$$\text{Total Revenue on Market 2} = 104.3313$$
$$\text{Total Monopolist Profit} = 76.0375$$
$$\text{Total Revenue} = 399.3168$$
$$\text{Plant Total Cost} = 323.2793$$

Demand and Prices for Market 1

$$\mathbf{x}_1 = \begin{bmatrix} x_{11} = 0.6869 \\ x_{21} = 0.0000 \\ x_{31} = 7.1723 \\ x_{41} = 10.6062 \end{bmatrix}, \quad \mathbf{p}_1 = \begin{bmatrix} p_{11} = 14.9579 \\ p_{21} = 17.5346 \\ p_{31} = 10.4624 \\ p_{41} = 19.7688 \end{bmatrix}$$

Demand and Prices for Market 2

$$\mathbf{x}_2 = \begin{bmatrix} x_{12} = 0.0211 \\ x_{22} = 0.0000 \\ x_{32} = 3.5876 \\ x_{42} = 1.9924 \end{bmatrix}, \quad \mathbf{p}_2 = \begin{bmatrix} p_{12} = 14.4579 \\ p_{22} = 14.3656 \\ p_{32} = 14.9624 \\ p_{42} = 25.2688 \end{bmatrix}$$

Supply and Shadow Prices from the Plant

$$\mathbf{x} = \begin{bmatrix} x_1 = 0.7080 \\ x_2 = 4.6973 \\ x_3 = 10.7599 \\ x_4 = 12.5986 \end{bmatrix}, \quad \mathbf{y} = \begin{bmatrix} y_1 = 8.4153 \\ y_2 = 3.2495 \\ y_3 = 7.0821 \end{bmatrix}$$

Numerical Example 5: Discriminating Monopolist with Two Physical Plants and Two Markets

Example 5 deals with a monopolist who owns two production plants where she produces her outputs and discriminates on two markets for her final commodities. This is the problem discussed in model (8.28), which is reproduced here for convenience:

Primal

$$\max \; TR = \mathbf{c}_1'\mathbf{x}_1 - \mathbf{x}_1' D_1\mathbf{x}_1 + \mathbf{c}_2'\mathbf{x}_2 - \mathbf{x}_2' D_2\mathbf{x}_2 \tag{8.28}$$

subject to
$$A_1\mathbf{v}_1 \le \mathbf{b}_1 \qquad \text{technology at plant 1}$$
$$A_2\mathbf{v}_2 \le \mathbf{b}_2 \qquad \text{technology at plant 2}$$
$$\mathbf{x}_1 + \mathbf{x}_2 \le \mathbf{v}_1 + \mathbf{v}_2 \qquad \text{market clearing}$$
$$\mathbf{x}_1 \ge 0, \; \mathbf{x}_2 \ge 0, \; \mathbf{v}_1 \ge 0, \; \mathbf{v}_1 \ge 0$$

The relevant data are given as:

$$\text{Plant 1:} \quad \mathbf{b}_1 = \begin{bmatrix} 7 \\ 5 \\ 10 \end{bmatrix}, \quad A_1 = \begin{bmatrix} 2.5 & -2 & 0.5 & 1.0 \\ 1.0 & 3 & -2.1 & 3.0 \\ -2.0 & 1 & 0.5 & 0.9 \end{bmatrix}$$

$$\text{Plant 2:} \quad \mathbf{b}_2 = \begin{bmatrix} 10 \\ 24 \\ 8.5 \end{bmatrix}, \quad A_2 = \begin{bmatrix} 0.7 & -1 & 0.5 & 3.0 \\ 1.0 & 3 & 0.2 & 3.0 \\ 0.5 & 1 & 2.0 & 0.9 \end{bmatrix}$$

Market 1: $\quad \mathbf{c}_1 = \begin{bmatrix} 24 \\ 36 \\ 20 \\ 15 \end{bmatrix}, \quad D_1 = \begin{bmatrix} 5.0 & 1 & 3 & -1.5 \\ 1.0 & 4 & 1 & 1.0 \\ 3.0 & 1 & 4 & -2.0 \\ -1.5 & 1 & -2 & 1.0 \end{bmatrix}$

Market 2: $\quad \mathbf{c}_2 = \begin{bmatrix} 23 \\ 31 \\ 34 \\ 30 \end{bmatrix}, \quad D_2 = \begin{bmatrix} 8 & -5 & 4 & -3 \\ -5 & 7 & 3 & 3 \\ 4 & 3 & 5 & -2 \\ -3 & 3 & -2 & 4 \end{bmatrix}.$

The GAMS solution of this problem is given for each market, for each plant, and for the overall monopolistic firm

$$\text{Monopolist Profit on Market 1} = 67.7497$$
$$\text{Total Revenue on Market 1} = 185.5321$$
$$\text{Monopolist Profit on Market 2} = 97.8309$$
$$\text{Total Revenue on Market 2} = 182.6955$$
$$\text{Total Monopolist Profit} = 165.5805$$
$$\text{Total Revenue} = 368.2276$$
$$\text{Total Cost at Plant 1} = 120.1199$$
$$\text{Total Cost at Plant 2} = 82.5272$$
$$\text{Total Cost} = 202.6471$$

Output Demand and Prices for Market 1

$$\mathbf{x}_1 = \begin{bmatrix} x_{11} = 0.9029 \\ x_{21} = 1.8574 \\ x_{31} = 3.4967 \\ x_{41} = 5.7207 \end{bmatrix}, \quad \mathbf{p}_1 = \begin{bmatrix} p_{11} = 14.3688 \\ p_{21} = 18.0000 \\ p_{31} = 11.0884 \\ p_{41} = 16.6697 \end{bmatrix}$$

Output Demand and Prices for Market 2

$$\mathbf{x}_2 = \begin{bmatrix} x_{12} = 0.4148 \\ x_{22} = 0.0000 \\ x_{32} = 4.4474 \\ x_{42} = 3.9924 \end{bmatrix}, \quad \mathbf{p}_2 = \begin{bmatrix} p_{12} = 13.8688 \\ p_{22} = 7.7547 \\ p_{32} = 18.0884 \\ p_{42} = 24.1697 \end{bmatrix}$$

Input Supply and Shadow Prices from Plant 1

$$\mathbf{v}_1 = \begin{bmatrix} v_{11} = 0.5132 \\ v_{21} = 1.9505 \\ v_{31} = 8.3941 \\ v_{41} = 5.4209 \end{bmatrix}, \quad \mathbf{y}_1 = \begin{bmatrix} y_{11} = 6.3319 \\ y_{21} = 2.0336 \\ y_{31} = 6.5628 \end{bmatrix}$$

Input Supply and Shadow Prices from Plant 2

$$\mathbf{v}_2 = \begin{bmatrix} v_{12} = 0.8046 \\ v_{22} = 3.4397 \\ v_{32} = 0.0000 \\ v_{42} = 4.2922 \end{bmatrix}, \quad \mathbf{y}_2 = \begin{bmatrix} y_{12} = 4.5848 \\ y_{22} = 1.5282 \\ y_{32} = 0.0000 \end{bmatrix}$$

GAMS Command File: Numerical Example 5

We list a command file for the nonlinear package GAMS that solves the numerical problem presented in Example 5. Asterisks in column 1 relate to comments.

```
$title a discriminating monopolist: two plants and two
* markets
* with symmetric d matrices
*
$offsymlist offsymxref
    option limrow = 0
    option limcol = 0
    option iterlim = 100000
    option reslim = 200000
    option nlp = conopt3
    option decimals = 7 ;
*
    sets  j     output variables / x1, x2, x3, x4 /
          i     inputs / y1, y2, y3 /
*
    alias(i,k,kk);
    alias(j,jj) ;
*
    parameter c1(j)     intercept of demand functions
      on market 1

    /  x1    24
       x2    36
       x3    20
       x4    15   /
*
    parameter c2(j)     intercept of demand functions
      on market 2
```

```
/   x1     23
    x2     31
    x3     34
    x4     30   /
```
*

parameter b1(i)   intercept of input supply for
   plant 1

```
/   y1      7
    y2      5
    y3     10   /
```
*

parameter b2(i)   intercept of input supply for
   plant 2

```
/   y1     10.0
    y2     24.0
    y3      8.5   /
```
*

table a1(i,j)   technical coefficient matrix for
   plant 1

	x1	x2	x3	x4
y1	2.5	-2	0.5	1.0
y2	1.0	3	-2.1	3.0
y3	-2.0	1	0.5	0.9

*

table a2(i,j)   technical coefficient matrix for
   plant 2

	x1	x2	x3	x4
y1	0.7	-1	0.5	3.0
y2	1.0	3	0.2	3.0
y3	0.5	1	2.0	0.9

*

table d1(j,jj)   slopes of demand functions on
   market 1

	x1	x2	x3	x4
x1	5.0	1	3	-1.5
x2	1.0	4	1	1.0
x3	3.0	1	4	-2.0
x4	-1.5	1	-2	1.0

```
*
    table d2(j,jj)    slopes of demand functions on
      market 2

            x1    x2    x3    x4
       x1    8    -5    4    -3
       x2   -5     7    3     3
       x3    4     3    5    -2
       x4   -3     3   -2     4
*
* discriminating monopolist problem
*
    variables
    monopol    objective function
    v1(j)  primal variables: input supplies for plant 1
    v2(j)  primal variables: input supplies for plant 2
    x1(j)  primal variables: output demand on market 1
    x2(j)  primal variables: output demand on market 2 ;
*
    positive variables v1, v2, x1, x2 ;
*
    equations
    objeq  name of objective function equation
    techeq1(i)  name of technical constraints for
                plant 1
    techeq2(i)  name of technical constraints for
                plant 2
    mktequil(j)  market clearing conditions ;
    objeq.. monopol =e= sum(j, c1(j)*x1(j) )
                - sum((j,jj), x1(j)*d1(j,jj)*x1(jj) )
                + sum(j, c2(j)*x2(j) )
                - sum((j,jj), x2(j)*d2(j,jj)*x2(jj) );
*
    techeq1(i)..   sum(j, a1(i,j)*v1(j)) =l= b1(i) ;
*
    techeq2(i)..   sum(j, a2(i,j)*v2(j)) =l= b2(i) ;
*
    mktequil(j)..   x1(j) + x2(j) =l= v1(j) + v2(j) ;
*
* name and definition of the qp model
*
```

```
model aqpmonop / objeq, techeq1, techeq2,
  mktequil / ;
*
solve aqpmonop using nlp maximizing monopol ;
*
parameter prof1,prof2,totprof, totplc1, totplc2,
  totcost, p1(j), p2(j), totrev1, totrev2;
*
prof1 = sum((j,jj), x1.l(j)*d1(j,jj)*x1.l(jj) ) ;
prof2 = sum((j,jj), x2.l(j)*d2(j,jj)*x2.l(jj) ) ;
totprof = prof1 + prof2 ;
totrev1 = sum(j, c1(j)*x1.l(j) )- sum((j,jj),
  x1.l(j)*d1(j,jj)*x1.l(jj) ) ;
totrev2 = sum(j, c2(j)*x2.l(j) )- sum((j,jj),
  x2.l(j)*d2(j,jj)*x2.l(jj) ) ;
totplc1 = sum(i,b1(i)*techeq1.m(i)) ;
totplc2 = sum(i,b2(i)*techeq2.m(i)) ;
totcost = totplc1 + totplc2 ;
p1(j) = c1(j) - sum(jj, d1(j,jj)*x1.l(jj) ) ;
p2(j) = c2(j) - sum(jj, d2(j,jj)*x2.l(jj) ) ;
*
display monopol.l, prof1, totrev1, prof2, totrev2 ,
  totprof, totplc1, totplc2, totcost, p1, p2,
  x1.l, x2.l, v1.l, v2.l, techeq1.m, techeq2.m ;
```

Exercises

8.1 Develop the programming model of a pure monopolist facing three or more inverse demand functions given by vector $\mathbf{p} = \mathbf{c} - D\mathbf{x}$, where D is an asymmetric positive semidefinite matrix of price/quantity slopes, and a linear technology $A\mathbf{x} \leq \mathbf{b}, \mathbf{x} \geq \mathbf{0}$.

(a) Can this problem be set up as dual pair of optimization models? Explain thoroughly.

(b) Formulate the problem as an LC problem.

8.2 Develop the programming model of a perfectly discriminating monopolist facing three or more inverse demand functions $\mathbf{p} = \mathbf{c} - D\mathbf{x}$, where D is an asymmetric positive semidefinite matrix of price/quantity slopes, and a linear technology $A\mathbf{x} \leq \mathbf{b}, \mathbf{x} \geq \mathbf{0}$.

(a) Can this problem be set up as dual pair of optimization models? Explain thoroughly.

(b) Formulate the problem as an LC problem.

8.3 A pure monopolist faces the following system of inverse demand functions and technology:

$$p_1 = 2$$
$$p_2 = 3 - 2x_2 + x_3, \quad A = \begin{bmatrix} 2 & -1 & 1 \\ 1 & 3 & 1 \end{bmatrix}, \quad b = \begin{bmatrix} 10 \\ 8 \end{bmatrix}$$
$$p_3 = 5 + x_2 - 3x_3$$

(a) Formulate the corresponding primal and dual problems.
(b) Formulate the corresponding LC problem.
(c) Solve the LC problem by Lemke computer program and interpret all the results according to the model set up in (a).

8.4 Given the following information:

$$D = \begin{bmatrix} 13 & -4 & 3 \\ -4 & 5 & -2 \\ 3 & -2 & 3 \end{bmatrix}, \quad c = \begin{bmatrix} 1 \\ 2 \\ 3 \end{bmatrix}$$

(a) Solve the following problem

$$\max (c'x - x'Dx)$$

subject to $$x \geq 0.$$

(b) Derive the dual problem and solve it.
(c) Derive the dual of the dual. Show that (for positive definite D matrices) the Lagrange multipliers are identically equal to the primal variables.
(d) With the knowledge obtained in (c), rederive the dual of the dual and solve it. Discuss the primal and dual solution vectors thus obtained. Justify the conclusion that the dual specification and the dual of the dual as obtained here form a pair of symmetric quadratic programming structures.

8.5 A discriminating monopolist produces the output vector x with a single technology A and plant b and faces the opportunity of two distinct markets in which to sell her three or more products. Markets 1 and 2 are represented by the inverse demand functions $p_1 = c_1 - D_1 x_1$ and $p_2 = c_2 - D_2 x_2$, respectively, where D_1 and D_2 are asymmetric positive semidefinite matrices.

(a) Set up the appropriate primal specification for this entrepreneur assuming that she wishes to maximize profits. Explain every component of the primal problem.
(b) Derive the dual problem and give a complete economic interpretation.

8.6 Given the system of inverse demand functions $\mathbf{p} = \mathbf{c} - D\mathbf{x}$, where D is a symmetric positive definite matrix, a pure monopolist, who operates a linear technology A and plant $\mathbf{b}$, wishes to set up his profit-maximizing problem in terms of prices $\mathbf{p}$ rather than quantities $\mathbf{x}$. Formulate the desired specification and explain clearly every step of the process.

8.7 Given the LC problem where M and $\mathbf{q}$ have the following structure:

$$M = \begin{bmatrix} D_1 & 0 & A' \\ 0 & D_2 & A' \\ -A & -A & 0 \end{bmatrix}, \quad \mathbf{q} = \begin{bmatrix} -\mathbf{c}_1 \\ -\mathbf{c}_2 \\ \mathbf{b} \end{bmatrix}$$

where D_1 and D_2 are symmetric positive semidefinite matrices,
(a) What kind of monopolistic behavior is implied by this LCP?
(b) State the corresponding problem in a primal and dual specification. Explain and interpret economically each component of your dual pair of QP problems.

8.8 Given the LC problem where M and $\mathbf{q}$ have the following structure:

$$M = \begin{bmatrix} D_1 & 0 & 0 & 0 & I \\ 0 & D_2 & 0 & 0 & I \\ 0 & 0 & 0 & A' & -I \\ 0 & 0 & -A & 0 & 0 \\ -I & -I & I & 0 & 0 \end{bmatrix}, \quad \mathbf{q} = \begin{bmatrix} -\mathbf{c}_1 \\ -\mathbf{c}_2 \\ 0 \\ \mathbf{b} \\ 0 \end{bmatrix}$$

where D_1 and D_2 are asymmetric positive semidefinite matrices,
(a) What kind of monopolistic behavior is implied by this LCP?
(b) State the corresponding economic specification and give a complete interpretation.

8.9 Explain the integrability problem. In what kind of monopolistic behavior does it become a problem, and why? How is this kind of behavior modeled?

8.10 Is it possible to claim that the traditional quadratic programming problem representing the behavior of a pure monopolist

$$\max TR = \mathbf{c}'\mathbf{x} - \mathbf{x}'D\mathbf{x}$$

subject to $\qquad\qquad A\mathbf{x} \le \mathbf{b}, \qquad \mathbf{x} \ge 0$

where D is a symmetric positive semidefinite matrix is equivalent to the bilinear programming problem

$$\max TR = \mathbf{p}'\mathbf{x}$$

$$\text{subject to} \qquad A\mathbf{x} \le \mathbf{b}$$

$$\mathbf{p} \le \mathbf{c} - D\mathbf{x}$$

$$\mathbf{x} \ge \mathbf{0}, \mathbf{p} \ge \mathbf{0}\,?$$

(a) Discuss thoroughly and explain your thought process. Support your discussion with an analytical demonstration.
(b) What is the reason for stating the price constraint as an inequality?

8.11 Within the context of monopolistic behavior, indicate specifically what type of monopolist is represented by the following structures of the LC problem:

$$M = \begin{bmatrix} D & A' \\ -A & 0 \end{bmatrix}, \quad D \text{ asymmetric}$$

$$M = \begin{bmatrix} D & A' \\ -A & 0 \end{bmatrix}, \quad D \text{ symmetric}$$

$$M = \begin{bmatrix} (D + D') & A' \\ -A & 0 \end{bmatrix}, \quad D \text{ asymmetric}$$

$$M = \begin{bmatrix} 2D & A' \\ -A & 0 \end{bmatrix}, \quad D.$$

Explain each matrix M and state the corresponding programming problem explicitly (using the familiar complements $\mathbf{c}$ and $\mathbf{b}$).

8.12 A pure monopolist produces two commodities regulated by the public utilities commission, which imposes a ceiling on the price of one commodity. Set up an appropriate programming model using the familiar notation. Discuss the consequences of this imposition by the public utility commission.

8.13 Compare the structure of the pure and of the perfectly discriminating monopolists as described in exercises (8.1) and (8.2), where, however, matrices D are symmetric positive semidefinite. Does it mean that a pure monopolist makes twice as much profit as a perfectly discriminating monopolist? Explain thoroughly.

9

The Monopsonist

An economic agent who is the sole buyer of all the available supply of an input is called a *monopsonist*. We discuss two categories of monopsonists: the pure monopsonist and the perfectly discriminating monopsonist.

Pure Monopsonist

In analogy to the monopolist treatment, we discuss the pure monopsonist's behavior assuming that she will be the sole buyer of a vector of inputs. Let $\mathbf{p}_s = \mathbf{g} + G\mathbf{s}$ be such a vector of inverse linear supply functions, where $\mathbf{s}$ is a $(m \times 1)$ vector of quantities of inputs purchased by (supplied to) the monopsonist, the matrix G is a $(m \times m)$ matrix of price/quantity slopes in the input supply functions, the vector $\mathbf{g}$ contains intercept coefficients and $\mathbf{p}_s$ is a $(m \times 1)$ vector of input prices. We assume that the matrix G is symmetric and positive definite. In analogy to the monopolist, the monopsonist "owns" the input supply functions.

In order to concentrate on the pure monopsonist's behavior, we assume that this economic agent is a price taker on the output markets and produces her outputs by means of a linear technology. The decision of the pure monopsonist is to find the optimal quantities of inputs to purchase on the market and to find the optimal quantity of outputs to produce in such a way to maximize profit. Total revenue of the price-taking entrepreneur is defined as $TR = \mathbf{c}'\mathbf{x}$, where $\mathbf{c}$ is a $(n \times 1)$ vector of market prices for the outputs, which are represented by the vector $\mathbf{x}$, conformable to the vector $\mathbf{c}$. Total cost of the pure monopsonist is defined as $TC = \mathbf{p}_s'\mathbf{s} = \mathbf{g}'\mathbf{s} + \mathbf{s}'G\mathbf{s}$. Hence, the primal specification of the price taker and the pure

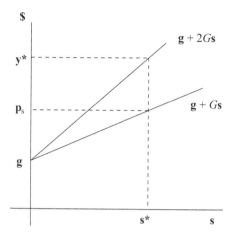

Figure 9.1. The pure monopsonist.

monopsonist can be stated as the maximization of profit subject to a linear technology:

Primal $$\max_{\mathbf{x},\mathbf{s}} \pi = \mathbf{c}'\mathbf{x} - [\mathbf{g}'\mathbf{s} + \mathbf{s}'G\mathbf{s}] \qquad (9.1)$$

subject to $$A\mathbf{x} \le \mathbf{s} \qquad (9.2)$$

$$\mathbf{x} \ge \mathbf{0}, \mathbf{s} \ge \mathbf{0}.$$

The economic interpretation of this model proceeds as in previous chapters. The primal constraints (9.2) represent the input quantity equilibrium conditions according to which the demand of inputs, $A\mathbf{x}$, must be less than or equal to the input supply, $\mathbf{s}$. The primal objective function represents the pure monopsonist's profit defined as total revenue minus total cost.

A diagrammatic illustration of the discussion related to model [(9.1), (9.2)] is given in Figure 9.1.

The pure monopsonist equilibrium is given by the equality between the marginal factor cost, $\mathbf{g} + 2G\mathbf{s}$, and the shadow price of inputs, $\mathbf{y}^*$, also called the vector of marginal revenue products of the inputs.

The dual specification of the pure monopsonist's problem, as stated in [(9.1), (9.2)] is achieved via KKT theory. For this purpose, the Lagrangean function corresponding to the primal problem [(9.1), (9.2)] is specified as

$$L(\mathbf{x}, \mathbf{s}, \mathbf{y}) = \mathbf{c}'\mathbf{x} - \mathbf{g}'\mathbf{s} - \mathbf{s}'G\mathbf{s} + \mathbf{y}'[\mathbf{s} - A\mathbf{x}] \qquad (9.3)$$

where the $\mathbf{y}$ vector represents Lagrange multipliers or, equivalently, shadow prices of the limiting inputs. The KKT conditions derived from (9.3) are

$$\frac{\partial L}{\partial \mathbf{x}} = \mathbf{c} - A'\mathbf{y} \leq \mathbf{0} \tag{9.4}$$

$$\mathbf{x}'\frac{\partial L}{\partial \mathbf{x}} = \mathbf{x}'[\mathbf{c} - A'\mathbf{y}] = 0 \tag{9.5}$$

$$\frac{\partial L}{\partial \mathbf{s}} = -\mathbf{g} - 2G\mathbf{s} + \mathbf{y} \leq \mathbf{0} \tag{9.6}$$

$$\mathbf{s}'\frac{\partial L}{\partial \mathbf{s}} = \mathbf{s}'[-\mathbf{g} - 2G\mathbf{s} + \mathbf{y}] = 0 \tag{9.7}$$

$$\frac{\partial L}{\partial \mathbf{y}} = \mathbf{s} - A\mathbf{x} \geq \mathbf{0} \tag{9.8}$$

$$\mathbf{y}'\frac{\partial L}{\partial \mathbf{y}} = \mathbf{y}'[\mathbf{s} - A\mathbf{x}] = 0 \tag{9.9}$$

together with the nonnegativity of all vectors, $\mathbf{x} \geq \mathbf{0}$, $\mathbf{s} \geq \mathbf{0}$, $\mathbf{y} \geq \mathbf{0}$.

KKT conditions (9.4) and (9.6) constitute the dual constraints of the pure monopsonist's problem. Constraint (9.4) states that the marginal cost of producing outputs $\mathbf{x}$ must be greater than or equal to the corresponding marginal revenue, $\mathbf{c}$. Constraint (9.6) states that the marginal expenditure on inputs (also traditionally called the marginal factor cost), $\mathbf{g} + 2G\mathbf{s}$, must be greater than or equal to the marginal valuation of those inputs, $\mathbf{y}$, also called the marginal revenue product or (in the case of a price taker on the output markets) the value marginal product. For the pure monopsonist's behavior, the marginal factor cost (MFC) is greater than the price for the inputs paid by her, which is $\mathbf{p}_s = \mathbf{g} + G\mathbf{s}$.

The statement of the dual specification of the pure monopsonist's problem, as stated in the primal [(9.1), (9.2)], takes advantage of the information found in KKT conditions (9.5) and (9.7) where $\mathbf{c}'\mathbf{x} = \mathbf{x}'A'\mathbf{y}$ and $\mathbf{s}'\mathbf{y} = \mathbf{g}'\mathbf{s} + 2\mathbf{s}'G\mathbf{s}$, respectively. By using these equations in the Lagrangean function (9.3), the dual specification of the pure monopsonist's problem results in

Dual $\qquad\qquad \min_{\mathbf{s},\mathbf{y}} TCMO = \mathbf{s}'G\mathbf{s} \tag{9.10}$

subject to $\qquad\qquad A'\mathbf{y} \geq \mathbf{c} \tag{9.11}$

$$\mathbf{g} + 2G\mathbf{s} \geq \mathbf{y} \tag{9.12}$$

$$\mathbf{s} \geq \mathbf{0}, \mathbf{y} \geq \mathbf{0}.$$

The objective function (9.10) specifies that an entrepreneur wishing to take over the monopsonist's firm will attempt to minimize the total cost of market options, (*TCMO*), represented by the producer surplus of the pure monopsonist. The quantity $s'Gs$ is the pure monopsonist's profit for the entrepreneur who owns the firm, as can be deduced by equating the primal and the dual objective functions (equivalently, by using KKT conditions (9.5), (9.7), and (9.9)) to produce

$$\pi = c'x - [g's + s'Gs] = s'Gs. \tag{9.13}$$

The linear complementarity structure corresponding to this specification of the price taker on the output markets and the pure monopsonist's problem is stated as

$$M = \begin{bmatrix} 0 & 0 & A' \\ 0 & 2G & -I \\ -A & I & 0 \end{bmatrix}, \quad q = \begin{bmatrix} -c \\ g \\ 0 \end{bmatrix}, \quad z = \begin{bmatrix} x \\ s \\ y \end{bmatrix} \tag{9.14}$$

which represents the KKT conditions [(9.4) through (9.9)] in compact form. The matrix M is rather sparse, with several null matrices and two noninformative identity matrices. One of the objectives of the analysis in this chapter is to reduce the number of null and noninformative matrices in the M matrix of the LC problem.

Perfectly Discriminating Monopsonist

Whereas the pure monopsonist must pay the same price for all the input units that she purchases, the perfectly discriminating monopsonist is capable of offering a different price for each unit of input that is purchased on the market. Hence, her total expenditure on inputs is the integral under the input supply functions. As in a previous section, the vector of input supply functions is assumed to be $\mathbf{p}_s = \mathbf{g} + G\mathbf{s}$, where $\mathbf{s}$ is a $(m \times 1)$ vector of quantities of inputs purchased by (supplied to) the monopsonist, the matrix G is a $(m \times m)$ matrix of price slopes in the input supply functions, and $\mathbf{p}_s$ is a $(m \times 1)$ vector of input prices. We assume that the matrix G is symmetric and positive definite. Total input cost for the perfectly discriminating monopsonist, therefore, is computed as

$$TC = \int_0^{s^*} (\mathbf{g} + G\mathbf{s})\, d\mathbf{s} = \mathbf{g}'\mathbf{s}^* + \tfrac{1}{2}\mathbf{s}^{*\prime} G\mathbf{s}^*. \tag{9.15}$$

The necessary condition for the existence of the integral as stated in (9.15) is that the matrix G be symmetric, as we have assumed previously.

We are now ready to state the primal problem of the price taker on the output market and of the perfectly discriminating monopsonist:

Primal $$\max_{x,s} \pi = c'x - [g's + \tfrac{1}{2}s'Gs] \qquad (9.16)$$

subject to $$Ax \le s \qquad (9.17)$$

$$x \ge 0, s \ge 0.$$

Except for the factor $\tfrac{1}{2}$, the primal problem [(9.16), (9.17)] has the same structure as the primal problem [(9.1), (9.2)] that deals with the pure monopsonist's problem. The primal constraints (9.17) state that the demand for inputs, Ax, must be less than or equal to the input supply, s. Hence, by analogy, the dual specification of the perfectly discriminating monopsonist can be stated as

Dual $$\min_{s,y} TCMO = \tfrac{1}{2}s'Gs \qquad (9.18)$$

subject to $$A'y \ge c \qquad (9.19)$$

$$g + Gs \ge y \qquad (9.20)$$

$$s \ge 0, y \ge 0.$$

The left-hand side of the dual constraint (9.20) is the vector of input supply functions. Hence, if any positive amount of inputs is purchased by the perfectly discriminating monopsonist, that is, if $s > 0$, then the dual constraint (9.20) will be fulfilled as an equation (via complementary slackness conditions) with the result that

$$p_s = g + Gs = y, \qquad s > 0. \qquad (9.21)$$

Constraints (9.19) state the economic equilibrium conditions according to which the output marginal cost, $A'y$, must be greater than or equal to marginal revenue, c.

A diagrammatic illustration of the discussion related to the dual pair of models (9.16) through (9.20) is given in Figure 9.2.

The equilibrium of the perfectly discriminating monopsonist is established by the equality between the marginal revenue product, y^*, and the input supply function, $g + Gs$. At that point, the input price, p_s equals the marginal revenue product.

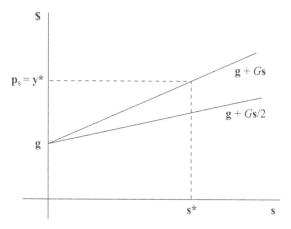

Figure 9.2. The perfectly discriminating monopsonist.

The linear complementarity structure corresponding to this specification of the price taker and the perfectly discriminating monopsonist's problem is stated as

$$
M = \begin{bmatrix} 0 & 0 & A' \\ 0 & G & -I \\ -A & I & 0 \end{bmatrix}, \quad q = \begin{bmatrix} -c \\ g \\ 0 \end{bmatrix}, \quad z = \begin{bmatrix} x \\ s \\ y \end{bmatrix}. \quad (9.22)
$$

The matrix M is as sparse as the matrix M in (9.14), with several null matrices and two noninformative identity matrices.

Perfectly Discriminating Monopsonist Respecified

It turns out that it is possible to achieve a considerable economy and elegance in the specification of the problem involving the behavior of the perfectly discriminating monopsonist. The economy involves the elimination of the vector of input quantities, s, from the primal and dual specifications of problems [(9.16), (9.17)] and [(9.18) through (9.20)], respectively. The corresponding LC problem given in (9.22), therefore, will be reduced by the dimension of the s vector. Furthermore, the primal problem will contain primal and dual variables, as will soon be apparent, while the dual problem will contain only dual variables. In this case, therefore, the structure of asymmetric quadratic programming (AQP), as discussed in Chapter 5, can be used for the specification of the behavior of an economic agent who is a price taker on the output markets and a perfectly discriminating monopsonist on the input markets.

Let us assume that a positive amount of all inputs will be purchased by the perfectly discriminating monopsonist and, thus, $\mathbf{p}_s = \mathbf{g} + G\mathbf{s} = \mathbf{y}$, as stated in (9.21). That is, the dual variable vector $\mathbf{y}$ of the technical constraints in the primal problem [(9.16), (9.17)] is equal to the input price vector $\mathbf{p}_s$. In other words, we can take $\mathbf{y} = \mathbf{g} + G\mathbf{s}$ to be the vector of inverse input supply functions facing the perfectly discriminating monopsonist. With the further assumption that the matrix G is symmetric positive definite, we can invert the system of inverse input supply functions to read

$$\mathbf{s} = -G^{-1}\mathbf{g} + G^{-1}\mathbf{y} \qquad (9.23)$$
$$= \mathbf{b} + E\mathbf{y}$$

where $E \equiv G^{-1}$ and $\mathbf{b} \equiv -G^{-1}\mathbf{g}$. We recall that the inverse matrix G^{-1} exists because G is positive definite, by assumption.

The present goal, therefore, is to transform the primal and the dual problems of the perfectly discriminating monopsonist as given in [(9.16), (9.17)] and [(9.18) through (9.20)] into equivalent specifications that do not include (explicitly) the $\mathbf{s}$ vector of input quantities. We begin the transformation with the total cost function in (9.16) by replacing the vector $\mathbf{s}$ with its equivalent expression in (9.23):

$$TC = \mathbf{g}'\mathbf{s} + \tfrac{1}{2}\mathbf{s}'G\mathbf{s} \qquad (9.24)$$
$$= \mathbf{g}'[\mathbf{b} + E\mathbf{y}] + \tfrac{1}{2}[\mathbf{b}' + \mathbf{y}'E]E^{-1}[\mathbf{b} + E\mathbf{y}]$$
$$= \mathbf{g}'\mathbf{b} + \mathbf{g}'E\mathbf{y} + \tfrac{1}{2}\mathbf{b}'E^{-1}\mathbf{b} + \mathbf{b}'\mathbf{y} + \tfrac{1}{2}\mathbf{y}'E\mathbf{y}$$
$$= -\mathbf{b}'E^{-1}\mathbf{b} - \mathbf{b}'\mathbf{y} + \tfrac{1}{2}\mathbf{b}E^{-1}\mathbf{b} + \mathbf{b}'\mathbf{y} + \tfrac{1}{2}\mathbf{y}'E\mathbf{y}$$
$$= -\tfrac{1}{2}\mathbf{b}'E^{-1}\mathbf{b} + \tfrac{1}{2}\mathbf{y}'E\mathbf{y}.$$

Similarly, the dual objective function (9.18) can be rewritten as

$$TCMO = \tfrac{1}{2}\mathbf{s}'G\mathbf{s} \qquad (9.25)$$
$$= \tfrac{1}{2}\mathbf{b}'E^{-1}\mathbf{b} + \mathbf{b}'\mathbf{y} + \tfrac{1}{2}\mathbf{y}'E\mathbf{y}.$$

The expression $\tfrac{1}{2}\mathbf{b}'E^{-1}\mathbf{b}$ is a fixed (constant) quantity that does not enter in the optimization process. Hence, it is possible to restate the dual pair of quadratic programming problems [(9.16), (9.17)] and [(9.18) through (9.20)] describing the behavior of a price taker on the output markets and of a perfectly discriminating monopsonist on the input markets by the following and equivalent dual pair of problems:

Primal $$\max_{\mathbf{x},\mathbf{y}} \pi = \mathbf{c}'\mathbf{x} - \tfrac{1}{2}\mathbf{y}'E\mathbf{y} \tag{9.26}$$

subject to $$A\mathbf{x} \le \mathbf{b} + E\mathbf{y} \tag{9.27}$$

$$\mathbf{x} \ge 0, \mathbf{y} \ge 0$$

Dual $$\min_{\mathbf{y}} TCMO = \mathbf{b}'\mathbf{y} + \tfrac{1}{2}\mathbf{y}'E\mathbf{y} \tag{9.28}$$

subject to $$A'\mathbf{y} \ge \mathbf{c} \tag{9.29}$$

$$\mathbf{y} \ge 0.$$

The linear complementarity structure corresponding to this specification of the price taker and the perfectly discriminating monopsonist's problem is stated as

$$M = \begin{bmatrix} 0 & A' \\ -A & E \end{bmatrix}, \quad \mathbf{q} = \begin{bmatrix} -\mathbf{c} \\ \mathbf{b} \end{bmatrix}, \quad \mathbf{z} = \begin{bmatrix} \mathbf{x} \\ \mathbf{y} \end{bmatrix}. \tag{9.30}$$

The M matrix has now only one null matrix, indicating the direction for achieving the full information of the matrix M.

Perfectly Discriminating Monopolist and Monopsonist by SQP

In this section we combine the behavior of an economic agent who behaves as a perfectly discriminating monopolist on the output markets and as a perfectly discriminating monopsonist on the input markets using the symmetric quadratic programming (SQP) structure discussed in Chapter 5. This symmetric structure achieves all the objectives of the economic analysis presented in previous sections without loss of information.

Therefore, combining the primal specification of the perfectly discriminating monopolist stated in Chapter 8, problem (8.13), with the primal specification of the perfectly discriminating monopsonist stated in [(9.26), (9.27)] we can write

Primal $\quad\quad\quad \max_{x,y} \pi = c'x - \frac{1}{2}x'Dx - \frac{1}{2}y'Ey$ (9.31)

subject to $\quad\quad\quad\quad\quad Ax \le b + Ey$ (9.32)

$$x \ge 0, y \ge 0$$

Dual $\quad\quad\quad \min_{x,y} TCMO = b'y + \frac{1}{2}y'Ey + \frac{1}{2}x'Dx$ (9.33)

subject to $\quad\quad\quad\quad\quad A'y \ge c - Dx$ (9.34)

$$y \ge 0, x \ge 0.$$

The economic interpretation of the dual pair of problems [(9.31), (9.32)] and [(9.33), (9.34)] follows established guidelines. The primal objective function (9.31) represents the profit of the given entrepreneur after adjusting it by the quantity $\frac{1}{2}b'E^{-1}b$ that was left out of the optimization specification because it is a known fixed quantity. Thus, total revenue of the perfectly discriminating monopolist is $(c'x - \frac{1}{2}x'Dx)$ whereas the total cost of the inputs purchased by the perfectly discriminating monopsonist is $(-\frac{1}{2}b'E^{-1}b + \frac{1}{2}y'Ey)$, as given by (9.24). The primal constraints (9.32) state that the demand for inputs, Ax, must be less than or equal to the quantity of inputs purchased on the market, that is, $s = b + Ey$, as given by (9.23).

The dual objective function (9.33) represents the combined total cost of market options for the perfectly discriminating monopolist, $\frac{1}{2}x'Dx$, and for the perfectly discriminating monopsonist, $b'y + \frac{1}{2}y'Ey$, after adjusting it by the same quantity $\frac{1}{2}b'E^{-1}b$ as stated in (9.25). The dual constraints (9.34) state the familiar condition according to which the output marginal cost, $A'y$, must be greater than or equal to output price, $p = c - Dx$, for the perfectly discriminating monopolist.

The linear complementarity structure corresponding to this SQP specification of the perfectly discriminating monopolist and the perfectly discriminating monopsonist's problem is stated as

$$M = \begin{bmatrix} D & A' \\ -A & E \end{bmatrix}, \quad q = \begin{bmatrix} -c \\ b \end{bmatrix}, \quad z = \begin{bmatrix} x \\ y \end{bmatrix}. \quad (9.35)$$

The matrix M has achieved full information without null matrices.

Pure Monopolist and Pure Monopsonist by SQP

There remains to discuss the treatment of the pure monopolist and the pure monopsonist in a symmetric quadratic programming framework. To achieve this goal we must first recognize a technical aspect of quadratic programming: the relationship between the quadratic form in the objective function and its derivative, appearing in the appropriate constraint, must be in the ratio of 1 to 2. This fact is not surprising and, in fact, it is a natural consequence of the differentiation process. The pure monopsonist purchases the amount of inputs represented by the vector $\mathbf{s}$ on the input supply function $\mathbf{p_s} = \mathbf{g} + G\mathbf{s}$ and pays $\mathbf{p_s}$ for each unit of the purchased input vector. Thus, $\mathbf{s} = -G^{-1}\mathbf{g} + G^{-1}\mathbf{p_s}$, assuming that G is symmetric and positive definite.

According to KKT condition (9.6) (assuming $\mathbf{s} > 0$), however, the marginal expenditure (marginal factor cost) of inputs at the pure monopsonist equilibrium, $\mathbf{y}$, is higher than the price paid by the pure monopsonist in the amount of

$$\mathbf{y} = \mathbf{g} + 2G\mathbf{s} = \mathbf{p_s} + G\mathbf{s} \qquad (9.36)$$
$$= \mathbf{p_s} + G[-G^{-1}\mathbf{g} + G^{-1}\mathbf{p_s}]$$
$$= \mathbf{p_s} - \mathbf{g} + \mathbf{p_s} = -\mathbf{g} + 2\mathbf{p_s}.$$

Thus, the input price vector paid by the pure monopsonist is

$$\mathbf{p_s} = \tfrac{1}{2}\mathbf{y} + \tfrac{1}{2}\mathbf{g}. \qquad (9.37)$$

Finally, we can express the supply function in terms of $\mathbf{y}$, the marginal factor cost, instead of the input price vector $\mathbf{p_s}$, by noticing that

$$\mathbf{s} = -G^{-1}\mathbf{g} + G^{-1}\mathbf{p_s} \qquad (9.38)$$
$$= -G^{-1}\mathbf{g} + G^{-1}[\tfrac{1}{2}\mathbf{y} + \tfrac{1}{2}\mathbf{g}]$$
$$= -\tfrac{1}{2}G^{-1}\mathbf{g} + \tfrac{1}{2}G^{-1}\mathbf{y}$$
$$= \bar{\mathbf{b}} + \bar{E}\mathbf{y}$$

where $\bar{\mathbf{b}} = -\tfrac{1}{2}G^{-1}\mathbf{g}$ and $\bar{E} = \tfrac{1}{2}G^{-1}$.

The total cost of the pure monopsonist is given in the objective function
(9.1) as $TC = \mathbf{g}'\mathbf{s} + \mathbf{s}'G\mathbf{s}$, which can be transformed in terms of the vector
$\mathbf{y}$ by replacing $\mathbf{s}$ with its equivalent expression of (9.38):

$$TC = \mathbf{g}'\mathbf{s} + \mathbf{s}'G\mathbf{s} \qquad (9.39)$$
$$= \mathbf{g}'[\bar{\mathbf{b}} + \bar{E}\mathbf{y}] + [\bar{\mathbf{b}} + \bar{E}\mathbf{y}]'G[\bar{\mathbf{b}} + \bar{E}\mathbf{y}]$$
$$= -\bar{\mathbf{b}}'G\bar{\mathbf{b}} + \tfrac{1}{2}\mathbf{y}'\bar{E}\mathbf{y}.$$

Similarly, the total cost of market options of the pure monopsonist is
given by the objective function (9.10), and it can be transformed in the dual
variables $\mathbf{y}$ as

$$TCMO = \mathbf{s}'G\mathbf{s} \qquad (9.40)$$
$$= [\bar{\mathbf{b}} + \bar{E}\mathbf{y}]'G[\bar{\mathbf{b}} + \bar{E}\mathbf{y}]$$
$$= \bar{\mathbf{b}}'G\bar{\mathbf{b}} + \bar{\mathbf{b}}'\mathbf{y} + \tfrac{1}{2}\mathbf{y}'\bar{E}\mathbf{y}.$$

Notice that the quantity $\bar{\mathbf{b}}'G\bar{\mathbf{b}}$ is a constant (fixed) quantity that does not
affect the optimization process.

We are now ready to state the dual pair of problems of an economic agent
who behaves as a pure monopolist and as a pure monopsonist using the
SQP framework.

Primal	$\max\limits_{\mathbf{x},\mathbf{y}} \pi = \mathbf{c}'\mathbf{x} - \mathbf{x}'D\mathbf{x} - \tfrac{1}{2}\mathbf{y}'\bar{E}\mathbf{y}$	(9.41)
subject to	$A\mathbf{x} \leq \bar{\mathbf{b}} + \bar{E}\mathbf{y}$	(9.42)
	$\mathbf{x} \geq \mathbf{0}, \mathbf{y} \geq \mathbf{0}$	

Dual	$\min\limits_{\mathbf{x},\mathbf{y}} TCMO = \bar{\mathbf{b}}'\mathbf{y} + \tfrac{1}{2}\mathbf{y}'\bar{E}\mathbf{y} + \mathbf{x}'D\mathbf{x}$	(9.43)
subject to	$A'\mathbf{y} \geq \mathbf{c} - 2D\mathbf{x}$	(9.44)
	$\mathbf{y} \geq \mathbf{0}, \mathbf{x} \geq \mathbf{0}$	

where it should be recalled that $\bar{\mathbf{b}} = -\tfrac{1}{2}G^{-1}\mathbf{g}$ and $\bar{E} = \tfrac{1}{2}G^{-1}$.

The economic interpretation of the dual pair of problems [(9.41), (9.42)]
and [(9.43), (9.44)] follows the same outline given for the perfectly discriminating monopolist and monopsonist.

The linear complementarity structure corresponding to this SQP model
of the pure monopolist and pure monopsonist's problem is stated as

$$M = \begin{bmatrix} 2D & A' \\ -A & \bar{E} \end{bmatrix}, \quad \mathbf{q} = \begin{bmatrix} -\mathbf{c} \\ \bar{\mathbf{b}} \end{bmatrix}, \quad \mathbf{z} = \begin{bmatrix} \mathbf{x} \\ \mathbf{y} \end{bmatrix}. \qquad (9.45)$$

The matrix M has the full information structure without null matrices.

Pure Monopolist and Pure Monopsonist with Asymmetric D and G Matrices

When the matrices D and G of the output demand functions $\mathbf{p} = \mathbf{c} - D\mathbf{x}$ facing the pure monopolist and the input supply functions $\mathbf{p_s} = \mathbf{g} + G\mathbf{s}$ facing the pure monopsonist are asymmetric (the empirically more realistic case), it is still possible to formulate the problem of this economic agent as a dual pair of optimization models. Let us assume that the matrices D and G are asymmetric positive semidefinite. Then, the primal problem is

$$\text{Primal} \qquad \max_{\mathbf{x,s}} \pi = \mathbf{c'x} - \mathbf{x'}D\mathbf{x} - [\mathbf{g's} + \mathbf{s'}G\mathbf{s}] \qquad (9.46)$$

$$\text{subject to} \qquad A\mathbf{x} \le \mathbf{s} \qquad (9.47)$$

$$\mathbf{x} \ge \mathbf{0}, \mathbf{s} \ge \mathbf{0}$$

The Lagrangean function is

$$L(\mathbf{x, s, y}) = \mathbf{c'x} - \mathbf{x'}D\mathbf{x} - \mathbf{g's} - \mathbf{s'}G\mathbf{s} + \mathbf{y'}[\mathbf{s} - A\mathbf{x}] \qquad (9.48)$$

where the $\mathbf{y}$ vector represents Lagrange multipliers or, equivalently, shadow prices of the limiting inputs. The KKT conditions derived from (9.48) are

$$\frac{\partial L}{\partial \mathbf{x}} = \mathbf{c} - (D + D')\mathbf{x} - A'\mathbf{y} \le \mathbf{0} \qquad (9.49)$$

$$\mathbf{x'}\frac{\partial L}{\partial \mathbf{x}} = \mathbf{x'}[\mathbf{c} - (D + D')\mathbf{x} - A'\mathbf{y}] = 0 \qquad (9.50)$$

$$\frac{\partial L}{\partial \mathbf{s}} = -\mathbf{g} - (G + G')\mathbf{s} + \mathbf{y} \le \mathbf{0} \qquad (9.51)$$

$$\mathbf{s'}\frac{\partial L}{\partial \mathbf{s}} = \mathbf{s'}[-\mathbf{g} - (G + G')\mathbf{s} + \mathbf{y}] = 0 \qquad (9.52)$$

$$\frac{\partial L}{\partial \mathbf{y}} = \mathbf{s} - A\mathbf{x} \ge \mathbf{0} \qquad (9.53)$$

$$\mathbf{y'}\frac{\partial L}{\partial \mathbf{y}} = \mathbf{y'}[\mathbf{s} - A\mathbf{x}] = 0 \qquad (9.54)$$

together with the nonnegativity of all vectors, $\mathbf{x} \ge \mathbf{0}, \mathbf{s} \ge \mathbf{0}, \mathbf{y} \ge \mathbf{0}$. The marginal revenue of the pure monopolist is $MR = \mathbf{c} - (D + D')\mathbf{x}$ and the marginal factor cost of the pure monopsonist is $MFC = \mathbf{g} + (G + G')\mathbf{s}$. Hence, the dual problem corresponding to $[(9.46), (9.47)]$ is

$$\textbf{Dual} \qquad \min_{\mathbf{x},\mathbf{s},\mathbf{y}} TCMO = \mathbf{x}'D\mathbf{x} + \mathbf{s}'G\mathbf{s} \qquad (9.55)$$

$$\text{subject to} \qquad A'\mathbf{y} \geq \mathbf{c} - (D + D')\mathbf{x} \qquad (9.56)$$

$$\mathbf{g} + (G + G')\mathbf{s} \geq \mathbf{y} \qquad (9.57)$$

$$\mathbf{x} \geq 0, \mathbf{s} \geq 0, \mathbf{y} \geq 0.$$

The linear complementarity structure corresponding to this specification of the pure monopolist and the pure monopsonist's problem is stated as

$$M = \begin{bmatrix} (D + D') & 0 & A' \\ 0 & (G + G') & -I \\ -A & I & 0 \end{bmatrix}, \quad \mathbf{q} = \begin{bmatrix} -\mathbf{c} \\ \mathbf{g} \\ 0 \end{bmatrix}, \quad \mathbf{z} = \begin{bmatrix} \mathbf{x} \\ \mathbf{s} \\ \mathbf{y} \end{bmatrix}. \quad (9.58)$$

The matrix M is rather sparse, with several null matrices and two noninformative identity matrices. This specification of the pure monopolist and pure monopsonist (with asymmetric D and G matrices) can be reformulated as an SQP structure for achieving a reduction in dimension and full information of the matrix M. Borrowing from the discussion and development of the LC problem stated in (9.45), the SQP specification corresponding to (9.58) can be stated as

$$M = \begin{bmatrix} (D + D') & A' \\ -A & \frac{1}{2}(\bar{E} + \bar{E}') \end{bmatrix}, \quad \mathbf{q} = \begin{bmatrix} -\mathbf{c} \\ \bar{\mathbf{b}} \end{bmatrix}, \quad \mathbf{z} = \begin{bmatrix} \mathbf{x} \\ \mathbf{y} \end{bmatrix} \quad (9.59)$$

where the definition of the matrix $\bar{E}$ and vector $\bar{\mathbf{b}}$ retain the previous specification, that is, $\bar{\mathbf{b}} = -\frac{1}{2}G^{-1}\mathbf{g}$ and $\bar{E} = \frac{1}{2}G^{-1}$.

Perfectly Discriminating Monopolist and Perfectly Discriminating Monopsonist with Asymmetric D and G Matrices

In Chapter 8 we discussed the fact that the case of a perfectly discriminating monopolist facing output demand functions $\mathbf{p} = \mathbf{c} - D\mathbf{x}$ with an asymmetric D matrix cannot be formulated as a dual pair of optimization problems because KKT theory would lead to the "wrong" marginal revenue condition. For a similar reason, the case of a perfectly discriminating monopsonist associated with an asymmetric G (or E) matrix cannot be stated as a dual pair of optimization problems. The decision problem of this entrepreneur, however, can be formulated as an equilibrium problem that takes on the following structure (using previous and appropriate KKT conditions as guidelines):

Equilibrium Problem

Input Demand/Supply	$Ax \leq s$	(9.60)
Quantity Complementary Slackness	$y'(s - Ax) = 0$	
Economic Equilibrium Output Market	$A'y \geq c - Dx$	
Economic Complementary Slackness	$x'(A'y - c + Dx) = 0$	
Economic Equilibrium Input Market	$y \leq g + Gs$	
Economic Complementary Slackness	$s'(g + Gs - y) = 0.$	

The LC problem corresponding to (9.60) is given as

$$M = \begin{bmatrix} D & 0 & A' \\ 0 & G & -I \\ -A & I & 0 \end{bmatrix}, \quad q = \begin{bmatrix} -c \\ g \\ 0 \end{bmatrix}, \quad z = \begin{bmatrix} x \\ s \\ y \end{bmatrix}. \quad (9.61)$$

This equilibrium problem can be reformulated as an LC problem and solved by Lemke's pivot algorithm, discussed in Chapter 6. The matrix M is rather sparse, with several null matrices and two noninformative identity matrices.

This specification of the equilibrium problem for the perfectly discriminating monopolist and the perfectly discriminating monopsonist can be reformulated as an equivalent SQP structure for achieving a reduction in dimension and full information of the matrix M. Borrowing directly from the primal and dual constraints (9.32) and (9.34), the SQP equilibrium problem of a perfectly discriminating monopolist and a perfectly discriminating monopsonist facing demand functions for outputs and supply functions for inputs with asymmetric D and E matrices can be stated as

Symmetric Equilibrium Problem

Input Demand/Supply	$Ax \leq b + Ey$	(9.62)
Quantity Complementary Slackness	$y'(b + Ey - Ax) = 0$	
Economic Equilibrium Output Market	$A'y \geq c - Dx$	
Economic Complementary Slackness	$x'(A'y - c + Dx) = 0$	

with an LCP specification as

$$M = \begin{bmatrix} D & A' \\ -A & E \end{bmatrix}, \quad q = \begin{bmatrix} -c \\ b \end{bmatrix}, \quad z = \begin{bmatrix} x \\ y \end{bmatrix}. \tag{9.63}$$

The LC problem (9.63) is structurally different from the LC problem (9.35) because the matrices D and E in (9.63) are asymmetric.

Numerical Example 1: Price Taker and Pure Monopsonist

In this example, we illustrate the case of an entrepreneur who is a price taker on the output markets and a pure monopsonist on the input markets. This corresponds to the scenario discussed in the traditional model [(9.1),(9.2)], which is reproduced here for convenience:

Primal $\qquad \max_{x,s} \pi = c'x - [g's + s'Gs] \tag{9.1}$

$\qquad$ subject to $\qquad Ax \leq s \tag{9.2}$

$$x \geq 0, s \geq 0.$$

The required data are given as

$$c = \begin{bmatrix} 15 \\ 8 \\ 13 \\ 16 \end{bmatrix}, \quad g = \begin{bmatrix} 1 \\ 3 \\ 3 \end{bmatrix}, \quad A = \begin{bmatrix} 3 & -2 & 1.0 & 1.0 \\ 1 & 3 & -2.1 & -3.0 \\ -2 & 1 & 0.5 & 0.9 \end{bmatrix},$$

$$G = \begin{bmatrix} 13 & -4 & 3 \\ -4 & 5 & -2 \\ 3 & -2 & 3 \end{bmatrix}.$$

The solution of the problem was obtained by GAMS with the following numerical results:

$$\text{Pure Monopsonist Profit} = 48.2915$$
$$\text{Total Revenue} = 117.2943$$
$$\text{Total Cost} = 69.0028$$

$$x = \begin{bmatrix} x_1 = 1.5764 \\ x_2 = 4.0895 \\ x_3 = 0.0000 \\ x_4 = 3.8082 \end{bmatrix}, \quad s = \begin{bmatrix} s_1 = 0.3585 \\ s_2 = 2.4202 \\ s_3 = 4.3641 \end{bmatrix}, \quad y = \begin{bmatrix} y_1 = 17.1439 \\ y_2 = 6.8777 \\ y_3 = 21.6547 \end{bmatrix}.$$

The foregoing numerical solution of the price taker/pure monopsonist entrepreneur was achieved with a traditional textbook representation of the monopsonistic behavior. We wish to illustrate now how to achieve the same solution using a programming specification adapted for the price-taking entrepreneur from model $[(9.41),(9.42)]$, which is also reproduced here, for convenience:

$$\text{Primal} \qquad \max_{x,y} \pi = c'x - \tfrac{1}{2}y'\bar{E}y \qquad (9.64)$$

$$\text{subject to} \qquad Ax \le \bar{b} + \bar{E}y \qquad (9.65)$$

$$x \ge 0, y \ge 0$$

The relationship between the given elements of problem $[(9.1),(9.2)]$ and those of problem $[(9.64),(9.65)]$ have been established in previous sections as $\bar{b} = -\tfrac{1}{2}G^{-1}g$ and $\bar{E} = \tfrac{1}{2}G^{-1}$. The numerical espression of $\bar{b}$ and $\bar{E}$ are as follows:

$$\bar{b} = \begin{bmatrix} -0.0408163 \\ -0.7040816 \\ -0.9285714 \end{bmatrix}, \quad \bar{E} = \begin{bmatrix} 0.0561224 & 0.0306122 & -0.0357143 \\ 0.0306123 & 0.1530612 & 0.0714286 \\ -0.0357143 & 0.0714286 & 0.2500000 \end{bmatrix}$$

The solution of problem $[(9.64),(9.65)]$ is

$$\text{AQP Pure Monopsonist Profit} = 48.2915$$
$$\text{AQP Total Revenue} = 117.2943$$
$$\text{AQP Total Cost} = 69.0028$$

$$x = \begin{bmatrix} x_1 = 1.5764 \\ x_2 = 4.0895 \\ x_3 = 0.0000 \\ x_4 = 3.8082 \end{bmatrix}, \quad y = \begin{bmatrix} y_1 = 17.1439 \\ y_2 = 6.8777 \\ y_3 = 21.6547 \end{bmatrix}$$

which is identical to the solution achieved solving the traditional textbook problem given in $[(9.1),(9.2)]$. Notice that profit must be computed as Profit $= \bar{b}'G\bar{b} + \bar{b}'y + \tfrac{1}{2}y'\bar{E}y$, whereas total cost is $TC = -\bar{b}'G\bar{b} + \tfrac{1}{2}y'\bar{E}y$, as explained in (9.40) and (9.39), respectively.

GAMS Command File: Numerical Example 1

This command file contains the code for solving the problem of a price taker on the output side and of a pure monopsonist on the input side in two versions: the traditional textbook formulation of problem $[(9.1),(9.2)]$ and the reformulation of problem $[(9.64),(9.65)]$. The solutions are identical.

```
$title a price taker on the output market and a pure
* monopsonist on in the input market. Two versions.
*
$offsymlist offsymxref
   option limrow = 0
   option limcol = 0
   option iterlim = 100000
   option reslim = 200000
   option nlp = conopt3
   option decimals = 7 ;
*
   sets  j   output variables / x1, x2, x3, x4 /
         i   inputs / y1, y2, y3 /
*
   alias(i,k,kk) ;
*
   parameter c(j)    intercept of demand functions

   /  x1    15
      x2     8
      x3    13
      x4    16 /
*
   parameter gi(i)    intercept of input supply

   /  y1    1
      y2    3
      y3    3 /
*
   table a(i,j)    technical coefficient matrix

            x1     x2      x3      x4
   y1        3   -2.0     1.0     1.0
   y2        1    3.0    -2.1    -3.0
   y3       -2    1.0     0.5     0.9
*
   table g(i,k)    slopes of supply functions

           y1   y2   y3
   y1      13   -4    3
   y2      -4    5   -2
   y3       3   -2    3
*
```

```
    scalar scale  parameter to define economic agents /
      1.0 /;
*
    variables
    monopsobj   traditional monopsonist's objective
      function
    qx(j)   output quantities
    is(i)   traditional monopsonist's input supplies ;
*
    positive variables qx, is ;
*
    equations
    objequ  traditional monopsonist's objective
            function equation
    techno(i)   traditional monopsonist's technical
                constraints;
*
    objequ..   monopsobj =e= sum(j, c(j)*qx(j) )
                            - ( sum(i,gi(i)*is(i))
                            + scale*sum((k,i),
                            is(k)*g(i,k)*is(i)) ) ;
*
    techno(i)..   sum(j, a(i,j)*qx(j)) - is(i) =l= 0 ;
*
* model name and definition
*
    model puremonops /objequ, techno /;
*
    solve puremonops using nlp maximizing monopsobj ;
*
* compute profit, total cost of physical resources
* of the traditional
* monopsonist's,
    parameter profit, totcost, totrev ;
    totrev = sum(j, c(j)*qx.l(j) ) ;
    profit = monopsobj.l ;
    totcost = ( sum(i,gi(i)*is.l(i) ) +
      scale*sum((k,i), is.l(k)*g(i,k)*is.l(i)) ) ;
*
* inverse of the matrix g
*
    parameter identity(i,k)  identity matrix ;
      identity(i,k)$(ord(i) eq ord(k) ) = 1 ;
```

```
*
    parameter zero(i) auxiliary vector of coefficients;
      zero(i) = 0 ;
    parameter compident(i,k)  check on computed
      inverse ;
*
    variables
    invx(i,k)    inverse matrix
    obj    objective function for the inverse
           computation ;
*
    equations
    eq(i,k)  equation for inverse computation
    objfunc   objective function's equation for
              inverse ;
*
    objfunc..    obj =e= sum((i,k), zero(i)*invx(i,k)
              *zero(k) ) ;
    eq(i,k)..    sum(kk, g(i,kk)*invx(kk,k) ) =e=
                 identity(i,k) ;
*
* inverse model's name and definition
*
    model inver / objfunc, eq /;
*
    solve inver using nlp minimizing obj;
*
* check on inverse computation
    compident(i,k) = sum(kk, g(i,kk)*invx.l(kk,k) ) ;
*
* computation of bbar = -invg*g/2, ebar = -invg /2
*
    parameter bbar(i)    intercept of supply function in
                         aqp from sqp
    ebar(i,k)   matrix in aqp from sqp ;
    ebar(i,k) = invx.l(i,k)/2 ;
    bbar(i) = - sum(k, invx.l(i,k)*gi(k) )/2 ;
*
* aqp from sqp model for the monopsonistic problem
*
    variables
    sqpmonops  objective function for sqp model of
               monopsonist
    sqpx(j)  output quantities in sqp model
```

```
   sqpy(i)    input constraints in sqp model;
*
   positive variables sqpx, sqpy ;
*
   equations
   sqpobjeq  sqp model's objective function equation
   techeq(i)  sqp model's technical constraints
             equations ;
*
   sqpobjeq..   sqpmonops =e= sum(j, c(j)*sqpx(j) )
                     - (1/2)*sum((i,k), sqpy(i)*
                       ebar(i,k)*sqpy(k) ) ;
   techeq(i)..   sum(j, a(i,j)*sqpx(j)) =l= bbar(i)
                     + sum(k,ebar(i,k)*sqpy(k)) ;
*
* sqp model name and definition
*
   model sqpmonips / sqpobjeq, techeq / ;
   solve sqpmonips using nlp maximizing sqpmonops ;
*
   parameter bgb, tcmo, tc, profsqp ;
   bgb = sum((i,k), bbar(i)*g(i,k)*bbar(k) ) ;
   tc = - bgb + (1/2)* sum((i,k), sqpy.l(i)*
                     ebar(i,k)*sqpy.l(k) ) ;
   tcmo = bgb + sum(i, bbar(i)*sqpy.l(i)) +
                (1/2)* sum((i,k), sqpy.l(i)
                *ebar(i,k)*sqpy.l(k) ) ;
   profsqp = sqpmonops.l + bgb ;
*
   display monopsobj.l, qx.l, is.l, techno.m ;
   display profit, totcost, totrev ;
*
   display identity, invx.l , compident ;
   display bbar, ebar ;
*
   display sqpmonops.l, profsqp, tc, tcmo,
                sqpx.l, sqpy.l, techeq.m ;
```

Numerical Example 2: Pure Monopolist and Pure Monopsonist by SQP with Asymmetric D and E Matrices

This numerical example deals with an entrepreneur who is a pure monopolist on the output market and a pure monopsonist on the input market. This scenario has been discussed in problem [(9.41),(9.42)], which we reproduce here for convenience:

Primal $\qquad\qquad\qquad \max_{\mathbf{x},\mathbf{y}} \pi = \mathbf{c}'\mathbf{x} - \mathbf{x}'D\mathbf{x} - \frac{1}{2}\mathbf{y}'\bar{E}\mathbf{y}$ $\qquad$ (9.41)

subject to $\qquad\qquad\qquad A\mathbf{x} \le \bar{\mathbf{b}} + \bar{E}\mathbf{y}$ $\qquad$ (9.42)

$$\mathbf{x} \ge \mathbf{0}, \mathbf{y} \ge \mathbf{0}.$$

The added feature is that we choose matrices D and E that are asymmetric. The definitions of vector $\bar{\mathbf{b}} = -G^{-1}\mathbf{g}/2$ and matrix $\bar{E} = G^{-1}/2$ depend on matrix G and vector $\mathbf{g}$ as given later.

The relevant data are

$$\mathbf{c} = \begin{bmatrix} 15 \\ 8 \\ 13 \\ 16 \end{bmatrix}, \quad \bar{\mathbf{b}} = \begin{bmatrix} -0.1551742 \\ -0.5258621 \\ -0.8189655 \end{bmatrix}, \quad A = \begin{bmatrix} 3 & -2 & 0.5 & 1.0 \\ 1 & 3 & -2.1 & -3.0 \\ -2 & 1 & 0.5 & 0.9 \end{bmatrix}$$

$$\bar{E} = \begin{bmatrix} 0.0517241 & 0.0517241 & -0.0172414 \\ 0.0086207 & 0.1336207 & 0.0387931 \\ -0.0603448 & 0.0646552 & 0.2284483 \end{bmatrix}$$

$$D = \begin{bmatrix} 8 & -4 & 2 & -1 \\ -2 & 6 & 5 & 3 \\ 4 & 1 & 4 & -2 \\ -2 & 1 & -2 & 1 \end{bmatrix}.$$

The GAMS solution of the SQP problem is given as

$$\text{SQP Pure Monopsonist Profit} = 13.0851$$
$$\text{SQP Total Revenue} = 21.2988$$
$$\text{SQP Total Cost} = 8.2137$$

$$\mathbf{x} = \begin{bmatrix} x_1 = 0.4438 \\ x_2 = 1.0532 \\ x_3 = 0.2237 \\ x_4 = 0.8301 \end{bmatrix}, \quad \mathbf{y} = \begin{bmatrix} y_1 = 1.7235 \\ y_2 = 6.7157 \\ y_3 = 6.6237 \end{bmatrix}.$$

Notice that, in this case, all final commodities are produced at positive levels, in contrast to the preceding numerical example 1 dealing with a price taker on the output market.

In order to recover the structure of the traditional textbook specification of the pure monopsonist, it is sufficient to compute: $G = 2\bar{E}^{-1}, \mathbf{g} = -\bar{E}^{-1}\bar{\mathbf{b}}$

and $s = \bar{b} + \bar{E}y$. Here are the results:

$$G = \begin{bmatrix} 13 & -6 & 2 \\ -2 & 5 & -1 \\ 4 & -3 & 3 \end{bmatrix}, \quad g = \begin{bmatrix} 1 \\ 3 \\ 3 \end{bmatrix}, \quad s = \begin{bmatrix} s_1 = 0.1671 \\ s_2 = 0.6433 \\ s_3 = 1.0244 \end{bmatrix}.$$

Numerical Example 3: Price Taker and Perfectly Discriminating Monopsonist

This numerical example assumes the structure discussed in model [(9.16), (9.17)], reproduced here for convenience:

$$\textbf{Primal} \qquad \max_{\mathbf{x,s}} \pi = \mathbf{c'x} - [\mathbf{g's} + \tfrac{1}{2}\mathbf{s'Gs}] \qquad (9.16)$$

$$\text{subject to} \qquad \mathbf{Ax} \le \mathbf{s} \qquad (9.17)$$

$$\mathbf{x} \ge 0, \, \mathbf{s} \ge 0.$$

This problem is very similar to the problem discussed in example 1 and, indeed, we will use the same numerical information to assess some differences between the two types of economic behavior displayed by the monopsonistic entrepreneur.

The required data are given as

$$\mathbf{c} = \begin{bmatrix} 15 \\ 8 \\ 13 \\ 16 \end{bmatrix}, \quad \mathbf{g} = \begin{bmatrix} 1 \\ 3 \\ 3 \end{bmatrix}, \quad A = \begin{bmatrix} 3 & -2 & 1.0 & 1.0 \\ 1 & 3 & -2.1 & -3.0 \\ -2 & 1 & 0.5 & 0.9 \end{bmatrix},$$

$$G = \begin{bmatrix} 13 & -4 & 3 \\ -4 & 5 & -2 \\ 3 & -2 & 3 \end{bmatrix}.$$

The solution of the problem was obtained by GAMS with the following numerical results:

Perfectly Discriminating Monopsonist Profit = 96.5829

Total Revenue = 234.5885

Total Cost = 138.0056

$$\mathbf{x} = \begin{bmatrix} x_1 = 3.1528 \\ x_2 = 8.1790 \\ x_3 = 0.0000 \\ x_4 = 7.6165 \end{bmatrix}, \quad \mathbf{s} = \begin{bmatrix} s_1 = 0.7170 \\ s_2 = 4.8405 \\ s_3 = 8.7281 \end{bmatrix}, \quad \mathbf{y} = \begin{bmatrix} y_1 = 17.1439 \\ y_2 = 6.8777 \\ y_3 = 21.6547 \end{bmatrix} 0.$$

We know that this problem has an equivalent reformulation in terms of a symmetric specification as discussed in relation to problem [(9.26),(9.27)], reproduced here for convenience:

Primal $\max\limits_{\mathbf{x},\mathbf{y}} \pi = \mathbf{c}'\mathbf{x} - \frac{1}{2}\mathbf{y}'E\mathbf{y}$ (9.26)

subject to $A\mathbf{x} \le \mathbf{b} + E\mathbf{y}.$ (9.27)

$$\mathbf{x} \ge \mathbf{0}, \mathbf{y} \ge \mathbf{0}.$$

The relationship between the given elements of problem [(9.16),(9.17)] and those of problem [(9.26),(9.27)] has been established in previous sections as $\mathbf{b} = -G^{-1}\mathbf{g}$ and $E = G^{-1}$. The numerical espression of $\mathbf{b}$ and E is as follows:

$$\mathbf{b} = \begin{bmatrix} -0.0816327 \\ -1.4081633 \\ -1.8571429 \end{bmatrix}, \quad E = \begin{bmatrix} 0.1122449 & 0.0612245 & -0.0714286 \\ 0.0612245 & 0.3061224 & 0.1428571 \\ -0.0714286 & 0.1428571 & 0.5000000 \end{bmatrix}.$$

The GAMS solution of problem [(9.26),(9.27)] is:

AQP Perfectly Discriminating Monopsonist Profit $= 96.5829$
AQP Total Revenue $= 234.5885$
AQP Total Cost $= 138.0056$

$$\mathbf{x} = \begin{bmatrix} x_1 = 3.1528 \\ x_2 = 8.1790 \\ x_3 = 0.0000 \\ x_4 = 7.6165 \end{bmatrix}, \quad \mathbf{y} = \begin{bmatrix} y_1 = 17.1439 \\ y_2 = 6.8777 \\ y_3 = 21.6547 \end{bmatrix},$$

which is identical to the solution achieved solving the traditional textbook problem given in [(9.16),(9.17)]. Notice that the output quantities, the total revenue, total profit, and total cost of the perfectly discriminating monopsonist of example 3 are exactly double the same quantities that resulted in numerical Example 1 for the price taker and the pure monopsonist.

GAMS Command File: Numerical Example 3

We list the GAMS command file for solving the numerical problem presented in Example 3. Asterisks in column 1 relate to comments.

```
$title a traditional textbook perfectly discriminating
* monopsonist
*
$offsymlist offsymxref
```

```
    option limrow = 0
    option limcol = 0
    option iterlim = 100000
    option reslim = 200000
    option nlp = conopt3
    option decimals = 7 ;
*
    sets j    output variables / x1, x2, x3, x4 /
        i     inputs / y1, y2, y3 /
*
    alias(i,k,kk) ;
*
    parameter c(j)    intercept of demand functions

     /  x1   15
        x2   ·8
        x3   13
        x4   16  /
*
    parameter gi(i)    intercept of input supply

     /  y1   1
        y2   3
        y3   3  /
*
    table a(i,j)     technical coefficient matrix

              x1    x2   x3      x4
        y1     3  -2.0  1.0     1.0
        y2     1   3.0 -2.1    -3.0
        y3    -2   1.0  0.5     0.9
*
    table g(i,k)    slopes of supply functions

             y1    y2   y3
        y1    13   -4    3
        y2    -4    5   -2
        y3     3   -2    3
*
    scalar scale       parameter to define economic
                       agents / 0.5 /;
*
    variables
    monopsobj       objective function's name
```

```
    qx(j)          primal variables: output
                   quantities
    is(i)           primal variables: input quantities ;
*
    positive variables qx, is ;
*
    equations
    objequ         name of the objective function's
                   equation
    techno(i)      name of the technical contraints ;
*
    objequ..   monopsobj =e= sum(j, c(j)*qx(j) )
                          - ( sum(i,gi(i)*is(i)) +
                          scale*sum((k,i), is(k)*
                          g(i,k)*is(i)) ) ;
*
    techno(i)..   sum(j, a(i,j)*qx(j)) - is(i) =l= 0 ;
*
    model puremonops /objequ, techno /;
*
    solve puremonops using nlp maximizing monopsobj ;
*
* compute profit, total cost of physical resources,
* total revenue
*
    parameter profit, totcost, totrev ;
*
    totrev = sum(j, c(j)*qx.l(j) ) ;
    profit = monopsobj.l ;
    totcost = ( sum(i,gi(i)*is.l(i) ) +
        scale*sum((k,i), is.l(k)*g(i,k)*is.l(i)) ) ;
*
* inverse of the matrix g
*
    parameter identity(i,k)      identity matrix;
    identity(i,k)$(ord(i) eq ord(k) ) = 1 ;
    parameter zero(i) ;
    zero(i) = 0 ;
    parameter compident(i,k) ;
*
    variables
    invx(i,k)    inverse of the g matrix
```

```
    obj    name of the objective function in the
    inverse problem;
*
    equations
    eq(i,k)  equation for the inverse's computation
    objfunc  auxiliary objective function ;
*
    objfunc..   obj =e= sum((i,k), zero(i)*invx(i,k)*
                zero(k) ) ;
*
    eq(i,k)..   sum(kk, g(i,kk)*invx(kk,k) ) =e=
                identity(i,k) ;
*
    model inver / objfunc, eq /;
*
    solve inver using nlp minimizing obj;
*
    compident(i,k) = sum(kk, g(i,kk)*invx.l(kk,k) ) ;
*
* computation of bbar = -invg*g, ebar = -invg
*
    parameter bbar(i)   intercept of supply function
                         in sqp
    ebar(i,k) matrix ebar in sqp ;
    ebar(i,k) = invx.l(i,k) ;
    bbar(i) = - sum(k, invx.l(i,k)*gi(k) ) ;
*
* sqp for the monopsonistic problem
*
    variables
    sqpmonops    name of the objective function in
                 the sQp model
    sqpx(j)   primal variables: x vector
    sqpy(i)   primal variables: y vector ;
*
    positive variables sqpx, sqpy ;
*
    equations
    sqpobjeq    name of the objective function equation
                in sQp
    techeq(i)   name of the constraints' ;
*
```

```
sqpobjeq..    sqpmonops =e= sum(j, c(j)*sqpx(j) )
              - (1/2)* sum((i,k), sqpy(i)*
              ebar(i,k)*sqpy(k) ) ;
techeq(i)..   sum(j, a(i,j)*sqpx(j)) =l=
              bbar(i) + sum(k,ebar(i,k)*sqpy(k)) ;
```

*

```
model sqpmonips / sqpobjeq, techeq / ;
solve sqpmonips using nlp maximizing sqpmonops ;
```

*

```
parameter bgb, tcmo, tc, profsqp, totrevaqp ;
bgb = sum((i,k), bbar(i)*g(i,k)*bbar(k) ) ;
tc = - bgb/2 + (1/2)* sum((i,k), sqpy.l(i)
*ebar(i,k)*sqpy.l(k) ) ;
tcmo = bgb/2 + sum(i, bbar(i)*sqpy.l(i)) +
          (1/2)* sum((i,k), sqpy.l(i)
          *ebar(i,k)*sqpy.l(k) ) ;
profsqp = sqpmonops.l + bgb/2 ;
totrevaqp = sum(j, c(j)*sqpx.l(j) ) ;
```

*

```
display monopsobj.l, qx.l, is.l, techno.m ;
display profit, totcost, totrev ;
display identity, invx.l , compident ;
display bbar, ebar ;
display sqpmonops.l, profsqp, tc, tcmo, totrevaqp,
  sqpx.l, sqpy.l, techeq.m ;
```

Exercises

9.1 The textbook discussion of monopsonistic behavior begins with stating the system of inverse input supply functions, $\mathbf{p}_s = \mathbf{g} + G\mathbf{s}$, where G is a symmetric positive semidefinite matrix. Assuming that a pure monopsonist is a price taker on the market for final commodities, with commodity prices $\mathbf{p} = \mathbf{c}$, and that he operates a single plant using a linear technology A,

(a) Set up and justify the corresponding primal problem.

(b) Derive the dual problem and explain its meaning as a whole and of each component.

(c) In particular, show the entrepreneur's profit and give an appropriate economic explanation of the dual objective function.

(d) Cast the problem as a linear complementarity problem.

9.2 Symmetric quadratic programming (SQP) is suitable for analyzing monopolistic and monopsonistic behavior. Assume that the entrepreneur is a perfectly discriminating monopolist and a perfectly discriminating monopsonist. Given final commodity prices $\mathbf{p} = \mathbf{c} - D\mathbf{x}$ and input prices $\mathbf{p}_s = \mathbf{g} + G\mathbf{s}$, where D is a symmetric positive semidefinite matrix and G is a symmetric positive definite matrix, and given that the entrepreneur operates a linear technology A,

(a) Set up the appropriate symmetric quadratic programming specification and describe your work in detail.

(b) Derive the dual specification and give an accurate economic interpretation of each component.

(c) State the problem as an LCP specification.

9.3 Consider all the information of exercise (9.2) but, now, model the economic behavior of a pure monopolist and a pure monospsonist and execute steps (a), (b), (c) and, furthermore, answer the question:

(d) Compare the SQP models in exercises 9.2 and 9.3 and explain the differences.

9.4 Within the context of monopolistic and monopsonistic behavior, indicate what type of monopolist and monopsonist is represented by the following structures of the LC problem (the vector $\mathbf{q}$ has the usual components, $(-\mathbf{c}, \mathbf{b})'$:

$$M = \begin{bmatrix} D & A' \\ -A & E \end{bmatrix}, \quad D \text{ and } E \text{ asymmetric}$$

$$M = \begin{bmatrix} D & A' \\ -A & E \end{bmatrix}, \quad D \text{ and } E \text{ symmetric}$$

$$M = \begin{bmatrix} (D + D') & A' \\ -A & E/2 \end{bmatrix}, \quad \begin{matrix} D \text{ asymmetric} \\ E \text{ symmetric} \end{matrix}$$

$$M = \begin{bmatrix} 2D & A' \\ -A & E \end{bmatrix}, \quad D\,?\,E\,?$$

$$M = \begin{bmatrix} 0 & A' \\ -A & E \end{bmatrix}, \quad E \text{ symmetric.}$$

Explain each matrix M and state the corresponding programming problem explicitly (using the familiar complements $\mathbf{c}$ and $\mathbf{b}$).

9.5 Decode the type of monopolistic and monopsonistic behavior implied by the following LCP specification:

$$M = \begin{bmatrix} 2D & 0 & A' \\ 0 & G & -I \\ -A & I & 0 \end{bmatrix}, \quad q = \begin{bmatrix} -c \\ g \\ 0 \end{bmatrix}.$$

Explain your reasoning.

9.6 A price taker on the final commodity market faces prices $p = c$. On the input side he behaves as a perfectly discriminating monopsonist on two distinct and separated markets. The input supply functions on each market are $s_1 = b_1 + E_1 y_1$ and $s_2 = b_2 + E_2 y_2$, respectively, where the E_i matrices are symmetric positive semidefinite, $i = 1, 2$. This entrepreneur uses a linear technology A to produce his output.
   (a) Formulate the appropriate primal specification giving a meaningful interpretation to each component.
   (b) Derive the dual problem and interpret each component.
   (c) Restate the problem in an LCP structure.

9.7 Given the input supply functions of a pure monopsonist, $p_s = g + Gs$, where G is a symmetric positive semidefinite matrix, and given the following primal problem:

$$\min\ TCMO = s'Gs$$

$$\text{subject to} \qquad A'y \geq c$$

$$g + 2Gs \geq y$$

$$s \geq 0, y \geq 0$$

   (a) Derive the dual problem and give a complete economic interpretation (use the symbols x and s for the dual variables of the primal constraints).
   (b) Now, interpret the primal in economic terms.

9.8 A pure monopolist on two distinct and separated final commodity markets faces prices $p_1 = c_1 - D_1 x_1$ and $p_2 = c_2 - D_2 x_2$, respectively, where D_i are asymmetric positive semidefinite matrices, $i = 1, 2$. On the input side he behaves as a perfectly discriminating monopsonist on two distinct and separated markets. The input supply functions on each market are $s_1 = b_1 + E_1 y_1$ and $s_2 = b_2 + E_2 y_2$, respectively, where the E_i matrices are symmetric positive semidefinite, $i = 1, 2$. This entrepreneur uses a linear technology A to produce his output.

(a) Formulate the appropriate primal specification, giving a meaningful interpretation to each component.
(b) Derive the dual problem and interpret each component.
(c) Restate the problem in an LCP structure.

9.9 Within the context of monopolistic and monopsonistic behavior, indicate what type of monopolist and monopsonist is represented by the following structures of the LC problem (the vector $\mathbf{q}$ has the usual components, $(-\mathbf{c}, \mathbf{b})'$:

$$M = \begin{bmatrix} (D + D') & A' \\ -A & (E + E')/2 \end{bmatrix}, \quad D \text{ and } E \text{ asymmetric}$$

$$M = \begin{bmatrix} D & A' \\ -A & (E + E')/4 \end{bmatrix}, \quad \begin{matrix} D \text{ asymmetric} \\ E \text{ symmetric} \end{matrix}$$

Explain each matrix M and state the corresponding programming problem explicitly (using the familiar complements $\mathbf{c}$ and $\mathbf{b}$).

10

Risk Programming

In previous chapters, the information available to an economic agent was assumed to be certain. In general, this assumption is not realistic. Market prices of commodities, supplies of limiting inputs, and technical coefficients are types of information subject to uncertainty, to either a small or large degree. Consider a farmer who, in the fall season, must plant crops to be harvested in the spring and for which a market price is not known in the fall. On the basis of his past experience, he may be able to form some expectations about those prices and use these expected prices for making his planning decisions in the fall. On the limiting input side, the effective supply of family labor may depend on seasonal weather, which is a stochastic event. Therefore, in order to proceed to form a production plan, the farmer will also have to form expectations for the uncertain quantities of limiting inputs. Technical coefficients form a third category of information that, generally, is subject to uncertainty. In any given county, agricultural extension personnel knows the "average" input requirements for producing one unit of any crop. However, when that information is transferred to a given farm, the result may not be as suggested by the extension counselor. Again, therefore, a farmer may realistically regard technical coefficients with some uncertainty.

In discussing uncertain commodity market prices, limiting inputs and technical coefficients, we admit that all the information necessary for making rational decisions by an economic agent must be subject to expectation formation about these aleatory prospects. The ability of an economic agent to form expectations about uncertain prospects falls under the analysis of risk.

A risky event can properly be analyzed by means of utility theory. In a famous paper, Pratt (1964) discussed the twin notions of risk aversion and risk premium. Following his notation, let $u(x)$ be a utility function for money. Then, local risk aversion, ra, is defined as

Local Risk Aversion $\qquad ra(x) = -\dfrac{u''(x)}{u'(x)} \qquad$ (10.1)

where $u'(x)$ and $u''(x)$ are first and second derivatives of the utility function evaluated at assets x.

Let $\tilde{z}$ be a random variable representing a risky prospect. Then, the risk premium **RP** is defined as the amount of money that would render a decision maker indifferent between receiving a risk $\tilde{z}$ and receiving a non-random amount $(E(\tilde{z}) - \mathbf{RP})$, where $E(\tilde{z})$ is the mathematical expectation of $\tilde{z}$. Thus, the definition of risk premium is given by

$$u(x + \tilde{z}) = u(x + E(\tilde{z}) - \mathbf{RP}). \qquad (10.2)$$

The quantity $(E(\tilde{z}) - \mathbf{RP})$ is also called the *certainty equivalent*.

To take advantage of a quadratic programming framework, we limit the discussion of risk programming to a strictly concave utility function with constant risk aversion.

Risky Output Prices

Freund was among the first researchers to introduce risk analysis into a programming model by means of expected utility theory. Following his discussion, suppose total revenue $\tilde{r}$ is stochastic due to the assumption that the vector of market prices of commodity outputs, $\tilde{c}$, is stochastic, that is, $\tilde{r} = \tilde{c}'\mathbf{x}$. The vector $\mathbf{x}$ represents the output levels decided by the economic agent, which, therefore, are not stochastic. Suppose also that the economic agent's utility function for money, where r stands for revenue, is

$$u(r) = 1 - e^{-\phi r} \qquad (10.3)$$

and where $\phi = [-u''(r)/u'(r)] > 0$ is a constant risk aversion coefficient corresponding to the assumption that the economic agent is risk averse. We assume also that stochastic commodity prices, $\tilde{c}$, are distributed normally as

$$\tilde{c} \sim N[E(\tilde{c}), \Sigma_c] \qquad (10.4)$$

where Σ_c is the variance-covariance matrix of the commodity price vector $\tilde{c}$ and $E(\tilde{c})$ is the mathematical expectation of the random vector $\tilde{c}$. Given these assumptions, revenue $\tilde{r}$ is distributed normally as

$$\tilde{r} \sim N(\mu_r, \sigma_r^2) = N[E(\tilde{c})'\mathbf{x}, \mathbf{x}'\Sigma_c\mathbf{x}] \qquad (10.5)$$

and expected utility is

$$E[u(\tilde{r})] = \int_{-\infty}^{+\infty} (1 - e^{-\phi\tilde{r}}) \frac{1}{\sigma_r\sqrt{2\pi}} e^{-(\tilde{r}-\mu_r)^2/2\sigma_r^2} d\tilde{r} \qquad (10.6)$$

$$= 1 - e^{-\phi(E(\tilde{c})'\mathbf{x} - \frac{\phi}{2}\mathbf{x}'\Sigma_c\mathbf{x})}.$$

The integration of (10.6) can be carried out by completing the square in the exponent:

$$E[u(\tilde{r})] = \int_{-\infty}^{+\infty} (1 - e^{-\phi\tilde{r}}) \frac{1}{\sigma_r\sqrt{2\pi}} e^{-(\tilde{r}-\mu_r)^2/2\sigma_r^2} d\tilde{r}$$

$$= 1 - \int_{-\infty}^{+\infty} \frac{1}{\sigma_r\sqrt{2\pi}} e^{[-\phi\tilde{r}-(\tilde{r}-\mu_r)^2/2\sigma_r^2]} d\tilde{r}$$

$$= 1 - e^{-\phi(\mu_r - \frac{\phi}{2}\sigma_r^2)} \int_{-\infty}^{+\infty} \frac{1}{\sigma_r\sqrt{2\pi}} e^{[-(\tilde{r}-\mu_r+\phi\sigma_r^2)^2/2\sigma_r^2]} d\tilde{r}$$

$$= 1 - e^{-\phi(E(\tilde{c})'\mathbf{x} - \frac{\phi}{2}\mathbf{x}'\Sigma_c\mathbf{x})}$$

because the integral in the third row corresponds to the density function of a normal random variable with mean $(\mu_r - \phi\sigma_r^2)$ and variance σ_r^2.

The maximization of expected utility, therefore, is equivalent to maximizing the exponent in the second row of (10.6) with respect to the vector $\mathbf{x}$ that represents the output decisions of the economic agent.

Given Pratt's discussion about risk premium, we notice that the quantity $\frac{\phi}{2}\mathbf{x}'\Sigma_c\mathbf{x}$ is precisely the risk premium corresponding to the environment of stochastic commodity prices. This is verified by using Pratt's definition of risk premium, resulting in

$$1 - e^{-\phi(E(\tilde{c})'\mathbf{x} - RP)} = 1 - e^{-\phi(E(\tilde{c})'\mathbf{x} - \frac{\phi}{2}\mathbf{x}'\Sigma_c\mathbf{x})}.$$

In common language, the risk premium may be interpreted as the insurance premium that an economic agent is willing to pay in order to avoid the risky consequences of an uncertain event. Hence, we can regard the risk premiun $\frac{\phi}{2}\mathbf{x}'\Sigma_c\mathbf{x}$ as the total cost of uncertainty due to the stochastic nature of commodity prices, $\tilde{c}$.

In general, the dimension of the risk aversion parameter ϕ is rather small. Its meaning, in terms of monetary units, can be established more intuitively by noticing that its own units are $\phi = 1/\$$. The reciprocal of the risk aversion coefficient is called the *risk tolerance* coefficient, as it may represent the amount of monetary loss that an economic agent may be able to sustain before bankrupcy.

Thus, for the economic agent described in this section (who is assumed to operate using a nonstochastic linear technology), the decision problem under risky output prices corresponds to the solution of the following asymmetric quadratic programming problem:

Primal $$\max_{\mathbf{x}} ENR = E(\tilde{\mathbf{c}})'\mathbf{x} - \tfrac{\phi}{2}\mathbf{x}'\Sigma_c\mathbf{x} \qquad (10.7)$$

subject to $$A\mathbf{x} \le \mathbf{b} \qquad (10.8)$$

$$\mathbf{x} \ge \mathbf{0}.$$

ENR stands for expected net revenue. The first term in the objective function, $E(\tilde{\mathbf{c}})'\mathbf{x}$, is the expected total revenue of the economic agent. The second term, $\tfrac{\phi}{2}\mathbf{x}'\Sigma_c\mathbf{x}$, is the risk premium that this agent is willing to pay for insuring his firm against the consequences of stochastic output prices. The primal constraints (10.8) represent the demand, $A\mathbf{x}$, and supply, $\mathbf{b}$, of limiting inputs.

On the basis of the mathematical experience acquired in Chapters 8 and 9, the dual specification of this risky program corresponds to

Dual $$\min_{\mathbf{x},\mathbf{y}} TC = \mathbf{b}'\mathbf{y} + \tfrac{\phi}{2}\mathbf{x}'\Sigma_c\mathbf{x} \qquad (10.9)$$

subject to $$A'\mathbf{y} + \phi\Sigma_c\mathbf{x} \ge E(\tilde{\mathbf{c}}) \qquad (10.10)$$

$$\mathbf{x} \ge \mathbf{0}, \quad \mathbf{y} \ge \mathbf{0}.$$

The interpretation of the dual objective function follows an already established outline. An external entrepreneur, wishing to take over the given firm, will want to minimize the cost of acquiring the physical plant, $\mathbf{b}'\mathbf{y}$, and to minimize the cost of reimbursing the risk premium paid by the owner of the firm. The dual constraints contain the marginal costs of producing the various outputs, $A'\mathbf{y}$, and the marginal costs of uncertainty in the output prices, $\phi\Sigma_c\mathbf{x}$. The vector $E(\tilde{\mathbf{c}})$ is the vector of expected marginal revenues.

The linear complementarity problem $(M, \mathbf{q})$ corresponding to the risky scenario discussed in this section is defined by the following M matrix and vectors $\mathbf{q}$ and $\mathbf{z}$:

$$M = \begin{bmatrix} \phi\Sigma_c & A' \\ -A & 0 \end{bmatrix}, \qquad \mathbf{q} = \begin{bmatrix} -E(\tilde{\mathbf{c}}) \\ \mathbf{b} \end{bmatrix}, \qquad \mathbf{z} = \begin{bmatrix} \mathbf{x} \\ \mathbf{y} \end{bmatrix}.$$

The matrix M is positive semidefinite because the variance-covariance matrix Σ_c is symmetric positive semidefinite by construction and the risk aversion coefficient ϕ is assumed to be positive.

An alternative, but equivalent, formulation of the risk problem stated by the dual pair of problems [(10.7),(10.8)] and [(10.9),(10.10)] is given by the following structure:

$$\textbf{Primal} \qquad \min_{\mathbf{x}} RP = \tfrac{\phi}{2}\mathbf{x}'\Sigma_c\mathbf{x} \qquad\qquad (10.11)$$

$$\text{subject to} \qquad\qquad A\mathbf{x} \le \mathbf{b} \qquad\qquad (10.12)$$

$$E(\tilde{\mathbf{c}})'\mathbf{x} \ge L \qquad\qquad (10.13)$$

$$\mathbf{x} \ge \mathbf{0}$$

where L is a given level of expected income and RP stands for risk premium. To demonstrate the equivalence of the two versions, we set up the appropriate Lagrangean function and derive the associated KKT conditions. Observe that the primal problem (10.11) requires a minimization. Furthermore, we state only the derivatives with respect to the primal variables. The Lagrangean function is

$$\mathcal{L} = \tfrac{\phi}{2}\mathbf{x}'\Sigma_c\mathbf{x} + \mathbf{y}'[A\mathbf{x} - \mathbf{b}] + \lambda[L - E(\tilde{\mathbf{c}})'\mathbf{x}]. \qquad (10.14)$$

Relevant KKT conditions are

$$\frac{\partial\mathcal{L}}{\partial\mathbf{x}} = \phi\Sigma_c\mathbf{x} + A'\mathbf{y} - \lambda E(\tilde{\mathbf{c}}) \ge \mathbf{0} \qquad\qquad (10.15)$$

$$\mathbf{x}'\frac{\partial\mathcal{L}}{\partial\mathbf{x}} = \phi\mathbf{x}'\Sigma_c\mathbf{x} + \mathbf{x}'A'\mathbf{y} - \lambda\mathbf{x}'E(\tilde{\mathbf{c}}) = 0. \qquad (10.16)$$

From (10.16), $\lambda\mathbf{x}'E(\tilde{\mathbf{c}}) = \phi\mathbf{x}'\Sigma_c\mathbf{x} + \mathbf{x}'A'\mathbf{y}$, which, when substituted into the Lagrangean function (10.14), will result in

$$\mathcal{L} = \tfrac{\phi}{2}\mathbf{x}'\Sigma_c\mathbf{x} + \mathbf{y}'A\mathbf{x} - \mathbf{y}'\mathbf{b} + \lambda L - \phi\mathbf{x}'\Sigma_c\mathbf{x} - \mathbf{y}'A\mathbf{x}$$

$$= \lambda L - \mathbf{y}'\mathbf{b} - \tfrac{\phi}{2}\mathbf{x}'\Sigma_c\mathbf{x}. \qquad (10.17)$$

Hence, the dual specification of primal problem [(10.11),(10.13)] can be stated as

$$\textbf{Dual} \qquad \max_{\lambda,\mathbf{x},\mathbf{y}} \{\lambda L - \mathbf{y}'\mathbf{b} - \tfrac{\phi}{2}\mathbf{x}'\Sigma_c\mathbf{x}\} \qquad (10.18)$$

$$\text{subject to} \qquad A'\mathbf{y} + \phi\Sigma_c\mathbf{x} \ge \lambda E(\tilde{\mathbf{c}}) \qquad (10.19)$$

$$\mathbf{x} \ge \mathbf{0}, \mathbf{y} \ge \mathbf{0}, \lambda \ge 0.$$

The two versions of the risk problem will yield the same solutions, identically, for a value of $\lambda = 1$. Notice, in fact, that the dual constraints (10.19) exhibit the same structure of dual constraints (10.10). The primal constraints (10.12) are identically equal to primal constraints (10.8). Primal constraints (10.13) can be interpreted as the defining level of expected revenue achieved in both specifications when L will be set equal to the level of expected revenue achieved in the primal problem (10.7).

Risky Output Prices and Input Supplies

The supply of limiting inputs may also be stochastic. Examples relevant to an agricultural environment may be given by the amount of family labor determined by the number of workdays in the field allowed by weather conditions, groundwater for irrigation as determined by drought conditions, timing of custom operations as determined by service availability, and machine availability as determined by the probability of breakdown. The extension of the expected utility approach to deal with limiting input supplies follows the E-V (Expectation-Variance) framework developed in the previous section and an SQP specification.

Let output prices and limiting input supplies be stochastic variables $\tilde{c}$ and $\tilde{s}$, respectively. Then, with $\mathbf{x}$ and $\mathbf{y}$ representing the output levels and the shadow input prices, stochastic profit is given by $\tilde{\pi} = \tilde{c}'\mathbf{x} - \tilde{s}'\mathbf{y}$. Assuming multivariate normal distributions for both $\tilde{c}$ and $\tilde{s}$, that is,

$$\tilde{c} \sim N[E(\tilde{c}), \Sigma_c], \qquad \tilde{s} \sim N[E(\tilde{s}), \Sigma_s] \tag{10.20}$$

profit, $\tilde{\pi}$, is also normally distributed as

$$\tilde{\pi} \sim [E(\tilde{c})'\mathbf{x} - E(\tilde{s})'\mathbf{y}, \mathbf{x}'\Sigma_c\mathbf{x} + \mathbf{y}'\Sigma_s\mathbf{y}] \tag{10.21}$$

The use of the same utility function for money given in (10.3) and the assumption that all the random variables are normally distributed allow for the specification of expected utility function of profit as

$$E u(\tilde{\pi}) = 1 - e^{-\phi\{E(\tilde{\pi}) - \frac{\phi}{2} Var(\tilde{\pi})\}}$$

$$= 1 - e^{-\phi\{E(\tilde{c})'\mathbf{x} - E(\tilde{s})'\mathbf{y} - \frac{\phi}{2}(\mathbf{x}'\Sigma_c\mathbf{x} + \mathbf{y}'\Sigma_s\mathbf{y})\}} \tag{10.22}$$

which is maximized by maximizing the exponent with respect to the vectors $\mathbf{x}$ and $\mathbf{y}$, the decisions of the risk-averse entrepreneur. We will show that the following dual pair of symmetric quadratic programming models will maximize the expected utility function in (10.22):

Primal $$\max_{\mathbf{x},\mathbf{y}} ENR = E(\tilde{c})'\mathbf{x} - \frac{\phi}{2}\mathbf{x}'\Sigma_c\mathbf{x} - \frac{\phi}{2}\mathbf{y}'\Sigma_s\mathbf{y} \tag{10.23}$$

subject to $$A\mathbf{x} \leq E(\tilde{s}) + \phi\Sigma_s\mathbf{y} \tag{10.24}$$

$$\mathbf{x} \geq 0, \quad \mathbf{y} \geq 0$$

Dual $\min_{\mathbf{x},\mathbf{y}} TC = E(\bar{\mathbf{s}})'\mathbf{y} + \frac{\phi}{2}\mathbf{y}'\Sigma_s\mathbf{y} + \frac{\phi}{2}\mathbf{x}'\Sigma_c\mathbf{x}$ (10.25)

subject to $A'\mathbf{y} + \phi\Sigma_c\mathbf{x} \geq E(\bar{\mathbf{c}})$ (10.26)

$$\mathbf{x} \geq 0, \quad \mathbf{y} \geq 0.$$

The economic interpretation of the dual pair of problems is based on the E-V approach. The primal objective function (10.23) requires the maximization of the firm's expected revenue minus the risk premium that a risk-averse entrepreneur may be willing to pay for insuring his firm against the consequences of risky output prices and input supplies. The risk premium is composed of two elements reflecting the double source of uncertainty: $(\phi/2)\mathbf{x}'\Sigma_c\mathbf{x}$ is the subjective risk premium the entrepreneur is willing to pay as a consequence of uncertainty in output prices; $(\phi/2)\mathbf{y}'\Sigma_s\mathbf{y}$ is the risk premium associated with uncertain input supplies.

The primal constraints (10.24) represent the technical possibilities of the firm under a risky environment (with a nonstochastic technology): The input requirements, $A\mathbf{x}$, must be less than or equal to expected supplies, $E(\mathbf{s})$, modified by a term $\phi\Sigma_s\mathbf{y}$ that constitutes a marginal risk adjustment directly related to the uncertain input supplies. In general, nothing can be said regarding the sign of this term, implying that risky input supplies and risk aversion may dictate either a larger or a smaller procurement of inputs.

The dual objective function (10.25) can be regarded as the goal of an entrepreneur who wishes to buy out the original owner of the firm. In this case, the entrepreneur's objective is to minimize the total expected cost of the firm's stochastic input supplies, $E(\bar{\mathbf{s}})'\mathbf{y}$, and the amount of money that he should reimburse the original owner of the firm for the payment of the risk premium on the two sources of uncertainty.

The dual constraints (10.26) state that marginal output cost, $A'\mathbf{y}$, plus the marginal risk premium involving the uncertain output prices, $\phi\Sigma_c\mathbf{x}$, must be greater than or equal to expected marginal revenue, $E(\bar{\mathbf{c}})$.

The specification of the dual problem [(10.25), (10.26)] is obtained by applying KKT theory to the primal problem [(10.23), (10.24)]. Thus, the Lagrangean function is specified as

$$L = E(\bar{\mathbf{c}})'\mathbf{x} - \frac{\phi}{2}\mathbf{x}'\Sigma_c\mathbf{x} - \frac{\phi}{2}\mathbf{y}'\Sigma_s\mathbf{y} + \mathbf{y}'[E(\bar{\mathbf{s}}) + \phi\Sigma_s\mathbf{y} - A\mathbf{x}]$$ (10.27)

whereas the corresponding KKT conditions are

$$\frac{\partial L}{\partial \mathbf{x}} = E(\bar{\mathbf{c}}) - \phi\Sigma_c\mathbf{x} - A'\mathbf{y} \leq 0$$ (10.28)

$$\mathbf{x}'\frac{\partial L}{\partial \mathbf{x}} = \mathbf{x}'E(\bar{\mathbf{c}}) - \phi\mathbf{x}'\Sigma_c\mathbf{x} - \mathbf{x}'A'\mathbf{y} = 0$$ (10.29)

$$\frac{\partial L}{\partial \mathbf{y}} = -\phi \Sigma_s \mathbf{y} + E(\tilde{\mathbf{s}}) + 2\phi \Sigma_s \mathbf{y} - A\mathbf{x} \geq 0$$

$$= E(\tilde{\mathbf{s}}) + \phi \Sigma_s \mathbf{y} - A\mathbf{x} \geq 0 \qquad (10.30)$$

$$\mathbf{y}'\frac{\partial L}{\partial \mathbf{y}} = \mathbf{y}' E(\tilde{\mathbf{s}}) + \phi \mathbf{y}' \Sigma_s \mathbf{y} - \mathbf{y}' A\mathbf{x} = 0 \qquad (10.31)$$

and the nonnegativity of vectors $\mathbf{x}$ and $\mathbf{y}$.

Relations (10.28) are the dual constraints. Furthermore, using equation (10.29) in the form $E(\tilde{\mathbf{c}})'\mathbf{x} = \phi \mathbf{x}' \Sigma_c \mathbf{x} + \mathbf{x}' A' \mathbf{y}$ in the Lagrangean function (10.27), we obtain the final form of the dual objective function as expressed in (10.25). Finally, subtracting the complementary slackness condition (10.31) from (10.29), we obtain

$$E(\tilde{\mathbf{c}})'\mathbf{x} - E(\tilde{\mathbf{s}})'\mathbf{y} - \tfrac{\phi}{2}(\mathbf{x}' \Sigma_c \mathbf{x} + \mathbf{y}' \Sigma_s \mathbf{y}) = \tfrac{\phi}{2}(\mathbf{x}' \Sigma_c \mathbf{x} + \mathbf{y}' \Sigma_s \mathbf{y}). \qquad (10.32)$$

The left-hand-side expression corresponds to the exponent of the expected utility function in (10.22), as intended and stated earlier. The right-hand-side expression corresponds to the risk premium.

The linear complementarity problem $(M, \mathbf{q})$ corresponding to the risky environment discussed in this section is defined by the following M matrix and vectors $\mathbf{q}$ and $\mathbf{z}$:

$$M = \begin{bmatrix} \phi \Sigma_c & A' \\ -A & \phi \Sigma_s \end{bmatrix}, \quad \mathbf{q} = \begin{bmatrix} -E(\tilde{\mathbf{c}}) \\ E(\tilde{\mathbf{s}}) \end{bmatrix}, \quad \mathbf{z} = \begin{bmatrix} \mathbf{x} \\ \mathbf{y} \end{bmatrix}. \qquad (10.33)$$

The matrix M is positive semidefinite because the variance-covariance matrices are symmetric positive semidefinite by construction and the risk aversion coefficient is assumed to be positive. The matrices A' and $(-A)$ will drop out of the quadratic form in $\mathbf{z}$ and are not involved in determining the definiteness of the M matrix.

Chance-Constrained Interpretation of Risk Programming

Chance-constrained programming is an approach pioneered by Charnes and Cooper that can be used to further justify the dual pair of risky programs developed in previous sections. Consider the following probability constraint:

$$\text{Prob}(\tilde{\mathbf{c}}'\mathbf{x} \leq \mathbf{y}' A\mathbf{x}) \leq 1 - \beta. \qquad (10.34)$$

This probabilistic constraint is associated, in some sense, to the dual constraints (10.26) and their corresponding complementary slackness conditions. Its economic interpretation may be regarded as representing an entrepreneur who is willing to accept events in which total revenue, $\tilde{c}'x$, could be less than or equal to total imputed cost, $y'Ax$, with a probability of $(1 - \beta)$, or smaller.

By normalizing the random variable $\tilde{c}'x$, we can write

$$\text{Prob}(\tilde{c}'x \leq y'Ax) \leq 1 - \beta \tag{10.35}$$

$$\text{Prob}\left(\frac{\tilde{c}'x - E(\tilde{c})'x}{(x'\Sigma_c x)^{1/2}} \leq \frac{y'Ax - E(\tilde{c})'x}{(x'\Sigma_c x)^{1/2}}\right) \leq 1 - \beta$$

$$\text{Prob}\left(\tau_c \leq \frac{y'Ax - E(\tilde{c})'x}{(x'\Sigma_c x)^{1/2}}\right) \leq 1 - \beta$$

$$\text{Prob}(E(\tilde{c})'x + \tau_c(x'\Sigma_c x)^{1/2} \leq y'Ax) \leq 1 - \beta$$

where τ_c is a standard normal variable and $(x'\Sigma_c x)^{1/2}$ is the standard deviation of $\tilde{c}'x$. Therefore, with a choice of τ_c, say $\bar{\tau}_c$, that will satisfy the probability statement (10.35) with the equality sign, the stochastic constraint (10.34) is equivalent to the nonstochastic constraint

$$E(\tilde{c})'x + \bar{\tau}_c(x'\Sigma_c x)^{1/2} \leq y'Ax. \tag{10.36}$$

The relationship between the value of $\bar{\tau}_c$ and the risk aversion coefficient ϕ can be established using the complementary slackness condition associated with the dual constraint (10.26). In other words, by multiplying and dividing the standard deviation in (10.36) by $(x'\Sigma_c x)^{1/2}$ we obtain the first row of (10.37), whereas the second row comes from the complementary slackness condition (10.29):

$$E(\tilde{c})'x + \left(\frac{\bar{\tau}_c}{(x'\Sigma_c x)^{1/2}}\right)(x'\Sigma_c x) \leq y'Ax \tag{10.37}$$

$$E(\tilde{c})'x - \phi(x'\Sigma_c x) = y'Ax.$$

Finally, subtracting the second row of (10.37) from the first relation, we obtain

$$\left(\frac{\bar{\tau}_c}{(x'\Sigma_c x)^{1/2}}\right) + \phi \leq 0. \tag{10.38}$$

It follows that, for a risk-averse entrepreneur, the probability of an event such that revenue is less than or equal to total cost will be rather small, that is, $(1 - \beta)$ will be small, and the critical value of $\bar{\tau}_c$ will be negative. This condition is required to satisfy relation (10.38) where ϕ and $(\mathbf{x}'\Sigma_c\mathbf{x})^{1/2}$ are positive quantities.

Relation (10.38) suggests a possible way to determine the dimension of the risk aversion coefficient using empirical information. Suppose that the entrepreneur in question chooses a probability $(1 - \beta) = 0.05$, or 1 year in 20 that revenue will be smaller than total cost. From the standard normal table the value of $\bar{\tau}_c = -1.65$, approximately. Furthermore, if realized output levels of the products produced by the firm are available from previous years, say $\bar{\mathbf{x}}$, the determination of a risk aversion coefficient that is consistent with expected utility theory and the E-V framework presented earlier can be computed as

$$\phi = -\frac{-1.65}{(\bar{\mathbf{x}}'\Sigma_c\bar{\mathbf{x}})^{1/2}}. \tag{10.39}$$

The value of the risk aversion coefficient computed using (10.39) depends on the output and price units selected to represent the data series. For sound computational reasons, it is suggested to scale all the data series to lie between 0 and 10.

Risky Output Prices and Input Supplies with Covariance

The discussion of risky output prices and risky limiting input supplies developed in previous sections was carried out assuming zero covariances between output prices and limiting inputs. This assumption has allowed the specification of the risky environment as a dual pair of symmetric quadratic programming models as presented in [(10.23) through (10.26)]. In other words, the presence of a covariance relation between output prices and limiting inputs prevents the specification of the risky environment as a pair of optimization problems.

For the sake of clarity, we respecify here all the components of the risky environment to be dealt with. Now, output prices and limiting inputs are assumed to be stochastic and distributed normally with mean $E(\tilde{c})$ and $E(\tilde{s})$, respectively, and variance-covariance matrix

$$\Sigma = \begin{bmatrix} \Sigma_c & -\Sigma_{cs} \\ -\Sigma_{sc} & \Sigma_s \end{bmatrix}. \tag{10.40}$$

Profit, therefore, is also stochastic, $\tilde{\pi} = \tilde{c}'\mathbf{x} - \tilde{s}'\mathbf{y}$, and distributed normally with mean $E(\tilde{\pi}) = E(\tilde{c})'\mathbf{x} - E(\tilde{s})'\mathbf{y}$ and variance $Var(\tilde{\pi}) = \mathbf{x}'\Sigma_c\mathbf{x} + \mathbf{y}'\Sigma_s\mathbf{y} - 2\mathbf{x}'\Sigma_{cs}\mathbf{y}$. Let $\mathbf{z}' = (\mathbf{x}', \mathbf{y}')$ and $\tilde{\mathbf{d}}' = (\tilde{c}', -\tilde{s}')$. Then, assuming that the economic agent possesses a utility function as in (10.3), his expected utility corresponds to

$$E[u(\tilde{\pi})] \propto [E(\tilde{\pi}) - \tfrac{\phi}{2}Var(\tilde{\pi})] \tag{10.41}$$

$$= [E(\tilde{d})'z - \tfrac{\phi}{2}z'\Sigma z]$$

$$= [E(\tilde{c})'x - E(\tilde{s})'y - \tfrac{\phi}{2}(x'\Sigma_c x + y'\Sigma_s y - 2x'\Sigma_{cs}y)].$$

Relation (10.41) remains a concave function because the variance of $\tilde{\pi}$, $z'\Sigma z$, is a positive semidefinite quadratic form. The quantity $\tfrac{\phi}{2}(x'\Sigma_c x + y'\Sigma_s y - 2x'\Sigma_{cs}y)$ is the risk premium of the more complex environment. The presence of the bilinear term $2x'\Sigma_{cs}y$ precludes the formulation of this economic agent's risky problem as an optimization model because the KKT conditions resulting from any plausible specification of the primal model do not correspond to the structure of the given problem. It is possible, however, to state this risky problem as an equilibrium model: find $x \geq 0$ and $y \geq 0$ such that

Symmetric Equilibrium Problem

$$Ax + \phi\Sigma_{sc}x \leq E(\tilde{s}) + \phi\Sigma_s y \tag{10.42}$$

$$A'y + \phi\Sigma_c x \geq E(\tilde{c}) + \phi\Sigma_{cs}y \tag{10.43}$$

$$y'[E(\tilde{s}) + \phi\Sigma_s y - Ax - \phi\Sigma_{sc}x] = 0 \tag{10.44}$$

$$x'[A'y - \phi\Sigma_{cs}y + \phi\Sigma_c x - E(\tilde{c})] = 0. \tag{10.45}$$

An effective criterion for establishing the correct structure of this symmetric equilibrium problem is that the covariance matrices must be positioned in constraints (10.42) and (10.43) according to the conformability of the other terms. Notice that no negative sign appears in either relation.

The difference between this set of equilibrium relations (10.42) through (10.45) and the KKT conditions associated with problem [(10.23) through (10.26)] is that the covariance term Σ_{sc} appears either to impose further restrictions on the input use or to relax their binding availabilities, depending on the sign of the term $\Sigma_{sc}x$. More explicitly, the primal constraints (10.42) may be restated as $(A + \phi\Sigma_{sc})x \leq E(\tilde{s}) + \phi\Sigma_s y$. The left-hand side indicates that the input use, Ax, must now be properly adjusted to account for the interaction between output prices and input quantities. The level of output, x, will be either larger or smaller than the one corresponding to the case where $\Sigma_{sc} = 0$ depending on the sign of $\Sigma_{sc}x$. Although the technology A is originally assumed to be nonstochastic, the quantity $(A + \phi\Sigma_{sc})$ reflects the "trasmission" of uncertainty between input supplies and output prices (or vice versa). The matrix $(A + \phi\Sigma_{sc})$ can thus be regarded as the "effective technology" utilized in this risky environment.

In a similar restatement of the dual constraints (10.43), $(A' - \phi\Sigma_{cs})\mathbf{y} + \phi\Sigma_c\mathbf{x} \geq E(\bar{c})$, the marginal cost of outputs, $A'\mathbf{y}$, must be adjusted by the marginal risk factor $\phi\Sigma_{cs}\mathbf{y}$, which expresses the stochastic interrelations between output prices and input quantities. Using analogous reasoning developed for the primal constraints, the quantity $(A' - \phi\Sigma_{cs})\mathbf{y}$ may be regarded as the "effective marginal output cost." Notice that $(A + \phi\Sigma_{sc}) \neq (A' - \phi\Sigma_{cs})'$. This is why it is not possible to state this risky problem as a dual pair of optimization models.

Furthermore, subtracting relation (10.45) from (10.44), we obtain

$$E(\bar{c})'\mathbf{x} - E(\bar{s})'\mathbf{y} - \tfrac{\phi}{2}(\mathbf{x}'\Sigma_c\mathbf{x} + \mathbf{y}'\Sigma_s\mathbf{y} - 2\mathbf{x}'\Sigma_{cs}\mathbf{y}) \qquad (10.46)$$
$$= \tfrac{\phi}{2}(\mathbf{x}'\Sigma_c\mathbf{x} + \mathbf{y}'\Sigma_s\mathbf{y} - 2\mathbf{x}'\Sigma_{cs}\mathbf{y}).$$

The first term of (10.46) corresponds to the expected utility in (10.41) whereas the second term is the risk premium.

The solution of the symmetric equilibrium problem in (10.42) through (10.45) may be attained by solving the corresponding LC problem $(M, \mathbf{q})$, where

$$M = \begin{bmatrix} \phi\Sigma_c & (A' - \phi\Sigma_{cs}) \\ -(A + \phi\Sigma_{sc}) & \phi\Sigma_s \end{bmatrix}, \quad \mathbf{q} = \begin{bmatrix} -E(\bar{c}) \\ E(\bar{s}) \end{bmatrix}, \quad \mathbf{z} = \begin{bmatrix} \mathbf{x} \\ \mathbf{y} \end{bmatrix}. \qquad (10.47)$$

The M matrix in (10.47) is positive semidefinite because the variance-covariance matrix Σ is positive semidefinite by construction, that is, $\mathbf{z}'M\mathbf{z} = \mathbf{z}'\Sigma\mathbf{z} \geq 0$. Notice that the off-diagonal matrices of the M matrix are not the negative transpose of each other, as in previous LCP specifications that admitted a dual pair of optimization models. This fact is another indication of the impossibility of stating this risky problem (with nonzero covariances) as a dual pair of optimization models.

Risky Technology

The discussion of a stochastic technology requires a technical treatment that combines various elements already presented in this book. In particular, it will be convenient to combine the chance-constrained formulation of the risky technical coefficients with the LCP framework.

Suppose that the chance-constrained problem

$$\text{maximize } c'x \tag{10.48}$$

$$\text{subject to} \quad \text{Prob}\left\{ \tilde{a}_i'x \le b_i \right\} \ge \alpha_i \quad i = 1, \ldots, m$$

$$x \ge 0$$

represents the problem faced by a price-taking entrepreneur who faces uncertain knowledge of the vector of technical coefficients, $\tilde{a}_i$, in the ith constraint. To simplify the discussion, we assume that the market prices, c, and the limiting input availabilities, b_i, $i = 1, \ldots, m$, are not stochastic.

Vectors c, x, and $\tilde{a}_i'$ are n-dimensional vectors, and α_i is the minimum level of acceptable probability associated with the solution of the stochastic constraint of (10.48). Within the framework of the firm's theory, $c'x$ may be interpreted as a nonstochastic revenue, whereas the constraints specify the acceptable, subjective level of probability by which the stochastic input demand $\tilde{a}_i'x$ must satisfy the physical quantity equilibrium relation expressed as the usual *demand* $\le$ *supply*. Another way to interpret the stochastic constraint is to imagine that an entrepreneur, facing a stochastic technology $\tilde{a}_i'$, $i = 1, \ldots, m$, desires to formulate a production plan x that will satisfy the stochastic constraint $\text{Prob}(\tilde{a}_i'x \le b_i)$ at least with a probability α_i.

In order to solve problem (10.48), it is necessary to convert the probabilistic constraints into their deterministic equivalents using properties of random variables. No particular assumption is necessary for the development that follows except the existence of finite moments of the probability distribution associated with the random vector variable $\tilde{a}_i'$. Then, using elementary statistical rules, the probability of the standardized random variable $\tilde{a}_i'x$ can be restated as

$$\alpha_i \le \text{Prob}\left\{ \tilde{a}_i'x \le b_i \right\} = \text{Prob}\left\{ \frac{\tilde{a}_i'x - E(\tilde{a}_i)'x}{(x'\Sigma_{a_i}x)^{1/2}} \le \frac{b_i - E(\tilde{a}_i)'x}{(x'\Sigma_{a_i}x)^{1/2}} \right\} \tag{10.49}$$

$$= \text{Prob}\left\{ \tau_i \le \frac{b_i - E(\tilde{a}_i)'x}{(x'\Sigma_{a_i}x)^{1/2}} \right\}$$

$$= \text{Prob}\left\{ \tilde{a}_i'x \le E(\tilde{a}_i)'x + \tau_i(x'\Sigma_{a_i}x)^{1/2} \le b_i \right\} \ge \alpha_i$$

where τ_i is the standardized random variable defined according to a given distribution and E is the expectation operator. With a choice of τ_i, say $\bar{\tau}_i$, that satisfies the probability statement (10.49) with equality, the stochastic constraint (10.49) is equivalent to the nonstochastic constraint

$$E(\tilde{\mathbf{a}}_i)'\mathbf{x} + \bar{\tau}_i(\mathbf{x}'\Sigma_{a_i}\mathbf{x})^{1/2} \le b_i. \tag{10.50}$$

A solution $\mathbf{x}$ satisfying (10.50) corresponds to a solution of the constraint $\text{Prob}\{\tilde{\mathbf{a}}_i'\mathbf{x} \le b_i\} \ge \alpha_i$ for all values of $\tilde{\mathbf{a}}_i'\mathbf{x}$ that are less than or equal to $E(\tilde{\mathbf{a}}_i)'\mathbf{x} + \bar{\tau}_i(\mathbf{x}'\Sigma_{a_i}\mathbf{x})^{1/2}$, which is less than or equal to b_i. Constraint (10.50) is called the deterministic equivalent of the corresponding probabilistic constraint, and the original problem (10.48) is replaced by

$$\text{maximize } \mathbf{c}'\mathbf{x} \tag{10.51}$$

$$\text{subject to} \quad E(\tilde{\mathbf{a}}_i)'\mathbf{x} + \bar{\tau}_i(\mathbf{x}'\Sigma_{a_i}\mathbf{x})^{1/2} \le b_i \quad i = 1, \ldots, m$$

$$\mathbf{x} \ge 0.$$

The constraints of (10.51) are nonlinear in the $\mathbf{x}$ vector and present nonnegligible computational difficulties. The algorithm presented in this section, therefore, linearizes the constraints and attempts to reach a solution of (10.51) by a sequence of linear complementarity problems.

The proposed algorithm is relatively simple. However, the complexity of the initial specification and structure of the necessary KKT conditions associated with problem (10.51) suggests that we should approach the introduction of such an algorithm by means of a simple numerical example.

Thus, let us consider the following chance-constrained problem (already converted into the form of (10.51)):

$$\text{maximize } R = x_1 + 0.8x_2 \tag{10.52}$$
$$\text{subject to}$$

$$E(\tilde{a}_{11})x_1 + E(\tilde{a}_{12})x_2 + \bar{\tau}_1\left[var(\tilde{a}_{11})x_1^2 + var(\tilde{a}_{12})x_2^2\right]^{1/2} \le 3.0$$

$$x_1 + \quad x_2 \qquad\qquad\qquad\qquad\qquad\qquad \le 3.5$$

$$x_1 + \quad 1.667x_2 \qquad\qquad\qquad\qquad\qquad \le 5.0$$

$$x_1 \ge 0, \quad x_2 \ge 0$$

where var stands for the variance of the corresponding coefficient. In this example, only the technical coefficients $\tilde{a}_{11}$ and $\tilde{a}_{12}$ are assumed stochastic and to have a zero covariance, $cov(\tilde{a}_{11}, \tilde{a}_{12}) = 0$.

The dual problem associated with (10.52) can be derived from the corresponding Lagrangean function stated as

$$L(\mathbf{x}, \mathbf{y}) = x_1 + 0.8x_2 + y_1\Big\{3.0 - E(\tilde{a}_{11})x_1 - E(\tilde{a}_{12})x_2 \quad (10.53)$$

$$- \bar{\tau}_1\Big[var(\tilde{a}_{11})x_1^2 + var(\tilde{a}_{12})x_2^2\Big]^{1/2}\Big\}$$

$$+ y_2\{3.5 - x_1 - x_2\} + y_3\{5.0 - x_1 - 1.667x_2\}.$$

The relevant Karush-Kuhn-Tucker conditions are (we derive only the dual relations)

$$\frac{\partial L}{\partial x_1} = 1 - E(\tilde{a}_{11})y_1 - \bar{\tau}_1 var(\tilde{a}_{11})y_1 x_1[\ldots]^{-1/2} - y_2 - y_3 \leq 0 \quad (10.54)$$

$$\frac{\partial L}{\partial x_2} = 0.8 - E(\tilde{a}_{12})y_1 - \bar{\tau}_1 var(\tilde{a}_{12})y_1 x_2[\ldots]^{-1/2} - y_2 - 1.667y_3 \leq 0$$

$$x_1\frac{\partial L}{\partial x_1} = x_1 - x_1 E(\tilde{a}_{11})y_1 - \bar{\tau}_1 var(\tilde{a}_{11})y_1 x_1^2[\ldots]^{-1/2} - x_1 y_2 - x_1 y_3 = 0$$

$$x_2\frac{\partial L}{\partial x_2} = 0.8x_2 - x_2 E(\tilde{a}_{12})y_1 - \bar{\tau}_1 var(\tilde{a}_{12})y_1 x_2^2[\ldots]^{-1/2}$$

$$- x_2 y_2 - 1.667x_2 y_3 = 0.$$

By replacing x_1 and $0.8x_2$ in the Lagrangean function with their equivalent expressions from the last two relations of (10.54), we obtain a simplified expression for the dual objective function:

$$L(\mathbf{x}, \mathbf{y}) = x_1 E(\tilde{a}_{11})y_1 + \bar{\tau}_1 var(\tilde{a}_{11})y_1 x_1^2[\ldots]^{-1/2} + x_1 y_2 + x_1 y_3 \quad (10.55)$$

$$+ x_2 E(\tilde{a}_{12})y_1 + \bar{\tau}_1 var(\tilde{a}_{12})y_1 x_2^2[\ldots]^{-1/2} + x_2 y_2 + 1.667x_2 y_3$$

$$+ 3.0y_1 - y_1 E(\tilde{a}_{11})x_1 - y_1 E(\tilde{a}_{12})x_2 - \bar{\tau}_1 y_1[\ldots]^{1/2}$$

$$+ 3.5y_2 - x_1 y_2 - x_2 y_2 + 5.0y_3 - x_1 y_3 - 1.667x_2 y_3$$

$$= 3.0y_1 + 3.5y_2 + 5.0y_3 - \bar{\tau}_1 y_1[\ldots]^{1/2} + \bar{\tau}_1 y_1[\ldots][\ldots]^{-1/2}$$

$$= 3.0y_1 + 3.5y_2 + 5.0y_3.$$

Therefore, the dual of the chance-constrained problem (10.52) is

$$\text{minimize } TC = 3.0y_1 + 3.5y_2 + 5.0y_3 \quad (10.56)$$

$$\text{subject to} \quad E(\tilde{a}_{11})y_1 + y_2 + y_3 + \bar{\tau}_1 var(\tilde{a}_{11})y_1 x_1[\ldots]^{-1/2} \geq 1$$

$$E(\tilde{a}_{12})y_1 + y_2 + 1.667y_3 + \bar{\tau}_1 var(\tilde{a}_{12})y_1 x_2[\ldots]^{-1/2} \geq 0.8$$

$$x_1 \geq 0, \ x_2 \geq 0, \ y_1 \geq 0, \ y_2 \geq 0, \ y_3 \geq 0.$$

Both primal (10.52) and dual (10.56) problems exhibit nonlinear constraints. The proposed algorithm, therefore, evaluates the nonlinear part of the constraints at the previous solution and solves the resulting linear complementarity problem created by combining primal and dual constraints as well as the associated complementary slackness conditions. To achieve this formulation explicitly, we first define the primal and dual adjustment coefficients as

$$(Padj)_1 = \bar{\tau}_1 [var(\tilde{a}_{11})x_1^2(k-1) + var(\tilde{a}_{12})x_2^2(k-1)]^{1/2} \tag{10.57}$$

$$(Dadj)_1 = \bar{\tau}_1 y_1(k-1)[var(\tilde{a}_{11})x_1^2(k-1) + var(\tilde{a}_{12})x_2^2(k-1)]^{-1/2}$$

$$(Dadj)_2 = \bar{\tau}_1 y_1(k-1)[var(\tilde{a}_{12})x_1^2(k-1) + var(\tilde{a}_{12})x_2^2(k-1)]^{-1/2}$$

where $x_j(k-1)$ and $y_i(k-1)$ are the elements of the primal and dual solutions obtained at the $(k-1)$ iteration.

The term $(Padj)_1$ is the adjustment coefficient for primal constraint 1. Similarly, the term $(Dadj)_1$ is the adjustment coefficient for dual constraint 1, and so forth. With these definitions, the specification of the linearized structure of the new algorithm is the following primal-dual problem stated in an LCP form:

maximize $PD = x_1 + 0.8x_2$ (10.58)

$$- (3.0 - (Padj)_1)y_1 - 3.5y_2 - 5.0y_3$$

$$- (Dadj)_1 x_1^2 - (Dadj)_2 x_2^2 = 0$$

subject to

$$E(\tilde{a}_{11})x_1 + E(\tilde{a}_{12})x_2 \leq 3.0 - (Padj)_1$$

$$x_1 + \quad x_2 \leq 3.5$$

$$x_1 + \quad 1.667x_2 \leq 5.0$$

$$E(\tilde{a}_{11})y_1 + y_2 + \quad y_3 + (Dadj)_1 x_1 \quad \geq 1.0$$

$$E(\tilde{a}_{12})y_1 + y_2 + 1.667y_3 \quad + (Dadj)_2 x_2 \geq 0.8$$

$$\mathbf{x} \geq 0, \ \mathbf{y} \geq 0.$$

The optimal value of the objective function PD is equal to zero because the function represents the primal and dual complementary slackness conditions of the given numerical example.

The first iteration of the algorithm is performed by choosing initial conditions for $\mathbf{x}$ and $\mathbf{y}$ as follows: $x_j(0) = 0$, $y_i(0) = 0$ for all i's and j's. This implies that, at iteration 0, problem (10.58) is the primal-dual specification of an LP problem. At the second iteration, we use the LP solution to evaluate

Table 10.1. *The solution sequence of problem (10.58)*

Cycle	x_1	x_2	y_1	y_2	y_3
LP	2.250	1.250	0.500	0.500	0.000
1	0.000	1.749	1.151	0.000	0.000
2	0.884	2.089	0.203	0.000	0.000
3	0.000	2.897	1.144	0.000	0.000
4	0.477	1.822	0.742	0.000	0.000
5	0.684	2.225	0.650	0.000	0.000
6	0.415	2.281	0.852	0.000	0.000
7	0.572	2.087	0.720	0.000	0.000
8	0.546	2.202	0.765	0.000	0.000
9	0.533	2.151	0.765	0.000	0.000
10	0.556	2.159	0.750	0.000	0.000
11	0.579	2.102	0.746	0.000	0.000
12	0.552	2.177	0.756	0.000	0.000
13	0.537	2.162	0.765	0.000	0.000
14	0.551	2.157	0.753	0.000	0.000
15	0.543	2.167	0.761	0.000	0.000
16	0.545	2.160	0.758	0.000	0.000
17	0.546	2.163	0.758	0.000	0.000
18	0.545	2.162	0.759	0.000	0.000

the primal and dual adjustment coefficients and solve problem (10.58). We iterate the process until a convergence criterion based on the discrepancy of successive solutions is satisfied. For example, we would declare problem (10.58) successfully solved if we can find vectors $\mathbf{x}(k)$ and $\mathbf{y}(k)$ such that

$$\left| x_j(k) - x_j(k-1) \right| < \epsilon \qquad (10.59)$$

$$\left| y_i(k) - y_i(k-1) \right| < \epsilon$$

for all i's and j's and for an arbitrarily small and positive number ϵ.

Problem (10.58) was solved for the following values of the parameters: $E(\tilde{a}_{11}) = 1.0$, $E(\tilde{a}_{12}) = 0.6$, $var(\tilde{a}_{11}) = 0.25$, $var(\tilde{a}_{12}) = 0.09$, $\bar{\tau}_i = 1.645$ (corresponding to a standardized normal random variable for a level of $\alpha_i = .95$). The sequence of iterations leading to an optimal solution of (10.58) is given in Table 10.1. The tolerance parameter was set at $\epsilon = 0.001$.

Generalization

In the preceding numerical example, only the coefficients of the first primal constraint were assumed to be stochastic and, furthermore, the covariance between them was equal to zero. We intend now to generalize the chance-constrained specification of problem (10.52) with all the $\tilde{a}_{ij}$ coefficients being stochastic and exhibiting nonzero covariances. The primal, deterministic-equivalent problem is now

$$\text{maximize } R = c_1 x_1 + c_2 x_2 \tag{10.60}$$

subject to

$$E(\tilde{a}_{11})x_1 + E(\tilde{a}_{12})x_2 + \bar{\tau}_1[v_{11}x_1^2 + v_{12}x_2^2 + 2w_{112}x_1x_2]^{1/2} \le b_1$$

$$E(\tilde{a}_{21})x_1 + E(\tilde{a}_{22})x_2 + \bar{\tau}_2[v_{21}x_1^2 + v_{22}x_2^2 + 2w_{212}x_1x_2]^{1/2} \le b_2$$

$$E(\tilde{a}_{31})x_1 + E(\tilde{a}_{32})x_2 + \bar{\tau}_3[v_{31}x_1^2 + v_{32}x_2^2 + 2w_{312}x_1x_2]^{1/2} \le b_3$$

$$x_1 \ge 0, \ x_2 \ge 0, \quad i = 1, \ldots, m, \quad j = 1, \ldots, n$$

where $v_{ij} = var(\tilde{a}_{ij})$ and $w_{ijj'} = cov(\tilde{a}_{ij}, \tilde{a}_{ij'})$ for $j \ne j'$.
In matrix notation, (10.60) can be restated as

$$\text{maximize } R = \mathbf{c}'\mathbf{x} \tag{10.61}$$

$$\text{subject to} \quad E(\tilde{\mathbf{a}})_i'\mathbf{x} + \bar{\tau}_i\left(\mathbf{x}'\Sigma_{a_i}\mathbf{x}\right)^{1/2} \le b_i \quad i = 1, \ldots, m$$

$$\mathbf{x} \ge 0.$$

The Lagrangean function of (10.60) is

$$L(\mathbf{x}, \mathbf{y}) = c_1 x_1 + c_2 x_2 \tag{10.62}$$

$$+ y_1\{b_1 - E(\tilde{a}_{11})x_1 - E(\tilde{a}_{12})x_2 - \bar{\tau}_1[v_{11}x_1^2 + v_{12}x_2^2 + 2w_{112}x_1x_2]^{1/2}\}$$

$$+ y_2\{b_2 - E(\tilde{a}_{21})x_1 - E(\tilde{a}_{22})x_2 - \bar{\tau}_2[v_{21}x_1^2 + v_{22}x_2^2 + 2w_{212}x_1x_2]^{1/2}\}$$

$$+ y_3\{b_3 - E(\tilde{a}_{31})x_1 - E(\tilde{a}_{32})x_2 - \bar{\tau}_3[v_{31}x_1^2 + v_{32}x_2^2 + 2w_{312}x_1x_2]^{1/2}\}$$

or, in matrix notation,

$$L(\mathbf{x}, \mathbf{y}) = \mathbf{c}'\mathbf{x} + \mathbf{y}'\left[\mathbf{b} - E(\tilde{A})\mathbf{x} - \bar{\tau}(\mathbf{x}'\Sigma_A\mathbf{x})^{1/2}\right]. \tag{10.63}$$

The KKT conditions involving the primal variables are

$$\frac{\partial L}{\partial x_1} = c_1 - y_1 E(\tilde{a}_{11}) - 1/2 y_1 \bar{\tau}_1[\ldots]^{-1/2}[2v_{11}x_1 + 2w_{112}x_2] \tag{10.64}$$

$$- y_2 E(\tilde{a}_{21}) - 1/2 y_2 \bar{\tau}_2[\ldots]^{-1/2}[2v_{21}x_1 + 2w_{212}x_2]$$

$$- y_3 E(\tilde{a}_{31}) - 1/2 y_3 \bar{\tau}_3[\ldots]^{-1/2}[2v_{31}x_1 + 2w_{312}x_2] \le 0$$

or, in a more general and compact notation,

$$\frac{\partial L}{\partial x_j} = c_j - E(\tilde{\mathbf{a}}_j)'\mathbf{y} - \left\{ \sum_i \bar{\tau}_i y_i \left[\mathbf{x}'\Sigma_{a_i}\mathbf{x}\right]^{-1/2} \Sigma_{a_{ij}} \right\}\mathbf{x}. \quad (10.65)$$

The dual problem of (10.61) is, therefore,

$$\text{minimize } TC = \mathbf{b}'\mathbf{y} \quad (10.66)$$

$$\text{subject to} \quad E(\tilde{\mathbf{a}}_j)'\mathbf{y} + \left\{ \sum_i \bar{\tau}_i y_i \left[\mathbf{x}'\Sigma_{a_i}\mathbf{x}\right]^{-1/2} \Sigma_{a_{ij}} \right\}\mathbf{x} \geq c_j$$

$$j = 1\ldots, n \text{ and } \mathbf{x} \geq 0, \ \mathbf{y} \geq 0.$$

Finally, the general primal-dual structure of the algorithm for solving chance-constrained problems involving a stochastic technology is

$$\text{maximize } PD = \mathbf{c}'\mathbf{x} - \sum_{i=1}^{m} \left[b_i - \bar{\tau}_i \left(\mathbf{x}'(k-1)\Sigma_{a_i}\mathbf{x}(k-1)\right)^{1/2} \right] y_i \quad (10.67)$$

$$- \mathbf{x}'\left[\sum_{i=1}^{m} \bar{\tau}_i y_i(k-1)\left(\mathbf{x}'(k-1)\Sigma_{a_i}\mathbf{x}(k-1)\right)^{1/2} \Sigma_{a_{ij}} \right]\mathbf{x} = 0$$

subject to

$$E(\tilde{\mathbf{a}})_i'\mathbf{x} \leq b_i - \bar{\tau}_i\left(\mathbf{x}'(k-1)\Sigma_{a_i}\mathbf{x}(k-1)\right)^{1/2}$$

$$E(\tilde{\mathbf{a}}_j)'\mathbf{y} + \left[\sum_i \bar{\tau}_i y_i(k-1)\left(\mathbf{x}'(k-1)\Sigma_{a_i}\mathbf{x}(k-1)\right)^{-1/2} \Sigma_{a_{ij}} \right]\mathbf{x} \geq c_j$$

$$j = 1\ldots, n \text{ and } \mathbf{x} \geq 0, \ \mathbf{y} \geq 0.$$

The optimal value of the objective function *PD* (Primal-Dual) of problem(10.67) is equal to zero because it corresponds to the complementary slackness conditions of the associated LC problem.

Extension of the Primal-Dual Algorithm to Concave Programs

The absence of any explicit direction's projection and search for the optimal step length makes the proposed algorithm a particularly simple procedure. This simplicity suggests that it may be successfully applicable to nonlinear specifications other than the chance-constrained problem.

Consider the following concave nonlinear problem:

$$\text{maximize } f(\mathbf{x}) \tag{10.68}$$

$$\text{subject to} \qquad g_i(\mathbf{x}) \le b_i \qquad\qquad i = 1, \ldots, m$$

$$\mathbf{x} \ge 0$$

where $f(\mathbf{x})$ and $g_i(\mathbf{x})$ are strictly concave and convex differentiable functions, respectively. The dual of (10.68) can be stated as the minimization of the Lagrangean function subject to its derivative with respect to $\mathbf{x}$:

$$\text{minimixe } L(\mathbf{x}, \mathbf{y}) = f(\mathbf{x}) + \mathbf{y}'[\mathbf{b} - \mathbf{g}(\mathbf{x})] \tag{10.69}$$

$$\text{subject to} \qquad \frac{\partial f}{\partial \mathbf{x}} - \left(\frac{\partial \mathbf{g}}{\partial \mathbf{x}}\right)\mathbf{y} \le 0, \qquad \mathbf{x} \ge 0, \quad \mathbf{y} \ge 0.$$

The extension of the primal-dual algorithm to a problem such as (10.68) is based on a Stirling-Maclaurin series expansion of the functions $f(\mathbf{x})$ and $g_i(\mathbf{x})$. Let us recall that a Stirling-Maclaurin expansion of the function $h(x)$ is a special case of a Taylor series expansion where the various derivatives are evaluated at zero:

$$h(x) = h(0) + h'(0)x + \frac{h''(0)}{2!}x^2 + \cdots + \frac{h^n(0)}{n!}x^n + \cdots \tag{10.70}$$

Then, the two functions $f(\mathbf{x})$ and $g_i(\mathbf{x})$ can be approximated by their first two expansion terms as

$$f(\mathbf{x}) \approx f(\mathbf{0}) + \nabla_x f(\mathbf{0})\mathbf{x} + \frac{\mathbf{x}'\nabla_{xx} f(\mathbf{0})\mathbf{x}}{2} \tag{10.71}$$

$$g_i(\mathbf{x}) \approx g_i(\mathbf{0}) + \nabla_x g_i(\mathbf{0})\mathbf{x} + \frac{\mathbf{x}'\nabla_{xx} g_i(\mathbf{0})\mathbf{x}}{2}. \tag{10.72}$$

Using these expansions, the primal and dual constraints of (10.68) can be respecified in an approximate form as

$$\nabla_x g(\mathbf{0})\mathbf{x} \le \mathbf{b} - g(\mathbf{0}) - \frac{\mathbf{x}'\nabla_{xx} g(\mathbf{0})\mathbf{x}}{2} \tag{10.73}$$

$$\nabla_x g(\mathbf{0})'\mathbf{y} + \left[\mathbf{y}'\nabla_{xx} g(\mathbf{0}) - \nabla_{xx} f(\mathbf{0})\right]\mathbf{x} \ge \nabla_x f(\mathbf{0}) \tag{10.74}$$

The formulation of the LCP structure suitable for implementing the primal dual algorithm can finally be stated as

$$\max PD = \mathbf{x}'\nabla_x f(\mathbf{0}) - \mathbf{y}'\left[\mathbf{b} - g(\mathbf{0}) - \frac{\mathbf{x}'(k-1)\nabla_{xx} g(\mathbf{0})\mathbf{x}(k-1)}{2}\right]$$

$$- \mathbf{x}'\left[\mathbf{y}'(k-1)\nabla_{xx} g(\mathbf{0}) - \nabla_{xx} f(\mathbf{0})\right]\mathbf{x} = 0 \tag{10.75}$$

Table 10.2. *The technology matrix A*

Limiting resources	Potatoes x_1	Corn x_2	Beef x_3	Cabbage x_4	Resource availability
Land					
Jan-June	1.199	1.382	2.776	0.000	60.
July-Dec	0.000	1.382	2.776	0.482	60.
Capital					
Jan-Apr	1.064	0.484	0.038	0.000	24.
May-Aug	−2.064	0.020	0.107	0.229	12.
Sept-Dec	−2.064	−1.504	−1.145	−1.229	0.0
Labor					
Period 1	5.276	4.836	0.000	0.000	799.
Period 2	2.158	4.561	0.000	4.198	867.
Period 3	0.000	4.146	0.000	13.606	783.
Unit Prices	100.0	100.0	100.0	100.0	

subject to

$$\nabla_x g(0)x \leq b - g(0) - \frac{x'(k-1)\nabla_{xx}g(0)x(k-1)}{2} \tag{10.76}$$

$$\nabla_x g(0)'y + \left[y'(k-1)\nabla_{xx}g(0) - \nabla_{xx}f(0) \right]x \geq \nabla_x f(0) \tag{10.77}$$

$$x \geq 0, \quad y \geq 0.$$

As in the chance-constrained problem, the initial iteration solves a linear programming problem, and the process continues until a convergence criterion is satisfied. The concavity/convexity assumption guarantees the finding of a global optimal solution, if one exists.

Freund's Numerical Example of Risk Programming

In 1956, Rudolf Freund presented the first discussion of risk programming cast in the structure of a quadratic programming problem, as given by the primal problem [(10.7),(10.8)]. By permission of the Econometric Society, we reproduce his numerical illustration dealing with a farm scenario of eastern North Carolina.

The required input data concern the technical coefficients of the technology matrix A, the resource availabilities expressed by the supply vector b, the expected output prices given by the vector $E(\bar{c})$, the variance-covariance matrix of output prices, and the risk aversion coefficient, ϕ.

Table 10.2 presents the technical coefficients of the matrix A and resource availabilities of vector b. Land is measured in acres, capital in units of $100,

Table 10.3. *Price variance-covariance matrix* Σ_c

Crop		Potatoes x_1	Corn x_2	Beef x_3	Cabbage x_4
Potatoes,	x_1	7304.69	903.89	−688.73	−1862.05
Corn,	x_2		620.16	−471.14	110.43
Beef,	x_3			1124.64	750.69
Cabbage,	x_4				3689.53

and labor (managerial labor) in hours. The risk aversion coefficient chosen by Freund is equal to $\phi = 0.0008$, which corresponds to a risk tolerance coefficient of $1/0.0008 = 1250$ dollars.

Table 10.3 presents the variance-covariance matrix of output prices. Potatoes and cabbage exhibit the largest variances. The positive and negative covariances interact to reduce the level of the risk premium.

This numerical problem was solved using the GAMS application. A no-risk program, corresponding to a LP specification, was also computed for comparison. Table 10.4 presents the two primal optimal solutions. The no-risk (LP) program is less diversified than the risk (QP) program, with potatoes and cabbage produced in larger quantities. By taking into account the variances and covariances of prices, the risk program spreads the risk over all the activities and reduces the level of those ones (potatoes and cabbage) that are associated with the largest variances.

The expected net revenue and the associated standard deviations reflect the risk-averse attitude of the two specifications. The higher expected net

Table 10.4. *Risk and no-risk optimum programs*

Item		Risk program	No-risk program
Crop			
Potatoes,	x_1	10.289	22.141
Corn,	x_2	26.757	0.000
Beef,	x_3	2.676	11.622
Cabbage,	x_4	32.350	57.548
Expected Net Revenue	$	7207.25	9131.11
Expected Utility	$	5383.09	4388.58
Standard Deviation of			
Expected Net Revenue	$	2135.51	3443.31
Risk Premium	$	1824.16	4742.55

Table 10.5. *Resource shadow values*

Constraint	Risk program	No-risk program
Land		
Jan-June	0.00	0.00
July-Dec	32.93	34.74
Capital		
Jan-Apr	65.97	93.99
May-Aug	0.00	0.00
Sept-Dec	0.00	0.00
Labor		
Period 1	0.00	0.00
Period 2	0.00	0.0
Period 3	0.00	6.12

return of the LP model is associated with a higher standard deviation. In this sense, the so-called no-risk program (a name chosen by Freund) is actually more risky than the QP program. The risk premium is also smaller for the risk program as compared to the risk premium of the "no-risk" LP model. The expected utility of the QP model is higher than the expected utility of the LP model, justifying its preference over the "no-risk" program.

Table 10.5 exhibits the shadow prices of the limiting resources. In each case, the shadow prices are lower for the risk-program, reflecting the reduced level of the objective functions corresponding to the QP and the LP models. In the no-risk program, three constraints are binding as opposed to only two in the risk specification.

It remains to explore the frontier between expected revenue and the standard deviation of expected revenue. This is done by keeping constant the variance-covariance matrix of prices and allowing a parametric variation of the expected prices in what is usually defined as a spread-preserving mean variation. In symbolic form, this parametric exploration is stated as the variation of parameter μ:

$$\max \left(\mu E(\tilde{c})'\mathbf{x} - \frac{\phi}{2}\mathbf{x}'\Sigma_c\mathbf{x} \right)$$

subject to the linear technological constraints.

The result of this analysis is displayed in Figure 10.1. As the expected output prices increase according to the increase in parameter μ, the standard deviation of total expected revenue increases to the point where the program selects the production plan associated with maximum risk, which

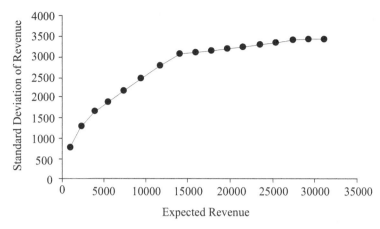

Figure 10.1. Risk Frontier of the Freund's Farm.

corresponds to the LP solution. Table 10.6 reports the production plans corresponding to the associated level of the parameter μ.

The bold rows in Table 10.6 correspond to the production plans of the risk and no-risk programs discussed earlier. Potatoes and cabbage are the riskiest crops. Hence, with low expected prices, the program gives a relative preference to corn. As expected prices increase, the risky crops are gradually preferred until the LP solution prevails, given the technological constraints.

Table 10.6. *Parametric solution sequence of Freund's farm*

μ	Potatoes	Corn	Beef	Cabbage
0.20	1.82	24.09	8.84	4.52
0.40	5.28	30.64	4.08	13.15
0.60	8.11	31.58	2.39	20.17
0.80	9.57	28.31	3.01	26.00
1.00	**10.29**	**26.76**	**2.68**	**32.35**
1.20	11.01	25.21	2.35	38.70
1.40	11.72	23.65	2.02	45.05
1.60	12.05	21.96	1.85	50.86
1.80	13.80	18.99	3.17	51.76
2.00	15.11	16.02	4.49	52.67
2.20	16.41	13.05	5.81	53.57
2.40	17.72	10.08	7.14	54.48
2.60	19.02	7.11	8.46	55.38
2.80	20.32	4.14	9.78	56.29
3.00	21.63	1.17	11.10	57.19
3.20	**22.14**	**0**	**11.62**	**57.55**

GAMS Command File: Freund's Example of Risk Programming

This file contains the code for computing the optimal solution of a risk programming problem as discussed by Freund and its twin model of no-risk as presented in this section. The risk frontier is implemented via a GAMS loop. The results are copied, at the end of the code, in a special Excel file.

```
$title risk programming a la freund (econometrica
* 1956, p. 253)
*
$offsymlist offsymxref
    option limrow = 0
    option limcol = 0
    option iterlim = 100000
    option reslim = 200000
    option nlp = conopt3
    option decimals = 7 ;
*
    sets   j    output variables / potatoes, corn, beef,
                  cabbage /
           i    resources / landj-j, landj-d, capitalp1,
                  capitalp2, capitalp3, laborp1, laborp2,
                  laborp3 /
           ll   loop /1*20 /
*
    alias(k,j) ;
*
    parameter c(j)  unit level "profit" ;
    c(j) = 100 ;
*
    parameter b(i)  resource availability

        /  landj-j      60
           landj-d      60
           capitalp1    24
           capitalp2    12
           capitalp3     0
           laborp1     799
           laborp2     867
           laborp3     783   /
*
```

```
    table a(i,j)    technical coefficients (table 1
                    page 257)
                    potatoes    corn   beef     cabbage
        landj-j       1.199    1.382   2.776     0.000
        landj-d       0.000    1.382   2.776     0.482
      capitalp1       1.064    0.484   0.038     0.000
      capitalp2      -2.064    0.020   0.107     0.229
      capitalp3      -2.064   -1.504  -1.145    -1.229
       laborp1        5.276    4.836   0.000     0.000
       laborp2        2.158    4.561   0.000     4.198
       laborp3        0.000    4.146   0.000    13.606
*
    table sigma(k,j)   variance-covariance matrix of
              unit levels (of revenue) page 258
                    potatoes    corn   beef      cabbage
      potatoes      7304.69   903.89 -688.73  -1862.05
          corn                620.16 -471.14    110.43
          beef                       1124.64    750.69
       cabbage                                  3689.53
*
    sigma(k,j) = sigma(j,k) + sigma(k,j) ;
    sigma(j,j) = sigma(j,j)/2 ;
    display sigma ;
*
    scalar phi  risk aversion coefficient / 0.0008 / ;
    display phi ;
*
    scalar expr  expected revenue /7207.245 / ;
*
* quadratic program for risk
* also linear program for no-risk
*
    variables
    eu   objective function under risk (qp)
    rev  objective function without risk (lp)
    xqp(j)  decision variables for risk program
    xlp(j)  decision variables for lp program
    minrisk  objective function for the minimization
             version of risk
    xmin(j)  decision variables for the minimization
             version of risk
```

```
*
   positive variable xqp, xlp, xmin ;
*

   equations
   qpobjeq    qp objective function equation
   lpobjeq    lp objective function equation
   qprhseq(i) resource constraints for qp
   lprhseq(i)  resource constraints for lp
   minriskobj  objective function for minimization of
               risk
   minreseq(i) resources for minimization of risk
   exreveq    expected revenue equation ;
*

   qpobjeq..  eu =e= sum(j, c(j)*xqp(j) )
                      - (phi/2)*sum((k,j), xqp(k)*
                      sigma(k,j)*xqp(j));
   lpobjeq..  rev =e= sum(j, c(j)*xlp(j) ) ;
   minriskobj..  minrisk =e= (phi/2)*sum((k,j),
                      xmin(k)*sigma(k,j)*xmin(j));
   minreseq(i)..  sum(j, a(i,j)*xmin(j) ) =l= b(i) ;
   exreveq..  sum(j, c(j)*xmin(j) ) =g= expr ;
   qprhseq(i)..  sum(j, a(i,j)*xqp(j) ) =l= b(i) ;
   lprhseq(i)..  sum(j, a(i,j)*xlp(j) ) =l= b(i) ;
* qp eu maximization of risk
   model risk / qpobjeq, qprhseq / ;
* lp program
   model norisk / lpobjeq, lprhseq / ;
* qp minimization version of risk
   model minprob / minriskobj, minreseq, exreveq /;
*

   solve norisk using lp maximizing rev ;
*

   solve risk using nlp maximizing eu ;
*

   solve minprob using nlp minimizing minrisk ;
*
* conputation of frontier between expected revenue and
* variance
* loop on mu parameter *
   parameter mu ;
   mu = .2 ;
*
```

```
   variables
   euf   objective function of frontier
   xf(j)  variables of frontier ;
*
   positive variables xf ;
*
   equations efeq   objective function equation of
                    frontier
   feq(i)  frontier constraints ;
*
   efeq..   euf =e= mu*sum(j, c(j)*xf(j) )
   - (phi/2)*sum((k,j), xf(k)*sigma(k,j)*xf(j)) ;
   feq(i)..   sum(j, a(i,j)*xf(j) ) =l= b(i) ;
* frontier model
   model frontier /efeq, feq /;
*
   parameter exprevfr(ll), stdfr(ll), expxf(j,ll),
             expfeq(i,ll), expeuf(ll), stddevr(ll);
*
* loop on frontier
*
   loop(ll,
   solve frontier using nlp maximizing euf ;
   expeuf(ll) = euf.l ;
   expxf(j,ll) = xf.l(j) ;
   expfeq(i,ll) = feq.M(i) ;
   exprevfr(ll) = mu*sum(j, c(j)*xf.l(j) ) ;
   stdfr(ll) = sqrt( sum((k,j), xf.l(k)*sigma(k,j)*
     xf.l(j)) );
   stddevr(ll) = sqrt( (2/phi)*exprevfr(ll) ) ;
   mu = mu + .2 ;
   );
* close loop
*
   parameter dualqp, duallp ;
   dualqp = sum(i,b(i)*qprhseq.M(i))
           + (phi/2)*sum((k,j), xqp.l(k)*sigma(k,j)*
             xqp.l(j));
   duallp = sum(i,b(i)*lprhseq.M(i)) ;
*
* verify freund's results, page 259 of econometrica
* 1956
*
```

```
    parameter exprevqp    expected revenue of risk
                          program,
    exputilqp   expected utility of risk program,
    Stddevrevqp Standard deviation of risk program,
    exprevlp    expected revenue of No-risk program,
    exputillp   expected utility of No-risk program,
    Stddevrevlp Standard deviation of No-risk program;
*
    exprevqp = sum(j, c(j)*xqp.l(j) );
    exputilqp = eu.l ;
    exprevlp = rev.l ;
    exputillp = sum(j, c(j)*xlp.l(j) )
              - (phi/2)*sum((k,j), xlp.l(k)*
                sigma(k,j)*xlp.l(j));
    Stddevrevqp = sqrt( sum((k,j), xqp.l(k)*
                sigma(k,j)*xqp.l(j)) ) ;
    Stddevrevlp = sqrt( sum((k,j), xlp.l(k)*
                sigma(k,j)*xlp.l(j)) ) ;
    display eu.l, dualqp, xqp.l, qprhseq.M ;
    display rev.l, duallp, xlp.l, lprhseq.M ;
    display exprevqp, exputilqp, Stddevrevqp, exprevlp,
            exputillp, Stddevrevlp ;
    display expeuf, expxf, expfeq, exprevfr, stdfr ;
*
* create an excel file with results
*
    file freuexcel /freund.xls / ;
    put freuexcel ;
*
    put " expeuf stddevr exp rev std front ", put / ;
    put/;
    loop(ll,
    put expeuf(ll), stddevr(ll), exprevfr(ll),
      stdfr(ll) :11:2;
    put /; );
*
    put///;
    loop(ll, put" ", put ll.tl:11);
    loop(ll, put/,
    loop(j, put expxf(j,ll):11:2);
    );
*
```

```
put///;
loop(ll, put" ", put ll.tl:11);
loop(ll, put/,
loop(i, put expfeq(i,ll):11:2); );
```

Exercises

10.1 What are the assumptions that allow the formulation of risk analysis about output price and input quantities as a quadratic programming model?
(a) Explain the notion of risk premium.
(b) Explain the notion of certainty equivalent.
(c) Explain the notion of risk aversion.
(d) Explain the specification of the corresponding QP model.

10.2 Consider the quadratic programming formulation of output price risk. Discuss how to obtain a measure of the risk aversion coefficient by using a chance-constrained approach.

10.3 Explain why a nonzero covariance between output prices and limiting input quantities prevents the formulation of the corresponding risk analysis as a pair of optimization models. What can be done in this case?

10.4 Derive the dual problem of the following risk model:

$$\min \frac{\phi}{2}\mathbf{x}'\Sigma_c\mathbf{x}$$

$$\text{subject to} \qquad \mathbf{c}'\mathbf{x} \geq R$$

$$A\mathbf{x} \leq \mathbf{b}, \qquad \mathbf{x} \geq 0$$

where R is revenue, $\phi > 0$, and all the other symbols retain the usual meaning. Show that this primal model is equivalent to the original Freund's specification.

10.5 Consider the following chance constraint:

$$\text{Prob}(\bar{\mathbf{c}}'\mathbf{x} \leq \mathbf{x}' A\mathbf{y}) \leq 1 - \beta$$

where $\bar{\mathbf{c}}$ is a vector of stochastic output prices and A is a nonstochastic linear technology. This specification can be regarded as dealing with the dual constraints of an LP problem. It can be read as: the probability that stochastic revenue is less than or equal to total cost is less than or equal to $(1 - \beta)$.

(a) Derive the deterministic equivalent of the given chance constraint.

(b) Is it possible and meaningful to derive the deterministic equivalent of the chance constraint

$$\text{Prob}(x' Ay \le \tilde{b}'y) \ge \alpha$$

where $\tilde{b}$ is the stochastic quantity of limiting inputs?

10.6 Consider the following LC problem (M, q), where $M = \phi \Sigma + \bar{A}$ and

$$\Sigma = \begin{bmatrix} \Sigma_c & 0 \\ 0 & \Sigma_s \end{bmatrix}, \quad \bar{A} = \begin{bmatrix} 0 & A' \\ -A & 0 \end{bmatrix}, \quad q = \begin{bmatrix} -E(\tilde{c}) \\ E(\tilde{s}) \end{bmatrix}$$

where $\tilde{c}$ and $\tilde{s}$ are random variables with mean $E(c)$, $E(\tilde{s})$ and variance-covariance matrices Σ_c, Σ_s, respectively. Furthermore, ϕ is a positive risk aversion coefficient. Given the foregoing information, provide a chance-constraint interpretation of the following relation:

$$\text{Prob}(z' \bar{A} z \ge -z' \tilde{q}) \le 1 - \beta$$

where $z' = [x, y]'$ and $\tilde{q}' = [-\tilde{c}, \tilde{s}]$ and $\beta = 0.95$.
    What is the economic meaning of the probabilistic constraint?

10.7 Consider the following information:

$$E(\bar{p}) = \begin{bmatrix} 3 \\ 2.2 \end{bmatrix}, \quad E(\tilde{s}) = 2, \quad A = [2 \quad 1.5]$$

$$\Sigma_p = \begin{bmatrix} 4 & 1 \\ 1 & 2 \end{bmatrix}, \quad \Sigma_s = 2, \quad \Sigma_{ps} = \begin{bmatrix} 1.0 \\ 0.5 \end{bmatrix}, \phi = .1$$

Compare the expected utilities generated by the following risky programs:

(a) The generalized risk program with nonzero covariances between prices and limiting inputs.

(b) The symmetric quadratic program (risky prices and risky limiting inputs without covariances between prices and limiting inputs).

(c) The asymmetric quadratic program (risky prices and certain limiting inputs).

(d) Give your comments about the relationship among the computed expected utilities.

10.8 With respect to the symmetric quadratic programming specification of a risk problem, it was written: "If the primal objective function is viewed as maximizing expected utility, the results lead to the conclusion that greater expected utility will be obtained if input supplies are stochastic than if they are known with certainty." Using the following information:

$$E(\tilde{p}) = \begin{bmatrix} 4 \\ 10 \end{bmatrix}, \quad E(\tilde{s}) = \begin{bmatrix} 5 \\ 10 \\ 8 \end{bmatrix}, \quad A = \begin{bmatrix} 0.1 & 1.0 \\ 1.0 & 1.0 \\ 1.0 & 0.1 \end{bmatrix}$$

$$\Sigma_p = \begin{bmatrix} 2 & -1 \\ -1 & 41 \end{bmatrix}, \quad \Sigma_s = \begin{bmatrix} 0 & 0 & 0 \\ 0 & 0 & 0 \\ 0 & 0 & 48 \end{bmatrix}$$

compute the expected utility of the symmetric quadratic programming specification and the expected utility of the asymmetric quadratic programming model for the following values of the risk aversion coefficient: $\phi = 0.08, 0.12, 0.14, 0.18$. After solving the eight problems, comment on the statement given in quotation marks.

10.9 Given the utility function $\tilde{u} = 1 - e^{-\phi\tilde{r}}$, where $\phi > 0$ is a constant risk aversion coefficient and $\tilde{r}$ is stochastic revenue distributed as $\tilde{r} \sim N[E(\tilde{r}), Var(\tilde{r})]$, ($N \equiv$ normal density),
   (a) Find an explicit expression for the expected utility. (Hint: complete the square.)
   (b) Show that the maximization of expected utility is equivalent to the maximization of $[E(\tilde{r}) - \frac{\phi}{2}Var(\tilde{r})]$.

10.10 A pure monopolist operates in a market where he faces stochastic inverse demand functions, $\tilde{p} = \tilde{c} - Dx$, where D is an asymmetric positive semidefinite matrix and the random vector $\tilde{c}$ is distributed according to a normal density with mean $E(\tilde{c})$ and variance $Var(\tilde{c})$. This entrepreneur's preferences are expressed by the utility function $\tilde{u} = 1 - e^{-\phi\tilde{r}}$, where $\phi > 0$ is a constant risk aversion coefficient and $\tilde{r}$ is stochastic revenue.
   (a) Set up and justify an appropriate model to represent the pure monopolist's behavior.
   (b) Derive the dual specification and give a complete economic interpretation.
   (c) Reformulate the problem as a linear complementarity problem.

References

Charnes, A., and Cooper, W. W. (1959). "Chance-Constrained Programming," *Management Science*, 6, 73–9.

Freund, R. J. (1956). "The Introduction of Risk into a Programming Model," *Econometrica*, 24, 253–63.

Pratt, J. W. (1964). "Risk Aversion in the Small and the Large," *Econometrica*, 32, 122–36.

11

Comparative Statics and
Parametric Programming

A main objective of economics analysis consists in the derivation of demand
and supply functions for the purpose of establishing market equilibria and
predicting their response in relation to the displacement of some parameters
(either prices or quantities). Such a variation of parameters corresponds to
a comparative statics analysis common to theoretical investigations. When
the available information allows it, the derivation of demand and supply
functions can be obtained by econometric methods. In that case, the appropriate methodology consists of two phases: estimation and prediction. The
estimation phase corresponds to a calibration of the econometric model
and includes hypothesis testing. The prediction phase analyzes the behavior
of the model outside the sample information and provides a measure of
response induced by parameter variations.

When the available information is insufficient for a proper application of
econometric procedures, mathematical programming admits the exploita-
tion of limited information and a complete analysis of the given scenario.
Problems of environmental economics, natural resources, economic development, and many others often defy econometric analysis because the necessary time series of information are too short for a meaningful employment
of those procedures.

The outline of this chapter is articulated in various sections. The first
development deals with the relations of comparative statics proper of the
theory of the firm operating in conditions of certainty. Such conditions
are known as the Hicksian relations of the competitive firm. The second
section discusses the parametric programming of a general LP model. It
will be shown that demand and supply schedules derived from a linear
programming model are nonincreasing and nondecreasing, respectively,
but exhibit an undesirable staircase structure. Demand and supply functions that exhibit such a property are not responsive to changes of relevant

parameters within intervals of variation that may be quite large. The third section establishes the analogy between the conditions of comparative statics of the theory of the firm and the parametric programming of QP. It demonstrates the pointwise responsiveness of the schedules derived from a QP framework.

Comparative Statics of the Competitive Firm

The theory of the firm operating under conditions of perfect competition has produced a set of comparative statics relations known as the Hicksian conditions. In 1939, John Hicks presented a complete discussion of output supply and input demand functions associated with a short-run profit-maximizing firm and characterized the response of demands and supplies with respect to variations of the corresponding prices.

Let $\mathbf{x} = \mathbf{f}(\mathbf{b})$ be the concave multiproduct and multi-input technology of a competitive firm, where $\mathbf{x}$ and $\mathbf{b}$ are output and input vectors of dimensions n and m, respectively, and $\mathbf{f}$ is a vector-valued function. Furthermore, let $\mathbf{p_x}$ and $\mathbf{p_b}$ be the vectors of output and input prices, respectively. Then, the profit-maximizing objective of the firm can be stated as $\max \pi = \mathbf{p'_x}\mathbf{f}(\mathbf{b}) - \mathbf{p'_b}\mathbf{b}$. The solution of this problem results in output supply functions $\mathbf{x}^* = \mathbf{x}(\mathbf{p_x}, \mathbf{p_b})$ and input demand functions $\mathbf{b}^* = \mathbf{b}(\mathbf{p_x}, \mathbf{p_b})$, which are characterized by the following relations of comparative statics:

$$\frac{\partial \mathbf{x}}{\partial \mathbf{p_x}} \equiv \text{symmetric positive semidefinite matrix} \qquad (11.1)$$

$$\frac{\partial \mathbf{b}}{\partial \mathbf{p_b}} \equiv \text{symmetric negative semidefinite matrix} \qquad (11.2)$$

$$\frac{\partial \mathbf{x}}{\partial \mathbf{p_b}} = -\left(\frac{\partial \mathbf{b}}{\partial \mathbf{p_x}}\right)'. \qquad (11.3)$$

The remainder of the chapter is dedicated to showing how to derive comparative statics relations similar to those in (11.1) and (11.2) from linear and quadratic programming models.

Parametric Programming in LP Models

After achieving primal and dual optimal solutions of a linear programming model, it is of interest to study how those solutions change as a result of variations of some or all the parameters of the model. For this reason, parametric programming is also called postoptimality analysis. Within the economic interpretation of LP models given in this book, parametric programming corresponds to the analysis of comparative statics associated with the theory of the competitive firm where entrepreneurs are regarded as price takers.

Let us consider a dual pair of LP models interpreted within the context of such a theory:

$$\max_{\mathbf{x}} TR = \mathbf{c}'\mathbf{x} \qquad \min_{\mathbf{y}} TC = \mathbf{b}'\mathbf{y} \qquad (11.4)$$

$$\text{subject to} \qquad A\mathbf{x} \leq \mathbf{b} \qquad \text{subject to} \qquad A'\mathbf{y} \geq \mathbf{c}$$

$$\mathbf{x} \geq 0 \qquad \qquad \mathbf{y} \geq 0.$$

The correspondence with the notation of the previous section is straightforward if one admits the following interpretation of the various symbols: $\mathbf{y} \equiv \mathbf{p_b}$, $\mathbf{c} \equiv \mathbf{p_x}$, and $A \equiv \mathbf{f}^{-1}$. Let us assume that optimal solutions to problem (11.4) were obtained, and let us indicate such solutions as $\mathbf{x}_B^* = B^{-1}\mathbf{b}$ and $\mathbf{y}^* = (B')^{-1}\mathbf{c}_B$, where B is the optimal basis. Furthermore, the relationship between the optimal values of the dual objective functions is $TR^* = \mathbf{c}_B'\mathbf{x}_B^* = \mathbf{y}^{*'}\mathbf{b} = TC^*$. From the structure of the primal solution, it is clear that output prices $\mathbf{c}_B$ do not directly affect the output quantities $\mathbf{x}_B^*$. Similarly, input quantities $\mathbf{b}$ do not have a direct relation with input prices $\mathbf{y}^*$. In other words, as long as the optimal basis B does not change, a variation in the jth output price c_{Bj} has no effect on the optimal level of the corresponding output quantity x_{Bj}^*, and a variation on the ith input quantity b_i has no effect on the corresponding input price y_i^*.

With a linear technology, an optimal production plan (optimal basis) remains optimal within a discrete interval of input variations, as illustrated in Figure 11.1, where the cone generated by vectors $(\mathbf{a}_2, \mathbf{a}_3)$ is assumed to form the initial optimal basis B. As long as the input vector $\mathbf{b}$ lies in the cone $(\mathbf{a}_2, \mathbf{a}_3)$, the initial basis B remains primal feasible and optimal and need not change in response to variations (either increment or decrement) of the initial vector $\mathbf{b}$ that do not position the resulting vector outside the original cone $(\mathbf{a}_2, \mathbf{a}_3)$.

A change of vector from $\mathbf{b}$ to, say, $\mathbf{b}^{**}$ is obtained by adding to the original vector $\mathbf{b}$ an arbitrary vector $\mathbf{r}$ multiplied by a nonnegative scalar θ, that is, $\mathbf{b}^{**} = \mathbf{b} + \theta\mathbf{r}$. For the increment of one component of input vector $\mathbf{b}$, say b_1, the arbitrary vector $\mathbf{r}$ is defined as a unit vector with one unit element in the first position and zero everywhere else. For a decrement of the same component, the definition will be $\mathbf{r}' = [-1, 0, \ldots, 0]$. The objective of the analysis is to find the level of the scalar θ that will take the initial input vector $\mathbf{b}$ to the edge (or face) of the cone $(\mathbf{a}_2, \mathbf{a}_3)$ in Figure 11.1, and, therefore, will

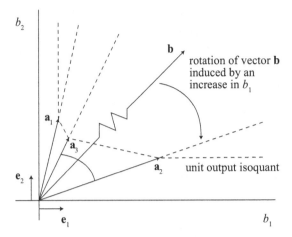

Figure 11.1. Parametric programming of input b_1.

make the resulting vector $\mathbf{b}^{**} = \mathbf{b} + \theta\mathbf{r}$ coincident with either vector $\mathbf{a}_2$ or vector $\mathbf{a}_3$.

The computation of the desired level of θ is performed by recalling that the product of the new input vector $\mathbf{b}^{**}$ with the inverse of the original basis $B = (\mathbf{a}_2, \mathbf{a}_3)$ produces a new solution vector of optimal output levels $\mathbf{x}_B^{**}$ that must be nonnegative for the reason that the new solution must be primal feasible, as it corresponds to a production plan. We thus have

$$\mathbf{x}_B^{**} = B^{-1}\mathbf{b}^{**} = B^{-1}(\mathbf{b} + \theta\mathbf{r}) \geq \mathbf{0} \tag{11.5}$$
$$= B^{-1}\mathbf{b} + \theta B^{-1}\mathbf{r} \geq \mathbf{0}$$
$$= \mathbf{x}_B^* + \theta\mathbf{w} \geq \mathbf{0}$$

where $\mathbf{w} = B^{-1}\mathbf{r}$. The components of vectors $\mathbf{x}_B^*$ and $\mathbf{w}$ are known. The nonnegativity condition required for the new level of outputs $\mathbf{x}_B^{**}$, therefore, dictates that the critical level of the scalar θ be computed according to the following minimum ratio criterion: $\theta_c = \min_i = \{\frac{x_{Bi}^*}{-w_i} \mid -w_i > 0\}$.

Notice that the derivatives of the optimal value of the objective function with respect to the parameters $\mathbf{b}$ and $\mathbf{c}_B$ are $\frac{\partial TR^*}{\partial \mathbf{c}_B} = \mathbf{x}_B^*$ and $\frac{\partial TR^*}{\partial \mathbf{b}} = \mathbf{y}^*$. Furthermore, from economic theory we know that the revenue function is concave in input quantities and is convex in output prices. These properties of the revenue function together with the nonresponsiveness of its derivatives (within the limits discussed earlier) are sufficient for establishing the

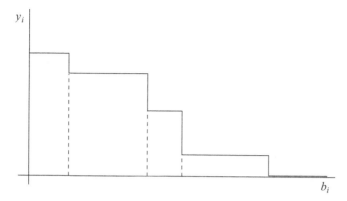

Figure 11.2. LP-derived demand function for input b_i.

fact that in linear programming the demand function for inputs assumes a staircase structure as illustrated in Figure 11.2.

For policy analysis, the staircase structure of the input demand functions derived from LP models is unsatisfactory because it is simply a technical feature of the LP model whose solution may be unresponsive within large interval variations of the input quantity.

An analogous conclusion can be derived for the output supply function. To variations of the vector of output prices c_B there may be unresponsiveness of the corresponding output quantities because, in linear programming, the vector of output prices c_B is not directly related to the vector of optimal output levels x^* but is related indirectly to it via the choice of the optimal basis (optimal technology). From economic theory, the revenue function is convex in output prices, and the output supply schedule of an LP model is nondecreasing as illustrated in Figure 11.3.

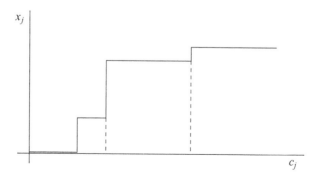

Figure 11.3. LP supply function for output x_j.

Comparative Statics in QP Models

This section shows that QP generates demand and supply functions that are pointwise responsive to exogenous variations of all parameters within the range of the given optimal basis. With a change of the optimal basis (optimal technology) induced by changes in parameters, the slopes of the demand and supply functions will also change.

The primal and dual constraints of an AQP model correspond to an LC problem whose matrix M and vector $\mathbf{q}$ are defined as

$$M = \begin{bmatrix} Q & A' \\ -A & 0 \end{bmatrix}, \quad \mathbf{q} = \begin{bmatrix} \mathbf{c} \\ -\mathbf{b} \end{bmatrix}, \quad \mathbf{z} = \begin{bmatrix} \mathbf{x} \\ \mathbf{y} \end{bmatrix}. \tag{11.6}$$

Let us suppose that M constitutes a feasible and complementary basis for the LC problem. Then the vector $\mathbf{z}^* = M^{-1}\mathbf{q}$ is a feasible and complementary solution for the same problem. Assuming now that Q is a positive definite matrix, the solution can be stated explicitly in terms of the quadratic programming structure of the AQP model:

$$\tag{11.7}$$

$$\begin{bmatrix} \mathbf{x}^* \\ \mathbf{y}^* \end{bmatrix} = \begin{bmatrix} Q^{-1} - Q^{-1}A'(AQ^{-1}A')^{-1}AQ^{-1} & -Q^{-1}A'(AQ^{-1}A')^{-1} \\ (AQ^{-1}A')^{-1}AQ^{-1} & (AQ^{-1}A')^{-1} \end{bmatrix} \begin{bmatrix} \mathbf{c} \\ -\mathbf{b} \end{bmatrix}$$

which corresponds to

$$\tag{11.8}$$

$$\mathbf{x}^* = \left[Q^{-1} - Q^{-1}A'(AQ^{-1}A')^{-1}AQ^{-1} \right]\mathbf{c} + Q^{-1}A'(AQ^{-1}A')^{-1}\mathbf{b}$$

$$\mathbf{y}^* = (AQ^{-1}A')^{-1}AQ^{-1}\mathbf{c} - (AQ^{-1}A')^{-1}\mathbf{b}. \tag{11.9}$$

Equations (11.8) and (11.9) demonstrate that optimal output levels $\mathbf{x}^*$ and input prices $\mathbf{y}^*$ are direct functions of output price parameters $\mathbf{c}$ and input quantities $\mathbf{b}$. These relationships determine the pointwise responsiveness of all decision functions, as asserted.

It is well known that the inverse of a positive definite matrix is positive definite. Furthermore, any principal submatrix of a positive definite matrix is positive definite. Hence, the slopes of the supply and demand functions given in (11.8) and (11.9) are

$$\frac{\partial \mathbf{x}^*}{\partial \mathbf{c}} = \left[Q^{-1} - Q^{-1}A'(AQ^{-1}A')^{-1}AQ^{-1} \right] \equiv \text{symmetric positive definite}$$

$$\tag{11.10}$$

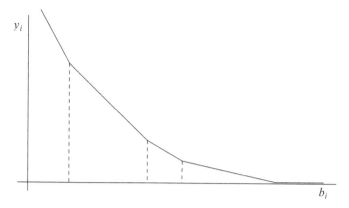

Figure 11.4. Derived demand function for input b_i under AQP.

$$\frac{\partial \mathbf{y}^*}{\partial \mathbf{b}} = -(AQ^{-1}A')^{-1} \equiv \text{symmetric negative definite} \tag{11.11}$$

$$\frac{\partial \mathbf{x}^*}{\partial \mathbf{b}} = Q^{-1}A'(AQ^{-1}A')^{-1} = [(AQ^{-1}A')^{-1}AQ^{-1}]' = \frac{\partial \mathbf{y}^*}{\partial \mathbf{c}}. \tag{11.12}$$

On the basis of the discussion developed in this section, the input demand and the output supply functions under AQP exhibit the curvature illustrated in Figures 11.4 and 11.5.

LP Parametric Programming: Variation in Input Quantity b_1

This section presents a numerical example of parametric programming for deriving the input demand schedule (also called function) for a limiting

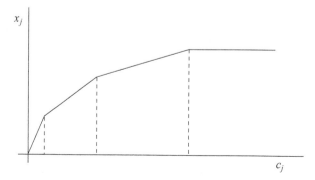

Figure 11.5. Supply function for output x_j under AQP.

input. As illustrated later, this exercise requires a series of iterations involving the dual simplex algorithm. Let us consider the following LP primal problem:

$$\max Z = 3x_1 + 8x_2 + 5x_3$$

$$= c_1 x_1 + c_2 x_2 + c_3 x_3$$

$$\text{subject to} \quad x_1 + 4x_2 + x_3 \leq 12 \equiv b_1, \quad\quad y_1$$

$$6x_1 + 2x_2 + 3x_3 \leq 18 \equiv b_2, \quad\quad y_2$$

$$x_j \geq 0, \quad j = 1, 2, 3.$$

We assume that the foregoing LP problem was succesfully solved using the primal simplex algorithm, as illustrated in Chapter 7, and display its first optimal tableau:

First Optimal Tableau

Z	x_1	x_2	x_3	x_{s1}	x_{s2}	P sol	BI
0	$-\frac{3}{10}$	1	0	$\frac{3}{10}$	$-\frac{1}{10}$	$\frac{9}{5}$	x_2
0	$\frac{11}{5}$	0	1	$-\frac{1}{5}$	$\frac{2}{5}$	$\frac{24}{5}$	x_3
1	$\frac{28}{5}$	0	0	$\frac{7}{5}$	$\frac{6}{5}$	$\frac{192}{5}$	Z
D sol	y_{s1}	y_{s2}	y_{s3}	y_1	y_2	R	

We talk about a first optimal tableau because, in the process of deriving the demand function for input b_1, we will generate other optimal tableaux. We select input b_1 as an example of the parametric programming analysis. The same process can, obviously, be applied to any other input.

The variation of the original quantity of input b_1 can be studied in the input requirement space as illustrated by Figure 11.1. We are interested in drawing an inverse demand schedule diagram (similar to Figure 11.2) between the shadow price of input 1 and its quantity. Hence, the pair of coordinates derivable from the first optimal tableau is given by ($y_1 = \frac{7}{5}$, $b_1 = 12$).

From the first optimal tableau just presented, we see also that the optimal basis is given by vectors $[\mathbf{a}_2, \mathbf{a}_3]$ whose cone (in Figure 11.1) includes the original vector of limiting inputs, $\mathbf{b}$. An increase of the original quantity of input b_1 (keeping constant all the other coefficients of the given LP problem) rotates the vector $\mathbf{b}$ toward the ray emanating from $\mathbf{a}_2$. As long as the modified vector **b** remains in the cone generated by the optimal basis $[\mathbf{a}_2, \mathbf{a}_3]$, the primal solution (x_2, x_3) will be primal feasible and optimal. For a certain critical increment of the quantity of input b_1, the vector **b** will coincide with the ray generated by the vector $\mathbf{a}_2$. A further increment will bring the vector **b** outside the cone generated by the basis $[\mathbf{a}_2, \mathbf{a}_3]$, which then will no longer be feasible in a primal sense and therefore will not be optimal. Thus, it will be wise to choose that critical increment of input b_1 that will make the vector **b** coincident with the ray corresponding to vector $\mathbf{a}_2$ and then change the original optimal basis to choose the next optimal basis for the purpose of continuing the parametric analysis.

To restate the discussion in symbolic terms, and with reference to input 1, we desire to find the largest allowable increment of input b_1 (and a new total quantity of it) such that the current optimal basis and optimal solution's activities remain optimal, that is, find the largest $\Delta b_1 \geq 0$, where

$$\text{new } b_1 = \text{old } b_1 + \Delta b_1$$

and such that
$$\text{new } x_2 \geq 0 \tag{11.13}$$

$$\text{new } x_3 \geq 0. \tag{11.14}$$

To execute the program, it is necessary to consider the optimal tableau and to realize that slack variable x_{s1} is another name for the increment Δb_1. Hence, by selecting the current optimal solution and the coefficients of the column corresponding to input 1 (that is, corresponding to slack variable x_{s1}), relations (11.13) and (11.14) are restated as follows.

First Increment of b_1

$$\text{new } x_2 = x_2 + \tfrac{3}{10}(\Delta b_1 \equiv x_{s1}) = \tfrac{9}{5} + \tfrac{3}{10}\Delta b_1 \geq 0 \tag{11.15}$$

$$\text{new } x_3 = x_3 - \tfrac{1}{5}(\Delta b_1 \equiv x_{s1}) = \tfrac{24}{5} - \tfrac{1}{5}\Delta b_1 \geq 0. \tag{11.16}$$

From the two relations (11.15) and (11.16), the largest allowable increment is

$$\Delta b_1 = \tfrac{24/5}{1/5} = 24, \quad \text{with new } b_1 = 12 + 24 = 36. \tag{11.17}$$

By replacing the value of $(\Delta b_1 = 24)$ into relations (11.15) and (11.16), the new optimal solution is computed as

$$\text{new } x_2 = \tfrac{9}{5} + (\tfrac{3}{10})24 = 9 \tag{11.18}$$

$$\text{new } x_3 = \tfrac{24}{5} - (\tfrac{1}{5})24 = 0. \tag{11.19}$$

The new optimal solution is degenerate, as expected from the discussion of Figure 11.1, and activity a_3 must leave the basis to allow for the next allowable increment of input b_1. At this stage, the shadow price of input b_1 remains the same because there has been no change of basis, as yet. Hence, we can record the new pair of coordinates $(y_1 = \tfrac{7}{5}, b_1 = 36)$. Total revenue is equal to $Z = c_2 x_2 = 72$.

Before computing the second increment of input 1, it is necessary to perform the change of the original optimal basis, as discussed previously. This task requires the use of the dual simplex algorithm by pivoting on the element at the intersection of the row of x_3 (the index of the activity that must leave the current basis) and the column of input 1 (indicated by the slack variable x_{s1}, according to the rules of the dual simplex algorithm). In the next two tableaux, the desired change of basis will be executed. In the first optimal tableau, the solution has been replaced with the new solution computed in relations (11.18) and (11.19).

Second Increment of b_1

First Optimal Tableau

$$\begin{bmatrix} 1 & \tfrac{3}{2} & \vdots & 0 \\ 0 & -5 & \vdots & 0 \\ 0 & 7 & \vdots & 1 \end{bmatrix}$$

	Z	x_1	x_2	x_3	x_{s1}	x_{s2}	P sol	BI
	0	$-\tfrac{3}{10}$	1	0	$\tfrac{3}{10}$	$-\tfrac{1}{10}$	9	x_2
	0	$\tfrac{11}{5}$	0	1	$\left(-\tfrac{1}{5}\right)$	$\tfrac{2}{5}$	0	$x_3 \rightarrow$
	1	$\tfrac{28}{5}$	0	0	$\tfrac{7}{5}$	$\tfrac{6}{5}$	72	Z

$\uparrow$

Second Optimal Tableau (for $b_1 \uparrow$)

	Z	x_1	x_2	x_3	x_{s1}	x_{s2}	P sol	BI
	0	3	1	$\tfrac{3}{2}$	0	$\tfrac{1}{2}$	9	x_2
	0	-11	0	-5	1	-2	0	x_{s1}
	1	21	0	7	0	4	72	Z

D sol	y_{s1}	y_{s2}	y_{s3}	y_1	y_2	R

Activity $\mathbf{a}_3$ was replaced (following the rules of the dual simplex algorithm) by the surplus activity $\mathbf{e}_1$, corresponding to input 1. The shadow price if this input has gone to zero with a quantity of $b_1 = 36$. This means that any quantity of input 1 above 36 will remain unused and, therefore, its shadow price will remain equal to zero. Therefore, another point in the demand schedule's diagram is $(y_1 = 0, b_1 = 36)$. The parametric analysis for increments of input b_1 is completed.

There remains to explore the demand schedule for decrements of input b_1 from the original level of $b_1 = 12$. To accomplish this objective, we must return to the first optimal tableau and state the relevant relations for a decrement of b_1 that we indicate as $(-\Delta b_1)$.

First Decrement of b_1

$$\text{new } x_2 = \tfrac{9}{5} + \tfrac{3}{10}(-\Delta b_1) \geq 0 \qquad (11.20)$$

$$\text{new } x_3 = \tfrac{24}{5} - \tfrac{1}{5}(-\Delta b_1) \geq 0 \qquad (11.21)$$

and the largest admissible decrement is computed from relation (11.20) as $-\Delta b_1 = -6$ with the new $b_1 = 12 - 6 = 6$. The optimal solution corresponding to $b_1 = 6$ is

$$\text{new } x_2 = \tfrac{9}{5} + \left(\tfrac{3}{10}\right)(-6) = 0 \qquad (11.22)$$

$$\text{new } x_3 = \tfrac{24}{5} - \left(\tfrac{1}{5}\right)(-6) = 6 \qquad (11.23)$$

and the value of the objective function is $Z = 30$. The coordinates of this point in the demand schedule's diagram is, thus, $(y_1 = \tfrac{7}{5}, b_1 = 6)$.

A further decrement in the quantity of input 1 requires a change of the original optimal basis for reasons that are analogous to those in the discussion developed for the second increment of b_1.

Second Decrement of b_1

First Optimal Tableau

		Z		x_1	x_2	x_3	x_{s1}	x_{s2}		P sol	BI
-10	0	0	0	$-\tfrac{3}{10}$	1	0	$\tfrac{3}{10}$	$\boxed{-\tfrac{1}{10}}$		0	$x_2 \rightarrow$
4	1	0	0	$\tfrac{11}{5}$	0	1	$-\tfrac{1}{5}$	$\tfrac{2}{5}$		6	x_3
12	0	1	1	$\tfrac{28}{5}$	0	0	$\tfrac{7}{5}$	$\tfrac{6}{5}$		30	Z

$\uparrow$

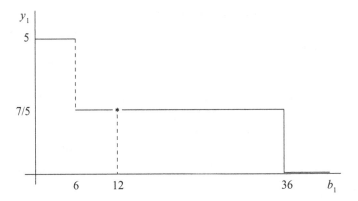

Figure 11.6. The demand schedule of b_1 in an LP environment.

Third Optimal Tableau (for $b_1 \downarrow$)

Z	x_1	x_2	x_3	x_{s1}	x_{s2}	P sol	BI
0	3	−10	0	−3	1	0	x_{s2}
0	1	4	1	1	0	6	x_3
1	2	12	0	5	0	30	Z
D sol	y_{s1}	y_{s2}	y_{s3}	y_1	y_2	R	

From the third optimal tableau, we have another pair of coordinates for the relationship between the shadow price of input 1 and its corresponding quantity, that is, $(y_1 = 5, b_1 = 6)$. There remains to find the largest decrement of input 1 starting at $b_1 = 6$. This task requires repeating the procedure developed previously using the latest information:

$$\text{new } x_{s2} = 0 - 3(-\Delta b_1) \geq 0 \qquad (11.22)$$

$$\text{new } x_3 = 6 + (-\Delta b_1) \geq 0 \qquad (11.23)$$

from where the largest decrement of b_1 is equal to $-\Delta b_1 = -6$. Hence, new $b_1 = 6 - 6 = 0$. The parametric analysis of the desired input is complete, and all the pairs of coordinates result in the demand schedule illustrated in Figure 11.6.

LP Parametric Programming: Variation in Output Price c_2

The parametric programming analysis of an objective function coefficient – usually indicated with the symbol c_j – corresponds to the development of

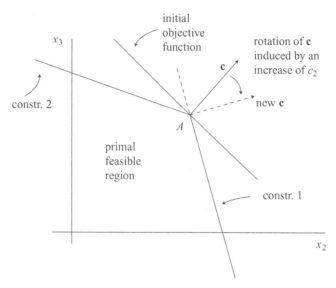

Figure 11.7. The output space and variations of c_2.

the supply schedule for an LP output activity. To illustrate this case we use the same numerical example and first optimal tableau that were analyzed for deriving the demand schedule of input 1.

The optimal solution of that example exhibits positive coordinates for commodities x_2 and x_3. Hence, the relevant output space can be represented as in Figure 11.7, where the original objective function is a supporting line of the feasible region of the output space at the extreme point A.

Beginning the parametric analysis with variations in the c_2 coefficient, the original objective function is rotated clockwise for an increase in the value of c_2, the price of commodity 2. For a critical increment of c_2, the objective function will become parallel to and coincident with the face of the feasible region determined by constraint 1. Further increments of c_2 will cause the objective function to cut through the feasible region and, therefore, the extreme point A will no longer be optimal. Hence, it will be wise to find the largest allowable increment of c_2 that will correspond to a rotation of the objective function that makes it parallel to constraint 1, as indicated in Figure 11.7. At that stage, an appropriate change of basis will allow the continuation of the parametric analysis of c_2. The symbolic and algebraic execution of this discussion will proceed along a path that is analogous to the discussion developed for the input demand schedule. But, whereas in that case the focus was on maintaining the feasibility of the primal optimal solution, now the focus is on maintaining the optimality of the primal feasible solution, and therefore, the dual solution becomes the crucial component of the analysis.

For convenience, we reproduce next the first optimal tableau of the LP example with emphasis on variations of c_2. The increment of c_2 is indicated as Δc_2, which corresponds to the dual slack variable y_{s2}. The location of the increment Δc_2 signifies that we wish to analyze the supply relation between commodity x_2 and its price c_2. Therefore, the relevant information to be extracted from the optimal tableau deals with the positive components of the dual solution in the last row of the tableau and the technical coefficients in the first row corresponding to commodity x_2. We are interested in drawing an inverse supply schedule diagram (similar to Figure 11.3) between the output quantity x_2 and its price c_2. Hence, the pair of coordinates derivable from the first optimal tableau is given by $(x_2 = \frac{9}{5}, c_2 = 8)$.

	Z	x_1	x_2	x_3	x_{s1}	x_{s2}	P sol	BI
$\Delta c_2 \equiv y_{s2}$	0	$\frac{-3}{10}$	1	0	$\frac{3}{10}$	$\frac{-1}{10}$	$\frac{9}{5}$	x_2
y_{s3}	0	$\frac{11}{5}$	0	1	$\frac{-1}{5}$	$\frac{2}{5}$	$\frac{24}{5}$	x_3
	1	$\frac{28}{5}$	0	0	$\frac{7}{5}$	$\frac{6}{5}$	$\frac{192}{5}$	Z
D sol	y_{s1}	y_{s2}	y_{s3}	y_1	y_2	R	

We begin the relevant computations of the desired parametric programming analysis by seeking the largest allowable increment of c_2, that is $\Delta c_2 \geq 0$, where new $c_2 = $ old $c_2 + \Delta c_2$, and such that the following applies.

First Increment of c_2

$$\text{new } y_{s1} = \frac{28}{5} + (\frac{-3}{10})\Delta c_2 \geq 0 \ \Rightarrow \Delta c_2 \leq \frac{28/5}{3/10} = \frac{56}{3} \tag{11.24}$$

$$\text{new } y_1 = \frac{7}{5} + (\frac{3}{10})\Delta c_2 \geq 0 \tag{11.25}$$

$$\text{new } y_2 = \frac{6}{5} + (\frac{-1}{10})\Delta c_2 \geq 0, \ \Rightarrow \Delta c_2 \leq \frac{6/5}{1/10} = 12. \tag{11.26}$$

The admissible increment of c_2 is the minimum value of the two ratios, that is, $\Delta c_2 = 12$. Hence, the new dual solution, for new $c_2 = 8 + 12 = 20$, corresponds to

New solution A:
$$\text{new } y_{s1} = \frac{28}{5} + (\frac{-3}{10})12 = 2$$
$$\text{new } y_1 = \frac{7}{5} + (\frac{3}{10})12 = 5$$
$$\text{new } y_2 = \frac{6}{5} + (\frac{-1}{10})12 = 0^*$$

with a value of the objective function of $Z = 60$. An asterisk characterizes the degeneracy of the dual solution indicated by a zero value of the new y_2 in order to distinguish it from other zero values in the optimal tableau. The next pair of coordinates for the supply schedule is $(x_2 = \frac{9}{5}, c_2 = 20)$.

Second Increment of c_2

Before seeking a new increment Δc_2, we must change the primal basis in order to preserve the optimality of the new primal solution. This goal can be achieved by starting with the original optimal tableau as just presented, replacing the opportunity costs with the new dual solution A, exploiting the dual degeneracy, and using the primal simplex algorithm for another iteration.

		Z	x_1	x_2	x_3	x_{s1}	x_{s2}		P sol	BI
Transfor-		0	$\frac{-3}{10}$	1	0	$\frac{3}{10}$	$\frac{-1}{10}$		$\frac{9}{5}$	x_2
mation		0	$\frac{11}{5}$	0	1	$\frac{-1}{5}$	$\textcircled{\frac{2}{5}}$		$\frac{24}{5}$	$x_3 \rightarrow$
Matrix		1	2	0	0	5	0^*		60	Z

$\uparrow$

0		$\frac{1}{4}$	1	$\frac{1}{4}$	$\frac{1}{4}$	0		3	x_2
0		$\frac{11}{2}$	0	$\frac{5}{2}$	$\frac{-1}{2}$	1		12	x_{s2}
1		2	0	0	5	0^*		60	Z

In the second tableau, commodity 2 reaches the level $x_2 = 3$. Hence, the next pair of coordinates for the supply schedule's diagram becomes $(x_2 = 3, c_2 = 20)$. At this point, we can proceed to determine the second increment Δc_2 that is consistent with the optimal solution of the last tableau, following the familiar procedure:

$$\text{new } y_{s1} = 2 + (\tfrac{1}{4})\Delta c_2 \geq 0 \tag{11.27}$$

$$\text{new } y_{s3} = 0^* + (\tfrac{1}{4})\Delta c_2 \geq 0 \tag{11.28}$$

$$\text{new } y_1 = 5 + (\tfrac{1}{4})\Delta c_2 \geq 0. \tag{11.29}$$

The three inequalities do not provide any obstacle for the increment Δc_2 to achieve the value of $+\infty$. Hence, there is no need to change the current basis and, beyond the price of $c_2 = 20$, the output supply will remain constant at the level of $x_2 = 3$.

There remains to compute the decrements of c_2 starting at the original value of $c_2 = 8$ and the information contained in the first optimal tableau.

First Decrement of c_2

$$\text{new } y_{s1} = \tfrac{28}{5} + (\tfrac{-3}{10})(-\Delta c_2) \geq 0 \qquad\qquad (11.30)$$

$$\text{new } y_1 = \tfrac{7}{5} + (\tfrac{3}{10})(-\Delta c_2) \geq 0 \qquad \Rightarrow \Delta c_2 \leq \tfrac{7/5}{3/10} = \tfrac{14}{3} \qquad (11.31)$$

$$\text{new } y_2 = \tfrac{6}{5} + (\tfrac{-1}{10})(-\Delta c_2) \geq 0. \qquad\qquad (11.32)$$

Only inequality (11.31) is relevant for determining the admissible level of Δc_2, because the other two inequalities would allow a Δc_2 of infinite magnitude. With the largest admissible decrement of $(-\Delta c_2) = -\tfrac{14}{3}$, the new value of c_2 becomes new $c_2 = 8 - \tfrac{14}{3} = \tfrac{10}{3}$, and the dual solution results in

$$\text{new } y_{s1} = \tfrac{28}{5} + (\tfrac{-3}{10})(-\tfrac{14}{3}) = 7 \qquad\qquad (11.33)$$

$$\text{new } y_1 = \tfrac{7}{5} + (\tfrac{3}{10})(-\tfrac{14}{3}) = 0^* \qquad\qquad (11.34)$$

$$\text{new } y_2 = \tfrac{6}{5} + (\tfrac{-1}{10})(-\tfrac{14}{3}) = \tfrac{5}{3} \qquad\qquad (11.35)$$

with a value of the objective function equal to $Z = 30$. The pair of relevant coordinates is $(x_2 = \tfrac{9}{5}, c_2 = \tfrac{10}{3})$.

Second Decrement of c_2
The computation of a further decrement of c_2 requires a change of basis in order to guarantee the optimality of the primal solution. Thus,

		Z	x_1	x_2	x_3	x_{s1}	x_{s2}	P sol	BI
$\Delta c_2 \equiv y_{s2}$		0	$\tfrac{-3}{10}$	1	0	$\left(\tfrac{3}{10}\right)$	$\tfrac{-1}{10}$	$\tfrac{9}{5}$	$x_2 \rightarrow$
		0	$\tfrac{11}{5}$	0	1	$\tfrac{-1}{5}$	$\tfrac{2}{5}$	$\tfrac{24}{5}$	x_3
		1	7	0	0	0^*	$\tfrac{5}{3}$	30	Z

$$\uparrow$$

The application of the primal simplex algorithm (using the dual degeneracy) indicates that in the next tableau commodity x_2 will be reduced to a zero level. Hence, the analysis of the output supply schedule of commodity x_2 is completed. The diagram reproducing the supply function is given in Figure 11.8.

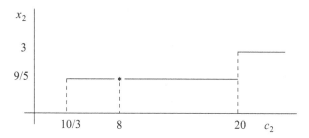

Figure 11.8. The output schedule of commodity x_2.

Parametric Quadratic Programming by LCP

In principle, parametric analysis of quadratic programming models can be regarded as an extension of the LP procedure discussed in previous sections, except for the added complexity resulting from the fact that a variation in a given parameter (either of the objective function or of the right-hand-side constraints) may cause a concurrent change in both the primal and the dual solution. This is a direct consequence of the structure of these solutions as indicated by relations (11.8) and (11.9). Another way to see this complexity is to realize that in a quadratic programming problem, the complementary slackness relations must be met purposely, whereas in an LP model they are met automatically.

The LC problem is also a convenient structure for developing this important analysis. Consider the following SQP problem:

$$\max Z = \mathbf{c}'\mathbf{x} - \tfrac{1}{2}\mathbf{x}'D\mathbf{x} - \tfrac{1}{2}\mathbf{y}'E\mathbf{y} \qquad (11.36)$$

$$\text{subject to} \qquad A\mathbf{x} - E\mathbf{y} \leq \mathbf{b} \qquad (11.37)$$

$$\mathbf{x} \geq \mathbf{0}, \mathbf{y} \geq \mathbf{0}$$

where D and E are symmetric and semidefinite matrices. From the discussion in Chapter 5 and subsequent chapters, this SQP problem can be restated as the following LCP structure: find $\mathbf{z} \geq \mathbf{0}$ and $\mathbf{w} \geq \mathbf{0}$ such that

$$\mathbf{w} - M\mathbf{z} = \mathbf{q} \qquad (11.38)$$

$$\mathbf{w}'\mathbf{z} = 0 \qquad (11.39)$$

where
$$M = \begin{bmatrix} D & A' \\ -A & E \end{bmatrix}, \quad \mathbf{q} = \begin{bmatrix} \mathbf{c} \\ -\mathbf{b} \end{bmatrix}.$$

The linear constraints (11.38) have the structure of a simplex tableau, as discussed in Chapter 7. There is, however, no objective function that has been resolved into the complementary slackness conditions (11.39). Vector q contains all the coefficients of vectors c and b that will be subject to parametric variations. This fact suggests the use of an algorithm akin to the dual simplex algorithm, as it was applied to the RHS vector b in the earlier parametric analysis of an LP model.

We discuss the parametric programming of an LC problem such as [(11.38), (11.39)] by a series of numerical examples following the directions of the dual simplex algorithm for linear programming.

Example 1: Let us reconsider the AQP example given in Chapter 6, which is reproduced here for convenience:

$$\text{maximize } Z = c'x - x'Dx \qquad (6.5)$$

$$\text{subject to} \qquad Ax \le b, \qquad x \ge 0$$

where A is a matrix of dimensions $(m \times n)$, the matrix D is a symmetric positive semidefinite matrix of order n, and all the other vectors are conformable to the given matrices. In this numerical example, the given parameter values are $c' = [4, 3]$, $A = [1, 2]$, $b = 4$ and $D = \begin{bmatrix} 2 & 1 \\ 1 & 0 \end{bmatrix}$. Hence, the M matrix and the vectors q, z and w of the LC problem corresponding to the KKT conditions of the asymmetric quadratic programming (6.5) can be stated as

$$M = \begin{bmatrix} 2D & A' \\ -A & 0 \end{bmatrix} = \begin{bmatrix} 4 & 2 & 1 \\ 2 & 0 & 2 \\ -1 & -2 & 0 \end{bmatrix},$$

$$q = \begin{bmatrix} -c \\ b \end{bmatrix} = \begin{bmatrix} -4 \\ -3 \\ 4 \end{bmatrix}, \quad z = \begin{bmatrix} x \\ y \end{bmatrix}, \quad w = \begin{bmatrix} v \\ u \end{bmatrix}.$$

The solution tableau of the given LC problem was computed in Chapter 6 as

	w_1	w_2	w_3	z_1	z_2	z_3	q	BI	(11.40)
		$-\frac{1}{2}$		1		1	$\frac{3}{2}$	z_3	
	0	$\frac{1}{2}$	$\frac{1}{2}$	1			2	z_2	
	1	$-\frac{1}{2}$	1	-2			$\frac{3}{2}$	w_1	

First Increment of b. We seek the largest admissible increment, $\Delta b \ge 0$, which is compatible with the feasible and complementary basis in tableau

(11.40). This objective corresponds to finding the largest increment Δb such that new $b =$ old $b + \Delta b$, without changing the feasible and complementary basis in tableau (11.40). As for parametric LP, the relevant vector's coefficients to consider are those corresponding to slack variable $w_3 \equiv$ slack variable of input constraint. Hence, the operational relations are stated in system (11.41):

$$\text{new } z_3 = \tfrac{3}{2} + 0(\Delta b) \geq 0$$
$$\text{new } z_2 = 2 + \tfrac{1}{2}(\Delta b) \geq 0 \tag{11.41}$$
$$\text{new } w_1 = \tfrac{3}{2} + (\Delta b) \geq 0$$

from which we deduce that $\Delta b = +\infty$.

First Decrement of b. As before, we signify a decrement with the symbol $(-\Delta b)$. Hence, we repeat the search of the largest admissible decrement using the same coefficients used in (11.41):

$$\text{new } z_3 = \tfrac{3}{2} + 0(-\Delta b) \geq 0$$
$$\text{new } z_2 = 2 + \tfrac{1}{2}(-\Delta b) \geq 0 \quad \Rightarrow \Delta b = 4 \tag{11.42}$$
$$\text{new } w_1 = \tfrac{3}{2} + (-\Delta b) \geq 0 \quad \Rightarrow \Delta b = \tfrac{3}{2}.$$

The largest admissible value of Δb is the minimum of the two values in (11.42), that is, $\tfrac{3}{2}$. Hence, new $b = b + (-\Delta b) = 4 - \tfrac{3}{2} = \tfrac{5}{2}$, and the corresponding feasible and complementary solution is

$$\text{new } z_3 = \tfrac{3}{2} + 0(-\tfrac{3}{2}) = \tfrac{3}{2}$$
$$\text{new } z_2 = 2 + \tfrac{1}{2}(-\tfrac{3}{2}) = \tfrac{5}{4} \tag{11.43}$$
$$\text{new } w_1 = \tfrac{3}{2} + (-\tfrac{3}{2}) = 0.$$

In order to verify that the solution in (11.43) is both feasible and complementary, it is convenient to multiply the new vector $\mathbf{q}' = [-4, -3, \tfrac{5}{2}]$ by the inverse of the current feasible and complementary basis. As stated many times in previous chapters, the inverse of a matrix is found under the initial identity matrix, in correspondence of the slack variables. Hence, $\bar{M}^{-1}\mathbf{q} = \bar{\mathbf{q}}$, where $\bar{M}^{-1}$ is the inverse of the current feasible complementary basis and $\bar{\mathbf{q}}$ is the feasible and complementary solution:

$$\begin{bmatrix} 0 & -\tfrac{1}{2} & 0 \\ 0 & 0 & \tfrac{1}{2} \\ 1 & -\tfrac{1}{2} & 1 \end{bmatrix} \begin{bmatrix} -4 \\ -3 \\ \tfrac{5}{2} \end{bmatrix} = \begin{bmatrix} \tfrac{3}{2} \\ \tfrac{5}{4} \\ 0 \end{bmatrix}. \tag{11.44}$$

Second Decrement of b. In order to explore a further decrement of b, below its current value of $b = \frac{5}{2}$, it is necessary first to find another feasible and complementary basis. This is done by replacing the solution in tableau (11.40) with the new solution in (11.44) and choosing a complementary pivot by exiting the degenerate variable $w_1 = 0$ and replacing it with its complement z_1. This is done by following the rules of the dual simplex algorithm.

$$\downarrow$$

T	w_1	w_2	w_3	z_1	z_2	z_3	q	BI	(11.45)

$$
\begin{bmatrix} 1 & & \tfrac{1}{2} \\ & 1 & \tfrac{1}{4} \\ & & -\tfrac{1}{2} \end{bmatrix}
\begin{bmatrix} & -\tfrac{1}{2} & & 1 & & 1 & \tfrac{3}{2} \\ & 0 & \tfrac{1}{2} & \tfrac{1}{2} & 1 & & \tfrac{5}{4} \\ 1 & -\tfrac{1}{2} & 1 & \boxed{-2} & & & 0 \end{bmatrix}
\begin{array}{l} z_3 \\ z_2 \\ w_1 \rightarrow \end{array}
$$

$$
\begin{bmatrix} \tfrac{1}{2} & -\tfrac{3}{4} & \tfrac{1}{2} & & & 1 & \tfrac{3}{2} \\ \tfrac{1}{4} & -\tfrac{1}{8} & \tfrac{3}{4} & & 1 & & \tfrac{5}{4} \\ \tfrac{-1}{2} & \tfrac{1}{4} & \tfrac{-1}{2} & 1 & & & 0 \end{bmatrix}
\begin{array}{l} z_3 \\ z_2 \\ z_1 \end{array}
$$

Now we can proceed with the computation of the second largest admissible decrement of b using the coefficients of the last tableau under the slack variable $w_3 \equiv \Delta b$:

$$\text{new } z_3 = \tfrac{3}{2} + \tfrac{1}{2}(-\Delta b) \geq 0 \Rightarrow \Delta b = 3$$
$$\text{new } z_2 = \tfrac{5}{4} + \tfrac{3}{4}(-\Delta b) \geq 0 \Rightarrow \Delta b = \tfrac{5}{3} \qquad (11.46)$$
$$\text{new } z_1 = 0 - \tfrac{1}{2}(-\Delta b) \geq 0.$$

Hence, the largest admissible decrement is $\Delta b = \frac{5}{3}$, the new $b = \frac{5}{2} - \frac{5}{3} = \frac{5}{6}$, and the new feasible and complementary solution corresponding to (11.46) is

$$\text{new } z_3 = \tfrac{3}{2} + \tfrac{1}{2}(-\tfrac{5}{3}) = \tfrac{2}{3}$$
$$\text{new } z_2 = \tfrac{5}{4} + \tfrac{3}{4}(-\tfrac{5}{3}) = 0 \qquad (11.47)$$
$$\text{new } z_1 = 0 - \tfrac{1}{2}(-\tfrac{5}{3}) = \tfrac{5}{6}.$$

The feasibility and complementarity of the solution in (11.47) can be further verified by postmultiplying the inverse matrix in the last tableau of (11.45) by the vector $\mathbf{q}' = [-4, -3, \frac{5}{6}]$. This check serves as an important verification that the computations have been carried out correctly.

Third Decrement of b. The computation of a third decrement of b (in general, it is of interest to conduct parametric programming of the various coefficients from 0 to $+\infty$) requires a change of the current feasible and complementary basis given in the last tableau of (11.45) by replacing the newly found feasible and complementary solution of (11.47) and to proceed with another round of the dual simplex algorithm while identifying the complementary pivot with the exiting basic and degenerate variable z_2 and the incoming complementary variable w_2.

$$\downarrow$$

$$
\begin{array}{ccccccccc}
T & w_1 & w_2 & w_3 & z_1 & z_2 & z_3 & \mathbf{q} & BI \qquad (11.48)
\end{array}
$$

$$
\begin{bmatrix} 1 & -6 \\ & -8 \\ & 2 & 1 \end{bmatrix}
\begin{bmatrix} \frac{1}{2} & -\frac{3}{4} & \frac{1}{2} & & & 1 & \frac{2}{3} \\ \frac{1}{4} & \boxed{-\frac{1}{8}} & \frac{3}{4} & & 1 & & 0 \\ \frac{-1}{2} & \frac{1}{4} & \frac{-1}{2} & 1 & & & \frac{5}{6} \end{bmatrix}
\begin{matrix} z_3 \\ z_2 \rightarrow \\ z_1 \end{matrix}
$$

$$
\begin{bmatrix} -1 & & -4 & & & 1 & \frac{2}{3} \\ -2 & 1 & -6 & & 1 & & 0 \\ 0 & & 1 & 1 & & & \frac{5}{6} \end{bmatrix}
\begin{matrix} z_3 \\ w_2 \\ z_1 \end{matrix}
$$

The search for the third and largest admissible decrement of b proceeds as before:

$$\text{new } z_3 = \tfrac{2}{3} - 4(-\Delta b) \geq 0$$
$$\text{new } w_2 = 0 - 6(-\Delta b) \geq 0 \qquad (11.49)$$
$$\text{new } z_1 = \tfrac{5}{6} + \ (-\Delta b) \geq 0 \ \Rightarrow \Delta b = \tfrac{5}{6}.$$

Therefore, the value of $b = 0$ has been reached, and the parametric analysis of the constraint b is completed. The new feasible and complementary solution corresponding to $b = 0$ is as follows:

$$\text{new } z_3 = \tfrac{2}{3} - 4(-\tfrac{5}{6}) = 4$$
$$\text{new } w_2 = 0 - 6(-\tfrac{5}{6}) = 5 \qquad (11.50)$$
$$\text{new } z_1 = \tfrac{5}{6} + (-\tfrac{5}{6}) = 0.$$

The variable $z_3 \equiv y_1$ does not have a monotonic behavior with respect to changes in the b constraint within the range of $(0, +\infty)$ (Cottle).

Example 2: The next parametric analysis deals with a coefficient of the linear part of the objective function, say c_2. We use the same QP numerical example and start with the LC feasible and complementary basis and solution displayed in tableau (11.40).

First Increment of c_2. We seek the largest admissible increment of c_2 that will not require a change of the feasible and complementary basis in tableau (11.40). Notice that the relevant incoming vector is now identified by w_2, the complement of $z_2 \equiv x_2$, the output variable directly associated with its price c_2. The feasible increment is found by analyzing the following relations:

$$\text{new } z_3 = \tfrac{3}{2} - \tfrac{1}{2}(\Delta c_2) \geq 0 \quad \Rightarrow \Delta c_2 = 3$$
$$\text{new } z_2 = 2 + 0(\Delta c_2) \geq 0 \qquad\qquad\qquad (11.51)$$
$$\text{new } w_1 = \tfrac{3}{2} - \tfrac{1}{2}(\Delta c_2) \geq 0 \quad \Rightarrow \Delta c_2 = 3.$$

A tie occurs in (11.51). Ties can be broken using a lexicographic criterion (Graves). This is the most satisfactory theoretical approach. A much simpler and often workable procedure is the flip of a coin. In this case, there is no need to break the tie, because the new value of the coefficient of interest is new $c_2 = -3 + 3 = 0$. The corresponding new feasible and complementary solution is

$$\text{new } z_3 = \tfrac{3}{2} - \tfrac{1}{2}(3) = 0$$
$$\text{new } z_2 = 2 + 0(3) = 2 \qquad\qquad\qquad (11.52)$$
$$\text{new } w_1 = \tfrac{3}{2} - \tfrac{1}{2}(3) = 0$$

First Decrement of c_2. A similar analysis with the decrement symbolized by $(-\Delta c_2)$ results in $(-\Delta c_2) = -\infty$.

Example 3: Parametric variation of c_1. The starting point is again tableau (11.40). This time the relevant column of coefficients is identified by w_1. Therefore the increment $\Delta c_1 = +\infty$ (we leave it to the reader to find out why).

First Decrement of c_1. The relevant relations to determine the decrement are:

$$\text{new } z_3 = \tfrac{3}{2} + 0(-\Delta c_1) \geq 0$$
$$\text{new } z_2 = 2 + 0(-\Delta c_1) \geq 0 \qquad\qquad\qquad (11.53)$$
$$\text{new } w_1 = \tfrac{3}{2} + (-\Delta c_1) \geq 0 \quad \Rightarrow \Delta c_1 = \tfrac{3}{2}$$

with new $c_1 = -4 - \tfrac{3}{2} = -\tfrac{11}{2}$ and corresponding feasible and complementary solution as

$$\text{new } z_3 = \tfrac{3}{2}$$
$$\text{new } z_2 = 2 \qquad\qquad\qquad (11.54)$$
$$\text{new } w_1 = 0.$$

Second Decrement of c_1. Before proceeding with the determination of the second decrement of c_1, we need to change the feasible and complementary basis using the newly found feasible and complementary solution (11.54).

The complementary pivot is identified by the exiting variable w_1 and the incoming complement z_1.

$$\downarrow$$

$$
\begin{array}{ccccccccc}
T & w_1 & w_2 & w_3 & z_1 & z_2 & z_3 & q & BI & (11.55)
\end{array}
$$

$$
\begin{bmatrix} 1 & & \\ & 1 & \\ & & 1 \end{bmatrix}
\begin{bmatrix} \frac{1}{2} \\ \frac{1}{4} \\ -\frac{1}{2} \end{bmatrix}
\left[
\begin{array}{ccc|ccc|c}
 & & -\frac{1}{2} & 1 & & 1 & \frac{3}{2} \\
 & & 0 & \frac{1}{2} & \frac{1}{2} & 1 & 2 \\
1 & -\frac{1}{2} & 1 & \boxed{-2} & & & 0
\end{array}
\right]
\begin{array}{l} z_3 \\ z_2 \\ w_1 \rightarrow \end{array}
$$

$$
\left[
\begin{array}{ccc|ccc|c}
\frac{1}{2} & -\frac{3}{4} & \frac{1}{2} & & & 1 & \frac{3}{2} \\
\frac{1}{4} & -\frac{1}{8} & \frac{3}{4} & & 1 & & 2 \\
\frac{-1}{2} & \frac{1}{4} & \frac{-1}{2} & 1 & & & 0
\end{array}
\right]
\begin{array}{l} z_3 \\ z_2 \\ z_1 \end{array}
$$

Using the relevant information from the last tableau of (11.55) (coefficients of the solution and of the w_1 column), we establish that

$$\text{new } z_3 = \tfrac{3}{2} + \tfrac{1}{2}(-\Delta c_1) \geq 0 \quad \Rightarrow \Delta c_1 = 3$$
$$\text{new } z_2 = 2 + \tfrac{1}{4}(-\Delta c_1) \geq 0 \quad \Rightarrow \Delta c_1 = 8 \quad (11.56)$$
$$\text{new } z_1 = 0 - \tfrac{1}{2}(-\Delta c_1) \geq 0$$

with the largest admissible decrement identified as $(-\Delta c_1) = -3$. Thus, the new $c_1 = -\frac{11}{2} - 3 = -\frac{17}{2}$ and the corresponding feasible and complementary solutions given by

$$\text{new } z_3 = 0$$
$$\text{new } z_2 = \tfrac{5}{4} \quad (11.57)$$
$$\text{new } z_1 = \tfrac{3}{2}.$$

The correctness of computations is verified, as usual, by postmultiplying the inverse of the current feasible and complementary basis by the vector $\mathbf{q}' = [-\frac{17}{2}, -3, 4]$ which corresponds to

$$
\begin{bmatrix}
\frac{1}{2} & -\frac{3}{4} & \frac{1}{2} \\
\frac{1}{4} & -\frac{1}{8} & \frac{3}{4} \\
-\frac{1}{2} & \frac{1}{4} & -\frac{1}{2}
\end{bmatrix}
\begin{bmatrix}
-\frac{17}{2} \\
-3 \\
4
\end{bmatrix}
=
\begin{bmatrix}
0 \\
\frac{5}{4} \\
\frac{3}{2}
\end{bmatrix}
\quad (11.58)
$$

as desired and expected.

Third Decrement of c_1. First, we must attempt to change the current feasible and complementary basis by exchanging, according to the rules of the dual simplex algorithm, variable z_3 with its complement w_3. Unfortunately, the coefficient candidate for the pivot is positive [as verified in the second tableau of (11.55)], a condition that violates the rules of the dual simplex algorithm.

Hence, a pivot cannot be found and the algorithm breaks down (Murty). This example demonstrates the complexity of LC parametric programming for which a complete and satisfactory algorithm is yet to be found.

Exercises

11.1 Given the LP problem

$$\max Z = 3x_1 + 8x_2 + 5x_3$$

$$= c_1 x_1 + c_2 x_2 + c_3 x_3$$

$$\text{subject to} \qquad x_1 + 4x_2 + x_3 \le 12 \equiv b_1, \qquad y_1$$

$$6x_1 + 2x_2 + 3x_3 \le 18 \equiv b_2, \qquad y_2$$

$$x_j \ge 0, \quad j = 1, 2, 3$$

(a) Derive the input demand schedule for input 2. Draw an appropriate diagram.

11.2 Given the LP problem in exercise 11.1,
   (b) Derive the output supply schedule for commodity 3. Draw an appropriate diagram.

11.3 Given the LP problem in exercise 11.1,
   (c) Derive the output supply schedule for commodity 1. Draw an appropriate diagram.

11.4 Parametric quadratic programming (Wang). Given the following QP problem:

$$\min Z = (-2 + t)x_1 - 2x_2 + x_1^2 + \tfrac{1}{2}x_2^2$$

$$\text{subject to} \qquad x_1 \qquad\qquad \le 1$$

$$x_2 \le 1$$

$$x_1 \qquad\qquad \ge 0$$

$$x_2 \ge 0$$

solve the given QP problem for $t < 0$, $t = 0$ and $0 < t \le 2$. Draw an appropriate diagram.

References

Best, M. J. (1996). "An Algorithm for the Solution of the Parametric Quadratic Programming Problem." In *Applied Mathematics and Parallel Computing: Festschrift for Klaus Ritter*, Ritter, K., Fisher, H., Riedmuller, B., and Schaffler, S., editors (Heidelberg: Physica-Verlag), pp. 57–76.

Churilov, L., Ralph, D., and Sniedovich, M. (1998). "A Note on Composite Concave Quadratic Programming," *Operations Research Letters*, 163–9.

Cottle, R. W. (1972). "Monotone Solutions of the Parametric Linear Complementarity Problem," *Mathematical Programming*, 3, 210–24.

Graves, R. L. (1967). "A Principal Pivoting Simplex Algorithm for Linear and Quadratic Programming," *Operations Research*, 15, 482–94.

Hicks, J. R. (1939). *Value and Capital: An Inquiry into Some Fundamental Principles of Economic Theory* (Oxford: Clarendon Press).

Murty, K. G. (1988). *Linear Complementarity, Linear and Nonlinear Programming* (Berlin: Heldermann Verlag).

Wang, X. (2004). *Resolution of Ties in Parametric Quadratic Programming*, masters thesis, University of Waterloo, Ontario, Canada.

12

General Market Equilibrium

A scenario of general economic equilibrium may be articulated according to various degrees of detail and complexity. The essential feature of a general equilibrium, however, is the existence of economic agents gifted with endowments and the will to appear on the market either as consumers or as producers in order to take advantage of economic opportunities expressed in the form of offers to either buy or sell.

In this chapter, we discuss a series of general equilibrium models characterized by an increasing degree of articulation and generality. The minimal requirement for a genuine general equilibrium model is the presence of demand and supply functions for some of the commodities.

Model 1: Final Commodities

A general market equilibrium requires consumers and producers. We assume that consumers have already maximized their utility function subject to their budget constraints and have expressed their decisions by means of an aggregate set of demand functions for final commodities. On the producers' side, the industry is atomistic in the sense that there are many producers of final commodities, each of whom cannot affect the overall market behavior with his decisions. It is the typical environment of a perfectly competitive industry.

Hence, consider the following scenario. There exists a set of inverse demand functions for final commodities expressed by $\mathbf{p} = \mathbf{c} - D\mathbf{x}$, where D is a symmetric positive semidefinite matrix of dimension $(n \times n)$, $\mathbf{p}$ is an n-vector of prices, $\mathbf{c}$ is an n-vector of intercept coefficients, and $\mathbf{x}$ is an n-vector of quantities. There also exists a set of aggregate supply functions for inputs defined as $\mathbf{s} = \mathbf{b} + E\mathbf{y}$, where E is a symmetric positive semidefinite matrix of dimension $(m \times m)$, $\mathbf{s}$ is an m-vector of quantities, $\mathbf{b}$ is an m-vector of intercept coefficients, and $\mathbf{y}$ is an m-vector of prices. This specification of the input supply functions leads directly to a symmetric structure of the market equilibrium problem, as seen in the monopsonist case. Finally, there exists a large number of firms, say K, that transform inputs into final commodities by means of individualized linear technologies A_k, $k = 1, \ldots, K$. Each firm is too small to influence prices appreciably and, therefore, it is considered as a price taker on the output as well as on the input markets.

This specification of the model provides one of the most stylized representations of a general equilibrium problem. Strictly speaking, it is more correct to view this model as a market equilibrium problem that allows the reader to focus on a few essential features of a general equilibrium. In this model, consumers are represented by the set of inverse demand functions for final commodities. These relations are aggregate functions representing the maximization of utility functions subject to a given level of income made by individual consumers and collectively rendered by the set of inverse demand functions just mentioned. The aggregation problem involved is assumed to be solved consistently. The assumption of symmetry associated with the matrix D is not necessary, but it circumvents the integrability problem and will be relaxed in subsequent models. Furthermore, the consumer demand functions specified earlier are conditional on a predetermined level of income. In order to reconcile theory with empirical modeling (for example, to satisfy the assumption of zero-degree homogeneity in prices and income of demand functions), it is convenient to think that the general specification of inverse demand functions is $\mathbf{p} = \mathbf{d}I - D\mathbf{x}$, where $\mathbf{d}$ is the vector of income coefficients associated with an aggregate level of income, I. By fixing income at a given level, say $\bar{I}$, the vector $\mathbf{c} = \mathbf{d}\bar{I}$ becomes the vector of intercepts in the original formulation of the inverse demand functions.

The final objective of a general equilibrium specification is that of finding commodity prices and quantities that clear input and output markets. The atomistic structure of the economy and the information given earlier guarantee that, under the working of the "invisible hand," this objective is equivalent to maximizing consumer (CS) and producer (PS) surpluses.

Figure 12.1 illustrates the geometric structure of this problem. In the output diagram (Figure 12.1A), the consumer surplus ($\frac{1}{2}\mathbf{x}' D\mathbf{x}$) is the triangle above the economy's marginal cost ($A_k'\mathbf{y}_k$) and below the aggregate demand function ($\mathbf{c} - D\mathbf{x}$). The input diagram (Figure 12.1B) exhibits inverted axes with respect to the traditional textbook representation and, therefore, the producer surplus, ($\mathbf{b}'\mathbf{y} + \frac{1}{2}\mathbf{y}' E\mathbf{y}$), is the trapezoid below the inverse input supply function. This specification of the producers' side is based on the

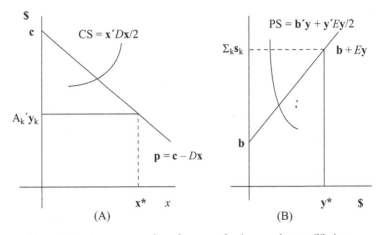

Figure 12.1. Consumer and producer surplus in a market equilibrium.

technical discussion of the perfectly discriminating monopsonist's input supply carried out in Chapter 9.

To justify the structure of the primal objective function as stated in Figure 12.1, we review the consumer and producer surpluses in an auxiliary single diagram where the demand is $(\mathbf{c} - D\mathbf{x})$ and the supply is $(\mathbf{h} + H\mathbf{x})$. This auxiliary specification allows plotting demand and supply functions on the same diagram.

Matrices D and H are assumed to be symmetric positive definite. The consumer and the producer surpluses are represented in Figure 12.2 by the area (triangle) under the demand function $(\mathbf{c} - D\mathbf{x})$ and above the supply

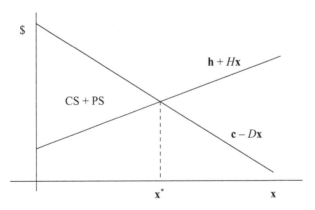

Figure 12.2. Auxiliary diagram for consumer and producer surpluses.

function $(\mathbf{h} + H\mathbf{x})$ and are measured as the difference between the integral under the demand function and the integral under the supply function.

Hence, in analytical form,

$$(CS + PS) = \int_0^{\mathbf{x}^*} (\mathbf{c} - D\mathbf{x})' d\mathbf{x} - \int_0^{\mathbf{x}^*} (\mathbf{h} + H\mathbf{x})' d\mathbf{x}$$

$$= [\mathbf{c}'\mathbf{x}^* - \tfrac{1}{2}\mathbf{x}^{*'} D\mathbf{x}^*] - [\mathbf{h}'\mathbf{x}^* + \tfrac{1}{2}\mathbf{x}^{*'} H\mathbf{x}^*].$$

We must now consider the fact that the supply functions in the general equilibrium problem of this section deal with inputs, and not final commodities. As computed for the perfectly discriminating monopsonist in Chapter 9, the second integral has the familiar specification $[\mathbf{g}'\mathbf{s} + \tfrac{1}{2}\mathbf{s}' G\mathbf{s}]$, where $(\mathbf{g} + G\mathbf{s})$ is the vector of inverse input supply functions. By letting $\mathbf{y} = \mathbf{g} + G\mathbf{s}$, as done in Chapter 9, we can write $\mathbf{s} = \mathbf{b} + E\mathbf{y}$ and, finally, $[\mathbf{g}'\mathbf{s} + \tfrac{1}{2}\mathbf{s}' G\mathbf{s}] = -\tfrac{1}{2}\mathbf{b}' E\mathbf{b} + \tfrac{1}{2}\mathbf{y}' E\mathbf{y}$, (compare equation (9.24)). In Appendix 12.1, we discuss this topic in more detail. The term $\tfrac{1}{2}\mathbf{b}' E\mathbf{b}$ is a constant and does not enter into the optimization process. Therefore, it can be disregarded. We can, thus, state the primal specification of the general market equilibrium as done in the following paragraph.

The dual pair of symmetric problems representing the market equilibrium for final commodities described in this section begins with the specification of the primal problem:

Primal

$$\max (CS + PS) = \mathbf{c}'\mathbf{x} - \tfrac{1}{2}\mathbf{x}' D\mathbf{x} - \tfrac{1}{2}\mathbf{y}' E\mathbf{y} \qquad (12.1)$$

$$\text{subject to} \qquad A_k\mathbf{x}_k - \mathbf{s}_k \qquad \leq 0 \qquad (12.2)$$

$$-\sum_{k=1}^{K} \mathbf{x}_k \qquad + \mathbf{x} \qquad \leq 0 \qquad (12.3)$$

$$\sum_{k=1}^{K} \mathbf{s}_k \qquad - E\mathbf{y} \leq \mathbf{b} \qquad (12.4)$$

$$\mathbf{y} \geq 0, \ \mathbf{x}_k \geq 0, \ \mathbf{s}_k \geq 0, \ \mathbf{x} \geq 0$$

for $k = 1, \ldots, K$. The first constraint (12.2) represents the technological relations of the kth firm. The individual entrepreneur must make decisions regarding the purchase of inputs $\mathbf{s}_k$ and the production of outputs $\mathbf{x}_k$ in a way to respect the physical equilibrium conditions according to which the kth firm's input demand $(A_k\mathbf{x}_k)$ must be less than or equal to its input supply $\mathbf{s}_k$.

Notice, therefore, that the quantity s_k is viewed both as a demand (when the entrepreneur faces the input market) and as a supply (when the entrepreneur faces his output opportunities, or input requirements, $(A_k x_k)$). The second constraint (12.3) represents the market clearing condition for the final commodity outputs. The total demand for final commodities x must be less than or equal to their total supply $\sum_{k=1}^{K} x_k$ as generated by the K firms. The third constraint (12.4) represents the market clearing condition for the commodity inputs. The total demand of inputs in the economy $\sum_{k=1}^{K} s_k$ must be less than or equal to the total (aggregate) input supply $(b + Ey)$.

The dual of model [(12.1) through (12.4)] is obtained as an application of KKT theory according to the familiar Lagrangean procedure. Let y_k, f, and y be the vectors of dual variables associated with the three primal constraints in [(12.2) through (12.4)] respectively. Then, the Lagrangean function of problem [(12.1) through (12.4)] is

$$L = c'x - \tfrac{1}{2}x'Dx - \tfrac{1}{2}y'Ey + \sum_{k=1}^{K} y_k'(s_k - A_k x_k) \tag{12.5}$$

$$+ f'\left(\sum_{k=1}^{K} x_k - x\right) + y'\left(b + Ey - \sum_{k=1}^{K} s_k\right).$$

Karush-Kuhn-Tucker conditions from (12.5) are the nonnegativity of all the variables involved ($y \geq 0$, $x_k \geq 0$, $s_k \geq 0$, $x \geq 0$) and

$$\frac{\partial L}{\partial x_k} = -A_k' y_k + f \leq 0 \tag{12.6}$$

$$\sum_{k=1}^{K} x_k' \frac{\partial L}{\partial x_k} = -\sum_{k=1}^{K} x_k' A_k' y_k + \sum_{k=1}^{K} x_k' f = 0 \tag{12.7}$$

$$\frac{\partial L}{\partial x} = c - Dx - f \leq 0 \tag{12.8}$$

$$x' \frac{\partial L}{\partial x} = x'c - x'Dx - x'f = 0 \tag{12.9}$$

$$\frac{\partial L}{\partial s_k} = y_k - y \leq 0 \tag{12.10}$$

$$\sum_{k=1}^{K} s_k' \frac{\partial L}{\partial s_k} = \sum_{k=1}^{K} s_k' y_k - \sum_{k=1}^{K} s_k' y = 0 \tag{12.11}$$

$$\frac{\partial L}{\partial y} = -Ey + b + 2Ey - \sum_{k=1}^{K} s_k \geq 0 \tag{12.12}$$

$$= \mathbf{b} + E\mathbf{y} - \sum_{k=1}^{K} \mathbf{s}_k \geq 0$$

$$\mathbf{y}' \frac{\partial L}{\partial \mathbf{y}} = \mathbf{y}'\mathbf{b} + \mathbf{y}'E\mathbf{y} - \mathbf{y}' \sum_{k=1}^{K} \mathbf{s}_k = 0. \tag{12.13}$$

The derivatives with respect to dual variables $\mathbf{y}_k$ and $\mathbf{f}$ were omitted because of their simplicity and the fact that they do not contribute to the definition of the dual constraints. Relations (12.6), (12.8), and (12.10) are the constraints of the dual problem associated to the primal problem [(12.1) through (12.4)]. Using (12.7), (12.9), and (12.11) in the Lagrangean function (12.5), it is possible to simplify the dual objective function in such a way that the dual problem in its final form reads as

Dual

$$\min C\,OA = \mathbf{b}'\mathbf{y} + \tfrac{1}{2}\mathbf{y}'E\mathbf{y} + \tfrac{1}{2}\mathbf{x}'D\mathbf{x} \tag{12.14}$$

$$\text{subject to} \qquad A_k'\mathbf{y}_k - \mathbf{f} \qquad\qquad \geq 0 \tag{12.15}$$

$$-\mathbf{y}_k \qquad + \mathbf{y} \qquad \geq 0 \tag{12.16}$$

$$\mathbf{f} \quad + D\mathbf{x} \geq \mathbf{c} \tag{12.17}$$

$$\mathbf{y} \geq 0, \ \mathbf{y}_k \geq 0, \ \mathbf{f} \geq 0, \ \mathbf{x} \geq 0.$$

The objective function of the dual problem states that the market as a whole minimizes the cost of achieving an optimal allocation ($C\,OA$). The dual objective function consists of two components identified with the consumer and producer surpluses, as shown in Figure 12.1. It would be inappropriate, however, to interpret the dual objective function as minimizing the sum of the consumer and producer surpluses. From the point of view of producers and consumers, these measures should be clearly maximized. A more suitable interpretation of the dual objective function, therefore, is that of an abstract general planner (or invisible hand) whose objective is to minimize the expenditure necessary to make the market economy operate as a competitive institution. In order to entice producers and consumers toward a general equilibrium as articulated by the primal constraints, it is necessary to quote prices of inputs ($\mathbf{y}$, $\mathbf{y}_k$, $\mathbf{f}$) and of outputs ($\mathbf{p} = \mathbf{c} - D\mathbf{x}$) such that, at the optimal solution of [(12.1) through (12.4)] and [(12.14) through (12.17)], the two objective functions are equal and, thus, the optimal level of expenditure is equal to the optimal level of producer and consumer surpluses.

The first set of dual constraints in (12.15) states that the marginal cost of each firm $(A'_k y_k)$ must be greater than or equal to an overall marginal cost for the entire economy, $\mathbf{f}$. Assuming that, at the optimum, every firm produces some positive level of output, the first dual constraint (12.15) is equivalent to saying that every firm must exhibit the same marginal activity cost. The third set of dual constraints (12.17) links this marginal cost to the output prices $(\mathbf{p} = \mathbf{c} - D\mathbf{x})$. Economic equilibrium requires that output prices be less than or equal to output marginal cost. Finally, the second set of dual constraints (12.16) asserts that the valuation of resources at the firm level, y_k, cannot exceed the marginal value of the same resources at the economy level.

Model 1 can be reformulated as a linear complementarity problem by following the usual procedure, which requires the simultaneous consideration of all the KKT conditions. The structure of the LC problem, therefore, can be stated as

$$
M =
\begin{array}{c}
(\ \mathbf{x} \quad \ \mathbf{x}_k \quad \ \mathbf{s}_k \quad \ \mathbf{y}_k \quad \ \mathbf{f} \quad \ \mathbf{y} \ ) \\
\begin{bmatrix}
D & 0 & 0 & 0 & I & 0 \\
0 & 0 & 0 & A'_k & -I & 0 \\
0 & 0 & 0 & -I & 0 & I \\
0 & -A_k & I & 0 & 0 & 0 \\
-I & I & 0 & 0 & 0 & 0 \\
0 & 0 & -I & 0 & 0 & E
\end{bmatrix}
\end{array}
, \quad
\mathbf{q} =
\begin{bmatrix}
-\mathbf{c} \\
0 \\
0 \\
0 \\
0 \\
\mathbf{b}
\end{bmatrix}
, \quad
\mathbf{z} =
\begin{bmatrix}
\mathbf{x} \\
\mathbf{x}_k \\
\mathbf{s}_k \\
\mathbf{y}_k \\
\mathbf{f} \\
\mathbf{y}
\end{bmatrix}
$$

where $k = 1, \ldots, K$. The vector variables carrying the k subscript must be thought of as a series of K vectors associated with a similar number of matrices that have been omitted from the foregoing LC specification simply for reasons of space.

Model 2: Intermediate and Final Commodities

In model 1, the supply functions of resources $(\mathbf{b} + E\mathbf{y})$ are exogenous and bear no direct relation with either consumers or producers operating in that economy. Toward a fuller understanding of the structure of model 1, it is possible to interpret the vector $\mathbf{b}$ as the aggregate vector of resource endowments belonging to the economic agents, mainly consumers, operating in that scenario. More difficult is to explain how the other component of the input supply functions, $(E\mathbf{y})$, is generated. The discussion in this second model, therefore, is centered on a justification of the entire supply function for inputs.

Let the aggregate supply of resources in a given economy be the sum of initial endowments of resources belonging to consumers and of the additional amount of the same resources developed by firms operating in the economy. Let $\mathbf{b}_C$ represent the sum of all endowment vectors of resources belonging to consumers. In this model, the kth firm is allowed to produce either final commodities $\mathbf{x}_k$ or intermediate commodities (inputs) $\mathbf{v}_k$, or both. The firm's incentive to expand the supply of resources is given by a profitable level of input prices, which she takes as given. As for prices of final commodities, input prices are generated at the endogenous market level. We postulate, therefore, that the aggregate supply of inputs over and above the initial consumers' endowments is represented by $(\mathbf{b}_V + E\mathbf{y})$.

The mathematical programming specification of this scenario corresponds to a further elaboration of model 1 and is stated as follows:

Primal

$$\max\,(CS + PS) = \mathbf{c}'\mathbf{x} - \tfrac{1}{2}\mathbf{x}'D\mathbf{x} - \tfrac{1}{2}\mathbf{y}'E\mathbf{y} \qquad (12.18)$$

$$\text{subject to} \qquad A_k\mathbf{x}_k + B_k\mathbf{v}_k \quad - \mathbf{s}_k \qquad\qquad \leq \mathbf{0} \qquad (12.19)$$

$$-\sum_{k=1}^{K}\mathbf{x}_k \qquad\qquad + \mathbf{x} \qquad \leq \mathbf{0} \qquad (12.20)$$

$$\sum_{k=1}^{K}\mathbf{v}_k \qquad - E\mathbf{y} \leq \mathbf{b}_V \qquad (12.21)$$

$$-\sum_{k=1}^{K}\mathbf{v}_k + \sum_{k=1}^{K}\mathbf{s}_k \qquad\qquad \leq \mathbf{b}_C \qquad (12.22)$$

$$\mathbf{y} \geq \mathbf{0},\ \mathbf{x}_k \geq \mathbf{0},\ \mathbf{v}_k \geq \mathbf{0},\ \mathbf{s}_k \geq \mathbf{0},\ \mathbf{x} \geq \mathbf{0}$$

for $k = 1, \ldots, K$. The interpretation of this primal version of the model builds on the explanation offered for the various components of model 1. The objective function, thus, corresponds to the maximization of the consumer and producer surpluses. The first set of constraints in (12.19) articulates the assumption that any firm may produce either final or intermediate commodities, or both. The second set of constraints (12.20) describes the market clearing condition (demand, $\mathbf{x}$, is less than or equal to supply, $\sum_{k=1}^{K}\mathbf{x}_k$) for final commodities. The third set of constraints (12.21) defines the endogenous vector of input supply functions $(\mathbf{b}_V + E\mathbf{y})$ as the sum of input vectors $\mathbf{v}_k$ produced by all firms. The presence of an intercept such as $\mathbf{b}_V$ is justified by assuming that these functions also depend on other factors not accounted for in the model. The fourth set of constraints (12.22) represents the market clearing condition for inputs ($\sum_{k=1}^{K} \mathbf{s}_k \leq \mathbf{b}_C + \sum_{k=1}^{K} \mathbf{v}_k \leq [\mathbf{b}_C + \mathbf{b}_V] + E\mathbf{y}$).

The dual of [(12.18) through (12.22)] is obtained by applying KKT procedures. Let ($\mathbf{y}_k$, $\mathbf{f}$, $\mathbf{y}$) and $\mathbf{r}$ be the vectors of dual variables associated with the primal constraints [(12.19) through (12.22)], respectively. Then, the dual problem of [(12.18) through (12.22)] is

Dual

$$\min COA = \mathbf{b}_C' \mathbf{r} + \mathbf{b}_V' \mathbf{y} + \tfrac{1}{2} \mathbf{y}' E \mathbf{y} + \tfrac{1}{2} \mathbf{x}' D \mathbf{x} \qquad (12.23)$$

$$\text{subject to} \qquad \mathbf{f} \quad + D\mathbf{x} \geq \mathbf{c} \qquad (12.24)$$

$$A_k' \mathbf{y}_k - \mathbf{f} \qquad \geq \mathbf{0} \qquad (12.25)$$

$$-\mathbf{y}_k \qquad + \mathbf{r} \geq \mathbf{0} \qquad (12.26)$$

$$B_k' \mathbf{y}_k + \mathbf{y} - \mathbf{r} \geq \mathbf{0} \qquad (12.27)$$

$$\mathbf{y} \geq \mathbf{0}, \ \mathbf{y}_k \geq \mathbf{0}, \ \mathbf{f} \geq \mathbf{0}, \ \mathbf{x} \geq \mathbf{0}, \ \mathbf{r} \geq \mathbf{0}.$$

The economic interpretation of the dual specification begins with recognizing that the dual objective function minimizes the cost of achieving an optimal allocation. The terms in vectors $\mathbf{y}$ and $\mathbf{r}$ constitute the producer surplus whereas the quadratic form in $\mathbf{x}$ is the consumer surplus. The first set of constraints (12.24) establishes the familiar economic equilibrium conditions according to which marginal cost of final commodities must be greater than or equal to their market price, ($\mathbf{p} = \mathbf{c} - D\mathbf{x}$). The second set of dual constraints (12.25) asserts that the marginal cost of producing final commodities in any firm must be at least as great as the corresponding marginal cost for the entire economy. The third set of dual constraints (12.26) establishes that the value marginal product of the kth firm cannot be greater than the rent ($\mathbf{r}$) derived from the ownership of the initial endowment of resources. Finally, the fourth set of constraints (12.27) states that the marginal cost of producing intermediate commodities must be greater than or equal to ($\mathbf{r} - \mathbf{y}$), the difference between the marginal valuation of the initial endowment of resources and the shadow price of the resources developed by the firms. An alternative interpretation would be that ($\mathbf{r} \leq B_k' \mathbf{y}_k + \mathbf{y}$), that is, the rent ($\mathbf{r}$) derived from the ownership of the initial endowment of resources must not be greater than the combined marginal cost of producing additional intermediate commodities and the shadow price commanded by these resources in the economy. The rent on the initial endowment of resources, therefore, is bracketed by the value marginal product of any firm $\mathbf{y}_k$ (which forms a lower bound) and the marginal cost of producing additional resources (which forms an upper bound) as follows ($\mathbf{y}_k \le \mathbf{r} \le B'_k\mathbf{y}_k + \mathbf{y}$).

The structure of the linear complementarity problem corresponding to problems (12.18) and (12.23) can be stated as

$$
M = \begin{array}{c} (\;\mathbf{x} \quad \mathbf{x}_k \quad \mathbf{v}_k \quad \mathbf{s}_k \quad \mathbf{y}_k \quad \mathbf{f} \quad \mathbf{y} \quad \mathbf{r}\;) \\ \begin{bmatrix} D & 0 & 0 & 0 & 0 & I & 0 & 0 \\ 0 & 0 & 0 & 0 & A'_k & -I & 0 & 0 \\ 0 & 0 & 0 & 0 & B'_k & 0 & I & -I \\ 0 & 0 & 0 & 0 & -I & 0 & 0 & I \\ 0 & -A_k & -B_k & I & 0 & 0 & 0 & 0 \\ -I & I & 0 & 0 & 0 & 0 & 0 & 0 \\ 0 & 0 & -I & 0 & 0 & 0 & E & 0 \\ 0 & 0 & I & -I & 0 & 0 & 0 & 0 \end{bmatrix} \end{array}, \quad \mathbf{q} = \begin{bmatrix} -\mathbf{c} \\ 0 \\ 0 \\ 0 \\ 0 \\ 0 \\ \mathbf{b}_V \\ \mathbf{b}_C \end{bmatrix}, \quad \mathbf{z} = \begin{bmatrix} \mathbf{x} \\ \mathbf{x}_k \\ \mathbf{v}_k \\ \mathbf{s}_k \\ \mathbf{y}_k \\ \mathbf{f} \\ \mathbf{y} \\ \mathbf{r} \end{bmatrix}
$$

where $k = 1, \ldots, K$. As for the previous model, the subscript k indicates a series of components of the same nature for $k = 1, \ldots, K$.

Model 3: Endogenous Income

A complete general equilibrium model requires the specification of a process for the endogenous determination of consumers' income. Models 1 and 2 are deficient with respect to this important aspect. Suppose, therefore, that consumers' demand functions are respecified to include aggregate income I in an explicit way, that is, $\mathbf{p} = \mathbf{c} - D\mathbf{x} + \mathbf{g}I$, where $\mathbf{g}$ is an n-vector of income coefficients. Aggregate consumer income is assumed to be the sum of individual incomes, which, in turn, is generated as the rental value of resource endowments, that is, $I = \mathbf{b}'_C\mathbf{r}$, where $\mathbf{r}$ is the vector of rental prices for the consumers' endowments. In the process so specified, we assume that the associated aggregation problems are solved consistently.

It turns out that the consideration of endogenous income, as defined earlier, precludes the formulation of a dual pair of symmetric quadratic programming models. In other words, it is no longer possible to define primal and dual optimization problems that constitute a symmetric structure. The reason for this unexpected result can be articulated in several alternative explanations. The principal cause of the problem uncovered is the fact that income enters a general equilibrium model in an asymmetric way, as a determinant of consumers' demands but not of input supplies. A subordinate reason is that knowledge of the rental value of resources is required for defining income. This fact necessitates the simultaneous consideration of primal and dual constraints.

The impossibility of formulating this general equilibrium scenario as a pair of optimization models does not preclude its formulation as an equilibrium problem. The linear complementarity model is, thus, the natural framework for dealing with the problem of general equilibrium with endogenous income. The explicit statement of the LC model corresponding to this economic scenario will contribute a further clarification of the asymmetry uncovered in this section.

The formulation of endogenous income developed previously suggests that the difference between model 2 and model 3 consists of two elements: the expansion of the demand function for final commodities to include aggregate income, I, explicitly, $\mathbf{p} = \mathbf{c} - D\mathbf{x} + \mathbf{g}I$, and the definition of aggregate income $I = \mathbf{b}'_C \mathbf{r}$.

The relations that define the relevant equilibrium problem for this scenario are those of model 2 incremented by the income distribution:

$$
\begin{aligned}
D\mathbf{x} - \mathbf{g}I + \mathbf{f} &\geq \mathbf{c} &&\text{final commodity pricing} &&(12.28)\\
A'_k\mathbf{y}_k - \mathbf{f} &\geq \mathbf{0} &&\text{final commodity marginal cost}\\
B'_k\mathbf{y}_k + \mathbf{y} - \mathbf{r} &\geq \mathbf{0} &&\text{intermediate commodity marginal cost}\\
-\mathbf{y}_k + \mathbf{r} &\geq \mathbf{0} &&\text{resource valuation}\\
I - \mathbf{b}'_C\mathbf{r} &= 0 &&\text{aggregate income}\\
A_k\mathbf{x}_k + B_k\mathbf{v}_k - \mathbf{s}_k &\leq \mathbf{0} &&\text{technology constraints}\\
-\sum_{k=1}^{K}\mathbf{x}_k + \mathbf{x} &\leq \mathbf{0} &&\text{final commodity market clearing}\\
\sum_{k=1}^{K}\mathbf{v}_k - E\mathbf{y} &\leq \mathbf{b}_V &&\text{input supply function from firms}\\
-\sum_{k=1}^{K}\mathbf{v}_k + \sum_{k=1}^{K}\mathbf{s}_k &\leq \mathbf{b}_C &&\text{total input supply function}
\end{aligned}
$$

$\mathbf{x} \geq \mathbf{0}$, $\mathbf{x}_k \geq \mathbf{0}$, $\mathbf{v}_k \geq \mathbf{0}$, $\mathbf{s}_k \geq \mathbf{0}$, $I \geq 0$, $\mathbf{y}_k \geq \mathbf{0}$, $\mathbf{f} \geq \mathbf{0}$, $\mathbf{y}$ free, $\mathbf{r} \geq \mathbf{0}$.

The equilibrium problem is defined by the relations stated in (12.28) and the associated complementary slackness relations. The variables that multiply the relations in (12.28) to form the required complementary slackness conditions are stated in the appropriate order in the bottom line of (12.28). For the benefit of the reader, we recall that a linear complementarity problem is defined as a vector $\mathbf{z} \geq \mathbf{0}$ such that $M\mathbf{z} + \mathbf{q} \geq \mathbf{0}$ and $\mathbf{z}'M\mathbf{z} + \mathbf{z}'\mathbf{q} = \mathbf{0}$.

The structure of the linear complementarity problem associated with the equilibrium problem stated in (12.28) (and the associated complementary slackness conditions) corresponds to the following representation (symbol I in the M matrix represents the identity matrix):

$$
M = \begin{array}{c}
\begin{array}{ccccccccc} (\mathbf{x} & \mathbf{x}_k & \mathbf{v}_k & \mathbf{s}_k & I & \mathbf{y}_k & \mathbf{f} & \mathbf{y} & \mathbf{r}) \end{array} \\
\begin{bmatrix}
D & 0 & 0 & 0 & -\mathbf{g} & 0 & I & 0 & 0 \\
0 & 0 & 0 & 0 & 0 & A_k' & -I & 0 & 0 \\
0 & 0 & 0 & 0 & 0 & B_k' & 0 & I & -I \\
0 & 0 & 0 & 0 & 0 & -I & 0 & 0 & I \\
0^* & 0 & 0 & 0 & 1 & 0 & 0 & 0 & -\mathbf{b}_C' \\
0 & -A_k & -B_k & I & 0 & 0 & 0 & 0 & 0 \\
-I & I & 0 & 0 & 0 & 0 & 0 & 0 & 0 \\
0 & 0 & -I & 0 & 0 & 0 & 0 & E & 0 \\
0 & 0 & I & -I & 0^* & 0 & 0 & 0 & 0
\end{bmatrix},
\end{array}
\quad
\mathbf{q} = \begin{bmatrix} -\mathbf{c} \\ 0 \\ 0 \\ 0 \\ 0 \\ 0 \\ 0 \\ \mathbf{b}_V \\ \mathbf{b}_C \end{bmatrix},
\quad
\mathbf{z} = \begin{bmatrix} \mathbf{x} \\ \mathbf{x}_k \\ \mathbf{v}_k \\ \mathbf{s}_k \\ I \\ \mathbf{y}_k \\ \mathbf{f} \\ \mathbf{y} \\ \mathbf{r} \end{bmatrix}
$$

where $k = 1, \ldots, K$. The matrix M is not antisymmetric as are the corresponding LC matrices of models 1 and 2. The zero elements with an asterisk as superscript in the matrix M indicate the location of the missing terms that would make the matrix M antisymmetric and, therefore, suitable for expressing the problem as a dual pair of optimization models.

In the preceding specification, we glossed over a rather important property of consumers' demand functions, namely the fact that inverse demand functions satisfy the budget constraint: $\mathbf{x}'\mathbf{p}(\mathbf{x}, I) = I$. When applied to the linear demand functions specified earlier, this property implies the following conditions: $\mathbf{x}'\mathbf{p}(\mathbf{x}, I) = \mathbf{x}'\mathbf{c} - \mathbf{x}'D\mathbf{x} + \mathbf{x}'\mathbf{g}I = I$ and, therefore, $\mathbf{x}'\mathbf{g} = 1$ while $\mathbf{x}'\mathbf{c} - \mathbf{x}'D\mathbf{x} = 0$. The imposition of these two additional constraints can be performed in alternative ways.

Model 4: Spatial Equilibrium – One Commodity

The solution of a competitive equilibrium among spatially separated markets, in the case of linear demand and supply functions, was originally suggested by Enke (1951) using an electric analogue. Samuelson (1952) riformulated the problem in a linear programming model that minimizes the total transportation cost of the commodity flow among regions. Takayama and Judge (1964) reformulated the problem in a quadratic programming specification. Over the years, this problem has received much scrutiny with many empirical applications dealing with international trade issues.

In a stylized formulation, the problem of finding the competitive equilibrium involving one homogeneous commodity that is traded among many separated markets can be stated as follows. Assume R regions that represent

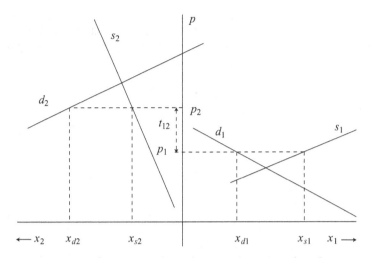

Figure 12.3. Competitive solution between two separated markets.

separated markets. For each region, the demand and the supply functions of a given commodity are given. Furthermore, the unit cost of transporting the commodity over all the routes connecting the R markets is also given. A competitive solution of this problem is constituted by the list of prices and quantities of the given commodity that are supplied and consumed in each market and the associated commodity flow among all the markets so that consumer and producer surpluses are maximized.

The competitive solution dealing with two markets is illustrated in the back-to-back diagram of Figure 12.3. In region 1, the given commodity is produced (supplied) in quantity x_{s1} but is consumed (demanded) in quantity x_{d1}. In region 2, the commodity is produced in quantity x_{s2} and consumed in quantity x_{d2}. To clear the markets, therefore, the excess supply $(x_{s1} - x_{d1})$ from region 1 will be shipped to region 2 in order to satisfy the excess demand $(x_{d2} - x_{s2})$. This event will happen at prices $p_2 = p_1 + t_{12}$, where t_{12} is the unit cost of transportation from region 1 to region 2. The consumer surplus of region 1 is the area under the demand function and above the price line. The producer surplus of market 1 is the area above the supply function and under the price line. Analogous inference can be made for market 2.

Before discussing a more general specification of spatial market equilibrium, we present the associated transportation problem, as analyzed by Samuelson. We assume that there are R regions endowed of a given quantity (availability, supply) of a commodity $\bar{x}_r^s$, $r = 1, \ldots, R$, and requesting a given quantity (demand) $\bar{x}_r^d$ for the same commodity. Furthermore, the available information regards the unit trasportation cost, $t_{r,r'}$, r, $r' = 1, \ldots, R$, over all the possible routes connecting any pair of regions. For $r = r'$, the unit transportation cost is, obviously, $t_{r,r} = 0$.

The problem is to satisfy the demand of each region while minimizing the total cost of transportation (total transaction costs) over all routes. This is a linear programming problem with two sets of constraints. The first set defines the requirement of supplying a given region with the quantity demanded. The second set guarantees the feasibility of that operation by preventing the supply schedule of each region from exceeding the available endowment. Indicating by $x_{r,r'}$ the nonnegative commodity flow between regions r and r', the resulting primal specification of the transportation problem is the minimization of the total transportation cost (TTC) subject to the given constraints, that is,

Primal

$$\min TTC = \sum_r \sum_{r'} t_{r,r'} x_{r,r'} \tag{12.29}$$

subject to

$$\sum_r x_{r,r'} \geq \bar{x}_{r'}^d \qquad \text{demand requirement} \tag{12.30}$$

$$\bar{x}_r^s \geq \sum_{r'} x_{r,r'} \qquad \text{supply availability.} \tag{12.31}$$

The dual specification of problem (12.29) through (12.31) can be stated as the maximization of the value added for the entire set of regions, that is,

Dual

$$\max VA = \sum_{r'} \bar{x}_{r'}^d p_{r'}^d - \sum_r \bar{x}_r^s p_r^s \tag{12.32}$$

subject to

$$p_{r'}^d \leq p_r^s + t_{r,r'}. \tag{12.33}$$

The dual problem, then, consists in finding nonnegative prices $p_{r'}^d$ and p_r^s, for each region, that maximize the value added (VA), that is, the difference between the total value of the commodity at all destination markets minus the total cost of the same commodity at all the supplying markets. The decision variables are the prices at the demand destinations, $p_{r'}^d$, and at the supply origins, p_r^s, r, $r' = 1, \ldots, R$. The economic interpretation of the dual, then, can be restated as follows: Suppose that a condition for winning the transport job requires purchasing the commodity at the supply markets (origins) and selling it at the various destinations (demand markets). A trucking firm, wishing to bid for the contract to transport the commodity flow over the entire network of regional routes, will wish to quote prices at destination markets and at supply origins that will maximize its value added. The dual constraint (12.33) states that the price of the commodity on the r'th demand market cannot exceed the price in the rth supply region augmented by the unit transportation cost between the two locations, $t_{r,r'}$ (marginal revenue $\leq$ marginal cost).

Notice that, in general, a transportation problem has multiple optimal solutions. That is, there are multiple networks of routes that satisfy the demand requirements of the various regions while achieving the same value of the total transportation cost. The reason is that the $(R \times R)$ matrix of flows, $X = [x_{r,r'}]$, has rank less than R, and the likelihood that, for some routes, the corresponding dual variable is degenerate.

Let us now formulate the spatial equilibrium problem in a more general specification. Instead of a fixed demand requirement and supply availability, as in the LP problem [(12.29) through (12.31)], each region is endowed with an inverse demand function, $p_r^d = a_r - D_r x_r^d$, and an inverse supply function for the same homogeneous commodity, $p_r^s = b_r + S_r x_r^s, r = 1, \ldots, R$. The parameters a_r, D_r, S_r are positive and known scalars. Parameter b_r can be either positive or negative. Therefore, the quantities x_r^d and x_r^s must now be determined as part of the equilibrium solution. This objective can be achieved by maximizing the sum of consumers' and producers' surpluses, CS and PS, in all markets, netted out of the total transportation cost, as illustrated in Figure 12.3. The analytical task is represented by the following quadratic programming problem, which is a direct extension of the LP problem discussed earlier.

Primal

$$\max N(CS + PS) = \sum_{r'} \left(a_{r'} - \tfrac{1}{2} D_r x_{r'}^d \right) x_{r'}^d - \sum_{r} \left(b_r + \tfrac{1}{2} S_r x_r^s \right) x_r^s$$

$$- \sum_{r} \sum_{r'} t_{r,r'} x_{r,r'} \qquad (12.34)$$

subject to $\qquad x_{r'}^d \leq \sum_{r} x_{r,r'} \quad$ demand requirement $\qquad (12.35)$

$$\sum_{r'} x_{r,r'} \leq x_r^s \qquad \text{supply availability.} \qquad (12.36)$$

A solution of the spatial equilibrium problem [(12.34) through (12.36)], which is regarded as a quantity formulation, is given by optimal values of all the primal decision variables (x_r^d, x_r^s, $x_{r,r'}$) and by the optimal values of the dual variables ($p_{r'}^d$, p_r^s), for $r, r' = 1, \ldots, R$.

The dual of problem [(12.34) through (12.36)] involves both primal and dual variables, as seen in all the quadratic programming problems discussed in previous chapters. However, in analogy to the demand and supply quantity-extension of the primal LP problem [(12.29) through (12.31)], we wish to define the demand and supply price-extension of the dual LP problem [(12.32), (12.33)]. To obtain this specification, it is sufficient to express the demand quantity $x_{r'}^d$ and the supply quantity x_r^s in terms of the respective prices. In other words, given the assumptions of the model, it is possible to invert the (inverse) demand and supply functions to obtain the desired information. Hence,

$$x_r^d = D^{-1}a_r - D_r^{-1}p_r^d = c_r - D_r^{-1}p_r^d \quad \text{demand function} \quad (12.37)$$

$$x_r^s = -S^{-1}b_r + S_r^{-1}p_r^s = h_r + S_r^{-1}p_r^s \quad \text{supply function.} \quad (12.38)$$

Replacing $x_{r'}^d p_{r'}^d$ and $x_r^s p_r^s$ (by appropriate integration) into the objective function of the dual LP of the transportation problem [(12.32), (12.33)], we obtain the "purified" dual of the spatial equilibrium problem [(12.34) through (12.36)], that is,

"Purified" Dual

$$\max VA = \sum_r \left(c_r - \tfrac{1}{2}D_r^{-1}p_r^d \right) p_r^d - \sum_r \left(h_r + \tfrac{1}{2}S_r^{-1}p_r^s \right) p_r^s \quad (12.39)$$

subject to $$p_{r'}^d \leq p_r^s + t_{r,r'}. \quad (12.40)$$

The terminology "purified duality" is due to Takayama and Woodland (1970). The solution of the "purified" dual problem provides the same solution of the primal problem in terms of prices p_r^d, p_r^s and quantities x_r^d, x_r^s. The quantity flow of commodities $x_{r,r'}$ obtained from the primal problem, however, may represent an alternative optimal solution to the flow obtained (as dual variables) from the "purified" dual problem. This is due to the way algorithmic codes for QP problems are written for computer applications and the initial values of the variables involved. It would be ideal to have solvers enumerate all the basic multiple optimal solutions but, to this day, this result is not attainable given the commercially availabe computer packages for solving nonlinear programming problems. A detailed discussion of this spatial equilibrium model is given in Appendix 12.2.

Model 5: Spatial Equilibrium – Many Commodities

Suppose that each region deals with M commodities. The extension of the spatial equilibrium model to this case is straightforward: it simply requires the inclusion of the commodity index $m = 1, \ldots, M$ into the primal and the "purified" dual models discussed in the previous section. Hence,

Primal

$$\max N(CS + PS) = \sum_{m,r'} \left(a_{m,r'} - \tfrac{1}{2} D_{m,r} x^d_{m,r'} \right) x^d_{m,r'}$$

$$- \sum_{m,r} \left(b_{m,r} + \tfrac{1}{2} S_{m,r} x^s_{m,r} \right) x^s_{m,r}$$

$$- \sum_{m,r} \sum_{m,r'} t_{m,r,r'} x_{m,r,r'} \tag{12.41}$$

subject to $\quad x^d_{m,r'} \leq \sum_{m,r} x_{m,r,r'} \quad$ demand requirement $\tag{12.42}$

$$\sum_{m,r'} x_{m,r,r'} \leq x^s_{m,r} \qquad \text{supply availability.} \tag{12.43}$$

Similarly,

"Purified" Dual

$$\max VA = \sum_{m,r'} \left(c_{m,r'} - \tfrac{1}{2} D^{-1}_{m,r'} p^d_{m,r'} \right) p^d_{m,r'}$$

$$- \sum_{m,r} \left(h_{m,r} + \tfrac{1}{2} S^{-1}_{m,r} p^s_{m,r} \right) p^s_{m,r} \tag{12.44}$$

subject to $\quad p^d_{m,r'} \leq p^s_{m,r} + t_{m,r,r'}. \tag{12.45}$

The possibility of multiple optimal solutions for the flow of commodities among regions, $x_{m,r,r'}$, also applies for this spatial equilibrium specification. It is possible also to conceive that the demand and supply functions of each commodity and each region may involve all the commodities in that region. In this case, the D and S parameters of the inverse demand and supply function stated earlier should be considered as symmetric positive definite matrices. Then, the analytical development just presented also applies to this more general scenario.

Numerical Example 1: General Market Equilibrium
Final Commodities

Example 1 deals with a scenario of general market equilibrium involving only final commodities and the allocation of resources among firms. This is the problem discussed in model [(12.1) through (12.4)], which is reproduced here for convenience:

Primal

$$\max (CS + PS) = \mathbf{c}'\mathbf{x} - \tfrac{1}{2}\mathbf{x}'D\mathbf{x} - \tfrac{1}{2}\mathbf{y}'E\mathbf{y} \tag{12.1}$$

$$\text{subject to} \qquad A_k\mathbf{x}_k - \mathbf{s}_k \qquad\qquad \le 0 \tag{12.2}$$

$$-\sum_{k=1}^{K}\mathbf{x}_k \qquad + \mathbf{x} \qquad \le 0 \tag{12.3}$$

$$\sum_{k=1}^{K}\mathbf{s}_k \qquad - E\mathbf{y} \le \mathbf{b} \tag{12.4}$$

$$\mathbf{y} \ge 0, \ \mathbf{x}_k \ge 0, \ \mathbf{s}_k \ge 0, \ \mathbf{x} \ge 0.$$

The relevant data are given as:

Technology of firm 1: $\quad A_1 = \begin{bmatrix} 2.5 & -2.0 & 0.5 & 1.0 \\ 1.0 & 3.0 & -2.1 & 3.0 \\ -2.0 & 1.0 & 0.5 & 0.9 \end{bmatrix}$

Technology of firm 2: $\quad A_2 = \begin{bmatrix} 1.0 & -1.0 & 0.5 & 0.3 \\ 0.5 & 3.0 & 2.0 & 0.3 \\ 2.0 & 1.0 & 0.2 & 9.0 \end{bmatrix}$

Technology of firm 3: $\quad A_3 = \begin{bmatrix} 0.7 & -1.0 & 5 & 2.0 \\ 1.0 & 3.0 & 4 & 1.0 \\ -0.5 & 1.0 & 6 & 0.6 \end{bmatrix}$

Market demands: $\quad \mathbf{c} = \begin{bmatrix} 23 \\ 40 \\ 34 \\ 30 \end{bmatrix}, \quad D = \begin{bmatrix} 8 & -5 & 4 & -3 \\ -5 & 7 & 3 & 3 \\ 4 & 3 & 5 & -2 \\ -3 & 3 & -2 & 4 \end{bmatrix}$

Total input supply: $\quad \mathbf{b} = \begin{bmatrix} 10 \\ 24 \\ 8 \end{bmatrix}, \quad E = \begin{bmatrix} 1.3 & -0.4 & 0.2 \\ -0.4 & 0.8 & -0.3 \\ 0.2 & -0.3 & 0.4 \end{bmatrix}.$

The GAMS solution of this problem is given for each firm, for the final commodity market as a whole, and for the total input supply.

$$\text{Consumer surplus} = 201.6512$$
$$\text{Producer surplus} = 148.3685$$
$$\text{Total surplus} = 350.0197$$
$$\text{Total cost of resources} = 179.9459$$

Demand and prices for final commodity market

$$\mathbf{x} = \begin{bmatrix} x_1 = 6.4941 \\ x_2 = 4.9629 \\ x_3 = 1.4109 \\ x_4 = 6.9597 \end{bmatrix}, \quad \mathbf{p} = \begin{bmatrix} p_1 = 11.0976 \\ p_2 = 12.6181 \\ p_3 = 0.0000 \\ p_4 = 9.5763 \end{bmatrix}$$

Outputs and inputs from firm 1

$$\mathbf{x}_1 = \begin{bmatrix} x_{11} = 0.4010 \\ x_{21} = 0.8539 \\ x_{31} = 1.4109 \\ x_{41} = 0.0000 \end{bmatrix}, \quad \mathbf{s}_1 = \begin{bmatrix} s_{11} = 0.0000 \\ s_{21} = 0.0000 \\ s_{31} = 0.7574 \end{bmatrix}$$

Outputs and inputs from firm 2

$$\mathbf{x}_2 = \begin{bmatrix} x_{12} = 0.0000 \\ x_{22} = 0.0735 \\ x_{32} = 0.0000 \\ x_{42} = 0.2449 \end{bmatrix}, \quad \mathbf{s}_2 = \begin{bmatrix} s_{12} = 0.0000 \\ s_{22} = 0.2939 \\ s_{32} = 2.2774 \end{bmatrix}$$

Outputs and inputs from firm 3

$$\mathbf{x}_3 = \begin{bmatrix} x_{13} = 6.0931 \\ x_{23} = 4.0355 \\ x_{33} = 0.0000 \\ x_{43} = 6.7149 \end{bmatrix}, \quad \mathbf{s}_3 = \begin{bmatrix} s_{13} = 13.6594 \\ s_{23} = 24.9145 \\ s_{33} = 5.0179 \end{bmatrix}$$

Quantity and shadow prices of total input supply

$$\mathbf{s} = \begin{bmatrix} s_1 = 13.6594 \\ s_2 = 25.2034 \\ s_3 = 8.0527 \end{bmatrix}, \quad \mathbf{y} = \begin{bmatrix} y_1 = 3.8262 \\ y_2 = 3.8337 \\ y_3 = 1.0938 \end{bmatrix}.$$

GAMS Command File: Numerical Example 1

We list a command file for the nonlinear package GAMS that solves the numerical problem presented in Example 1. Asterisks in column 1 relate to comments.

```
$title a general market equilibrium: three firms and
* one market
* with symmetric d and e matrices - sqp
*
$offsymlist offsymxref
    option limrow = 0
    option limcol = 0
    option iterlim = 100000
    option reslim = 200000
    option nlp = conopt3
    option decimals = 7 ;
*
    sets   j  output variables / x1, x2, x3, x4 /
            i   inputs / y1, y2, y3 /
*
    alias(i,k,kk);
    alias(j,jj) ;
*
    parameter c(j)    intercept of demand functions

    /  x1  23
       x2  40
       x3  34
       x4  30  /
*
    parameter b(i)    intercept of total input supply

    /  y1  10
       y2  24
       y3   8  /
*
    table a1(i,j)  technical coefficient matrix in
                      firm 1

             x1    x2     x3    x4
       y1    2.5   -2    0.5   1.0
       y2    1.0    3   -2.1   3.0
       y3   -2.0    1    0.5   0.9
*
    table a2(i,j)  technical coefficient matrix in
                      firm 2

            x1    x2    x3    x4
       y1   1.0   -1   0.5   0.3
       y2   0.5    3   2.0   0.3
       y3   2.0    1   0.2   9.0
```

```
*
    table a3(i,j)    technical coefficient matrix in
                     firm 3

          x1   x2   x3    x4
    y1    0.7  -1    5   2.0
    y2    1.0   3    4   1.0
    y3   -0.5   1    6   0.6
*
    table d(j,jj)  slopes of demand functions

          x1   x2   x3   x4
    x1     8   -5    4   -3
    x2    -5    7    3    3
    x3     4    3    5   -2
    x4    -3    3   -2    4
*
    table e(i,k)  slopes of the input supply function

          y1     y2     y3
    y1    1.3   -0.4    0.2
    y2   -0.4    0.8   -0.3
    y3    0.2   -0.3    0.4
*
    scalar scale  parameter to define economic
                  agents / .5 /;
*
* general equilibrium problem - final commodities
*
    variables
    csps  consumers and produces' surpluses
    s1(i)  input of firm 1 - demand/supply
    s2(i)  input of firm 2 - demand/supply
    s3(i)  input of firm 3 - demand/supply
    x1(j)  output of firm 1 - supply
    x2(j)  output of firm 2 - supply
    x3(j)  output of firm 3 - supply
    x(j)  output aggregate demand
    y(i)  input shadow prices ;
*
    positive variables s1, s2, s3, x1, x2, x3, x, y ;
*
    equations
```

```
    objeq   objective function equation
    techeq1(i)  technology constraints of firm 1
    techeq2(i)  technology constraints of firm 2
    techeq3(i)  technology constraints of firm 3
    mktequil(j)  output market clearing conditions
    inputsup(i)  input market clearing conditions
    peq(j)  positive price condition ;
*
    objeq.. csps =e= sum(j, c(j)*x(j) )
              - scale*sum((j,jj), x(j)*d(j,jj)*x(jj) )
              - scale*sum((i,k), y(i)*e(i,k)*y(k) ) ;
*
    techeq1(i)..    sum(j, a1(i,j)*x1(j)) =l= s1(i) ;
    techeq2(i)..    sum(j, a2(i,j)*x2(j)) =l= s2(i) ;
    techeq3(i)..    sum(j, a3(i,j)*x3(j)) =l= s3(i) ;
    mktequil(j)..   x1(j) + x2(j) + x3(j) =e= x(j) ;
    inputsup(i)..   s1(i) + s2(i) +s3(i) =l= b(i) +
                    sum(k, e(i,k)*y(k) ) ;
    peq(j)..  c(j) - sum(jj, d(j,jj)*x(jj) ) =g= 0 ;
*
* name and definition of primal general equilibrium
* model
*
    model genmktequil / objeq, techeq1, techeq2,
      techeq3, mktequil, inputsup, peq / ;
*
    solve genmktequil using nlp maximizing csps ;
*
    parameter cs, ps, totsurplus, totsupply(i),
      totcost, p(j);
*
    cs = scale*sum((j,jj), x.l(j)*d(j,jj)*x.l(jj) ) ;
    ps = sum(i, b(i)*y.l(i)) + scale*sum((i,k),
      y.l(i)*e(i,k)*y.l(k) ) ;
    totsurplus = cs + ps ;
    totcost = (1/2)*sum((i,k), b(i)*e(i,k)*b(k)) +
              scale*sum((i,k), y.l(i)*e(i,k)*y.l(k) ) ;
    totsupply(i) = b(i) + sum(k, e(i,k)*y.l(k)) ;
    p(j) = c(j) - sum(jj, d(j,jj)*x.l(jj) ) ;
*
    display cs, ps, totsurplus, totcost, p,
```

```
        x1.1, x2.1, x3.1, x.1, s1.1, s2.1, s3.1,
    techeq1.m, techeq2.m , techeq3.m, inputsup.m,y.1,
    totsupply;
```

Numerical Example 2: General Market Equilibrium Intermediate and Final Commodities

Example 2 deals with a scenario of general market equilibrium involving both the production of final as well as intermediate commodities and the allocation of resources among firms. Furthermore, this scenario includes a beginning stock of resource endowments held by consumers. This is the problem discussed in model [(12.18) through (12.22)], which is reproduced here for convenience:

Primal

$$\max{(CS + PS)} = \mathbf{c}'\mathbf{x} - \tfrac{1}{2}\mathbf{x}'D\mathbf{x} - \tfrac{1}{2}\mathbf{y}'E\mathbf{y} \qquad (12.18)$$

$$\text{subject to} \qquad A_k\mathbf{x}_k + B_k\mathbf{v}_k \quad - \mathbf{s}_k \qquad\qquad \leq 0 \qquad (12.19)$$

$$-\sum_{k=1}^{K}\mathbf{x}_k \qquad\qquad + \mathbf{x} \qquad \leq 0 \qquad (12.20)$$

$$\sum_{k=1}^{K}\mathbf{v}_k \qquad\qquad - E\mathbf{y} \leq \mathbf{b}_V \qquad (12.21)$$

$$-\sum_{k=1}^{K}\mathbf{v}_k + \sum_{k=1}^{K}\mathbf{s}_k \qquad\qquad \leq \mathbf{b}_C \qquad (12.22)$$

$$\mathbf{y} \geq 0, \; \mathbf{x}_k \geq 0, \; \mathbf{v}_k \geq 0, \; \mathbf{s}_k \geq 0, \; \mathbf{x} \geq 0.$$

The relevant data are given as:

Technology for final and intermediate goods of firm 1

$$A_1 = \begin{bmatrix} 2.5 & -2.0 & 0.5 & 1.0 \\ 1.0 & 3.0 & -2.1 & 3.0 \\ -2.0 & 1.0 & 0.5 & 0.9 \end{bmatrix}, \quad B_1 = \begin{bmatrix} 0.25 & 0.2 & 0.50 \\ 0.10 & 0.3 & 0.21 \\ 0.20 & 0.1 & 0.50 \end{bmatrix}$$

Technology for final and intermediate goods of firm 2

$$A_2 = \begin{bmatrix} 1.0 & -1.0 & 0.5 & 0.3 \\ 0.5 & 0.3 & 2.0 & 0.3 \\ 2.0 & 1.0 & 0.2 & 9.0 \end{bmatrix}, \quad B_2 = \begin{bmatrix} 0.25 & 0.2 & 0.50 \\ 0.10 & 0.3 & 0.21 \\ 0.20 & 0.1 & 0.50 \end{bmatrix}$$

Technology for final and intermediate goods of firm 3

$$A_3 = \begin{bmatrix} 0.7 & -1.0 & 5.0 & 2.0 \\ 1.0 & 3.0 & 0.4 & 1.0 \\ -0.5 & 1.0 & 0.6 & 0.6 \end{bmatrix}, \qquad B_3 = \begin{bmatrix} 0.25 & 0.2 & 0.50 \\ 0.10 & 0.3 & 0.21 \\ 0.20 & 0.1 & 0.50 \end{bmatrix}$$

Market demands for final commodities

$$\mathbf{c} = \begin{bmatrix} 9 \\ 40 \\ 34 \\ 30 \end{bmatrix}, \qquad D = \begin{bmatrix} 8 & -5 & 4 & -3 \\ -5 & 7 & 3 & 3 \\ 4 & 3 & 5 & -2 \\ -3 & 3 & -2 & 4 \end{bmatrix}$$

$$\text{Total input supply: } \mathbf{b}_V = \begin{bmatrix} -.10 \\ .02 \\ .50 \end{bmatrix}, \qquad E = \begin{bmatrix} 1.3 & -0.4 & 0.2 \\ -0.4 & 0.8 & -0.3 \\ 0.2 & -0.3 & 0.4 \end{bmatrix}$$

Consumers' initial endowment of resources: $\quad \mathbf{b}_C = \begin{bmatrix} 7 \\ 5 \\ 3 \end{bmatrix}$.

The GAMS solution of this problem is given for each firm, for the final commodity market as a whole, and for the total input supply.

$$\text{Consumer surplus} = 145.8201$$
$$\text{Producer surplus} = 5.3914$$
$$\text{Total surplus} = 151.2114$$
$$\text{Total cost of resources} = 4.7704$$

Demand and prices for final commodity market

$$\mathbf{x} = \begin{bmatrix} x_1 = 2.1636 \\ x_2 = 3.1372 \\ x_3 = 4.2646 \\ x_4 = 3.4029 \end{bmatrix}, \qquad \mathbf{p} = \begin{bmatrix} p_1 = 0.5277 \\ p_2 = 5.8549 \\ p_3 = 1.4169 \\ p_4 = 21.9966 \end{bmatrix}$$

Outputs, inputs, and shadow prices from firm 1

$$\mathbf{x}_1 = \begin{bmatrix} x_{11} = 2.1636 \\ x_{21} = 2.5583 \\ x_{31} = 4.2646 \\ x_{41} = 0.0000 \end{bmatrix}, \qquad \mathbf{v}_1 = \begin{bmatrix} v_{11} = 2.9742 \\ v_{21} = 0.0000 \\ v_{31} = 0.0000 \end{bmatrix}$$

$$\mathbf{s}_1 = \begin{bmatrix} s_{11} = 3.1683 \\ s_{21} = 1.1803 \\ s_{31} = 0.9582 \end{bmatrix}, \qquad \mathbf{y}_1 = \begin{bmatrix} y_{11} = 6.5649 \\ y_{21} = 3.1550 \\ y_{31} = 9.5198 \end{bmatrix}$$

Outputs, inputs, and shadow prices from firm 2

$$\mathbf{x}_2 = \begin{bmatrix} x_{12} = 0.0000 \\ x_{22} = 0.5789 \\ x_{32} = 0.0000 \\ x_{42} = 0.0000 \end{bmatrix}, \quad \mathbf{v}_2 = \begin{bmatrix} v_{12} = 0.0000 \\ v_{22} = 0.0000 \\ v_{32} = 1.1578 \end{bmatrix}$$

$$\mathbf{s}_2 = \begin{bmatrix} s_{12} = 0.0000 \\ s_{22} = 0.4168 \\ s_{32} = 1.1578 \end{bmatrix}, \quad \mathbf{y}_2 = \begin{bmatrix} y_{12} = 4.6113 \\ y_{22} = 3.1550 \\ y_{32} = 9.5198 \end{bmatrix}$$

Outputs, inputs, and shadow prices from firm 3

$$\mathbf{x}_3 = \begin{bmatrix} x_{13} = 0.0000 \\ x_{23} = 0.0000 \\ x_{33} = 0.0000 \\ x_{43} = 3.4030 \end{bmatrix}, \quad \mathbf{v}_3 = \begin{bmatrix} v_{13} = 0.0000 \\ v_{23} = 0.0000 \\ v_{33} = 0.0000 \end{bmatrix}$$

$$\mathbf{s}_3 = \begin{bmatrix} s_{13} = 6.8059 \\ s_{23} = 3.4030 \\ s_{33} = 2.0418 \end{bmatrix}, \quad \mathbf{y}_3 = \begin{bmatrix} y_{13} = 6.5649 \\ y_{23} = 3.1550 \\ y_{33} = 9.5198 \end{bmatrix}$$

Quantity and shadow prices of total input supply

$$\mathbf{s} = \begin{bmatrix} s_1 = 2.9742 \\ s_2 = 0.0000 \\ s_3 = 1.1578 \end{bmatrix}, \quad \mathbf{y} = \begin{bmatrix} y_1 = 2.7042 \\ y_2 = 1.9990 \\ y_3 = 1.7917 \end{bmatrix}.$$

GAMS Command File: Numerical Example 2

We list a command file for the nonlinear package GAMS that solves the numerical problem presented in Example 2. Asterisks in column 1 relate to comments.

```
$title a general market equilibrium: three firms and
* one market
* four commodities and three inputs with symmetric d
* and e matrices
* sqp and intermediate commodities
*
$offsymlist offsymxref
    option limrow = 0
    option limcol= 0
    option iterlim = 100000
    option reslim = 200000
    option nlp = conopt3
    option decimals = 7 ;
```

```
*
   sets   j   output variables / x1, x2, x3, x4 /
          i   inputs / y1, y2, y3 /
*
   alias(i,k,kk);
   alias(j,jj) ;
*
   parameter c(j)   intercept of demand functions

   /  x1    9
      x2    40
      x3    34
      x4    30  /
*
   parameter bv(i)   intercept of total input supply
                     functions

   /  y1   -0.10
      y2    0.02
      y3    0.50  /
*
   parameter bc(i)   initial consumers' endowment of
                     resources

   /  y1  7
      y2  5
      y3  3  /
*
   table a1(i,j)  technology of final commodities
                  of firm 1

            x1   x2    x3    x4
      y1   2.5   -2   0.5   1.0
      y2   1.0    3  -2.1   3.0
      y3  -2.0    1   0.5   0.9
*
   table b1(i,k)  technology of intermediate
                  commodities of firm 1

            y1     y2    y3
      y1   0.25   0.2   0.50
      y2   0.10   0.3   0.21
      y3   0.20   0.1   0.50
```

*

```
table a2(i,j)  technology of final commodities of
               firm 2

        x1   x2    x3    x4
   y1  1.0   -1   0.5   0.3
   y2  0.5    3   2.0   0.3
   y3  2.0    1   0.2   9.0
```

*

```
table b2(i,k)   technology of intermediate
                commodities of firm 2

        y1     y2     y3
   y1  0.25   0.2   0.50
   y2  1.00   0.3   0.21
   y3  0.20   0.1   0.50
```

*

```
table a3(i,j)   technology of final commodities of
                firm 3

        x1   x2   x3    x4
   y1   0.7   -1   5.0   2.0
   y2   1.0    3   0.4   1.0
   y3  -0.5    1   0.6   0.6
```

*

```
table b3(i,k)  technology of intermediate
               commodities in firm 3

        y1     y2     y3
   y1  0.25   0.2   0.50
   y2  1.00   0.3   0.21
   y3  0.20   0.1   0.50
```

*

```
table d(j,jj)  slopes of final commodities' demand
               functions

        x1   x2   x3   x4
   x1    8   -5    4   -3
   x2   -5    7    3    3
   x3    4    3    5   -2
   x4   -3    3   -2    4
```

*

```
table e(i,k)    slopes of the input supply functions
```

```
           y1     y2     y3
     y1    1.3   -0.4    0.2
     y2   -0.4    0.8   -0.3
     y3    0.2   -0.3    0.4
*
   scalar scale   parameter to define economic
                  agents / .5 /;
*
* general equilibrium problem - intermediate and final
* commodities
*
   variables
   csps  consumers and producers' surplus
   s1(i)  input supply of firm 1
   s2(i)  input supply of firm 2
   s3(i)  input supply of firm 3
   v1(i)  intermediate commodities' output of firm 1
   v2(i)  intermediate commodities' output of firm 2
   v3(i)  intermediate commodities' output of firm 3
   x1(j)  final commodities' output of firm 1
   x2(j)  final commodities' output of firm 2
   x3(j)  final commodities' output of firm 3
   x(j)   total quantity of final commodities' demand
   y(i)   shadow prices of total resources ;
*
   positive variables  s1, s2, s3, v1,v2,v3, x1, x2,
     x3, x, y ;
*
   equations
   objeq name of objective function
   techeq1(i)  name of technical constraints of firm 1
   techeq2(i)  name of technical constraints of firm 2
   techeq3(i)  name of technical constraints of firm 3
   mktequil(j)  name of market clearing of final
                commodities
   inputsup(i)]  name of market clearing of resources
   consendow(i)  consumers' endowment and intermediate
                 outputs ;
*
   objeq..   csps =e= sum(j, c(j)*x(j) )
             - scale*sum((j,jj), x(j)*d(j,jj)*x(jj) )
             - scale*sum((i,k), y(i)*e(i,k)*y(k) ) ;
*
```

```
   techeq1(i)..   sum(j, a1(i,j)*x1(j)) +
                  sum(k,B1(i,k)*v1(k)) =e= s1(i) ;
   techeq2(i)..   sum(j, a2(i,j)*x2(j))+
                  sum(k,B2(i,k)*v2(k)) =e= s2(i) ;
   techeq3(i)..   sum(j, a3(i,j)*x3(j)) +
                  sum(k,B3(i,k)*v3(k)) =e= s3(i) ;
   mktequil(j)..  x1(j) + x2(j) + x3(j) =e= x(j) ;
   inputsup(i)..  v1(i) + v2(i) +v3(i) =e= bv(i) +
                  sum(k, e(i,k)*y(k) ) ;
   consendow(i)..  -v1(i)-v2(i)-v3(i)
                  +s1(i)+s2(i)+s3(i) =e= bc(i) ;
*
* name and definition of general equilibrium model
* with intermediate commodities
*
   model genmktequil / objeq, techeq1, techeq2,
     techeq3, mktequil, inputsup, consendow / ;
*
   solve genmktequil using nlp maximizing csps ;
*
   parameter cs, ps, totsurplus, totcost,
     totsupply(i), p(j);
   cs = scale*sum((j,jj), x.l(j)*d(j,jj)*x.l(jj) ) ;
   ps = sum(i, bv(i)*y.l(i)) + scale*sum((i,k),
     y.l(i)*e(i,k)*y.l(k) ) ;
   totsurplus = cs + ps ;
   totcost = (1/2)*sum((i,k), bv(i)*e(i,k)*bv(k)) +
           scale*sum((i,k), y.l(i)*e(i,k)*y.l(k) ) ;
   totsupply(i) = bv(i) + sum(k, e(i,k)*y.l(k)) ;
   p(j) = c(j) - sum(jj, d(j,jj)*x.l(jj) ) ;
*
   display cs, ps, totsurplus, totcost, p,
       x1.l, x2.l, x3.l, x.l, s1.l, s2.l, s3.l,
        v1.l, v2.l, v3.l,
       techeq1.m, techeq2.m , techeq3.m,
       inputsup.m,y.l, totsupply ;
```

Numerical Example 3: Spatial Equilibrium – One Commodity

Example 3 deals with the computation of the spatial equilibrium among four regions (A, B, U, and E) and involves only one homogeneous commodity.

The equilibrium will be computed twice using the quantity and the price formulations. In this way, the possibility of multiple optimal solutions of the commodity flow among regions will be illustrated. The relevant models are the primal [(12.34) through (12.36)] for the quantity specification and the "purified" dual [(12.39), (12.40)] for the price representation. They are reproduced here for convenience:

Primal

$$\max\,(CS + PS) = \sum_{r'} \left(a_{r'} - \tfrac{1}{2}D_r x_{r'}^d\right) x_{r'}^d - \sum_{r} \left(b_r + \tfrac{1}{2}S_r x_r^s\right) x_r^s$$

$$- \sum_{r}\sum_{r'} t_{r,r'} x_{r,r'} \tag{12.34}$$

subject to $\qquad x_{r'}^d \le \sum_{r} x_{r,r'}$ demand requirement $\qquad$ (12.35)

$$\sum_{r'} x_{r,r'} \le x_r^s \qquad\qquad \text{supply availability.} \tag{12.36}$$

"Purified" Dual

$$\max\,VA = \sum_{r'} \left(c_{r'} - \tfrac{1}{2}D_{r'}^{-1}p_{r'}^d\right) p_{r'}^d - \sum_{r} \left(h_r + \tfrac{1}{2}S_r^{-1}p_r^s\right) p_r^s \tag{12.39}$$

subject to $\qquad\qquad\qquad p_{r'}^d \le p_r^s + t_{r,r'}.$ $\qquad\qquad$ (12.40)

The relevant data are as follows:
    Regions: A, B, U, E

Demand intercepts		Demand slopes	
A	15.0	A	1.2
B	22.0	B	1.8
U	25.0	U	2.1
E	28.0	E	1.1

Supply intercepts		Supply slopes	
A	0.4	A	1.4
B	0.2	B	2.4
U	0.6	U	1.9
E	0.5	E	0.6

Unit cost of transportation between regions

	A	B	U	E
A	0.00	1.50	1.0	0.5
B	1.50	0.00	0.2	0.8
U	0.75	2.25	0.0	0.6
E	3.00	5.00	4.0	0.0

The GAMS solution of this numerical example is given for the price model and the quantity model, in that order.

Price Model

Demand and supply prices		Regional supply		Regional demand	
A	7.129	A	10.380	A	6.445
B	6.829	B	16.589	B	9.708
U	7.029	U	13.955	U	10.240
E	7.629	E	5.077	E	19.608

Interregional trade

	A	B	U	E
A	6.445			3.935
B		9.708	6.881	
U			3.359	10.596
E				5.077

Implied demand elasticities		Implied supply elasticities	
A	−1.327	A	0.961
B	−1.266	B	0.988
U	−1.442	U	0.957
E	−0.428	E	0.902

Total transportation cost   9.701

Objective function   321.972.

Quantity Model

Demand and supply prices		Regional supply		Regional demand	
A	7.129	A	10.380	A	6.445
B	6.829	B	16.589	B	9.708
U	7.029	U	13.955	U	10.240
E	7.629	E	5.077	E	19.608

Interregional trade

	A	B	U	E
A	6.445			3.935
B		9.708	5.216	1.665
U			5.023	8.931
E				5.077

Total transportation cost	9.701
Objective function	411.764

Consumer surplus   Producer surplus

A	17.310	A	38.483
B	26.180	B	57.333
U	24.964	U	51.246
E	174.766	E	21.482

Total consumer and producer surplus   411.764.

Notice that the interregional trade flow is different in the price model and in the quantity model, but that the total transportation cost is the same in the two models. This occurrence is an example of multiple optimal solutions in spatial equilibrium analysis. Furthermore, the value of the two objective functions differ by constants K_r^d and K_r^s, $r = 1, \ldots, R$, as explained in Appendix 12.2. As expected, demand and supply prices and regional demand and supply quantities are the same in the two models.

GAMS Command File: Numerical Example 3

We list a command file for the nonlinear package GAMS that solves the numerical problem presented in Example 3. Asterisks in column 1 relate to comments.

```
$title world commodity trade - one commodity
$offsymlist offsymxref
    option limrow = 0
    option limcol = 0
    option iterlim =2500
    option nlp = conopt3
*
    sets  r     regions /a, b, u, e/
```

```
*
    alias (r,rr) ;
*
    parameters aa(r)        demand intercepts

    /   a    15
        b    22
        u    25
        e    28   /
*
    parameters dd(r)        demand slopes

    /   a    1.2
        b    1.8
        u    2.1
        e    1.1   /
*
    parameters bb(r)        supply intercepts

    /   a    0.4
        b    0.2
        u    0.6
        e    0.5   /
*
    parameters ss(r)        supply slopes

    /   a    1.4
        b    2.4
        u    1.9
        e    0.6   /
*
    table t(r,rr)       unit cost of transportation

                a     b      u      e
        a     0.00  1.50   1.0    0.5
        b     1.50  0.00   0.2    0.8
        u     0.75  2.25   0.0    0.6
        e     3.00  5.00   4.0    0.0
*
* price dependent form
*
    variables
    pd(r)      demand price (price model)
    ps(r)      supply price (price model)
```

```
    obj     objective function
*
    positive variables     pd, ps;
*
    equations
    va      objective function equation
    trade(r,rr)     trade between regions equations
                    (price model);
*
    va..   sum(r, (aa(r)-.5*dd(r)*pd(r))* pd(r) )
              -sum(r, (bb(r)+.5*ss(r)* ps(r))* ps(r) )
              =e= obj ;
*
    trade(r,rr)..   pd(rr) =l= ps(r) + t(r,rr)) ;
*
    model interreg /all/ ;
*
    solve interreg using nlp maximizing obj;
*
    parameter
    regdem(rr)      regional demand quantity
    regsup(r)       regional supply quantity
    demelas(rr)     implied demand elasticities
    supelas(r)      implied supply elasticities;
*
    regdem(rr) = sum(r, trade.m(r,rr) ) ;
    regsup(r) = sum(rr, trade.m(r,rr) ) ;
*
    demelas(rr) = -dd(rr) * (pd.l(rr)/regdem(rr)) ;
    supelas(r) = ss(r) * (ps.l(r)/regsup(r)) ;
*
    display pd.l, ps.l, trade.l, obj.l , regdem,
      regsup, demelas, supelas ;
*
* quantity dependent form
*
    parameters
    a(rr)   pd demand intercepts
    d(rr)   pd demand slopes
    h(r)    pd supply intercepts
    s(r)    pd supply slopes ;
*
* parameter inversion
```

```
*
    a(rr) = aa(rr)/dd(rr);
    d(rr) = 1/dd(rr) ;
    h(r) = -bb(r)/ss(r);
    s(r) = 1/ss(r) ;
*
    display a, d, h, s ;
*
    variables
    qd(rr)   demand quantity (quantity model)
    qs(r)   supply quantity (quantity model)
    x(r,rr)   quantity trade (quantity model)
    obj2   objective function (quantity model)
*
    positive variable   qd, qs, x;
*
    equations
    nsb      objective function equation
    aggd(rr)     aggregate regional demand
    aggs(r)      aggregate regional supply ;
*
    nsb..   sum(rr, (a(rr)-.5*d(rr)*qd(rr))* qd(rr) )
               -sum(r, (h(r)+.5*s(r)* qs(r))* qs(r) )
               -sum((r,rr), t(r,rr)*x(r,rr)) =e= obj2 ;
*
    aggd(rr)..   qd(rr)=1= sum(r, x(r,rr) );
*
    aggs(r)..   sum(rr, x(r,rr) ) =1= qs(r);
*
    model interreg2 /nsb, aggd, aggs / ;
*
    solve interreg2 using nlp maximizing obj2;
*
    parameter
    pd2(rr)   demand prices (quantity model)
    ps2(r)   supply prices (quantity model)
    transcostx   total transportation cost (quantity
                 model)
    transcostt   total transportation cost (price
                 model)
    consur(rr)   consumer surplus
    prosur(r)   producer surplus
    totsur   total surplus;
```

```
*
   pd2(rr) = a(rr)-d(rr)*qd.l(rr) ;
   ps2(r) = h(r)+s(r)*qs.l(r) ;
   transcostx = sum((r,rr), t(r,rr)*x.l(r,rr));
   transcostt = sum((r,rr), t(r,rr)*trade.m(r,rr));
   consur(rr) = 0.5* (a(rr)-pd2(rr))* qd.l(rr) ;
   prosur(r) = 0.5*(ps2(r)-h(r))*qs.l(r) ;
   totsur = sum(rr, consur(rr))+ sum(r, prosur(r)) ;
*
   display consur, prosur, totsur;
   display qd.l, qs.l, x.l, obj2.l, aggd.m, aggs.m ;
   display pd.l, pd2, ps.l, ps22, trade.m , x.l,
     obj.l, obj2.l,
   transcostx, transcostt ;
```

Numerical Example 4: Spatial Equilibrium – Many Commodities

Example 4 deals with the computation of the spatial equilibrium among four regions (A, B, U, and E) and involves three homogeneous commodities. The equilibrium will be computed twice using the quantity and the price formulations. In this way, the possibility of multiple optimal solutions of the commodity flow among regions will be illustrated. The relevant models are the primal [(12.41) through (12.43)] for the quantity specification and the "purified" dual [(12.44), (12.45)] for the price representation. They are reproduced here for convenience:

Primal

$$
\max (CS + PS) = \sum_{m,r'} \left(a_{m,r'} - \tfrac{1}{2} D_{m,r} x^d_{m,r'} \right) x^d_{m,r'}
$$

$$
- \sum_{m,r} \left(b_{m,r} + \tfrac{1}{2} S_{m,r} x^s_{m,r} \right) x^s_{m,r}
$$

$$
- \sum_{m,r} \sum_{m,r'} t_{m,r,r'} x_{m,r,r'} \tag{12.41}
$$

subject to $\quad x^d_{m,r'} \leq \sum_{m,r} x_{m,r,r'} \quad$ demand requirement $\tag{12.42}$

$$
\sum_{m,r'} x_{m,r,r'} \leq x^s_{m,r} \qquad \text{supply availability.} \tag{12.43}
$$

"Purified" Dual

$$\max VA = \sum_{m,r'} \left(c_{m,r'} - \tfrac{1}{2} D_{m,r'}^{-1} p_{m,r'}^d \right) p_{m,r'}^d$$

$$- \sum_{m,r} \left(h_{m,r} + \tfrac{1}{2} S_{m,r}^{-1} p_{m,r}^s \right) p_{m,r}^s \qquad (12.44)$$

subject to $\qquad p_{m,r'}^d \leq p_{m,r}^s + t_{m,r,r'}. \qquad (12.45)$

The relevant data are as follows:

Regions: $A, \ B, \ U, \ E$

Commodities: 1, 2, 3

Demand intercepts

	1	2	3
A	15.0	25.0	10.0
B	22.0	18.0	15.0
U	25.0	10.0	18.0
E	28.0	20.0	19.0

Supply intercepts

	1	2	3
A	0.4	0.1	0.7
B	0.2	0.4	0.3
U	0.6	0.2	0.4
E	0.5	0.6	0.2

Demand slopes

	1	2	3
A.1	1.2		
A.2		2.1	
A.3			1.1
B.1	1.8		
B.2		1.6	
B.3			2.6
U.1	2.1		
U.2		0.9	
U.3			1.7
E.1	1.1		
E.2		0.8	
E.3			1.9

Supply slopes

	1	2	3
A.1	1.4		
A.2		2.1	
A.3			1.7
B.1	2.4		
B.2		1.6	
B.3			1.8
U.1	1.9		
U.2		2.8	
U.3			2.1
E.1	0.6		
E.2		2.1	
E.3			1.2

Unit cost of transportation between regions

	A	B	U	E
A	0.00	1.50	1.0	0.5
B	1.50	0.00	0.2	0.8
U	0.75	2.25	0.0	0.6
E	3.00	5.00	4.0	0.0

The cost of transportation is the same for all the three commodities.
The solution of this numerical example is given for the price model and the
quantity model, in that order.

Price Model

Demand and supply prices

	1	2	3
A	7.129	5.306	4.294
B	6.829	5.500	3.994
U	7.029	4.556	4.194
E	7.629	5.156	4.794

Regional supply

	1	2	3
A	10.380	11.244	8.000
B	16.589	9.200	7.490
U	13.955	12.958	9.208
E	5.077	11.429	5.953

Regional demand

	1	2	3
A	6.445	13.856	5.276
B	9.708	9.200	4.615
U	10.240	5.899	10.870
E	19.608	15.875	9.891

Interregional trade

		A	B	U	E
commodity 1:	A	6.445			3.935
	B		9.708	6.881	
	U			3.359	10.596
	E				5.077

		A	B	U	E
commodity 2:	A	11.244			
	B		9.200	6.881	
	U	2.613		5.899	4.446
	E				11.429

		A	B	U	E
	A	5.276			2.724
commodity 3:	B		4.615	1.662	1.213
	U			9.208	
	E				5.953

Total transportation cost	16.994
Objective function	643.732.

Quantity Model

Demand and supply prices

	1	2	3
A	7.129	5.306	4.294
B	6.829	5.500	3.994
U	7.029	4.556	4.194
E	7.629	5.156	4.794

Regional Supply

	1	2	3
A	10.380	11.244	8.000
B	16.589	9.200	7.490
U	13.955	12.958	9.208
E	5.077	11.429	5.953

Regional demand

	1	2	3
A	6.445	13.856	5.276
B	9.708	9.200	4.615
U	10.240	5.899	10.870
E	19.608	15.875	9.891

Interregional trade

		A	B	U	E
	A	6.445			3.935
commodity 1:	B		9.708	5.761	1.120
	U			4.478	9.476
	E				5.077

		A	B	U	E
	A	11.244			
commodity 2:	B		9.200	6.881	
	U	2.613		5.899	4.446
	E				11.429

		A	B	U	E
	A	5.276			2.724
commodity 3:	B		4.615	2.875	
	U			7.995	1.213
	E				5.953

Total transportation cost   16.994

Objective function   925.006.

Notice that the interregional trade flow is different in the price and quantity models for commodity 1 and 3 but that the total transportation cost is the same in the two models. This occurrence is an example of multiple optimal solutions in spatial equilibrium analysis.

GAMS Command File: Numerical Example 4

We list a command file for the nonlinear package GAMS that solves the numerical problem presented in Example 4. Asterisks in column 1 relate to comments.

```
$title world commodity trade. multi-region multi-
* commodity
*
$offsymlist offsymxref
    option limrow = 0
    option limcol = 0
    option iterlim = 2500
    option nlp = conopt3
*
* 3 commodities, 4 regions
*
    sets   r    regions /a, b, u, e/
           m    commodities /1,2,3/
*
    alias(r,rr) ;
    alias(m,mm) ;
*
    table aa(r,m)    demand intercepts

            1    2    3
        a   15   25   10
        b   22   18   15
        u   25   10   18
        e   28   20   19
```

```
*
     table dd(r,m,mm)   demand slopes

            1    2    3
     a.1  1.2
     a.2       2.1
     a.3            1.1

            1    2    3
     b.1  1.8
     b.2       1.6
     b.3            2.6

            1    2    3
     u.1  2.1
     u.2       0.9
     u.3            1.7

            1    2    3
     e.1  1.1
     e.2       0.8
     e.3            1.9

*
     table bb(r,m)   supply intercepts

            1    2    3
       a  0.4  0.1  0.7
       b  0.2  0.4  0.3
       u  0.6  0.2  0.4
       e  0.5  0.6  0.2
*
     table ss(r,m,mm)    supply slopes

            1    2    3
     a.1  1.4
     a.2       2.1
     a.3            1.7

            1    2    3
     b.1  2.4
     b.2       1.6
     b.3            1.8
```

```
        1    2    3
  u.1  1.9
  u.2       2.8
  u.3            2.1

        1    2    3
  e.1  0.6
  e.2       2.1
  e.3            1.2
```

*

```
table t(r,rr)   unit costs of transportation

          a     b     u     e
    a   0.00  1.50  1.0   0.5
    b   1.50  0.00  0.2   0.8
    u   0.75  2.25  0.0   0.6
    e   3.00  5.00  4.0   0.0
```

*
* price dependent form
*

```
variables
pd(r,m)   demand prices (price model)
ps(r,m)   supply prices (price model)
obj   objective function
```

*

```
positive variables     pd, ps;
```

*

```
equations
va   objective function equation
trade(r,rr,m)    trade between regions equations
                 (price model) ;
```

*

```
va..  sum((r,m), aa(r,m)*pd(r,m))
   - sum((r,m,mm),.5*pd(r,m)*dd(r,m,mm)*pd(r,mm))
   - sum((r,m), bb(r,m)*ps(r,m))
   - sum((r,m,mm), .5*ps(r,m)*ss(r,m,mm)*ps(r,mm))
     =e= obj ;
```

*

```
trade(r,rr,m)..  pd(rr,m) =l= ps(r,m) + t(r,rr) ;
```

*

```
model interreg /all/ ;
```

*

```
   solve interreg using nlp maximizing obj ;
*
   parameter
   regdem(rr,m)    regional demand quantity
   regsup(r,m)    regional supply quantity
   demelas(rr,m,mm)  implied demand elasticities
   spelas(r,m,mm)   implied supply elasticities;
*
   regdem(rr,m) = sum(r, trade.m(r,rr,m) ) ;
   regsup(r,m) = sum(rr, trade.m(r,rr,m) ) ;
*
   demelas(rr,m,m) = -dd(rr,m,m) *
     (pd.l(rr,m)/regdem(rr,m)) ;
   supelas(r,m,m) = ss(r,m,m) *
     (ps.l(r,m)/regsup(r,m)) ;
   display pd.l,ps.l, trade.m, obj.l , regdem,
     regsup, demelas, supelas ;
*
* quantity dependent form
*
   parameter
   a(rr,m)   pd demand intercepts
   d(r,m,mm)  pd demand slopes
   h(r,m)   ps supply intercepts
   s(r,m,mm)  ps supply slopes ;
*
* demand and supply inversion
*
   a(rr,m) = aa(rr,m)/dd(rr,m,m);
   d(rr,m,m) = 1/ dd(rr,m,m) ;
   h(r,m) = -bb(r,m)/ ss(r,m,m);
   s(r,m,m) = 1/ ss(r,m,m) ;
*
   display a, d, h, s ;
*
   variables
   qd(rr,m)   demand quantity (quantity model)
   qs(r,m)   supply quantity (quantity model)
   x(r,rr,m)   quantity trade (quantity model)
   obj2   objective function (quantity model)
*
   positive variable   qd, qs, x;
*
```

```
     equations
     nsb   objective function equation
     aggd(rr,m)   aggregate regional demand equations
     aggs(r,m)   aggregate regional supply equations;
*
     nsb..   sum((r,m), a(r,m)*qd(r,m))
             - sum((r,m,mm),.5*qd(r,m)*d(r,m,mm)*qd(r,mm))
             - sum((r,m),h(r,m)*qs(r,m))
             - sum((r,m,mm),.5*qs(r,m)*s(r,m,mm)*
                 qs(r,mm))
             - sum((r,rr,m), t(r,rr)*x(r,rr,m)) =e= obj2;
*
     aggd(rr,m)..   qd(rr,m) =l= sum(r, x(r,rr,m) );
*
     aggs(r,m).. sum(rr, x(r,rr,m) ) =l= qs(r,m);
*
     model interreg2 /nsb,aggd, aggs / ;
*
     solve interreg2 using nlp maximizing obj2;
*
     parameter
     pd2(rr,m)     demand prices (quantity model)
     ps2(r,m)     supply prices (quantity model)
     transcostx     total transportation cost (quantity
                    model)
     transcostt     total transportation cost (price
                    model)
     consur(rr,m)     consumer surplus
     prosur(r,m)     producer surplus
     totsur     total surplus;
*
     pd2(rr,m) = a(rr,m)- sum(mm,
                 d(rr,m,mm)*qd.l(rr,mm) ) ;
     ps2(r,m) = h(r,m) + sum(mm, d(r,m,mm)*
                 qs.l(r,mm) ) ;
     transcostx = sum((r,rr,m), t(r,rr)*x.l(r,rr,m));
     transcostt = sum((r,rr,m),
                 t(r,rr)*trade.m(r,rr,m));
     consur(rr,m) = 0.5* (a(rr,m)-pd2(rr,m))*
                 qd.l(rr,r) ;
     prosur(r,m) = 0.5*(ps2(r,m)-h(r,m))*qs.l(r,m) ;
     totsur = sum((rr,m), cpnsur(rr,m))+ sum((r,m),
             prosur(r,m)) ;
```

```
*
    display consur, prosur, totsur;
    display aggd.m, aggs.m ;
    display pd.l, pd2, ps.l, ps2, qd.l, qs.l, trade.m ,
        x.l, obj.l, obj2.l, transcostx, transcostt ;
```

APPENDIX 12.1: ALTERNATIVE SPECIFICATION OF GME

In this appendix, we discuss an alternative specification of the General Market Equilibrium (GME) presented in Model 1: Final Commodities, at the beginning of this chapter.

The known elements of this problems are as follows. There exists a set of inverse demand functions for final commodities expressed by $\mathbf{p} = \mathbf{c} - D\mathbf{x}$, where D is a symmetric positive semidefinite matrix of dimensions $(n \times n)$, $\mathbf{p}$ is an n-vector of prices, $\mathbf{c}$ is an n-vector of intercept coefficients, and $\mathbf{x}$ is an n-vector of quantities demanded. There also exists a set of inverse supply functions for inputs defined as $\mathbf{p}_s = \mathbf{g} + G\mathbf{s}$, where G is a symmetric positive definite matrix of dimensions $(m \times m)$ and where $\mathbf{p}_s, \mathbf{g}, \mathbf{s}$ are m-vectors of prices, intercepts, and quantities supplied, respectively. Finally, the production system is represented by a large number K of competitive firms, each of which uses an individualized linear technology represented by A_k, $k = 1, \ldots, K$. The unknown (quantity, or primal) elements of the problems are $\mathbf{x}, \mathbf{x}_k, \mathbf{s}_k, \mathbf{s}$, that is, the total quantity of final commodities demanded by the market, the quantity of final commodities supplied by the kth firm, the quantity of inputs demanded by the kth firm, and the total quantity of inputs supplied by the market, respectively.

A competitive market equilibrium, therefore, is a production and consumption allocation of commodities (inputs and outputs), and their corresponding prices, that satisfies consumers and producers.

A competitive equilibrium can be achieved (when technical conditions allow it) by maximizing the sum of consumers' and producers' surpluses subject to technology constraints that establish the transformation of inputs into outputs and the associated market clearing conditions. Hence, given the demand and supply functions stated earlier, the primal specification that is suitable to represent the described scenario can be stated as

Primal

$$\max (CS + PS) = \left[\mathbf{c}'\mathbf{x} - \tfrac{1}{2}\mathbf{x}' D\mathbf{x}\right] - \left[\mathbf{g}'\mathbf{s} + \tfrac{1}{2}\mathbf{s}' G\mathbf{s}\right] \quad (A12.1.1)$$

$$\text{subject to} \qquad - A_k\mathbf{x}_k + \mathbf{s}_k \qquad\qquad \geq \mathbf{0} \qquad (A12.1.2)$$

$$\sum_{k=1}^{K} \mathbf{x}_k \quad - \mathbf{x} \qquad \geq \mathbf{0} \qquad (A12.1.3)$$

$$-\sum_{k=1}^{K} \mathbf{s}_k \quad + \mathbf{s} \geq \mathbf{0} \qquad (A12.1.4)$$

$$\mathbf{x} \geq \mathbf{0}, \ \mathbf{x}_k \geq \mathbf{0}, \ \mathbf{s}_k \geq \mathbf{0}, \ \mathbf{s} \geq \mathbf{0}$$

for $k = 1, \ldots, K$. The first constraint (A12.1.2) represents the technological relations of the kth firm. The individual entrepreneur must make decisions regarding the purchase of inputs $\mathbf{s}_k$ and the production of outputs $\mathbf{x}_k$ in a way that respects the physical equilibrium conditions according to which the kth firm's input demand ($A_k\mathbf{x}_k$) must be less than or equal to its input supply $\mathbf{s}_k$. Notice, therefore, that the quantity $\mathbf{s}_k$ is viewed both as a demand (when the entrepreneur faces the input market) and as a supply (when the entrepreneur faces his output opportunities, or input requirements, ($A_k\mathbf{x}_k$)). The second constraint (A12.1.3) represents the market clearing condition for the final commodity outputs. The total demand for final commodities $\mathbf{x}$ must be less than or equal to their total supply $\sum_{k=1}^{K} \mathbf{x}_k$ as generated by the K firms. The third constraint (A12.1.4) represents the market clearing condition for the commodity inputs. The total demand of inputs in the economy $\sum_{k=1}^{K} \mathbf{s}_k$ must be less than or equal to the total input supply ($\mathbf{s}$).

With a choice of Lagrange multipliers (dual variables) for the primal constraints in the form of $\mathbf{y}_k$, $\mathbf{f}$, $\mathbf{y}$, respectively, the Lagrangean function is stated as

$$L = \mathbf{c}'\mathbf{x} - \tfrac{1}{2}\mathbf{x}'D\mathbf{x} - \mathbf{g}'\mathbf{s} - \tfrac{1}{2}\mathbf{s}'G\mathbf{s} + \sum_{k=1}^{K} \mathbf{y}_k'(\mathbf{s}_k - A_k\mathbf{x}_k) \qquad (A12.1.5)$$

$$+ \mathbf{f}'\left(\sum_{k=1}^{K} \mathbf{x}_k - \mathbf{x}\right) + \mathbf{y}'\left(\mathbf{s} - \sum_{k=1}^{K} \mathbf{s}_k\right).$$

The relevant KKT conditions (for deriving the dual problem) are those associated with the primal variables. Hence,

$$\frac{\partial L}{\partial \mathbf{x}} = \mathbf{c} - D\mathbf{x} - \mathbf{f} \leq \mathbf{0} \qquad (A12.1.6)$$

$$\mathbf{x}'\frac{\partial L}{\partial \mathbf{x}} = \mathbf{x}'\mathbf{c} - \mathbf{x}'D\mathbf{x} - \mathbf{x}'\mathbf{f} = 0 \qquad (A12.1.7)$$

$$\frac{\partial L}{\partial \mathbf{x}_k} = -A'_k \mathbf{y}_k + \mathbf{f} \leq \mathbf{0} \qquad (A12.1.8)$$

$$\mathbf{x}'_k \frac{\partial L}{\partial \mathbf{x}_k} = -\mathbf{x}'_k A'_k \mathbf{y}_k + \mathbf{x}'_k \mathbf{f} = 0 \qquad (A12.1.9)$$

$$\frac{\partial L}{\partial \mathbf{s}} = -\mathbf{g} - G\mathbf{s} + \mathbf{y} \leq \mathbf{0} \qquad (A12.1.10)$$

$$\mathbf{s}' \frac{\partial L}{\partial \mathbf{s}} = -\mathbf{s}'\mathbf{g} - \mathbf{s}'G\mathbf{s} + \mathbf{s}'\mathbf{y} = 0 \qquad (A12.1.11)$$

$$\frac{\partial L}{\partial \mathbf{s}_k} = \mathbf{y}_k - \mathbf{y} \leq \mathbf{0} \qquad (A12.1.12)$$

$$\mathbf{s}'_k \frac{\partial L}{\partial \mathbf{s}_k} = \mathbf{s}'_k \mathbf{y}_k - \mathbf{s}'_k \mathbf{y} = 0. \qquad (A12.1.13)$$

The simplification of the Lagrangean function, as the objective function of the dual problem, takes place, as already discussed on many other occasions, by using the information contained in the complementary slackness conditions $(A12.1.7)$, $(A12.1.9)$, $(A12.1.11)$, and $(A12.1.13)$ associated with the dual constraints. The final result is that all the linear terms disappear from the Lagrangean function and, therefore, the dual problem can be stated as

Dual

$$\min \ TCMO = \tfrac{1}{2}\mathbf{s}'G\mathbf{s} + \tfrac{1}{2}\mathbf{x}'D\mathbf{x} \qquad (A12.1.14)$$

$$\text{subject to} \quad A'_k \mathbf{y}_k \qquad\qquad \geq \mathbf{f} \qquad (A12.1.15)$$

$$+ \mathbf{y} \quad \geq \mathbf{y}_k \qquad (A12.1.16)$$

$$\mathbf{f} \quad \geq \mathbf{c} - D\mathbf{x} \qquad (A12.1.17)$$

$$\mathbf{g} + G\mathbf{s} \geq \mathbf{y} \qquad (A12.1.18)$$

$$\mathbf{y} \geq \mathbf{0}, \ \mathbf{y}_k \geq \mathbf{0}, \ \mathbf{f} \geq \mathbf{0}, \ \mathbf{x} \geq \mathbf{0}, \ \mathbf{s} \geq \mathbf{0}.$$

The dual objective function is interpreted as the minimization of the total cost of market options (*TCMO*) which, on the primal side, correspond to the sum of the consumers' and producers' surplus. Constraint $(A12.1.15)$ states that the marginal cost of the kth firm, $A'_k \mathbf{y}_k$, must be greater than or equal to the marginal cost found in the entire economy, $\mathbf{f}$. Constraint $(A12.1.16)$ states that marginal valuation of the resources for the entire economy, $\mathbf{y}$, must be greater than or equal to the marginal valuation of the same resources for the kth firm, $\mathbf{y}_k$. Constraint $(A12.1.17)$ means that the marginal cost of producing the final commodities in the entire economy must be greater than or equal to the market price, $\mathbf{p} = \mathbf{c} - D\mathbf{x}$, of those commodities. Finally, constraint $(A12.1.18)$ states that the marginal valuation of the resources in the entire economy, $\mathbf{y}$, must be less than or equal to the market price of resources, $\mathbf{p}_s = \mathbf{g} + G\mathbf{s}$.

We reiterate that the dual pair of problems discussed in this appendix refers to a general market equilibrium scenario that was already discussed in Model 1 of this chapter. We, therefore, wish to establish a direct connection between the two equivalent specifications, one of which (model 1) corresponds to a symmetric quadratic programming problem whereas the second one (Appendix 12.1) corresponds to an asymmetric quadratic programming problem.

KKT condition $(A12.1.10)$ and the mild assumption that $\mathbf{s} > \mathbf{0}$, that is the economy needs at least a minuscule positive amount of each resource, allow us to state that $\mathbf{y} = \mathbf{g} + G\mathbf{s} = \mathbf{p}_s$. Therefore, we can express the vector of resource supply functions in the form of quantity as a function of price (recalling the assumption of positive definiteness of the G matrix)

$$\mathbf{s} = -G^{-1}\mathbf{g} + G^{-1}\mathbf{y} \qquad (A12.1.19)$$

$$= \mathbf{b} + E\mathbf{y}$$

where $\mathbf{b} = -G^{-1}\mathbf{g}$ and $E = G^{-1}$. Then, the producers' surplus in the dual objective function $(A12.1.14)$ in terms of input quantities, $\mathbf{s}$, can be reformulated in terms of the resource price, $\mathbf{y}$:

$$\tfrac{1}{2}\mathbf{s}'G\mathbf{s} = \tfrac{1}{2}(\mathbf{b} + E\mathbf{y})'E^{-1}(\mathbf{b} + E\mathbf{y}) \qquad (A12.1.20)$$

$$= \tfrac{1}{2}\mathbf{b}'E^{-1}\mathbf{b} + \mathbf{b}'\mathbf{y} + \tfrac{1}{2}\mathbf{y}'E\mathbf{y}.$$

Analogously, the total cost function (in terms of resource quantities, $\mathbf{s}$) in the primal objective function $(A12.1.1)$ can be restated in terms of input prices, $\mathbf{y}$:

$$\mathbf{g}'\mathbf{s} + \tfrac{1}{2}\mathbf{s}'G\mathbf{s} = \mathbf{g}'(\mathbf{b} + E\mathbf{y}) + \tfrac{1}{2}\mathbf{b}'E^{-1}\mathbf{b} + \mathbf{b}'\mathbf{y} + \tfrac{1}{2}\mathbf{y}'E\mathbf{y} \qquad (A12.1.21)$$

$$= \mathbf{g}'\mathbf{b} + \mathbf{g}'E\mathbf{y} + \tfrac{1}{2}\mathbf{b}'E^{-1}\mathbf{b} + \mathbf{b}'\mathbf{y} + \tfrac{1}{2}\mathbf{y}'E\mathbf{y}$$

$$= -\mathbf{b}'E^{-1}\mathbf{b} - \mathbf{b}'E^{-1}E\mathbf{y} + \tfrac{1}{2}\mathbf{b}'E^{-1}\mathbf{b} + \mathbf{b}'\mathbf{y} + \tfrac{1}{2}\mathbf{y}'E\mathbf{y}$$

$$= -\tfrac{1}{2}\mathbf{b}'E^{-1}\mathbf{b} + \tfrac{1}{2}\mathbf{y}'E\mathbf{y}$$

because $\mathbf{g} = -E^{-1}\mathbf{b}$ and $G = E^{-1}$, by definition.

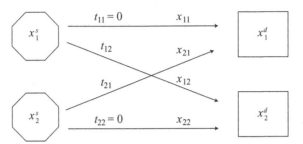

Figure 12.4. Network of trade flow between two regions.

By replacing $\mathbf{s}$ and $\mathbf{g's} + \frac{1}{2}\mathbf{s}'G\mathbf{s}$ in the primal problem and $\frac{1}{2}\mathbf{s}'G\mathbf{s}$ in the dual problem with their equivalent expressions in terms of input prices, $\mathbf{y}$, we obtain the dual pair of symmetric quadratic programming models presented in model 1.

APPENDIX 12.2: A DETAILED DISCUSSION OF SPATIAL EQUILIBRIUM

To facilitate the understanding of the spatial equilibrium model presented in this chapter, we discuss a two-region example in detail.

Each region is endowed with a demand and a supply function for a final and homogeneous commodity:

$$p_r^d = a_r - D_r x_r^d \qquad \text{demand function} \qquad (A12.2.1)$$

$$p_r^s = b_r + S_r x_r^s \qquad \text{supply function} \qquad (A12.2.2)$$

where p_r is the regional price, x_r is the regional quantity and $r = 1, 2$. Each region may either import or export the final commodity and requires the satisfaction of the demand expressed by its regional consumers. The unit transportation cost matrix is known and stated as

$$T = \begin{bmatrix} 0 & t_{12} \\ t_{21} & 0 \end{bmatrix} \qquad (A12.2.3)$$

where it is assumed that the unit transportation cost within a region is equal to zero. Figure 12.4 presents the diagram of the possible trade flows between the two regions. With the help of this diagram, the necessary primal constraints of the spatial equilibrium problem will be easily established.

The objective function of such a problem is to maximize the sum of the consumers' and producers' surpluses minus the total cost of transporting the commodity from one region to the other. The formal specification is

$$\max N(CS+PS) = \left[a_1 x_1^d - \tfrac{1}{2} D_1\left(x_1^d\right)^2\right] + \left[a_2 x_2^d - \tfrac{1}{2} D_2\left(x_2^d\right)^2\right] \quad (A12.2.3)$$
$$- \left[b_1 x_1^s + \tfrac{1}{2} S_1\left(x_1^s\right)^2\right] - \left[b_2 x_2^s + \tfrac{1}{2} S_2\left(x_2^s\right)^2\right]$$
$$- t_{12} x_{12} - t_{21} x_{21}$$

subject to	Dual Variables
$x_1^d \leq x_{11} + x_{21}$	p_1^d
$x_2^d \leq x_{12} + x_{22}$	p_2^d
$x_{11} + x_{12} \leq x_1^s$	p_1^s
$x_{21} + x_{22} \leq x_2^s$	$p_2^s.$

The symbol $N(CS+PS)$ stands for the net sum of the consumers' and producers' surpluses that have been netted out of the total cost of transportation. The first set of two primal constraints states that the regional demand must be satisfied with an adequate supply of the final commodity supplied by the two regions. The second set of the other two primal constraints states that the total shipment to the two regions from the same location cannot exceed the available supply at that location.

On the way to specifying the dual problem, the Lagrangean function is stated as

$$L = \left[a_1 x_1^d - \tfrac{1}{2} D_1\left(x_1^d\right)^2\right] + \left[a_2 x_2^d - \tfrac{1}{2} D_2\left(x_2^d\right)^2\right] \quad (A12.2.4)$$
$$- \left[b_1 x_1^s + \tfrac{1}{2} S_1\left(x_1^s\right)^2\right] - \left[b_2 x_2^s + \tfrac{1}{2} S_2\left(x_2^s\right)^2\right]$$
$$- t_{12} x_{12} - t_{21} x_{21}$$
$$+ p_1^d \left(x_{11} + x_{21} - x_1^d\right) + p_2^d \left(x_{12} + x_{22} - x_2^d\right)$$
$$+ p_1^s \left(x_1^s - x_{11} - x_{12}\right) + p_2^s \left(x_2^s - x_{21} - x_{22}\right).$$

The relevant KKT conditions deal with all the primal variables:

$$\frac{\partial L}{\partial x_1^d} = a_1 - D_1 x_1^d - p_1^d \leq 0 \qquad (A12.2.5)$$

$$\frac{\partial L}{\partial x_2^d} = a_2 - D_2 x_2^d - p_2^d \leq 0 \qquad (A12.2.6)$$

$$\frac{\partial L}{\partial x_1^s} = -b_1 - S_1 x_1^s + p_1^s \leq 0 \qquad (A12.2.7)$$

$$\frac{\partial L}{\partial x_2^s} = -b_2 - S_2 x_2^s + p_2^s \leq 0 \qquad (A12.2.8)$$

$$\frac{\partial L}{\partial x_{11}} = p_1^d - p_1^s \leq 0 \qquad (A12.2.9)$$

$$\frac{\partial L}{\partial x_{12}} = -t_{12} + p_2^d - p_1^s \leq 0 \qquad (A12.2.10)$$

$$\frac{\partial L}{\partial x_{21}} = -t_{21} + p_1^d - p_2^s \leq 0 \qquad (A12.2.11)$$

$$\frac{\partial L}{\partial x_{22}} = p_2^d - p_2^s \leq 0. \qquad (A12.2.12)$$

The corresponding complementary slackness conditions can be stated ready to use for the simplification of the Lagrangean function:

$$a_1 x_1^d = D_1 \left(x_1^d\right)^2 + p_1^d x_1^d \qquad (A12.2.13)$$

$$a_2 x_2^d = D_2 \left(x_2^d\right)^2 + p_2^d x_2^d \qquad (A12.2.14)$$

$$b_1 x_1^s = -S_1 \left(x_1^s\right)^2 + p_1^s x_1^s \qquad (A12.2.15)$$

$$b_2 x_2^s = -S_2 \left(x_2^s\right)^2 + p_2^s x_2^s \qquad (A12.2.16)$$

$$x_{11} p_1^d = x_{11} p_1^s \qquad (A12.2.17)$$

$$x_{12} p_2^d = x_{12} p_1^s + x_{12} t_{12} \qquad (A12.2.18)$$

$$x_{21} p_1^d = x_{21} p_2^s + x_{21} t_{21} \qquad (A12.2.19)$$

$$x_{22} p_2^d = x_{22} p_2^s. \qquad (A12.2.20)$$

By replacing the terms on the left-hand side of the foregoing complementary slackness conditions in the Lagrangean function, all the linear terms disappear from it and the final result is the following simplified dual objective function

$$\min L = \tfrac{1}{2} D_1 \left(x_1^d\right)^2 + \tfrac{1}{2} D_2 \left(x_2^d\right)^2 + \tfrac{1}{2} S_1 \left(x_1^s\right)^2 + \tfrac{1}{2} S_2 \left(x_2^s\right)^2. \quad (A12.2.21)$$

The dual problem of the spatial equilibrium example discussed in this appendix is given by the minimization of the objective function $(A12.2.21)$ subject to constraints $(A12.2.5)$ through $(A12.2.12)$.

There exists, however, a further and convenient simplification of the dual problem that was suggested by Takayama and Woodland, who called it "purified duality." The "purification" stems from the elimination of all the primal quantity variables from the dual specification in such a way that the resulting equivalent dual model is written exclusively in terms of price variables.

Consider the demand functions (which is equivalent to using the first two KKT conditions (A12.2.5), (A12.2.6)), assuming that $x_r^d > 0, r = 1, 2$:

$$p_r^d = a_r - D_r x_r^d, \quad r = 1, 2$$

and the corresponding inverse functions

$$x_r^d = D_r^{-1} a_r - D_r^{-1} p_r^d, \quad r = 1, 2. \qquad (A12.2.22)$$

Then, the first two terms of the dual objective function (A12.2.21) can be written as

$$\frac{1}{2} D_r \left(x_r^d \right)^2 = \frac{1}{2} D_r \left[D_r^{-1} a_r - D_r^{-1} p_r^d \right]^2 \qquad (A12.2.23)$$

$$= \frac{1}{2} D_r \left[D_r^{-2} a_r^2 - 2 D_r^{-2} a_r p_r^d + D_r^{-2} \left(p_r^d \right)^2 \right]$$

$$= \frac{1}{2} D_r^{-1} a_r^2 - D_r^{-1} a_r p_r^d + \frac{1}{2} D_r^{-1} \left(p_r^d \right)^2$$

$$= K_r^d - \left[c_r p_r^d - \frac{1}{2} D_r^{-1} \left(p_r^d \right)^2 \right], \qquad r = 1, 2$$

where $c_r \equiv D_r^{-1} a_r$ and the K_r^d parameters are constant coefficients.

Similarly, consider the supply functions (which is equivalent to using the KKT conditions (A12.2.7), (A12.2.8)), assuming that $x_r^s > 0, r = 1, 2$:

$$p_r^s = b_r + S_r x_r^s, \quad r = 1, 2$$

and the corresponding inverse functions

$$x_r^s = -S_r^{-1} b_r + S_r^{-1} p_r^s, \quad r = 1, 2. \qquad (A12.2.24)$$

Then, the last two terms of the dual objective function (A12.2.21) can be written as

$$\frac{1}{2} S_r (x_r^s)^2 = \frac{1}{2} S_r \left[-S_r^{-1} b_r + S_r^{-1} p_r^s \right]^2 \qquad (A12.2.25)$$

$$= \frac{1}{2} S_r \left[S_r^{-2} b_r^2 - 2 S_r^{-2} b_r p_r^s + S_r^{-2} \left(p_r^s \right)^2 \right]$$

$$= \frac{1}{2} S_r^{-1} b_r^2 - S_r^{-1} b_r p_r^s + \frac{1}{2} S_r^{-1} \left(p_r^s \right)^2$$

$$= K_r^s + \left[h_r p_r^s + \frac{1}{2} S_r^{-1} \left(p_r^s \right)^2 \right], \qquad r = 1, 2$$

where $h_r \equiv -S_r^{-1} b_r$ and the K_r^s parameters are constant coefficients.

By replacing the quadratic terms in the dual objective function $(A12.2.4)$ with their equivalent expressions in equations $(A12.2.23)$ and $(A12.2.25)$, we obtain

$$\min L = -\sum_{r=1}^{2}\left[c_r\, p_r^d - \tfrac{1}{2} D_r^{-1}\left(p_r^d\right)^2\right] \qquad (A12.2.26)$$

$$+\sum_{r=1}^{2}\left[h_r\, p_r^s + \tfrac{1}{2} S_r^{-1}\left(p_r^s\right)^2\right] + \sum_{r=1}^{2} K_r^d + \sum_{r=1}^{2} K_r^s$$

and finally, because the constant parameters K_r^d and K_r^s do not enter the optimization process, the purified duality specification of spatial equilibrium is stated as

Purified Dual

$$\max L^* = \min\,(-L) = \sum_{r=1}^{2}\left[c_r\, p_r^d - \tfrac{1}{2} D_r^{-1}\left(p_r^d\right)^2\right] \quad (A12.2.27)$$

$$-\sum_{r=1}^{2}\left[h_r\, p_r^s + \tfrac{1}{2} S_r^{-1}\left(p_r^s\right)^2\right]$$

subject to

$$p_r^d \le p_{r'}^s + t_{r,r'}.$$

This purified dual model is stated in more general terms in equations (12.39) and (12.40).

APPENDIX 12.3: SPATIAL EQUILIBRIUM, MANY COMMODITIES

When a trade analysis involves R regions and M commodities ($M \ge 3$), the corresponding systems of demand and supply functions may or may not exhibit price/quantity-slope matrices that are symmetric. In fact, consumer theory establishes that a system of M Marshall-Antonelli demand functions does not exhibit a symmetric price/quantity-slope matrix. The corresponding Slutsky-Antonelli matrix, which is symmetric and negative semidefinite, is the sum of the Marshall-Antonelli price/quantity-slope matrix and the matrix of income effects. In this appendix, therefore, we assume that the systems of demand and supply functions of each region involved in trade exhibit price/quantity-slope matrices that are not symmetric.

This assumption prevents the integration of the system of demand functions in order to represent the consumers' surplus. It also prevents the integration of the system of supply functions in order to represent the producers' surplus. Without these two integrals, there is no objective function to maximize and there is no meaning in setting up primal and dual problems as if they were connected by a Lagrangean function. The analysis of this scenario requires the direct application of the Equilibrium Problem's structure, as defined in Chapter 3 and reproduced here for convenience.

Equilibrium Problem

Quantity side

$S \geq D$ *Supply $\geq$ Demand*

$P \geq 0$ *Nonnegative Price*

$(S - D)P = 0$ *Complementary Slackness.*

Price side

$MC \geq P$ *Marginal Cost $\geq$ Price*

$Q \geq 0$ *Nonnegative Quantity*

$(MC - P)Q = 0$ *Complementary Slackness.*

The usual "marginal revenue" term has been replaced by "price," P, because a revenue function does not exist.

The available information of this trade problem regards the regional system of demand functions, $\mathbf{p}_r^d = \mathbf{c}_r - D_r \mathbf{x}_r^d$, the regional system of supply functions, $\mathbf{p}_r^s = \mathbf{b}_r + S_r \mathbf{x}_r^s$, and the vector of unit transportation costs, $\mathbf{t}_{r,r'}$, $r, r' = 1, \ldots, R$. Vectors $\mathbf{p}_r^d$, $\mathbf{p}_r^s$, $\mathbf{t}_{r,r'}$ are nonnegative and of dimension $(M \times 1)$.

The application of the Equilibrium Problem's structure to a trade scenario, as specified earlier, begins with the quantity relations that, in this case, involve the demand and supply inequalities and complementary slackness conditions of the transportation components of the problem, that is:

$$\mathbf{x}_r^d \leq \sum_{r'} \mathbf{x}_{r,r'} \qquad (A12.3.1)$$

$$\sum_r \mathbf{x}_{r,r'} \leq \mathbf{x}_{r'}^s \qquad (A12.3.2)$$

$$\left(\mathbf{p}_r^d\right)' \left[\sum_{r'} \mathbf{x}_{r,r'} - \mathbf{x}_r^d\right] = 0 \qquad (A12.3.3)$$

$$\left(\mathbf{p}_{r'}^s\right)'\left[\mathbf{x}_{r'} - \sum_r \mathbf{x}_{r,r'}\right] = 0, \quad r, r' = 1, \ldots, R \quad (A12.3.4)$$

together with the nonnegativity of all the price and quantity variables. Vector $\mathbf{x}_{r,r'}$ represents the quantities of the M commodities that are traded between region r and region r'. Constraint ($A12.3.1$) states that the demand of commodities in region r must be fulfilled by the supply of commodities coming from all the regions. Constraint ($A12.3.2$) states that region r' cannot ship out more quantities of commodities that are produced in that region.

The price relations and the corresponding complementary slackness conditions of the Equilibrium Problem are stated as:

$$\mathbf{p}_r^d \geq \mathbf{c}_r - D_r\mathbf{x}_r^d \qquad (A12.3.5)$$

$$\mathbf{b}_r + S_r\mathbf{x}_r^s \geq \mathbf{p}_r^s \qquad (A12.3.6)$$

$$\mathbf{p}_{r'}^s + \mathbf{t}_{r.r'} \geq \mathbf{p}_r^d \qquad (A12.3.7)$$

$$\left(\mathbf{x}_r^d\right)'\left[\mathbf{p}_r^d - \mathbf{c}_r + D_r\mathbf{x}_r^d\right] = 0 \qquad (A12.3.8)$$

$$\left(\mathbf{x}_r^s\right)'\left[\mathbf{b}_r + S_r\mathbf{x}_r^s - \mathbf{p}_r^s\right] = 0 \qquad (A12.3.9)$$

$$\mathbf{x}_{r,r'}'\left[\mathbf{p}_{r'} + \mathbf{t}_{r,r'} - \mathbf{p}_r^d\right] = 0, \quad r, r' = 1, \ldots, R. \quad (A12.3.10)$$

Constraints ($A12.3.5$) and ($A12.3.6$) represent the systems of demand and supply functions, respectively. Constraint ($A12.3.7$) states that the marginal cost of commodities shipped from region r' to region r must be greater than or equal to the price of those commodities in region r. The marginal cost is composed by the price in region r' plus the unit transportation cost for shipping commodities from region r' to region r. Relationships ($A12.3.1$) through ($A12.3.10$), together with the nonnegativity of all the variables, constitute the Equilibrium Problem of the trade scenario.

The numerical solution of this Equilibrium Problem using commercially available applications for mathematical programming such as GAMS takes advantage of all the complementary slackness conditions that can be added together to constitute the objective function of the numerical model. Given the statement of these conditions as given earlier, the terms in each product between the quantities in the squared brackets and the corresponding complementary variable are nonnegative. Hence, the newly defined auxiliary objective function (AOF) should be minimized subject to the linear constraints represented by relations ($A12.3.1$), ($A12.3.2$),

$(A12.3.5)$, $(A12.3.6)$, $(A12.3.7)$:

$$\min AOF = \sum_r \left(\mathbf{p}_r^d\right)' \left[\sum_{r'} \mathbf{x}_{r,r'} - \mathbf{x}_r^d\right] + \sum_{r'} \left(\mathbf{p}_{r'}^s\right)' \left[\mathbf{x}_{r'} - \sum_r \mathbf{x}_{r,r'}\right]$$

$$+ \sum_r (\mathbf{x}_r^d)' \left[\mathbf{p}_r^d - \mathbf{c}_r + D_r \mathbf{x}_r^d\right] + \sum_r (\mathbf{x}_r^s)' \left[\mathbf{b}_r + S_r \mathbf{x}_r^s - \mathbf{p}_r^s\right]$$

$$+ \sum_r \sum_{r'} \mathbf{x}_{r,r'}' \left[\mathbf{p}_{r'} + \mathbf{t}_{r,r'} - \mathbf{p}_r^d\right] = 0 \qquad (A12.3.11)$$

subject to constraints

$$\mathbf{x}_r^d \leq \sum_{r'} \mathbf{x}_{r,r'} \qquad (A12.3.1)$$

$$\sum_r \mathbf{x}_{r,r'} \leq \mathbf{x}_{r'}^s \qquad (A12.3.2)$$

$$\mathbf{p}_r^d \geq \mathbf{c}_r - D_r \mathbf{x}_r^d \qquad (A12.3.5)$$

$$\mathbf{b}_r + S_r \mathbf{x}_r^s \geq \mathbf{p}_r^s \qquad (A12.3.6)$$

$$\mathbf{p}_{r'}^s + \mathbf{t}_{r,r'} \geq \mathbf{p}_r^d, \qquad r, r' = 1, \ldots, R \qquad (A12.3.7)$$

and the nonnegativity of all variables involved.

Although it is not possible to compute correct measures of regional consumer and producer surpluses (because there is no proper objective function), it is possible to measure regional revenue and cost of selling and buying the M commodities traded under equilibrium. Furthermore, it is possible to measure the total cost of transporting these commodities from all regions to region r. After solving the Equilibrium Problem, these measures are given by $(\mathbf{p}_r^d)' \mathbf{x}_r^d$, $(\mathbf{p}_r^s)' \mathbf{x}_r^s$, $\sum_{r'} \mathbf{t}_{r,r'}' \mathbf{x}_{r,r'}$, respectively. When $\mathbf{t}_{r,r} = \mathbf{0}$, that is, when the unit cost of transporting commodities within region r is equal to zero (zero transaction costs), $\mathbf{p}_r^d = \mathbf{p}_r^s$, that is, the demand price of any commodity is equal to the supply price of the same commodity (assuming that some quantity of all the commodities involved is consumed within region r).

Exercises

12.1 The traditional components of a stylized and general market equilibrium problem are (i) final demand functions, $\mathbf{p} = \mathbf{c} - D\mathbf{x}$, where D is an asymmetric positive semidefinite matrix; (ii) total input supply functions, $\mathbf{s} = \mathbf{b} + E\mathbf{y}$, where E is a symmetric positive semidefinite matrix; (ii) technologies for the individual sectors, A_k, $k = 1, \ldots, K$. Formulate a meaningful specification of the given problem and provide an economic interpretation of all its components.

12.2 Paul Samuelson (*Foundations of Economic Analysis*, p. 5) wrote: "In this study I attempt to show that ... the conditions of equilibrium are equivalent to the maximization (minimization) of some magnitude. ... However, when we leave single economic units, the determinination of unknowns is found unrelated to an extremum position. In even the simplest business cycle theories there is lacking symmetry in the condition of equilibrium so that there is no possibility of directly reducing the problem to that of a maximum or a minimum." Discuss the Samuelson statement in view of the discussion about symmetry, integrability, and equilibrium developed in this book.

12.3 The traditional components of a general market equilibrium problem are (i) final commodity demand functions, (ii) input supply functions, and (iii) technologies of the individual sectors. Let the final commodities be specified by two sets of demand functions representing the rich (R) and the poor (P) consumers in the economy: $\mathbf{p}_R = \mathbf{c}_R - D_R \mathbf{x}_R$ and $\mathbf{p}_P = \mathbf{c}_P - D_P \mathbf{x}_P$, where D_R and D_P are symmetric positive semidefinite matrices. Let the total input supply functions be: $\mathbf{s} = \mathbf{b} + E\mathbf{y}$, where E is a symmetric positive semidefinite matrix. Technologies for the individual sectors are A_k, $k = 1, \ldots, K$.

  (a) Formulate a meaningful specification of the corresponding general equilibrium problem and provide an economic interpretation of all its components. Set up the corresponding LC problem.

  (b) How would your stated specification change if matrices D_R and D_P were asymmetric?

12.4 In both the general market equilibrium scenario and in the case of an entrepreneur who is a perfectly discriminating monopolist and a perfectly discriminating monopsonist, the objective function is identical.

  (a) Let the demand functions for final commodities be $\mathbf{p} = \mathbf{c} - D\mathbf{x}$, where D is a symmetric positive demidefinite matrix; let the input supply function be $\mathbf{s} = \mathbf{b} + E\mathbf{y}$, where E is a symmetric positive definite matrix. Define the primal objective function of a general market equilibrium scenario and of an entrepreneur who is a perfectly discriminating monopolist and a perfectly discriminating monopsonist.

  (b) Explain the difference between the two economic scenarios.

12.5 Consider the general equilibrium scenario in an economy that produces final and intermediate commodities. The final commodities' demands and the input supplies are expressed by the familiar $\mathbf{p} = \mathbf{c} - D\mathbf{x}$, where D is a symmetric positive semidefinite matrix and $\mathbf{s} = \mathbf{b} + E\mathbf{y}$, where E is a symmetric positive definite matrix. The technologies for producing final commodities are A_k, $k = 1, \ldots, K$, whereas the technologies for producing intermediate commodities are B_k, $k = 1, \ldots, K$.

(a) Formulate a meaningful primal specification and give an appropriate economic interpretation.

(b) Derive the dual specification and give a complete economic interpretation.

References

Enke, S. (1951). "Equilibrium among Spatially Separated Markets: Solution by Electrical Analogue," *Econometrica*, 19, 40–7.

Samuelson, P. A. (1947). *Foundation of Economic Analysis* (Boston: Harvard University Press).

Samuelson, P. A. (1952). "Spatial Price Equilibrium and Linear Programming," *American Economic Review*, 42, 283–303.

Takayama, T., and Judge, G. G. (1964). "Equilibrium among Spatially Separated Markets: A Reformulation," *Econometrica*, 32, 510–24.

Takayama, T., and Woodland, A. D. (1970). "Equivalence of Price and Quantity Formulations of Spatial Equilibrium: Purified Duality in Quadratic and Concave Programming," *Econometrica* 38, 889–906.

13

Two-Person Zero- and Non-Zero-Sum Games

Game theory deals with conflicts of interest between (among) persons. A game is a situation of conflict in which two or more persons interact by choosing an admissible set of actions while knowing the reward associated with each action. The persons who interact are called *players*, the set of actions are called *strategies*, and the rewards are called *payoffs*. Hence, a game is a set of rules describing all the possible actions available to each player in correspondence with the associated payoff. In a game, it is assumed that each player will attempt to optimize his/her (expected) payoff.

In this chapter, we discuss two categories of games that involve two players, player 1 and player 2. The first category includes zero-sum games, in which the total payoff awarded the two players is equal to zero. In other words, the "gain" of one player is equal to the "loss" of the other player. This type of games assumes the structure of a dual pair of linear programming problems. The second category includes games for which the total payoff is not equal to zero and each player may have a positive payoff. This type of games requires the structure of a linear complementarity problem in what is called a bimatrix game.

The notion of strategy is fundamental in game theory. A strategy is the specification of all possible actions that a player can take for each move of the other player. In general, a player has available a large number of strategies. In this chapter we will assume that this number is finite. Player 1 and player 2 may have a different number of strategies. A set of strategies describes all the alternative ways to play a game.

There are *pure* strategies and *mixed* strategies. Pure strategies occur when chance does not influence the outcome of the game, that is, the outcome of the game is entirely determined by the choices of the two players. In the case of a game with pure strategies, a_{ij} indicates the payoff of the game when player 1 chooses pure strategy i and player 2 chooses pure strategy j. Mixed strategies occur when chance influences the outcome of a game. In this case it is necessary to talk about an *expected* outcome in the form of an *expected* payoff.

Two-Person Zero-Sum Games

In a two-person zero-sum game, it is possible to arrange the payoffs corresponding to all the available finite strategies in a matrix A exhibiting m rows and n columns:

$$\text{Player 2} \Rightarrow j$$

$$\text{Player 1} \Rightarrow i \begin{pmatrix} a_{11} & a_{12} & \cdots & a_{1j} & \cdots & a_{1n} \\ a_{21} & a_{22} & \cdots & a_{2j} & \cdots & a_{2n} \\ \cdots & \cdots & \cdots & \cdots & \cdots & \cdots \\ a_{i1} & a_{i2} & \cdots & a_{ij} & \cdots & a_{in} \\ \cdots & \cdots & \cdots & \cdots & \cdots & \cdots \\ a_{m1} & a_{m2} & \cdots & a_{mj} & \cdots & a_{mn} \end{pmatrix} = A.$$

We will say that player 1, or row player, or P1, has m strategies available to him, whereas player 2, or column player, or P2, has n strategies available to her. It is assumed that player 1 attempts to win as much as possible, that is, he wishes to maximize his payoff, while player 2 will attempt to minimize the payoff of player 1. This assumption corresponds to the *MaxiMin-MiniMax* principle. This principle may be described as follows. If P1 will choose the i strategy, he will be assured of winning at least

$$\min_{j} a_{ij} \tag{13.1}$$

regardless of the choice of P2. Therefore, the goal of player 1 will be to choose a strategy that will maximize this amount, that is,

$$\max_{i} \min_{j} a_{ij}. \tag{13.2}$$

Player 2 will act to limit the payoff of player 1. By choosing strategy j, P2 will be assured that P1 will not gain more than

$$\max_{i} a_{ij} \tag{13.3}$$

regardless of the choice of P1. Therefore – given that P1's gain corresponds to P2's loss, according with the stipulation of the game – P2 will choose a strategy to minimize her own loss, that is,

$$\min_{j} \max_{i} a_{ij}. \tag{13.4}$$

The following discussion borrows from Hadley. There are several ways to restate the behavior of the two players. The expression in (13.1) is a lower bound, or a floor, on the payoff of player 1. Hence, expression (13.2) can be interpreted as a maximization of the payoff lower bound. Analogously, expression (13.3) may be interpreted as an upper bound, or ceiling, on the amount lost by player 2. Hence, expression (13.4) may be regarded as the minimization of that ceiling.

If there exists a payoff amount, say, a_{rk}, that will correspond to

$$a_{rk} = \max_i \min_j a_{ij} = \min_j \max_i a_{ij} \tag{13.5}$$

the game is said to have a *saddle point*. Clearly, in this case, the best course of action for P1 will be to choose strategy r, whereas P2 will optimize her performance by choosing strategy k. As an example, and given the following payoff matrix A,

$$
\text{Player 1} \Rightarrow i \quad
\begin{array}{c}
\text{Player 2} \Rightarrow j \\[4pt]
\begin{pmatrix}
7 & 2 & 1 \\
2 & 2 & 3 \\
5 & 3 & 4 \\
3 & 2 & 6
\end{pmatrix}
\end{array}
$$

$\min_j a_{ij}$

$$
\begin{array}{c}
1 \\
2 \\
3 \\
2
\end{array}
$$

$\max_i a_{ij}$

$$7 \qquad 3 \qquad 6$$

Hence,

$$a_{32} = \max_i \min_j a_{ij} = 3 = \min_j \max_i a_{ij} = 3$$

and this game has a saddle point. A remarkable property of pure strategy games with a saddle point is that security measures of secrecy are not necessary. In other words, any player can reveal his choice of strategy, and the other player will be unable to take advantage of this information.

In contrast, if

$$\max_i \min_j a_{ij} < \min_j \max_i a_{ij} \tag{13.6}$$

the game does not have a saddle point and the game is not stable. This event is given by the following payoff matrix A:

$$
\text{Player 1} \Rightarrow i \quad
\begin{pmatrix}
7 & 4 & 1 \\
2 & 2 & 3 \\
5 & 3 & 4 \\
3 & 2 & 6
\end{pmatrix}
$$

Player 2 $\Rightarrow j$

$$
\min_{j} a_{ij}
$$

1	
2	
3	
2	

$$
\max_{i} a_{ij}
$$

$$
7 \quad 4 \quad 6
$$

Hence,

$$
\max_{i} \min_{j} a_{ij} = 3 \quad < \quad \min_{j} \max_{i} a_{ij} = 4
$$

and this game does not have a saddle point. Both players feel that they could do better by choosing a different criterion for choosing their strategy.

In order to solve this problem, von Neumann introduced the notion of mixed strategy and proved the famous Minimax theorem. A mixed strategy is a selection of pure strategies weighted by fixed probabilities. That is, suppose that player 1 chooses pure strategy i with probability $x_i \geq 0$ and $\sum_{i=1}^{m} x_i = 1$. This selection can be realized using an appropriate chance device. Similarly, player 2 chooses pure strategy j with probability $y_j \geq 0$ and $\sum_{j=1}^{n} y_j = 1$. This is a situation in which a player knows his/her strategy only after using a chance device, such as a die. As a consequence, we can only speak of an expected payoff for the game, stated as $E(\mathbf{x}, \mathbf{y}) = \mathbf{x}' A \mathbf{y} = \sum_{ij} x_i a_{ij} y_j$, assuming that player 1 uses mixed strategy $\mathbf{x}$ and player 2 uses mixed strategy $\mathbf{y}$. The expected payoff $E(\mathbf{x}, \mathbf{y})$ is also called the value of the game.

The focus of the analysis, therefore, is shifted to the determination of the probability vectors $\mathbf{x}$ and $\mathbf{y}$. As before, player 1 is aware that his opponent will attempt to minimize the level of his winnings. In other words, player 2 is expected to choose a mixed strategy $\mathbf{y}$ such that, as far as she is concerned, the expected payoff (which is a cost to player 2) will turn out to be as small as possible, that is,

$$
\min_{\mathbf{y}} E(\mathbf{x}, \mathbf{y}).
$$

Hence, the best course of action for player 1 will be to choose a mixed strategy **x** such that

$$V_1^* = \max_{\mathbf{x}} \min_{\mathbf{y}} E(\mathbf{x}, \mathbf{y}). \qquad (13.7)$$

Analogously, player 2 expects that player 1 will attempt to maximize his own winnings, that is, she expects that player 1 will choose a mixed strategy such that, from his point of view,

$$\max_{\mathbf{x}} E(\mathbf{x}, \mathbf{y}).$$

Therefore, the best course of action of player 2 will be to choose a mixed strategy **y** such that

$$V_2^* = \min_{\mathbf{y}} \max_{\mathbf{x}} E(\mathbf{x}, \mathbf{y}). \qquad (13.8)$$

Von Neumann has shown that there always exist optimal mixed strategies $\mathbf{x}^*$ and $\mathbf{y}^*$ such that $V_1^* = V_2^*$. This is called the fundamental theorem of two-person zero-sum games. It turns out that a two-person zero-sum game can be always formulated as a dual pair of linear programming problems. Remarkably, the primal problem corresponds to the behavior of player 1, whereas the dual problem expresses the behavior of player 2. This LP specification is also due to von Neumann, and it represents the most elegant proof of the fundamental theorem of two-person zero-sum games.

The justification of the LP format is based on the observation that player 1, when choosing mixed strategy **x**, can expect his payoff to be

$$\sum_{i=1}^{m} a_{ji} x_i \qquad j = 1, \ldots, n. \qquad (13.9)$$

It will be in his interest, therefore, to make this amount as large as possible among the n selections available to player 2. In other words, player 1 will attempt to maximize a lower bound L on the admissible n levels of payoff accruable to him and as expressed by (13.9). Given this justification, the primal linear programming specification that will represent this type of behavior is given by the problem of finding a vector $\mathbf{x} \geq \mathbf{0}$ such that

Primal: Player 1

$$\max_{\mathbf{x}, L} L \qquad (13.10)$$

subject to $$\mathbf{s}_n L - A'\mathbf{x} \leq \mathbf{0}$$

$$\mathbf{s}'_m \mathbf{x} = 1$$

where $\mathbf{s}_n$ and $\mathbf{s}_m$ are vectors of unit elements of dimension $(n \times 1)$ and $(m \times 1)$, respectively. Vectors $\mathbf{s}_n$ and $\mathbf{s}_m$ are also called *sum vectors*. The first constraint of (13.10) states a floor (lower bound) on each possible strategy choice of player 2. Player 1 wishes to make this floor as high as possible. The second constraint of (13.10) is simply the adding-up condition of probabilities.

By selecting symbols $\mathbf{y}$ and R as dual variables of the primal constraints in (13.10), we can state the corresponding dual problem as finding a vector $\mathbf{y} \geq \mathbf{0}$ such that

Dual: Player 2

$$\min_{\mathbf{y}, R} R \tag{13.11}$$

subject to
$$\mathbf{s}_m R - A\mathbf{y} \geq \mathbf{0}$$

$$\mathbf{s}_n' \mathbf{y} = 1.$$

The dual problem (13.11) represents the optimal behavior of player 2. She will want to minimize the ceiling (upper bound) of any possible strategy chosen by player 1.

Let us assume that there exist feasible vectors $\mathbf{x}^*$ and $\mathbf{y}^*$. Then, from the primal constraints

$$\mathbf{y}^{*\prime} \mathbf{s}_n L - \mathbf{y}^{*\prime} A' \mathbf{x}^* \leq 0 \tag{13.12}$$

$$L \leq \mathbf{y}^{*\prime} A' \mathbf{x}^*.$$

Similarly, from the dual constraints

$$\mathbf{x}^{*\prime} \mathbf{s}_m R - \mathbf{x}^{*\prime} A\mathbf{y}^* \geq 0 \tag{13.13}$$

$$R \geq \mathbf{x}^{*\prime} A\mathbf{y}^*.$$

Hence, $L^* = \max L = \mathbf{x}^{*\prime} A\mathbf{y}^* = \min R = R^*$ and the value of the game is $V^* = L^* = R^*$, according to the duality theory of linear programming.

An alternative, but equivalent way, to establish the saddle-point property of a two-person zero-sum game is to derive and analyze the KKT conditions of the LP problem (13.10). In this case, the corresponding Lagrangean function, $\mathcal{L}$, is specified as

$$\mathcal{L} = L + \mathbf{y}'(A'\mathbf{x} - \mathbf{s}_n L) + R(1 - \mathbf{s}_m' \mathbf{x}) \tag{13.14}$$

with the following KKT conditions:

$$\frac{\partial \mathcal{L}}{\partial L} = 1 - \mathbf{s}_n' \mathbf{y} \leq 0 \tag{13.15}$$

$$L\frac{\partial \mathcal{L}}{\partial L} = L(1 - \mathbf{s}'_n\mathbf{y}) = 0 \tag{13.16}$$

$$\frac{\partial \mathcal{L}}{\partial \mathbf{x}} = A\mathbf{y} - \mathbf{s}_m R \leq \mathbf{0} \tag{13.17}$$

$$\mathbf{x}'\frac{\partial \mathcal{L}}{\partial \mathbf{x}} = \mathbf{x}'A\mathbf{y} - \mathbf{x}'\mathbf{s}_m R = 0 \tag{13.18}$$

$$\frac{\partial \mathcal{L}}{\partial R} = 1 - \mathbf{s}'_m\mathbf{x} \geq 0 \tag{13.19}$$

$$R\frac{\partial \mathcal{L}}{\partial R} = R(1 - \mathbf{s}'_m\mathbf{x}) = 0 \tag{13.20}$$

$$\frac{\partial \mathcal{L}}{\partial \mathbf{y}} = A'\mathbf{x} - \mathbf{s}_n L \geq \mathbf{0} \tag{13.21}$$

$$\mathbf{y}'\frac{\partial \mathcal{L}}{\partial \mathbf{y}} = \mathbf{y}'A'\mathbf{x} - \mathbf{y}'\mathbf{s}_n L = 0. \tag{13.22}$$

Using the information of KKT conditions (13.16), (13.18), (13.20), and (13.22), we reach the conclusion that, for $(L \neq 0)$ and $(R \neq 0)$, $L = \mathbf{y}'A'\mathbf{x} = R$, as expected.

The condition that $(L \neq 0)$ and $(R \neq 0)$ can always be fulfilled. In fact, the value of the game can always be regarded as a positive amount. This means that the solution of a game, represented by vectors $\mathbf{x}^*$ and $\mathbf{y}^*$, is the same when a payoff matrix A with positive and negative elements is augmented by a matrix C with constant positive elements.

To demonstrate this assertion, let the $(m \times n)$ matrix C be defined by a constant scalar k and vectors $\mathbf{s}_m$ and $\mathbf{s}_n$ such that $C = k\mathbf{s}_m\mathbf{s}'_n$. This means that $C\mathbf{y} = k\mathbf{s}_m\mathbf{s}'_n\mathbf{y} = k\mathbf{s}_m$ and $\mathbf{x}'C\mathbf{y} = k\mathbf{x}'\mathbf{s}_m = k$. Now we may augment the original payoff matrix A by the matrix C to make any payoff element a strictly positive amount. The corresponding LP problem now becomes

Primal: Player 1

$$\max_{\mathbf{x}, L} L \tag{13.23}$$

subject to $\qquad \mathbf{s}_n L - (A' + C')\mathbf{x} \leq \mathbf{0}$

$$\mathbf{s}'_m\mathbf{x} = 1.$$

We will show that the primal problem (13.23) is equivalent to primal problem (13.10), and therefore their solutions, in terms of mixed strategies $(\mathbf{x}, \mathbf{y})$, are identical. Notice that the structure of matrix C allows the redefinition of the primal constraints in (13.23) as follows:

Primal: Player 1

$$\max_{\mathbf{x}, L} L \qquad (13.24)$$

subject to
$$\mathbf{s}_n L - A'\mathbf{x} \leq k\mathbf{s}_n$$

$$\mathbf{s}'_m \mathbf{x} = 1.$$

The dual specification of problem (13.24) is

Dual: Player 2

$$\min_{\mathbf{y}, R} R + k \qquad (13.25)$$

subject to
$$\mathbf{s}_m R - A\mathbf{y} \geq \mathbf{0}$$

$$\mathbf{s}'_n \mathbf{y} = 1.$$

Recall that the symbol k is a constant scalar and, thus, does not affect the optimization process. This dual problem (13.25) has exactly the same structure as problem (13.11), which, in turn, corresponds to the dual specification of problem (13.10). Hence, the primal problem (13.23), with regard to mixed strategies, is equivalent to problem (13.10), as asserted.

Two-Person Non-Zero-Sum Games

Two-person non-zero-sum games are also called *bimatrix* games because they are characterized by two distinct payoff matrices, A and B, one for each player. Both matrices A and B have m rows and n columns. Elements a_{ij} and b_{ij} are the payoffs to player 1 and player 2, respectively, when player 1 plays pure strategy i, $i = 1, \ldots, m$ and player 2 plays pure strategy j, $j = 1, \ldots, n$.

Mixed strategies are pure strategies played according to probability distributions denoted by the vector $\mathbf{x}$ for player 1 and by the vector $\mathbf{y}$ for player 2. Hence, vectors $\mathbf{x}$ and $\mathbf{y}$ have m and n nonnegative elements, respectively, adding up to unity. Therefore, in matrix form, a pair of mixed strategies $(\mathbf{x}, \mathbf{y})$ is written as

$$\mathbf{x}'\mathbf{s}_m = 1, \quad \mathbf{x} \geq \mathbf{0} \qquad \mathbf{y}'\mathbf{s}_n = 1, \quad \mathbf{y} \geq \mathbf{0} \qquad (13.26)$$

with expected payoffs to player 1 and player 2, respectively,

$$\mathbf{x}' A \mathbf{y} \qquad \mathbf{x}' B \mathbf{y}. \qquad (13.27)$$

As in the case of the two-person zero-sum game discussed in the preceding section, we can assume that all the elements of matrices A and B are strictly positive without affecting the vectors of mixed strategies, as Lemke and Howson have demonstrated. A bimatrix game is completely specified by the pair of matrices $[A, B]$.

The solution of a bimatrix game consists in finding the vectors of mixed strategies $(\mathbf{x}, \mathbf{y})$ such that they lead to an equilibrium of the game. A characteristic of a bimatrix game is that it cannot be expressed as an optimization problem. In other words, there is no dual pair of optimization problems that can be used to solve a bimatrix game, as there is for a two-person zero-sum game.

The following discussion is taken from Lemke and Howson, who used an algebraic proof to demonstrate the existence of an equilibrium point of a bimatrix game. Originally, Nash demonstrated, using a fixed-point argument, that an *equilibrium point* for the game $[A, B]$ is a pair of mixed strategies $(\bar{\mathbf{x}}, \bar{\mathbf{y}})$ such that, for all pairs of mixed strategies $(\mathbf{x}, \mathbf{y})$ satisfying (13.26),

$$\bar{\mathbf{x}}' A \bar{\mathbf{y}} \leq \mathbf{x}' A \bar{\mathbf{y}}, \qquad \text{and} \qquad \bar{\mathbf{x}}' B \bar{\mathbf{y}} \leq \bar{\mathbf{x}}' B \mathbf{y}. \tag{13.28}$$

The interpretation of $\mathbf{x}' A \mathbf{y}$ and $\mathbf{x}' B \mathbf{y}$ is the expected loss to player 1 and player 2, respectively, if player 1 plays according to probabilities $\mathbf{x}$ and player 2 plays according to probabilities $\mathbf{y}$. Each player attempts to minimize his own expected loss under the assumption that each player knows the equilibrium strategies of his opponent.

To further analyze system (13.28), let $\mathbf{e}_j$ be a unit vector with all components being equal to zero and only the jth component being equal to 1. It is clear that $\mathbf{e}_j$ is a mixed strategy called *pure strategy*. Hence, system (13.28) holds if and only if it holds for all pure strategies $(\mathbf{x}, \mathbf{y}) = (\mathbf{e}_i, \mathbf{e}_j)$, $i = 1, \ldots, m$ and $j = 1, \ldots, n$. Then, in vector form, system (13.28) can be expressed as

$$
\begin{array}{llll}
(\bar{\mathbf{x}}' A \bar{\mathbf{y}}) & \leq & \mathbf{e}_1' A \bar{\mathbf{y}} & \qquad (\bar{\mathbf{x}}' B \bar{\mathbf{y}}) \leq \bar{\mathbf{x}}' B \mathbf{e}_1 \\
(\bar{\mathbf{x}}' A \bar{\mathbf{y}}) & \leq & \mathbf{e}_2' A \bar{\mathbf{y}} & \qquad (\bar{\mathbf{x}}' B \bar{\mathbf{y}}) \leq \bar{\mathbf{x}}' B \mathbf{e}_2 \\
& \vdots & & \qquad \qquad \vdots \\
(\bar{\mathbf{x}}' A \bar{\mathbf{y}}) & \leq & \mathbf{e}_m' A \bar{\mathbf{y}} & \qquad (\bar{\mathbf{x}}' B \bar{\mathbf{y}}) \leq \bar{\mathbf{x}}' B \mathbf{e}_n
\end{array}
\tag{13.29}
$$

or, in more compact form and with reference only to the first system based on the A matrix,

$$
(\bar{\mathbf{x}}' A \bar{\mathbf{y}})
\begin{bmatrix} 1 \\ 1 \\ \vdots \\ 1 \end{bmatrix}
\leq
\begin{bmatrix}
1 & 0 & \cdots & 0 \\
0 & 1 & \cdots & 0 \\
\cdots & \cdots & \cdots & \cdots \\
0 & 0 & \cdots & 1
\end{bmatrix}
A \bar{\mathbf{y}}
$$

and, furthermore,

$$(\bar{\mathbf{x}}' A \bar{\mathbf{y}}) \mathbf{s}_m \leq A \bar{\mathbf{y}}. \tag{13.30}$$

A similar discussion, with respect to the system based on the B matrix, leads to the following relation:

$$(\bar{\mathbf{x}}' B \bar{\mathbf{y}}) \mathbf{s}'_n \leq \bar{\mathbf{x}}' B. \tag{13.31}$$

The goal is now to restate systems (13.30) and (13.31) in the form of a linear complementarity problem. Therefore, the constraints

$$\phi_1 \mathbf{s}_m \leq A \bar{\mathbf{y}} \qquad \bar{\mathbf{x}}'(A \bar{\mathbf{y}} - \phi_1 \mathbf{s}_m) = 0 \tag{13.32}$$

$$\phi_2 \mathbf{s}_n \leq B' \bar{\mathbf{x}} \qquad \bar{\mathbf{y}}'(B' \bar{\mathbf{x}} - \phi_2 \mathbf{s}_n) = 0 \tag{13.33}$$

where $\phi_1 = (\bar{\mathbf{x}}' A \bar{\mathbf{y}}) > 0$ and $\phi_2 = (\bar{\mathbf{x}}' B \bar{\mathbf{y}}) > 0$, are equivalent to (13.30) and (13.31).

Finally, by defining new vector variables $\mathbf{x} = \bar{\mathbf{x}}/\phi_2$ and $\mathbf{y} = \bar{\mathbf{y}}/\phi_1$ and introducing slack vectors $\mathbf{v}$ and $\mathbf{u}$, systems (13.32) and (13.33) can be rewritten in the form of an LC problem $(M, \mathbf{q})$:

$$\begin{bmatrix} 0 & A \\ B' & 0 \end{bmatrix} \begin{bmatrix} \mathbf{x} \\ \mathbf{y} \end{bmatrix} + \begin{bmatrix} -\mathbf{s}_m \\ -\mathbf{s}_n \end{bmatrix} = \begin{bmatrix} \mathbf{v} \\ \mathbf{u} \end{bmatrix}, \qquad \begin{bmatrix} \mathbf{v} \\ \mathbf{u} \end{bmatrix} \geq \mathbf{0}, \begin{bmatrix} \mathbf{x} \\ \mathbf{y} \end{bmatrix} \geq \mathbf{0} \tag{13.34}$$

$$\begin{bmatrix} \mathbf{v} \\ \mathbf{u} \end{bmatrix}' \begin{bmatrix} \mathbf{x} \\ \mathbf{y} \end{bmatrix} = 0 \tag{13.35}$$

$$\text{where } M = \begin{bmatrix} 0 & A \\ B' & 0 \end{bmatrix}, \quad \mathbf{q} = \begin{bmatrix} -\mathbf{s}_m \\ -\mathbf{s}_n \end{bmatrix}.$$

A solution $(\mathbf{x}, \mathbf{y})$ to the LC problem (13.34) and (13.35) can be transformed into a solution of the original bimatrix problem (13.30) and (13.31) by the following computations:

$$A\mathbf{y} \geq \mathbf{s}_m \quad \rightarrow \quad \mathbf{x}' A\mathbf{y} = \mathbf{x}' \mathbf{s}_m \quad \rightarrow \quad \frac{\bar{\mathbf{x}}'}{\phi_2} \frac{A}{} \frac{\bar{\mathbf{y}}}{\phi_1} = \mathbf{x}' \mathbf{s}_m \tag{13.36}$$

$$\frac{1}{\phi_2} = \mathbf{x}' \mathbf{s}_m \quad \rightarrow \quad \phi_2 = \frac{1}{\mathbf{x}' \mathbf{s}_m}$$

because $\phi_1 = \bar{\mathbf{x}}' A \bar{\mathbf{y}}$ by definition. Therefore, a solution for the bimatrix game will be achieved by retracing the steps from the definitions given previously: $\bar{\mathbf{x}} = \mathbf{x}\phi_2 = \mathbf{x}/\mathbf{x}' \mathbf{s}_m$. Analogous computations will lead to the second part of the solution, that is, $\bar{\mathbf{y}} = \mathbf{y}\phi_1 = \mathbf{y}/\mathbf{y}' \mathbf{s}_n$.

Algorithm for Solving a Bimatrix Game

The description of this algorithm, as given by Lemke (p. 106), is reproduced below. The bimatrix game, as articulated in (13.34) and (13.35), may be expressed in the form:

$$\text{I.} \quad \mathbf{u} = -\mathbf{s}_n + B'\mathbf{x}, \quad \mathbf{u} \geq 0, \quad \mathbf{x} \geq 0 \qquad (13.37)$$

$$\text{II.} \quad \mathbf{v} = -\mathbf{s}_m + A\mathbf{y}, \quad \mathbf{v} \geq 0, \quad \mathbf{y} \geq 0 \qquad (13.38)$$

together with the complementary conditions

$$\mathbf{u}'\mathbf{y} = 0 \quad \text{and} \quad \mathbf{v}'\mathbf{x} = 0. \qquad (13.39)$$

Hence, (v_i, x_i), $i = 1, \ldots, m$ and (u_j, y_j), $j = 1, \ldots, n$ are complementary pairs, that is, $v_i x_i = 0$, $i = 1, \ldots, m$ and $u_j y_j = 0$, $j = 1, \ldots, n$.

The two systems **I** and **II** are, seemingly, disjoint, if it were not for conditions (13.39). Hence, the complementary pivot algorithm for a bimatrix game is a variant of the algorithm discussed in Chapter 6 and consists of the following sequence:

1. *First pivot.* In system **I**, increase x_1 to obtain a feasible solution of system **I**. That is, pivot on the pair (u_r, x_1), with index r automatically defined by feasibility conditions.
2. *Second pivot.* Having determined the index r on the first pivot, in system **II** increase y_r (complement of u_r) to obtain the initial feasibility of system **II**. Let (v_s, y_r) be the pivot pair.

Then, if $s = 1$, the resulting basic points satisfy (13.39), and the pivoting terminates. If not, it continues.

The algorithm consists of alternating pivots in systems **I** and **II**, always increasing the complement of the variable that, on the immediately previous pivot, became nonbasic. This pivoting scheme is automatic. Furthermore, the algorithm will always terminate in a complementary solution (Lemke, p. 107, Theorem III).

It is convenient to restate the complementary pivot algorithm for a bimatrix game in a compact form as allowed by the LC problem. This is the form adopted by the computer program described in Chapter 16, problem 7. Hence,

$$\mathbf{w} - M\mathbf{z} = \mathbf{q}, \quad \mathbf{w} \geq 0, \quad \mathbf{z} \geq 0 \qquad (13.40)$$

together with the complementary condition

$$\mathbf{z}'\mathbf{w} = 0 \qquad (13.41)$$

where

$$M = \begin{bmatrix} 0 & A \\ B' & 0 \end{bmatrix}, \quad \mathbf{q} = \begin{bmatrix} -\mathbf{s}_m \\ -\mathbf{s}_n \end{bmatrix}, \quad \mathbf{z} = \begin{bmatrix} \mathbf{x} \\ \mathbf{y} \end{bmatrix}, \quad \mathbf{w} = \begin{bmatrix} \mathbf{v} \\ \mathbf{u} \end{bmatrix}.$$

The initial basis of system (13.40) is the identity matrix associated with the slack vector $\mathbf{w}$. Thus, $\mathbf{z} = \mathbf{0}$ and the complementary condition (13.41) is satisfied. Notice that, at this initial step, the indexes of the basic variables constitute an uninterrupted series from 1 to $(m + n)$. The first step of the complementary pivot algorithm, then, consists in increasing the variable z_1, by introducing the corresponding vector into the new basis. Presumably, the vector associated with variable w_r will be eliminated from the current basis. Now, if $r \neq 1$, the complementary condition is violated because $z_1 w_1 \neq 0$. At this stage, the basic index series is interrupted because variable z_1 and its complement w_1 have become basic variables.

The pivoting scheme of the algorithm continues by choosing to increase the complementary variable (z_r, in this case) and keeping track of the variable that is reduced to zero. The algorithm terminates when either the variable w_1 or z_1 is reduced to zero, following the automatic pivoting scheme. At this stage, the index series of basic variables has become uninterrupted again.

A Numerical Example of a Bimatrix Game

The numerical example of a two-person non-zero-sum game is defined by the following two payoff matrices:

$$A = \begin{bmatrix} 1 & 4 \\ 3 & 1 \\ 2 & 2 \end{bmatrix}, \quad B = \begin{bmatrix} 3 & 2 \\ 1 & 2 \\ 4 & 1 \end{bmatrix}.$$

Hence, the payoffs to player 1 and player 2 are, respectively:

$$\phi_1 = \bar{\mathbf{x}}' A \bar{\mathbf{y}}, \quad \phi_2 = \bar{\mathbf{y}}' B' \bar{\mathbf{x}}$$

where $\bar{\mathbf{x}} \geq \mathbf{0}$, $\bar{\mathbf{y}} \geq \mathbf{0}$, $\mathbf{s}'_m \bar{\mathbf{x}} = 1$ and $\mathbf{s}'_n \bar{\mathbf{y}} = 1$.

The transformation of the game into an LC problem follows the structure of relations (13.32) and (13.33), where $\mathbf{x} = \bar{\mathbf{x}}/\phi_2$ and $\mathbf{y} = \bar{\mathbf{y}}/\phi_1$. The corresponding LC problem, therefore, takes on the following configuration, according to relations (13.34) and (13.35):

$$M = \begin{bmatrix} & & & 1 & 4 \\ & & & 3 & 1 \\ & & & 2 & 2 \\ 3 & 1 & 4 & & \\ 2 & 2 & 1 & & \end{bmatrix}, \quad q = \begin{bmatrix} -1 \\ -1 \\ -1 \\ -1 \\ -1 \end{bmatrix}, \quad z = \begin{bmatrix} x \\ y \end{bmatrix}, \quad w = \begin{bmatrix} v \\ u \end{bmatrix}.$$

In order to simplify the illustration and the understanding of the complementary pivot algorithm, we will use the compact form in terms of vectors **z** and **w** rather than the more articulated specification illustrated in relations (13.37), (13.38), and (13.39). The recovery of the information in terms of vectors **x**, **y**, **u**, and **v** is straightforward.

In the following three tableaux, the specification of the LC problem assumes the following rearrangement: **w** − *M***z** = **q**. Blank entries correspond to zero values.

↓ initial step

$$\begin{bmatrix} \\ \\ \\ -\tfrac{3}{2} \\ -\tfrac{1}{2} \end{bmatrix}$$

T_0	w_1	w_2	w_3	w_4	w_5	z_1	z_2	z_3	z_4	z_5	q	BI
	1								−1	−4	−1	w_1
		1							−3	−1	−1	w_2
			1						−2	−2	−1	w_3
				1		−3	−1	−4			−1	w_4
					1	(−2)	−2	−1			−1	$w_5 \to$

complement of w_5 ↓

$$\begin{bmatrix} -4 \\ -1 \\ -2 \\ \\ \end{bmatrix}$$

T_1	w_1	w_2	w_3	w_4	w_5	z_1	z_2	z_3	z_4	z_5	q	BI
	1								−1	−4	−1	w_1
		1							−3	(−1)	−1	$w_2 \to$
			1						−2	−2	−1	w_3
				1	$-\frac{3}{2}$	0	2	$-\frac{5}{2}$			$\frac{1}{2}$	w_4
					$-\frac{1}{2}$	1	1	$\frac{1}{2}$			$\frac{1}{2}$	z_1

↓ complement of w_2

$$\begin{bmatrix} \\ \\ \\ \tfrac{1}{2} \\ -\tfrac{1}{2} \end{bmatrix}$$

T_2	w_1	w_2	w_3	w_4	w_5	z_1	z_2	z_3	z_4	z_5	q	BI
	1	−4							11	0	3	w_1
		−1							3	1	1	z_5
		−2	1						4	0	1	w_3
				1	$-\frac{3}{2}$	0	(2)	$-\frac{5}{2}$			$\frac{1}{2}$	$w_4 \to$
					$-\frac{1}{2}$	1	1	$\frac{1}{2}$			$\frac{1}{2}$	z_1

The initial step of the complementary pivot algorithm, in its variant for dealing with a bimatrix game, is to turn all the values of the **q** vector into nonnegative elements in order to achieve feasibility of the solution. Given the seemingly disjoint nature of the overall system of equations, as stated in relations (13.37) and (13.38), this goal is achieved in the third tableau, after two iterations that are guided by a special choice of the pivot element.

In the initial tableau, the basic variables are all slack variables, that is, $\mathbf{w} = \mathbf{q}$ and $\mathbf{z} = \mathbf{0}$. The complementarity condition $\mathbf{w}'\mathbf{z} = 0$ is satisfied, but the solution is not feasible because all the elements of the $\mathbf{q}$ vector are negative. Notice that the index series of the basic variables, w_j, $j = 1, 2, 3, 4, 5$, is uninterrupted. The algorithm begins by introducing the column vector associated with the variable z_1 into the basis. The choice of z_1 is arbitrary but, once executed, the selection of all the successive column vectors to enter the basis is automatically determined by the complementary condition.

In the first tableau, the choice of the pivot element is determined by the following criterion: pivot $= \max(q_i/m_{i1})$, $i = 1, \ldots, N$ for $m_{i1} < 0$ and where m_{i1} are the coefficients of the first column in the $[-M]$ matrix. In the first tableau, the pivot corresponds to (-2) and it is indicated by the circling of this value. The updating of the $\mathbf{q}$ vector and the basis inverse eliminates the w_5 variable from the set of basic variables and replaces it with the z_1 variable (second tableau). Hence, the next candidate vector to enter the basis is associated with variable z_5, the complement of w_5. The updating of each tableau is done by premultiplying the entire current tableau by the transformation matrix T_k, where k is the iteration index, as explained in Chapter 4.

The second step of the algorithm follows the same criterion in the choice of the pivot element and achieves the feasibility of the solution in the third tableau. Notice that feasibility of the solution has been achieved at the (temporary) expense of the complementarity condition. That is, in the third tableau (as in the second tableau), the complementarity condition is violated because $w_1 z_1 \neq 0$, indicating precisely that the solution is *almost* complementary. A visual way to assess the violation of the complementarity condition is given by the index series of the basic variables, which is now interrupted, with a gap between indices. For example, in the third tableau, the series of the basic variables (under the *BI* heading) is 1, 5, 3, 4, 1, missing the index 2.

The algorithm proceeds in the next three tableaux with the goal of maintaining the feasibililily of the solution while striving to achieve its full complementarity. Beginning with the third tableau, the choice of the pivot element must be modified in order to maintain the feasibility of the solution. From now on, the choice of the pivot is determined as pivot $= \min(q_i / m_{ir})$, $i = 1, \ldots, N$, for $m_{ir} > 0$, where the r index refers to the vector selected to enter the basis.

From the preceding third tableau   ↓ complement to w_4

Left vector: $\begin{bmatrix} -\frac{11}{4} \\ -\frac{3}{4} \\ \frac{1}{4} \end{bmatrix}$

T_3	w_1	w_2	w_3	w_4	w_5	z_1	z_2	z_3	z_4	z_5	q	BI
	1	-4							11	0	3	w_1
		-1							3	1	1	z_5
		-2	1						④	0	1	$w_3 \rightarrow$
				$\frac{1}{2}$	$\frac{-3}{4}$	0	1	$\frac{-5}{4}$			$\frac{1}{4}$	z_2
				$\frac{-1}{2}$	$\frac{1}{4}$	1	0	$\frac{7}{4}$			$\frac{1}{4}$	z_1

T_4 ↓ complement of w_3

Left vector: $\begin{bmatrix} \frac{5}{7} \\ \frac{4}{7} \end{bmatrix}$

T_4	w_1	w_2	w_3	w_4	w_5	z_1	z_2	z_3	z_4	z_5	q	BI
	1	$\frac{3}{2}$	$\frac{-11}{4}$						0	0	$\frac{1}{4}$	w_1
		$\frac{1}{2}$	$\frac{-3}{4}$						0	1	$\frac{1}{4}$	z_5
		$\frac{-1}{2}$	$\frac{1}{4}$						1	0	$\frac{1}{4}$	z_4
				$\frac{1}{2}$	$\frac{-3}{4}$	0	1	$\frac{-5}{4}$			$\frac{1}{4}$	z_2
				$\frac{-1}{2}$	$\frac{1}{4}$	1	0	⑦⁄₄			$\frac{1}{4}$	$z_1 \rightarrow$

final tableau : solution

	w_1	w_2	w_3	w_4	w_5	z_1	z_2	z_3	z_4	z_5	q	BI
	1	$\frac{3}{2}$	$\frac{-11}{4}$						0	0	$\frac{1}{4}$	w_1
		$\frac{1}{2}$	$\frac{-3}{4}$						0	1	$\frac{1}{4}$	z_5
		$\frac{-1}{2}$	$\frac{1}{4}$						1	0	$\frac{1}{4}$	z_4
				$\frac{1}{7}$	$\frac{-4}{7}$	$\frac{5}{7}$	1	0			$\frac{3}{7}$	z_2
				$\frac{-2}{7}$	$\frac{1}{7}$	$\frac{4}{7}$	0	1			$\frac{1}{7}$	z_3

The solution of the bimatrix game is achieved in the last tableau. Notice that the index series of the basic variables has been reconstituted with indices 1, 5, 4, 2, 3, without any gap. This is a visual indication that the current solution is both feasible and complementary.

The reading of the LC problem's solution from the final tableau and the conversion of this solution into a solution of the bimatrix game proceeds as follows:

$$z = \begin{bmatrix} \mathbf{x} \\ \mathbf{y} \end{bmatrix} = \begin{bmatrix} z_1 \equiv x_1 \\ z_2 \equiv x_2 \\ z_3 \equiv x_3 \\ z_4 \equiv y_1 \\ z_5 \equiv y_2 \end{bmatrix} = \begin{bmatrix} 0 \\ 3/7 \\ 1/7 \\ 1/4 \\ 1/4 \end{bmatrix}, \quad \mathbf{w} = \begin{bmatrix} \mathbf{v} \\ \mathbf{u} \end{bmatrix} = \begin{bmatrix} w_1 \equiv v_1 \\ w_2 \equiv v_2 \\ w_3 \equiv v_3 \\ w_4 \equiv u_1 \\ w_5 \equiv u_2 \end{bmatrix} = \begin{bmatrix} 1/4 \\ 0 \\ 0 \\ 0 \\ 0 \end{bmatrix}.$$

From the discussion of the previous section, the solution of the bimatrix game, corresponding to the mixed strategies of player 1 and player 2, is extracted from the relations: $\bar{\mathbf{x}} = \mathbf{x}/s'_m\mathbf{x}$ and $\bar{\mathbf{y}} = \mathbf{y}/s'_n\mathbf{y}$. Hence,

$$s'_m\mathbf{x} = \begin{bmatrix} 1 & 1 & 1 \end{bmatrix}\begin{bmatrix} 0 \\ 3/7 \\ 1/7 \end{bmatrix} = \frac{4}{7}, \quad s'_n\mathbf{y} = \begin{bmatrix} 1 & 1 \end{bmatrix}\begin{bmatrix} 1/4 \\ 1/4 \end{bmatrix} = \frac{2}{4}.$$

Therefore, the vectors of mixed strategies for player 1 and player 2, respectively, are

$$\text{Player 1:} \quad \bar{\mathbf{x}} = \mathbf{x}/s'_m\mathbf{x} = \begin{bmatrix} 0 \\ 3/7 \\ 1/7 \end{bmatrix} \Big/ \frac{4}{7} = \begin{bmatrix} 0 \\ 3/4 \\ 1/4 \end{bmatrix}$$

$$\text{Player 2:} \quad \bar{\mathbf{y}} = \mathbf{y}/s'_n\mathbf{y} = \begin{bmatrix} 1/4 \\ 1/4 \end{bmatrix} \Big/ \frac{2}{4} = \begin{bmatrix} 1/2 \\ 1/2 \end{bmatrix}.$$

Finally, the payoff values are

$$\text{Player 1:} \quad \phi_1 = \bar{\mathbf{x}}' A \bar{\mathbf{y}} = \begin{bmatrix} 0 & \frac{3}{4} & \frac{1}{4} \end{bmatrix}\begin{bmatrix} 1 & 4 \\ 3 & 1 \\ 2 & 2 \end{bmatrix}\begin{bmatrix} \frac{1}{2} \\ \frac{1}{2} \end{bmatrix} = \frac{1}{\mathbf{y}'s_n} = 2$$

$$\text{Player 2:} \quad \phi_2 = \bar{\mathbf{x}}' B \bar{\mathbf{y}} = \begin{bmatrix} 0 & \frac{3}{4} & \frac{1}{4} \end{bmatrix}\begin{bmatrix} 3 & 2 \\ 1 & 2 \\ 4 & 1 \end{bmatrix}\begin{bmatrix} \frac{1}{2} \\ \frac{1}{2} \end{bmatrix} = \frac{1}{\mathbf{x}'s_m} = \frac{7}{4}.$$

This concludes the discussion of the numerical example of a bimatrix game.

Lemke's Complementary Pivot Algorithm for bimatrix games requires that the payoff matrices A and B have all positive elements. This requirement does not affect the solution of a bimatrix game. This statement can be demonstrated by the following reasoning.

Let us suppose that the payoff matrices A, B contain some negative elements and that there exists an equilibrium point $(\bar{\mathbf{x}}, \bar{\mathbf{y}})$ for the game $[A, B]$.

Now, let $C = s_m s'_n$ be the matrix with all unitary elements, and let the scalar k be large enough so that the matrices $(kC + A) > 0$ and $(kC' + B') > 0$, that is, they have all positive elements. Consider now the solution $\mathbf{x}, \mathbf{y}$ to the following relations:

$$(kC + A)\mathbf{y} \geq s_m, \quad \mathbf{y} \geq 0 \quad \text{and} \quad \mathbf{x}'[(kC + A)\mathbf{y} - s_m] = 0 \quad (13.42)$$

$$(kC' + B')\mathbf{x} \geq s_n, \quad \mathbf{x} \geq 0 \quad \text{and} \quad \mathbf{y}'[(kC' + B')\mathbf{x} - s_n] = 0. \quad (13.43)$$

The solution $\mathbf{x}, \mathbf{y}$ does not, in general, satisfy the adding-up conditions $\mathbf{x}'\mathbf{s}_m = 1$ and $\mathbf{y}'\mathbf{s}_n = 1$ because no such constraints are involved in relations (13.42) and (13.43).

Now, consider relation (13.42). By expanding the complementary condition, we write

$$\mathbf{x}'[(kC + A)\mathbf{y} - \mathbf{s}_m] = 0 \qquad (13.44)$$

$$k\mathbf{x}'C\mathbf{y} + \mathbf{x}'A\mathbf{y} - \mathbf{x}'\mathbf{s}_m = 0$$

$$\frac{k\mathbf{x}'C\mathbf{y}}{\mathbf{x}'\mathbf{s}_m\mathbf{s}_n'\mathbf{y}} + \frac{\mathbf{x}'}{\mathbf{x}'\mathbf{s}_m}A\frac{\mathbf{y}}{\mathbf{s}_n'\mathbf{y}} - \frac{1}{\mathbf{s}_n'\mathbf{y}} = 0$$

$$k + \bar{\mathbf{x}}'A\bar{\mathbf{y}} - \frac{1}{\mathbf{s}_n'\mathbf{y}} = 0$$

where

$$\bar{\mathbf{x}} = \frac{\mathbf{x}'}{\mathbf{x}'\mathbf{s}_m} \quad \text{and} \quad \bar{\mathbf{y}} = \frac{\mathbf{y}'}{\mathbf{y}'\mathbf{s}_n} \qquad (13.45)$$

which are the same relations presented in (13.36).

The correspondence between the payoff is

$$\bar{\mathbf{x}}'A\bar{\mathbf{y}} = \frac{1}{\mathbf{s}_n'\mathbf{y}} - k. \qquad (13.46)$$

A similar calculation can be done for relation (13.43), with the result that

$$\bar{\mathbf{y}}'B'\bar{\mathbf{x}} = \frac{1}{\mathbf{s}_m'\mathbf{x}} - k. \qquad (13.47)$$

This discussion establishes that the augmentation of the payoff matrices A and B by a constant matrix kC, as defined earlier, does not affect the equilibrium point of the bimatrix game.

Finally, what happens, or may happen, if there are ties in the columns of either the payoff matrix A or B'? Ties may cause the bimatrix game to be degenerate in the sense that the Complementary Pivot Algorithm may cycle between two successive entries/exit operations without reaching an equilibrium point. Without entering in the technical discussion of ties and degeneracy, we point out that the presence of degeneracy may signal the presence of multiple equilibrium points. A simple procedure for breaking ties is to add a small arbitrary positive constant to one of the tie elements. This is the procedure implemented in the Lemke computer program presented in Chapter 17.

Maximizing Expected Gain

The preceding discussion of a bimatrix game, including the numerical example, was conducted under the assumption that players wish to minimize their expected loss. If the game involves the maximization of expected gain, the corresponding Nash equilibrium for the game $[A, B]$ must be stated as a pair of mixed strategies $(\bar{\mathbf{x}}, \bar{\mathbf{y}})$ such that, for all pairs of mixed strategies $(\mathbf{x}, \mathbf{y})$ satisfying (13.26),

$$\bar{\mathbf{x}}' A \bar{\mathbf{y}} \geq \mathbf{x}' A \bar{\mathbf{y}}, \quad \text{and} \quad \bar{\mathbf{x}}' B \bar{\mathbf{y}} \geq \bar{\mathbf{x}}' B \mathbf{y}. \tag{13.48}$$

The interpretation of $\mathbf{x}' A \mathbf{y}$ and $\mathbf{x}' B \mathbf{y}$ is now the expected gain to player 1 and player 2, respectively, if player 1 plays according to probabilities $\mathbf{x}$ and player 2 plays according to probabilities $\mathbf{y}$. Each player attempts to maximize his own expected gain under the assumption that each player knows the equilibrium strategies of his opponent.

The Complementary Pivot Algorithm, however, must also be implemented as presented in the preceding sections for this form of the bimatrix game. Let us suppose, therefore, that the same matrices A and B used for the foregoing numerical example (with all positive elements) are now the payoff matrices for a game formulated as in (13.48). In order to reformulate the game (13.48) in the form suitable for submission to the Complementary Pivot Algorithm, it is necessary to invert the inequalities of (13.48) and write

$$\bar{\mathbf{x}}'(-A)\bar{\mathbf{y}} \leq \mathbf{x}'(-A)\bar{\mathbf{y}}, \quad \text{and} \quad \bar{\mathbf{x}}'(-B)\bar{\mathbf{y}} \leq \bar{\mathbf{x}}'(-B)\mathbf{y}. \tag{13.49}$$

Furthermore, we must add a suitable positive factor, k, to each element of the matrices $(-A)$ and $(-B)$ so that the resulting matrices have all positive elements, that is, $A^* = (k\mathbf{s}_m\mathbf{s}'_n - A) > 0$ and $B^* = (k\mathbf{s}_m\mathbf{s}'_n - B) > 0$. Application of this transformation to the matrices A and B used in the previous numerical example results in the following matrices A^* and B^*:

$$A^* = \begin{bmatrix} 5 & 5 \\ 5 & 5 \\ 5 & 5 \end{bmatrix} - \begin{bmatrix} 1 & 4 \\ 3 & 1 \\ 2 & 2 \end{bmatrix} = \begin{bmatrix} 4 & 1 \\ 2 & 4 \\ 3 & 3 \end{bmatrix}$$

$$B^* = \begin{bmatrix} 5 & 5 \\ 5 & 5 \\ 5 & 5 \end{bmatrix} - \begin{bmatrix} 3 & 2 \\ 1 & 2 \\ 4 & 1 \end{bmatrix} = \begin{bmatrix} 2 & 3 \\ 4 & 3 \\ 1 & 4 \end{bmatrix}$$

where the factor, $k = 5$, was chosen for implementing the positivity of all the elements of matrices A^* and B^*.

The solution of a bimatrix game $[A, B]$ in the form of (13.48), requiring the maximization of expected gain by each player, is thus carried out using matrices A^* and B^* and the Complementary Pivot Algorithm as illustrated in the following tableaux.

↓ initial step

T_0

Left matrix:

1
$\frac{-1}{2}$
$\frac{-3}{2}$

	w_1	w_2	w_3	w_4	w_5	z_1	z_2	z_3	z_4	z_5	q	BI
	1								-4	-1	-1	w_1
		1							-2	-4	-1	w_2
			1						-3	-3	-1	w_3
				1		(−2)	-4	-1			-1	$w_4 \rightarrow$
					1	-3	-3	-4			-1	w_5

T_1 ↓ complement of w_4

Left matrix:

-2
$\frac{-1}{2}$
$\frac{-3}{2}$

	w_1	w_2	w_3	w_4	w_5	z_1	z_2	z_3	z_4	z_5	q	BI
	1								-4	-1	-1	w_1
		1							(−2)	-4	-1	$w_2 \rightarrow$
			1						-3	-3	-1	w_3
				$\frac{-1}{2}$		1	2	$\frac{1}{2}$			$\frac{1}{2}$	z_1
				$\frac{-3}{2}$	1		3	$\frac{-5}{2}$			$\frac{1}{2}$	w_5

T_2 ↓ complement of w_2

Left matrix:

1	-2
	$\frac{-1}{2}$
	$\frac{-3}{2}$
$\frac{-2}{3}$	
$\frac{1}{3}$	

	w_1	w_2	w_3	w_4	w_5	z_1	z_2	z_3	z_4	z_5	q	BI
	1	-2							0	7	1	w_1
		$\frac{-1}{2}$							1	2	$\frac{1}{2}$	z_4
		$\frac{-3}{2}$	1						0	3	$\frac{1}{2}$	w_3
				$\frac{-1}{2}$		1	2	$\frac{1}{2}$			$\frac{1}{2}$	z_1
				$\frac{-3}{2}$	1		(3)	$\frac{-5}{2}$			$\frac{1}{2}$	$w_5 \rightarrow$

T_3 complement of w_5 ↓

Left matrix:

$\frac{1}{7}$	
$\frac{-2}{7}$	
$\frac{-3}{7}$	

	w_1	w_2	w_3	w_4	w_5	z_1	z_2	z_3	z_4	z_5	q	BI
	1	-2							0	(7)	1	$w_1 \rightarrow$
		$\frac{-1}{2}$							1	2	$\frac{1}{2}$	z_4
		$\frac{-3}{2}$	1						0	3	$\frac{1}{2}$	w_3
				$\frac{1}{2}$	$\frac{-2}{3}$	1		$\frac{13}{6}$			$\frac{1}{6}$	z_1
				$\frac{-1}{2}$	$\frac{1}{3}$		1	$\frac{-5}{6}$			$\frac{1}{6}$	z_2

final tableau : solution

Left matrix:

$\frac{1}{7}$	$\frac{-2}{7}$
$\frac{-2}{7}$	$\frac{1}{14}$
$\frac{-3}{7}$	$\frac{-9}{14}$
$\frac{1}{2}$	$\frac{-2}{3}$
$\frac{-1}{2}$	$\frac{1}{3}$

	w_1	w_2	w_3	w_4	w_5	z_1	z_2	z_3	z_4	z_5	q	BI
									0	1	$\frac{1}{7}$	z_5
									1	0	$\frac{3}{14}$	z_4
			1						0	0	$\frac{1}{14}$	w_3
				$\frac{1}{2}$	$\frac{-2}{3}$	1		$\frac{13}{6}$			$\frac{1}{6}$	z_1
				$\frac{-1}{2}$	$\frac{1}{3}$		1	$\frac{-5}{6}$			$\frac{1}{6}$	z_2

The solution of the bimatrix game (13.48) is achieved in the last tableau. Notice that the index series of the basic variables has been reconstituted with indices 5, 4, 3, 1, 2, without any gap. This is a visual indication that the current solution is both feasible and complementary.

The reading of the LC problem's solution from the final tableau and the conversion of this solution into a solution of the bimatrix game proceeds as follows:

$$
\mathbf{z} = \begin{bmatrix} \mathbf{x} \\ \mathbf{y} \end{bmatrix} = \begin{bmatrix} z_1 \equiv x_1 \\ z_2 \equiv x_2 \\ z_3 \equiv x_3 \\ z_4 \equiv y_1 \\ z_5 \equiv y_2 \end{bmatrix} = \begin{bmatrix} 1/6 \\ 1/6 \\ 0 \\ 3/14 \\ 2/14 \end{bmatrix}, \quad
\mathbf{w} = \begin{bmatrix} \mathbf{v} \\ \mathbf{u} \end{bmatrix} = \begin{bmatrix} w_1 \equiv v_1 \\ w_2 \equiv v_2 \\ w_3 \equiv v_3 \\ w_4 \equiv u_1 \\ w_5 \equiv u_2 \end{bmatrix} = \begin{bmatrix} 0 \\ 0 \\ 1/14 \\ 0 \\ 0 \end{bmatrix}.
$$

From the discussion of previous sections, the solution of the bimatrix game, corresponding to the mixed strategies of player 1 and player 2, is extracted from the relations $\bar{\mathbf{x}} = \mathbf{x}/s'_m\mathbf{x}$ and $\bar{\mathbf{y}} = \mathbf{y}/s'_n\mathbf{y}$. Hence,

$$
\mathbf{s}'_m\mathbf{x} = \begin{bmatrix} 1 & 1 & 1 \end{bmatrix} \begin{bmatrix} 1/6 \\ 1/6 \\ 0 \end{bmatrix} = \frac{2}{6}, \quad \mathbf{s}'_n\mathbf{y} = \begin{bmatrix} 1 & 1 \end{bmatrix} \begin{bmatrix} 3/14 \\ 2/14 \end{bmatrix} = \frac{5}{14}.
$$

Therefore, the vectors of mixed strategies for player 1 and player 2, respectively, are

$$
\text{Player 1:} \quad \bar{\mathbf{x}} = \mathbf{x}/s'_m\mathbf{x} = \begin{bmatrix} 1/6 \\ 1/6 \\ 0 \end{bmatrix} \bigg/ \frac{2}{6} = \begin{bmatrix} 1/2 \\ 1/2 \\ 0 \end{bmatrix}
$$

$$
\text{Player 2:} \quad \bar{\mathbf{y}} = \mathbf{y}/s'_n\mathbf{y} = \begin{bmatrix} 3/14 \\ 2/14 \end{bmatrix} \bigg/ \frac{5}{14} = \begin{bmatrix} 3/5 \\ 2/5 \end{bmatrix}.
$$

Finally, the payoff values are

$$
\text{Player 1:} \quad \phi_1 = \bar{\mathbf{x}}' A \bar{\mathbf{y}} = \begin{bmatrix} \frac{1}{2} & \frac{1}{2} & 0 \end{bmatrix} \begin{bmatrix} 1 & 4 \\ 3 & 1 \\ 2 & 2 \end{bmatrix} \begin{bmatrix} \frac{3}{5} \\ \frac{2}{5} \end{bmatrix} = \frac{1}{\mathbf{y}'s_n} = 2.2
$$

$$
\text{Player 2:} \quad \phi_2 = \bar{\mathbf{x}}' B \bar{\mathbf{y}} = \begin{bmatrix} \frac{1}{2} & \frac{1}{2} & 0 \end{bmatrix} \begin{bmatrix} 3 & 2 \\ 1 & 2 \\ 4 & 1 \end{bmatrix} \begin{bmatrix} \frac{3}{5} \\ \frac{2}{5} \end{bmatrix} = \frac{1}{\mathbf{x}'s_m} = 2.0.
$$

From the two versions of the bimatrix game discussed in this chapter (minimization of expected loss and maximization of expected gain), it is clear that different mixed strategies and expected values of the games are obtained using the same pair of matrices.

Exercises

13.1 Given the $(m \times n)$ payoff matrix A,
  (a) Set up the linear programming specification to find the mixed strategy that will maximize the value of the game for player 1.
  (b) Derive the dual specification and give a meaningful interpretation in terms of the behavior of player 2.
  (c) Show that, if the payoff matrix A has some negative coefficients, the addition of a constant matrix $C = K\mathbf{s}_m\mathbf{s}'_n$, where K is a suitable positive scalar and vectors $\mathbf{s}_m$, $\mathbf{s}_n$ have all unitary coefficients, does not change the value of the game.

13.2 Find the mixed strategies for the given payoff matrix
$$A = \begin{bmatrix} 3 & -1 & 4 \\ -2 & 5 & 1 \end{bmatrix}.$$
Explain your rationale and your work.

13.3 Find the mixed strategies for the given payoff matrix
$$A = \begin{bmatrix} 2 & 1 & -4 \\ -2 & 1 & 3 \\ 5 & -3 & 2 \\ 1 & 4 & 1 \end{bmatrix}.$$
Explain your rationale and your work.

13.4 Find the mixed strategies and the values of the game for the following two-person non-zero-sum game:
$$A = \begin{bmatrix} 2 & 1 & -4 \\ -2 & 1 & 3 \end{bmatrix}, \quad B = \begin{bmatrix} 5 & -3 & 2 \\ 1 & 4 & 1 \end{bmatrix}.$$
Explain your rationale and your work.

13.5 Find the mixed strategies and the values of the game for the following two-person non-zero-sum game:
$$A = \begin{bmatrix} 2 & 1 \\ -2 & 1 \\ 5 & -3 \end{bmatrix}, \quad B = \begin{bmatrix} 1 & -4 \\ 1 & 3 \\ -3 & 2 \end{bmatrix}.$$
Explain your rationale and your work.

13.6 Find the mixed strategies and the values of the game for the following two-person non-zero-sum game:

$$A = \begin{bmatrix} 2 & 1 & -4 \\ -2 & 1 & 3 \\ 1 & 4 & 1 \end{bmatrix}, \quad B = \begin{bmatrix} 5 & -3 & -1 \\ 1 & 4 & -2 \\ 2 & 2 & 3 \end{bmatrix}.$$

Explain your rationale and your work.

References

Hadley, G. (1962). *Linear Programming* (Reading, MA: Addison-Wesley).

Lemke, C. E. (1968). "On Complementary Pivot Theory." In Dantzig, G. B., and Veinott, A. F. Jr., editors, *Mathematics of Decision Sciences*, Part I (Providence, RI: American Mathematical Society).

Lemke, C. E., and Howson, J. T. (1964). "Equilibrium Points of Bimatrix Games," *Journal of the Social of Industrial on Applied Mathematics*, 12, 413–23.

Nash, J. (1951). "Non-cooperative Games," *Annals of Mathematics*, 54, 286–95.

14

Positive Mathematical Programming

Positive Mathematical Programming (PMP) is an approach to empirical analysis that uses all the available information, no matter how scarce. It uses sample and user-supplied information in the form of expert opinion. This approach is especially useful in situations where only short time series are available as, for example, in sectoral analyses of developing countries and environmental economics analyses. PMP is a policy-oriented approach. By this characterization we mean that, although the structure of the PMP specification assumes the form of a mathematical programming model, the ultimate objective of the analysis is to formulate policy recommendations. In this regard, PMP is not different from a traditional econometric analysis.

PMP grew out of two distinct dissatisfactions with current methodologies: first, the inability of standard econometrics to deal with limited and incomplete information and, second, the inability of linear programming (LP) to approximate, even roughly, realized farm production plans and, therefore, to become a useful methodology for policy analysis. The original work on PMP is due to Howitt. After the 1960s, a strange idea spread like a virus among empirical economists: only traditional econometric techniques were considered to be legitimate tools for economic analysis. In contrast, mathematical programming techniques, represented mainly by LP (which had flourished alongside traditional econometrics in the previous decade), were regarded as inadequate tools for interpreting economic behavior and for policy analysis. In reality, the emphasis on linear programming applications during the 1950s and 1960s provided ammunitions to the critics of mathematical programming who could not see the analytical potential of quadratic and, in general, nonlinear programming.

It is well known that LP specializes a model's solution beyond the economic reality observed in any sample of firms. To restate the same idea using the dimensions of an LP model, the number of production activities that are operated at a positive level cannot exceed the number of constraints. If the constraints are only a few – as in the case of commercial agriculture – an LP model may result in a solution with even fewer production activities operated at positive levels that will be very different from those observed in reality. Furthermore, an LP model is articulated in such a manner that all the net revenue is allotted to the limiting inputs, leaving a farm entrepreneur, identically and unrealistically, with zero profit.

A second methodological dissatisfaction was identified with the perceived dichotomy between econometrics and mathematical programming. During the 1960s and 1970s, a questionable characterization of econometrics and mathematical programming took place in the literature. Econometrics was seen as a "positive" methodology, whereas mathematical programming was labeled as a "normative" approach.

Without entering into a deep philosophical discussion, a "positive" approach is one that observes (measures) "facts" as consequences of economic agents' decisions and uses a methodological apparatus that avoids recommendations suggesting actions based on verbs such as "ought to, must, should." A "positive" approach is based on observed data, whereas in a "normative" approach an economic agent must actively follow a recommendation in order to achieve a given objective. For example, in a traditional mathematical programming analysis that attempts to maximize an objective function subject to a set of constraints, the recommendation would be that the economic agent who desires to maximize the specified objective function *ought to* implement the plan resulting from the solution of the model. The "positive" aspect of econometrics, instead, could be illustrated by the fact that the main objective of the methodology deals with the utilization and analysis of information contained in a sample of data representing the realized decisions of economic agents facing specific technological, environmental, and market information.

In order to illustrate the difference between the econometric approach and a traditional mathematical programming model, we will study the anatomy of each stylized model in terms of the given (known) and unknown information associated with each specification. First, let us suppose that an econometrician is interested in estimating a supply function for a given commodity using a vector of sample information on output quantity, $\mathbf{y}$, and a matrix of output and input prices, $\mathbf{X}$. Let us assume also that she chooses a linear model to represent the supply function as

$$\mathbf{y} = \mathbf{X}\boldsymbol{\beta} + \mathbf{u} \tag{14.1}$$

where β is a vector of unknown parameters that – according to the econometrician – define the structure of the supply function, and **u** is a vector of (unknown) random disturbances. This linear model and the methodology to estimate it are called "positive" because they are based on the sample information (**y**, **X**). Little or no attention is paid to the fact that a supply function is the result of a profit-maximizing assumption requiring an implicit statement such as "in order to maximize profit, a price-taking economic agent must (ought to, should) equate the value marginal product of each input to the corresponding input price."

On the contrary, mathematical programming is viewed as a "normative" approach because a typical model – but, we remind the reader, not an equilibrium problem – requires an explicit optimization operator such as either "maximize" or "minimize." Let us consider the following linear programming model that refers to, say, a farmer who is a price-taking entrepreneur and wishes to maximize profit, precisely like those entrepreneurs associated with the econometric model (14.1):

$$\text{maximize} \quad TNR = \mathbf{p}'\mathbf{x} - \mathbf{v}'\mathbf{x} \qquad (14.2)$$

$$\text{subject to} \quad A\mathbf{x} \leq \mathbf{b}$$

$$\mathbf{x} \geq \mathbf{0}.$$

In the LP model (14.2), the vector **p** represents known output prices, the vector **v** represents known (variable) accounting costs per unit of output, and the matrix A represents the known technology available to the price-taking entrepreneur. This technology articulates the structure of the problem analogously to the β vector of the econometric model (14.1) and is usually obtained in consultation with experts in the field. The vector **b** represents the known quantities of available and limiting resources. Finally, the vector **x** represents the unknown output levels of the profit-maximizing farmer. An example of accounting costs may be fertilizer and pesticide expenses. *TNR* stands for total net revenue, because $\mathbf{p}'\mathbf{x}$ is total revenue and $\mathbf{v}'\mathbf{x}$ is total variable cost. Hence, when mathematical programming is used to select the production plan of a firm, the methodology can certainly be regarded as "normative." We are interested, however, in using the methodology of mathematical programming for policy analysis. This is the reason for comparing it to the econometric methodology and integrating it in those missing parts that make econometrics a positive methodology.

The essential difference between the two models (14.1) and (14.2) is that the output levels are known in the econometric model (14.1) and are unknown in the LP model (14.2). Hence, we conclude that, if the "positive" character of the econometric model (14.1) depends on the utilization of the sample information $\mathbf{y}$, the same "positive" characterization will apply to the LP model (14.2) as soon as one will associate the known output levels with the structure of model (14.2).

Notice that in the econometric model (14.1) the information given by $\mathbf{y}$ is represented by $\mathbf{x}_{obs}$ in model (14.3). To homogenize the different notation used in the two models for indicating the same information, let $\mathbf{x}_{obs} \equiv \mathbf{y}$, and $\mathbf{X} \equiv (\mathbf{p}, \mathbf{v})$ represents the information in question, where $\mathbf{x}_{obs}$ is the "observed" level of output that may be part of the sample information. Then, the following LP model contains essentially the same information that defines the econometric model (14.1) and, thus, can be regarded as a Positive Mathematical Programming model:

$$\text{maximize } TNR = \mathbf{p}'\mathbf{x} - \mathbf{v}'\mathbf{x} \tag{14.3}$$

Dual variables

subject to $\quad A\mathbf{x} \leq \mathbf{b} \qquad\qquad \mathbf{y} \geq 0$

$\mathbf{x} \leq \mathbf{x}_{obs} \qquad\qquad \mathbf{r} \geq 0$

$\mathbf{x} \geq 0.$

Constraints ($A\mathbf{x} \leq \mathbf{b}$) are called structural constraints, whereas constraints ($\mathbf{x} \leq \mathbf{x}_{obs}$) are called calibrating constraints. The meaning of calibration is the adjustment of the value of a reading by comparison to a standard: the reading is the vector $\mathbf{x}$, and the standard is the vector $\mathbf{x}_{obs}$.

The dual variables $\mathbf{y}$ and $\mathbf{r}$ are associated, respectively, with the limiting resources, $\mathbf{b}$, and the observed output levels, $\mathbf{x}_{obs}$. Here, the symbol $\mathbf{y}$ no longer represents the sample information of the econometric model but rather the vector of dual variables of limiting resources, as in previous chapters. The novel constraint $\mathbf{x} \leq \mathbf{x}_{obs}$ constitutes the characterizing element of the PMP model. Any dual variable (or Lagrange multiplier) is interpreted as the marginal sacrifice associated with the corresponding constraint. Hence, the direction of the inequality is justified by the meaning of the corresponding dual variable, $\mathbf{r}$, as the marginal cost of the corresponding observed output levels. Without the specified direction of the inequality constraint, the marginal cost would not be guaranteed to be nonnegative.

An important comment, which anticipates an expected criticism of the PMP model, regards the apparent tautology of model (14.3) where it is clear, by inspection, that an optimal solution will occur at $\mathbf{x}_{opt} = \mathbf{x}_{obs}$. The expected question: what is the use of an LP model for which one knows in advance the optimal solution? The answer rests on the measurement of the

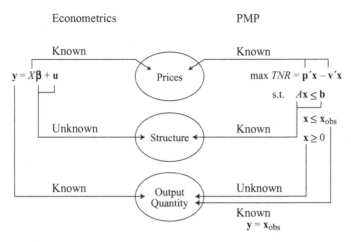

Figure 14.1. Relationship between econometric and PMP information.

marginal costs of the observed output levels, $\mathbf{r}$. This type of information is missing in the econometric model (14.1) but it constitutes an essential piece of economic information about the behavior of any economic agent.

As to the tautology associated with the PMP model (14.3), that is, $\mathbf{x}_{opt} = \mathbf{x}_{obs}$, we observe that any statistical and econometric model, such as (14.1), attempts to reach the same type of tautology. In fact, it will be easily recognized that the goodness of fit of any econometric model such as (14.1) hinges on the residual vector $\hat{\mathbf{u}} = \mathbf{y} - \hat{\mathbf{y}}$ being as small as possible in all its components, preferably equal to zero. Hence, a successful econometrician would like to get as close as possible (albeit without ever achieving it) to a tautology similar to the tautology achieved in a PMP model.

A schematic representation of the relationship between econometric and PMP information is given in Figure 14.1. Without the double arrow in the bottom part of the PMP section, the structure and the output quantity exhibits opposite known and unknown elements of the respective econometric and PMP specifications. It is precisely the double arrow that distinguishes traditional mathematical programming models from PMP models and confers on them the desired "positive" character.

An alternative view of the PMP methodology, which is complementary to the "positive" characterization presented earlier, can be stated as an approach that uses all the available information, whether of the sample and/or expert kind. Hence, in the limit, PMP can also be used in the presence of one single sample observation. We are not advocating the use of one observation if other observations are available. We wish to emphasize only that information should not be discarded only because it is scarce.

This admittedly unorthodox view of a data sample opens up the use of any amount of available sample information and establishes a continuum in the analysis of data samples. In contrast, the traditional econometric methodology requires the availability of a sufficiently large number of degrees of freedom before any estimation is carried out. What should be done, then, when these degrees of freedom are not available? Wait until more observations somehow become available? In situations such as environmental analyses, development economics, and resource economics, it is often difficult to find readily available information in the form of substantial samples. Thus, it is necessary to resort to surveys that will produce only a limited amount of information. In these situations, PMP represents a methodology that should not be overlooked.

Econometric analysis is articulated in two phases: estimation and testing being the first phase, and out-of-sample prediction or policy analysis the second phase. PMP follows a similar path although – in its original formulation – it requires three phases: estimation of the output marginal cost, estimation of the cost function or calibration of the nonlinear model, and policy analysis.

To justify the use of a nonlinear model in the calibration phase of PMP, let us consider first the dual specification of the LP model (14.3):

$$\text{minimize} \quad TC = \mathbf{b}'\mathbf{y} + \mathbf{r}'\mathbf{x}_{\text{obs}} \tag{14.4}$$

$$\text{subject to} \quad A'\mathbf{y} + \mathbf{r} \geq \mathbf{p} - \mathbf{v}$$

$$\mathbf{y} \geq \mathbf{0}, \mathbf{r} \geq \mathbf{0}.$$

The meaning of $\mathbf{b}'\mathbf{y}$ is the usual total cost associated with the limiting resources, whereas $\mathbf{r}'\mathbf{x}_{\text{obs}}$ is the additional total variable cost, above the total accounting cost $\mathbf{v}'\mathbf{x}_{\text{obs}}$, that varies indeed with the output level. Rearranging the dual constraint

$$A'\mathbf{y} + (\mathbf{r} + \mathbf{v}) \geq \mathbf{p} \tag{14.5}$$

the marginal cost of the limiting resources, $A'\mathbf{y}$, will be added to the variable marginal cost of the output level, $(\mathbf{r} + \mathbf{v})$. Hence, for achieving economic equilibrium, total marginal cost must be greater than or equal to marginal revenue, $\mathbf{p}$.

At this point, it is convenient to recall that a typical dual pair of Quadratic Programming models takes on the following structure:

$$\text{Primal} \qquad\qquad \text{Dual} \qquad\qquad (14.6)$$

$$\max\ TNR = \mathbf{p'x} - \mathbf{x'}Q\mathbf{x}/2 \qquad \min\ TC = \mathbf{b'y} + \mathbf{x'}Q\mathbf{x}/2$$

$$\text{subject to}\qquad A\mathbf{x} \le \mathbf{b} \qquad\qquad A'\mathbf{y} + Q\mathbf{x} \ge \mathbf{p}.$$

Comparing the dual constraint in (14.6) with the dual constraint in (14.5), we conclude that, if $(\mathbf{r} + \mathbf{v}) = Q\mathbf{x}$, the dual pair of LP problems (14.3) and (14.4) is equivalent (in the sense that it achieves the same solution) to the dual pair of QP problems (14.6).

To implement this conclusion in the PMP approach, we simply restate the equivalence as

$$\mathbf{r}_{LP} + \mathbf{v} = Q\mathbf{x}_{\text{obs}} \qquad\qquad (14.7)$$

where the only unknown quantity is the matrix Q. The main justification for postulating relation (14.7) is to allow the variable marginal cost to vary with output. The dimensions of the symmetric matrix Q are the same as the number of outputs. Notice that the total cost function is the integral under of the marginal cost function, and thus

$$C(\mathbf{x}) = \int_{0}^{\mathbf{x}_{\text{obs}}} (Q\mathbf{x})'\, d\mathbf{x} = \mathbf{x}'_{\text{obs}} Q\mathbf{x}_{\text{obs}}/2$$

which corresponds to the structure of the cost function in the QP model (14.6).

The estimation of the coefficients of the Q matrix will be the subject of an extended discussion involving several methodologies, including maximum entropy, as discussed in the next sections. For the moment, and given that we are dealing with only one firm, the simplest approach is to assume that the matrix Q is diagonal. Hence, the jth diagonal coefficient of the Q matrix, Q_{jj}, can be estimated as

$$\hat{Q}_{jj} = \frac{r_{LP\,j} + v_j}{x_{\text{obs}\,j}}. \qquad\qquad (14.8)$$

The purpose of transferring the information from the marginal cost level $(\mathbf{r}_{LP} + \mathbf{v})$ estimated in the linear programming model (14.3) to the matrix Q of the total cost function $\mathbf{x'}Q\mathbf{x}/2$ is to eliminate the calibrating constraint $\mathbf{x} \le \mathbf{x}_{\text{obs}}$, therefore making the resulting nonlinear model more flexible with respect to the parametric analysis that follows. It could be argued that this parametric analysis is akin to the evaluation of the out-of-sample prediction in a traditional econometric analysis. In fact, out-of-sample prediction requires choosing the value of explanatory variables outside the sample and measuring the response on the dependent variable. In a similar vein, parametric programming (or policy analysis) requires choosing the desired values of the model's parameters (usually either **p** or **b**, or both) and measuring the response on the model's new solution.

Therefore, the calibrating model of the PMP methodology is stated as

$$\text{maximize } TNR = \mathbf{p}'\mathbf{x} - \mathbf{x}'\hat{Q}\mathbf{x}/2 \tag{14.9}$$

$$\text{subject to} \quad A\mathbf{x} \le \mathbf{b}$$

$$\mathbf{x} \ge \mathbf{0}.$$

Given the equivalence stated by equation (14.7), the solution of the QP problem (14.9) is identical to the solution of the LP problem (14.3), that is, $\mathbf{x}_{LP} = \mathbf{x}_{QP}$ and $\mathbf{y}_{LP} = \mathbf{y}_{QP}$. This is the result and the meaning of the calibration process.

After the calibration phase there comes the policy analysis phase. A parametric change in either output prices or resource availability will produce a response of interest to the policy analyst.

To summarize, the PMP methodology was developed for a policy analysis that utilizes all the available information, no matter how scarce. It is especially suitable in agricultural economics where there is the possibility of combining agronomic and economic data using experts' information. It is often easier to collect information about the output levels produced on a farm (or by the agricultural sector) than information about the cost of production. Surely, the entrepreneur who decided to produce those output levels must have taken into account the available technology, the market environment, and the risky nature of the enterprise. The observed levels of output, therefore, are the result of a complex decision based on a cost function that is known to (or perceived by) the entrepreneur but that is difficult to observe directly.

In general, therefore, the traditional PMP approach consists, first, of estimating the marginal costs of producing the observed levels of outputs. Second, there comes the estimation of a parametrically specified cost function. This phase is analogous to the specification of an econometric model. The task here is to select an appropriate functional form for the cost function, an appropriate specification of the distributional assumptions of the various stochastic elements, and an appropriate estimator. Third, the calibrated nonlinear model is used for assessing the response due to parameter variations (prices, resource availability) of interest from a policy viewpoint. Hence, in a stylized fashion:

1. Phase I – Estimation of the output marginal costs
2. Phase II – Estimation of the cost function
3. Phase III – Specification of the calibrating model and policy analysis

These are the traditional three phases of the PMP methodology. In a subsequent section we discuss a methodology that combines the first two phases.

PMP with More Than One Observation

In the previous section, the PMP methodology was introduced through a discussion of its application to a single firm, or sample observation. This introduction was done mainly with pedagogical reasons in mind. We acknowledge that the event of a single observation is of limited interest, as a few observations of a given phenomenon are often available to the researcher. When N observations (firms) are available, the PMP methodology assumes a slightly more elaborate specification, but it maintains the same objectives and structure.

Phase I – Estimation of Output Marginal Cost

Suppose that the sample at hand represents a group of N homogeneous firms. By homogeneous firms we intend firms that belong to the same statistical distribution. Hence, those firms need not be identical, only reasonably similar. We assume the existence of J outputs in the sample, $j = 1, \ldots, J$. Using the same notation as before for prices, resources, and technologies, the phase I model of the nth firm assumes the following structure:

$$\max \ TNR_n = \mathbf{p}'_n\mathbf{x}_n - \mathbf{v}'_n\mathbf{x}_n \qquad (14.10)$$

$$\text{subject to} \qquad A_n\mathbf{x}_n \leq \mathbf{b}_n$$

$$x_{nj} \leq x_{\text{obs}nj} \quad \text{if } x_{\text{obs}nj} > 0$$

$$x_{nj} \leq 0 \qquad \text{if } x_{\text{obs}nj} = 0$$

$$\mathbf{x}_n \geq 0$$

where $\mathbf{p}_n$ is the vector of output prices associated with the nth firm, $\mathbf{v}_n$ is the vector of variable accounting costs (for unit of output), A_n is the matrix of technical coefficients, $\mathbf{b}_n$ is the vector of limiting resources, and $\mathbf{x}_{\text{obs}n}$ is the vector of observed levels of output. There are N such LP programs,

$n = 1, \ldots, N$. The only unknown quantity is the vector of output levels $\mathbf{x}_n$. This specification admits self-selection among firms, that is, not all firms must produce all outputs. The explicit recognition of this realistic event avoids biased estimates of the desired parameters (Heckman). Furthermore, firms are not required to use the same inputs, and the technology is individualized to each firm.

Under the hypothesis of nondegeneracy, we partition the vectors of model (14.10) between their produced or "realized," R and "not realized" NR components. Then, the dual problem of the nth firm can be stated as

$$\min TC_n = \mathbf{b}'_n\mathbf{y}_n + \mathbf{r}'_{Rn}\mathbf{x}_{Rn} \tag{14.11}$$

subject to

$$A'_{Rn}\mathbf{y}_n + \mathbf{r}_{Rn} + \mathbf{v}_{Rn} = \mathbf{p}_{Rn} \qquad \text{for } \mathbf{x}_{Rn} > 0$$

$$A'_{NRn}\mathbf{y}_n + \mathbf{r}_{NRn} + \mathbf{v}_{NRn} > \mathbf{p}_{NRn} \qquad \text{for } \mathbf{x}_{NRn} = 0$$

where the vectors $\mathbf{y}$, $\mathbf{r}_{Rn}$ and $\mathbf{r}_{NRn}$ contain the dual variables of the primal constraints in model (14.10). For the realized (produced) outputs, the dual constraint, representing the corresponding marginal cost and marginal revenue, is satisfied with an equality sign. For the nonrealized (not produced) outputs (in the nondegenerate case), the marginal cost is strictly greater than the marginal revenue, and this is precisely the reason why the entrepreneur has chosen not to produce the corresponding output. This relatively simple LP model, therefore, accounts for the self-selection process that characterizes each unit in a typical sample of firms, no matter how homogeneous. Its dual specification shows explicitly the latent marginal cost of producing or not producing the outputs that are present in the sample as a whole.

The peculiarity of the specification discussed earlier is that each sample observation (firm) is characterized by its own LP model. This is not generally true in an econometric model that relies heavily on "average" assumptions. An "average" or, better, an overall sample model is a convenient framework also in the PMP methodology for conducting policy analysis. In particular, by specifying an overall sample model it is possible to define a frontier cost function from which each individual firm's cost function may deviate by a nonnegative amount.

Hence, let us define the various sample vectors as follows:

$\mathbf{p} \equiv$ vector of average output prices,
$\mathbf{v} \equiv$ vector of average (variable) accounting costs per unit of output,
$A \equiv$ matrix of average technical coefficients,
$\mathbf{b} \equiv$ vector of total sample limiting resources,
$\mathbf{x}_R \equiv$ vector of total sample output production.

All the components of the vector $\mathbf{x}_R$ are positive by construction. Hence, the overall model for the sample is not represented by an average firm but, rather, the sample information is considered as one global firm that produces the total sample output using the availability of total resources in the sample. This choice is a matter of researcher's preference and affects neither the methodology nor the empirical outcome.

Thus, the overall sample LP problem can be stated as

$$\max \; TNR = \mathbf{p}'\mathbf{x} - \mathbf{v}'\mathbf{x} \tag{14.12}$$

$$\text{subject to} \qquad A\mathbf{x} \leq \mathbf{b}$$

$$\mathbf{x} \leq \mathbf{x}_R$$

$$\mathbf{x} \geq \mathbf{0}$$

It should be emphasized that the PMP methodology treats the sample information with maximum care. It does not resort to unnecessary aggregation before estimating any model. On the other hand, it strives to follow the guidelines of econometrics by estimating models for the ultimate purpose of policy analysis.

From the solution of the $(N + 1)$ LP models specified in (14.10) and (14.12), we obtain an estimate of the marginal cost levels associated with the observed output quantities, whether realized or not realized. This completes phase I of the PMP methodology.

Phase II – Estimation of the Cost Function

With the information obtained from the LP models of phase I, the marginal cost function for the sample as a whole is stated as

$$\mathbf{r}_{LP} + \mathbf{v} = Q\mathbf{x}_R \tag{14.13}$$

where Q is a symmetric, positive semidefinite matrix. The choice of this particular functional form for the marginal cost function is dictated by simplicity. Numerous other functional forms can be selected as discussed in a subsequent section. The choice of a functional form at this stage of the PMP methodology is akin to a model specification in econometrics. If the number of sample observations allows it, any traditional test of model specification and selection can be implemented during this phase. The known quantities of relation (14.13) are the vector of marginal costs $(\mathbf{r}_{LP} + \mathbf{v})$ and the vector of realized output levels $\mathbf{x}_R$, whereas the matrix Q is unknown and must be estimated.

Analogously, the marginal cost function for the nth firm is stated as

$$\mathbf{r}_{LPn} + \mathbf{v}_n = Q\mathbf{x}_{Rn} + \mathbf{u}_n \tag{14.14}$$

where the matrix Q is the same as in equation (14.13) and $\mathbf{u}_n$ is a nonnegative vector that indexes the marginal cost function of the nth firm. In other words, the vector $\mathbf{u}_n$ can be regarded as a deviation from the most efficient marginal cost function corresponding to the overall sample marginal cost function. The nonnegativity of the $\mathbf{u}_n$ vector is established by the frontier character of the overall sample marginal cost function.

For simplicity, the estimator of choice of this rather demanding econometric problem is a least squares estimator defined as

$$\min \Sigma_{n=1}^{N} \mathbf{u}'_n \mathbf{u}_n / 2 \tag{14.15}$$

subject to
$$\mathbf{r}_{LP} + \mathbf{v} = Q\mathbf{x}_R$$

$$\mathbf{r}_{LPn} + \mathbf{v}_n = Q\mathbf{x}_{Rn} + \mathbf{u}_n$$

$$n = 1, \ldots, N.$$

The matrix Q is supposed to be a symmetric, positive semidefinite matrix, according to microeconomic theory. In general, without taking special precautions, the estimates of the Q matrix derived from the solution of the least-squares problem (14.15) cannot be expected to satisfy the symmetry and the positive semidefiniteness properties.

In order to achieve this goal, the Cholesky factorization (Benoit; see also Appendix 14.1) will be adopted. According to this efficient decomposition, the Q matrix can be stated as

$$Q = LHL' \tag{14.16}$$

where L is a unit lower triangular matrix and H is a diagonal matrix with nonnegative elements. It can be shown that the Q matrix is symmetric, positive semidefinite (definite) if and only if the diagonal elements of H are nonnegative (positive). These diagonal elements are called Cholesky values (Lau). Therefore, the complete estimator of the matrix Q (and indexes $\mathbf{u}_n$) is given by problem (14.15) subject to condition (14.16). A suitable computer application for estimating this least-squares problem with side constraints is, once again, the GAMS application.

The total cost function of the overall sample model can be recovered by integrating the marginal cost function from zero to $\mathbf{x}_R$ to yield

$$C(\mathbf{x}) = \int_0^{\mathbf{x}_R} (Q\mathbf{x})' d\mathbf{x} = \mathbf{x}'_R Q\mathbf{x}_R / 2.$$

Similarly, the cost function of the nth firm will take on the following specification:

$$C_n(\mathbf{x}_n) = \int_0^{\mathbf{x}_{\text{obs}}} (Q\mathbf{x}_n + \mathbf{u}_n)' d\mathbf{x}_n = \mathbf{x}_{\text{obs}}' Q\mathbf{x}_{\text{obs}}/2 + \mathbf{u}_n'\mathbf{x}_{\text{obs}}.$$

By comparing the two cost functions just derived, we can conclude that, if $\mathbf{u}_n$ were a nonnegative vector, the overall sample cost function would represent a frontier cost function, whereas the nth firm cost function would deviate from the former by the positive amount $\mathbf{u}_n'\mathbf{x}_n$. If $\mathbf{u}_n$ is unrestricted, the overall cost function represents a sample "average," whereas the the nth firm cost function may lie either above or below it. This concludes phase II of the PMP methodology.

Phase III – Calibrating Model and Policy Analysis
The least-squares estimates of the matrix Q and vectors $\mathbf{u}_n$, $n = 1, \ldots, N$, which are indicated as $\hat{Q}$ and $\hat{\mathbf{u}}_n$, allow for the formulation of a calibrating quadratic programming model that forms the basis for the desired policy analysis. Indeed, there is the possibility of conducting a policy analysis at two levels of response. The first level is at the overall sample, as in a typical econometric study. The second level of policy analysis, better regarded as an extension service analysis, is at the firm level.

Let us begin with the policy analysis at the level of the overall sample. The QP model of interest is stated as

$$\max \ TNR = \mathbf{p}'\mathbf{x} - \mathbf{x}'\hat{Q}\mathbf{x}/2 \qquad (14.17)$$

$$\text{subject to} \qquad A\mathbf{x} \leq \mathbf{b}$$

$$\mathbf{x} \geq \mathbf{0}.$$

This model produces primal and dual solutions that are identical to the LP solutions obtained in phase I with model (14.12). This is the essence of calibration. The model can now be used to measure the response on output levels and shadow prices of limiting resources of a variation in either output prices $\mathbf{p}$ or input quantities $\mathbf{b}$. This parametric programming was discussed in Chapter 11 and corresponds to the policy analysis envisaged for the PMP methodology from the beginning.

Another calibrating model deals with each sample unit. Because the cost function matrix Q is assumed to be common to each firm in the homogeneous group of sample units, and because the nth $\mathbf{u}_n$ vector represents the specific characteristics of the nth firm that force the entrepreneur to deviate from the most efficient cost, the nth firm's QP calibrating model is stated as

$$\max \; TNR_n = \mathbf{p}'_n\mathbf{x}_n - (\mathbf{x}'_n\hat{Q}\mathbf{x}_n/2 + \hat{\mathbf{u}}'_n\mathbf{x}_n) \qquad (14.18)$$

$$\text{subject to} \qquad A_n\mathbf{x}_n \leq \mathbf{b}_n$$

$$\mathbf{x}_n \geq \mathbf{0}.$$

A calibrating model such as (14.18), taken in isolation, is likely to be of limited interest for a policy analysis that involves an entire sector or region. Yet, it is specified in order to reinforce the calibrating power of the PMP methodology and to reemphasize the fact that PMP treats information without the necessity of making elaborate and aggregate data series before starting the estimation of a model. In principle, the N calibrating models specified by (14.18) could be used in conjunction to the overall model (14.17) for a policy analysis that produces an aggregate response at the sample level and also a consistent disaggregated response at the level of each sample unit.

Empirical Implementation of PMP

In the model of phase I, the typical LP specification contains more constraints than decision variables. This is a cause for dual degeneracy. Assuming I structural constraints, $i = 1, \ldots, I$, it will happen that either some dual variable y_i, associated with the structural constraint, $\mathbf{a}'_i\mathbf{x} \leq b_i$, or some dual variable r_j, associated with the calibrating constraints $x_j \leq x_{\text{obs}j}$, will be equal to zero.

Let us suppose that the vector of resources $\mathbf{b}$ represents inputs such as land, labor, and capital. In general, it will be of interest to ensure that the corresponding dual variables are not equal to zero when the constraints are binding. To accomplish this goal, the option of the researcher is to "transfer" the inevitable degeneracy to the dual variable of some output level. We recall that, if a dual variable such as r_j is equal to zero, it follows that $r_j = p_j - (v_j + a'_j y) = 0$ or, in economic terms, $r_j = MR_j - MC_j(\mathbf{b}) = 0$, where we wish to emphasize that the marginal cost $MC_j(\mathbf{b})$ depends on the vector of limiting resources $\mathbf{b}$. Because, in a price-taking firm, the marginal revenue is given by the market conditions, the fact that for the specific jth commodity the marginal cost, $MC_j(\mathbf{b})$, is as high as the corresponding marginal revenue means that that commodity is less profitable than other commodities.

To accomplish the desired objective (a nonzero dual variable, $y_i > 0$, for the structural resources), the phase I LP model will be implemented using an arbitrarily small parameter ϵ in the following fashion:

$$\text{maximize } TNR = \mathbf{p}'\mathbf{x} - \mathbf{v}'\mathbf{x} \qquad\qquad (14.19)$$

$$\text{subject to} \qquad A\mathbf{x} \leq \mathbf{b}, \qquad\qquad \mathbf{y}$$

$$\mathbf{x} \leq \mathbf{x}_{\text{obs}}(1 + \epsilon), \qquad\qquad \mathbf{r}$$

$$\mathbf{x} \geq \mathbf{0}.$$

The dimension of the parameter ϵ has to be commensurate to the units of measurement of the data series. In general, it can be as small as (0.000001) but, in order to fulfill the desired goal, its specific dimension must be chosen in relation to the measurement units of the sample information.

Recovering Revenue and Cost Functions

The original specification of PMP, as presented in previous sections, was focused on the supply side of the production process. The main objective, in other words, was the recovering of a cost function.

It turns out that, using the same information as specified earlier, it is also possible to recover a revenue function. This achievement may allow a more articulated and flexible parametric analysis in the final policy phase.

The economic scenario that is envisioned in this case considers the analysis of an entire sector, region, or state where the sector or region is subdivided into many subsectors (or areas). The agricultural sector, with its regional dimension, provides a useful reference point for the scenario discussed here.

Let us suppose, therefore, that we now deal with an extended agricultural region and J products. We assume that it is possible to subdivide the overall region into N subregions that can be regarded as extended farms. We suppose that the observed information consists of output prices $\mathbf{p}_n$ and quantities $\bar{\mathbf{x}}_n$ at the farm level, the subsidies per unit of output $\mathbf{s}_n$, the farm unit (accounting) variable costs $\mathbf{v}_n$, the specific farm technology A_n, and the availability of the farm limiting inputs $\mathbf{b}_n$. With this information, it is possible to extend the scope of the PMP methodology to include the estimation of a set of farm-level demand functions for the agricultural outputs of the region. To do this, the list of phases of the original PMP methodology must be extended to include a fourth one. We thus have:

1. Phase I: Estimation of the regional set of farm-level demand functions
2. Phase II: Estimation of the output marginal costs
3. Phase III: Estimation of the cost function
4. Phase IV: Specification of the calibration model and policy analysis

Phase I – Estimation of the Revenue Function

We postulate that the set of farm-level demand functions of the J agricultural outputs are specified as the following linear inverse functions:

$$\mathbf{p}_n = \mathbf{d} - D\bar{\mathbf{x}}_n + \mathbf{e}_n \tag{14.20}$$

where $\mathbf{d}$ is a vector of intercepts, D is a symmetric positive semidefinite matrix, and $\mathbf{e}_n$ is a vector of deviations of the nth farm prices, $\mathbf{p}_n$, from the regional demand functions. Vector $\bar{\mathbf{x}}_n$ represents the observed nth firm's output levels. The estimation of the demand functions is obtained by a restricted least-squares approach specified as

$$\min \ \sum_n \mathbf{e}'_n \mathbf{e}_n / 2 \tag{14.21}$$

$$\text{subject to} \qquad \mathbf{p}_n = \mathbf{d} - D\bar{\mathbf{x}}_n + \mathbf{e}_n \tag{14.22}$$

$$D = LGL' \tag{14.23}$$

$$\sum_n \mathbf{e}_n = \mathbf{0}. \tag{14.24}$$

Constraint (14.24) guarantees the recovery of the regional demand function $\mathbf{p} = \mathbf{d} - D\bar{\mathbf{x}}$, where $\mathbf{p}$ is interpreted as the vector of average prices of the agricultural products prevailing in the region and $\bar{\mathbf{x}}$ is the vector of average outputs.

The revenue function of the nth farm is obtained by integrating the estimated demand function as

$$R_n(\mathbf{x}_n) = \int_0^{\bar{\mathbf{x}}_n} (\hat{\mathbf{d}} - \hat{D}\mathbf{x}_n + \hat{\mathbf{e}}_n)' d\mathbf{x}_n$$

$$= \hat{\mathbf{d}}'\bar{\mathbf{x}}_n - \bar{\mathbf{x}}'_n \hat{D}\bar{\mathbf{x}}_n / 2 + \hat{\mathbf{e}}'_n \bar{\mathbf{x}}_n. \tag{14.25}$$

This process completes phase I of the novel PMP extension.

Phase II – Estimation of Marginal Costs

The estimated revenue function (14.25) is used in phase II to recover the marginal costs of all the N farms, one at a time. This step is similar to model (14.10) but, in this case, the programming problem of the nth farm becomes a quadratic model:

$$\max \ TNR_n = \hat{\mathbf{d}}'\mathbf{x}_n - \mathbf{x}'_n \hat{D}\mathbf{x}_n / 2 + \hat{\mathbf{e}}'_n \mathbf{x}_n - \mathbf{v}'_n \mathbf{x}_n \tag{14.26}$$

$$\text{Dual Variables}$$

$$\text{subject to} \quad A_n \mathbf{x}_n \leq \mathbf{b}_n \qquad \mathbf{y}$$

$$\mathbf{x}_n \leq \bar{\mathbf{x}}_n (1 + \epsilon) \qquad \mathbf{r}$$

$$\mathbf{x}_n \geq \mathbf{0}.$$

The entire series of marginal costs of all the N farms, $(\hat{\mathbf{r}}_n + \mathbf{v}_n)$, $n = 1, \ldots, N$, forms the basis for the estimation of the cost function in the next phase.

Phase III – Estimation of the Cost Function

The specification of the marginal cost function follows the strategy presented in previous sections, with a variation to admit a vector of intercepts $\mathbf{a}$:

$$\hat{\mathbf{r}}_{QP\,n} + \mathbf{v}_n = \mathbf{a} + Q\bar{\mathbf{x}}_n + \mathbf{u}_n \tag{14.27}$$

where Q is a symmetric, positive semidefinite matrix. The chosen estimator may be a restricted least squares, as in phase I. Hence,

$$\min \; \sum_n \mathbf{u}_n' \mathbf{u}_n / 2 \tag{14.28}$$

$$\text{subject to} \quad \hat{\mathbf{r}}_{QP\,n} + \mathbf{v}_n = \mathbf{a} + Q\bar{\mathbf{x}}_n + \mathbf{u}_n \tag{14.29}$$

$$Q = L H L'$$

$$\sum_n \mathbf{u}_n = \mathbf{0}. \tag{14.30}$$

The cost function of the nth farm is obtained by integration of the estimated marginal cost function, as before:

$$C_n(\mathbf{x}_n) = \int_0^{\bar{\mathbf{x}}_n} (\hat{\mathbf{a}} + \hat{Q}\mathbf{x}_n + \hat{\mathbf{u}}_n)' d\mathbf{x}_n$$

$$= \hat{\mathbf{a}}' \bar{\mathbf{x}}_n + \bar{\mathbf{x}}_n' \hat{Q} \bar{\mathbf{x}}_n / 2 + \hat{\mathbf{u}}_n' \bar{\mathbf{x}}_n. \tag{14.31}$$

Phase IV – Calibrating Model

The final assembly of the calibrating model is done by defining an objective function that is the difference between the revenue and the cost functions estimated earlier:

$$\max \; TNR_n = \hat{\mathbf{d}}' \mathbf{x}_n - \mathbf{x}_n' \hat{D} \mathbf{x}_n / 2 + \hat{\mathbf{e}}_n' \mathbf{x}_n$$

$$- (\hat{\mathbf{a}}' \mathbf{x}_n + \mathbf{x}_n' \hat{Q} \mathbf{x}_n / 2 + \hat{\mathbf{u}}_n' \mathbf{x}_n) \tag{14.32}$$

$$\text{subject to} \quad A_n \mathbf{x}_n \leq \mathbf{b}_n$$

$$\mathbf{x}_n \geq \mathbf{0}.$$

This model can now be used to evaluate policy changes involving, for example, the limiting inputs $\mathbf{b}_n$ or the intercepts of demand and/or supply functions.

Symmetric Positive Equilibrium Problem – SPEP

In previous sections, the specification of the PMP methodology involved essentially one limiting input, say land. This restriction has to do with the degeneracy caused in recovering the input and outputs marginal costs. With more constraints than decision variables, the estimation of marginal cost of previous sections produces a zero value of either the dual variable of the single limiting input, y, or (at least) one zero value in the vector of marginal costs, $\mathbf{r}$. The specification of an appropriate dimension of the ϵ parameter of the calibrating constraints allows us to obtain a positive value of the dual variable associated with the single structural constraint, as we would like to achieve for a constraint such as land. When multiple structural constraints are present, the degeneracy of some of the dual variables associated with them cannot be avoided.

To circumvent this "pitfall" of PMP, it is necessary to state a symmetric structure and formulate the economic problem as an equilibrium model. In order to grasp the meaning of the relevant symmetric structure and the associated equilibrium problem, we review the primal and dual constraints of model (14.3), which, we now know, admit only one limiting input b:

$$A\mathbf{x} \le b \qquad\qquad y \qquad\qquad (14.33)$$

$$\mathbf{x} \le \bar{\mathbf{x}} \qquad\qquad \mathbf{r} \qquad\qquad (14.34)$$

$$A'y + (\mathbf{r} + \mathbf{v}) \ge \mathbf{p} \qquad\qquad \mathbf{x} \qquad\qquad (14.35)$$

$$y \ge 0 \qquad\qquad\qquad (14.36)$$

The economic meaning of all the foregoing terms remains as before. The vector $\bar{\mathbf{x}}$ stands now for the realized (observed) quantities of the firm's outputs. The structure of problem (14.33) through (14.36) is asymmetric because the primal constraints exhibit only one set of primal variables, $\mathbf{x}$, whereas the dual constraints include two sets of dual variables, $(y, \mathbf{r})$.

As stated earlier, the introduction of multiple limiting inputs induces a degeneracy of the associated dual variables. To avoid this occurrence, we assume that information on the regional market price of all limiting inputs is available and observable. Let vector $\mathbf{w}$ represent this information. Then, the Symmetric Positive Equilibrium Problem (SPEP) can be stated as

$$Ax + \beta \leq b \qquad\qquad y \qquad\qquad (14.37)$$

$$x \leq \bar{x} \qquad\qquad r \qquad\qquad (14.38)$$

$$A'y + (r + v) \geq p \qquad\qquad x \qquad\qquad (14.39)$$

$$y \geq w \qquad\qquad \beta \qquad\qquad (14.40)$$

The preceding four constraints have a symmetric formulation. The first two constraints, (14.37) and (14.38), are quantity constraints representing, respectively, the demand and supply of limiting inputs and output calibration. Constraints (14.39) and (14.40) represent marginal costs and marginal revenues of outputs and inputs, respectively. Notice the symmetric position and role of the two vector variables designated with symbols, r and β. Both vectors have the meaning of dual variables of the corresponding constraints. The r vector variable also appears in the output marginal cost constraint (14.39) and, together with vector v, takes on the meaning of variable marginal cost. The β dual vector variable appearing in the input constraint (14.37) defines the effective supply of limiting inputs $(b - \beta)$, as opposed to the fixed input and nominal supply represented by the vector b. The vector β enables a generalization of the limiting input supply that allows for a more flexible specification of allocatable inputs. The vector b can be thought of as an upper limit on the quantity of allocatable inputs that does not imply a zero implicit marginal cost for quantities of allocatable inputs used in amounts less than b, as in the usual asymmetric specification $Ax \leq b$. Furthermore, the vector β is not to be regarded as a slack variable. The symbols to the right of the four constraints are their corresponding dual variables.

To complete the specification of the equilibrium problem we must state the associated complementary slackness conditions:

$$y'(b - Ax - \beta) = 0 \qquad\qquad (14.41)$$

$$r'(\bar{x} - x) = 0 \qquad\qquad (14.42)$$

$$x'(A'y + r + v - p) = 0 \qquad\qquad (14.43)$$

$$\beta'(y - w) = 0 \qquad\qquad (14.44)$$

The solution of the foregoing Symmetric Positive Equilibrium Problem represented by the set of constraints [(14.37) through (14.44)] generates estimates of output levels, x, the effective supply of limiting inputs, $(b - \beta)$, the total marginal cost of production activities, $(A'\mathbf{y} + \mathbf{r} + \mathbf{v})$, and the marginal cost of limiting inputs, $\mathbf{y}$.

In order to solve the preceding SPEP by means of a suitable computer code such as GAMS, it is convenient to introduce slack vector variables in each constraint [(14.37) through (14.40)]. Let $\mathbf{z}_{P1}$, $\mathbf{z}_{P2}$, $\mathbf{z}_{D1}$, $\mathbf{z}_{D2}$ be nonnegative slack vectors of the primal and dual constraints of the SPEP structure. Then, a computable specification of SPEP can be stated as

$$\min \{\mathbf{z}'_{P1}\mathbf{y} + \mathbf{z}'_{P2}\mathbf{r} + \mathbf{z}'_{D1}\mathbf{x} + \mathbf{z}'_{D2}\beta\} = 0 \qquad (14.45)$$

subject to

$$A\mathbf{x} + \beta + \mathbf{z}_{P1} = \mathbf{b} \qquad (14.46)$$

$$\mathbf{x} + \mathbf{z}_{P2} = \bar{\mathbf{x}} \qquad (14.47)$$

$$A'\mathbf{y} + (\mathbf{r} + \mathbf{v}) = \mathbf{p} + \mathbf{z}_{D1} \qquad (14.48)$$

$$\mathbf{y} = \mathbf{w} + \mathbf{z}_{D2}. \qquad (14.49)$$

In this structure of SPEP, the complementary slackness conditions [(14.41) through (14.44)] have been added together to form the auxiliary objective function (14.45) that, we know, must obtain a zero value at the equilibrium solution because all the variables are nonnegative. Hence, an equilibrium solution $(\mathbf{x}, \mathbf{y}, \mathbf{r}, \beta)$ is achieved when the objective function (14.45) reaches a value of zero and the solution vector $(\mathbf{x}, \mathbf{y}, \mathbf{r}, \beta)$ is feasible.

Phase II of SPEP – the Total Cost Function

In previous versions of the traditional PMP methodology, phase II (or phase III) of the estimation process dealt with the recovery of a *variable* cost function, that is, a function concerned with variable costs. SPEP, however, will recover a *total* cost function. Let us recall that the total marginal cost is represented by $[A'\mathbf{y} + (\mathbf{r} + \mathbf{v})]$, with component $(\mathbf{r} + \mathbf{v})$ representing the variable marginal cost while $A'\mathbf{y}$ has the meaning of marginal cost due to limiting inputs.

By definition, a total cost function is a function of output levels and input prices, $C(\mathbf{x}, \mathbf{y})$. The properties of a cost function require it to be concave and linear homogeneous in input prices. The functional form selected to represent input prices is a generalized Leontief specification with nonnegative and symmetric off-diagonal terms. For the outputs, the functional form is a quadratic specification in order to avoid the imposition of a linear technology. Furthermore, we must allow sufficient flexibility to fit the available empirical data. For this reason we add an unrestricted intercept term, with the proviso to guarantee the linear homogeneity of the entire cost function. All these considerations lead to the following functional form:

$$C(\mathbf{x}, \mathbf{y}) = \mathbf{u}'\mathbf{y}(\mathbf{f}'\mathbf{x}) + \mathbf{u}'\mathbf{y}(\mathbf{x}' Q\mathbf{x})/2 + (\mathbf{y}^{1/2})' S\mathbf{y}^{1/2} \qquad (14.50)$$

where $\mathbf{u}$ is a vector of unit elements. Many different functional forms could have been selected. The matrix Q is symmetric positive semidefinite, whereas the S matrix is symmetric with nonnegative off-diagonal terms.

The marginal cost function is the derivative of equation (14.50) with respect to the output vector $\mathbf{x}$, that is,

$$\frac{\partial C}{\partial \mathbf{x}} = (\mathbf{u}'\mathbf{y})\mathbf{f} + (\mathbf{u}'\mathbf{y}) Q\mathbf{x} = A'\mathbf{y} + \mathbf{r} + \mathbf{v} \qquad (14.51)$$

and, by the Shephard lemma, the limiting input-derived demand functions are

$$\frac{\partial C}{\partial \mathbf{y}} = (\mathbf{f}'\mathbf{x})\mathbf{u} + \mathbf{u}(\mathbf{x}' Q\mathbf{x})/2 + \Delta_{\mathbf{y}^{-1/2}} S\mathbf{y}^{1/2} = A\mathbf{x} = \mathbf{b} - \boldsymbol{\beta}. \qquad (14.52)$$

The matrix $\Delta_{\mathbf{y}^{-1/2}} S\mathbf{y}^{1/2}$ is diagonal with elements of the vector $\mathbf{y}^{-1/2}$ on the diagonal.

The objective of phase II is to estimate the parameters of the cost function $\mathbf{f}$, Q, S. This estimation can be performed by a maximum entropy estimator (Golan et al.). The relevant relations are stated as follows:

$$A'\hat{\mathbf{y}} + \hat{\mathbf{r}} + \mathbf{v} = (\mathbf{u}'\hat{\mathbf{y}})\mathbf{f} + (\mathbf{u}'\hat{\mathbf{y}}) Q\bar{\mathbf{x}} \qquad (14.53)$$

$$A\bar{\mathbf{x}} = (\mathbf{f}'\bar{\mathbf{x}})\mathbf{u} + \mathbf{u}(\bar{\mathbf{x}}' Q\bar{\mathbf{x}})/2 + \Delta_{\mathbf{y}^{-1/2}} S\hat{\mathbf{y}}^{1/2}. \qquad (14.54)$$

Equation (14.53) represents output marginal costs. Equation (14.54) is the vector of derived demands for inputs. The sample information is given by the left-hand-side expressions of equations (14.53) and (14.54), where $\bar{\mathbf{x}}$ is the realized level of outputs and $(\hat{\mathbf{y}}, \hat{\mathbf{r}})$ are the computed shadow variables from phase I.

Phase III of SPEP – Calibrating Model for Policy Analysis

With the estimated parameters of the total cost function, $\hat{\mathbf{f}}$, $\hat{Q}$, $\hat{S}$, it is possible to set up a calibrating specification that takes the structure of an equilibrium problem:

$$\min \{\mathbf{z}'_{P1}\mathbf{y} + \mathbf{z}'_{D1}\mathbf{x} + \mathbf{z}'_{D2}\boldsymbol{\beta}\} = 0 \qquad (14.55)$$

subject to

$$(\hat{\mathbf{f}}'\mathbf{x})\mathbf{u} + \mathbf{u}(\mathbf{x}'\hat{Q}\mathbf{x})/2 + \Delta_{\mathbf{y}^{-1/2}}\hat{S}\mathbf{y}^{1/2} + \boldsymbol{\beta} + \mathbf{z}_{P1} = \mathbf{b} \qquad (14.56)$$

$$(\mathbf{u}'\mathbf{y})\hat{\mathbf{f}} + (\mathbf{u}'\mathbf{y})\hat{Q}\mathbf{x} = \mathbf{p} + \mathbf{z}_{D1} \qquad (14.57)$$

$$\mathbf{y} = \mathbf{w} + \mathbf{z}_{D2} \qquad (14.58)$$

where all the unknown variables are nonnegative. The linear technology in equation (14.46) is now replaced by the Shephard lemma's equation (14.52) in constraint (14.56). Similarly, the marginal cost in equation (14.48) is replaced by the marginal output cost equation (14.51). In addition, the calibration constraints in equation (14.47) are removed since the calibration of output levels is now guaranteed by the cost function. Constraint (14.56), when rearranged as $\{(\hat{\mathbf{f}}'\mathbf{x})\mathbf{u} + \mathbf{u}(\mathbf{x}'\hat{Q}\mathbf{x})/2 + \Delta_{\mathbf{y}^{-1/2}}\hat{S}\mathbf{y}^{1/2} \leq \mathbf{b} - \boldsymbol{\beta}\}$, states the quantity equilibrium condition according to which the demand for limiting inputs must be less than or equal to the effective supply of those inputs. The quantity $(\mathbf{b} - \boldsymbol{\beta})$ is the effective supply by virtue of the endogenous parameter $\boldsymbol{\beta}$ that is part of the solution. The SPEP specification given earlier neither implies nor excludes an optimizing behavior. Hence, it removes from the original PMP methodology the last vestige of a normative behavior. Furthermore, the nonlinear cost function implies a nonlinear technology and, therefore, it removes the restriction of fixed production coefficients.

Dynamic Positive Equilibrium Problem – DPEP

The methodology of the Symmetric Positive Equilibrium Problem is extended in this section to include a dynamic structure. Dynamic models of economic problems can take on different specifications in relation to different sources of dynamic information. When dealing with farms whose principal output is derived from orchards, for example, the equation of motion is naturally represented by the difference between standing orchard acreage in two successive years plus new planting and minus culling. In more general terms, the investment model provides a natural representation of stocks and flows via the familiar investment equation

$$K_t = K_{t-1} + I_t - \delta K_{t-1} \qquad (14.59)$$

where K_t represents the capital stock at time t, I_t is the investment flow at time t, and δ is the fixed depreciation rate. This dynamic framework, expressed by an equation of motion, becomes operational only when explicit information about investment, initial stock, and depreciation is available.

Annual crops are also dynamically connected through decisions that involve price expectations and some inertia of the decision-making process. We observe that farmers who produce field crops, for example, will produce these activities year after year with an appropriate adjustment of both acreage and yields. In this section, therefore, we consider economic units (farms, regions, sectors) that produce annual crops: that is, production activities that, in principle, may have neither technological antecedents nor market consequences but, nevertheless, are observed to be connected through time. We postulate that the underlying dynamic connection is guided by a process of output price expectations.

The Dynamic Framework
We assume that output price expectations of the decision maker are governed by an adaptive process such as

$$\mathbf{p}_t^* - \mathbf{p}_{t-1}^* = \Gamma(\mathbf{p}_{t-1} - \mathbf{p}_{t-1}^*) \tag{14.60}$$

where the starred vectors are interpreted as expected output prices and Γ is a diagonal matrix with unrestricted elements. In general, the elements of the Γ matrix are required to be positive and less than 1 in order to guarantee the stability of the difference equation in an infinite series of time periods. The case discussed here, however, considers a finite horizon of only a few years, and no stability issue is at stake. It is as if we were to model an arbitrarily small time interval of an infinite horizon. Within such a small interval, the relation expressed by equation (14.60) can be either convergent or explosive without negating the stability of the infinite process. A further assumption is that the expected output supply function is specified as

$$\mathbf{x}_t = B\mathbf{p}_t^* + \mathbf{w}_t \tag{14.61}$$

where B is a positive diagonal matrix and $\mathbf{w}_t$ is a vector of intercepts. Then, equation (14.60) can be rearranged as

$$\Gamma\mathbf{p}_{t-1} = \mathbf{p}_t^* - [I - \Gamma]\mathbf{p}_{t-1}^* \tag{14.62}$$

while, by lagging one period the supply function, multiplying it by the matrix $[I - \Gamma]$, and subtracting the result from equation (14.61), we obtain

$$\mathbf{x}_t - [I - \Gamma]\mathbf{x}_{t-1} = B\{\mathbf{p}_t^* - [I - \Gamma]\mathbf{p}_{t-1}^*\} + \mathbf{w}_t - [I - \Gamma]\mathbf{w}_{t-1} \tag{14.63}$$

$$= B\Gamma\mathbf{p}_{t-1} + \mathbf{v}_t$$

where $\mathbf{v}_t = \mathbf{w}_t - [I - \Gamma]\mathbf{w}_{t-1}$. Hence, the equation of motion involving annual crops and resulting from the assumption of adaptive expectations for output prices is

$$\mathbf{x}_t = [I - \Gamma]\mathbf{x}_{t-1} + B\Gamma\mathbf{p}_{t-1} + \mathbf{v}_t. \tag{14.64}$$

It is important to emphasize that this equation of motion is different from the more traditional dynamic relation where the state variable is usually interpreted as a stock and the control is under the jurisdiction of the decision maker. Equation of motion (14.64) emerges from an assumption of adaptive expectations about output prices. Prices are not under the control of the decision maker and, furthermore, the state variable is not a stock but a flow variable as it represents yearly output levels. Nevertheless, relation (14.64) is a legitimate equation of motion that relates entrepreneur's decisions from year to year.

Phase I of DPEP – Estimation of Marginal Costs

Before proceeding further in the development of the Dynamic Positive Equilibrium Problem, it is necessary to estimate matrices B and Γ and vector $\mathbf{v}_t$ that define the equation of motion. One approach to this problem is to use the maximum entropy methodology as presented in Golan et al. and modified by van Akkeren and Judge. In this section, therefore, we assume that the estimation of the relevant matrices was performed, $(\hat{B}, \hat{\Gamma}, \hat{\mathbf{v}}_t)$, and proceed to the discussion of phase I of DPEP.

We begin with a specification of the optimization problem for the entire horizon $t = 1, \ldots, T$ and the statement of a salvage function. We assume that the economic agent wishes to maximize the discounted stream of profit (or net revenue) over the horizon T. After T periods, it is assumed that the objective function consists of the discounted value of profit from period $(T + 1)$ to infinity, which is realized under a condition of steady state. Furthermore, the given information refers to input and output prices, $\mathbf{r}_t, \mathbf{p}_t$, the discount rate, ρ, the matrix of technical coefficients, A_t, and the available supply of limiting inputs, $\mathbf{b}_t$.

Analytically, then, the discrete Dynamic Positive Equilibrium Problem takes on the following specification:

$$\max V = \sum_{t=1}^{T} [\mathbf{p}'_t \mathbf{x}_t - \mathbf{r}'_t(\mathbf{b}_t - \boldsymbol{\beta}_t)]/(1+\rho)^{(t-1)} \tag{14.65}$$

$$+ \sum_{\tau=T+1}^{+\infty} [\mathbf{p}'_{T+1}\mathbf{x}_{T+1} - \mathbf{r}'_{T+1}(A_{T+1}\mathbf{x}_{T+1})]\left[\frac{1}{1+\rho}\right]^{\tau-1}$$

subject to

$$A_t \mathbf{x}_t + \boldsymbol{\beta} \leq \mathbf{b}_t, \qquad\qquad t = 1, \ldots, T \qquad (14.66)$$

$$\mathbf{x}_t = [I - \hat{\Gamma}]\mathbf{x}_{t-1} + \hat{B}\hat{\Gamma}\mathbf{p}_{t-1} + \hat{\mathbf{v}}_t, \qquad t = 1, \ldots, T + 1 \quad (14.67)$$

Constraint (14.66) espresses the technological requirements for producing the vector of crop activities $\mathbf{x}_t$ given the limiting resource availability $\mathbf{b}_t$. The objective function is stated in two parts. The first component expresses the discounted profit over the entire horizon T. The second component is the salvage function. By defining $d^\tau \overset{\text{def}}{=} [\frac{1}{1+\rho}]^\tau$, under the assumption of steady state, the salvage function may be written as

$$\sum_{\tau=T+1}^{+\infty} [\mathbf{p}'_{T+1}\mathbf{x}_{T+1} - \mathbf{r}'_{T+1}(A_{T+1}\mathbf{x}_{T+1})] \left[\frac{1}{1+\rho}\right]^{\tau-1}$$

$$= [\mathbf{p}'_{T+1}\mathbf{x}_{T+1} - \mathbf{r}'_{T+1}(A_{T+1}\mathbf{x}_{T+1})] \sum_{\tau=T+1}^{+\infty} d^{\tau-1}$$

$$= [\mathbf{p}'_{T+1}\mathbf{x}_{T+1} - \mathbf{r}'_{T+1}(A_{T+1}\mathbf{x}_{T+1})][d^T + d^{T+1} + d^{T+2} + \cdots]$$

$$= d^T[\mathbf{p}'_{T+1}\mathbf{x}_{T+1} - \mathbf{r}'_{T+1}(A_{T+1}\mathbf{x}_{T+1})][1 + d^1 + d^2 + \cdots]$$

$$= \left[\frac{d^T}{1-d}\right][\mathbf{p}'_{T+1}\mathbf{x}_{T+1} - \mathbf{r}'_{T+1}(A_{T+1}\mathbf{x}_{T+1})]$$

$$= \frac{1}{\rho}\left[\frac{1}{1+\rho}\right]^{T-1}[\mathbf{p}'_{T+1}\mathbf{x}_{T+1} - \mathbf{r}'_{T+1}(A_{T+1}\mathbf{x}_{T+1})].$$

As stated previously, we assume that in period $(T + 1)$, the period after planning ceases, the variables are at their steady-state values.

With these stipulations, the Lagrangean function of problem [(14.65) through (14.67)] is stated as

$$L = \sum_{t=1}^{T}\{\mathbf{p}'_t\mathbf{x}_t - \mathbf{r}'_t(\mathbf{b}_t - \boldsymbol{\beta}_t)\}/(1 + \rho)^{(t-1)} \qquad (14.68)$$

$$+ [\mathbf{p}'_{T+1}\mathbf{x}_{T+1} - \mathbf{r}'_{T+1}(A_{T+1}\mathbf{x}_{T+1})]/\rho(1 + \rho)^{(T-1)}$$

$$+ \sum_{t=1}^{T}(\mathbf{b}_t - \boldsymbol{\beta}_t - A_t\mathbf{x}_t)'\mathbf{y}_t$$

$$+ \sum_{t=1}^{T+1}\{[I - \hat{\Gamma}]\mathbf{x}_{t-1} + \hat{B}\hat{\Gamma}\mathbf{p}_{t-1} + \hat{\mathbf{v}}_t - \mathbf{x}_t\}'\boldsymbol{\lambda}_t.$$

The corresponding KKT conditions are

$$\frac{\partial L}{\partial \mathbf{x}_t} = \mathbf{p}_t/(1+\rho)^{t-1} - A'_t\mathbf{y}_t - \boldsymbol{\lambda}_t + [I - \hat{\Gamma}]\boldsymbol{\lambda}_{t+1} \leq \mathbf{0} \quad (14.69)$$

$$\frac{\partial L}{\partial \mathbf{x}_{T+1}} = (\mathbf{p}_{T+1} - A'_{T+1}\mathbf{r}_{T+1})/\rho(1+\rho)^{(T-1)} - \boldsymbol{\lambda}_{T+1} = \mathbf{0} \quad (14.70)$$

$$\frac{\partial L}{\partial \boldsymbol{\beta}_t} = \mathbf{r}_t/(1+\rho)^{t-1} - \mathbf{y}_t \leq \mathbf{0} \quad (14.71)$$

$$\frac{\partial L}{\partial \boldsymbol{\lambda}_t} = [I - \hat{\Gamma}]\mathbf{x}_{t-1} + \hat{B}\hat{\Gamma}\mathbf{p}_{t-1} + \hat{\mathbf{v}}_t - \mathbf{x}_t \geq \mathbf{0} \quad (14.72)$$

$$\frac{\partial L}{\partial \mathbf{y}_t} = \mathbf{b}_t - \boldsymbol{\beta}_t - A_t\mathbf{x}_t \geq \mathbf{0} \quad (14.73)$$

where $\mathbf{y}_t \geq \mathbf{0}$ and $\boldsymbol{\lambda}_t \geq \mathbf{0}$ together with the associated complementary slackness conditions.

This discrete dynamic problem can be solved, year by year, using a backward solution approach on the system of KKT conditions [(14.69) through (14.73)]. The key to this strategy is the realizazion that the equation of motion calibrates exactly the sample information, $\bar{\mathbf{x}}_t$, for any year, that is, $\bar{\mathbf{x}}_t = [I - \hat{\Gamma}]\bar{\mathbf{x}}_{t-1} + \hat{B}\hat{\Gamma}\mathbf{p}_{t-1} + \hat{\mathbf{v}}_t$ and, therefore, the left-hand-side quantity $\bar{\mathbf{x}}_t$ can replace the corresponding right-hand-side expression. In other words, we can equivalently use the available and contemporaneous information about the economic agent's decisions. Furthermore, from KKT condition (14.70), the costate variable $\boldsymbol{\lambda}_{T+1}$, for the time period outside the horizon is equal to the derivative of the salvage function with respect to the decisions at time $(T+1)$, $\hat{\boldsymbol{\lambda}}_{T+1} = (\mathbf{p}_{T+1} - A'_{T+1}\mathbf{r}_{T+1})/\rho(1+\rho)^{(T-1)}$.

Then, at time T, the equilibrium problem to be solved is given by the following structural relations:

$$A_T\mathbf{x}_T + \boldsymbol{\beta}_T \leq \mathbf{b}_T \qquad\qquad \mathbf{y}_T \geq \mathbf{0} \qquad (14.74)$$

$$\mathbf{x}_T \leq \bar{\mathbf{x}}_T = [I - \hat{\Gamma}]\bar{\mathbf{x}}_{T-1} + \hat{B}\hat{\Gamma}\mathbf{p}_{T-1} + \hat{\mathbf{v}}_T \qquad\qquad \boldsymbol{\lambda}_T \geq \mathbf{0} \qquad (14.75)$$

$$A'_T\mathbf{y}_T + \boldsymbol{\lambda}_T \geq \mathbf{p}_T d^{(T-1)}/\rho + [I - \hat{\Gamma}]\hat{\boldsymbol{\lambda}}_{T+1} \qquad\qquad \mathbf{x}_T \geq \mathbf{0} \qquad (14.76)$$

$$\mathbf{y}_T \geq \mathbf{r}_T d^{(T-1)} \qquad\qquad \boldsymbol{\beta}_T \geq \mathbf{0} \qquad (14.77)$$

and by the associated complementary slackness conditions. Knowledge of the realized levels of output at time t, $\bar{\mathbf{x}}_t$, and of the costate variables $\hat{\boldsymbol{\lambda}}_{t+1}$, estimated at time $t+1$, allows for the solution of the dynamic problem as a sequence of T equilibrium problems. Hence, the dynamic linkage between successive time periods is established through the vector of costate variables

λ_t. In this way, the equilibrium problem [(14.74) through (14.77)] can be solved backward to time ($t = 1$) without the need to specify initial conditions for the vector of state variables $\mathbf{x}_0$ and the price vector $\mathbf{p}_0$. This dynamic problem arises exclusively from the assumption of adaptive price expectations and, given the DPEP as stated earlier, the costate variable λ_t does not depend explicitly on the state variable $\mathbf{x}_t$. This implies that the positive character of the problem, with the concomitant use of the realized levels of activity outputs $\bar{\mathbf{x}}_t$, avoids the usual two-part solution of a dynamic problem where the backward solution is carried out in order to find the sequence of costate variables λ_t, and the forward solution is devoted to finding the optimal level of the state variables $\mathbf{x}_t$. In the context specified here, the solution regarding the state variable $\mathbf{x}_t$ is obtained contemporaneously with the solution of the costate variable λ_t.

The objective of DPEP during phase I, therefore, is to solve T equilibrium problems starting at the end point of the time horizon $t = T, T - 1, \ldots, 2, 1$ and having the following structure:

$$\min \{\mathbf{z}'_{P1t}\mathbf{y}_t + \mathbf{z}'_{P2t}\lambda_t + \mathbf{z}'_{D1t}\mathbf{x}_t + \mathbf{z}'_{D2t}\boldsymbol{\beta}_t\} = 0 \qquad (14.78)$$

subject to

$$A_t\mathbf{x}_t + \boldsymbol{\beta}_t + \mathbf{z}_{P1t} = \mathbf{b}_t \qquad (14.79)$$

$$\mathbf{x}_t + \mathbf{z}_{P2t} = \bar{\mathbf{x}}_t \qquad (14.80)$$

$$A'_t\mathbf{y}_t + \lambda_t = \mathbf{p}_t d^{(t-1)} + [I - \hat{\Gamma}]\hat{\lambda}_{t+1} + \mathbf{z}_{D1t} \qquad (14.81)$$

$$\mathbf{y}_t = \mathbf{r}_t d^{(t-1)} + \mathbf{z}_{D2t}. \qquad (14.82)$$

The objective function is the sum of all the complementary slackness conditions. A solution of the equilibrium problem is achieved when the objective function reaches the zero value. The main objective of phase I is the recovery of the costate variables, λ_t, for the entire horizon and of the dual variables for the structural primal constraints, $\mathbf{y}_t$, to serve as information in the estimation of the cost function during the next phase. The fundamental reason for estimating a cost function to represent the economic agent's decision process is to relax the fixed-coefficient technology represented by the A_t matrix and to introduce the possibility of a more direct substitution between products and limiting inputs. In other words, the observation of output and input decisions at time t provides only a single point in the technology and cost spaces. The process of eliciting an estimate of the latent marginal cost levels and the subsequent recovery of a consistent cost function that rationalizes the available data is akin to the process of fitting an isocost through the observed output and input decisions.

Phase II of DPEP – Estimation of the Cost Function

By definition, total cost is a function of output levels and input prices. In a dynamic problem, the total cost function is defined period by period as in a static problem and represented as $C(\mathbf{x}_t, \mathbf{y}_t, t) \equiv C_t(\mathbf{x}_t, \mathbf{y}_t)$. The properties of the cost function of a dynamic problem follow the same properties specified for a static case (Stefanou): it must be concave and linearly homogeneous in input prices in each time period. Borrowing, therefore, from the SPEP specification discussed in previous sections, the functional form of the cost function for DPEP is stated as

$$C_t(\mathbf{x}_t, \mathbf{y}_t) = \mathbf{u}'\mathbf{y}_t(\mathbf{f}_t'\mathbf{x}_t) + \mathbf{u}'\mathbf{y}_t(\mathbf{x}_t' Q_t \mathbf{x}_t)/2 + \left(\mathbf{y}_t^{1/2}\right)' S_t \mathbf{y}_t^{1/2} \quad (14.83)$$

where $\mathbf{u}$ is a vector of unitary elements. The matrix Q_t is symmetric positive semidefinite, whereas the S_t matrix is symmetric with nonnegative elements on and off the main diagonal.

The marginal cost function at time t is the derivative of equation (14.83) with respect to the output level at time t, that is,

$$\frac{\partial C_t}{\partial \mathbf{x}_t} = (\mathbf{u}'\mathbf{y}_t)\mathbf{f}_t + (\mathbf{u}'\mathbf{y}_t) Q_t \mathbf{x}_t = A_t'\mathbf{y}_t \quad (14.84)$$

whereas, by the Shephard lemma, the limiting input derived demand functions are

$$\frac{\partial C_t}{\partial \mathbf{y}_t} = (\mathbf{f}_t'\mathbf{x}_t)\mathbf{u} + \mathbf{u}(\mathbf{x}_t' Q_t \mathbf{x}_t)/2 + \Delta_{\mathbf{y}_t^{-1/2}} S_t \mathbf{y}_t^{1/2} = A_t \mathbf{x}_t. \quad (14.85)$$

The matrix $\Delta_{\mathbf{y}^{-1/2}} S \mathbf{y}^{1/2}$ is diagonal with elements of the vector $\mathbf{y}^{-1/2}$ on the diagonal.

There is a significant difference between the marginal cost of the static equilibrium problem and the short-run (period by period) marginal cost of the dynamic equilibrium problem. If one considers the static equilibrium specification formulated in model [(14.37) through (14.40)], the marginal cost is given in relation (14.39) as $MC(\mathbf{x}, \mathbf{y}) \equiv A'\mathbf{y} + (\mathbf{r} + \mathbf{v})$. In other words, without a time dimension, the marginal cost is equal to the sum of the marginal cost attributable to the limiting inputs, $A'\mathbf{y}$, plus the variable marginal cost attributable to the output levels, $(\mathbf{r} + \mathbf{v})$. In the dynamic context specified earlier, the Lagrange multiplier λ_t assumes the meaning of costate variable and signifies the marginal valuation of the state variable $\mathbf{x}_t$. Its forward-looking nature is expressed by the relation $\lambda_{T-n} = \sum_{s=0}^{n+1} [I - \hat{\Gamma}]^s (\mathbf{p}_{T-n+s} - A'_{T-n+s}\mathbf{y}_{T-n+s})$, where $n = -1, 0, 1, \ldots. T$. In a dynamic context, therefore, the costate variable λ_t cannot be used to define the period-by-period marginal cost (as is done in a static equilibrium problem, where the symbol $\mathbf{r}$ is interpreted simply as variable marginal cost) because it incorporates the long-run notion of a trajectory associated with a multiperiod horizon. In the dynamic equilibrium problem discussed earlier, the period-by-period marginal cost is defined as $MC(\mathbf{x}_t, \mathbf{y}_t) \equiv A_t'\mathbf{y}_t$, as indicated in relation (14.84).

The objective of phase II is to estimate the parameters of the cost function given in equation (14.83), $\mathbf{f}_t$, Q_t, S_t. This estimation can be performed with a maximum entropy approach (Golan et al.).

Phase III of DPEP – Calibration and Policy Analysis

The estimated cost function can now be used to replace the marginal cost levels and the demand for inputs in the dynamic equilibrium problem of phase I. This replacement ensures the calibration of the model, relaxes the fixed-coefficient technology, and allows direct substitution among inputs and outputs. At this stage, therefore, it is possible to implement policy scenarios based on the variation of output and input prices.

The structure of the calibrating DPEP is given next. With knowledge of the costate variables $\hat{\boldsymbol{\lambda}}_t$ and $\hat{\boldsymbol{\lambda}}_{t+1}$ obtained from the solution of the DPEP of phase I, the following specification calibrates the output decisions and the input dual variables for any period:

$$\min \ \{\mathbf{z}_{P1t}'\mathbf{y}_t + \mathbf{z}_{D1t}'\mathbf{x}_t + \mathbf{z}_{D2t}'\boldsymbol{\beta}_t\} = 0 \tag{14.86}$$

subject to

$$(\hat{\mathbf{f}}_t'\mathbf{x}_t)\mathbf{u} + \mathbf{u}(\mathbf{x}_t'\hat{Q}_t\mathbf{x}_t)/2 + \Delta_{\mathbf{y}^{-1/2}}\hat{S}_t\mathbf{y}_t^{1/2} + \boldsymbol{\beta}_t + \mathbf{z}_{P1t} = \mathbf{b}_t \tag{14.87}$$

$$(\mathbf{u}'\mathbf{y}_t)\hat{\mathbf{f}}_t + (\mathbf{u}'\mathbf{y}_t)\hat{Q}_t\mathbf{x}_t = \mathbf{p}_t d^{t-1} + [I - \hat{\Gamma}]\hat{\boldsymbol{\lambda}}_{t+1} - \hat{\boldsymbol{\lambda}}_t + \mathbf{z}_{D1t} \tag{14.88}$$

$$\mathbf{y}_t = \mathbf{r}_t d^{t-1} + \mathbf{z}_{D2t}. \tag{14.89}$$

The use of the costate values obtained during phase I is required for eliminating the constraint on the decision variables, $\mathbf{x}_t \leq \bar{\mathbf{x}}_{Rt}$, which were employed in phase I specification precisely for eliciting the corresponding values of the costates. As observed earlier, the costate variables are the dynamic link between any two periods, and their determination requires a backward solution approach. If we were to require their measurement for a second time during the calibrating and policy analysis phase, we would need to add also the equation of motion in its explicit form, because the constraint $\mathbf{x}_t \leq \bar{\mathbf{x}}_t$ would no longer be sufficient. In this case, the T problems would be all linked together and ought to be solved as a single large-scale model. The calibration phase, therefore, is conditional on the knowledge of the costate variables obtained during phase I and involves the period-by-period determination of the output decisions and dual variables of the limiting inputs.

Given the dynamic structure of the model, a policy scenario becomes a prediction at the end of the T-period horizon. All the model components at period T are known, and the researcher wishes to obtain a solution of the DPEP for the $(T + 1)$ period. The parameters of the cost function are assumed constant and equal to those at time T. The costate variables at times $(T + 2)$ and $(T + 1)$, $\hat{\lambda}_{T+2}$, $\hat{\lambda}_{T+1}$, are taken to be equal to the steady-state marginal values of the salvage function. The remaining parameters, $\mathbf{b}_{T+1}$, $\mathbf{r}_{T+1}$, and $\mathbf{p}_{T+1}$, will assume the value of interest under the desired policy scenario. More explictly, the relevant structure of the dynamic positive equilibrium problem during the policy analysis phase takes on the following specification:

$$\min \; \{\mathbf{z}'_{P1,T+1}\mathbf{y}_{T+1} + \mathbf{z}'_{D1,T+1}\mathbf{x}_{T+1} + \mathbf{z}'_{D2,T+1}\boldsymbol{\beta}_{T+1}\} = 0 \qquad (14.90)$$

subject to

$$(\hat{\mathbf{f}}'_{T+1}\mathbf{x}_{T+1})\mathbf{u} + \mathbf{u}(\mathbf{x}'_{T+1}\hat{Q}_{T+1}\mathbf{x}_{T+1})/2 + \Delta_{\mathbf{y}^{-1/2}}\hat{S}_{T+1}\mathbf{y}_{T+1}^{1/2}$$
$$+ \boldsymbol{\beta}_{T+1} + \mathbf{z}_{P1,T+1} = \mathbf{b}_{T+1} \qquad (14.91)$$

$$(\mathbf{u}'\mathbf{y}_{T+1})\hat{\mathbf{f}}_{T+1} + (\mathbf{u}'\mathbf{y}_{T+1})\hat{Q}_{T+1}\mathbf{x}_{T+1} = \mathbf{p}_{T+1}d^T$$
$$+ [I - \hat{\Gamma}]\hat{\lambda}_{T+2} - \hat{\lambda}_{T+1} + \mathbf{z}_{D1,T+1} \qquad (14.92)$$

$$\mathbf{y}_{T+1} = \mathbf{r}_{T+1}d^T + \mathbf{z}_{D2,T+1}. \qquad (14.93)$$

Projected policy prices, on either the input or output side, will induce responses in output and input decisions that are consistent with a process of output price expectations articulated in previous sections.

Numerical Example 1: Dynamic Positive Equilibrium Problem

In order to show the empirical feasibility of the Dynamic Positive Equilibrium Problem, as presented in the previous section, we discuss in detail a sizable example pertaining to California agriculture. This example also illustrates a procedure for handling the apparent complexity of the Dynamic Positive Equilibrium Problem.

California agriculture is divided into 21 regions. We have selected a region of the Central Valley that produces seven annual crops: rice, fodder crops, field crops, grains, tomatoes, sugarbeets, and truck crops. Eight years of reporting have been selected, from 1985 to 1992; hence the horizon is $T = 8$. The annual output levels are measured in tons. Data on crop

Table 14.1. *Input quantities per crop, table ha(g,j,i,tt)*

Region.crop.input	85	86	87	88	89	90	91	92
v04.drce.land	79.9600	69.5100	70.8900	82.7500	80.1300	70.8300	62.1000	52.9000
v04.drce.water	514.1428	446.9493	455.8227	532.0825	515.2359	455.4369	399.3030	468.7470
v04.drce.other	2.088e3	1.234e3	1.468e3	1.395e3	1.623e3	1.633e3	1.191e3	1.568e3
v04.fddr.land	17.6121	18.2015	16.6464	16.1069	16.3141	16.0903	17.0182	14.5607
v04.fddr.water	69.5678	71.8959	65.7533	63.6223	64.4407	63.5567	67.2219	57.5148
v04.fddr.other	229.5511	154.1838	181.1784	111.6153	130.7117	176.6630	147.7467	119.7645
v04.mfld.land	63.3575	58.2090	55.9120	49.4045	50.9370	55.1215	44.2930	50.2785
v04.mfld.water	162.8288	149.5971	143.6938	126.9696	130.9081	141.6623	113.8330	129.2157
v04.mfld.other	360.7526	125.6173	272.7480	272.7480	218.1732	383.0192	142.3306	291.7824
v04.mgrn.land	47.7740	36.4238	25.6052	23.7786	32.3138	29.6750	23.9126	28.1348
v04.mgrn.water	42.5189	32.4172	22.7886	21.1630	28.7593	26.4108	21.2822	25.0400
v04.mgrn.other	50.0000	50.0000	50.0000	50.0000	50.0000	50.0000	50.0000	50.0000
v04.ptom.land	21.8100	21.0700	20.1300	21.6300	25.0700	26.4700	33.4400	27.6400
v04.ptom.water	66.9567	64.6849	61.7991	66.4041	76.9649	81.2629	102.6608	84.8548
v04.ptom.other	1.836e3	1.358e3	1.356e3	1.315e3	1.708e3	2.054e3	2.424e3	1.963e3
v04.sbts.land	9.0200	8.9100	10.3900	11.6900	10.9100	8.3600	8.7900	6.3300
v04.sbts.water	30.3072	29.9376	34.9104	39.2784	36.6576	28.0896	29.5344	21.2688
v04.sbts.other	334.8205	250.9828	306.4505	309.9139	325.4047	285.3777	279.6574	197.1944
v04.trck.land	12.7400	12.9400	10.3700	9.3600	9.2200	11.3100	11.2500	12.1500
v04.trck.water	23.9512	24.3272	19.4956	17.5968	17.3336	21.2628	21.1500	22.8420
v04.trck.other	424.9481	299.9607	283.5550	209.2171	245.3396	347.9399	288.0432	299.7690

prices, cultivated areas, and yields are based on annual county agricultural commissioner reports. Three limiting inputs are also recorded: land, water, and other inputs. Crop land is measured in acres and water in acre-feet. The other inputs represent the annual operating costs of irrigation and are measured in dollars. The operating cost of irrigation includes labor, management, and capital costs referred to a given irrigation technology. The available information deals with total supply of limiting inputs, their prices, total realized output production and the associated prices. These series are reported in Tables 14.1 through 14.4.

In the command file reported later, all data series have been scaled appropriately, for computational reason, to lie in a range between 0 and 10. A

Table 14.2. *Per acre yields, table yb(g,j,tt)*

Region.crop	85	86	87	88	89	90	91	92
v04.drce	3.7300	3.8300	3.7700	3.5300	4.0700	3.7700	4.0300	4.2700
v04.fddr	6.9394	6.0303	6.4343	6.3636	6.2929	6.1616	6.6667	6.8990
v04.mfld	4.1000	4.4000	4.7300	4.3300	4.1700	4.1000	4.3700	4.5000
v04.mgrn	3.0581	2.3605	2.5930	2.9884	2.9419	2.6744	2.9884	2.9070
v04.ptom	27.0000	30.6300	30.0700	27.5000	30.0300	28.7700	30.6300	34.0700
v04.sbts	19.6700	21.1000	23.8000	22.0700	23.8300	22.6000	23.1300	24.7300
v04.trck	7.6000	7.0000	7.8000	7.9000	7.5000	7.4000	7.6000	7.9000

Table 14.3. *Input prices, table w(g,j,i,tt)*

Region.crop.input	85	86	87	88	89	90	91	92
v04.drce.land	139.0000	131.0000	115.0000	123.0000	123.0000	139.0000	154.0000	124.0000
v04.drce.water	4.9435	3.8123	3.9799	3.6029	4.0218	4.5664	4.2732	4.1894
v04.drce.other	10.0000	10.0000	10.0000	10.0000	10.0000	10.0000	10.0000	10.0000
v04.fddr.land	139.0000	123.0000	108.0000	127.0000	139.0000	139.0000	146.0000	146.0000
v04.fddr.water	4.9435	3.8123	3.9799	3.6029	4.0218	4.5664	4.2732	4.1894
v04.fddr.other	10.0000	10.0000	10.0000	10.0000	10.0000	10.0000	10.0000	10.0000
v04.mfld.land	185.0000	165.0000	146.0000	146.0000	154.0000	154.0000	177.0000	147.0000
v04.mfld.water	4.9435	3.8123	3.9799	3.6029	4.0218	4.5664	4.2732	4.1894
v04.mfld.other	10.0000	10.0000	10.0000	10.0000	10.0000	10.0000	10.0000	10.0000
v04.mgrn.land	185.0000	165.0000	146.0000	146.0000	154.0000	154.0000	177.0000	147.0000
v04.mgrn.water	4.9435	3.8123	3.9799	3.6029	4.0218	4.5664	4.2732	4.1894
v04.mgrn.other	10.0000	10.0000	10.0000	10.0000	10.0000	10.0000	10.0000	10.0000
v04.ptom.land	200.0000	200.0000	200.0000	200.0000	200.0000	200.0000	200.0000	200.0000
v04.ptom.water	4.9435	3.8123	3.9799	3.6029	4.0218	4.5664	4.2732	4.1894
v04.ptom.other	10.0000	10.0000	10.0000	10.0000	10.0000	10.0000	10.0000	10.0000
v04.sbts.land	200.0000	200.0000	200.0000	200.0000	200.0000	200.0000	200.0000	200.0000
v04.sbts.water	4.9435	3.8123	3.9799	3.6029	4.0218	4.5664	4.2732	4.1894
v04.sbts.other	10.0000	10.0000	10.0000	10.0000	10.0000	10.0000	10.0000	10.0000
v04.trck.land	216.0000	192.0000	169.0000	177.0000	181.0000	200.0000	219.0000	219.0000
v04.trck.water	4.9435	3.8123	3.9799	3.6029	4.0218	4.5664	4.2732	4.1894
v04.trck.other	10.0000	10.0000	10.0000	10.0000	10.0000	10.0000	10.0000	10.0000

technical coefficient matrix is defined, in the command file, in terms of input per unit of output.

The crop indexes appearing in the various tables are coded as follows: drce $\equiv$ rice, fddr $\equiv$ fodder crops, mfld $\equiv$ field crops, mgrn $\equiv$ grain crops, ptom $\equiv$ processing tomatoes, sbts $\equiv$ sugarbeets, trck $\equiv$ truck crops.

The presentation of the empirical results begins with the diagonal matrices Γ and B that characterize the process of adaptive expectations, as in equation (14.60), and the output supply functions in equations (14.61), respectively. This information is reported in Table 14.5. The diagonality of both matrices is required for guaranteeing the specification of the equation of motion as given in (14.64). The estimation of both matrices was performed by a maximum entropy estimator as illustrated by van Akkeren

Table 14.4. *Output prices, table pri(g,j,tt)*

Region.crop	85	86	87	88	89	90	91	92
v04.drce	151.0000	161.0000	159.0000	154.0000	141.0000	153.0000	166.0000	155.0000
v04.fddr	85.0000	77.0000	71.7000	87.3000	92.3000	100.7000	83.3000	74.7000
v04.mfld	96.7000	77.0000	79.3000	101.3000	102.7000	106.0000	109.3000	98.3000
v04.mgrn	96.7000	80.7000	80.3000	107.0000	119.7000	98.3000	101.7000	110.3000
v04.ptom	51.0000	51.0000	46.0000	48.0000	52.0000	55.0000	54.7000	48.7000
v04.sbts	35.0000	34.3000	33.3000	37.3000	38.7000	39.0000	37.3000	38.3000
v04.trck	178.0000	158.0000	168.0000	198.0000	188.0000	195.0000	205.0000	196.0000

Table 14.5. *Diagonal matrices* Γ *and B*

Matrix	drce	fddr	mfld	mgrn	ptom	sbts	trck
Γ	−0.0118	0.0059	−0.0271	0.0295	0.1032	−0.0113	0.0111
B	0.0771	0.0008	0.0774	0.0143	5.0006	0.1410	0.0111

and Judge. A stylized presentation of the procedure is commented on in the GAMS command file presented later.

Phase I of DPEP deals with the estimation of the costate variables λ_t and of the dual variables $\mathbf{y}_t$ of the structural primal constraints, as specified in equations (14.78) through (14.82). The estimation of the costate variables requires a backward solution for $t = T, T - 1, T - 2, \dots, 2, 1$. To achieve this order of the data series, it is necessary to multiply the input data by a matrix *Hor*, which reverses the order of the time index and has the structure given in Table 14.6. We recall that the costate variables at time $(T + 1)$ are given by $\hat{\lambda}_{T+1} = (\mathbf{p}_{T+1} - A'_{T+1}\mathbf{r}_{T+1})/\rho(1 + \rho)^{(T-1)}$, where all the terms on the right-hand side of the equality sign are known and are specified in a previous section.

The estimates of the dual variables $\mathbf{y}_t$ obtained by solving the phase I problem [(14.78) through (14.82)] are reported in Table 14.7. The value of the discount rate, ρ, selected for this empirical example is equal to 0.03.

Table 14.8 presents the estimates of the costate variables obtained in the execution of phase I of the DPEP specification. It turns out that the costate variable for rice is equal to zero in all the years of the horizon. This event corresponds to a case of primal degeneracy in the primal constraints

Table 14.6. *Reverse time index matrix, table hor(tt,tt)*

Time	85	86	87	88	89	90	91	92
85								1
86							1	
87						1		
88					1			
89				1				
90			1					
91		1						
92	1							

Table 14.7. *Dual variables,* $\mathbf{y}_t$, *phase I of DPEP*

Region.input	85	86	87	88	89	90	91	92
v04.land	1.5803	1.4113	1.2351	1.3794	1.4521	1.4162	1.4399	1.4043
v04.water	0.0494	0.1409	0.1434	0.0346	0.0357	0.0394	0.0358	0.0341
v04.other	1.4300	2.0671	1.6868	2.0007	1.6870	1.4340	2.0505	1.2761

of model [(14.78) through (14.82)]. The estimate of the costate variable for year 93 corresponds to the first derivative of the salvage function with respect to the decision at time $(T + 1)$.

Phase II of the DPEP specification deals with the estimation of the yearly cost function that is reproduced here for convenience:

$$C_t(\mathbf{x}_t, \mathbf{y}_t) = \mathbf{u}'\mathbf{y}_t(\mathbf{f}'_t\mathbf{x}_t) + \mathbf{u}'\mathbf{y}_t(\mathbf{x}'_t Q_t\mathbf{x}_t)/2 + \left(\mathbf{y}_t^{1/2}\right)' S_t\mathbf{y}_t^{1/2} \quad (14.83)$$

where $\mathbf{u}$ is a vector of unitary elements and $t = 1, \ldots, T - 1$. The observations for year $(T = 92)$ were not used in the estimation process but were kept in reserve for an out-of-sample prediction test. The matrix Q_t is symmetric positive semidefinite, whereas the S_t matrix is symmetric with nonnegative elements on and off the main diagonal. The parameters to be estimated are the vector $\mathbf{f}_t$ and matrices Q_t, S_t. The given information is represented by the realized output series $\bar{\mathbf{x}}_t$, the dual variables $\mathbf{y}_t$ estimated in phase I, and the vector $\mathbf{u}$ of unitary values. A generalized maximum entropy (GME) approach developed by Golan et al. was used to obtain estimates of the parameters of interest as they appear in the first derivatives of the cost function with respect to $\mathbf{x}_t$, illustrated in equation (14.84) and with respect to $\mathbf{y}_t$, as given by equation (14.85). Table 14.9 reports the estimated S_t matrix

Table 14.8. *Costate variables,* $\boldsymbol{\lambda}_t$, *phase I of DPEP*

Region.crop	85	86	87	88	89	90	91	92	93 = T + 1
v04.drce	0.0000	0.0000	0.0000	0.0000	0.0000	0.0000	0.0000	0.0000	0.0248
v04.fddr	2.0136	1.6981	1.5765	1.4748	1.1387	0.7913	0.4359	0.2439	0.0118
v04.mfld	2.9596	2.5387	2.2348	1.9475	1.4601	1.0623	0.7409	0.3183	0.0147
v04.mgrn	1.8896	1.5483	1.5827	1.5233	1.1918	0.7434	0.5445	0.3387	0.0137
v04.ptom	0.0000	0.0000	0.0000	0.0000	0.0636	0.0405	0.0070	0.0946	0.0099
v04.sbst	0.2153	0.2215	0.2509	0.2158	0.1805	0.1125	0.0605	0.0965	0.0072
v04.trck	6.7582	5.8913	5.3405	4.5921	3.5687	2.7297	1.8658	1.0497	0.0409

Table 14.9. *Estimates of the S_t matrix, phase II of DPEP*

Region.input	Year 85			Year 91		
	Land	Water	Other	Land	Water	Other
v04.land	2.9986	0.9824	3.5696	2.9591	0.8088	3.7642
v04.water	0.9824	3.7268	0.7191	0.8088	3.9347	0.5359
v04.other	3.5696	0.7191	5.4832	3.7642	0.5359	6.8683

for the years 85 and 91. Both matrices are positive definite, as verified by the computation of the corresponding eigenvalues.

Table 14.10 reports the estimates of the Q_t matrix for the years 85 and 91. Both matrices are positive definite, as verified by the computation of the corresponding eigenvalues. The estimates of the linear part of the cost function, $\mathbf{f}_t$, are not reported here but can be retrieved by running the GAMS command file presented later. The parameter estimates of $\mathbf{f}_t$ are negative for the entire horizon and range from -0.3 to -1.5.

With the estimates of the cost function it is possible to derive output and input demand functions and the corresponding elasticities. In Table 14.11 and for the year 91, we present the input elasticities in the form of derived demand and Morishima specifications. The derived demand elasticities are computed in the usual format, whereas the Morishima elasticities are

Table 14.10. *Estimates of the Q_t matrix, years 85 and 91*

Year.crop.	drce	fddr	mfld	mgrn	ptom	sbts	trck
85.drce	0.7310	−0.0390	0.0025	−0.1938	0.0078	0.0064	−0.1763
85.fddr	−0.0390	0.7243	0.0046	−0.0536	0.0038	0.0035	−0.0442
85.mfld	0.0025	0.0046	0.3627	−0.0085	0.0037	0.0039	0.0013
85.mgrn	−0.1938	−0.0536	−0.0085	1.1901	0.0059	0.0037	−0.2305
85.ptom	0.0078	0.0038	0.0037	0.0059	0.1215	0.0018	0.0125
85.sbts	0.0064	0.0035	0.0039	0.0037	0.0018	0.2320	0.0068
85.trck	−0.1763	−0.0442	0.0013	−0.2305	0.0125	0.0068	1.5991
91.drce	0.7062	−0.0567	0.0022	−0.0928	0.0002	−0.0055	−0.2024
91.fddr	−0.0567	0.7230	0.0032	−0.0146	−0.0008	−0.0007	−0.0709
91.mfld	0.0022	0.0032	0.3645	0.0250	0.0018	0.0020	−0.0059
91.mgrn	−0.0928	−0.0146	0.0250	1.1728	0.0075	0.0071	−0.0910
91.ptom	0.0002	−0.0008	0.0018	0.0075	0.0988	0.0001	0.0003
91.sbts	−0.0055	−0.0007	0.0020	0.0071	0.0001	0.2250	−0.0001
91.trck	−0.2024	−0.0709	−0.0059	−0.0910	0.0003	−0.0001	1.5477

Table 14.11. *Derived demand and Morishima elasticities*

| Region.input | Derived Demand | | | Morishima | | |
	Land	Water	Other	Land	Water	Other
v04.land	−1.1503	0.0317	1.1185		0.6401	1.4750
v04.water	0.3397	−0.6084	0.2686	1.4900		0.6252
v04.other	0.3487	0.0078	−0.3565	1.4990	0.6162	

defined as the difference between the cross and own expenditure price elasticities (Blackorby and Russell). Only the land input is elastic. Notice that all cross-elasticities are positive, signifying that the three factors of production are considered as substitute inputs.

The inversion of the marginal cost function as expressed in equation (14.84) allows for the computation of the output supply elasticities that, for the year 91, are reported in Table 14.12. All crops show an inelastic supply and nearly zero cross-elasticities, a probable result of considering crop cultivation of an entire region of California.

The phase III implementation of the DPEP model consists in specifying the calibrating equilibrium stated in equations [(14.90) through (14.93)]. The difference between the phase I and phase III models is twofold: the calibrating constraints (equation of motion) have been removed in the phase III specification and the fixed coefficient technology, $A_t \mathbf{x}_t$, has been replaced by the first derivative of the cost function with respect to the limiting input prices, $\mathbf{y}_t$. This substitution removes one of the main criticisms of PMP dealing with a fixed coefficient technology. The phase III calibrating model reproduces exactly all the realized output levels and the input dual prices estimated in phase I.

Table 14.12. *Output supply elasticities, year 91*

Crop	drce	fddr	mfld	mgrn	ptom	sbts	trck
drce	0.2614	0.0123	−0.0019	0.0146	−0.0007	0.0013	0.0453
fddr	0.0511	0.2539	−0.0034	0.0078	0.0009	0.0006	0.0378
mfld	−0.0033	−0.0014	0.3566	−0.0072	−0.0029	−0.0010	0.0010
mgrn	0.0775	0.0100	−0.0220	0.3008	−0.0121	−0.0030	0.0492
ptom	−0.0006	0.0002	−0.0013	−0.0018	0.1531	0.0000	−0.0004
sbts	0.0076	0.0008	−0.0034	−0.0033	0.0000	0.2282	0.0010
trck	0.0896	0.0180	0.0012	0.0183	−0.0010	−0.0010	0.3565

GAMS Command File for Numerical Example 1

The following GAMS file executes the numerical example of the DPEP model presented previously. It requires an additional input file, called *calv0.dat*, which contains the data reported in Tables 14.1 to 14.4 according to the following format: table ha(g,j,i,tt), acres; table yb(g,j,tt), acre yields; table w(g,j,i,tt), input prices; table pri(g,j,tt), output prices. It requires a second input file called *Tmatrix.dat* that is used to reverse the time horizon as in Table 14.6:

```
$title dynamic pep model with price adaptive
* expectations and supply function
* quadratic-generalized leontief cost function model
* v04 region of california
* c(x,y) = u'y(f'x) + u'y(x'qx)/2 +(y**.5sy**.5)
* no more linear technology in phase 3
*
$offsymlist offsymxref
    option limrow = 0
    option limcol = 0
    option iterlim = 20000
    option reslim = 10000
    option nlp = conopt3
    option decimals = 7 ;
*
    sets
    q    full set /drce,fddr,ftom, mfld,mgrn,orch,
        ptom,sbts,trck,land,water,other/
    j(q)    production processes /drce,fddr,mfld,
            mgrn,ptom,sbts,trck/
    i(q)    resources /land,water,other /
    gg    regions / v04 /
    g(gg)    run regions / v04/
    ttt    horizon /85*93/
    tt(ttt)    horizon years /85*92/
    t(tt)    calibration years / 85*91 /
    t2(tt)    run years / 85*92 /
    t1(tt)    / 86*92 /
*
    p    probability grid / 1*3 /
*
    alias (t,t5,t6)
    alias(t2,t3)
```

```
    alias(t1,t7,t8,t9)
    alias (j,jj,k,kk)
    alias(q,qq)
    alias(qq,qq2)
    alias(q,q2)
    alias (i,ii,i2,ii2)
    alias (p,l)
    alias (p,ll)
*
    parameter flag(q) ordinal index ;
    flag(q) = ord(q) ;
*
$include calv04.dat
$include tmatrix.dat
    parameter xbar(g,j,tt)   total output production
    a(g,j,i,tt)   input per unit output
    cc(g,i,tt)   input prices
    b(g,i,tt)   total inputs;
* scaling
    ha(g,j,i,tt) = ha(g,j,i,tt)/100 ;
    ha(g,j,"other",tt) = ha(g,j,"other",tt)/10 ;
    pri(g,j,tt) = pri(g,j,tt)/100 ;
    pri(g,"sbts",tt) = pri(g,"sbts",tt)/1 ;
    yb(g,"sbts",tt) = yb(g,"sbts",tt)*1 ;
    cc(g,i,tt) = w(g,"fddr",i,tt)/100 ;
    xbar(g,j,tt) = ha(g,j,"land",tt)* yb(g,j,tt) ;
    a(g,j,i,tt) = ha(g,j,i,tt)/xbar(g,j,tt) ;
    b(g,i,tt) = sum(j, ha(g,j,i,tt) ) ;
* display ha, yb, pri, cc, xbar, a, b ;
*
* estimation of the supply function x = w + bp* using
* dbit (van akkeren and judge)
* approach and of the price expectation matrix gg
* the equation of motion is x(t) = b*gg(t)*p(t-1) +
    (i-gg(t))*x(t-1) + v(t)
*
    parameter xxbar(j,tt), ppri(j,tt), ident(j,jj),
      xdelay(j,t1), pridelay(j,t1), r(i,t1) ;
*
    loop(g,
    xxbar(j,tt) = xbar(g,j,tt) ;
    ppri(j,tt) = pri(g,j,tt) ;
    xdelay(j,t1) = xbar(g,j,t1-1) ;
```

```
    xdelay(j,"86") =xbar(g,j,"85") ;
    pridelay(j,t1) = pri(g,j,t1-1) ;
    pridelay(j,"86") = pri(g,j,"85") ;
    r(i,t1) = cc(g,i,t1-1) ;
    r(i,"86") = cc(g,i,"85") ;
    );
* close loop
    ident(j,jj)$(ord(j) eq ord(jj)) = 1. ;
    ident(j,jj)$(ord(j) ne ord(jj)) = 0 ;
* definition of average and deviation equations of
    motion for implementing the entropy
* approach of van akkeren and judge, see references
    parameter avex(j), avexdelay(j), avepri(j),
      avepridel(j), dxt(j,t1), dxdelay(j,t1),
      dpridelay(j,t1) ;
    avex(j) = sum(t1, xxbar(j,t1) )/7 ;
    avepri(j) = sum(t1, ppri(j,t1))/7 ;
    avepridel(j) = sum(t1, pridelay(j,t1) )/7 ;
    avexdelay(j) = sum(t1, xdelay(j,t1) ) /7 ;
    dxt(j,t1) = xxbar(j,t1) - avex(j) ;
    dxdelay(j,t1) = xdelay(j,t1) - avexdelay(j) ;
    dpridelay(j,t1) = pridelay(j,t1) - avepridel(j) ;
    display ha, yb, a, b ;
    display xbar, xdelay, pri, pridelay, cc, r ;
    display avex, avexdelay, avepri, avepridel, dxt,
      dxdelay, dpridelay ;
*
    parameter
    zb(j,j,t9) z value range for bs diag matrix
    zg(j,j,t9) z values for the gg matrix
    zv(j,t1,t9) z value for the intercept of the
      equation of motion;
*
* definition of probability supports according to van
* akkeren and judge
*
    zb(j,j,t9) = 3*dxt(j,t9)*dxdelay(j,t9) ;
    zb(j,jj,t9)$(flag(j) ne flag(jj)) = 0 ;
    zg(j,j,t9) = 3*dxt(j,t9)*dpridelay(j,t9) ;
    zg(j,jj,t9)$(flag(j) ne flag(jj)) = 0 ;
    zv(j,t1,t9) = 5*dxt(j,t9) ;
*
```

```
* estimation of b (supply functions) and gamma
* matrices
*
   variables
   cent    entropy level objective function
   pb(j,j,t9)  probability of b diagonal matrix -
               supply functions
   pg(j,j,t9)   probability of the gamma matrix
   pv(j,t1,t9)  prob of linear part of motion
               equation ;
*
   positive variable pb, pg, pv ;
*
   equations
   gentrop   entropy measure objective function
   motion(j,t1)    equation of motion in deviations
                   from the mean
   avemotio(j)    average equation of motion
   pbsum(j,jj)    probability sum on b matrix
   pgsum(j,jj)    probability sum on g matrix
   pvsum(j,t1)    probability sum on v vector ;
*
   gentrop..   cent =e= - sum((j,t9), pb(j,j,t9)*
               log((pb(j,j,t9)) +.00001))
               - sum((j,t9),pg(j,j,t9)*log((pg(j,j,t9))
               +.00001)) - sum((j,t1,t9), pv(j,t1,t9)*
               log((pv(j,t1,t9)) +.00001)) ;
*
   motion(j,t1)..   dxt(j,t1) =e= sum(k$(ord(j)
            eq ord(k)), sum(t9, pb(j,k,t9)
            *zb(j,k,t9))* sum(kk$(ord(k) eq ord(kk)),
            sum(t9, pg(k,kk,t9) *zg(k,kk,t9))
            *dpridelay(kk,t1) ) ) + sum(k$(ord(j)
            eq ord(k)), (ident(j,k)-sum(t9,
            pg(j,k,t9) *zg(j,k,t9)))*dxdelay(k,t1) )
            + sum(t9, pv(j,t1,t9)*zv(j,t1,t9))
         - sum((t8,t9), pv(j,t8,t9)*zv(j,t8,t9))/7 ;
*
   avemotio(j)..   avex(j) =e= sum(k$(ord(j)
               eq ord(k)), sum(t9, pb(j,k,t9)
               *zb(j,k,t9)) * sum(kk$(ord(k)
               eq ord(kk)),sum(t9, pg(k,kk,t9)
               *zg(k,kk,t9))*avepridel(kk) ) )
```

```
                        + sum(k$(ord(j) eq ord(k)), (ident(j,k)
                        -sum(t9, pg(j,k,t9)*zg(j,k,t9)))
                        *avexdelay(k)) + sum((t1,t9),
                        pv(j,t1,t9)*zv(j,t1,t9))/7 ;
*
    pbsum(j,j)..    sum(t9, pb(j,j,t9)) =e= 1. ;
    pgsum(j,j)..    sum(t9, pg(j,j ,t9)) =e= 1. ;
    pvsum(j,t1)..   sum(t9, pv(j,t1,t9)) =e= 1. ;
*
* name and definition of model for estimating b and
* gamma matrices
*
    model equmotion /gentrop, motion, avemotio, pbsum,
        pgsum, pvsum / ;
* initial values
    pb.l(j,j,t9) = 1/7 ;
    pb.fx(j,jj,t9)$(flag(j) ne flag(jj)) = 1/7 ;
    pg.l(j,j,t9) = 1/7 ;
    pg.fx(j,jj,t9)$(flag(j) ne flag(jj)) = 1/7 ;
    pv.l(j,t1,t9) = 1/7 ;
*
    equmotion.workspace=10.0 ;
    solve equmotion using nlp maximizing cent ;
* calculating the expected parameter values
    parameter v(j,t1), bs(j,jj), ge(j,jj), avev(j),
        vv(j,t1) ;
    v(j,t1) = sum(t9, pv.l(j,t1,t9)*zv(j,t1,t9)) ;
    avev(j) = sum(t1, v(j,t1))/7 ;
    vv(j,t1) = v(j,t1) - avev(j) ;
    bs(j,j) = sum(t9, pb.l(j,j,t9)*zb(j,j,t9) ) ;
    bs(j,jj)$(flag(j) ne flag(jj)) = 0 ;
    ge(j,j) = sum(t9, pg.l(j,j,t9)* zg(j,j,t9) ) ;
    ge(j,jj)$(flag(j) ne flag(jj)) = 0 ;
*
    parameter xthat(j,t1)    equation of motion,
    comparxt(j,t1)    percent difference xbart1
                        -xthatt1 ;
    xthat(j,t1) = sum(jj, bs(j,jj)* sum(kk$(ord(jj)
            eq ord(kk)),ge(jj,kk) *pridelay(kk,t1) ) )
            + sum(kk$(ord(j) eq ord(kk)), (ident(j,kk)
            -ge(j,kk))*xdelay(kk,t1) ) + v(j,t1) ;
    comparxt(j,t1) = ((xxbar(j,t1) - xthat(j,t1) )/
        xxbar(j,t1) )* 100 ;
```

```
    display v, vv, bs, ge, comparxt ;
*
* compute phase 1 of dpep. backward solution from t to
* 1 realized using the
* hor matrix
    scalar epsilon /.000001/ ;
*
* loop parameters defined
*
    parameter
    la(j,i)   a matrix of fixed technical coefficients
    lb(i)   supply of limiting inputs
    lxbar(j)   realized output levels
    lpri(j)   output prices
    lc(j)   unit variable costs
    lcc(i)   prices of limiting inputs
    llam1(j)   costate at time t+1
    lxl(g,j,tt)   loop lp values
    nxl(g,q,tt) loop nlp output values
    lyl(g,i,tt)   loop nlp shadwow prices
    lamu(g,j,ttt)   time pmp values
    labet(g,i,tt)   lp dual variables of limiting
                    prices constraints
    shadres(g,i,tt)   resources shadow price
    lfxcost(g,j,tt)   limiting marginal cost
    d   discount factor
    rho   discount rate
    nt   time index for discount
    salcost(j)   stores the costate for t+1 ;
*
* dynamic equilibrium program to calculate resource
* duals and costates phase 1 dpep
*
    variables lx(j)   lp output allocated
    ly(i)   lp dual variables
    llam(j)   lp calibration dual variables quantities
    bet(i)   lp calibration dual variables limprices
    lp1(i)   lp primal 1 slack variables
    lvp2(j)   lp primal 2 slack variables
    lvd(j)   lp dual 1 slack variables
    lvd2(i)   lp dual 2 slack variables
    equil   lp fake objective function ;
*
```

```
     positive variable lx, ly, lvp1, lvp2, lvd, lvd2,
       llam, bet ;
*
     equations
     resource(i)    constrained resources
     calibu(j)      upper primal calibration constraints
     ldual(j)       dual constraints
     limpri(i)      lower dual calibration constraints
     equilequ       equilibrium objective function ;
*
     resource(i)..    sum(j,la(j,i)*lx(j)) + bet(i)
                        + lvp1(i) =e= lb(i) ;
     calibu(j)..      lx(j) + lvp2(j) =e= lxbar(j)
                        * (1+epsilon) ;
     ldual(j)..       sum(i, la(j,i)*ly(i) ) + llam(j)
                        =e= lpri(j)/d + sum(jj, (ident(j,jj)
                        - ge(j,jj) )*llam1(jj) ) + lvd(j) ;
     limpri(i)..      ly(i) =e= lcc(i)/d + lvd2(i) ;
     equilequ..       sum(j, lx(j) *lvd(j) )
                        + sum(i, lvp1(i)*ly(i) ) + sum(j,
                        llam(j)*lvp2(j)) + sum(i, bet(i)
                        *lvd2(i) ) =e= equil ;
*
* name and definition of phase 1 model
*
     model calibrate /resource,calibu, ldual, limpri,
       equilequ /;
*
     rho = .03 ;
     llam1(j) = (pri("v04",j,"92") -
     sum(i, a("v04",j,i,"92")*cc("v04",i,"92" ) ))
       *(rho*exp(-rho*8) ) ;
     salcost(j) = llam1(j) ;
*
* loop on years to reverse time index
*
     loop( g, loop( t2,
     nt = 93 - (ord(t2) + 85 ) ;
     d = (1 + rho)**nt ;
* the following trick reverses the time index in the
* data series
       la(j,i) = sum(tt, a(g,j,i,tt)*hor(tt,t2)) ;
       lb(i) = sum(tt, b(g,i,tt)*hor(tt,t2)) ;
       lxbar(j) = sum(tt, xbar(g,j,tt)*hor(tt,t2)) ;
```

```
    lpri(j) = sum(tt, pri(g,j,tt)*hor(tt,t2)) ;
    lcc(i) = sum(tt, cc(g,i,tt)*hor(tt,t2)) ;
    lvd.fx(j) = 0 ;
    lvp2.fx(j) = 0 ;
*
    solve calibrate using nlp minimizing equil ;
    lxl(g,j,t2) = lx.l(j) ;
    llam1(j) = llam.l(j) ;
    lamu(g,j,t2) = llam.l(j) ;
    shadres(g,i,t2) = resource.m(i) ;
    lyl(g,i,t2) = ly.l(i) ;
    labet(g,i,t2) = bet.l(i) ;
    lfxcost(g,j,t2) = sum(i,la(j,i)*ly.l(i)) ;
    ) ; ) ;
* close loops
    lamu("v04",j,"93") = salcost (j) ;
    display xbar, lxl, lyl, labet, lamu, shadres,
      lfxcost ;
*
* time index is restored in the data series by the
* following operations
*
    parameter
    invlxl(g,j,tt)
    invlamu(g,j,tt)
    invshad(g,i,tt)
    invlyl(g,i,tt)
    invlabet(g,i,tt)
    invlfcos(g,j,tt) ;
    invlxl("v04",j,t2) = sum(tt, lxl("v04",j,tt)
      *hor(tt,t2)) ;
    invlamu("v04",j,t2) = sum(tt, lamu("v04",j,tt)
      *hor(tt,t2)) ;
    invshad("v04",i,t2) = sum(tt, shadres("v04",i,tt)
      *hor(tt,t2)) ;
    invlyl("v04",i,t2) = sum(tt, lyl("v04",i,tt)
      *hor(tt,t2)) ;
    invlabet("v04",i,t2) = sum(tt, labet("v04",i,tt)
      *hor(tt,t2)) ;
    invlfcos("v04",j,t2) = sum(tt, lfxcost("v04",j,tt)
      *hor(tt,t2)) ;
    display xbar, invlxl, invlyl, invlabet, invlamu,
      invshad , invlfcos;
* end of phase 1
```

```
* beginning of phase 2: estimation of cost function
* parameter
   gam(g,q)   prior for cost slope
   avc(g,t)   average variable cost
*
* note — change numcrp later for zero acres
   numcrp   number of crops
   numt    number of time periods
   prid(j,jj,p)   prior probs for zeta values of d
   pril(j,jj,p)  prior probs for zeta values of lt
   pris(i,ii,p)   prior probs for the s matrix
   prifs(j,p)   prior on linear part ;
   numcrp = smax(j, ord(j) ) ;
   numt = smax(t, ord(t) ) ;
   avc(g,t) = sum(j, invlfcos(g,j,t)) / numcrp ;
   gam(g,j) = sum(t, invlfcos(g,j,t)/xbar(g,j,t) )/
     numt ;
   gam(g,i) = sum(t, b(g,i,t) )/ numt;
*
   pril(j,jj,p) = 1/3 ;
   prid(j,jj,p) = 1/3 ;
   pris(i,ii,p) = 1/3 ;
   prifs(j,p) = 1/3 ;
   display gam , calibu.m, lamu ;
* definition of the probability supports from pmp
* values in phase 2
   parameter zwgt(p)    z weights

   / 1   0.0
     2   1.5
     3   3.0  /
   parameter zwgt2(p)    z weights

   / 1   -2.5
     2    0.0
     3    2.5  /
*
   parameter
   zd(j,jj,p)   z value range for cholesky d matrix
   zl(j,jj,p)   z value range for cholesky lt matrix
   zs(i,ii,p)   z values for the s matrix
   zfs(j,p)   z values for f vector
   maco(g,j,t)   marginal costs of outputs
```

```
    lmaco(j)   entropy marginal cost
    insup(g,i,t)   input supply-derived demand
    linsup(i)   entropy quantity of limiting inputs;
*
    parameter
    lprod(j)   entropy levels of production
    prodx(g,j,t)   production
    inpri(g,i,t)   limiting input prices
    linpri(i)   entropy market price of limiting inputs
    zetaq(g,j,jj,tt)   expected marginal cost
                       coefficients ;
*
    parameter
    lzetaq(j,jj)   loop zeta value
    zetas(g,i,ii,tt)   leontief matrix for limiting
                       inputs
    lzetas(i,ii)   nlp matrix of limiting inputs
    u(i)   sum vector
    cfs(g,j,tt)   linear part of cost function
    ncfs(j)   linear part of cost function in nlp
    rrs(i)   market rentals of limiting inputs
    effecb(g,i,tt)   effective b(i) ;
*
    maco(g,j,t) = invlfcos(g,j,t) ;
    insup(g,i,t) = b(g,i,t) - invlabet(g,i,t) ;
    prodx(g,j,t) = invlxl(g,j,t) ;
    inpri(g,i,t) = invlyl(g,i,t) ;
    u(i) = 1 ;
*
    display maco, insup, prodx, inpri ;
*
* solving the generalized entropy problem - phase 2
* estimating a generalized leontief-quadratic cost
* function
* c(x,y) = u'y(f'x) + u'y(x'qx)/2 +(y**.5sy**.5)
*
    variables
    cent   entropy level objective function
    cx   definition of quadratic form in x
    cy   definition of leontief part of cost function
    qp(j,jj)   qp matrix qp'qp = zeta
    pd(j,jj,p)   probability of cholesky's values
    pl(j,jj,p)   probability of lower triangular matrix
```

```
    ps(i,ii,p)   probabilities of the s matrix
    pfs(j,p)     probability of the linear part of cost
                 function ;
*
    positive variable pd, pl, ps, pfs ;
*
    equations
    gentrop2   entropy measure
    mc(j)    marginal cost of outputs
    is(i)    implicit supply of limiting inputs
    defqp(j,jj)   definition of qp
    defcx    equation for the quadratic form oin x
    pdsum(j,jj)   probability sum on d matrix
    plsum(j,jj)   probability sum on lt matrix
    lteq(j,jj)    unit values on lower triangular
                   diagonal
    lteq2(j,jj)   zero value on upper triangle of lower
                   traingular matrix
    pssum(i,ii)   probability on s matrix
    pfssum(j)   probability of f vector
    symms(i,ii)   symmetry of s matrix
    pos(i,ii)   nonnegativity of s matrix ;
*
    gentrop2..   cent =e= sum((j,jj,p),pl(j,jj,p)
            *log((pl(j,jj,p)/pril(j,jj,p)) +.00001))
             + sum((j,jj,p), pd(j,jj,p)*log((pd(j,jj,p)/
             prid(j,jj,p)) +.00001))+ sum((i,ii,p),
             ps(i,ii,p)*log((ps(i,ii,p)/pris(i,ii,p))
             +.00001)) + sum((j,p), pfs(j,p)
             *log((pfs(j,p)/prifs(j,p))+.00001)) ;
*
  mc(j)..    lmaco(j) =e= sum(i, u(i)*linpri(i) )
             * sum(k, sum(jj, qp(j,jj)*qp(k,jj))
             *lprod(k))+ sum(i, u(i)*linpri(i) )
             * sum(p, pfs(j,p)*zfs(j,p)) ;
*
    defqp(j,jj)..   qp(j,jj) =e= sum(k, sum(p, pl(j,k,p)
             *zl(j,k,p)) * (sum(l,
             pd(k,jj,1)*zd(k,jj,1)))**0.5 );
*
    lteq(j,jj)$(ord(j) eq ord(jj))..  sum(p,pl(j,jj,p)
                               *zl(j,jj,p)) =e= 1 ;
*
```

```
    lteq2(j,jj)$(ord(j) lt ord(jj))..   sum(p,
                             pl(j,jj,p)* zl(j,jj,p) )
                             =e= 0 ;
*
    is(i)..   linsup(i) =e= cx + sum(ii,
            sum(p, ps(i,ii,p) *zs(i,ii,p))*
             (linpri(ii)**.5)/(linpri(i)**.5 +.00001) )
        + sum(j, sum(p, pfs(j,p)*zfs(j,p))*lprod(j) );
*
    defcx..  cx =e= sum((j,k), lprod(j)
             *sum(jj, qp(j,jj)*qp(k,jj))*lprod(k))/2 ;
*
    pos(i,ii)$(flag(i) ne flag(ii))..
                 sum(p, ps(i,ii,p)*zs(i,ii,p)) =g= 0 ;
*
    symms(i,ii)$(flag(i) ne flag(ii))..   sum(p,
             ps(i,ii,p)*zs(i,ii,p)) =e=
              sum(p, ps(ii,i,p)*zs(ii,i,p)) ;
*
    pdsum(j,jj)..   sum(p, pd(j,jj,p)) =e= 1. ;
    plsum(j,jj)..   sum(p, pl(j,jj,p)) =e= 1. ;
    pssum(i,ii)..   sum(p, ps(i,ii,p)) =e= 1. ;
    pfssum(j)..   sum(p, pfs(j,p)) =e= 1. ;
*
* name and definition of phase 2 model
*
    model maxent / mc, defqp, lteq, lteq2, pos, is,
      defcx, symms, pdsum, plsum, pssum, pfssum,
      gentrop2 / ;
    parameter cd(j,jj,t) cholesky values,
        lowert(j,jj) cholesky lower triangular matrix ;
*
* loop on horizon years, 85-91, for estimating the
* cost function
*
    loop(g, loop( t,
    zd(j,jj,p)$(flag(j) eq flag(jj)) = gam(g,j)
      * zwgt(p) ;
    zl(j,jj,p)$(flag(j) eq flag(jj)) = zwgt(p) ;
    zl(j,jj,p)$(flag(j) ne flag(jj)) = (gam(g,j))
      * zwgt2(p) ;
```

```
      zs(i,ii,p)$(flag(i) ne flag(ii)) = zwgt(p)
        *gam(g,i) ;
      zs(i,ii,p)$(flag(i) eq flag(ii)) = gam(g,i)
        *zwgt(p) ;
      zfs(j,p) = zwgt2(p) ;
      lmaco(j) = maco(g,j,t) ;
      lprod(j) = prodx(g,j,t) ;
      linsup(i) = insup(g,i,t) ;
      linpri(i) = inpri(g,i,t) ;
* initial values
      pd.l(j,jj,p) = 1/3 ;
      pl.l(j,jj,p) = 1/3 ;
      ps.l(i,ii,p) = 1/3 ;
      pfs.l(j,p) = 1/3 ;
*
      solve maxent using nlp minimizing cent ;
* calculating the expected parameter values
      cd(j,jj,t)= sum(1,pd.l(j,jj,1) * zd(j,jj,1));
      lowert(j,jj) = sum(p, pl.l(j,jj,p)* zl(j,jj,p) ) ;
      cfs(g,j,t) = sum(p, pfs.l(j,p)*zfs(j,p)) ;
      zetaq(g,j,jj,t) = sum(k, qp.l(j,k)*qp.l(jj,k) ) ;
      zetas(g,i,ii,t) = sum(p, ps.l(i,ii,p)* zs(i,ii,p));
* updating the priors
      pril(j,jj,p) = 0.0001 ;
      prid(j,jj,p) = 0.0001 ;
      pris(i,ii,p) = 0.0001 ;
      prifs(j,p) = 0.0001 ;
      pril(j,jj,p)$pl.l(j,jj,p) = pl.l(j,jj,p) ;
      prid(j,jj,p)$pd.l(j,jj,p) = pd.l(j,jj,p) ;
      pris(i,ii,p)$ps.l(i,ii,p) = ps.l(i,ii,p) ;
      prifs(j,p) = pfs.l(j,p) ;
      ) ; );
* close loops
* predicting the zeta values for 1992 from 1991
*
      zetaq(g,j,jj,"92") = zetaq(g,j,jj,"91") ;
      zetas(g,i,ii,"92") = zetas(g,i,ii,"91") ;
      cfs(g,j,"92") = cfs(g,j,"91") ;
      display zetaq, zetas, cd, lowert ;
*
* end of phase 2
* beginning of phase 3
*
```

```
    parameter llamt(j), llamt1(j) ;
* solution of calibrating dynamic equilibrium problem
* quadratic-leontiev for base year
*
    variables
    nx(j)    nonlinear outputs
    vp(i)    primal slacks
    ny(i)    nonlinear symmetric dual variables
    nbet(i)   nonlinear beta
    vd2(i)    dual slacks on input prices
    vd(j)    dual slacks on marginal costs
    nlequil   nonlinear equilibrium ;
*
    positive variable nx, vp, ny, vd, nbet, vd2 ;
*
    equations resourcen(i)   primal constrained
                             resources equations
    dualmc(j)   dual marginal cost equations
    betequ(i)   beta equations
    npequequ   nonlinear equilibrium objective
               function;
    resourcen(i)..   sum((j,jj), nx(j)
                *lzetaq(j,jj)*nx(jj) )/2
                + sum(ii, lzetas(i,ii)*(ny(ii)
                **.5)/(ny(i)**.5 +.00001) ) + nbet(i)
                + sum(j, ncfs(j)*nx(j))
                + vp(i) =e= lb(i) ;
    betequ(i)..   ny(i) =e= rrs(i)/d + vd2(i) ;
    dualmc(j)..   sum(jj, lzetaq(j,jj)
                *nx(jj) )*sum(i, u(i)*ny(i))
                + sum(i, u(i)*ny(i))*ncfs(j) =e=
                lpri(j)/d + vd(j) + (ident(j,j)
                - ge(j,j) )*llamt1(j) - llamt(j) ;
    npequequ..   sum((j), vd(j) * nx(j) )
                + sum(i, vp(i)*ny(i) )
                + sum(i, nbet(i)*vd2(i)) =e= nlequil ;
*
* name and definition of phase 3 equilibrium model
*
    model equilib /resourcen, dualmc, betequ,
      npequequ/ ;
*
    parameter bhat(g,i,t2), nyl(g,i,t2),
```

```
      nbeta(g,i,t2) ;
*
* loop on horizon years
*
    loop(g, loop( t2,
    nt = ord(t2) - 1 ;
    d = (1 + rho)**nt ;
    llamt(j) = invlamu(g,j,t2) ;
    llamt1(j) = invlamu(g,j,t2+1) ;
    lb(i) = b(g,i,t2);
    lpri(j) = pri(g,j,t2);
    lcc(i) = cc(g,i,t2) ;
    ncfs(j) = cfs(g,j,t2) ;
    rrs(i) = cc(g,i,t2) ;
    lzetaq(j,jj) = zetaq(g,j,jj,t2) ;
    lzetas(i,ii) = zetas(g,i,ii,t2) ;
    nx.l(j) = lxbar(j)*.95 ;
    ny.l(i) = cc(g,i,t2) ;
*
    solve equilib using nlp minimizing nlequil;
*
    nxl(g,j,t2) = nx.l(j) ;
    nyl(g,i,t2) = ny.l(i) ;
    bhat(g,i,t2) = sum((j,jj), nx.l(j)
               *lzetaq(j,jj)*nx.l(jj) )/2
               + sum(ii, lzetas(i,ii)*(ny.l(ii)**.5)/
               (ny.l(i)**.5 +.00001) )
               +sum(j, ncfs(j)*nx.l(j)) ;
    nbeta(g,i,t2) = nbet.l(i) ;
    effecb(g,i,t2) = lb(i) - nbet.l(i) ;
    ) ; ) ;
* close loops
*
    option decimals = 4;
* end of phase 3
* writing a report
*
    parameters
    diffx(g,j,t2)   percent difference in nlp x
    diffy(g,i,t2)   percent difference in nlp y
    firsto(q)    first order condition
    inputs(i)    nl input quantities
    tinput(i)    linear input quantities
```

```
    cropcost(g,j,t2)    crop cost
    tcost    total cost by cost function
    allen(i,ii)    allen elasticities
    morishima(i,ii)    morishima elasticities
    demelas(i,ii)    derived demand elasticity
    supplyx(j)    output supply function
    supelas(j,jj)    elasticity of supply
    parameter totcost    total cost by b'y
    profit91    profit in year 91 ;
*
    diffx(g,j,t2) = ((nxl(g,j,t2) - xbar(g,j,t2)) /
              xbar(g,j,t2))* 100 ;
    diffy(g,i,t2)$lyl(g,i,t2) = ((nyl(g,i,t2)
              - invlyl(g,i,t2) ) /nyl(g,i,t2) )* 100 ;
    firsto(j) = sum(i, u(i)*nyl("v04",i,"91") )*
                  sum(jj, zetaq("v04",j,jj,"91")
                  *nxl("v04",jj,"91")) ;
    inputs(i) = sum((j,jj), nxl("v04",j,"91")
                  *zetaq("v04",j,jj,"91")
                  *nxl("v04",jj,"91"))/2
                  + sum(ii, zetas("v04",i,ii,"91")
                  *(nyl("v04",ii,"91")**.5)
                  /(nyl("v04",i,"91")**.5 +.00001) )
                  + sum(j, nxl("v04",j,"91")
                  * cfs("v04",j,"91"));
*
* c(x,y) = u'y(f'x) + u'y(x'qx)/2 +(y**.5sy**.5)
*
    tcost = sum(i, u(i)*nyl("v04",i,"91"))
                  * sum((j,jj), nxl("v04",j,"91")
                  *zetaq("v04",j,jj,"91")
                  *nxl("v04",jj,"91"))/2 + sum((i,ii),
                  (nyl("v04",i,"91")**.5)
                  *zetas("v04",i,ii, "91")
                  *(nyl("v04",ii,"91")**.5) )
                  + sum(i, u(i)*nyl("v04",i,"91"))
                  *sum(j, cfs("v04",j,"91")
                  *nxl("v04",j,"91") ) ;
    totcost = sum(i, (nyl("v04",i,"91")*
      bhat("v04",i,"91")));
*
```

```
* computation of the inverse of the q matrix for
* deriving the output supply fuction
*
    parameter identity(j,k), qmat91(j,k), qmat90(j,k),
      qmat89(j,k),qmat85(j,k), smat91(i,ii),
      smat90(i,ii),smat89(i,ii), smat85(i,ii) ;
    identity(j,k)$(ord(j) eq ord(k) ) = 1 ;
    qmat91(j,k) = zetaq("v04",j,k,"91") ;
    qmat90(j,k) = zetaq("v04",j,k,"90") ;
    qmat89(j,k) = zetaq("v04",j,k,"89") ;
    qmat85(j,k) = zetaq("v04",j,k,"85") ;
    smat91(i,ii) = zetas("v04",i,ii,"91") ;
    smat90(i,ii) = zetas("v04",i,ii,"90") ;
    smat89(i,ii) = zetas("v04",i,ii,"89") ;
    smat85(i,ii) = zetas("v04",i,ii,"85") ;
    lpri(j) = pri("v04",j,"91") ;
    parameter zero(j) ;
    zero(j) = 0 ;
    parameter compident(j,k)  check on identity matrix;
*
* model for computing the inverse of the q91 matrix
*
    variables
    invx(j,k)    inverse matrix
    obj   objective function ;
*
    equations
    eq(j,k)    equations for q91*inverse = identity
    objfunc    objective function equation ;
    objfunc..    obj =e= sum((j,k), zero(j)*invx(j,k)
                 *zero(k) ) ;
    eq(j,k)..    sum(kk, qmat91(j,kk)*invx(kk,k) )
                 =e= identity(j,k) ;
*
    model inver / eq, objfunc /;
*
    solve inver using nlp minimizing obj;
    compident(j,k) = sum(kk, qmat91(j,kk)
      *invx.l(kk,k) ) ;
    display identity, invx.l , compident ;
*
* output supply function
*
```

```
    supplyx(j) = sum(k, invx.l(j,k)*lpri(k) )/
      sum(i, u(i)*nyl("v04",i,"91"))
      - sum(k, invx.l(j,k)*cfs("v04",k,"91") ) ;
*
* output supply elasticities for year 91
*
    supelas(j,jj) = invx.l(j,jj)*lpri(jj)/
      (sum(i, u(i)*nyl("v04",i,"91"))*supplyx(j)) ;
* profit for the year 91
    profit91 = sum(j, lpri(j)*supplyx(j) ) - tcost ;
*
* demand elasticities are computed twice for check.
* manuelast computes them element
* by element while demelas computes them in compact
* formula.
* the two computations check out.
*
    parameter manuelast(i,ii) derived demand
      elasticity ;
    manuelast("land","land") = -( zetas("v04","land",
                  "water","91")
                *(nyl("v04", "water","91")**.5)
                *(nyl("v04","land","91")**(-.5))
                + zetas("v04","land","other","91")
                *(nyl("v04","other","91")**.5)
                *(nyl("v04","land","91")**(-.5)))/
                (2*bhat("v04","land","91")) ;
    manuelast("water","water") =
                -(zetas("v04","water","land","91")
                *(nyl("v04","land","91")**.5)
                *(nyl("v04","water","91")**(-.5))
                + zetas("v04","water","other","91")
                *(nyl("v04", "other","91")**.5)
                *(nyl("v04","water","91")**(-.5)))/
                (2*bhat("v04","water","91")) ;
    manuelast("other","other") =
                -( zetas("v04","other","land","91")
                *(nyl("v04","land","91")**.5)
                *(nyl("v04","other","91")**(-.5))
                + zetas("v04","other","water","91")
                *(nyl("v04","water","91")**.5)
                *(nyl("v04","other","91")**(-.5)))/
                (2*bhat("v04","other","91")) ;
```

```
manuelast("land","water") =
          zetas("v04","land","water","91")
          *(nyl("v04","water","91")
          **(.5))*(nyl("v04","land","91")
          **(-.5))/
          (2*bhat("v04","land","91")) ;
manuelast("land","other") =
          zetas("v04","land","other","91")
           *(nyl("v04","other","91")
          **(.5))*(nyl("v04","land","91")
          **(-.5))/
          (2*bhat("v04","land","91")) ;
manuelast("water","land") =
          zetas("v04","water","land","91")
          *(nyl("v04","land","91")
          **(.5))*(nyl("v04","water","91")
          **(-.5))/
          (2*bhat("v04","water","91")) ;
manuelast("water","other") =
          zetas("v04","water","other","91")
          *(nyl("v04","other","91")
          **(.5))*(nyl("v04","water","91")
          **(-.5))/
          (2*bhat("v04","water","91")) ;
manuelast("other","land") =
          zetas("v04","other","land","91")
          *(nyl("v04","land","91")
          **(.5))*(nyl("v04","other","91")
          **(-.5))/
          (2*bhat("v04","other","91")) ;
manuelast("other","water") =
          zetas("v04","other","water","91")
          *(nyl("v04","water","91")
          **(.5))*(nyl("v04","other","91")
          **(-.5))/
          (2*bhat("v04","other","91")) ;
demelas(i,ii)$(flag(i) eq flag(ii)) =
          - (sum(ii2$(flag(i) ne flag(ii2)),
          zetas("v04",i,ii2,"91")
          *(nyl("v04",ii2,"91")**.5)
          *(nyl("v04",i,"91")**(-.5)) ))/
          (2*bhat("v04",i,"91")) ;
```

```
      demelas(i,ii)$(flag(i) ne flag(ii)) =
               zetas("v04",i,ii,"91")*
               (nyl("v04",ii,"91")
               **(.5))*(nyl("v04",i,"91")
               **(-.5))/(2*bhat("v04",i,"91")) ;
*
   parameter allen2(i,ii) allen elasticity of
      substitution;
   allen2(i,ii) = demelas(i,ii) * ( totcost/
               (nyl("v04",ii,"91")*inputs(ii))) ;
   allen(i,ii) = demelas(i,ii) * ( tcost/
               (nyl("v04",ii,"91")*inputs(ii))) ;
   morishima(i,ii) = demelas(i,ii) - demelas(ii,ii) ;
* profit derived input demand functions
   parameter proinput(i) ;
   proinput(i) = sum((j,k), lpri(j)*invx.l(j,k)
               *lpri(k))/(2*(sum(ii, u(ii)
               *nyl("v04",ii,"91") )**2))
               - sum((j,k), cfs("v04",j,"91")
               *invx.l(j,k) *cfs("v04",k,"91") ) /2
               + sum(ii, zetas("v04",i,ii,"91")
               *(nyl("v04",ii,"91")**.5) /
               (nyl("v04",i,"91")**.5) ) ;
*
   parameter identq(j,k), idents(i,i2), aq(j,k),
      as(i,i2) ;
   identq(j,k) = 0. ;
   identq(j,k)$(ord(j) eq ord(k) ) = 1. ;
   idents(i,i2) = 0. ;
   idents(i,i2)$(ord(i) eq ord(i2) ) = 1. ;
* solving the eigenvalue problem
   variables
   eigensobj  fake objective for eigenvalues of the
               s matrix
   eigenqobj  fake objective for eigenvalues of the
               q matrix
   pq(j,k)    orthogonal matrix for the q matrix
   elq(j,k)   eigenvalue matrix for the q matrix
   pps(i,i2)  orthogonal matrix for the s matrix
   els(i,i2)  eigenvalue matrix for the s matrix ;
*
* if the problem is infeasible comment out the
* following command
```

```
    positive variable elq, els ;
*
    equations
    eigobjqeq    eigenvalue fake obj function for the q
                 matrix
    eigobjseq    eigenvalue fake obj function for the s
                 matrix
    aeq(j,k)     equations for the q
                 matrix
    aes(i,i2)    equations for the s
                 matrix
    orthoq(j,k)  orthogonal conditions for the q
                 matrix
    orthos(i,i2) orthogonality conditions on the s
                 matrix ;
*
    aeq(j,k)..   aq(j,k) =e= sum(jj, pq(j,jj)
                 *sum(kk, elq(jj,kk)* pq(k,Kk)) ) ;
    orthoq(j,k)..   sum(jj, pq(j,jj)*pq(k,jj) ) =e=
                 identq(j,k) ;
    eigobjqeq..  eigenqobj =e= sum((j,K) ,
                 sqr (elq(j,k) ) ) ;
    aes(i,i2)..  as(i,i2) =e= sum(ii, pps(i,ii)
                 *sum(ii2, els(ii,ii2)* pps(i2,ii2)));
    orthos(i,i2)..   sum(ii, pps(i,ii)*pps(i2,ii) ) =e=
                 idents(i,i2) ;
    eigobjseq..  eigensobj =e= sum((i,i2) ,
                 sqr (els(i,i2) ) ) ;
*
    model eigenq /aeq, eigobjqeq, orthoq /;
*
    model eigens /aes, eigobjseq, orthos /;
*
    parameter eigeq(j,t2), eiges(i,t2) ;
* loop on horizon years
    loop(t2,
* initial values
    elq.l(j,k)$(flag(j) eq flag(k) ) = 1. ;
    elq.fx(j,k)$(flag(j) ne flag(k) ) = 0. ;
    pq.l(j,k) = 1. ;
    els.l(i,i2)$(flag(i) eq flag(i2) ) = 1. ;
    els.fx(i,i2)$(flag(i) ne flag(i2) ) = 0. ;
    pps.l(i,i2) = 1. ;
```

```
   aq(j,k) = zetaq("v04",j,k,t2) ;
   as(i,i2) = zetas("v04",i,i2,t2) ;
*
   solve eigenq using nlp minimizing eigenqobj ;
   solve eigens using nlp minimizing eigensobj ;
   eigeq(j,t2) = elq.l(j,j) ;
   eiges(i,t2) = els.l(i,i) ;
   ) ;
* close loop
   display invlxl, xbar, invlyl, nxl, nyl, cc, diffx,
     diffy, lamu,
   invlamu, invlfcos, tcost, totcost, profit91, b,
     bhat,
   effecb, inputs, proinput, labet, nbeta, cfs,
   firsto, manuelast,
   demelas, allen, allen2, morishima, supplyx,
     supelas, lzetaq, zetaq ;
   display qmat91, qmat90, qmat89,qmat85 ;
   display lzetas, zetas ;
   display smat91, smat90, smat89,smat85 ;
   display cd, lowert ;
   display identity, invx.l , compident ;
   display eigeq, eiges ;
   display ha, yb, a, b ;
   display xbar, xdelay, pri, pridelay, cc, r ;
   display avex, avexdelay, avepri, avepridel, dxt,
     dxdelay, dpridelay ;
   display bs, ge, comparxt ;
```

Revisiting the Three Phases of the Traditional PMP

One aspect of PMP that has left many people unconvinced deals with the specification of the calibration constraints such as $x \leq x_{obs}$, from problem (14.3), for example, where it is rather obvious that the optimal primal solution of the corresponding LP problem will occur precisely at $x = x_{obs}$. This issue, as the reader may recall, involves the "tautology problem" discussed in the introduction of PMP. The crucial question has always been: if one knows a priori the solution of the given LP problem, what is the meaning of setting up and solving a "pseudo" LP problem? Furthermore, phase I and phase II of the traditional methodology seem to be disconnected in the sense that phase I deals with N independent LP problems, whereas phase II estimates a cost function leading to the specification of a QP model. What setup may guarantee that the KKT conditions of the LP problems are consistent with the KKT conditions of the QP specification? An ingenious answer to both questions was given by Arfini and Donati.

In order to be clear, let us respecify the environment and the information leading to a PMP model. We assume a sample of N homogeneous farms and the availability of the following information for each farm: a K-vector of realized output levels, $\bar{\mathbf{x}}_n$; a K-vector of output prices, $\mathbf{p}_n$, faced by the nth entrepreneur; a technology matrix A_n of dimensions $(K \times 1)$; and total available land, b_n. We restrict our consideration to a single structural constraint to avoid the degeneracy of the dual variables, as discussed in a previous section.

To repeat, the main justification of the PMP methodology is the lack of information about the variable marginal costs of producing the output levels, $\bar{\mathbf{x}}_n$, selected by the entrepreneur. Letting, therefore, the output marginal cost vector be indicated by the symbol $\mathbf{r}_n$ and assuming a LP framework, profit is equal to zero. Furthermore, the estimation of a quadratic cost function gives flexibility to the model when used for exploring the effects of various policy scenarios. Hence, Arfini and Donati combined the estimation of the cost function for the N farms to the structure of a LP model in the following way:

$$\min \left\{ \sum_{n=1}^{N} \mathbf{u}_n' \mathbf{u}_n / 2 + \sum_{n=1}^{N} (b_n y_n + \mathbf{r}_n' \bar{\mathbf{x}}_n - \mathbf{p}_n' \bar{\mathbf{x}}_n) \right\} \tag{14.94}$$

$$\text{subject to} \qquad \mathbf{p}_n \leq A_n' y_n + \mathbf{r}_n \tag{14.95}$$

$$\mathbf{r}_n = Q\bar{\mathbf{x}}_n + \mathbf{u}_n \tag{14.96}$$

$n = 1, \ldots, N$ and where $y_n \geq 0$, $\mathbf{r}_n \geq \mathbf{0}$, Q is a symmetric positive semidefinite matrix representing the parameters of the quadratic cost function, the vector $\mathbf{u}_n$ is interpreted as a vector of deviations from the cost function that is specific to the nth farm, and the remaining symbols are as indicated earlier. Notice that, in the objective function (14.94), the quantity $(b_n y_n + \mathbf{r}_n' \bar{\mathbf{x}}_n - \mathbf{p}_n' \bar{\mathbf{x}}_n) = 0$ or, better, it is expected to be equal to zero as it represents the difference between total revenue, $\mathbf{p}_n' \bar{\mathbf{x}}_n$, and total cost, $b_n y_n + \mathbf{r}_n' \bar{\mathbf{x}}_n$, in an LP model. The estimation procedure adopted in problem (14.94) is a least-squares approach.

Before going further, let us summarize the known sample information and the unknown parameters to be estimated. For each farm, the known quantities are $b_n, \bar{\mathbf{x}}_n, \mathbf{p}_n, A_n$. The unknown parameters are $\mathbf{r}_n, y_n, Q, \mathbf{u}_n$. Notice the crucial characteristic of the setup in problem [(14.94) through

(14.96)]: the "tautological" relations $\mathbf{x}_n \leq \bar{\mathbf{x}}_n$ do not appear – explicitly – in the model and, therefore, the most contentious objection to PMP has been removed. Second, and using the marginal cost equation (14.96), the constraints (14.95) can be rewritten as $\mathbf{p}_n \leq A'_n y_n + Q\bar{\mathbf{x}}_n + \mathbf{u}_n$ which correspond to the dual constraints of a quadratic programming model such as (14.18). Thus, the purported disconnect between the traditional phase I and phase II has been eliminated.

Finally, to verify the calibrating property of model (14.94), we need to show that it can compute the output levels and that such quantities should be equal to the realized levels, $\bar{\mathbf{x}}_n$. To achieve this goal we define the Lagrangean function of model (14.94) to be

$$L = \sum_{n=1}^{N} \mathbf{u}'_n \mathbf{u}_n/2 + \sum_{n=1}^{N} (b_n y_n + \mathbf{r}'_n \bar{\mathbf{x}}_n - \mathbf{p}'_n \bar{\mathbf{x}}_n) \tag{14.97}$$

$$+ \sum_{n=1}^{N} \mathbf{w}'_n (\mathbf{p}_n - A'_n y_n - \mathbf{r}_n) + \sum_{n=1}^{N} \mathbf{z}'_n (\mathbf{r}_n - Q\bar{\mathbf{x}}_n - \mathbf{u}_n)$$

where $\mathbf{w}_n \geq \mathbf{0}$ and $\mathbf{z}_n$ unrestricted are the dual variables of constraints (14.95) and (14.96), respectively. The relevant KKT conditions for the nth farm take on the following structure:

$$\frac{\partial L}{\partial \mathbf{u}_n} = \mathbf{u}_n - \mathbf{z}_n = \mathbf{0} \tag{14.98}$$

$$\frac{\partial L}{\partial \mathbf{r}_n} = \bar{\mathbf{x}}_n - \mathbf{w}_n + \mathbf{z}_n \geq \mathbf{0} \tag{14.99}$$

$$\frac{\partial L}{\partial y_n} = b_n - A_n \mathbf{w}_n \geq 0. \tag{14.100}$$

The direction of the partial derivatives is dictated by the minimization operator in problem (14.94). KKT condition (14.98) establishes that the farm deviation $\mathbf{u}_n$ is equal to the dual variable of the cost function's equation (14.96). However, given the ill-posed nature of the problem, the deviation terms $\mathbf{u}_n$ will be always very close to zero (except for numerical imprecisions). In other words, the least-squares approach will attempt to minimize the sum of squared deviations and, when possible, the minimum value of this sum will be close to zero. Second, assuming that marginal costs are positive, $\mathbf{r}_n > \mathbf{0}$, for each output produced by the nth farm (definitely a weak assumption), KKT conditions (14.99) reduce to a set of equations, $\mathbf{w}_n - \mathbf{z}_n = \bar{\mathbf{x}}_n$. But, as we asserted a few lines earlier, the $\mathbf{z}_n$ vector variable will be always close to zero. Hence, the dual variables of the marginal cost constraints, $\mathbf{w}_n$, which simply by their nature must be interpreted as shadow output quantities, are equal to the realized level of activities, $\bar{\mathbf{x}}_n$, that is, $\mathbf{w}_n \approx \bar{\mathbf{x}}_n$, up to a desired level of accuracy. As a consequence, the complementary slackness conditions associated with KKT relations [(14.98) through (14.100)] can be shown to result in the zero value of the LP part of the objective function, that is, $(b_n y_n + \mathbf{r}'_n \bar{\mathbf{x}}_n - \mathbf{p}'_n \bar{\mathbf{x}}_n) \approx 0$. This discussion demonstrates that model [(14.94) through (14.96)] implies the calibration of the output activities, as required by the traditional PMP methodology. The result can hardly be considered a tautology, although it corresponds precisely to the principal setup of the original PMP specification.

To complete the discussion of the Arfini-Donati specification, we state the corresponding dual problem, which is obtained as an application of KKT theory:

$$\max \left\{ \sum_{n=1}^{N} \mathbf{p}'_n(\mathbf{w}_n - \bar{\mathbf{x}}_n) - \sum_{n=1}^{N} \mathbf{u}'_n \mathbf{u}_n / 2 - \sum_{n=1}^{N} \mathbf{z}'_n Q \bar{\mathbf{x}}_n \right\}$$

subject to
$$\mathbf{u}_n - \mathbf{z}_n = 0$$

$$\mathbf{w}_n - \mathbf{z}_n \leq \bar{\mathbf{x}}_n$$

$$A_n \mathbf{w}_n \leq b_n$$

where $\mathbf{w}_n \geq 0$ while $\mathbf{u}_n$ and $\mathbf{z}_n$ are unrestricted vector variables. Notice that, in this dual specification, the calibrating constraints reappear, as they should, slightly disguised in a "nontautological" format. Given the calibration of the model, however, the first term in the objective function will almost vanish.

Numerical Example 2: Arfini-Donati PMP Specification

The way to look at PMP suggested by Arfini and Donati warrants a detailed discussion of a numerical example of model [(14.94) through (14.96)] and the associated programming code. By kind permission of the authors, we present a sizable problem involving 20 farms and seven crops of the Emilia Romagna region of Italy. The relevant data refer to parameters b_n, $\mathbf{p}_n$, $\bar{\mathbf{x}}_n$, and arable land for each crop, measured in hectares, say $\mathbf{ha}_n$. The seven crops are sugarbeets (sube), durum-wheat (duwh), soft-wheat (sowh), corn (corn), tomatoes (toma), rice (rice), and soybeans (soyb).

The total cultivated acreage, b_n, is obtained from Table 14.13 by summing over all the hectares allocated to the various crops: $b_n = \sum_{k=1}^{K} (ha)_{kn}$. Table 14.16 lists the total available land, which shows a marked variability

Table 14.13. *Crop hectares,* ha_n

Farm	Sube	Duwh	Sowh	Corn	Toma	Rice	Soyb
130038			82.820	191.910	13.410	47.460	58.860
130426			17.900	22.500	15.010		7.000
133812	9.870		16.570	66.640	19.750		16.570
111972	13.570		14.810	3.090	17.730		
111973	6.090		12.440	10.400	16.590		
111998	4.040			29.110	14.130		
112003	2.300	12.000	31.650		59.250		
112970			44.700	1.990	51.960		
111511	3.970		9.200		0.500		
110371			13.330	14.590	6.500	16.570	
110494		12.920			28.400		90.700
111310	3.400			6.000	7.000		
111392			9.350	10.050	9.300		
111654			7.780	3.500	15.580		2.000
112399			9.550	12.070	7.830		
112431	515.050	104.940	1005.810	244.260	118.020	387.720	554.620
112432	82.600			458.470	36.400	437.580	127.890
112985	3.000	36.500			2.500		
111212		7.330			4.000		

among the 20 farms, an aspect that is not a deterrent for using the PMP procedure. Table 14.14 exhibits the realized levels of outputs in each farm. Table 14.15 shows the output prices faced by each farm. The typical element of the technical coefficients' matrix utilized in this example is obtained as $A_{nk} = (ha)_{nk}/\bar{x}_{nk}$, for $\bar{x}_{nk} > 0$. This sample of farms reflects the reality that not all farmers cultivate all the crops. In other words, farmers practice self-selection. This information turns out to be very important for achieving the calibration of all the farms' ouput levels and must be programmed into a set of inequality constraints, as indicated in the GAMS command file presented later.

The numerical solution of a nonlinear programming problem requires a careful scaling of the data series in order to better assist the algorithm in the search for a feasible and, then, for an optimal solution. Ideally, the data series should be scaled around the unit value. In this example, prices where scaled by a factor of 10 and the realized output levels by a factor of 1000, as indicated later in the GAMS command file.

The GAMS solution results in all the estimated deviations $\hat{u}_n$ being very close to zero and in a very precised calibration of the output levels that appear as dual variables of constraints (14.95), w_n. Furthermore,

Table 14.14. *Realized levels of output,* $\bar{\mathbf{x}}_n$

Farm	Sube	Duwh	Sowh	Corn	Toma	Rice	Soyb
130038			5933.5	14696.4	6212.2	2675.8	2545.45
130426			1190.0	2420.0	6800.0		280.00
133812	5763.0		1043.0	6284.0	11940.0		672.00
111972	7289.0		1293.0	320.0	8155.0		
111973	3200.0		850.0	800.0	11000.0		
111998	2480.0			4080.0	8765.0		
112003	1510.0	840.0	2492.0		38877.0		
112970			2790.0	120.0	25757.0		
111511	1600.0		500.0		193.0		
110371			959.0	1475.5	2184.0	2660.0	
110494		927.0			10224.0		3356.00
111310	1065.0			558.0	1933.0		
111392			612.0	805.0	4540.0		
111654			475.0	391.0	8590.0		107.00
112399			584.0	1008.0	2665.0		
112431	221088.0	9025.0	74238.0	18970.0	70034.0	13137.0	18897.00
112432	47490.0			42100.0	19253.0	26900.0	5440.00
112985	1853.0	1188.2			2318.0		
111212		304.0			3850.0		

Table 14.15. *Output prices,* $\mathbf{p}_n$

Farm	Sube	Duwh	Sowh	Corn	Toma	Rice	Soyb
130038			12.70	13.50	7.26	37.00	21.65
130426			13.03	11.10	7.00		21.00
133812	6.00		13.50	12.60	6.70		22.20
111972	5.07		12.70	11.62	8.46		
111973	4.39		12.39	12.39	7.23		
111998	4.97			13.15	5.56		
112003	4.70	14.58	15.49		7.75		
112970			12.00	12.00	4.50		
111511	5.00		8.40		8.03		
110371			14.04	13.00	4.50	35.10	
110494		11.73			5.80		21.99
111310	5.00			12.30	6.00		
111392			14.43	13.57	8.42		
111654			13.19	10.97	6.50		19.39
112399			12.37	12.23	4.34		
112431	6.02	14.50	13.00	12.50	5.31	24.55	22.05
112432	5.84			12.68	6.08	20.09	25.29
112985	5.50	15.00			6.44		
111212		14.42			5.77		

Table 14.16. *Total land, b_n, and shadow prices, y_n*

Farm	Total land, b_n	Shadow price, y_n
130038	394.46	0.091
130426	62.41	0.084
133812	129.40	0.085
111972	49.20	0.111
111973	45.52	0.085
111998	47.28	0.147
112003	105.20	0.102
112970	98.65	0.063
111511	13.67	0.046
110371	66.78	0.101
110494	132.02	0.081
111310	16.40	0.114
111392	28.70	0.094
111654	28.86	0.081
112399	29.45	0.076
112431	2930.42	0.075
112432	1142.94	0.108
112985	42.00	0.049
111212	11.33	0.060

and as expected, the LP profit relation is equal to zero, $(b_n \hat{y}_n + \hat{\mathbf{r}}'_n \bar{\mathbf{x}}_n - \mathbf{p}'_n \bar{\mathbf{x}}_n) = 0$.

The shadow price of land is shown in Table 14.16. In case some shadow price are equal to zero it would be sufficient to reduce the associated level of the land constraint by an arbitrarily (0.001) small positive number.

The estimated $\hat{Q}$ matrix is given in Table 14.17. This matrix is a crucial component of the calibrating model, together with the deviation from the regional cost function for each individual farm. We must emphasize the fact that, for verifying the calibrating property of the model using the individual quadrating programming specification of (14.18), it is crucial to estimate the Q matrix using the self-selection approach.

GAMS Command File for Numerical Example 2

The following GAMS file executes the numerical example of the Arfini-Donati model presented earlier. It requires an additional input file, called *ADdata.dat* that contains the data reported in Tables 14.13 to 14.15 according to the following format: table ha(az,proc), table xbar(az,proc), table

Table 14.17. *Estimated $\hat{Q}$ matrix*

Crop	Sube	Duwh	Sowh	Corn	Toma	Rice	Soyb
sube	0.0321	0.0022	−0.0730	0.0309	−0.0028	−0.1037	−0.0110
duwh	0.0022	0.0286	0.0003	0.0008	−0.0019	−0.0002	−0.0014
sowh	−0.0730	−0.0003	0.1960	−0.0828	−0.0070	0.2661	0.0246
corn	0.0309	0.0008	−0.0828	0.0411	0.0070	−0.1093	−0.0115
toma	−0.0028	−0.0019	−0.0070	0.0070	0.0214	−0.0006	0.0042
rice	−0.1037	−0.0002	0.2661	−0.1093	−0.0006	0.3674	0.0350
soyb	−0.0110	−0.0014	0.0246	−0.0115	0.0042	0.0350	0.0051

pr(az,proc), where "az" is the farm index and "proc" is the crop index. The command file requires a second input file, named *sets.prn*, which contains the definition of indices "az" and "proc". All the solution results and the input data are diplayed at the end of the list file. The verification of the calibration and the matrix Q are also reported in a separate file named *calib.prn*. The command file solves the Arfini-Donati specification and then uses the matrix $\hat{Q}$ and the farm deviations $\hat{u}_n$ to solve, for each farm, the quadratic programming model given in (14.18). It is a second way of verifying that this approach calibrates the levels of realized outputs, as asserted.

```
$title arfini and donati model.
* phase 1 and phase 2 of pmp combined
* through dual
*
$offsymlist offsymxref
    option limrow = 0
    option limcol = 0
    option reslim = 10000
    option nlp = conopt3;
*
$include sets.prn
$include addata.dat
*
    set i   input total land /land/
*
* the "proc" index is defined in the file sets.prn
* its range is reported here for convenience:
* sube,duwh,sowh,toma,
* corn,rice,soyb
*
```

```
    alias (proc,j,jv,jj,jjv,k,kv,kk)
    alias (i,ii) ;
*
* the dollar sign $ signifies the conditional "if"
* the parameters xbar, pr, ha are defined in the file
* addata.dat
* the meaning of xbar≡ x̄ₙ, pr≡ pₙ, ha≡ haₙ
*
    xbar(az,j)$(ha(az,j) eq 0)=0;
    pr(az,j)$(xbar(az,j) eq 0)=0;
    ha(az,j)$(xbar(az,j) eq 0)=0;
*
* definition of technical coefficient matrices and
* available resources
*
    parameter a(az,j,i), b(az,i) ;
    a(az,j,i)$xbar(az,j) = ha(az,j)/xbar(az,j) ;
    b(az,i) = sum(jv,ha(az,jv));
    display a, b, xbar, ha, pr ;
*
* the following two farms' total land was reduced by
* 0.001 hectare
* to avoid the degeneracy of the corresponding dual
* variable, yₙ
*
    b("112431","land") = 2930.419 ;
    b("112432","land") = 1142.939 ;
*
    scalar scale   scaling coefficient for xbar /1000/;
*
    xbar(az,j) = xbar(az,j)/scale;
    pr(az,j) = pr(az,j)/10;
    display a, b, pr, xbar;
*
* model ww (with least squares and lp objective
* functions)
*
    variables
    uvww(az,jv)   firm's deviation from cost function
    lamdanww(az,j)   dual variable - marginal cost
    pqvww(jv,kv)   p=lsqrt(d) definition square root
                   of cholesky
```

The meaning of $xbar\equiv \bar{\mathbf{x}}_n$, $pr\equiv \mathbf{p}_n$, $ha\equiv \mathbf{ha}_n$

```
    objww    objective function
    pdvww(jv,kv)    diagonal matrix of cholesky
    plvvww(jv,kv)    lower triangular matrix for
                     cholesky ;
*
    positive variables ypsilonww(az), lamdanww, pdvww;
*
    equations
    objequww    objective function equation
    definpvww(jv,jjv)    cholesky equation
    mcvww(az,jv)    marginal cost function equations
    mc1vww(az,jv)    marginal cost inequalities for self
                     selection
    dualquww(az,jv)    dual costraints ;
*
    mcvww(az,jv)$xbar(az,jv)..    lamdanww(az,jv) =e=
      scale*uvww(az,jv) + sum(kv, sum(jjv,
      pqvww(jv,jjv) *pqvww(kv,jjv))* xbar(az,kv) );
*
    mc1vww(az,jv)$(xbar(az,jv) eq 0)..
      lamdanww(az,jv) =l= scale* uvww(az,jv)
      + sum(kv, sum(jjv, pqvww(jv,jjv)*pqvww(kv,jjv))
      * xbar(az,kv) ) ;
*
    dualquww(az,jv)$xbar(az,jv)..    lamdanww(az,jv)
      + ypsilonww(az)*[ha(az,jv)/xbar(az,jv)]
      =g= pr(az,jv);
*
    objequww..    objww =e=
      - sum((az,j)$xbar(az,j),pr(az,j)*xbar(az,j))
      + sum((az,i), b(az,i)*ypsilonww(az) )
      + sum((az,j)$xbar(az,j),lamdanww(az,j)
      *xbar(az,j) ) + sum((az,jv)$xbar(az,jv),
      sqr(uvww(az,jv)))/2 ;
*
    definpvww(jv,jjv)..    pqvww(jv,jjv) =e=
      sum(kv, plvvww(jv,kv)*
      ((pdvww(kv,jjv)+0.000000001)**0.5) );
*
* initial values
*
    pdvww.l(jv,kv)$(ord(jv) eq ord(kv)) = .051 ;
    pdvww.fx(jv,kv)$(ord(jv) ne ord(kv)) = 0 ;
    plvvww.l(jv,kv)$(ord(jv) ne ord(kv)) = .05 ;
```

```
    plvvww.fx(jv,kv)$(ord(jv) eq ord(kv)) = 1. ;
    plvvww.fx(jv,kv)$(ord(jv) lt ord(kv)) = 0. ;
    pdvww.lo(jv,kv)$(ord(jv) eq ord(kv)) = .00000001 ;
    uvww.up(az,jv) = 200. ;
    uvww.lo(az,jv) = -100. ;
    ypsilonww.up(az) = 100000. ;
    lamdanww.up(az,jv) = 600 ;
*
* name and definition of the ad model
*
    model ww / objequww, definpvww, mcvww, mc1vww,
      dualquww / ;
*
    solve ww using nlp minimizing objww ;
*
* recovery of the q matrix and farm deviations
*
    parameter qmatv(jv,kv)   quadratic form matrix of
                               cost function
          fuv(az,jv)   farm deviations from cost
                        function;
    qmatv(jv,kv) = sum(jjv, pqvww.l(jv,jjv)*pqvww.l
      (kv,jjv) ) ;
    fuv(az,jv)= scale* uvww.l(az,jv);
*
    parameter checkww(az,j) ;
* percent check on dual variables of the dual
* constraints in model ww ;
    checkww(az,j)$xbar(az,j) =(( xbar(az,j)
      -(dualquww.m(az,j)+mcvww.m(az,j) )
      )/( xbar(az,j)) )*100 ;
*
* loop on farms of individual quadratic programming
* model
*
    parameter uu(j), nsolx(az,j), nsoly(az,i),
      nlobj(az), uuv(jv);
    parameter aa(j,i) , bb(i), ppr(j) , xxbar(j) ;
*
    variables
    nx(j)   output in qp individual model
    nlinprofit   qp net revenue ;
*
    positive variables nx ;
```

```
*
    equations
    resourcen(i)   resource constraint, land, in qp
        problem
    nlprofit   qp objective function ;
*
    resourcen(i)..   sum(jv,aa(jv,i)*nx(jv))
        =l= bb(i) ;
    nlprofit..   sum(j, ppr(j)*nx(j))
        - sum(jv,uuv(jv) * nx(jv))
        - .5* sum((jv,kv), nx(jv) * qmatv(jv,kv)
        * nx(kv)) =e= nlinprofit;
*
    model primal /resourcen, nlprofit /;
*
* loop on individual qp model
*
    loop((az)$b(az,"land"),
    aa(j,i)$xbar(az,j) = [ha(az,j)/xbar(az,j)] ;
    bb(i) = b(az,i) ;
    ppr(j) = pr(az,j) ;
    uuv(jv) = fuv(az,jv) ;
*
    solve primal using nlp maximizing nlinprofit ;
*
    nsolx(az,j) = nx.l(j) ;
    nsoly(az,i) = resourcen.m(i) ;
    nlobj(az) = nlinprofit.l ;  );
* close loop
    parameter contcal1(az,j)  percent difference of
        nsolx from xbar;
     contcal1(az,j)$xbar(az,j)=(nsolx(az,j)/
        xbar(az,j)*100)-100;
    parameter contcal2(az,j)  absolute difference of
        nsolx from xbar;
     contcal2(az,j)$xbar(az,j) = nsolx(az,j) -
        xbar(az,j);
*
    display contcal1, contcal2, uvww.l, dualquww.m ;
    display xbar, checkww ;
*
$include controlww.prn
*
* end of command file
```

```
* file controlww.prn
*
   file out /calib.prn/;
   out.pw=255;
   put out;
*
   put "*calibrating control "; put /;
   put/;
   put "* "; put system.title; put /;
   put/;
   put "* execution date (month/day/year): "; put
     system.date; put /;
   put /;
   put "* model ww " ; put system.ifile; put/;
   put /;
   put "* solver status: " ; put ww.solvestat/;
   put "* 1 - normal completion"; put /;
   put /;
   put "* model status: "; put ww.modelstat /;
   put "* 2 - locally optimal"; put /;
   put /;
*
   put "percent difference in calibration ad model",
   put /;
   put " ", loop (j, put j.tl :10); put /;
   loop (az, put az.tl :14 ; loop (j, put
     checkww(az,j):10:2; ); put /;
   );
   put/; put/;
*
   put/;
   put "matrix q-ad ", put /;
   put " ", loop (kv, put kv.tl :15); put /;
   loop (jv, put jv.tl :15 ; loop (kv, put
     qmatv(jv,kv):15:7; ); put /;
  );
   put ";"; put/; put/;
*
   put "marginal costs lambda", put /;
   put " ", loop (j, put j.tl :10); put /;
   loop (az, put az.tl :14 ; loop (j, put
     lamdanww.l(az,j):10:4; ); put /;
   );
   put/; put/;
```

APPENDIX 14.1: CHOLESKY FACTORIZATION

Definition: Given a symmetric, positive semidefinite matrix Q, its Cholesky factorization (decomposition) is stated as follows:

$$Q = LHL' \qquad (A14.1)$$

where L is a unit lower triangular matrix and H is a diagonal matrix with nonnegative elements. The elements of the H matrix are called Cholesky values.

Example: Consider a (3×3) SPSD (symmetric, positive semidefinite) matrix Q. Its Cholesky factorization is stated as

$$
\begin{bmatrix} q_{11} & q_{12} & q_{13} \\ q_{21} & q_{22} & q_{23} \\ q_{31} & q_{32} & q_{33} \end{bmatrix} = \begin{bmatrix} 1 & 0 & 0 \\ l_{21} & 1 & 0 \\ l_{31} & l_{32} & 1 \end{bmatrix} \begin{bmatrix} h_{11} & 0 & 0 \\ 0 & h_{22} & 0 \\ 0 & 0 & h_{33} \end{bmatrix} \begin{bmatrix} 1 & l_{21} & l_{31} \\ 0 & 1 & l_{32} \\ 0 & 0 & 1 \end{bmatrix}.
$$

It follows that:

$$
\begin{aligned}
q_{11} &= h_{11} \\
q_{12} &= h_{11} l_{12} \\
q_{13} &= h_{11} l_{13} \\
q_{22} &= h_{22} + h_{11}(l_{21})^2 \\
q_{23} &= h_{22} l_{32} + h_{11} l_{21} l_{31} \\
q_{33} &= h_{33} + h_{11}(l_{31})^2 + h_{22}(l_{32})^2.
\end{aligned}
$$

From the example, it is clear that, by knowing the coefficients of the Q matrix, it is possible to derive, one at a time, all the coefficients of the H and L matrices.

In the PMP methodology, however, the Cholesky factorization is used in a reverse mode. The Q matrix is not known and must be estimated in such a way that it should turn out to be symmetric and positive semidefinite. This is dictated by economic theory. Hence, a feasible approach to that task is to estimate the coefficients of the L and H matrices and make sure that the diagonal elements of the H matrix are nonnegative. This can easily be done with a computer program such as GAMS.

References

Arfini, F., and Donati, M. (2008). "Health check ed efficienza delle aziende agricole: una valutazione comparativa su quattro regioni agricole europee," *Rivista di Economia Agraria*, 63, 65–91.

Benoit, Commandant. (1924). "Notes sur une Méthode de Résolution des Équations Normales Provenant de l'Application de la Méthode des Moindres Carrés a un Système d'Équations Linéaires en Nombre Inférieur des Inconnues, – Application de la Méthode a la Résolution d'un Système Defini d'Équations Linéaires, (Procédé du Commandant Cholesky)," *Bulletin Géodésique*, 2, 67–77.

Blackorby, C., and Russell, R. R. (1981). "The Morishima Elasticity of Substitution; Symmetry, Constancy, Separability, and Its Relationship to the Hicks and Allen Elasticities," *Review of Economic Studies*, 48, 147–58.

Golan, A., Judge, G. G, and Miller, D. (1996). *Maximum Entropy Econometrics* (Chichester, UK: Wiley).

Heckman, J. J. (1979). "Sample Bias as a Specification Error," *Econometrica*, 47, 153–62.

Howitt, R. E. (1995). "Positive Mathematical Programming," *American Journal of Agricultural Economics*, 77, 329–42.

Lau, L. J. (1978). "Testing and Imposing Monotonicity Convexity and Quasi-Convexity Constraints," In Fuss, M., and McFadden, D., editors, *Production Economics: A Dual Approach to Theory and Applications* (Amsterdam: North-Holland), pp. 409–53.

Stefanou, S. E. (1989). "Returns to Scale in the Long-Run: The Dynamic Theory of Cost," *Southern Economic Journal*, 55, 570–9.

van Akkeren, M., and Judge, G. G. (1999). "Extended Empirical Likelihood Estimation and Inference," *Working Papers*, Department of Agricultural and Resource Economics, University of California, Berkeley, pp. 1–49.

15

Multiple Optimal Solutions

A large majority of empirical studies using either an LP or a QP specification has neglected the consequences of one important aspect of mathematical programming. Simply stated, the polyhedral nature of the solution set in LP and QP models may be responsible for multiple optimal solutions, if some plausible conditions are realized. If and when an empirical problem possesses alternative optimal solutions, why is only one of them usually selected for presentation in final reports which, often, make efficiency judgements and prescribe significant policy changes? In this chapter, we discuss, separately, the existence, the computation, and the consequences of multiple optimal solutions (MOS) in linear programming and in quadratic programming models.

MOS in Linear Programming

When LP is used for analyzing empirical problems, an explicit comparison is usually made between the activities actually chosen and operated by the economic agent under scrutiny and the optimal level of activities suggested by the model's solution. In some instance (Wicks), the use of LP for policy planning has inspired the use of Theil's U-inequality coefficient to assess formally the discrepancy between actual and optimal (predicted) activities. Desired values of the U coefficient are those close to zero, attained when the squared distance between actual and LP optimally predicted activities is small. Implicitly, minimum distance criteria have been used by many authors to assess the plausibility and performance of their LP models. In the presence of multiple optimal solutions, however, the selection of a specific solution for final analysis is crucial and should not be left to computer codes, as probably has been the case in all reported studies.

Furthermore, an LP problem is made even more complex by the existence of quasioptimal solutions; that is, solutions that change the optimal value of the objective function by only a fractional percentage. Because the information used to specify empirical problems is seldom exact, quasioptimal solutions may legitimately be considered as suitable candidates for reporting.

The conditions under which primal and dual multiple optimal solutions can occur are related to the phenomenon of degeneracy, a rather plausible event in empirical studies. Degeneracy of the primal LP solution occurs when a set of activities employs inputs in exactly the proportion that completely exhausts two or more available resources. Analogously, degeneracy of the dual LP solution is encountered when, given an optimal plan, the opportunity cost for some nonbasic activity happens to be the same (zero) as that of the activities included in the optimal plan. Hence, the likelihood of either primal or dual degeneracy increases rapidly with the size of the model. Baumol asserts that "computational experience indicates that such cases (primal and dual degeneracy) are encountered more frequently than might be expected in advance." Thus, a correct and informative report of empirical results generated by LP should include complete information about the problem's size and an explicit statement of whether the presented primal and dual solutions are indeed unique. Unfortunately, a search of the literature has revealed that a majority of studies fail to disclose even the number of columns and rows in the constraint matrix. No study mentioned whether or not the reported solutions were unique.

Example of Primal MOS in LP

How do we detect and derive multiple optimal solutions in LP models? By following either the primal or the dual simplex algorithm: First, determine whether there are degeneracies in either the dual or the primal solution. Second, execute a pivot operation (if a pivot exists) for the appropriate algorithm. The following numerical example exhibits three primal optimal solutions:

$$
\begin{aligned}
\max Z \; = \;\; & \tfrac{53}{22}x_1 \; + \; \tfrac{39}{22}x_2 \; + \; 5x_3 \; + \; 2x_4 \\
\text{subject to} \quad & 3x_1 \; + \; 2x_2 \; + \; x_3 \; + \; 4x_4 \; \leq \; 6 \\
& 2x_1 \; + \; x_2 \; + \; 5x_3 \; + \; x_4 \; \leq \; 4 \\
& x_1 \; + \; 3x_2 \; - \; 2x_3 \; + \; 4x_4 \; \leq \; 0
\end{aligned}
$$

with $x_i \geq 0$, $i = 1, \ldots, 4$. The three optimal tableaux are as follows:

First Optimal Tableau

Z	x_1	x_2	x_3	x_4	x_{s1}	x_{s2}	x_{s3}	sol	BI
0	$\frac{23}{22}$	$-\frac{25}{22}$	0	0	1	$-\frac{6}{11}$	$-\frac{19}{22}$	$\frac{42}{11}$	x_{s1}
0	$\frac{7}{22}$	$\frac{1}{22}$	1	0	0	$\frac{2}{11}$	$-\frac{1}{22}$	$\frac{8}{11}$	x_3
0	$\frac{9}{22}$	$\left(\frac{17}{22}\right)$	0	1	0	$\frac{1}{11}$	$\frac{5}{22}$	$\frac{4}{11}$	$x_4 \rightarrow$
1	0^*	0^*	0	0	0	$\frac{12}{11}$	$\frac{5}{22}$	$\frac{48}{11}$	Z

Second Optimal Tableau

Z	x_1	x_2	x_3	x_4	x_{s1}	x_{s2}	x_{s3}	sol	BI
0	$\frac{28}{17}$	0	0	$\frac{25}{17}$	1	$-\frac{7}{17}$	$-\frac{9}{17}$	$\frac{74}{17}$	x_{s1}
0	$\frac{5}{17}$	0	1	$-\frac{1}{17}$	0	$\frac{3}{17}$	$-\frac{1}{17}$	$\frac{12}{17}$	x_3
0	$\left(\frac{9}{17}\right)$	1	0	$\frac{22}{17}$	0	$\frac{2}{17}$	$\frac{5}{17}$	$\frac{8}{17}$	$x_2 \rightarrow$
1	0^*	0	0	0^*	0	$\frac{12}{11}$	$\frac{5}{22}$	$\frac{48}{11}$	Z

Third Optimal Tableau

Z	x_1	x_2	x_3	x_4	x_{s1}	x_{s2}	x_{s3}	sol	BI
0	0	$-\frac{28}{9}$	0	$-\frac{23}{9}$	1	$-\frac{7}{9}$	$-\frac{13}{9}$	$\frac{26}{9}$	x_{s1}
0	0	$-\frac{5}{9}$	1	$-\frac{7}{9}$	0	$\frac{1}{9}$	$-\frac{2}{9}$	$\frac{4}{9}$	x_3
0	1	$\frac{17}{9}$	0	$\left(\frac{22}{9}\right)$	0	$\frac{2}{9}$	$\frac{5}{9}$	$\frac{8}{9}$	$x_1 \rightarrow$
1	0	0^*	0	0^*	0	$\frac{12}{11}$	$\frac{5}{22}$	$\frac{48}{11}$	Z

The dual solution is degenerate in all three tableaux, and this event is signified by the asterisk that is associated with the zero opportunity costs of nonbasic activities in the last row of each tableau. Although the corresponding activity is not a part of the optimal production plan, it exhibits a marginal cost that is equal to its marginal revenue, causing the

Table 15.1. *LP Example*

Primal Solution	Extreme Point 1	Extreme Point 2	Extreme Point 3
x_1	0	0	$\frac{8}{9} = 0.8889$
x_2	0	$\frac{8}{17} = 0.4706$	0
x_3	$\frac{8}{11} = 0.7273$	$\frac{12}{17} = 0.7059$	$\frac{4}{9} = 0.4444$
x_4	$\frac{4}{11} = 0.3636$	0	0
x_{s1}	$\frac{42}{11} = 3.8182$	$\frac{74}{17} = 4.3529$	$\frac{26}{9} = 2.8889$
x_{s2}	0	0	0
x_{s3}	0	0	0

dual degeneracy. The complete analysis of the LP problem shows that there are three basic (extreme point) primal optimal solutions and a unique dual solution corresponding to an optimal value of the objective function equal to 48/11. In each optimal tableau, the dual solution exhibits the degeneracy of two opportunity costs, a property that permits the discovery of the other optimal solutions. The pivot in each tableau indicates the path chosen to go from one optimal extreme point to the next one. The third optimal tableau leads to the first optimal tableau, repeating the cycle of optimal solutions. The primal simplex algorithm was used to obtain the three optimal tableaux. The primal basic optimal solutions are reported in Table 15.1. Degeneracy of the primal solution is the gateway to multiple dual optimal solutions, if a proper pivot element can be identified using the dual simplex algorithm.

Dealing with MOS

Given the number of data and the substantial effort for organizing them usually involved in a specification of a large LP model, multiple optimal and quasioptimal solutions should not be regarded as a curse. They are merely processed information incorporated in the model from the start, for thoughtful researchers to be aware of. The curious reader, on the other hand, should know about them in order to evaluate the study properly and to appreciate the model's capabilities. Reporting of all optimal and quasioptimal solutions, therefore, does not seem, a priori, an excessive burden. The informational content of such reporting may easily outweigh the initial cost of assembling the model.

Two seemingly unrelated ideas provide a plausible criterion to help a researcher in choosing among various optimal solutions. The first one is that a convex combination of optimal LP solutions is itself an optimal solution. The idea can provide an unexplored flexibility for the application of LP methods to empirical problems. As is well known, the number of positive activity levels included in an extreme-point optimal solution cannot exceed the number of independent constraints. But this restriction is not applicable to convex combinations of extreme-point solutions. Hence, the possibility of more diversified LP optimal solutions should not be ignored. But it requires evaluation of all (or at least several) basic (extreme point) optimal solutions implied by the LP model at hand.

The second idea is that researchers have often judged the quality of their LP models by comparing their performance (in terms of an optimal solution) with actual behavior of the economic agent under study. In the presence of dual degeneracy, this criterion implies choosing the convex combination of primal optimal solutions in closest proximity to actually realized activity levels.

To combine these two ideas, a familiar minimum distance criterion based on minimizing a quadratic loss function can be used. Thus, consider the LP problem of choosing a nonnegative vector $\mathbf{x}$ to

$$\text{maximize } \mathbf{c}'\mathbf{x}, \quad \text{subject to} \quad A\mathbf{x} \leq \mathbf{b} \tag{15.1}$$

where A is an $(m \times n)$ matrix of known coefficients and the other elements are conformable to it. Suppose that problem (15.1) represents a regional production location problem and possesses k distinct extreme-point optimal solutions, $k < n$. Let P be the matrix whose column vectors are such k-extreme point optimal solutions. Let $\mathbf{x}_a$ be a vector of activity levels congruent to the given problem and actually operated in the region. Then, the problem of choosing a nonnegative vector $\mathbf{w}$ to

$$\text{minimize } (\mathbf{x}_a - P\mathbf{w})'(\mathbf{x}_a - P\mathbf{w}), \quad \text{subject to} \quad \mathbf{s}'\mathbf{w} = 1 \tag{15.2}$$

defines a procedure to estimate the weights $\mathbf{w}$ for the convex combination $P\mathbf{w}$ of the k-extreme point optimal solutions. The components of the vector $\mathbf{s}$ are all unitary. The optimality criterion stated in (15.2) is the least-squares problem of choosing that optimal LP solution, $P\hat{\mathbf{w}}$, which is closest to the activity levels actually operated in the region.

The formulation of problem (15.2) is appealing for several reasons. First, the objective function can be viewed as a measure of the loss incurred by the region for not producing according to the optimal activity levels that require minimal deviations from present practices. Second, the matrix P is of full column rank because the optimal solutions that define it are associated with extreme points and are, therefore, independent of each other. Hence, the solution vector of weights, $\hat{\mathbf{w}}$, is unique and, in turn, the projection $P\hat{\mathbf{w}}$ constitutes an optimal LP solution that itself is unique in the sense defined by problem (15.2). The components of the $\mathbf{w}$ vector are scalars without unit of measurement because they represent weights of a convex combination. Therefore, changes in the measurement units of the LP activities considered in the model do not affect the estimates of $\mathbf{w}$. In fact, the components of every column in the P matrix represent the same activities as in the $\mathbf{x}_a$ vector. If measurement units are changed for some activity in the model, they are changed in both the P matrix and the vector $\mathbf{x}_a$, offsetting each other. Therefore, when there are multiple optimal solutions, finding a plausible optimal solution of LP problems generally involves a two-stage optimization process. In the first stage, all extreme-point optimal solutions are generated. In the second stage, optimal weights are computed to collapse them into an optimal (least-distance) convex combination.

The two-stage optimization procedure just outlined is a blend of mathematical programming and inferential, statistical techniques. In mathematical programming, the researcher assumes knowledge of the problem's structure and asks: what is the optimal response associated with it? In statistical inference, one starts with the "real-world" observations and asks: what is the most likely structure that generated such observations?

This sharp dichotomy is useful only as a classification scheme. In reality, each approach shares some features of the other. Thus, on one hand, linear programming models are specified using real-world observations in their constraints, input-output coefficients, and revenue vector. Econometric models, on the other hand, assume some elements of the problem's structure that will constitute the maintained hypothesis. The additional link between mathematical programming and econometrics is represented by the vector of realized activity levels, $\mathbf{x}_a$, which allows a test of the null hypothesis whether or not the linear programming structure is suitable for the problem under investigation.

Approaching the problem of multiple optimal solutions by computing an optimal convex combination, indicated in problem (15.2), has the advantage of making the most use of all the information contained in the original LP specification. This does not imply that the best-fit solution is preferred to others. But, if a planned optimal solution is implemented by an economic agent, the solution that requires minimal adjustments from present practices ought to be carefully considered.

MOS in QP Models

Although conditions leading to multiple optimal solutions in LP have been known for a long time, knowledge of the structural causes underlying multiple optimal solutions in quadratic programming and criteria for their detection are limited.

The existence of either unique or multiple optimal solutions in QP models has significant consequences in the formulation of policy recommendations. Unfortunately, commercial computer programs are completely silent about this very important aspect and leave it to the enterprising researcher to find convenient ways for assessing the number of optimal solutions and their values.

For many years, references to uniqueness of solutions in QP models have been scant. A reference to a sufficient condition for uniqueness of a part of the solution vector in a QP model, namely the positive definiteness of the quadratic form, is found in Takayama and Judge. However, it is not necessary to have positive definite quadratic forms to have unique solutions. The relevant aspect of the problem is, therefore, to know both the necessary and sufficient conditions for uniqueness. Hence, a more interesting problem can be stated as follows: if the quadratic form in a QP model is positive semidefinite (as are the quadratic forms in many empirical problems presented in the literature), how do we come to know whether the given problem has a unique optimal solution or admits multiple optimal solutions? We will address this problem and present an algorithmic approach to its solution.

The algorithm is remarkable. An important aspect of the algorithm is that the set of multiple optimal solutions in positive semidefinite QP models is convex. After discussing this property, the algorithm will be applied to QP problems to illustrate its numerical feasibility. A remarkable feature of this algorithm is that, for finding all multiple optimal solutions of a QP problem, it is sufficient to solve an associated linear programming problem.

One promising way to gain insight into this rather complex problem is to regard the quadratic program as a linear complementarity problem. Hence, consider the following symmetric QP model:

$$\max \{ \mathbf{c}'\mathbf{x} - k_x \mathbf{x}' D\mathbf{x}/2 - k_y \mathbf{y}' E\mathbf{y}/2 \} \tag{15.3}$$

$$\text{subject to} \qquad A\mathbf{x} - k_y E\mathbf{y} \leq \mathbf{b}, \quad \mathbf{x} \geq 0, \mathbf{y} \geq 0$$

where A is an $(m \times n)$ matrix and D and E are symmetric positive semidefinite matrices of order n and m, respectively. Parameters k_x and k_y are nonnegative scalars suitable for representing various economic scenarios, from perfect and imperfect market equilibria to risk and uncertainty problems. In Chapter 5 it was shown that this problem can be rearranged in the form of an LC problem: $\mathbf{w} = M\mathbf{z} + \mathbf{q}$, and $\mathbf{z}'\mathbf{w} = 0$, $\mathbf{z} \geq \mathbf{0}$ and $\mathbf{w} \geq \mathbf{0}$, where $\mathbf{w}$ stands for an $[(n + m) \times 1]$ vector of slack variables, $\mathbf{q}' = [-\mathbf{c}', \mathbf{b}']$, $\mathbf{z}' = [\mathbf{x}', \mathbf{y}']$, and $M = \begin{bmatrix} k_x D & A' \\ -A & k_y E \end{bmatrix}$ is an $[(m + n) \times (m + n)]$ PSD matrix (for any A).

It is well known that when multiple optimal solutions exist in an LP problem, their set constitutes a face of the convex polytope of all feasible solutions. This property can be extended to the LC problem stated previously. First of all, notice that the linear inequalities (removing the slack variables) of the LC problem form a convex set of feasible solutions. Of course, we are not merely interested in the set of feasible solutions but in the set of feasible as well as complementary solutions, that is, those solutions $(\mathbf{z}, \mathbf{w})$ that satisfy the feasibility conditions $\mathbf{z} \geq \mathbf{0}$, $\mathbf{w} \geq \mathbf{0}$ and also the complementarity condition $\mathbf{z}'\mathbf{w} = 0$. All feasible and complementary solutions of the LC problem are optimal solutions for the QP problem (15.3).

The set of optimal solutions in QP problems is convex. To demostrate this proposition it is sufficient to prove that the set of feasible and complementary solutions of the LC problem is convex. The proof requires the results of the following:

Lemma: Suppose $(\hat{\mathbf{z}}, \hat{\mathbf{w}})$ and $(\bar{\mathbf{z}}, \bar{\mathbf{w}})$ are feasible and complementary solutions of the LC problem. Then, $\hat{\mathbf{w}}'\bar{\mathbf{z}} = \bar{\mathbf{w}}'\hat{\mathbf{z}} = (\hat{\mathbf{z}} - \bar{\mathbf{z}})' M(\hat{\mathbf{z}} - \bar{\mathbf{z}}) = 0$.

Proof: According to the statement of the LC problem, the definition of the $\hat{\mathbf{w}}$ and $\bar{\mathbf{w}}$ vectors is $\hat{\mathbf{w}} = M\hat{\mathbf{z}} + \mathbf{q}$ and $\bar{\mathbf{w}} = M\bar{\mathbf{z}} + \mathbf{q}$. Subtracting $\bar{\mathbf{w}}$ from $\hat{\mathbf{w}}$: $(\hat{\mathbf{w}} - \bar{\mathbf{w}}) = M(\hat{\mathbf{z}} - \bar{\mathbf{z}})$. Premultiplying the foregoing result by $(\hat{\mathbf{z}} - \bar{\mathbf{z}})'$ gives

$$(\hat{\mathbf{z}} - \bar{\mathbf{z}})'(\hat{\mathbf{w}} - \bar{\mathbf{w}}) = (\hat{\mathbf{z}} - \bar{\mathbf{z}})' M(\hat{\mathbf{z}} - \bar{\mathbf{z}}) \geq 0 \tag{15.4}$$

because the M matrix is PSD. Expanding the left-hand-side of (15.4):

$$\hat{\mathbf{z}}'\hat{\mathbf{w}} - \hat{\mathbf{z}}'\bar{\mathbf{w}} - \bar{\mathbf{z}}'\hat{\mathbf{w}} + \bar{\mathbf{z}}'\bar{\mathbf{w}} = -\hat{\mathbf{z}}'\bar{\mathbf{w}} - \bar{\mathbf{z}}'\hat{\mathbf{w}} \leq 0 \tag{15.5}$$

because $(\hat{\mathbf{z}}, \hat{\mathbf{w}})$ and $(\bar{\mathbf{z}}, \bar{\mathbf{w}})$ are complementary solutions by assumption and all the vectors involved are nonnegative. Hence, the two inequalities (15.4) and (15.5) establish the conclusion of the lemma.

We can now demonstrate the following important theorem.

Theorem: The set of all feasible and complementary solutions in a PSD-LC problem is convex.

Proof: Consider any two distinct pairs of feasible and complementary solutions to the LC problem, say $(\hat{z}, \hat{w})$ and $(\bar{z}, \bar{w})$. We need to show that (z, w), defined as a convex combination of $(\hat{z}, \hat{w})$ and $(\bar{z}, \bar{w})$, is also a feasible and complementary solution of the LC problem. Hence, let $z = \alpha\bar{z} + (1 - \alpha)\hat{z}$ and $w = \alpha\bar{w} + (1 - \alpha)\hat{w}$ for $0 \leq \alpha \leq 1$. Then, (z, w) is a feasible solution of the LC problem because $z \geq 0$, $w \geq 0$ and

$$Mz + q = M[\alpha\bar{z} + (1 - \alpha)\hat{z}] + q \qquad (15.6)$$
$$= \alpha M\bar{z} + (1 - \alpha)M\hat{z} + q$$
$$= \alpha(\bar{w} - q) + (1 - \alpha)(\hat{w} - q) + q$$
$$= \alpha\bar{w} + (1 - \alpha)\hat{w} = w.$$

To show that (z, w) is a complementary solution of the LC problem,

$$w'z = [\alpha\bar{w} + (1 - \alpha)\hat{w}]'[\alpha\bar{z} + (1 - \alpha)\hat{z}] \qquad (15.7)$$
$$= \alpha^2 \bar{w}'\bar{z} + (1 - \alpha)^2 \hat{w}'\hat{z} + \alpha(1 - \alpha)\bar{w}'\hat{z} + \alpha(1 - \alpha)\hat{w}'\bar{z} = 0$$

since $\bar{w}'\hat{z}$ and $\hat{w}'\bar{z}$ are equal to zero according to the preceding lemma.

An important corollary to this theorem is that the number of solutions to a PSD-LC problem is 0, 1, or ∞. This is so because the problem has no solution, or has a unique solution, or if it has more than one (basic) solution, by convexity, it has an infinite number of solutions.

Determining the Number of Solutions

Judging from the empirical literature, it has almost never been a concern of authors to state whether a QP problem possesses either a unique or multiple optimal solutions. Von Oppen and Scott present a rare passing reference of solution uniqueness of their QP model. They do not state, however, whether the associated quadratic form is positive definite or semidefinite, or how the uniqueness of the solution was determined. It is difficult, therefore, to downplay the importance of this aspect in empirical studies.

To reduce as much as possible the additional computations required by a complete report, a two-stage procedure seems convenient:

1. After achieving any extreme-point optimal solution of the QP (LC) problem, determine the number of solutions by means of a suggestion presented by Kaneko. If the result of the algorithm indicates that the solution is unique, stop.

2. If the number of solutions is infinite, it is possible to proceed to find all the extreme-point optimal solutions, which are finite in number for a finite number of linear inequalities, of the QP problem, through the combination of results obtained by Adler and Gale and by Mattheiss.

The algorithm suggested by Kaneko for finding the number of solutions of an LC problem is ingenious. The first step of the algorithm is to solve the LC problem (corresponding to the QP problem) by means of any suitable algorithm, for example, Lemke's complementary pivot algorithm. At this point, let $\rho = \{j\}$ be the set of all the j indexes for which $\bar{w}_j = \bar{z}_j = 0$, $j = 1, \ldots, m + n$, where $(\bar{z}, \bar{w})$ is a solution of the LC problem. In other words, consider all the degenerate components of the feasible and complementary solution.

2.1. If ρ is empty, $\rho = \emptyset$, stop because the solution is unique.
2.2. Otherwise, let $\bar{M}$ be the transformation of M in the final tableau of the Lemke's algorithm and solve the following PSD-QP problem:

$$\min R = \mathbf{u}' \bar{M}_{\rho\rho'} \mathbf{u}/2 \tag{15.8}$$

$$\text{subject to} \qquad \mathbf{s}'\mathbf{u} = 1, \quad \mathbf{u} \geq \mathbf{0}$$

where $\mathbf{s}$ is a vector of ones. This QP problem corresponds to the following PSD-LC problem:

$$L\mathbf{v} + \mathbf{d} \geq \mathbf{0}, \quad \mathbf{v} \geq \mathbf{0} \tag{15.9}$$

$$\mathbf{v}'(L\mathbf{v} + \mathbf{d}) = 0$$

where $L = \begin{bmatrix} \bar{M}_{\rho\rho'} & -\mathbf{s} \\ \mathbf{s}' & 0 \end{bmatrix}$, $\mathbf{d} = \begin{bmatrix} 0 \\ -1 \end{bmatrix}$, and $\mathbf{v} = \begin{bmatrix} \mathbf{u} \\ 2R \end{bmatrix}$.

Kaneko has demonstrated that if no solution exists or if a solution is found such that $R > 0$, then the solution of the original QP (LC) problem is unique. In contrast, if a solution exists such that $R = 0$, then the number of solutions to the original QP (LC) problem is infinite. In other words, the admissibility of multiple optimal solutions requires that the matrix $\bar{M}_{\rho\rho'}$ be positive semidefinite. Notice that the dimensions of the $\bar{M}_{\rho\rho'}$ matrix depend on the number of degeneracies present in the first optimal solution found in step 1. In many instances, $\bar{M}_{\rho\rho'}$ is also a rather small matrix for a large-scale model and problem (15.8) is easy to solve.

The rationale of Kaneko's algorithm is based on the fact that a degenerate solution of the LC problem opens the way for the linear dependence of the vectors of the submatrix $\bar{M}_{\rho\rho'}$ of the final optimal tableau of the LC problem. The constraint of problem (15.8) defines a convex combination, whereas the objective function tests the linear dependence (or independence) of the subset of vectors associated with the degenerate components of the original optimal solution of the QP problem. Hence, degeneracy of an optimal solution is a necessary but not a sufficient condition for multiple optimal solutions in QP problems: degeneracy and linear dependence of the associated submatrix $\bar{M}_{\rho\rho'}$ are necessary and sufficient conditions.

To illustrate this point and the working of Kaneko's algorithm, two numerical examples of asymmetric quadratic programs are discussed. Example 1 illustrates the necessary aspect of degeneracy (but not its sufficiency) for the existence of multiple optimal solutions. Example 2 shows that degeneracy of an optimal solution must be accompanied by linear dependence of the submatrix $\bar{M}_{\rho\rho'}$ for the existence of multiple solutions.

Example 1: Kaneko's Necessity but not Sufficiency

The information for the asymmetric QP problem is given as follows:

$$\max \{\mathbf{c}'\mathbf{x} - \mathbf{x}'D\mathbf{x}/2\} \qquad (15.10)$$

$$\text{subject to} \qquad A\mathbf{x} \le \mathbf{b}, \quad \mathbf{x} \ge 0$$

where $A = \begin{bmatrix} 6 & 4 & 2 \\ 4 & 3 & 1 \end{bmatrix}$, $\mathbf{b} = \begin{bmatrix} 18 \\ 12 \end{bmatrix}$, $D = \begin{bmatrix} 3 & 2 & \frac{3}{2} \\ 2 & \frac{4}{3} & 1 \\ \frac{3}{2} & 1 & \frac{3}{2} \end{bmatrix}$, $\mathbf{c} = \begin{bmatrix} 12 \\ 8 \\ \frac{11}{2} \end{bmatrix}$

The D matrix is symmetric PSD of rank 2. In order to formulate and solve this QP problem as an LC problem, we must set up a tableau following Lemke's instructions and having the structure $(I\mathbf{w} - M\mathbf{z} - \mathbf{s}z_0; \mathbf{q})$, where $\mathbf{s}$ is a vector of unitary elements and z_0 is the associated artificial variable, as explained in Chapter 6. All the other components of the problem are defined as in the LC specification given earlier. The layout of example 1 is given in tableau 1, whereas the final tableau, exhibiting a feasible and complementary solution, is given in tableau 2.

The feasible and complementary solution of tableau 2 translates into an optimal QP solution as $z_1 = x_1 = 3$; $z_4 = y_1 = \frac{1}{2}$, while all the other x and y variables are equal to zero. The optimal value of the QP objective function is equal to 22.5.

Tableau 1: Example 1 – Initial layout

w_1	w_2	w_3	w_4	w_5	z_1	z_2	z_3	z_4	z_5	z_0	q	BI
1					-3	-2	$-\frac{3}{2}$	-6	-4	-1	-12	w_1
	1				-2	$-\frac{4}{3}$	-1	-4	-3	-1	-8	w_2
		1			$-\frac{3}{2}$	-1	$-\frac{3}{2}$	-2	-1	-1	$-\frac{11}{2}$	w_3
			1		6	4	2	0	0	-1	18	w_4
				1	4	3	1	0	0	-1	12	w_5

Tableau 2 has been reordered in its rows and columns to achieve a natural sequence of indexes.

Tableau 2: Example 1 – Solution

$\bar{z}_1$	$\bar{w}_2$	$\bar{w}_3$	$\bar{z}_4$	$\bar{w}_5$	$\bar{w}_1$	$\bar{z}_2$	$\bar{z}_3$	$\bar{w}_4$	$\bar{z}_5$	q	BI
1					0	$\frac{2}{3}$	$\frac{1}{3}$	$\frac{1}{6}$	0	3	$\bar{z}_1$
	1				$-\frac{2}{3}$	0	0	0	$-\frac{1}{3}$	0	$\bar{w}_2$
		1			$-\frac{1}{3}$	0	$-\frac{5}{6}$	$\frac{1}{12}$	$\frac{1}{3}$	0	$\bar{w}_3$
			1		$-\frac{1}{6}$	0	$\frac{1}{12}$	$-\frac{1}{12}$	$\frac{2}{3}$	$\frac{1}{2}$	$\bar{z}_4$
				1	0	$\frac{1}{3}$	$-\frac{1}{3}$	$-\frac{2}{3}$	0	0	$\bar{w}_5$

Degeneracy appears in three pairs of complementary variables, that is, those variable $\bar{w}_j = \bar{z}_j = 0$ for $j = 2, 3, 5$. Hence, Kaneko's index set is $\rho = \{2, 3, 5\}$. This index set corresponds to the following $-\bar{M}_{\rho\rho'}$ matrix:

$$-\bar{M}_{\rho\rho'} = \begin{bmatrix} 0 & 0 & -\frac{1}{3} \\ 0 & -\frac{5}{6} & \frac{1}{3} \\ \frac{1}{3} & -\frac{1}{3} & 0 \end{bmatrix}.$$

To determine either the uniqueness or the multiplicity of solutions according to Kaneko's suggestions, one must solve problem (15.8), alternatively, problem (15.9). We choose the specification of problem (15.9), and tableaux 3 and 4 give the corresponding initial and final layouts.

Tableau 3: Example 1 – Initial tableau for problem (15.9)

w_1	w_2	w_3	w_4	v_1	v_2	v_3	v_4	z_0	q	BI
1				0	0	$-\frac{1}{3}$	1	-1	0	w_1
	1			0	$-\frac{5}{6}$	$\frac{1}{3}$	1	-1	0	w_2
		1		$\frac{1}{3}$	$-\frac{1}{3}$	0	1	-1	0	w_3
			1	-1	-1	-1	0	-1	-1	w_4

Tableau 4: Example 1 – Final tableau (reordered) for problem (15.9)

$\bar{w}_1$	$\bar{v}_2$	$\bar{v}_3$	$\bar{v}_4$	$\bar{v}_1$	$\bar{w}_2$	$\bar{w}_3$	$\bar{w}_4$	q	BI
1				$-\frac{8}{15}$	$\frac{4}{5}$	$-\frac{9}{5}$	$-\frac{1}{15}$	$\frac{1}{15}$	$\bar{w}_1$
	1			$\frac{4}{5}$	$-\frac{6}{5}$	$\frac{6}{5}$	$-\frac{2}{5}$	$\frac{2}{5}$	$\bar{v}_2$
		1		$\frac{1}{5}$	$\frac{6}{5}$	$-\frac{6}{5}$	$-\frac{3}{5}$	$\frac{3}{5}$	$\bar{v}_3$
			1	$\frac{3}{5}$	$-\frac{2}{5}$	$\frac{7}{5}$	$-\frac{2}{15}$	$\frac{2}{15}$	$\bar{v}_4$

From tableau 4 it can be observed that $\bar{v}_4 = 2R = \frac{2}{15} > 0$ and, therefore, in spite of its extended degeneracy, the QP problem in example 1 has a unique optimal solution, the one presented in tableau 2. Correspondingly, it can be observed that the matrix $\bar{M}_{\rho\rho'}$ is positive definite.

Example 2: Kaneko's Necessity and Sufficiency

In this example, a second QP problem is considered with the following coefficients that vary from those of example 1 in the D matrix and the $\mathbf{c}$ vector:

$$\max \{\mathbf{c}'\mathbf{x} - \mathbf{x}' D\mathbf{x}/2\} \tag{15.11}$$

$$\text{subject to} \qquad A\mathbf{x} \le \mathbf{b}, \qquad \mathbf{x} \ge \mathbf{0}$$

where $A = \begin{bmatrix} 6 & 4 & 2 \\ 4 & 3 & 1 \end{bmatrix}$, $\mathbf{b} = \begin{bmatrix} 18 \\ 12 \end{bmatrix}$, $D = \begin{bmatrix} 3 & 2 & 1 \\ 2 & \frac{4}{3} & \frac{2}{3} \\ 1 & \frac{2}{3} & \frac{1}{3} \end{bmatrix}$, $\mathbf{c} \begin{bmatrix} 12 \\ 8 \\ 4 \end{bmatrix}$.

The D matrix is symmetric PSD of rank 1. The initial and final tableaux corresponding to this example are presented in tableaux 5 and 6.

Tableau 5: Example 2 – Initial layout

w_1	w_2	w_3	w_4	w_5	z_1	z_2	z_3	z_4	z_5	z_0	q	BI
1					-3	-2	-1	-6	-4	-1	-12	w_1
	1				-2	$-\frac{4}{3}$	$-\frac{2}{3}$	-4	-3	-1	-8	w_2
		1			-1	$-\frac{2}{3}$	$-\frac{1}{3}$	-2	-1	-1	-4	w_3
			1		6	4	2	0	0	-1	18	w_4
				1	4	3	1	0	0	-1	12	w_5

Tableau 6: Example 2 – Solution (reordered)

$\bar{z}_1$	$\bar{w}_2$	$\bar{w}_3$	$\bar{z}_4$	$\bar{w}_5$	$\bar{w}_1$	$\bar{z}_2$	$\bar{z}_3$	$\bar{w}_4$	$\bar{z}_5$	$\mathbf{q}$	BI
1					0	$\frac{2}{3}$	$\frac{1}{3}$	$\frac{1}{6}$	0	3	$\bar{z}_1$
	1				$-\frac{2}{3}$	0	0	0	$-\frac{1}{3}$	0	$\bar{w}_2$
		1			$-\frac{1}{3}$	0	0	0	$\frac{1}{3}$	0	$\bar{w}_3$
			1		$-\frac{1}{6}$	0	0	$-\frac{1}{12}$	$\frac{2}{3}$	$\frac{1}{2}$	$\bar{z}_4$
				1	0	$\frac{1}{3}$	$-\frac{1}{3}$	$-\frac{2}{3}$	0	0	$\bar{w}_5$

The index set of degenerate feasible and complementary variables is, once again, $\rho = \{2, 3, 5\}$ and the corresponding $-\bar{M}_{\rho\rho'}$ matrix is

$$-\bar{M}_{\rho\rho'} = \begin{bmatrix} 0 & 0 & -\frac{1}{3} \\ 0 & 0 & \frac{1}{3} \\ \frac{1}{3} & -\frac{1}{3} & 0 \end{bmatrix}.$$

The $-\bar{M}_{\rho\rho'}$ matrix is, obviously, singular and PSD. Therefore, we can conclude that the QP example 2 has multiple optimal solutions. But we will want to follow Kaneko's setup of problem (15.9) in this case as well to determine that, indeed, example 2 has multiple optimal solutions. These computations are presented in tableaux 7 and 8.

Tableau 7: Example 2 – Initial tableau for problem (15.9)

w_1	w_2	w_3	w_4	v_1	v_2	v_3	v_4	z_0	$\mathbf{q}$	BI
1				0	0	$-\frac{1}{3}$	1	-1	0	w_1
	1			0	0	$\frac{1}{3}$	1	-1	0	w_2
		1		$\frac{1}{3}$	$-\frac{1}{3}$	0	1	-1	0	w_3
			1	-1	-1	-1	0	-1	-1	w_4

Tableau 8: Example 2 – Final tableau (reordered) for problem (15.9)

$\bar{w}_1$	$\bar{v}_2$	$\bar{v}_3$	$\bar{v}_4$	$\bar{v}_1$	$\bar{w}_2$	$\bar{w}_3$	$\bar{w}_4$	$\mathbf{q}$	BI
1				0	$-\frac{3}{2}$	$\frac{3}{2}$	$-\frac{1}{2}$	$\frac{1}{2}$	$\bar{w}_1$
	1			$\frac{3}{2}$	0	$-\frac{3}{2}$	$-\frac{1}{2}$	$\frac{1}{2}$	$\bar{v}_2$
		1		$-\frac{3}{2}$	$\frac{3}{2}$	0	0	0	$\bar{v}_3$
			1	$\frac{1}{2}$	$\frac{1}{2}$	0	0	0	$\bar{v}_4$

Tableau 8 shows that $\bar{v}_4 = 2R = 0$ and we conclude (following Kaneko) that the QP problem of example 2 possesses an infinite number of optimal solutions.

Computing All Basic Feasible and Complementary Solutions

Once it has been determined that the number of solutions of a given QP (LC) problem is infinite, it is of interest to compute all feasible and complementary solutions associated with the vertices of the corresponding convex set K. These solutions are finite in number. Let us recall that this set constitutes a face of the convex set of feasible solutions of the given LC problem. Adler and Gale have demonstrated that this face is defined by the following system of inequalities and equations:

$$\bar{M}_{.\rho'}\mathbf{z}_\rho + \bar{\mathbf{q}} \geq \mathbf{0}. \quad \mathbf{z}_\rho \geq \mathbf{0} \tag{15.12}$$

$$(\bar{M}_{\rho\rho'} + \bar{M}'_{\rho\rho'})\mathbf{z}_\rho = \mathbf{0} \tag{15.13}$$

where $\bar{M}$ is the complementary transform of the given LC problem obtained in the final tableau of Lemke's algorithm; ρ is the index set of subscripts corresponding to the degenerate complementary pairs of variables; $\bar{M}_{.\rho}$ is the submatrix of $\bar{M}$ with the columns defined by the index set ρ; $\bar{M}_{\rho\rho'}$ is the submatrix of $\bar{M}$ with both rows and columns defined by ρ; and $\bar{\mathbf{q}}$ is the transform of $\mathbf{q}$ in the final tableau.

Any solution of (15.12) and (15.13) constitutes a feasible and complementary solution of the original LC problem. At this point, an algorithm is required for evaluating all the vertices of problem [(15.12),(15.13)]. The work of Mattheiss provides such an algorithm that is both elegant and efficient.

Consider the system of linear inqualities $Ax \leq b$, which must also include all nonnegative constraints of the $\mathbf{x}$ variable vector. Let A be an $(m \times n)$ matrix, $m > n$. Let K be the n-convex set of solutions of the given system of inequalities. K is embedded in one-higher-dimensional space forming the convex $(n + 1)$ polytope C, which is the set of feasible solutions of the following linear program:

$$\max Z = y \tag{15.14}$$

subject to $\qquad Ax + ty + Is = b, \quad x \geq 0, \ y \geq 0, s \geq 0$

where $\mathbf{x}$ is an $(n \times 1)$ nonnegative vector variable, y is a scalar variable, $\mathbf{s}$ is a $(m \times 1)$ vector of slack variables, and $\mathbf{t}$ is an $(m \times 1)$ vector of coefficients defined as

$$t_i = \left(\sum_{j=1}^n a_{ij}^2\right)^{1/2}, \quad i = 1, \dots, m.$$

Mattheiss chose to represent slack variables with the symbol **s**, and for this reason, in this scenario, we maintain his notation in order to facilitate the reading of his work. The **t** vector is regarded as a generalized slack activity whose purpose is to define and construct the radius of the largest sphere inscribable in the set of feasible solutions K. The idea of embedding K in C is to make the convex set K be a face of the $(n + 1)$ polytope C. Then, by starting at the vertex of C where the radius y is maximum, it is possible to reach every vertex of K by simplex pivot operations that, it is well known, lead to adjacent vertices.

Every optimal solution to the linear program (15.14) is characterized by all x_j variables, $j = 1, \ldots, n$, and by y as basic variables. Otherwise, the problem is infeasible. Also, $(m - n - 1)$ slack variables will be basic while the remaining $(n - 1)$ slacks not in the basis ($s_i = 0$) identify the set of binding constraints H_p where p is the index of the solution.

In Mattheiss' algorithm, a crucial role is played by the structure of the primal tableau (patterned on the image of the LP problem (15.14)) of a basic solution that is reproduced below for convenience:

The Simplex Tableau

		Z	$\mathbf{x}$	y	$\mathbf{s}_B$		$\mathbf{s}_{NB}$	sol
Z	:	1				:	$\mathbf{w}'$	Z
$\mathbf{x}$	:		I			:	$U\mathbf{x}$	$B\mathbf{x}$
y	:			1		:	Uy	By
$\mathbf{s}_B$	:				I	:	$U\mathbf{s}_{NB}$	$B\mathbf{s}_B$

where

$\mathbf{s}_B \equiv$ slack variables in the basis, B.

$\mathbf{s}_{NB} \equiv$ slack variables not in the basis.

sol $\equiv$ the solution column. $B\mathbf{x}$ is a $(n \times 1)$ vector giving the values of $\mathbf{x}$; By is a scalar giving the value of y; $B\mathbf{s}_B$ is an $[(m - n - 1) \times 1]$ vector giving the solution values of the basic slack variables.

$\mathbf{w} \equiv$ the row of dual variables.

$Z \equiv$ the value of the objective function Z.

$U \equiv$ the $[m \times (n + 1)]$ block of coefficients partitioned in the $[n \times (n + 1)]$ block $U\mathbf{x}$, the $[1 \times (n + 1)]$ block Uy, and the $[(m - n - 1) \times (n + 1)]$ block $U\mathbf{s}_{NB}$ that corresponds to slack variables not in the basis.

A pivot in the $U\mathbf{x}$ block will be defined inadmissible because it would remove some x_j from the basis, thereby leaving K, the set of feasible solutions. A pivot executed in the Uy block will collapse the set C onto some vertex of $C \cap K$, that is, entering the hyperplane $y = 0$, one of the desired vertices. A pivot executed in the $U\mathbf{s}_{NB}$ block will exchange slack activities in the basis, providing another solution of the linear program.

The description of the Mattheiss algorithm for finding all vertices of a linear system of inequalities is complete. Some numerical examples should be of help in following and understanding the thread of reasoning and the required computations, which generate all the feasible and complementary solutions of a given LC problem.

Two numerical examples will be discussed. The first example is the same LP example analyzed earlier, in the section entitled "Example of Primal MOS in LP" which we reproduce here for convenience.

Example 3: LP Problem Revisited

Consider the following LP problem, which is essentially the same LP example analyzed in a previous section, although the first constraint does not appear here because it was always not binding.

$$\max Z \quad = \quad \tfrac{53}{22}x_1 \quad + \quad \tfrac{39}{22}x_2 \quad + \quad 5x_3 \quad + \quad 2x_4 \qquad (15.15)$$

$$\text{subject to} \quad 2x_1 \quad + \quad x_2 \quad + \quad 5x_3 \quad + \quad x_4 \quad \leq \quad 4$$
$$x_1 \quad + \quad 3x_2 \quad - \quad 2x_3 \quad + \quad 4x_4 \quad \leq \quad 0$$

with $x_i \geq 0, i = 1, \ldots, 4$.

We know already that this LP example has three optimal solutions, as reported in Table 15.1. The discussion in terms of Mattheiss's algorithm will allow an easy understanding of the procedure. Although Lemke's setup and algorithm is not the most convenient computational procedure to solve an LP problem, we choose this specification to maintain uniformity throughout the discussion of Mattheiss's method. Tableaux 9 and 10 present the initial and the final layouts of the LP example 3.

Tableau 9: Example 3 — Initial layout

w_1	w_2	w_3	w_4	w_5	w_6	z_1	z_2	z_3	z_4	z_5	z_6	z_0	$\mathbf{q}$	BI
1						0	0	0	0	-2	-1	-1	$-\frac{53}{22}$	w_1
	1					0	0	0	0	-1	-3	-1	$-\frac{39}{22}$	w_2
		1				0	0	0	0	-5	2	-1	-5	w_3
			1			0	0	0	0	-1	-4	-1	-2	w_4
				1		2	1	5	1	0	0	-1	4	w_5
					1	1	3	-2	4	0	0	-1	0	w_6

Tableau 10: Example 3 — Final tableau (reordered)

$\bar{w}_1$	$\bar{w}_2$	$\bar{z}_3$	$\bar{z}_4$	$\bar{z}_5$	$\bar{z}_6$	$\bar{z}_1$	$\bar{z}_2$	$\bar{w}_3$	$\bar{w}_4$	$\bar{w}_5$	$\bar{w}_6$	$\mathbf{q}$	BI
1						0	0	$-\frac{7}{22}$	$-\frac{9}{22}$	0	0	0	$\bar{w}_1$
	1					0	0	$-\frac{1}{22}$	$-\frac{17}{22}$	0	0	0	$\bar{w}_2$
		1				$\frac{7}{22}$	$\frac{1}{22}$	0	0	$\frac{2}{11}$	$-\frac{1}{22}$	$\frac{8}{11}$	$\bar{z}_3$
			1			$\frac{9}{22}$	$\frac{17}{22}$	0	0	$\frac{1}{11}$	$\frac{5}{22}$	$\frac{4}{11}$	$\bar{z}_4$
				1		0	0	$-\frac{2}{11}$	$-\frac{1}{11}$	0	0	$\frac{12}{11}$	$\bar{z}_5$
					1	0	0	$\frac{1}{22}$	$-\frac{5}{22}$	0	0	$\frac{5}{22}$	$\bar{z}_6$

The first primal optimal solution of the LP problem of example 3 and its dual solution are:

$$\begin{bmatrix} \text{Primal} \\ \text{Optimal} \\ \text{Solution} \end{bmatrix} = \begin{bmatrix} \bar{z}_1 = \bar{x}_1 = 0 \\ \bar{z}_2 = \bar{x}_2 = 0 \\ \bar{z}_3 = \bar{x}_3 = \frac{8}{11} \\ \bar{z}_4 = \bar{x}_4 = \frac{4}{11} \end{bmatrix}, \quad \begin{bmatrix} \text{Dual} \\ \text{Optimal} \\ \text{Solution} \end{bmatrix} = \begin{bmatrix} \bar{z}_5 = \bar{y}_1 = \frac{12}{11} \\ \bar{z}_6 = \bar{y}_2 = \frac{5}{11} \end{bmatrix}.$$

The index set of degenerate pairs of complementary variables is $\rho = \{1, 2\}$. The systems of linear inequalities and equations corresponding to the face of the convex set of multiple optimal solutions and represented by relations (15.12) and (15.13) are given, respectively, as

$$- \begin{bmatrix} 0 & 0 \\ 0 & 0 \\ \frac{7}{22} & \frac{1}{22} \\ \frac{9}{22} & \frac{17}{22} \\ 0 & 0 \\ 0 & 0 \end{bmatrix} \begin{bmatrix} x_1 \\ x_2 \end{bmatrix} + \begin{bmatrix} 0 \\ 0 \\ \frac{8}{11} \\ \frac{4}{11} \\ \frac{12}{11} \\ \frac{5}{11} \end{bmatrix} \geq \begin{bmatrix} 0 \\ 0 \\ 0 \\ 0 \\ 0 \\ 0 \end{bmatrix}, \quad \begin{bmatrix} x_1 \\ x_2 \end{bmatrix} \geq \begin{bmatrix} 0 \\ 0 \end{bmatrix} \qquad (15.12)'$$

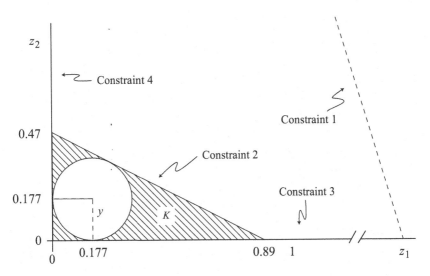

Figure 15.1. The set of solutions, K, of system (15.16).

$$\begin{bmatrix} 0 & 0 \\ 0 & 0 \end{bmatrix} \begin{bmatrix} x_1 \\ x_2 \end{bmatrix} = \begin{bmatrix} 0 \\ 0 \end{bmatrix}. \qquad (15.13)'$$

Hence, system (15.13)′ is vacuous, whereas system (15.12)′ can be reduced to the two central inequalities. Mattheiss's algorithm can thus be applied to the following reduced system expressed in the form of $A\mathbf{x} \le \mathbf{b}$:

$$\begin{bmatrix} \frac{7}{22} & \frac{1}{22} \\ \frac{9}{22} & \frac{17}{22} \\ -1 \\ & -1 \end{bmatrix} \begin{bmatrix} x_1 \\ x_2 \end{bmatrix} \le \begin{bmatrix} \frac{8}{11} \\ \frac{4}{11} \\ 0 \\ 0 \end{bmatrix}, \quad \begin{bmatrix} x_1 \\ x_2 \end{bmatrix} \ge \begin{bmatrix} 0 \\ 0 \end{bmatrix}. \qquad (15.16)$$

Mattheiss's algorithm requires embedding the inequality system (15.16) into an LP problem of the form specified in (15.14) where, in this case;

$$\mathbf{t} = \left[\left(\sum_{j=1}^{n} a_{ij}^2 \right)^{1/2} \right] = \begin{bmatrix} \{(\frac{7}{22})^2 + (\frac{1}{22})^2\}^{1/2} = 0.321412 \\ \{(\frac{9}{22})^2 + (\frac{17}{22})^2\}^{1/2} = 0.874336 \\ \{(-1)^2\} + (0)^2\}^{1/2} = 1.000000 \\ \{(0)^2\} + (-1)^2\}^{1/2} = 1.000000 \end{bmatrix}.$$

Prior to analyzing system (15.16) algebraically and proceeding with the implementation of Mattheiss's algorithm, it is convenient to graph it. Figure 15.1 indicates that the convex polytope K of feasible solutions to (15.16), whose vertices are sought, possesses three extreme points (0, 0), (0.89, 0.0), and (0.0, 0.47) and that constraint 1 is redundant. It also shows that the largest sphere inscribable in the convex set of feasible solutions K has a radius $y = 0.177$.

The initial and the final tableaux of Mattheiss's setup are presented in tableaux 11 and 12, respectively. The primal simplex algorithm is used for solving this part of the procedure.

Tableau 11: Example 3 – Initial tableau of Mattheiss's problem (15.16)

	Z	x_1	x_2	y	s_1	s_2	s_3	s_4	sol	BI
	1	0	0	-1	0	0	0	0	0	Z
		$\frac{7}{22}$	$\frac{1}{22}$	.3214	1				$\frac{8}{11}$	s_1
		$\frac{9}{22}$	$\frac{17}{22}$	.8743		1			$\frac{4}{11}$	s_2
		-1	0	1			1		0	s_3
		0	-1	(1)				1	0	s_4

The pivot element in tableau 11 is indicated by parentheses. The only "profitable" activity is the **t** vector associated with the y variable. There is a tie in the choice of the pivot in correspondence of basic variables s_3 and s_4 and the selection of the pivot in row s_4 was determined by flipping a coin. After three iterations of the primal simplex algorithm, the final tableau looks as in tableau 12 (rounding off to four decimal digits is reported for convenience):

Tableau 12: Example 3 — Final tableau (reordered) of problem (15.16)

	Z	$\bar{x}_1$	$\bar{x}_2$	$\bar{y}$	$\bar{s}_1$	s_2^*	s_3^*	s_4^*	sol	BI
	1					.4863	.1990	.3758	.1769	Z
		1				.4863	$-.8010$	.3758	.1769	$\bar{x}_1$
			1			.4863	.1990	$-.6242$	.1769	$\bar{x}_2$
				1		(.4863)	(.1990)	(.3758)	.1769	$\bar{y}$
					1	$-.3332$	.1819	$-.2120$	.6061	$\bar{s}_1$

Tableau 12 shows that, at this stage of the procedure, the basic variables are $\bar{x}_1$, $\bar{x}_2$, $\bar{y}$, and $\bar{s}_1$. The nonbasic variables are s_2^*, s_3^* and s_4^* which have been starred to indicate that the corresponding constraints are binding. The values of $\bar{x}_1$, $\bar{x}_2$, and $\bar{y}$ are all equal to .1769. They are interpreted as the coordinates of the center of the maximum circumference (sphere in higher dimensions) inscribed in the K-polytope, as illustrated in Figure 15.1.

Mattheiss's algorithm requires a thorough analysis of tableau 12. First of all, $H_1 = \{2, 3, 4\}$ defines the set of binding constraints for this tableau. A record, R_1, is defined by the value of the linear objective function, Z (the radius of the largest sphere) and by the set of binding constraints, hence,

$R_1 = \{.1769, (2, 3, 4)\}$. In the process of analyzing a record, either a new record or a set of vertices of K is obtained. A "*List*" is a set of records. When all the records have been analyzed and eliminated from the *List*, the algorithm terminates.

The analysis of a record is performed through a set of pivot operations. Recall that it is admissible to pivot only in the row corresponding to either $\bar{y}$ or slack variable $\bar{s}_1$. By choosing a pivot in the row of a basic slack variable, $\bar{s}_1$ (in such a way to maintaining the feasibility of the next solution), a new record is generated. A pivot executed in the $\bar{y}$ row generates a vertex of K.

Let us now proceed to the analysis of tableau 12, *List* $= (R_1)$.

Step 1. $H_1 = \{2, 3, 4\}$.

Step 2. The pivot in the first nonbasic column, s_2^* is a pivot in the $\bar{y}$ row (pivot in parentheses), alternatively in the Uy row of Mattheiss's Simplex Tableau, which generates the vertex of K equal to $V_1 = (0, 0)$. In fact, the solution column corresponding to the pivot execution is

$$\begin{bmatrix} 0.0 \\ 0.0 \\ 0.0 \\ 0.3636 \\ 0.7273 \end{bmatrix} \begin{matrix} Z \\ \bar{x}_1 \\ \bar{x}_2 \\ s_2^* \\ \bar{s}_1 \end{matrix}$$

Step 3. The pivot in column s_3^* is, again, a Uy pivot (from the Simplex Tableau of Mattheiss) corresponding to the vertex of K, $V_2 = (0.8889, 0.0)$. Recall that, according to the primal simplex algorithm, the pivot corresponds to the minimum ratio between nonnegative elements of the solution column and positive elements of the incoming column. The solution column corresponding to this pivot execution is:

$$\begin{bmatrix} 0.0 \\ 0.8889 \\ 0.0 \\ 0.8889 \\ 0.4444 \end{bmatrix} \begin{matrix} Z \\ \bar{x}_1 \\ \bar{x}_2 \\ s_3^* \\ \bar{s}_1 \end{matrix}$$

Step 4. The pivot in column s_4^* is also a Uy pivot corresponding to the vertex of K, $V_3 = (0.0, 0.4706)$. The solution column corresponding

Table 15.2. *LP Problem (15.15)*

Primal Solution	Vertex 1	Vertex 2	Vertex 3
x_1	0	0.8889	0
x_2	0	0	0.4706
x_3	0.7273	0.4444	0.7059
x_4	0.3636	0	0

to this pivot execution is:

$$\begin{bmatrix} 0.0 \\ 0.0 \\ 0.4706 \\ 0.4706 \\ 0.7059 \end{bmatrix} \begin{matrix} Z \\ \bar{x}_1 \\ \bar{x}_2 \\ s_4^* \\ \bar{s}_1 \end{matrix}$$

The analysis of record R_1 is complete, and R_1 is removed from the *List*. No other record is in the *List*, and the algorithm is terminated. All vertices of K have been identified together with the redundant constraint corresponding to the slack variable $\bar{s}_1$.

One final scrutiny of system (15.16) will reveal that slack variables s_1 and s_2 correspond to variables x_3 and x_4 of the LP constraints in problem (15.15):

$$\frac{7}{22}x_1 + \frac{1}{22}x_2 + s_1 \qquad = \frac{8}{11} \qquad (15.17)$$

$$\frac{9}{22}x_1 + \frac{17}{22}x_2 \qquad + s_2 = \frac{4}{11} \qquad (15.18)$$

Hence, Table 15.2 summarizes the three basic optimal solutions of the LP problem (15.15), which are identical to those of Table 15.1.

It can be verified that all three primal basic solutions in Table 15.2 generate the same optimal value of the linear objective function in example 3, that is, $Z = 48/11 \cong 4.3636$.

Example 4: QP Problem (15.11) Revisited

To complete the description of the algorithm for finding all the optimal solutions of a QP problem, example 2 of a previous section will be fully analyzed. That example was partially analyzed in tableau 6, which is reproduced here for convenience:

Tableau 6: Example 2 – Solution (reordered)

$\bar{z}_1$	$\bar{w}_2$	$\bar{w}_3$	$\bar{z}_4$	$\bar{w}_5$	$\bar{w}_1$	z_2	z_3	$\bar{w}_4$	z_5	q	BI
1					0	$\frac{2}{3}$	$\frac{1}{3}$	$\frac{1}{6}$	0	3	$\bar{z}_1$
	1				$-\frac{2}{3}$	0	0	0	$-\frac{1}{3}$	0	$\bar{w}_2$
		1			$-\frac{1}{3}$	0	0	0	$\frac{1}{3}$	0	$\bar{w}_3$
			1		$-\frac{1}{6}$	0	0	$-\frac{1}{12}$	$\frac{2}{3}$	$\frac{1}{2}$	$\bar{z}_4$
				1	0	$\frac{1}{3}$	$-\frac{1}{3}$	$-\frac{2}{3}$	0	0	$\bar{w}_5$

The index set of degeneracies is equal to $\rho = \{2, 3, 5\}$ and the $\bar{M}_{\rho\rho'}$ matrix is such that $(M_{\rho\rho'} + M'_{\rho\rho'})$ is a null matrix. In fact,

$$(M_{\rho\rho'} + M'_{\rho\rho'}) = \begin{bmatrix} 0 & 0 & -\frac{1}{3} \\ 0 & 0 & \frac{1}{3} \\ \frac{1}{3} & -\frac{1}{3} & 0 \end{bmatrix} + \begin{bmatrix} 0 & 0 & \frac{1}{3} \\ 0 & 0 & -\frac{1}{3} \\ -\frac{1}{3} & \frac{1}{3} & 0 \end{bmatrix}.$$

Therefore, in this example, constraints (15.13) will also be inoperative. The $\bar{M}_{.\rho}$ matrix of system (15.12) establishes the following relevant inequalities corresponding to (15.12):

$$-\begin{bmatrix} \frac{2}{3} & \frac{1}{3} & 0 \\ 0 & 0 & -\frac{1}{3} \\ 0 & 0 & \frac{1}{3} \\ 0 & 0 & \frac{2}{3} \\ \frac{1}{3} & -\frac{1}{3} & 0 \end{bmatrix} \begin{bmatrix} z_2 \\ z_3 \\ z_5 \end{bmatrix} + \begin{bmatrix} 3 \\ 0 \\ 0 \\ \frac{1}{2} \\ 0 \end{bmatrix} \geq \begin{bmatrix} 0 \\ 0 \\ 0 \\ 0 \\ 0 \end{bmatrix}, \quad \begin{bmatrix} z_2 \\ z_3 \\ z_5 \end{bmatrix} \geq \begin{bmatrix} 0 \\ 0 \\ 0 \end{bmatrix}. \quad (15.19)$$

Notice that, by inspection, one can immediately conclude that $z_5 = 0$. In fact, $z_5 = y_2 = 0$, in tableau 6. Thus, it is possible to reduce problem (15.19) to two inequalities as:

$$\begin{bmatrix} \frac{2}{3} & \frac{1}{3} \\ \frac{1}{3} & -\frac{1}{3} \end{bmatrix} \begin{bmatrix} x_2 \\ x_3 \end{bmatrix} \leq \begin{bmatrix} 3 \\ 0 \end{bmatrix}, \quad \begin{bmatrix} x_2 \equiv z_2 \\ x_3 \equiv z_3 \end{bmatrix} \geq \begin{bmatrix} 0 \\ 0 \end{bmatrix}. \quad (15.20)$$

The generalized slack vector for Mattheiss's specification of the LP problem (15.14) is computed as follows:

$$\mathbf{t} = \left[\left(\sum_{j=1}^{n} a_{ij}^2 \right)^{1/2} \right] = \begin{bmatrix} \{(\frac{2}{3})^2 + (\frac{1}{3})^2\}^{1/2} = 0.745356 \\ \{(\frac{1}{3})^2 + (-\frac{1}{3})^2\}^{1/2} = 0.471045 \\ \{(-1)^2 + (0)^2\}^{1/2} = 1.000000 \\ \{(0)^2 + (-1)^2\}^{1/2} = 1.000000 \end{bmatrix}.$$

The initial and optimal layouts of Mattheiss's algorithm are presented in tableaux 13 and 14, respectively.

Tableau 13: Example 4 — Initial tableau of Mattheiss' problem (15.20)

Z	x_1	x_2	y	s_1	s_2	s_3	s_4	sol	BI
1	0	0	-1	0	0	0	0	0	Z
	$\frac{2}{3}$	$\frac{1}{3}$	.7454	1				3	s_1
	$\frac{1}{3}$	$-\frac{1}{3}$	.4714		1			0	s_2
	-1	0	1			1		0	s_3
	0	-1	(1)				1	0	s_4

Tableau 14: Example 4 — Final tableau (reordered) of problem (15.20)

Z	$\bar{x}_2$	$\bar{x}_3$	$\bar{y}$	$\bar{s}_4$	s_1^*	s_2^*	s_3^*	sol	BI
1					.4511	.4511	.4511	1.3533	Z
	1				.4511	.4511	$-.5489$	1.3533	$\bar{x}_2$
		1			1.0891	-1.9109	.0891	3.2672	$\bar{x}_3$
			1		(.4511)	(.4511)	(.4511)	1.3533	$\bar{y}$
				1	(.6380)	-2.3620	$-.3620$	1.9139	$\bar{s}_4$

The analysis of tableau 14 starts with the three nonbasic slack variables s_1^*, s_2^*, s_3^*, corresponding to binding constraints. Pivots are in parentheses. From tableau 14, record R_1 is $R_1 = \{y, \rho\} = \{1.35, (1, 2, 3)\}$.

Figure 15.2 illustrates this record. It shows that the three vertices are $(0, 0)$, $(0, 9)$, $(3, 3)$, whereas the radius of the largest circumference is $\bar{y} \cong 1.35$. The distance of the circumference from constraint 4 is given by slack $\bar{s}_4 \cong 1.91$.

Step 1. The selection of pivot in column s_1^* indicates a tie with pivot elements in both the Uy row and the Us_{NB} block (of Mattheiss's Simplex Tableau). In this case, $(Us_{NB} \to \bar{s}_4)$. Execution of the pivot in the Uy row generates a vertex of K, $V_1 = (x_2 = 0, x_3 = 0)$. Execution of the pivot in the $(Us_{NB} \to \bar{s}_4)$ row creates a new record, $R_2 = \{0, (2, 3, 4)\}$ corresponding to tableau 15. The *List* of records comprises R_1 and R_2.

Step 2. Execution of pivot in column s_2^* generates a vertex in K, $V_2 = (0, 9)$.

Step 3. Execution of pivot in column s_3^* generates a vertex in K, $V_3 = (3, 3)$.

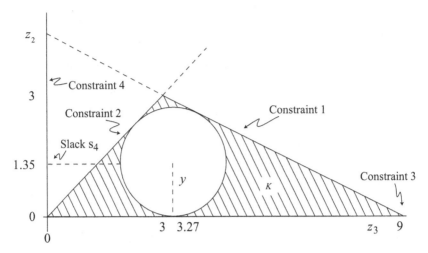

Figure 15.2. The set of solutions, K, of system (15.20).

Record R_1 is analyzed completely and is removed from the *List*.

Tableau 15: Example 4 – Record R_2 (reordered) of problem (15.20)

$$
\begin{array}{ccccccccccc}
& Z & \bar{x}_2 & \bar{x}_3 & \bar{y} & \bar{s}_1 & s_2^* & s_3^* & s_4^* & \text{sol} & BI \\
\begin{bmatrix}
1 & & & & & 2.1213 & .7058 & -.7070 & 0 \\
& 1 & & & & 2.1213 & -.2942 & -.7070 & 0 \\
& & 1 & & & 2.1213 & .7058 & -1.7070 & 0 \\
& & & 1 & & 2.1213 & .7058 & -.7070 & 0 \\
& & & & 1 & -3.7026 & -.5652 & 1.5674 & 3
\end{bmatrix}
& & & & & & & & &
\begin{matrix}
Z \\ \bar{x}_2 \\ \bar{x}_3 \\ \bar{y} \\ \bar{s}_1
\end{matrix}
\end{array}
$$

The analysis of record R_2 indicates that by pivoting in columns s_2^* and s_3^*, vertices already identified are generated. The pivot in column s_4^* is in the $(Us_{NB} \rightarrow \bar{s}_1)$ row, and its execution creates a new record $R_3 = R_1$, that was already analyzed. Hence, Mattheiss's algorithm terminates successfully, having identified all the vertices of K.

Notice that, in this example, slack s_1 corresponds to x_1 of the original QP problem (15.11). To summarize, the three optimal solutions of the QP problem (15.11) in examples 2 and 4 are exhibited in Table 15.3.

It can be easily verified that each of the three solutions corresponds to a value of the QP objective function of 22.5. Furthermore, any convex combination of these three basic optimal solutions corresponds to another optimal solution. The suggestion is to use the same least-distance framework

Table 15.3. *QP Problem (15.11)*

Primal Solution	Vertex 1	Vertex 2	Vertex 3
x_1	3	0	0
x_2	0	0	3
x_3	0	9	3

discussed in problem (15.2) for dealing with MOS of a LP problem. Hence, all three activities can be operated efficiently at positive levels.

Exercises

15.1 The following LP example

$$
\begin{aligned}
\max Z \quad = \quad & 4x_1 \; + \quad x_2 \; + \; 5x_3 \\
\text{subject to} \quad & 3x_1 \; + \; 2x_2 \; - \quad x_3 \; \leq \; 2 \\
& -x_1 \; + \quad x_2 \; + \; 5x_3 \; \leq \; 4 \\
& \; x_1 \qquad\qquad\quad + \quad x_3 \; \leq \; 2
\end{aligned}
$$

and $x_j \geq 0$, $j = 1, \ldots, n$, possesses dual multiple optimal solutions.
(a) Apply the appropriate algorithm and compute all the basic alternative optimal solutions.
(b) Explain and justify your procedure.

15.2 The following LP example

$$
\begin{aligned}
\max Z \quad = \quad & \tfrac{53}{22}x_1 \; + \; \tfrac{5}{3}x_2 \; + \; 5x_3 \; + \; 2x_4 \\
\text{subject to} \quad & \tfrac{43}{22}x_1 \; + \; 2x_2 \; + \quad x_3 \; + \; 4x_4 \; \leq \; \tfrac{24}{11} \\
& 2x_1 \; + \quad x_2 \; + \; 5x_3 \; + \quad x_4 \; \leq \; 4 \\
& \; x_1 \; + \; 3x_2 \; - \; 2x_3 \; + \; 4x_4 \; \leq \; 0
\end{aligned}
$$

and $x_j \geq 0$, $j = 1, \ldots, n$, possesses multiple primal and dual multiple optimal solutions.
(a) Using the appropriate algorithms, compute all the basic primal and dual alternative optimal solutions.
(b) Explain and justify your procedure.

15.3 The LP numerical example discussed in a previous section, and reproduced here for convenience,

$$\max Z = \tfrac{53}{22}x_1 + \tfrac{39}{22}x_2 + 5x_3 + 2x_4$$

$$\text{subject to} \quad 3x_1 + 2x_2 + x_3 + 4x_4 \le 6$$
$$2x_1 + x_2 + 5x_3 + x_4 \le 4$$
$$x_1 + 3x_2 - 2x_3 + 4x_4 \le 0$$

with $x_i \ge 0$, $i = 1, \ldots, 4$, has three basic primal optimal solutions as reported in Table 15.1. Suppose that the observed levels of production for the four activities are as follows: $\bar{x}_j$, $j = 1, \ldots, 4$, are: $\bar{x}_1 = \tfrac{4}{9}$, $\bar{x}_2 = \tfrac{2}{17}$, $\bar{x}_3 = \tfrac{977}{1683}$, $\bar{x}_4 = \tfrac{1}{11}$. Using the three basic optimal solutions exhibited in Table 15.1 and the weights $w_1 = \tfrac{1}{4}$, $w_2 = \tfrac{1}{4}$, $w_3 = \tfrac{1}{2}$, compute the convex combination of the three optimal solutions and show that the resulting, nonbasic, solution is also an optimal solution.

15.4 Often, in an LP model, the opportunity cost of some nonbasic activity is just a few cents away from a zero value. What can be done for discovering an alternative (quasi) optimal solution?

References

Adler, I., and Gale, D. (1975). "On the Solution of Positive Semi-definite Complementary Problems," Report ORC 75-12, Department of Industrial Engineering and Operations Research, University of California.

Baumol, W. J. (1977). *Economic Theory and Operations Analysis*, 4th ed. (Englewood Cliffs, NJ: Prentice-Hall).

Kaneko, I. (1979). "The Number of Solutions of a Class of Linear Complementarity Problems," *Mathematical Programming*, 17, 104–5.

Lemke, C. E. (1968). "On Complementary Pivot Theory." In *Mathematics for the Decision Sciences*, Part I, Dantzig, G.B. and Veinott, A.F. Jr., editors (Providence, RI: American Mathematical Society), pp. 95–114.

Mattheiss, T. H. (1973). "An Algorithm for Determining Irrelevant Constraints and All Vertices in Systems of Linear Inequalities," *Operations Research*, 21, 247–60.

Paris, Q. (1981). "Multiple Optimal Solutions in Linear Programming Models," *American Journal of Agricultural Economics*, 63, 724–27.

Paris, Q. (1983). "Multiple Optimal Solutions in Quadratic Programming Models," *Western Journal of Agricultural Economics*, 141–54.

Takayama, T., and Judge, G. G. (1971). *Spatial Temporal and Price Allocation Models* (Amsterdam: North-Holland).

von Oppen, M., and Scott, J. (1978). "A Spatial Equilibrium Model for Plant Location and Interregional Trade," *American Journal of Agricultural Economics*, 58, 437–45.

Wicks, J. A. (1979). "Alternative Approaches to Risk in Aggregative Programming: An Evaluation," *European Review of Agricultural Economics*, 5, 159–73.

16

Lemke Complementary Pivot Algorithm
User Manual

The LEMKE computer program is a modified and extended version of the SHARE LIBRARY PROGRAM NO. 360D-15.3.003 by A. Ravindran. The revisions were implemented by Q. Paris and E. Morgan, Department of Agricultural Economics, University of California, Davis, in 1977. Further extensions were implemented in 1986. In 2005 and 2007, the program was adapted to Fortran 77 by Q. Paris and K. Edgington, Department of Agricultural and Resource Economics, University of California, Davis. SHARE endorses neither the author nor the use of this work.

I. Purpose

This program solves Linear Complementarity (LC) problems of the form: find vectors $\mathbf{w}$ and $\mathbf{z}$ such that

$$\mathbf{w} = M\mathbf{z} + \mathbf{q}, \quad \mathbf{w} \geq \mathbf{0}, \ \mathbf{z} \geq \mathbf{0},$$

$$\mathbf{w}'\mathbf{z} = 0,$$

where M is an $(N \times N)$ matrix and $\mathbf{w}$, $\mathbf{z}$ and $\mathbf{q}$ are N-dimensional column vectors. In particular, it can solve the symmetric quadratic programming, the asymmetric quadratic programming, and the linear programming problems, as well as problems of equilibrium that cannot be formulated as a dual pair of optimization models, bimatrix games (two-person non-zero-sum games), and general Linear Complementarity problems.

(i) Symmetric Quadratic Programming (SQP)
It is the most general version of quadratic programming (QP) and possesses the following specification:

Primal $\max \{ \mathbf{c}'\mathbf{x} - k_d \mathbf{x}' D \mathbf{x} - k_e \mathbf{y}' E \mathbf{y} \}$ (16.1)

subject to $A\mathbf{x} - 2k_e E \mathbf{y} \le \mathbf{b}$

$$\mathbf{x} \ge \mathbf{0}, \ \mathbf{y} \ge \mathbf{0}.$$

where A is any $(m \times n)$ matrix, $\mathbf{b}$ is an $(m \times 1)$ vector, $\mathbf{c}$ is an $(n \times 1)$ vector, $\mathbf{x}$ is an $(n \times 1)$ vector of primal variables, $\mathbf{y}$ is an $(m \times 1)$ vector of dual variables, k_d and k_e are (nonnegative) scalars, and D and E are symmetric positive semidefinite matrices of order n and m, respectively. When these conditions are satisfied, the algorithm is guaranteed to find an optimal solution, if one exists. (The user may request the program to verify whether either D or E are positive definite or positive semidefinite by setting the optional parameters NCHKD, NCHKE to a value of 1, as explained later.

The dual problem corresponding to the primal problem (16.1) is

Dual $\min \{ \mathbf{b}'\mathbf{y} + k_e \mathbf{y}' E \mathbf{y} + k_d \mathbf{x}' D \mathbf{x} \}$ (16.2)

subject to $A'\mathbf{y} + 2k_d D \mathbf{x} \ge \mathbf{c}$

$$\mathbf{x} \ge \mathbf{0}, \ \mathbf{y} \ge \mathbf{0}.$$

If the primal problem requires minimization, the form of the dual (16.2) becomes that of the primal and vice versa. The user, however, is required to specify only if the primal problem is a maximization or a minimization by using the parameter MAX.

Equality constraints can be handled by changing them to inequalities. Suppose there are k equality constraints of the form

$$\sum_j a_{ij} x_j - 2k_e \sum_s e_{is} y_s = b_i, \quad i = 1, \ldots, k.$$

This set of k equations can be converted to an equivalent set of $(k+1)$ inequalities as follows:

$$\sum_j a_{ij} x_j - 2k_e \sum_s e_{is} y_s \ge b_i, \quad i = 1, \ldots, k; \ s = 1, \ldots, m$$

$$-\sum_{ij} a_{ij} x_j + 2k_e \sum_{is} e_{is} y_s \ge -\sum_i b_i.$$

(ii) Asymmetric Quadratic Programming (AQP)

There are two families of asymmetric quadratic programming problems. By setting either D or E equal to a null matrix in problem (16.1) and (16.2), the asymmetric versions of QP are obtained. Suppose $E \equiv$ null matrix. Then:

Primal $\qquad$ $\max \{\mathbf{c}'\mathbf{x} - k_d\mathbf{x}'D\mathbf{x}\}$ $\qquad$ (16.3)

$$\text{subject to} \qquad A\mathbf{x} \leq \mathbf{b}$$

$$\mathbf{x} \geq \mathbf{0}$$

with the corresponding dual problem stated as

Dual $\qquad$ $\min \{\mathbf{b}'\mathbf{y} + k_d\mathbf{x}'D\mathbf{x}\}$

$$\text{subject to} \qquad A'\mathbf{y} + 2k_d D\mathbf{x} \geq \mathbf{c}$$

$$\mathbf{x} \geq \mathbf{0}, \mathbf{y} \geq \mathbf{0}.$$

Suppose $D \equiv$ null matrix. Then:

Primal $\qquad$ $\max \{\mathbf{c}'\mathbf{x} - k_e\mathbf{y}'E\mathbf{y}\}$ $\qquad$ (16.4)

$$\text{subject to} \qquad A\mathbf{x} - 2k_e E\mathbf{y} \leq \mathbf{b}$$

$$\mathbf{x} \geq \mathbf{0} \, \mathbf{y} \geq \mathbf{0}$$

with the corresponding dual problem stated as

Dual $\qquad$ $\min \{\mathbf{b}'\mathbf{y} + k_e\mathbf{y}'E\mathbf{y}\}$

$$\text{subject to} \qquad A'\mathbf{y} \geq \mathbf{c}$$

$$\mathbf{y} \geq \mathbf{0}.$$

(iii) Linear Programming (LP)

When both D and E are null matrices, problems (16.1) and (16.2) reduce to a dual pair of linear programming problems, that is,

Primal $\qquad$ $\max \mathbf{c}'\mathbf{x}$, $\quad$ subject to $\quad A\mathbf{x} \leq \mathbf{b}$, and $\mathbf{x} \geq \mathbf{0}$ $\quad$ (16.5)

with the corresponding dual problem stated as

Dual $\qquad$ $\min \mathbf{b}'\mathbf{y}$, $\quad$ subject to $\quad A'\mathbf{y} \geq \mathbf{c}$, and $\mathbf{y} \geq \mathbf{0}$.

(iv) Symmetric and Asymmetric Equilibrium Problems (SEP, AEP)

Whereas all the optimization problems (when a feasible solution exists) can be viewed (stated) as equilibrium problems (via their Karush-Kuhn-Tucker conditions), not all the equilibrium problems can be stated as optimization problems. This event may occur when either the D and/or the E matrices are not symmetric.

Suppose the matrix D and the matrix E are *asymmetric* and positive semidefinite. Then, problems (16.1) and (16.2) are not logically consistent because they cannot represent a dual pair of optimization problems. However, the equilibrium problem of interest can be formulated directly as a Linear Complementarity problem:

$$Ax - 2k_e\,Ey \le b, \quad y \ge 0 \tag{16.6}$$

$$A'y + 2k_d\,Dx \ge c, \quad x \ge 0$$

and

$$y'[-Ax + 2k_e\,Ey + b] = 0$$

$$x'[A'y + 2k_d\,Dx - c] = 0.$$

The second set of equations are called *complementary slackness conditions*. Asymmetric equilibrium problems can be easily obtained from problem (16.6) by setting either the D matrix or the E matrix equal to the null matrix.

(v) Bimatrix Games: Two-Person Non-Zero-Sum Games

A two-person non-zero-sum game is a bimatrix game. Given a payoff matrix A associated with player I and a payoff matrix B associated with player II, where A and B are of dimension $(n \times m)$, the value of the game (corresponding to a Nash equilibrium) is found by solving the following problem:

$$B'x \ge e_n, \quad x \ge 0, \quad y'[B'x - e_n] = 0 \tag{16.7}$$

$$Ay \ge e_m \quad y \ge 0, \quad x'[Ay - e_m] = 0$$

where e_n and e_m are sum vectors (vectors whose components are all unitary) of dimension n and m, respectively. (Notice that a two-person zero-sum game corresponds to a dual pair of linear programming problems, as explained in Chapter 13.)

II. Method

The computer code is based on Lemke's Complementary Pivot Algorithms and Ravindran's computer routine (extended and rewritten by Q. Paris, E. Morgan, and K. Edgington in Fortran 77 over a period of years) to solve a linear complementarity problem of the form:

Find vectors **w** and **z** such that

$$\mathbf{w} = M\mathbf{z} + \mathbf{q}, \quad \mathbf{w} \geq \mathbf{0}, \mathbf{z} \geq \mathbf{0}, \tag{16.8}$$

$$\mathbf{w}'\mathbf{z} = 0,$$

where M is an $(N \times N) = [(n + m) \times (n + m)]$ matrix and **w**, **z** and **q** are N-dimensional column vectors. Problems (16.1) through (16.7) can easily be transformed into problem (16.8).

Symmetric QP. Consider the earlier problems (16.1) and (16.2). An optimal solution to these problems may be obtained by solving a Linear Complementarity problem of the form:

$$\begin{pmatrix} \mathbf{u} \\ \mathbf{v} \end{pmatrix} = \begin{bmatrix} k_d(D + D') & A' \\ -A & k_e(E + E') \end{bmatrix} \begin{pmatrix} \mathbf{x} \\ \mathbf{y} \end{pmatrix} + \begin{pmatrix} -\mathbf{c} \\ \mathbf{b} \end{pmatrix} \tag{16.9}$$

$$\mathbf{u} \geq \mathbf{0}, \ \mathbf{v} \geq \mathbf{0}, \ \mathbf{x} \geq \mathbf{0}, \ \mathbf{y} \geq \mathbf{0}$$

and

$$\mathbf{u}'\mathbf{x} + \mathbf{v}'\mathbf{y} = 0$$

where **u** and **v** are slack variables of the primal and dual systems of constraints, respectively. All the relations in (16.9) are based on the KKT conditions of problems (16.1) and (16.2). Comparing (16.9) with (16.8), it is clear that

$$\mathbf{w} = \begin{bmatrix} \mathbf{u} \\ \mathbf{v} \end{bmatrix}, \quad \mathbf{z} = \begin{bmatrix} \mathbf{x} \\ \mathbf{y} \end{bmatrix}, \quad \mathbf{q} = \begin{bmatrix} -\mathbf{c} \\ \mathbf{b} \end{bmatrix},$$

$$M = \begin{bmatrix} k_d(D + D') & A' \\ -A & k_e(E + E') \end{bmatrix}. \tag{16.10}$$

If the symmetric QP problem is one that requires minimization, the M matrix and the **q** vector of (16.10) will be defined as

$$M = \begin{bmatrix} k_d(D + D') & -A' \\ A & k_e(E + E') \end{bmatrix}, \quad \mathbf{q} = \begin{bmatrix} \mathbf{c} \\ -\mathbf{b} \end{bmatrix}. \tag{16.11}$$

The computer routine first transforms the given quadratic program into an equivalent complementarity problem using transformation (16.10) (or (16.11)), solves the complementarity problem by Lemke's algorithm, and retransforms the solution into the components of the original specification. It should be remarked that Lemke's algorithm is guaranteed to work whenever the M matrix exhibits certain properties such as positive semidefiniteness, all nonnegative components, and others. In systems (16.10) and (16.11), M is positive semidefinite if, and only if, the matrices D and E are both positive semidefinite, or one is positive definite and the other is positive semidefinite. The matrix A is irrelevant for the definiteness of the M matrix. Notice that some quadratic programming problems can handle asymmetric positive semidefinite matrices D and E, as long as the corresponding KKT conditions involve symmetric matrices in the form $(D + D')$ or $(E + E')$.

Equilibrium Problems with Asymmetric D and/or E Matrices. In the case of problem (16.6) with asymmetric D and/or E matrices, the elements of the corresponding Linear Complementarity problem assume the following structure:

$$\mathbf{q} = \begin{bmatrix} -\mathbf{c} \\ \mathbf{b} \end{bmatrix}, \quad M = \begin{bmatrix} k_d D & A' \\ -A & k_e E \end{bmatrix}.$$

The General Linear Complementarity Problem. The computer program is instructed to recognize a general M matrix of the LCP with the following symbols:

$$M = \begin{bmatrix} G & H \\ F & K \end{bmatrix}, \quad \mathbf{q} = \begin{bmatrix} -\mathbf{c} \\ \mathbf{b} \end{bmatrix}$$

where the matrices G, K, F, and H are declared in that order (columnwise). The matrix M must have some specified properties such as positive semidefiniteness, or other properties as stated by Lemke.

Bimatrix Game. For a bimatrix game, the structure of the corresponding LC problem is

$$M = \begin{bmatrix} 0 & H \\ F & 0 \end{bmatrix}, \quad \mathbf{q} = \begin{bmatrix} -\mathbf{e}_m \\ -\mathbf{e}_n \end{bmatrix}$$

where $F \equiv B'$ and $H \equiv A$ in the previous discussion. A payoff matrix can always be taken to be a positive matrix (all positive elements) without modifying the equilibrium solution of the game. Hence, if the original payoff matrix A (or B) contains positive and negative elements, it is sufficient to add a matrix with constant elements to obtain an equivalent payoff matrix with all positive elements without affecting the solution of the original equilibrium of the bimatrix game.

III. Limitations

1. In its present form, the program can handle problems of size $(m + n) = 99$. For larger problems, a change in the dimension statement and a change in the format statement $(7(2I,F8.4))$ for Ipack=1 (see Input Format) are required.
2. The program is guaranteed to solve any linear and convex/concave program. Concavity/convexity of the quadratic function is dependent on matrices D and E being positive definite or positive semidefinite. If either D or E does not satisfy this property, the program could either converge to a local optimum or terminate erroneously, indicating that there is no optimal solution. The user may request the program to verify whether D or E is positive definite or positive semidefinite by setting the optional parameters NCHKD and NCHKE in the input parameter line of the datafile to a value of 1. The program, however, also solves the general LC problem subject to the conditions specified by Lemke.
3. In this program, the property of positive semidefiniteness of D and E is checked by utilizing machine dependent subroutines for computing the eigenvalues of the relevant matrices. If this subroutine is not needed, the program could then be used as such by making sure that the integer variables NCHKD and NCHKE are set equal to zero or -1 in the appropriate input data line to avoid checking the property of definiteness of matrices D and E.

IV. Environment Requirements

1. In its present form, the program's core requirements are closed to 100,000 words. This can be reduced by reducing the size of the dimension statement.
2. In subroutine "SORT", the statement TOL $=$ AMAX$^{*}2.0^{**}(-21)$ should be changed according to the computer system available. In general, TOL $=$ AMAX$^{*}2.0^{**}(-NB)$ and NB should be replaced by $(B - 11)$, where B is the number of bits in the floating-point mantissa of the computer. This tolerance statement is needed to avoid complications caused by degeneracy in the solution.

V. Input

The user must prepare a ⟨datafile.dat⟩ file to submit to the main program. The program name is RUNLEMKE7 and, when executed, it will request the datafile name with extension (*.dat).

Input Format

1. The program will solve any number of problems in succession. The first line must contain the title for the problem in (20A4) format, 80 characters or less.

2. The second line contains the following information in *free format* (space delimited):

NVAR = number of primal (decision) variables

NCON = number of constraints

PROB = an integer variable indicating what type of problem is to be solved:

1 = symmetric QP (D and E matrices)

2 = asymmetric QP (D matrix only)

3 = asymmetric QP (E matrix only)

4 = LP (no D or E matrices)

5 = LCP with asymmetric D and E matrices (Equilibrium Problem)

6 = general LC problem (G, K, F, H matrices, $G \not\equiv 0$ and/or $K \not\equiv 0$)

7 = bimatrix game ($G \equiv 0$, $K \equiv 0$, F, H and $\mathbf{q}'=(-\mathbf{e}_n, \quad -\mathbf{e}_m)'$).

MAX = an integer variable indicating if problem is a maximization (1) or minimizaton (0)

XKD = a real variable used as a scale factor for the D matrix

XKE = a real variable used as a scale factor for the E matrix

IPACK = 0 or blank, if matrices D, E, and A are to be inputted in their entirety

= 1, if only the nonzero elements of D, E, and A are to beinputted in packed form,

NCHKD = −1, if D is already known to be positive definite (PD) or positive semidefinite (PSD);

= 0, if D is not known to be PD or PSD and no such determination is requested;

= 1, if a determination of definiteness of D is to be performed.

NCHKE = −1, if E is already known to be positive definite or semidefinite

= 0, if E is not known to be PD or PSD and no such determination is requested;

= 1, if a determination of definiteness of E is to be performed.

NPRNT = 1, if printout of input is desired

= 0, if it is not desired.

3. Use this section only if IPACK = 0.
   (i) The next set of lines contains the quadratic form matrix $D \equiv G$, columnwise, in free format.
   (ii) The next set of lines contains the quadratic form matrix $E \equiv K$, columnwise, in free format.
   (iii) The next set of lines contains the matrix $A \equiv F$ for problems 1 through 6; $B' \equiv F$ for problem 7, columnwise, in free format.
   (iv) For problems 6 and 7 only. The next set of lines contains the matrix $A \equiv H$, columnwise, in free format.
4. Use this section only if IPACK = 1.

   Use of packed input: The input data in this section are not in free format (not space delimited). For each column, in format 7(2I,F8.4), enter the row index in which the nonzero element occurs, followed by the element. Each column (including zero columns) must have at least one line. For a zero column, at least one row index with a zero should appear. The format 7(2I,F8.4) means that, on each line, the program reads seven fields, each one of 10 columns, where the first 2 columns of a field are reserved for the (right-adjusted) row index and the remaining 8 columns for the value of the coefficients. Within the 8-column field, the decimal point can appear in any column. If the decimal point does not appear explicitly, the program assumes that it will be located in column 6 of the 10-column field. See examples in problem 1 and problem 7.
   (i) The next set of lines contains the nonzero elements of the quadratic form matrix $D \equiv G$, columnwise, in packed form.
   (ii) The next set of lines contains the nonzero elements of the quadratic form $E \equiv K$, columnwise, in packed form.
   (iii) The next set of lines contains the nonzero elements of the matrix $A \equiv F$ for problems 1 through 6; $B' \equiv F$ for problem 7, columnwise, in packed form.
   (iv) For problems 6 and 7 only. The next set of lines contains the nonzero elements of the matrix $A \equiv H$, columnwise, in packed form.
5. The next set of lines contains the ENTIRE cost vector **c** in *free format*.
6. The next set of lines should contain the ENTIRE right-hand-side vector **b** in *free format*.
7. If there is another problem, repeat steps 1 through 6; otherwise, terminate with a blank line as the last line in the data deck.

VI. Output

In general, the output will contain the following information:

1. The first item printed is the title of the problem. The output of each problem starts on a new page;
2. Then comes a statement indicating what type of problem is dealt with;
3. The next statement indicates whether it is a maximization or a minimization (or an equilibrium) problem.
4. The next output is a statement pertaining to the definiteness of the quadratic form matrices D and E, respectively, unless NCHKD and NCHKE were set to a negative integer, in which case no statement is printed.
5. If NPRNT was set equal to 1 the input is then printed in the following order:
   (a) The quadratic form matrix, $D \equiv G$
   (b) The quadratic form matrix, $E \equiv K$
   (c) The matrix, $B' \equiv F$ (rowwise)
   (d) For problems 6 and 7 only: the matrix $A \equiv H$
   (e) The cost vector, $\mathbf{c}$
   (f) The right-hand-side vector, $\mathbf{b}$
   (g) For problems 6 and 7 only: the matrix M
   (h) For problems 6 and 7 only: the $\mathbf{q}$ vector
   (i) The primal solution, $X(j)$, and the number of iterations. (Note: If the problem does not have an optimal solution, the message "problem has no solution" and the "interation no." will be printed.)
   (j) Primal slack variables, $WP(i)$
   (k) Dual solution, $Y(i)$
   (l) Dual slack variables, $WD(j)$

   If the problem is one of those specified by the parameter PROB = 1, or 2, or 3, or 4, further output will be presented in the following format:
   (a) The optimal value of the primal objective function
   (b) The optimal value of the dual objective function (the equality between the values of the primal and of the dual objective functions constitutes a necessary check for the solution to be optimal)
   (c) The $A\mathbf{x}$ vector
   (d) The $A'\mathbf{y}$ vector

(e) The $\mathbf{y}'A\mathbf{x}$ value
(f) The $k_d\mathbf{x}'D\mathbf{x}$ value
(g) The $\mathbf{c} - k_d D\mathbf{x}$ vector for max; the $\mathbf{c} + k_d D\mathbf{x}$ vector for min
(h) The $\mathbf{c} - k_d(D + D')\mathbf{x}$ vector for max; the $\mathbf{c} + k_d(D + D')\mathbf{x}$ vector for min
(i) The $(\mathbf{c} - k_d D\{bfx\})'\mathbf{x}$ value for max; the $(\mathbf{c} + k_d D\mathbf{x})'\mathbf{x}$ value for min; $[\mathbf{c} - k_d(D + D')\mathbf{x}]'\mathbf{x}$ for max; $[\mathbf{c} + k_d(D + D')\mathbf{x}]'\mathbf{x}$ for min
(j) The $k_e\mathbf{y}'E\mathbf{y}$ value
(k) The $\mathbf{b} + k_e E\mathbf{y}$ vector for max; the $\mathbf{b} - k_e E\mathbf{y}$ vecor for min
(l) The $\mathbf{b} + k_e(E + E')\mathbf{y}$ vector for max; the $\mathbf{b} - k_e(E + E')\mathbf{y}$ vector for min
(m) The $(\mathbf{b} + k_e E\mathbf{y})'\mathbf{y}$ value for max; the $(\mathbf{b} - k_e E\mathbf{y})'\mathbf{y}$ value for min; $[\mathbf{b} + k_e(E + E')\mathbf{y}]'\mathbf{y}$ for max; $[\mathbf{b} - k_e(E + E')\mathbf{y}]'\mathbf{y}$ for min

VII. How to Use the Lemke Program

Because the entire program and its subroutines are given in Fortran 77, only the control lines for compiling and executing a Fortran program are needed. The data structure and a sample output for an illustrative problem is given below.

Consider the symmetric quadratic program (problem 1), a maximization:

Objective function

$$(0 \quad 1 \quad 2)\begin{pmatrix} x_1 \\ x_2 \\ x_3 \end{pmatrix} - (1/2)(x_1 \quad x_2 \quad x_3)\begin{bmatrix} 13 & -4 & 3 \\ -4 & 5 & -2 \\ 3 & -2 & 1 \end{bmatrix}\begin{pmatrix} x_1 \\ x_2 \\ x_3 \end{pmatrix}$$

$$- (1/2)(y_1 \quad y_2)\begin{bmatrix} 2 & 1 \\ 1 & 2 \end{bmatrix}\begin{pmatrix} y_1 \\ y_2 \end{pmatrix}$$

subject to $$\begin{bmatrix} 1 & 0 & -2 \\ 3 & 1 & 0 \end{bmatrix}\begin{pmatrix} x_1 \\ x_2 \\ x_3 \end{pmatrix} - \begin{bmatrix} 2 & 1 \\ 1 & 2 \end{bmatrix}\begin{pmatrix} y_1 \\ y_2 \end{pmatrix} \le \begin{pmatrix} 3 \\ -2 \end{pmatrix}$$

and $\quad x_1 \ge 0, x_2 \ge 0, x_3 \ge 0, \quad y_1 \ge 0, y_2 \ge 0.$

Comparing with notation used before,

$$\mathbf{c}' = (0 \quad 1 \quad 2), \qquad \mathbf{b} = \begin{pmatrix} 3 \\ -2 \end{pmatrix}, \qquad k_d = 1/2, \qquad k_e = 1/2,$$

$$D = \begin{bmatrix} 13 & -4 & 3 \\ -4 & 5 & -2 \\ 3 & -2 & 1 \end{bmatrix}, \qquad E = \begin{bmatrix} 2 & 1 \\ 1 & 2 \end{bmatrix}, \qquad A = \begin{bmatrix} 1 & 0 & -2 \\ 3 & 1 & 0 \end{bmatrix}.$$

Notice that the matrix D is positive semidefinite and the matrix E is positive definite. Hence, Lemke's algorithm is guaranteed to find an optimal solution, if one exists.

Example of SQP, Problem 1

INPUT DATA in Free Format
The input lines in the ⟨datafile.dat⟩ file can be typed as shown (here, the option IPACK = 0 was used):

```
Line No.    Typed Data
   1        AN EXAMPLE OF A SQP PROBLEM   - Title
   2        3 2 1 1 .5 .5 0 1 1 1 Parameter Indicators
   3           13.  -4.   3.
   4          - 4.   5.  -2.         D Matrix
   5           3.  -2.   1.
   6            2.  1.
   7            1.  2.                E Matrix
   8            1.  3.
   9            0.  1.                A Matrix
  10          - 2.  0.
  11            0.   1.   2.          COST vector c
  12            3.  -2.               RHS vector b
  13
           BLANK LINE
```

INPUT DATA in Packed Form
The input lines in the ⟨datafile.dat⟩ file can be typed as shown (here, the option IPACK = 1 was used):

```
Line No.    Typed Data (in packed form: Format
               7(2I,F8.4))
   1        AN EXAMPLE OF A SQP PROBLEM   - Title
   2        3 2 1 1 .5 .5 1 1 1 1    Parameter Indicators
```

```
          12345678901234567890123456789 - guide to fields
   3      1   13.   2      -4. 3     3.
   4      1   -4.   2       5. 3    -2.
   5      1    3.   2      -2. 3     1.
   6      1    2.   2       1.
   7      1    1.   2       2.
   8      1    1.   2       3.
   9      2    1.
  10      1   -2.
  11        0.  1.   2.      COST vector c
  12        3. -2.           RHS vector b
  13          BLANK LINE
```

Remember to eliminate the "guide to fields" line after positioning the data in the correct fields.

OUTPUT (obtained in a ⟨datafile.lis⟩ file)

```
AN EXAMPLE OF A SQP PROBLEM

This is a Symmetric QP Problem (D and E Matrices)

This is a MAXIMIZATION problem
D is a positive semidefinite matrix
E is a positive definite matrix

LEMKE's algorithm is guaranteed to find
an optimal solution, if one exists, and
the M matrix is positive semi-definite


Input Parameters
  Full matrix input specified
  kD parameter = 0.50
  kE parameter = 0.50
  NCHKD parameter for D matrix = 1
  NCHKE parameter for E matrix = 1
D Matrix:
   13.0000   -4.0000    3.0000
   -4.0000    5.0000   -2.0000
    3.0000   -2.0000    1.0000
E Matrix:
   2.0000  1.0000
   1.0000  2.0000
```

```
A Matrix :
  1.0000   0.0000  -2.0000
  3.0000   1.0000   0.0000
Cost vector:
  0.0000   1.0000   2.0000

RHS vector:
  3.0000  -2.0000

Primal solution - ITERATION NO. 4
  X( 1) =   0.000000
  X( 2) =   2.666667
  X( 3) =   7.333333
Primal Slacks
  WP( 1) =  20.000002
  WP( 2) =   0.000000
Dual solution
  Y( 1) =   0.000000
  Y( 2) =   2.333333
Dual Slacks
  WD( 1) =  18.333334
  WD( 2) =  -0.000002
  WD( 3) =   0.000000
The primal value of the objective function at the
optimal point is: 6.333334
The dual value of the objective function at the
optimal point is: 6.333333

AX vector:
  -16.666667   2.666667

ATY vector:
  7.000000   2.333333   0.000000

YTAX =       6.222222
(KD)ATDX =       5.555555
C - (KD)DX vector:

  -5.666667   1.666667   1.000000

C - (KD)(D + DT)X vector:

  -11.333333   2.333333  -0.000000

[C - (KD)DX]TX =      11.777778
[C - (KD)(D+DT)X]TX =       6.222223
(KE)YTEY =       5.444444
```

```
B + (KE)EY vector:
  4.166667   0.333333

B + (KE)(E + ET)Y vector:
  5.333333   2.666667

[B + (KE)EY]TY =      0.777778
[B + (KE)(E+ET)Y]TY =      6.222222

COPYRIGHT 1968 BY   A. Ravindran
                    School of Industrial Engineering
                    Purdue University
                    Lafayette, Indiana


Program expanded in 1977, 1986, 1993, and 2007
    by Quirino Paris, Ed Morgan and Kathy Edgington
    Department of Agricultural and Resource Economics
    University of California Davis,
    CA 95616
```

Example of an Equilibrium Problem (with asymmetric D and E matrices), Problem 5

INPUT DATA in Free Format

The input lines in the ⟨datafile.dat⟩ file can be typed as shown (here, the option IPACK = 0 was used):

```
Line No.    Typed Data
   1        A Symmetric Equilibrium Problem with
            Asymmetric D and E Matrices
   2        3 2 5 1 .5 .5 0 1 1 1    Parameter
                                     Indicators
   3        13.  −2.   4.  |
   4        − 6.   5.  −1.  |   D Matrix
   5         2.  −3.   1.  |
   6           2.  0.5  |
   7           1.5  2.  |      E Matrix
   8         1.  3.  |
   9         0.  1.  |         A Matrix
  10        − 2.  0.  |
  11         0.  1.   2.       COST vector c
  12         3.  −2.           RHS vector b
  13        BLANK LINE
```

OUTPUT (obtained in a ⟨datafile.lis⟩ file)

A Symmetric Equilibrium Problem with Asymmetric *D* and
E Matrices

This is an LC Problem (Asymmetric D and E Matrices)

This is an EQUILIBRIUM problem
D is a positive semidefinite matrix
E is a positive definite matrix

LEMKE's algorithm is guaranteed to find
an optimal solution, if one exists, and
the M matrix is positive semi-definite

Input Parameters
  Full matrix input specified
  kD parameter = 0.50
  kE parameter = 0.50
  NCHKD parameter for D matrix = 1
  NCHKE parameter for E matrix = 1

D Matrix:
   13.0000   −6.0000   2.0000
   −2.0000   5.0000   −3.0000
    4.0000   −1.0000   1.0000

E Matrix:
  2.0000 1.5000
  0.5000 2.0000

A Matrix :
  1.0000 0.0000 −2.0000
  3.0000 1.0000   0.0000

Cost vector:
  0.0000 1.0000 2.0000

RHS vector:
  3.0000 −2.0000

Primal solution - ITERATION NO. 4
  $X(\ 1) =$ 0.000000
  $X(\ 2) =$ 2.500000
  $X(\ 3) =$ 6.500000
Primal Slacks
  $WP(\ 1) =$ 19.375000
  $WP(\ 2) =$ 0.000000

```
Dual solution
  Y( 1) =  0.000000
  Y( 2) =  4.500000

Dual Slacks
  WD( 1) =  12.500001
  WD( 2) =   0.000000
  WD( 3) =   0.000000

AX vector:
  -13.00000  2.500000

ATY vector:
  13.500000  4.500000  0.000000

YTAX =      11.249999
(KD)ATDX =     4.250000
C - (KD)DX vector:

  1.000000  4.500000  0.000000

C - (KD)(D + DT)X vector:

  2.000000  8.000000  -2.000000

[C - (KD)DX]TX =       11.250000
[C - (KD)(D+DT)X]TX =      7.000000
(KE)YTEY =      20.250000
B + (KE)EY vector:

  6.375000  2.500000

B + (KE)(E + ET)Y vector:

  9.750000  7.000000

[B + (KE)EY]TY =       11.250000
[B + (KE)(E+ET)Y]TY =      31.500000

COPYRIGHT 1968 BY   A. Ravindran
                School of Industrial Engineering
                Purdue University Lafayette,
                Indiana


Program expanded in 1977, 1986, 1993, and 2007
      by Quirino Paris, Ed Morgan and Kathy Edgington
      Department of Agricultural and Resource Economics
      University of California
      Davis, CA 95616
```

Example of a General LC Problem, Problem 6

INPUT DATA in Free Format
The input lines in the ⟨datafile.dat⟩ file can be typed as shown (here, the option IPACK = 0 was used):

```
Line No.   Typed Data
   1       A General LC problem with G, K, F, H
                                       Matrices
   2       3 2 6 1 1 1 0 1 1 1   Parameter
                                  Indicators
   3       5.  0.  0.  |
   4       0.  3.  0.  |      D ≡ G Matrix
   5       0.  0.  1.  |
   6           2.  1.  |
   7           1.  2.  |      E ≡ K Matrix
   8       −.2   .2   |
   9        .1  −.2   |       F Matrix
  10        .4   .1   |
  11       1.  2.  1.  |
  12       2.  1.  1.  |      H Matrix
  13       1.  1.  1.      COST vector c
  14       -1.   -1.       RHS vector b
  15       BLANK LINE
```

OUTPUT (obtained in a ⟨datafile.lis⟩ file)

A General LC EXAMPLE

This is a General LC Problem (G, K, F and H Matrices)
G is a positive semidefinite matrix
K is a positive definite matrix

LEMKE's algorithm is guaranteed to find
an optimal solution, if one exits, and
the M matrix is positive semi-definite

Notation of the LCP

$$\begin{matrix} z' & M & z & + & z' & q \\ [x \quad y] & \begin{bmatrix} G & H \\ F & K \end{bmatrix} & \begin{bmatrix} x \\ y \end{bmatrix} & + & [x \quad y] & \begin{bmatrix} -COST \\ RHS \end{bmatrix} \end{matrix}$$

```
Input Parameters
  Full matrix input specified
  kG parameter = 1.000000
  kK parameter = 1.000000

G Matrix:
  5.0000  0.0000  0.0000
  0.0000  3.0000  0.0000
  0.0000  0.0000  1.0000

K Matrix:
  2.0000  1.0000
  1.0000  2.0000

F Matrix :
  -0.2000   0.1000  0.4000
   0.2000  -0.2000  0.1000

H Matrix:
  1.0000  2.0000
  2.0000  1.0000
  1.0000  1.0000

Cost vector:
  1.0000  1.0000  1.0000

RHS vector:
  -1.0000  -1.0000

M Matrix:
   5.0000   0.0000  0.0000  1.0000  2.0000
   0.0000   3.0000  0.0000  2.0000  1.0000
   0.0000   0.0000  1.0000  1.0000  1.0000
  -0.2000   0.1000  0.4000  2.0000  1.0000
   0.2000  -0.2000  0.1000  1.0000  2.0000

q vector:
  -1.0000  -1.0000  -1.0000  -1.0000  -1.0000

Solution -- ITERATION NO. 6
  Z( 1) ≡ X( 1) =  0.006019
  Z( 2) ≡ X( 2) =  0.054457
  Z( 3) ≡ X( 3) =  0.397822
  Z( 4) ≡ Y( 1) =  0.234451
  Z( 5) ≡ Y( 2) =  0.367727
```

```
Slacks
   WD ( 1) ≡ U ( 1) =   0.000000
   WD ( 2) ≡ U ( 2) =   0.000000
   WD ( 3) ≡ U ( 3) =   0.000000
   WP ( 1) ≡ V ( 1) =   0.000000
   WP ( 2) ≡ V ( 2) =   0.000000


   Xt(G) X =   0.1673
   Yt(K) Y =   0.5528
   Yt(F) X =   0.0494
   Xt(H) Y =   0.2910
```

```
COPYRIGHT 1968 BY   A. Ravindran
                    School of Industrial Engineering
                    Purdue University
                    Lafayette, Indiana

Program expanded in 1977, 1986, 1993, and 2007
        by Quirino Paris, Ed Morgan and Kathy Edgington
        Department of Agricultural and Resource Economics
        University of California
        Davis, CA 95616
```

Example of a Bimatrix Game, Problem 7

INPUT DATA in Free Format
The input lines in the ⟨datafile.dat⟩ file can be typed as shown (here, the option IPACK = 0 was used):

```
Line No.   Typed Data
    1      A Bimatrix Game with F, H Matrices.
           Null G and K
    2      3  2  7  0  1  1  0  1  1  1
                                Parameter Indicators
    3      0.  0.  0.   |
    4      0.  0.  0.   |        D ≡ G Matrix
    5      0.  0.  0.   |
    6          0.  0.   |        E ≡ K Matrix
    7          0.  0.   |
```

```
 8          3.  2.
 9          1.  2.                    F ≡ B' Matrix
10          4.  1.
11            1.  3.  2.
12            4.  1.  2.              H ≡ A Matrix
13          1.   1.   1.              COST vector c
14          -1.     -1.               RHS vector b
15          BLANK LINE
```

INPUT DATA in Packed Form

The input lines in the ⟨datafile.dat⟩ file can be typed as shown (here,
the option IPACK = 1 was used):

```
Line No.    Typed Data (in packed form: Format
            7(2I,F8.4))
   1          A Bimatrix Game with F, H Matrices.
              Null G and K
   2          3  2  7  0  1  1  1  1  1  1
                                   Parameter Indicators
   3          1    0.
   4          1    0.
   5          1    0.
   6          1    0.
   7          1    0.
   8          1    3.  2    2.
   9          1    1.  2    2.
  10          1    4.  2    1.
              12345678901234567890123456789 0 - guide
                                        to fields
  11          1    1.  2    3.  3    2.
  12          1    4.  2    1.  3    2.
  13          1.   1.   1.          COST vector c
  14          -1.     -1.           RHS vector b
  15          BLANK LINE
```
Remember to eliminate the ''guide to fields'' line
after positioning the data in the correct fields.

OUTPUT (obtained in a ⟨datafile.lis⟩ file)

```
A Bimatrix Game with F, H Matrices.  Null G and K

LEMKE's algorithm is guaranteed to find a solution.
```

Notation of the LCP

$$
\begin{array}{ccccc}
z' & M & z & + & z' & q
\end{array}
$$

$$
[x \quad y]
\begin{bmatrix}
0 & H \\
F & 0
\end{bmatrix}
\begin{bmatrix}
x \\
y
\end{bmatrix}
+
[x \quad y]
\begin{bmatrix}
-COST \\
RHS
\end{bmatrix}
$$

Input Parameters
  Full matrix input specified

G Matrix:
  0.0000   0.0000   0.0000
  0.0000   0.0000   0.0000
  0.0000   0.0000   0.0000

K Matrix:
  0.0000   0.0000
  0.0000   0.0000

F Matrix:
  3.0000   1.0000   4.0000
  2.0000   2.0000   1.0000

H Matrix:
  1.0000   4.0000
  3.0000   1.0000
  2.0000   2.0000

Cost vector = e(n):
  1.0000   1.0000   1.0000

RHS vector = -e(m):
  −1.0000   −1.0000

M Matrix:
  0.0000   0.0000   0.0000   1.0000   4.0000
  0.0000   0.0000   0.0000   3.0000   1.0000
  0.0000   0.0000   0.0000   2.0000   2.0000
  3.0000   1.0000   4.0000   0.0000   0.0000
  2.0000   2.0000   1.0000   0.0000   0.0000

q vector:

  −1.0000   −1.0000   −1.0000   −1.0000   −1.0000

```
Solution -- ITERATION NO. 5
   Z( 1) ≡ X( 1) =   0.000000
   Z( 2) ≡ X( 2) =   0.428571
   Z( 3) ≡ X( 3) =   0.142857
   Z( 4) ≡ Y( 1) =   0.250000
   Z( 5) ≡ Y( 2) =   0.250000

Slacks
   WD( 1) ≡ V( 1) =   0.250000
   WD( 2) ≡ V( 2) =   0.000000
   WD( 3) ≡ V( 3) =   0.000000
   WP( 1) ≡ U( 1) =   0.000000
   WP( 2) ≡ U( 2) =   0.000000

SOLUTION OF BIMATRIX GAME

   EXPECTED PAYOFF FOR PLAYER 1, PHI1   =   2.0000

   MIXED STRATEGY (MS) FOR PLAYER 1

                  MSX( 1)   =   0.0000
                  MSX( 2)   =   0.7500
                  MSX( 3)   =   0.2500

   EXPECTED PAYOFF FOR PLAYER 2, PHI2   =   1.7500

   MIXED STRATEGY (MS) FOR PLAYER 2

                  MSY( 1)   =   0.5000
                  MSY( 2)   =   0.5000


COPYRIGHT 1968 BY   A. Ravindran
                School of Industrial Engineering
                Purdue University
                Lafayette, Indiana

Program expanded in 1977, 1986, 1993, and 2007
     by Quirino Paris, Ed Morgan and Kathy Edgington
     Department of Agricultural and Resource Economics
     University of California
     Davis, CA 95616
```

A Bimatrix Game with Negative Payoffs, Problem 7

Sometime, a payoff matrix may contain negative elements. Lemke and Howson have shown that the addition of a constant matrix to ensure that all the payoff elements are positive does not influence the solution (mixed strategies) of the game. Lemke's complementary pivot algorithm is based on the assumption that all the payoff coefficients are positive. Hence, if the original payoff matrices contain negative elements, the Lemke program will add a suitable constant factor to all the original coefficients to ensure the positivity of all the payoff elements.

INPUT DATA in Free Format
The input lines in the ⟨datafile.dat⟩ file can be typed as shown (here, the option IPACK = 0 was used):

```
Line No.    Typed Data
   1        A Bimatrix Game with Negative Payoffs
   2        5  4  7  0  1  1  0  1  1  1 Parameter
                                         Indicators
   3        0. 0. 0. 0.  0.     ⎤
   4        0. 0. 0. 0.  0.     ⎥
   5        0. 0. 0. 0.  0.     ⎥    D ≡ G Matrix
   6        0. 0. 0. 0.  0.     ⎥
   7        0. 0. 0. 0.  0.     ⎦
   8           0. 0. 0. 0.      ⎤
   9           0. 0. 0. 0.      ⎥    E ≡ K Matrix
  10           0. 0. 0. 0.      ⎥
  11           0. 0. 0. 0.      ⎦
  12           3. .8  .5  10    ⎤
  13           1.  2  .3  .6    ⎥
  14           .4 .1   2  .8    ⎥    F ≡ B' Matrix
  15           .6  5  12  .3    ⎥
  16            2 .3  −1   2    ⎦
  17            .4 .1  1   2  .5   ⎤
  18            .7 −2  1.  .3  .4  ⎥    H ≡ A Matrix
  19            .5  3  2.  .4  .4  ⎥
  20             1  1 .3   2  1.   ⎦
  21        1.  1.  1.  1.  1.      COST vector c
  22        −1.  −1.  −1.  −1.      RHS vector b
  23        BLANK LINE
```

OUTPUT (obtained in a ⟨datafile.lis⟩ file)
A Bimatrix Game with Negative Payoffs.   Null G and K matrices.

```
LEMKE's algorithm is guaranteed to find a solution.

Notation of the LCP
```

$$
\begin{array}{cccccc}
z' & M & z & + & z' & q
\end{array}
$$

$$
\begin{bmatrix} x & y \end{bmatrix} \begin{bmatrix} 0 & H \\ F & 0 \end{bmatrix} \begin{bmatrix} x \\ y \end{bmatrix} + \begin{bmatrix} x & y \end{bmatrix} \begin{bmatrix} -COST \\ RHS \end{bmatrix}
$$

```
Input Parameters
  Full matrix input specified

G Matrix:
  0.0000  0.0000  0.0000  0.0000  0.0000
  0.0000  0.0000  0.0000  0.0000  0.0000
  0.0000  0.0000  0.0000  0.0000  0.0000
  0.0000  0.0000  0.0000  0.0000  0.0000
  0.0000  0.0000  0.0000  0.0000  0.0000

K Matrix:
  0.0000  0.0000  0.0000  0.0000
  0.0000  0.0000  0.0000  0.0000
  0.0000  0.0000  0.0000  0.0000
  0.0000  0.0000  0.0000  0.0000

F Matrix :
   3.0000  1.0000  0.4000   0.6000   2.0000
   0.8000  2.0000  0.1000   5.0000   0.3000
   0.5000  0.3000  2.0000  12.0000  -1.0000
  10.0000  0.6000  0.8000   0.3000   2.0000

H Matrix:
  0.4000   0.7000  0.5000  1.0000
  0.1000  -2.0000  3.0000  1.0000
  1.0000   1.0000  2.0000  0.3000
  2.0000   0.3000  0.4000  2.0000
  0.5000   0.4000  0.4000  1.0000

Cost vector = e(n):
  1.0000  1.0000  1.0000  1.0000  1.0000

RHS vector = -e(m):
  -1.0000  -1.0000  -1.0000  -1.0000

Adjusted F matrix, F* = F + KF, KF = 2.00
```

Adjusted H matrix, $H^* = H + KH, KH = 3.00$

Comment not included in the output file: Every element of the original payoff matrix $F \equiv B'$ was augmented by a constant factor of 2.00. Every element of the original payoff matrix $H \equiv A$ was augmented by a constant factor of 3.00.

M Matrix (The first 5 columns are followed by the last 4 columns):

0.0000	0.0000	0.0000	0.0000	0.0000
0.0000	0.0000	0.0000	0.0000	0.0000
0.0000	0.0000	0.0000	0.0000	0.0000
0.0000	0.0000	0.0000	0.0000	0.0000
0.0000	0.0000	0.0000	0.0000	0.0000
5.0000	3.0000	2.4000	2.6000	4.0000
2.8000	4.0000	2.1000	7.0000	2.3000
2.5000	2.3000	4.0000	14.0000	1.0000
12.0000	2.6000	2.8000	2.3000	4.0000

3.4000	3.7000	3.5000	4.0000
3.1000	1.0000	6.0000	4.0000
4.0000	4.0000	5.0000	3.3000
5.0000	3.3000	3.4000	5.0000
3.5000	3.4000	3.4000	4.0000
0.0000	0.0000	0.0000	0.0000
0.0000	0.0000	0.0000	0.0000
0.0000	0.0000	0.0000	0.0000
0.0000	0.0000	0.0000	0.0000

q vector:

-1.0000	-1.0000	-1.0000	-1.0000	-1.0000
-1.0000	-1.0000	-1.0000	-1.0000	

Solution - ITERATION NO. 9

$Z(\ 1) \equiv X(\ 1) = \ 0.000000$
$Z(\ 2) \equiv X(\ 2) = \ 0.059661$
$Z(\ 3) \equiv X(\ 3) = \ 0.000000$
$Z(\ 4) \equiv X(\ 4) = \ 0.048533$
$Z(\ 5) \equiv X(\ 5) = \ 0.183313$
$Z(\ 6) \equiv Y(\ 1) = \ 0.000000$
$Z(\ 7) \equiv Y(\ 2) = \ 0.144124$
$Z(\ 8) \equiv Y(\ 3) = \ 0.133038$
$Z(\ 9) \equiv Y(\ 4) = \ 0.014412$

```
Slacks
  WD( 1) ≡ V( 1) =   0.056541
  WD( 2) ≡ V( 2) =   0.000000
  WD( 3) ≡ V( 3) =   0.289246
  WD( 4) ≡ V( 4) =   0.000000
  WD( 5) ≡ V( 5) =   0.000000

  WP( 1) ≡ U( 1) =   0.038424
  WP( 2) ≡ U( 2) =   0.000000
  WP( 3) ≡ U( 3) =   0.000000
  WP( 4) ≡ U( 4) =   0.000000

SOLUTION OF BIMATRIX GAME

  EXPECTED PAYOFF FOR PLAYER 1, PHI1  =   0.429658

  MIXED STRATEGY (MS) FOR PLAYER 1

                MSX( 1) = 0.000000
                MSX( 2 = 0.204666
                MSX( 3 = 0.000000
                MSX( 4 = 0.166490
                MSX( 5 = 0.628844

  EXPECTED PAYOFF FOR PLAYER 2, PHI2  =   1.430440

  MIXED STRATEGY (MS) FOR PLAYER 2

                MSY( 1 = 0.000000
                MSY( 2 = 0.494297
                MSY( 2 = 0.456274
                MSY( 2 = 0.049430

COPYRIGHT 1968 BY   A. Ravindran
                School of Industrial Engineering
                Purdue University
                Lafayette, Indiana

Program expanded in 1977, 1986, 1993, and 2007
      by Quirino Paris, Ed Morgan and Kathy Edgington
      Department of Agricultural and Resource Economics
      University of California
      Davis, CA 95616
```

References

Lemke, C. E. (1968). "On Complementary Pivot Theory." In Dantzig, G. B., and Veinott, A. F. Jr., editors, *Mathematics of Decision Sciences*, Part I (Providence, RI: American Mathematical Society).

Lemke, C. E., and Howson, J. T. (1964). "Equilibrium Points of Bimatrix Games," *Journal of the Society of Industrial and Applied Mathematics*, 12, 413–23.

Ravindran, A. (1968). A Complementary Pivot Method for Solving Quadratic Programming Problems. SHARE Library Program, 360D–15.3.2003.

17

Lemke Fortran 77 Program

This chapter presents a list of subroutines for a Fortran 77 computer program that solves the Linear Complementarity Problem in its generality. It accompanies the User Manual of Chapter 16 that deals with the Lemke Complementary Pivot Algorithm. This program is an extension of the SHARE Library Fortran Program N.360D-15.3.003 originally written by A. Ravindran. It is published with the permission of Professor Ravindran and the SHARE Inc. SHARE endorses neither the authors of this extension nor the use of the extension. The source program can be readily compiled using the appropriate compiler.

The program is a self-contained application and is composed of a series of subroutines that address the various specifications of the Linear Complementarity Problem.

ReadMe

README File for Lemke7
Lemke7 consists of a Fortran program, lemke.f, and several subroutines:
 COMMON.FOR, initia.f, initia7.f, lemke.f, matprnt.f, matrd.f, matrix.f, newbas.f, newbas7.f, opnfil.f, pinput.f, pinput6.f, pivot.f, pprint.f, pprint5.f, pprint6.f, pprint7.f, scalam.f, sort.f, symval.f, vecprnt.f.

To compile (OS dependent) and create the executable, lem7.exe, cd to the subdirectory that contains the above files and type:

```
f77 -o lem7.exe *.f
```

You may find it useful to create a script that will prompt for input files and run Lemke7, for example:

```
#!/bin/csh -f
# Script to run Lemke7
#
echo " "
echo "                    Lemke7                          "
echo "    Checking for positivity of all elements
            of F and H        "
echo "Lemke's Algorithm for the Linear
      Complementarity Problem "
echo "---------------------------------------- "
echo " "
echo "Enter the name of your input file"
set infile=$<
#
   if (-e $infile) then # 'if the input file exists'
       set basename=$infile:r
       set outfile=$basename.lis
#
       echo " "
       echo "Input file: $infile"
       echo "Output file: $outfile"
       cp $infile fort.1
#
     if (-e $outfile) then # 'if the file exists'
       echo -n "Do you want to save a backup copy of
       $basename.lis?
            (y/n, default=n)? "
       set answer=$<
         if ($answer == 'y') then
       cp $outfile "$outfile.bak"
       echo "A copy of $outfile has been saved in
       $outfile.bak."
         endif
     endif
#
#
       /usr/local/lemke7/lem7.exe
#
       cp fort.11 $outfile
       rm fort.1
```

```
        rm -rf fort.10
        rm fort.11
  #
        echo "Lemke run finished"
        else
        echo "Input file does not exist, please try
        again"
   endif
------------
```

Attention: Fortran language requires indentation to column 7 for command lines, with symbol for continuation lines in column 6. The following pages do not respect these requirements.

COMMON.FOR Subroutine

```
C------------------------------------------------------
C        COMMON.FOR
C------------------------------------------------------
C This FORTRAN program solves the Linear
C Complementarity Problem
C (LCP) of Lemke in its generality.
C It was initially written by A. Ravindran
C who, however, used the LCP
C to solve only Asymmetric Quadratic
C Programming (AQP) problems.
C It was revised and extended by Quirino
C Paris, Ed Morgan, and Kathy
C Edgington in 1977, 1980, 1993, and 2007,
C to deal with the full linear
C complementarity problem including
C two-person non-zero sum games.
C------------------------------------------------------
C
      PARAMETER (MATSIZ = 75)
C
C Common definitions for LEMKE
C
C Common CTRL — Control variables
C
C     IPACK .... Type of matrix read
C        0 — Matrices are inputed in their entirety.
C        1 — Matrices are inputed in sparse notation
```

```
C                    (non-zero elements only).
C
C     IPRINT .... FORTRAN logical unit for printer file.
C
C     IPRNT .... Flag for output
C        0 — Suppress output of input data.
C        1 — Print input data.
C
C     IREAD .... FORTRAN logical unit for data.
C
C     MAX .... Flag for max or min problem type
C        0 — Minimize
C        1 — Maximize
C
C     N .... Problem size (NVAR + NCON)
C
C     NCHKD .... Control test if D is positive
C                     definite or positive semidefinite.
C            -1 — If D is already known to be positive
C                     definite or positive semidefinite.
C             0 — No determination is required.
C             1 — Determine if D is positive definite
C                     or positive semidefinite.
C
C     NCHKE .... Control test if E is positive definite
C                     or positive semidefinite.
C            -1 — If E is already known to be positive
C                     definite or positive semidefinite.
C             0 — No determination is required.
C             1 — Determine if E is positive definite
C                     or positive semidefinite.
C
C     NCON .... Number of constraints.
C
C     NVAR .... Number of primal (decision) variables.
C
C     NQP1 .... Used for loading arrays (NVAR + 1)
C
C     PROB .... Problem type (1 - 7).
C
C     START .... Time at beginning of program,
C     after file opens.
C
```

```
C     N2 .... Twice N
C
C     ITMAX .... Max Iter to avoid infinite loop =
C     5*(NVAR+NCON)
C
C
      INTEGER IPACK, IPRINT, IPRNT, IREAD, MAX, N,
     1 NCHKD, NCHKE, NCON, NVAR, NQP1, PROB,
     2 N2, ITMAX
      REAL START
      COMMON /CTRL/ IPACK, IPRINT, IPRNT, IREAD, MAX,
     1 N, NCHKD, NCHKE, NCON, NVAR, NQP1, PROB,
     2 START, N2, ITMAX
C
C   Common INPUT — Data as input
C
C     XKD .... Scale factor for D matrix
C
C     XKE .... Scale factor for E matrix
C
C     B1 .... Right hand side vector
C
C     C1 .... Cost vector
C
C     D .... Quadratic form matrix D
C
C     E .... Quadratic form matrix E
C
C     F .... For problem types 1 - 5 it is the -A
C            constraint matrix. For problems 6 and 7 it
C            is simply the F matrix.
C
C     H .... For problem types 1 - 5 it is the At
C            (t = transpose) constraint matrix. For
C            problems 6 and 7 it is simply the H matrix.
C
C     G .... For problem types 1 - 5 it is the D matrix.
C            For problems 6 and 7 it is simply the
C            G matrix.
C
C     K .... For problem types 1 - 5 it is the E matrix.
C            For problems 6 and 7 it is simply the
C            K matrix.
```

```
C
C    KF .... For adjusting F Matrix if negative values
C
C    KH .... For adjusting H Matrix if negative values
C
C    IDUP .... Flag for duplicate input values, Problem
C    Type 7
C    IDUPF .... Col & duplicate rows for F Matrix, Prob
C    Type 7
C    IDUPH .... Col & duplicate rows for H Matrix, Prob
C    Type 7
C
     REAL B1, C1, D, E, F, H, XKD, XKE, KF, KH, FF, HH
     COMMON /INPUT/ XKD, XKE, B1(MATSIZ), C1(MATSIZ),
    1 D(MATSIZ, MATSIZ), E(MATSIZ, MATSIZ),
    2 F(MATSIZ, MATSIZ), H(MATSIZ, MATSIZ),
    3 FF(MATSIZ, MATSIZ), HH(MATSIZ, MATSIZ),
    4 KF, KH, IDUP, IDUPF(3), IDUPH(3)
C
C  Common COMP — Computational variables
C
C    AM .... The composite matrix used by LEMKE's
C algorithm
C
C         + -     - +           + -     -+
C         | D   At |           | G    H |
C         | - A  E |    OR      | F    K |
C         + -     - +           + -     -+
C
C    Q .... The vector containing the cost and RHS.
C
C    AA .... Working matrix
C
C    CC .... Working matrix
C
C    BB .... Working matrix
C
C    B .... Working matrix
C
C    MBASIS .... A singly subscripted array for the
C               basic
C       variables. Two indicators are used for each
C       basic variable. One for whether it is a W
```

```
C          or Z, the other for what component of W or Z.
C
C     W,Z .... Vectors to represent LCP unknown
C               variables
C
C     L1 .... Iteration count.
C
C     IZR .... Used in INITIA, and PPRINTx
C
        REAL AM, Q, AA, CC, BB, B, A, W, X, Y, Z
        INTEGER MBASIS,IR,NL1,NL2,NE1,NE2,L1,IZR,EIR
        COMMON /COMP/ AM(MATSIZ, MATSIZ), Q(MATSIZ),
       1 AA(MATSIZ, MATSIZ), CC(MATSIZ), BB(MATSIZ),
       2 B(MATSIZ, MATSIZ), MBASIS(MATSIZ*2),
       3 A(MATSIZ), W(MATSIZ), X(MATSIZ), Y(MATSIZ),
       4 Z(MATSIZ), IR, NL1, NE1, NL2, NE2, L1, IZR, EIR
```

initia.f Subroutine

```
  SUBROUTINE INITIA
C
C  PURPOSE - TO FIND THE INITIAL ALMOST COMPLEMENTARY
C  SOLUTION BY ADDING AN ARTIFICIAL VARIABLE Z0.
C  FOR LCP WITH PSD M MATRIX
C
  INCLUDE 'COMMON.FOR'
C
C  SET Z0 EQUAL TO THE MOST NEGATIVE Q(I)
C
  I=1
  J=2
100  IF (Q(I) .LE. Q(J)) GO TO 110
  I=J
110 J=J+1
  IF (J .LE. N) GO TO 100
C
C  UPDATE Q VECTOR
C
  IR=I
  T1 = -(Q(IR))
  IF (T1 .LE. 0.0) GO TO 140
  DO 120 I=1,N
```

```
  Q(I)=Q(I)+T1
120  CONTINUE
  Q(IR)=T1
C
C  UPDATE BASIS INVERSE AND INDICATOR VECTOR OF BASIC
C  VARIABLES.
C
  DO 130 J=1,N
     B(J,IR) = -1.0
     W(J)=Q(J)
     Z(J)=0.0
     MBASIS(J)=1
     L=N+J
     MBASIS(L)=J
130  CONTINUE
C
  IZR=IR
  NL1=1
  L=N+IR
  NL2=IR
  MBASIS(IR)=3
  MBASIS(L)=0
  W(IR)=0.0
  Z0=Q(IR)
  L1=1
  RETURN
C
140  WRITE (IPRINT, 160)
  IR=1000
  RETURN
C
160  FORMAT (5X, 'Problem has a trivial solution
     with X = 0.0')
  END
```

initia7.f Subroutine

```
  SUBROUTINE INITIA7
C
C  PURPOSE - TO FIND AN INITIAL ALMOST COMPLEMENTARY
C  SOLUTION FOR 2-PERSON NON-ZERO-SUM GAMES BY
C  INCLUDING Z(1) VARIABLE AT STARTING POINT,
C  Z(1)W(1) ≠ 0
```

```
C
C  INITIA7 REQUIRES TWO BASIS UPDATES.
C  THERE IS NO Z0 VARIABLE
C
   INCLUDE 'COMMON.FOR'
   REAL AMAX, TOL
C
   IR = 0
   L = 0
   NL1 = 0
   NL2 = 0
   EIR = 0
C
C  DEFINE W(J), Z(J), A(J)
C
   DO 10 J=1,N
       W(J) = 0.0
       Z(J) = 0.0
       A(J) = AM(J,1)
       MBASIS(J) = 1
       L= N+J
       MBASIS(L) = J
10    CONTINUE
C
C  INSERT Z(1) INTO BASIS, THAT IS, FIND
C  A PIVOT ELEMENT IN
C  A(I). SIMILAR TO SUBROUTINE SORT
C
   AMAX = ABS(A(1))
   DO 20 I = 2, N
       IF(AMAX .LT. ABS(A(I))) AMAX = ABS(A(I))
20    CONTINUE
C
   TOL = AMAX*2.0**(-21)
C
   I = 1
40 IF (A(I) .GT. TOL) GO TO 60
   I = I + 1
   IF(I .GT. N) GO TO 140
   GO TO 40
60 T1 = -Q(I)/A(I)
   IR = I
80 I = I + 1
   IF (I .GT. N) GO TO 120
```

```
   IF (A(I) .GT. TOL) GO TO 100
   GO TO 80
100 T2 = -Q(I)/A(I)
    IF (T2 .LE. T1) GO TO 80
    IR = I
    T1 = T2
    GO TO 80
120   CONTINUE
C
C  IF ALL THE COMPONENTS OF A(I) ARE LESS THAN
C  TOLERANCE THERE IS NO SOLUTION
C
140   CONTINUE
C
   DO 90 I = 1,N
90 B(IR,I) = -B(IR,I)/A(IR)
     Q(IR) = -Q(IR)/A(IR)
   DO 115 I = 1,N
     IF (I .EQ. IR) GO TO 115
     Q(I) = Q(I) + Q(IR)*A(I)
   DO 125 J = 1,N
     B(I,J) = B(I,J) + B(IR,J)*A(I)
125   CONTINUE
115   CONTINUE
C
C UPDATE INDICATORS
C
  NL1 = MBASIS(IR)
  L = N + IR
  NL2 = MBASIS(L)
  MBASIS(1) = 31
  MBASIS(IR) = 32
  MBASIS(L) = 1
  EIR = IR
C
  NE1 = 2
  NE2 = NL2
C
  L1 = 1
C
C   SECOND STEP, REPEAT
C
  DO 225 I = 1,N
     A(I) = AM(I,NE2)
```

```
225  CONTINUE
C
  I = 1
240  IF(A(I) .GT. TOL) GO TO 260
  I = I + 1
  IF (I .GT. N) GO TO 220
  GO TO 240
260  T1 = -Q(I)/A(I)
  IR = I
280 I = I + 1
  IF (I .GT. N) GO TO 220
  IF (A(I) .GT. TOL) GO TO 200
  GO TO 280
200  T2 = -Q(I)/A(I)
  IF (T2 .LE. T1) GO TO 280
  IR = I
  T1 = T2
  GO TO 280
220  CONTINUE
C
C  IF ALL THE COMPONENTS OF A(I) ARE LESS THAN
C  TOLERANCE THERE IS NO SOLUTION
C
    DO 190 I = 1,N
      B(IR,I) = -B(IR,I)/A(IR)
190 CONTINUE
    Q(IR) = -Q(IR)/A(IR)
    DO 315 I = 1,N
      IF (I .EQ. IR) GO TO 315
      Q(I) = Q(I) + Q(IR)*A(I)
      DO 325 J = 1,N
        B(I,J) = B(I,J) + B(IR,J)*A(I)
325   CONTINUE
315 CONTINUE
C
C UPDATE INDICATORS
C
  NL1 = MBASIS(IR)
  L = N + IR
  NL2 = MBASIS(L)
  MBASIS(IR) = NE1
  MBASIS(L) = NE2
  IZR = IR
```

```
  W(IR) = 0
C
  L1 = L1 + 1
C
  IF (NL1 .EQ. 31) GO TO 500
  RETURN
C
500 CONTINUE
    MBASIS(EIR) = 2
    CALL PPRINT7
    IR=1000
    RETURN
    END
```

lemke.f Main

```
  PROGRAM LEMKE
C
C  LEMKE LCP PROGRAM (MODIFIED FROM SHARE PROGRAM
C  LIBRARY as originally developed by A. Ravindran).
C
C  This program uses Lemke's algorithm to solve the
C  symmetric QP
C  problem (SQP)... either max ctx - (kd)xtdx -
C  (ke)ytey subject to
C  ax - (ke)(e+et)y ≤ b or min ctx +
C  (kd)xtdx + (ke)ytey
C  subject to ax + (ke)(e+et)y ≥ b.
C  This program also solves all the asymmetric QP
C  cases implied in
C  the above formulation and derived by simply setting
C  either the
C  D or the E matrix equal to the null matrix. When
C  both the D and
C  the E matrices are null matrices, the above
C  specification
C  collapses into an LP problem. This program solves
C  also the two-
C  person non-zero sum game of Lemke.
C
    INCLUDE 'COMMON.FOR'
    CHARACTER TITLE*80
C
```

```
C   Problem titles
C   (Subscripted by PROB)
C
    CHARACTER*60 PRBNAM(7)
    DATA PRBNAM /
 &  'This is a Symmetric QP Problem (D=G & E=K
      Matrices)',
 &  'This is an Asymmetric QP Problem (D=G Matrix
      only)',
 &  'This is an Asymmetric QP Problem (E=K Matrix
      only)',
 &  'This is a LP Problem (No D=G or E=K Matrices) ',
 &  'This is a LC Problem (Asymmetric D=G and E=K
      Matrices)',
 &  'This is a General LC Problem (G, K, F, and
      H Matrices)',
 &  '2-Person Non-Zero-Sum Game (F and H Matrices)'/
C
C   OPNFIL opens the input and output files
C
   IREAD = 1
   IPRINT = 11
   CALL OPNFIL (IREAD, IPRINT)
C
20 CONTINUE
C
C READ IN THE TITLE FOR THE PROBLEM
C IF THE TITLE CARD IS A BLANK CARD, THEN STOP
C
    READ (IREAD, 180,END=120) TITLE
    IF (TITLE .EQ. ' ') GOTO 120
C
    WRITE (IPRINT,200) TITLE
C
C   Read parameters and problem type
C
     READ (IREAD, *, END=120) NVAR,NCON,PROB,MAX,XKD,
  & XKE,IPACK,NCHKD, NCHKE, IPRNT
C
   IF ((PROB .GE. 1) .AND. (PROB .LE. 7)) GOTO 60
C
C   Problem.type out of range
C
```

```
  WRITE (IPRINT, 140) PROB
  GOTO 120
C
C  Print problem type
C
60   CONTINUE
  WRITE (IPRINT, 160) PRBNAM(PROB)
C
C  Set maximum Iteration for the problem to avoid
C  infinite loop
  ITMAX = 5*(NVAR+NCON)
C
  IF (PROB .LT. 6) THEN
        IF (MAX .EQ. 0) WRITE(IPRINT, 220)
        IF (MAX .EQ. 1) WRITE(IPRINT, 240)
  END IF
  N = NVAR + NCON
  N2 = N * 2
C
C  Matrix reads the input matrices and sets up the
C  problem.
C  All info is passed in the various commons
C
  CALL MATRIX
C
C  If IPRNT = 1 then echo input parameters
C
  IF (IPRNT .EQ. 1) THEN
        IF (PROB .LT. 6) THEN
          CALL PINPUT
        ELSE
          CALL PINPUT6
        END IF
  END IF
C
  IF (IDUP .GT. 0) THEN DO
        WRITE(IPRINT,990)
        IF (IDUPF(1) .GT. 0) THEN
          WRITE(IPRINT,991) (IDUPF(I), I=1,3)
        ENDIF
        IF (IDUPH(1) .GT. 0) THEN
          WRITE(IPRINT,992) (IDUPH(I), I=1,3)
        ENDIF
```

```
      GOTO 120
      ENDIF
C
      IF (PROB .EQ. 7) THEN
          CALL INITIA7
      ELSE
          CALL INITIA
      ENDIF
C
C  Since for any problem, termination can occur in
C  INITIA, NEWBAS or
C  SORT subroutine, the value of IR is matched with
C  1000 to check
C  whether to continue or go on to next problem. IR is
C  elsewhere
C  used to denote the pivot row at each operation.
C
      IF (IR .EQ. 1000) GO TO 20
100   CONTINUE
C
      IF (PROB .EQ. 7) THEN
          CALL NEWBAS7
      ELSE
          CALL NEWBAS
      ENDIF
C
      IF (IR .EQ. 1000) GO TO 20
C
      CALL SORT
C
      IF (IR .EQ. 1000) GO TO 20
C
      CALL PIVOT
C
      GO TO 100
C
C  End of program
C
120   CONTINUE
      WRITE (IPRINT, 260)
C
C  Close files
C
```

```
   CLOSE (IPRINT)
   CLOSE (IREAD)
C
140  FORMAT(//,' Fatal error: Problem number', I5,
   &       ' is out of range.')
160  FORMAT (/, A60)
180  FORMAT (A80)
200  FORMAT (/, A80)
220  FORMAT (/, 'Minimization')
240  FORMAT (/, 'Maximization')
260  FORMAT (/,5X, 'COPYRIGHT 1968 BY', T29,
   & 'A. Ravindran',
   & /, 28X, 'School of Industrial Engineering',
   & /, 28X, 'Purdue University',
   & /, 28X, 'Lafayette, Indiana',
   & //,5X, 'Program expanded in 1977, 1986, 1993,
   & and 2007',/
   & 28X, 'by Quirino Paris, Ed Morgan, and Kathy
   & Edgington',/
   & 28X, 'Department of Agricultural and Resource
   & Economics'/,
   & 28X, 'University of California'/,
   & 28X, 'Davis, CA. 95616')
990  FORMAT (' Ties (duplicate values in columns of
   & the M matrix)',/
   & ' may cause cycling of the algorithm. Break
   & ties by',/
   & ' adding a small positive number to one of
   & the duplicate',/
   & ' values'/)
991  FORMAT (
   1 ' — Duplicate values found in F Matrix', /,
   2 ' — Col =',I4, ', Rows =',I4, ' and', I4,/,
   3 ' — Please adjust one of the values, check
   & for other',/,
   4 ' — duplicates, and resubmit'/)
992  FORMAT (
   1 ' — Duplicate values found in H Matrix', /,
   2 ' — Col =',I4, ', Rows =',I4, ' and', I4,/,
   3 ' — Please adjust one of the values, check
   & for other',/,
   4 ' — duplicates, and resubmit'/)
     END
```

matprnt.f Subroutine

```fortran
      SUBROUTINE MATPRNT (UNIT, MATRIX, SIZE, COL, ROW)
      INTEGER UNIT, SIZE, COL, ROW
      REAL MATRIX(SIZE, SIZE)
C
C  Prints any 2 dim. real array. Prints up to
C  5 columns across.
C
      INTEGER I, I_END, J_START
C
      J_START = 1
100   CONTINUE
      J_END = MIN(J_START + 4, COL)
      DO 200, I = 1, ROW
       WRITE (UNIT,'(2X,5(f12.4))') (MATRIX(I,J),
     & J=J_START,J_END)
200   CONTINUE
       WRITE (UNIT, '(A1)') ' '
       J_START = J_START + 5
       IF (J_START .LE. COL) GOTO 100
C
500   CONTINUE
      RETURN
      END
```

matrd.f Subroutine

```fortran
      SUBROUTINE MATRD (NREAD, IPACK, AM, ISIZ, IEND, JEND)
C
C  PURPOSE - TO READ IN THE VARIOUS INPUT DATA
C  Read column-wise
C
       INTEGER NREAD, IPACK, ISIZ, IEND, JEND
       REAL AM(ISIZ, ISIZ)
       INTEGER I, J, K(7)
       REAL TEMP(7)
C
C  NREAD — FORTRAN logical unit number
C  IPACK — Switch for format of input
C  AM — MATRIX to hold data
C  ISIZ — Size of Matrix AM (assumed to be square
C  ISIZ by ISIZ)
```

```
C  IEND — Ending I value
C  JEND — Ending J value
C
   IF (IPACK .GE. 1) GOTO 200
C
C  NB — FREE FORMAT READ
C
   DO 100, I = 1, JEND
       READ (NREAD, *) (AM(J, I), J=1, IEND)
100  CONTINUE
   RETURN
C
C  Read packed format
C
470  FORMAT (7(I2, F8.4))
200  CONTINUE
     DO 600, I = 1, JEND
300  CONTINUE
     DO 400, J = 1, 7
       K(J) = 0
       TEMP(J) = 0.0
400  CONTINUE
     READ (NREAD, 470) (K(J), TEMP(J), J=1, 7)
     DO 500, J = 1, 7
      IF (K(J) .LT. 1) GOTO 600
      KT = K(J)
      AM(KT, I) = TEMP(J)
500  CONTINUE
     GOTO 300
600  CONTINUE
     RETURN
     END
```

matrix.f Subroutine

```
   SUBROUTINE MATRIX
C
C  PURPOSE - TO INITIALIZE AND READ IN THE VARIOUS
C  INPUT DATA
C
   INCLUDE 'COMMON.FOR'
C
C  Local storage
```

```
C   DD .... Used to pass D to SYMVAL
C   EE .... Used to pass E to SYMVAL
C   EV .... Used to return the Eigenvalues
C   PDD .... Flag for SYMVAL test
C   PDE .... Flag for SYMVAL test
C   PD .... Flag for SYMVAL test
C
    REAL MR, MIN
    REAL DD(MATSIZ, MATSIZ), EE(MATSIZ, MATSIZ)
    REAL EV(MATSIZ), MINF(MATSIZ), MINH(MATSIZ)
    INTEGER PDD, PDE, PD
    DIMENSION MR(MATSIZ,MATSIZ), MIN(MATSIZ)
C
C   ACC is distance from zero for Min Eigenvalue to
C   still be considered zero
C
    ACC = 3.0E-4
    NQP1 = NVAR + 1
C
C   Initialize PDD, PDE, and PD
C
    PDD = 0.0
    PDE = 0.0
    PD = 0.0
C
C   Initialize IDUP (flag for duplicates in Problem
C   Type 7)
    IDUP = 0.0
C
C   Initialize Flags and MINF and MINH for Problem
C   type 7
C
    KF = 0.0
    KH = 0.0
    DO 15 J = 1,N
       MINF(J) = 0
       MINH(J) = 0
15     CONTINUE
C
C   Main switch is PROB — Problem type 1-7
C   each problem type a little bit differently
C
    GOTO (100, 200, 300, 400, 500, 600, 670) PROB
```

```
C
C  Problem type 1 — Symmetric QP (D & E Matrices)
C
100  CONTINUE
  GOTO 700
C
C  Problem type 2
C
200  CONTINUE
  NCHKE = 1
  PDE = 1
  GOTO 700
C
C  Problem type 3
C
300  CONTINUE
  NCHKD = 1
  PDD = 1
  GOTO 700
C
C  Problem type 4
C
400  CONTINUE
  NCHKD = 1
  NCHKE = 1
  PDD = 1
  PDE = 1
  GOTO 700
C
C  Problem type 5 — LCP (Asymmetric D & E)
C
500  CONTINUE
  GOTO 700
C
C  Problem type 6
C
600  CONTINUE
  GOTO 700
C
C  Problem type 7
C
670  CONTINUE
700  CONTINUE
```

```
C
C  Zero out AM matrix
   DO 710, I = 1, N
   DO 710, J = 1, N
      AM(I, J) = 0.0
710  CONTINUE
C
C  Read the matrices differently for each problem
C
   GOTO (1000, 2000, 3000, 4000, 5000, 6000, 6700) PROB
C
C  Problem type 1
C
1000 CONTINUE
C  Read D Matrix
     CALL MATRD(IREAD, IPACK, D, MATSIZ, NVAR, NVAR)
C  Read E Matrix
     CALL MATRD(IREAD, IPACK, E, MATSIZ, NCON, NCON)
C  Read Constraint Matrix
     CALL MATRD(IREAD, IPACK, F, MATSIZ,NCON, NVAR)
C
C  Setup AM matrix from various pieces
C  AM(1 to nvar, 1 to nvar) <-- (D + Dt)
     DO 1010, J = 1, NVAR
     DO 1010, I = 1, NVAR
        AM(I, J) = D(I, J) + D(J, I)
1010 CONTINUE
C  AM(ncon to ncon+nvar, ncon to ncon+nvar)
C  <-- (E + Et)
     DO 1030, J = 1, NCON
     DO 1030, I = 1, NCON
        AM(I + NVAR, J + NVAR) = E(I, J) + E(J, I)
1030 CONTINUE
C  AM(ncon to ncon+nvar, 1 to nvar) <-- (At)
C  AM(1 to ncon, nvar to nvar+ncon) <--  -(A)
     DO 1050, I = 1, NCON
     DO 1050, J = 1, NVAR
      AM(NVAR + I, J) = -(F(I, J))
      AM(J, NVAR + I) = F(I, J)
1050 CONTINUE
C  DD is used by SYMVAL
     DO 1060, I = 1, NVAR
     DO 1060, J = I, NVAR
```

```
        DD(I, J) = AM(I, J) * 0.5
        DD(J, I) = DD(I, J)
1060 CONTINUE
C   EE is used by SYMVAL
    DO 1070, I = NQP1, N
    DO 1070, J = I, N
        EE(I - NVAR, J - NVAR) = AM(I, J) * 0.5
        EE(J - NVAR, I - NVAR) = EE(I - NVAR, J - NVAR)
1070 CONTINUE
C
C   Scale AM
C
   IF (XKD .NE. 1.0) CALL SCALAM(XKD, 1, NVAR, 1, NVAR)
   IF (XKE .NE. 1.0) CALL SCALAM(XKE, NQP1, N, NQP1, N)
   GOTO 7000
C
C   Problem type 2
C
2000  CONTINUE
C   Read D Matrix
    CALL MATRD(IREAD, IPACK, D, MATSIZ, NVAR, NVAR)
C   Read Constraint Matrix
    CALL MATRD(IREAD, IPACK, F, MATSIZ, NCON, NVAR)
C
C   Setup AM matrix from various pieces
C   AM(1 to nvar, 1 to nvar) <-- (D + Dt)
    DO 2010, J = 1, NVAR
    DO 2010, I = 1, NVAR
     AM(I, J) = D(I, J) + D(J, I)
2010 CONTINUE
C   AM(ncon to ncon+nvar, 1 to nvar) <-- (At)
C   AM(1 to ncon, nvar to nvar+ncon) <--  -(A)
    DO 2050, I = 1, NCON
    DO 2050, J = 1, NVAR
       AM(NVAR + I, J) = -(F(I, J))
       AM(J, NVAR + I) = F(I, J)
2050 CONTINUE
C   DD is used by SYMVAL
    DO 2060, I = 1, NVAR
    DO 2060, J = I, NVAR
       DD(I, J) = AM(I, J) * 0.5
       DD(J, I) = DD(I, J)
2060 CONTINUE
```

```
C
C  Scale AM
C
   IF (XKD .NE. 1.0) CALL SCALAM(XKD, 1, NVAR, 1, NVAR)
   GOTO 7000
C
C Problem type 3
C
3000 CONTINUE
C  Read E Matrix
   CALL MATRD(IREAD, IPACK, E, MATSIZ, NCON, NCON)
C  Read Constraint Matrix
   CALL MATRD(IREAD, IPACK, F, MATSIZ, NCON, NVAR)
C
C  Setup AM matrix from various pieces
C  AM(ncon to ncon+nvar, ncon to ncon+nvar)
     <-- (E + Et)
   DO 3010, J = 1, NCON
   DO 3010, I = 1, NCON
      AM(I + NVAR, J + NVAR) = E(I, J) + E(J, I)
3010 CONTINUE
C  AM(ncon to ncon+nvar, 1 to nvar) <-- (At)
C  AM(1 to ncon, nvar to nvar+ncon) <--  -(A)
   DO 3030, I = 1, NCON
   DO 3030, J = 1, NVAR
     AM(NVAR + I, J) = -(F(I, J))
     AM(J, NVAR + I) = F(I, J)
3030 CONTINUE
C  EE is used by SYMVAL
   DO 3040, I = NQP1, N
   DO 3040, J = I, N
     EE(I - NVAR, J - NVAR) = AM(I, J) * 0.5
     EE(J - NVAR, I - NVAR) = EE(I - NVAR, J - NVAR)
3040 CONTINUE
C
C  Scale AM
C
   IF (XKE .NE. 1.0) CALL SCALAM(XKE, NQP1, N, NQP1, N)
   GOTO 7000
C
C  Problem type 4
C
4000 CONTINUE
```

```
C  Read Constraint Matrix
   CALL MATRD(IREAD, IPACK, F, MATSIZ, NCON, NVAR)
C
C  Setup AM matrix from various pieces
C  AM(ncon to ncon+nvar, 1 to nvar) <-- (At)
C  AM(1 to ncon, nvar to nvar+ncon) <--  -(A)
   DO 4010, I = 1, NCON
   DO 4010, J = 1, NVAR
      AM(NVAR + I, J) = -(F(I, J))
      AM(J, NVAR + I) = F(I, J)
4010 CONTINUE
  GOTO 7000
C
C  Problem type 5
C
5000 CONTINUE
C  Read D Matrix
   CALL MATRD(IREAD, IPACK, D, MATSIZ, NVAR, NVAR)
C  Read E Matrix
   CALL MATRD(IREAD, IPACK, E, MATSIZ, NCON, NCON)
C  Read Constraint Matrix
   CALL MATRD(IREAD, IPACK, F, MATSIZ, NCON, NVAR)
C
C  Setup AM matrix from various pieces
C  AM(1 to nvar, 1 to nvar) <-- (D)
   DO 5010, J = 1, NVAR
   DO 5010, I = 1, NVAR
      AM(I, J) = D(I, J)
5010 CONTINUE
C  AM(ncon to ncon+nvar, ncon to ncon+nvar) <-- (E)
   DO 5020, J = 1, NCON
   DO 5020, I = 1, NCON
      AM(I + NVAR, J + NVAR) = E(I, J)
5020 CONTINUE
C  AM(ncon to ncon+nvar, 1 to nvar) <-- (At)
C  AM(1 to ncon, nvar to nvar+ncon) <--  -(A)
   DO 5030, I = 1, NCON
   DO 5030, J = 1, NVAR
      AM(NVAR + I, J) = -(F(I, J))
      AM(J, NVAR + I) = F(I, J)
5030 CONTINUE
C
C  DD needs to be symmetrical for SYMVAL
```

```
C
   DO 5060, I = 1, NVAR
   DO 5060, J = 1, NVAR
   DD(I, J) = (D(I, J) + D(J, I)) / 2.0
5060 CONTINUE
C
C  EE needs to be symmetrical for SYMVAL
C
   DO 5070, I = NQP1, N
   DO 5070, J = I, N
      EE(I - NVAR, J - NVAR) = AM(I, J)
      EE(J - NVAR, I - NVAR) = EE(I - NVAR, J - NVAR)
      EE(I, J) = (E(I, J) + E(J, I)) / 2.0
5070 CONTINUE
C
C  Scale AM
C
  IF (XKD .NE. 1.0) CALL SCALAM(XKD, 1, NVAR, 1, NVAR)
  IF (XKE .NE. 1.0) CALL SCALAM(XKE, NQP1, N, NQP1, N)
  GOTO 7000
C
C  Problem type 6
C
6000 CONTINUE
C  Read D Matrix
   CALL MATRD(IREAD, IPACK, D, MATSIZ, NVAR, NVAR)
C Read E Matrix
   CALL MATRD(IREAD, IPACK, E, MATSIZ, NCON, NCON)
C  Read Constraint Matrix
   CALL MATRD(IREAD, IPACK, F, MATSIZ, NCON, NVAR)
C  Read second Constraint Matrix
   CALL MATRD(IREAD, IPACK, H, MATSIZ, NVAR, NCON)
C
C  Setup AM matrix from various pieces
C  AM(1 to nvar, 1 to nvar) <-- (D)
   DO 6010, J = 1, NVAR
   DO 6010, I = 1, NVAR
    AM(I, J) = D(I, J)
6010 CONTINUE
C  AM(ncon to ncon+nvar, ncon to ncon+nvar) <-- (E)
   DO 6020, J = 1, NCON
   DO 6020, I = 1, NCON
      AM(I + NVAR, J + NVAR) = E(I, J)
```

```
6020 CONTINUE
C
C  Copy to AM for computations
    DO 6030, I = 1, NCON
    DO 6030, J = 1, NVAR
       AM(NVAR + I, J) = F(I, J)
       AM(J, NVAR + I) = H(J, I)
6030 CONTINUE
C
C  DD needs to be symmetrical for SYMVAL
    DO 6060, I = 1, NVAR
    DO 6060, J = 1, NVAR
       DD(I, J) = (D(I, J) + D(J, I)) / 2.0
6060 CONTINUE
C
C  EE needs to be symmetrical for SYMVAL
    DO 6070, I = 1, NCON
    DO 6070, J = I, NCON
       EE(I, J) = (E(I, J) + E(J, I)) / 2.0
6070 CONTINUE
C
C  Scale AM
C
   IF (XKD .NE. 1.0) CALL SCALAM(XKD, 1, NVAR, 1, NVAR)
   IF (XKE .NE. 1.0) CALL SCALAM(XKE, NQP1, N, NQP1, N)
   GOTO 7000
C
C  Problem type 7
C
6700 CONTINUE
C  Read D Matrix
   CALL MATRD(IREAD, IPACK, D, MATSIZ, NVAR, NVAR)
C  Read E Matrix
   CALL MATRD(IREAD, IPACK, E, MATSIZ, NCON, NCON)
C  Read Constraint Matrix
   CALL MATRD(IREAD, IPACK, F, MATSIZ, NCON, NVAR)
C  Read second Constraint Matrix
   CALL MATRD(IREAD, IPACK, H, MATSIZ, NVAR, NCON)
C
C  Setup AM matrix from various pieces
C  AM(1 to nvar, 1 to nvar) <-- (D)
    DO 6710, J = 1, NVAR
    DO 6710, I = 1, NVAR
```

```
       AM(I, J) = D(I, J)
6710 CONTINUE
C  AM(ncon to ncon+nvar, ncon to ncon+nvar) <-- (E)
     DO 6720, J = 1, NCON
     DO 6720, I = 1, NCON
        AM(I + NVAR, J + NVAR) = E(I, J)
6720 CONTINUE
C
C  Check for duplicates in the rows. If you find
C  duplicates,
C  add .00001 to each one (for testing, add .0001)
     DO 13 I = 1, NVAR
     DO 12 J = 1, NCON
      DO 12 JJ = 1,J
      IF (JJ .NE. J) THEN
       IF (F(J,I) .EQ. F(JJ,I)) THEN
         IDUP = 1
         IDUPF(1) = I
         IDUPF(2) = JJ
         IDUPF(3) = J
         GOTO 14
       END IF
      END IF
12    CONTINUE
13    CONTINUE
14    CONTINUE
C
   DO 23 I = 1, NCON
   DO 22 J = 1, NVAR
     DO 22 JJ = 1,J
     IF (JJ .NE. J) THEN
       IF (H(J,I) .EQ. H(JJ,I)) THEN
         IDUP = 1
         IDUPH(1) = I
         IDUPH(2) = JJ
         IDUPH(3)= J
         GOTO 24
       END IF
      END IF
22    CONTINUE
23    CONTINUE
24    CONTINUE
C
```

```
C   CHECK THE POSITIVITY OF ALL THE ELEMENTS OF THE F
C   AND H MATRICES. FIND MINIMUM IN EACH COLUMN, THEN,
C   FIND MINIMUM IN THE VECTOR OF MINIMA
C   IF MIN-MIN IS NEGATIVE, ADD AN EQUIVALENT +
C   1 FACTOR
C   TO ALL ELEMENTS OF THE MATRICES
C
      DO 20 I = 1, NCON
      DO 20 J = 1, NVAR
         FF(I,J) = F(I,J)
         HH(J,I) = H(J,I)
20    CONTINUE
C
C   FIND MINIMUM OF F(I,K) FOR FIXED K
C
      DO 30 K = 1, NVAR
         I = 1
         J = 2
102   IF (F(I,K) .LE. F(J,K)) GO TO 103
      I = J
103   J = J + 1
      IF (J .LE. NCON) GO TO 102
         IR = I
         MINF(K) = F(IR,K)
30    CONTINUE
C
C   FIND MINIMUM OF MINF(K)
C
      I = 1
      J = 2
101   IF (MINF(I) .LE. MINF(J)) GO TO 111
      I = J
111   J = J + 1
      IF (J .LE. NVAR) GO TO 101
      IR = I
      IF (MINF(IR) .GT. 0) GO TO 129
C
C   ADJUST F(I,J)
C
      KF = -MINF(IR) + 1
      DO 116 I = 1, NCON
      DO 116 J = 1, NVAR
         F(I,J) = F(I,J) - MINF(IR) + 1
```

```
116  CONTINUE
C
129  CONTINUE
C
C  FIND MIN FOR H(J,K) FOR FIXED K
C
     DO 40 K = 1, NCON
       I = 1
       J = 2
122    IF (H(I,K) .LE. H(J,K)) GO TO 123
       I = J
123    J = J + 1
       IF (J .LE. NVAR) GO TO 122
       IR = I
       MINH(K) = H(IR,K)
40     CONTINUE
C
C  FIND MINIMUM OF MINH(K)
C
     I = 1
     J = 2
131  IF (MINH(I) .LE. MINH(J)) GO TO 135
     I = J
135 J = J + 1
     IF (J .LE. NCON) GO TO 131
     IR = I
     IF (MINH(IR) .GT. 0) GO TO 139
C
C ADJUST H(I,J)
C
     KH = -MINH(IR) + 1
     DO 118 I = 1, NCON
       DO 118 J = 1, NVAR
        H(J,I) = H(J,I) - MINH(IR) + 1
118  CONTINUE
C
139  CONTINUE
C------------------------------------------------------
C
C  Copy to AM for computations
C
     DO 6730, I = 1, NCON
     DO 6730, J = 1, NVAR
```

```
      AM(NVAR + I, J) = F(I, J)
      AM(J, NVAR + I) = H(J, I)
6730 CONTINUE
C
C  DD needs to be symmetrical for SYMVAL
C
   DO 6760, I = 1, NVAR
   DO 6760, J = 1, NVAR
      DD(I, J) = (D(I, J) + D(J, I)) / 2.0
6760 CONTINUE
C
C  EE needs to be symmetrical for SYMVAL
C
   DO 6770, I = 1, NCON
   DO 6770, J = I, NCON
      EE(I, J) = (E(I, J) + E(J, I)) / 2.0
6770 CONTINUE
C
C Scale AM
C
  IF (XKD .NE. 1.0) CALL SCALAM(XKD, 1, NVAR, 1, NVAR)
  IF (XKE .NE. 1.0) CALL SCALAM(XKE, NQP1, N, NQP1, N)
  GOTO 7000
C
7000 CONTINUE
C
C  Read the cost vector
C
   READ (IREAD, *) (Q(I), I = 1, NVAR)
   DO 7060, I = 1, NVAR
      C1(I) = Q(I)
7060 CONTINUE
C
C  Read the right hand side vector
C
   READ (IREAD, *) (Q(I), I = NQP1, N)
   DO 7070, I = NQP1, N
      B1(I - NVAR) = Q(I)
      Q(I) = -1.0 * Q(I)
7070 CONTINUE
C
   DO 7080, I = 1, N
      Q(I) = -1.0 * Q(I)
```

```
7080 CONTINUE
C
C  If requested, then we check that D and E are at
C  least
C  semi-positive definite.
C  If no D matrix then we can't check it.
C
    IF ((PROB .EQ. 3) .OR. (PROB .EQ. 4)) GOTO 7500
    IF (NCHKD .LT. 0) THEN
      PDD = 1
      GOTO 7500
    END IF
C
C  The names of the matrices D & E have been changed
C  to G & K for printing
C
    IF (NCHKD .EQ. 0) THEN
      WRITE (IPRINT, 7100) 'G'
      GOTO 7500
    END IF
C
    7100 FORMAT (/,
 1 'WARNING: ', /,
 2 'With no check on the positive (semi)
 & definiteness of ',
 3 A1, /,
 4 'there is no guarantee that any solution found is
 & optimal',
 5 /)
C
C  Skip to label 7500 if problem type 7 (print
C  statements not needed)
    IF (PROB .EQ. 7) GO TO 7500
C
C  Actually check it out
    NCHKD = 1
    CALL SYMVAL(MATSIZ, NVAR, DD, EV)
    IF (EV(1) .LT. -ACC) THEN
      WRITE (IPRINT, 7110) 'G'
    ELSE
      PDD = 1
      IF (EV(1) .GT. ACC) THEN
       WRITE (IPRINT, 7120) 'G'
```

```
      ELSE
        WRITE (IPRINT, 7130) 'G'
        END IF
      END IF
C
7110 FORMAT (A1, ' is neither positive definite
   & nor positive ', 'semidefinite matrix ')
7120 FORMAT (A1, ' is a positive definite matrix ')
7130 FORMAT (A1, ' is a positive semidefinite matrix')
C
C  Next section is for E matrices
C
7500 CONTINUE
C
C  If no E matrix then we can't check it. .
C
      IF ((PROB .EQ. 2) .OR. (PROB .EQ. 4)) GOTO 7800
      IF (NCHKE .LT. 0) THEN
        PDE = 1
        GOTO 7800
      END IF
      IF (NCHKE .EQ. 0) THEN
        WRITE (IPRINT, 7100) 'K'
        GOTO 7800
      END IF
C
C  Skip to label 7800 if problem type 7 (print
C  statements not needed)
      IF (PROB .EQ. 7) GO TO 7800
C
C  Actually check it out
      NCHKE = 1
      CALL SYMVAL(MATSIZ, NCON, EE, EV)
      IF (EV(1) .LT. -ACC) THEN
        WRITE (IPRINT, 7110) 'K'
      ELSE
        PDE = 1
        IF (EV(1) .GT. ACC) THEN
         WRITE (IPRINT, 7120) 'K'
        ELSE
          WRITE (IPRINT, 7130) 'K'
        END IF
      END IF
```

```
C
7800 CONTINUE
C
C  The results of the checks on both D and E
C
   PD = PDD + PDE
C
   IF (PROB .EQ. 7) THEN
      WRITE (IPRINT, 7825)
      GO TO 7830
   END IF
C
   IF (PD .EQ. 2) THEN
      WRITE (IPRINT, 7810)
   ELSE
      WRITE (IPRINT, 7820)
   END IF
C
7810 FORMAT (/,
  1 'LEMKE'S Algorithm is guaranteed to find ', /,
  2 'an optimal solution, if one exists, and ',/,
  3 'the M matrix is positive semi-definite. ')
7820 FORMAT (/,
  1 'LEMKE'S Algorithm is NOT guaranteed to find ', /,
  2 'an optimal solution, if one exists. ')
7825 FORMAT (/,
  1 'LEMKE'S Algorithm is guaranteed to find a
  2 solution.')
7830 CONTINUE
C
C  In Iteration 1; Basis inverse is an identity matrix
C
8000 CONTINUE
   DO 8110, I = NQP1, N
   DO 8110, J = 1, NVAR
      AA(I - NVAR, J) = AM(I, J)
8110 CONTINUE
   DO 8120, I = 1, N
      CC(I) = Q(I)
8120 CONTINUE
   DO 8130, I = NQP1, N
      BB(I - NVAR) = Q(I)
8130 CONTINUE
```

```
      DO 8140, J = 1, N
      DO 8140, I = 1, N
         IF (I .EQ. J) THEN
           B(I, J) = 1.0
         ELSE
           B(I, J) = 0.0
         END IF
8140 CONTINUE
      END
```

newbas.f Subroutine

```
  SUBROUTINE NEWBAS
C
C  PURPOSE - TO FIND THE NEW BASIS COLUMN TO ENTER IN
C  TERMS OF THE CURRENT BASIS.
C
   INCLUDE 'COMMON.FOR'
C
C  IF NL1 IS NEITHER 1 NOR 2 THEN THE VARIABLE Z0
C  LEAVES
C  THE BASIS INDICATING TERMINATION WITH
C  A COMPLEMENTARY SOLUTION
C
   IF (NL1 .EQ. 1) GO TO 100
   IF (NL1 .EQ. 2) GO TO 130
   IF (PROB .EQ. 5) THEN
     CALL PPRINT5
   ELSE
     IF (PROB .EQ. 6) THEN
      CALL PPRINT6
     ELSE
      CALL PPRINT
     END IF
   END IF
   IR = 1000
   RETURN
C
100 CONTINUE
   NE1 = 2
   NE2 = NL2
C
C  UPDATE NEW BASIC COLUMN BY MULTIPLYING
```

```
C  BY BASIS INVERSE.
C
    DO 120 I=1,N
      T1 = 0.0
      DO 110 J=1,N
       T1=T1-B(I,J)*AM(J,NE2)
110   CONTINUE
      A(I) = T1
120  CONTINUE
    RETURN
C
130  NE1= 1
    NE2=NL2
    DO 140 I= 1, N
      A(I)=B(I,NE2)
140  CONTINUE
    RETURN
C
C  Formats
C
200  FORMAT (A)
220  FORMAT (A, I3)
    END
```

newbas7.f Subroutine

```
  SUBROUTINE NEWBAS7
C
C  PURPOSE - TO FIND THE NEW BASIS COLUMN TO ENTER IN
C  TERMS OF THE CURRENT BASIS
C  FOR 2-PERSON NON-ZERO SUM GAMES
C
  INCLUDE 'COMMON.FOR'
C
C  IF NL1 IS NEITHER 1 OR 2 THEN IT MUST BE EITHER
C  31 OR 32
C
    IF (NL1 .EQ. 32) GO TO 150
    IF (NL1 .EQ. 31) GO TO 160
    IF (NL1 .EQ. 1) GO TO 100
    IF (NL1 .EQ. 2) GO TO 130
C
    CALL PPRINT7
```

```
      IR=1000
      RETURN
C
150 MBASIS(1) = 1
      CALL PPRINT7
      IR=1000
      RETURN
C
160 MBASIS(EIR) = 2
      CALL PPRINT7
      IR=1000
      RETURN
C
100 CONTINUE
      NE1 = 2
      NE2 = NL2
C
C UPDATE NEW BASIC COLUMN BY MULTIPLYING BY BASIS
C INVERSE
C
      DO 120 I = 1,N
         T1 = 0.0
         DO 110 J = 1,N
110        T1 = T1 - B(I,J)*AM(J,NE2)
         A(I) = T1
120 CONTINUE
      RETURN
C
130 CONTINUE
      NE1 = 1
      NE2 = NL2
      DO 140 I = 1,N
         A(I) = B(I,NE2)
140 CONTINUE
      RETURN
      END
```

opnfil.f Subroutine

```
   SUBROUTINE OPNFIL (IREAD, IPRINT)
C
C   This routine gets the input and output file
C   names, and
```

```
C  opens them on units IREAD, and IPRINT respectively.
C
      INTEGER IREAD, IPRINT
      OPEN (UNIT=IREAD, STATUS = 'OLD')
      OPEN (UNIT=IPRINT)
      END
```

pinput.f Subroutine

```
      SUBROUTINE PINPUT
C
C  This displays the inputs to LEMKE.
C
      INCLUDE 'COMMON.FOR'
      WRITE (IPRINT, 100)
C
      IF (IPACK .EQ. 1) THEN
        WRITE (IPRINT, 120)
      ELSE
        WRITE (IPRINT, 140)
      END IF
C
      IF (PROB .EQ. 4) GOTO 155
C
      WRITE (IPRINT, 145) (XKD), (XKE)
      WRITE (IPRINT, 147) NCHKD, NCHKE
C
      IF (NCHKD .EQ. -1) THEN
        WRITE (IPRINT, 260) 'D'
      ELSE IF (NCHKD .EQ. 0) THEN
        WRITE (IPRINT, 280) 'D'
      ELSE IF (NCHKD .EQ. 1) THEN
        WRITE (IPRINT, 300) 'D'
      END IF
C
      IF (NCHKE .EQ. -1) THEN
        WRITE (IPRINT, 260) 'E'
      ELSE IF (NCHKE .EQ. 0) THEN
        WRITE (IPRINT, 280) 'E'
      ELSE IF (NCHKE .EQ. 1) THEN
        WRITE (IPRINT, 300) 'E'
      END IF
C
```

```
155 CONTINUE
C
    WRITE (IPRINT, *)
    WRITE (IPRINT, 160) 'D'
    CALL MATPRNT (IPRINT, D, MATSIZ, NVAR, NVAR)
C
    WRITE (IPRINT, 160) 'E'
    CALL MATPRNT (IPRINT, E, MATSIZ, NCON, NCON)
C
    WRITE (IPRINT, 200)
    CALL MATPRNT (IPRINT, F, MATSIZ, NVAR, NCON)
C
    WRITE (IPRINT, 220)
    CALL VECPRNT (IPRINT, C1, MATSIZ, NVAR)
C
    WRITE (IPRINT, 240)
    CALL VECPRNT (IPRINT, B1, MATSIZ, NCON)
C
    WRITE (IPRINT, 160) 'M'
    CALL MATPRNT (IPRINT, AM, MATSIZ, N, N)
C
    WRITE (IPRINT, 250)
    CALL VECPRNT (IPRINT, Q, MATSIZ, N)
C
100  FORMAT (//, 'Input Parameters')
120  FORMAT (5X, 'Packed input specified')
140  FORMAT (5X, 'Full matrix input specified')
145  FORMAT (5X, 'kD parameter = ', F14.6, /
    1 5X, 'kE parameter = ', F14.6)
147  FORMAT (5X, 'Check requested on D matrix ', I5, /
    1 5x, 'Check requested on E matrix ', I5)
160  FORMAT (A1, ' Matrix: ')
200  FORMAT ('Constraint Matrix: ')
220  FORMAT ('Cost vector: ')
240  FORMAT ('RHS vector: ')
250  FORMAT ('q vector: ')
260  FORMAT (5X, A1, ' is already known to be positive
    & definite or',
    1 ' positive semidefinite. ')
280  FORMAT (5X, A1, ' is not known to be positive
    & definite or',
    1 ' positive semidefinite',/
    2 10x, 'and no such determination is requested for
```

```
     & this',
     3 ' problem.')
300  FORMAT (5X,'A determination of the definiteness
     & of ', A1,
     1 ' was requested. ')
     END
```

pinput6.f Subroutine

```
  SUBROUTINE PINPUT6
C
C  This displays the inputs to LEMKE for problems 6
C  and 7.
C
   INCLUDE 'COMMON.FOR'
C
   WRITE(IPRINT,12) ' '
   WRITE(IPRINT,10)
   WRITE(IPRINT,12) ' z'' M z z'' q '
   WRITE(IPRINT,12) '+ − −+ + − −+ + − −+ + − −+
   1   + − −+'
C
   IF (PROB .EQ. 7) THEN
   WRITE(IPRINT,12) '| x   y | | 0   H | | x |+
   1  | x   y | | − e(n) |'
   WRITE(IPRINT,12) '+ − −+|       | |       |+ − −
   1  +|      | = 0'
   WRITE(IPRINT,12) ' | F     0 | | y |    | − e(m) |'
   ELSE
   WRITE(IPRINT,12) '| x   y | | G   H | | x |  +
   1  | x   y | |− COST |'
   WRITE(IPRINT,12) '+ − −+|   | | |   + − −+|   |'
   WRITE(IPRINT,12) ' | F   K | | y |   | RHS |'
   ENDIF
C
   WRITE(IPRINT,12) ' + − −++ − −+    + − −+'
   WRITE(IPRINT,12) ' '
C
   WRITE (IPRINT, 100)
C
   IF (IPACK .EQ. 1) THEN
     WRITE (IPRINT, 120)
   ELSE
```

```
      WRITE (IPRINT, 140)
   ENDIF
C
   IF (PROB .NE. 7) THEN
      WRITE (IPRINT, 145) (XKD), (XKE)
   ENDIF
C
   WRITE (IPRINT, *)
   WRITE (IPRINT, 160) 'G'
   CALL MATPRNT (IPRINT, D, MATSIZ, NVAR, NVAR)
C
   WRITE (IPRINT, 160) 'K'
   CALL MATPRNT (IPRINT, E, MATSIZ, NCON, NCON)
C
   WRITE (IPRINT, 160) 'F'
   IF (KF .GT. 0) THEN
      CALL MATPRNT (IPRINT, FF, MATSIZ, NVAR, NCON)
   ELSE
      CALL MATPRNT (IPRINT, F, MATSIZ, NVAR, NCON)
   END IF
C
   WRITE (IPRINT, 160) 'H'
   IF (KH .GT. 0) THEN
      CALL MATPRNT (IPRINT, HH, MATSIZ, NCON, NVAR)
   ELSE
      CALL MATPRNT (IPRINT, H, MATSIZ, NCON, NVAR)
   END IF
C
   WRITE (IPRINT, 220)
   CALL VECPRNT (IPRINT, C1, MATSIZ, NVAR)
C
   WRITE (IPRINT, 240)
   CALL VECPRNT (IPRINT, B1, MATSIZ, NCON)
C
   IF (IDUP .GT. 0) THEN
      IR=1000
      RETURN
   END IF
C
C IF M MATRIX HAS BEEN ADJUSTED:
C
   IF (KF .GT. 0) THEN
      WRITE (IPRINT, 162) KF
   END IF
```

```
      IF (KH .GT. 0) THEN
        WRITE (IPRINT, 163) KH
      ENDIF
C
      WRITE (IPRINT, 160) 'M'
      CALL MATPRNT (IPRINT, AM, MATSIZ, N, N)
C
      WRITE (IPRINT, 250)
      CALL VECPRNT (IPRINT, Q, MATSIZ, N)
C
100   FORMAT ('Input Parameters')
120   FORMAT (5X, 'Packed input specified')
140   FORMAT (5X, 'Full matrix input specified')
145   FORMAT (5X, 'kG parameter = ', E12.4, /
     1 5X, 'kK parameter = ', E12.4)
160   FORMAT (A1, '  Matrix: ')
162   FORMAT ('ADJUSTED F MATRIX, F* = F+KF,
     1 KF =', F6.2)
163   FORMAT ('ADJUSTED H MATRIX, H* = H+KH,
     1 KH =', F6.2)
220   FORMAT ('Cost vector = e(n): ')
240   FORMAT ('RHS vector = -e(m): ')
250   FORMAT ('q vector: ')
260   FORMAT (5X, A1, '  is already known to be
     2 positive definite or',
     1 'positive semidefinite.')
280   FORMAT (5X, A1, '  is not known to be positive
     2 definite or',
     1 'positive semidefinite and no such
     3 determination',
     2 'is required for this problem,')
300   FORMAT (5X, 'A determination of the definiteness
     2 of ', A1,
     1 ' was requested.')
10    FORMAT ('Notation of the LCP: ' /)
12    FORMAT (10X, A)
      END
```

pivot.f Subroutine

```
  SUBROUTINE PIVOT
C
C PURPOSE - TO PERFORM THE PIVOT OPERATION BY
```

```
C UPDATING THE INVERSE OF THE BASIS AND Q VECTOR.
C
    INCLUDE 'COMMON.FOR'
C
    DO 100 I=1,N
      B(IR,I)=B(IR,I)/A(IR)
100 CONTINUE
    Q(IR)=Q(IR)/A(IR)
    DO 120 I=1,N
      IF (I .EQ. IR) GO TO 120
      Q(I)=Q(I)-Q(IR)*A(I)
      DO 110 J=1,N
      B(I,J)=B(I,J)-B(IR,J)*A(I)
110 CONTINUE
120 CONTINUE
C
C   UPDATE THE INDICATOR VECTOR OF BASIC VARIABLES
C
    NL1=MBASIS(IR)
    L=N+IR
    NL2=MBASIS(L)
    MBASIS(IR)=NE1
    MBASIS(L)=NE2
    L1=L1+1
C
    RETURN
    END
```

pprint.f Subroutine

```
  SUBROUTINE PPRINT
C
C PURPOSE - TO PRINT THE CURRENT SOLUTION TO THE
C LP/QP
C THE LAGRANGE MULTIPLIERS, THE OBJECTIVE FUNCTION
C VALUE, AND THE ITERATION NUMBER
C
    INCLUDE 'COMMON.FOR'
C
C Local Storage
C
    INTEGER IW
    DIMENSION AX(MATSIZ), WP(MATSIZ), AY(MATSIZ),
```

```
   1 EEY(MATSIZ),A1X(MATSIZ),A1Y(MATSIZ),EY(MATSIZ),
C
   2 DDX(MATSIZ),DX(MATSIZ),CDX(MATSIZ),BEEY(MATSIZ),
C
   3 CDDX(MATSIZ), BEY(MATSIZ), WD(MATSIZ)
C
     DO 20 I=1,NVAR
       X(I)=0.0
       WD(I) = 0.0
       AY(I) = 0.0
       A1Y(I) = 0.0
       DDX(I) = 0.0
       DX(I) = 0.0
 20 CONTINUE
C
     DO 40 I=NQP1,N
       J=I-NVAR
       WP(J) = 0.0
       AX(J) = 0.0
       A1X(J) = 0.0
       EEY(J) = 0.0
       EY(J) = 0.0
       Y(J)=0.0
 40 CONTINUE
C
     WRITE(IPRINT, 1060) L1
C
     I=N+1
     J=1
C-----------------------------------------------------------
 60 CONTINUE
     K1 = MBASIS(I)
     IF (K1 .EQ. 0) K1 = IZR
     K2 = MBASIS(J)
     IF (K2 .EQ. 1) THEN
        IF (K1 .GT. NVAR) THEN
         WP(K1 - NVAR) = Q(J)
        ELSE
         WD(K1) = Q(J)
        END IF
     END IF
     IF (K2 .EQ. 2) THEN
        IF (K1 .GT. NVAR) THEN
```

```
      Y(K1 - NVAR) = Q(J)
      ELSE
       X(K1) = Q(J)
      END IF
     END IF
     I=I+1
     J=J+1
     IF (J .LE. N) GO TO 60
C-----------------------------------------------------------
     DO 140 I=1,NCON
     DO 140 J=1,NVAR
      A1X(I)=A1X(I)+F(I,J)*X(J)
      AX(I)=AX(I)+AA(I,J)*X(J)
140 CONTINUE
C
     DO 180 I=1,NVAR
     DO 180 J=1,NCON
      A1Y(I)=A1Y(I)+F(J,I)*Y(J)
      AY(I)=AY(I)+AA(J,I)*Y(J)
180 CONTINUE
C
     GO TO (220,280,220,340), PROB
C
220  DO 240 I=1,NCON
     DO 240 J=1,NCON
      EEY(I)=EEY(I)+(E(I, J)+E(J, I))*Y(J)*XKE
      EY(I)=EY(I)+E(I,J)*Y(J)*XKE
240  CONTINUE
C
     IF (PROB .EQ. 3) GO TO 340
280  DO 300 I=1,NVAR
     DO 300 J=1,NVAR
      DDX(I)=DDX(I)+(D(I,J)+D(J,I))*X(J)*XKD
      DX(I)=DX(I)+D(I,J)*X(J)*XKD
300  CONTINUE
C
     IW = 1
340  DO 360 I=1,NVAR
      IF (I .GT. 9) IW = 2
     WRITE (IPRINT, 1000) I, (X(I))
360  CONTINUE
C
     WRITE (IPRINT, 1120)
```

```
      IW = 1
      DO 380 I=1,NCON
         IF (I .GT. 9) IW = 2
         WRITE (IPRINT, 1140) I, (WP(I))
 380  CONTINUE
C
      WRITE (IPRINT, 1080)
      IW = 1
      DO 400 I=1,NCON
         IF (I .GT. 9) IW = 2
         WRITE (IPRINT, 1020) I, (Y(I))
 400  CONTINUE
C
      WRITE (IPRINT, 1160)
      IW = 1
      DO 420 I=1,NVAR
         IF (I .GT. 9) IW = 2
         WRITE (IPRINT, 1180) I, (WD(I))
 420  CONTINUE
C
      WRITE (IPRINT, *) ' '
C
      OBJP=0.0
      OBJD=0.0
      DO 440 I=1,NVAR
         OBJP=OBJP+C1(I)*X(I)
 440  CONTINUE
C
      DO 460 I=1,NCON
         OBJD=OBJD+B1(I)*Y(I)
 460  CONTINUE
C
      TEMP1=0.0
      TEMP2=0.0
C
      GO TO (480, 480, 520, 600),PROB
C
 480  DO 500 I=1,NVAR
         TEMP1=TEMP1+X(I)*DX(I)
 500  CONTINUE
C
      IF (PROB .EQ. 2) GO TO 560
C
```

```
520   DO 540 I=1,NCON
         TEMP2=TEMP2+Y(I)*EY(I)
540   CONTINUE
C
560   IF (MAX .EQ. 1) GO TO 580
C
      OBJP=OBJP+TEMP1+TEMP2
      OBJD=OBJD-TEMP1-TEMP2
      GO TO 600
580   OBJP=OBJP-TEMP1-TEMP2
      OBJD=OBJD+TEMP1+TEMP2
600   WRITE (IPRINT, 1100) (OBJP), (OBJD)
      WRITE (IPRINT, 1200) 'AX'
      CALL VECPRNT (IPRINT, A1X, MATSIZ, NCON)
      WRITE (IPRINT, 1200) 'ATY'
      CALL VECPRNT (IPRINT, A1Y, MATSIZ, NVAR)
      DO 620 I=1,NCON
         YAX=YAX+Y(I)*A1X(I)
620   CONTINUE
      WRITE (IPRINT, 1220) 'YTAX=', (YAX)
      IF(PROB .EQ. 4) GO TO 820
      DO 640 I=1,NVAR
         XDX=XDX+X(I)*DX(I)
640 CONTINUE
      DO 660 I=1,NCON
         YEY=YEY+Y(I)*EY(I)
660   CONTINUE
      IF(MAX .EQ. 1) GO TO 720
      DO 680 I=1,NVAR
         CDX(I)=C1(I)+DX(I)
         CDDX(I)=C1(I)+DDX(I)
         CDXX=CDXX+CDX(I)*X(I)
         CDDXX=CDDXX+CDDX(I)*X(I)
680   CONTINUE
      DO 700 I=1,NCON
         BEEY(I)=B1(I)-EEY(I)
         BEY(I)=B1(I)-EY(I)
         BEYY=BEYY+BEY(I)*Y(I)
         BEEYY=BEEYY+BEEY(I)*Y(I)
700   CONTINUE
      GO TO 780
720   DO 740 I=1,NVAR
         CDX(I)=C1(I)-DX(I)
         CDDX(I)=C1(I)-DDX(I)
```

```
      CDXX=CDXX+CDX(I)*X(I)
      CDDXX=CDDXX+CDDX(I)*X(I)
740  CONTINUE
    DO 760 I=1,NCON
      BEEY(I)=B1(I)+EEY(I)
      BEY(I)=B1(I)+EY(I)
      BEYY=BEYY+BEY(I)*Y(I)
      BEEYY=BEEYY+BEEY(I)*Y(I)
760  CONTINUE
780  IF(PROB .EQ. 3) GO TO 800
    WRITE (IPRINT, 1220) '(KD)XTDX=', (XDX)
    IF(MAX .EQ. 0) WRITE (IPRINT, 1200) 'C+(KD)DX'
    IF(MAX .EQ. 1) WRITE (IPRINT, 1200) 'C-(KD)DX'
    CALL VECPRNT (IPRINT, CDX, MATSIZ, NVAR)
    IF(MAX .EQ. 0) WRITE (IPRINT, 1200) 'C+(KD)(D+DT)X'
    IF(MAX .EQ. 1) WRITE (IPRINT, 1200) 'C-(KD)(D+DT)X'
    CALL VECPRNT (IPRINT, CDDX, MATSIZ, NVAR)
    IF(MAX .EQ. 0) WRITE (IPRINT, 1220)
  & '[C+(KD)DX]TX=', (CDXX)
    IF(MAX .EQ. 1) WRITE (IPRINT, 1220)
  & '[C-(KD)DX]TX=', (CDXX)
    IF(MAX .EQ. 0) WRITE (IPRINT, 1220)
  & '[C+(KD)(D+DT)X]TX=', (CDDXX)
    IF(MAX .EQ. 1) WRITE(IPRINT, 1220)
  & '[C-(KD)(D+DT)X]TX=', (CDDXX)
    IF(PROB .EQ. 2) GO TO 820
800  WRITE (IPRINT, 1220) '(KE)YTEY=', (YEY)
    IF(MAX .EQ. 0) WRITE(IPRINT, 1200) 'B-(KE)EY'
    IF(MAX .EQ. 1) WRITE (IPRINT, 1220) 'B+(KE)EY'
    CALL VECPRNT (IPRINT, BEY, MATSIZ, NCON)
    IF(MAX .EQ. 0) WRITE (IPRINT, 1200) 'B-(KE)(E+ET)Y'
    IF(MAX .EQ. 1) WRITE (IPRINT, 1220) 'B+(KE)(E+ET)Y'
    CALL VECPRNT (IPRINT, BEEY, MATSIZ, NCON)
    IF(MAX .EQ. 0) WRITE (IPRINT, 1220)
  & '[B-(KE)EY]TY=', (BEYY)
    IF(MAX .EQ. 1) WRITE(IPRINT, 1220)'[B+(KE)EY]TY=',
  & (BEYY)
    IF(MAX .EQ. 0) WRITE (IPRINT, 1220)
  & '[B-(KE)(E+ET)Y]TY=',
  & (BEEYY)
    IF(MAX .EQ. 1) WRITE (IPRINT, 1220)
  & '[B+(KE)(E+ET)Y]TY=',
  & (BEEYY)
820 CONTINUE
```

```
      RETURN
C
C Formats
C
1000  FORMAT (10X, 'X(',I2,')= ', E14.6)
1020  FORMAT (10X, 'Y(',I2,')= ', E14.6)
1060  FORMAT (/ 'Primal solution — ITERATION NO.', I4)
1080  FORMAT (/ 'Dual solution')
1100  FORMAT (/ 'The primal value of the objective',
     1 function at the optimal point is:', E14.6, /
     2'The dual value of the objective',
     3' function at the optimal point is:', E14.6, /)
1120  FORMAT (/5X, 'Primal Slacks')
1140  FORMAT (10X, 'WP(',I2,')=', E14.6)
1160  FORMAT (/5X, 'Dual Slacks')
1180  FORMAT (10X, 'WD(',I2,')=', E14.6)
1200  FORMAT (A, ' vector:')
1220  FORMAT (A, T31, E14.6)
      END
```

pprint5.f Subroutine

```
   SUBROUTINE PPRINT5
C
C  Prints the current solution to the LP/QP, the
C  Lagrange multipliers, the objective function value,
C  and the iteration number
C
   INCLUDE 'COMMON.FOR'
C
C  LOCAL STORAGE
C
   REAL AX, WP, AY, WD, EEY, A1X, A1Y
   REAL EY, DDX, DX, CDX, BEEY, CDDX, BEY, WDDX, WEEY
   DIMENSION AX(MATSIZ), WP(MATSIZ), AY(MATSIZ)
   DIMENSION EEY(MATSIZ), A1X(MATSIZ), A1Y(MATSIZ)
   DIMENSION DDX(MATSIZ), DX(MATSIZ), CDX(MATSIZ)
   DIMENSION CDDX(MATSIZ), BEY(MATSIZ), WDDX(MATSIZ)
   DIMENSION WD(MATSIZ), EY(MATSIZ), BEEY(MATSIZ)
   DIMENSION WEEY(MATSIZ)
C
   DO 20 I=1,NVAR
     X(I) = 0.0
```

```
      WD(I) = 0.0
      AY(I) = 0.0
      A1Y(I) = 0.0
      DDX(I) = 0.0
      DX(I) = 0.0
20 CONTINUE
C
   DO 40, J = 1, NCON
      WP(J) = 0.0
      AX(J) = 0.0
      A1X(J) = 0.0
      EEY(J) = 0.0
      EY(J) = 0.0
      Y(J) = 0.0
40 CONTINUE
C
C Write iteration count
C
   WRITE (IPRINT, 1060) L1
C
   I = N + 1
   J = 1
C-------------------------------------------------------
60 CONTINUE
   K1 = MBASIS(I)
   IF (K1 .EQ. 0) K1 = IZR
   K2 = MBASIS(J)
   IF (K2 .EQ. 1) THEN
      IF (K1 .GT. NVAR) THEN
        WP(K1 - NVAR) = Q(J)
      ELSE
        WD(K1) = Q(J)
      END IF
   END IF
C
   IF (K2 .EQ. 2) THEN
      IF (K1 .GT. NVAR) THEN
        Y(K1 - NVAR) = Q(J)
      ELSE
        X(K1) = Q(J)
      END IF
   END IF
   I = I + 1
```

```
      J = J + 1
      IF (J .LE. N) GO TO 60
C------------------------------------------------------
      IF (Q(J) .LT. 0.0) Q(J) = 0.0
      IF (K2 .NE. 1) THEN
        IF (K1 .GT. NVAR) THEN
          Y(K1 - NVAR) = Q(J)
        ELSE
          X(K1) = Q(J)
        END IF
      END IF
C
      I = I + 1
      J = J + 1
      IF (J .LE. N) GO TO 60
C
      DO 80, I = 1, NCON
      DO 80, J = 1, NVAR
        A1X(I) = A1X(I) + F(I,J) * X(J)
        AX(I) = AX(I) + AA(I,J) * X(J)
   80 CONTINUE
C
      DO 120, I = 1, NVAR
      DO 120, J = 1, NCON
        A1Y(I) = A1Y(I) + F(J,I) * Y(J)
        AY(I) = AY(I) + AA(J,I) * Y(J)
  120 CONTINUE
C
C Problem type 5
C
  160 CONTINUE
      DO 180, I = 1, NCON
      DO 180, J = 1, NCON
        EEY(I) = EEY(I) + (E(I,J) + E(J,I)) * Y(J) * XKE
        EEY(I) = EEY(I) + 2.0 * E(I,J) * Y(J) * XKE
        WEEY(I) = WEEY(I) + E(I,J) * Y(J) * XKE
        EY(I) = EY(I) + E(I,J) * Y(J) * XKE
  180 CONTINUE
C
      DO 220, I = 1, NVAR
      DO 220, J = 1, NVAR
        DDX(I) = DDX(I) + (D(I, J) + D(J, I)) * XKD
        DDX(I) = DDX(I) + 2.0 * D(I,J) * X(J) * XKD
```

```
      WDDX(I) = WDDX(I) + D(I,J) * X(J) * XKD
      DX(I) = DX(I) + D(I,J) * X(J) * XKD
220 CONTINUE
C
   IW = 1
   DO 260, I = 1, NVAR
      IF (I .GT. 10) IW = 2
      WRITE(IPRINT, 1000) I, (X(I))
260 CONTINUE
C
   WRITE(IPRINT, 1120)
   IW = 1
   DO 280 I=1,NCON
      IF(I .GT. 10) IW = 2
      WRITE (IPRINT, 1140) I, (WP(I))
280 CONTINUE
C
   WRITE(IPRINT, 1080)
   IW = 1
   DO 300 I=1,NCON
      IF (I .GT. 10) IW = 2
      WRITE (IPRINT, 1020) I, (Y(I))
300 CONTINUE
C
   WRITE (IPRINT, 1160)
   IW = 1
   DO 320 I=1,NVAR
      IF (I .GT. 10) IW = 2
      WRITE (IPRINT, 1180) I, (WD(I))
320 CONTINUE
C
   WRITE (IPRINT, *) ' '
C
C Compute Xt * D * X
C
   RESULT = 0
   DO 460, I = 1, NVAR, 1
   DO 460, J = 1, NVAR, 1
      RESULT = RESULT + X(I) * D(I,J) * X(J)
460 CONTINUE
   WRITE (IPRINT, 1200) 'Xt(G)X = ', (RESULT)
C
C Compute Yt * E * Y
```

```
C
   RESULT = 0
   DO 480, I = 1, NCON, 1
   DO 480, J = 1, NCON, 1
      RESULT = RESULT + Y(I) * E(I, J) * Y(J)
480 CONTINUE
   WRITE (IPRINT, 1200) 'Yt(K)Y = ', (RESULT)
C
C Compute Yt * F * X
C
   RESULT = 0
   DO 500, I = 1, NCON, 1
   DO 500, J = 1, NVAR, 1
      RESULT =RESULT + Y(I) * AA(I,J) * X(J)
500 CONTINUE
   WRITE (IPRINT, 1200) 'Yt(F)X = ', (RESULT)
C
C Compute Xt * H * Y
C
   RESULT = 0
   DO 520, I = 1, NCON, 1
   DO 520, J = 1, NVAR, 1
      RESULT = RESULT + X(J) * AA(J, I) * Y(I)
520 CONTINUE
   WRITE (IPRINT, 1200) 'Xt(H)Y = ', (RESULT)
C
   RETURN
C
C Formats
C
1000 FORMAT (10X, 'X(',I6,') =', E14.6)
1020 FORMAT (10X, 'Y(',I6,') =', E14.6)
1060 FORMAT (/ 'Primal solution — ITERATION NO.', I4)
1080 FORMAT(/'Dual solution')
1100 FORMAT(/'The primal value of the objective',
   1 ' function at the optimal point is:', E14.6,
   2 /'The dual value of the objective',
   3 ' function at the optimal point is: ', E14.6)
1120 FORMAT(/5X,'Primal slacks')
1140 FORMAT(10X, 'WP(',I6,') =', E14.6)
1160 FORMAT(/5X,'Dual slacks')
1180 FORMAT(10X,'WD(',I6,') =', E14.6)
1200 FORMAT (10X, A, E14.6)
```

```
1220 FORMAT(A, T31, E14.6)
     END
```

pprint6.f Subroutine

```
  SUBROUTINE PPRINT6
C
C Report for problem type 6
C
C Iteration count
C X(), Y(), WP(), WD()
C Primal and Dual Objective values
C Xt * D * X
C Yt * E * X
C Yt * F * Y
C Xt * H * Y
C
    INCLUDE 'COMMON.FOR'
C
C Local storage
C
    INTEGER IW
    REAL WD, WP
    DIMENSION WD(MATSIZ), WP(MATSIZ)
    DIMENSION AX(MATSIZ), AY(MATSIZ),
   1 EEY(MATSIZ), EY(MATSIZ), DDX(MATSIZ), DX(MATSIZ)
C
    DO 20 I = 1, NVAR
       X(I) = 0.0
       WD(I) = 0.0
       AY(I) = 0.0
       DDX(I) = 0.0
       DX(I) = 0.0
20 CONTINUE
C
    DO 40 I = NQP1, N
       J = I - NVAR
       WP(J) = 0.0
       AX(J) = 0.0
       EEY(J) = 0.0
       EY(J) = 0.0
       Y(J) = 0.0
40 CONTINUE
```

```
C
    WRITE (IPRINT, 1060) L1
    I = N + 1
    J = 1
C-------------------------------------------------------------
60 CONTINUE
    K1 = MBASIS(I)
    IF (K1 .EQ. 0) K1 = IZR
    K2 = MBASIS(J)
    IF (K2 .EQ. 1) THEN
       IF (K1 .GT. NVAR) THEN
         WP(K1 - NVAR) = Q(J)
       ELSE
         WD(K1) = Q(J)
       END IF
    END IF
    IF (K2 .EQ. 2) THEN
       IF (K1 .GT. NVAR) THEN
         Y(K1 - NVAR) = Q(J)
       ELSE
         X(K1) = Q(J)
       END IF
    END IF
    I =I + 1
    J =J + 1
    IF (J .LE. N) GO TO 60
C-------------------------------------------------------------
C
C Print X()
C
    IW = 1
360   DO 380 I = 1, NVAR
    IF (I .GT. 9) IW = 2
    WRITE (IPRINT, 1000) I, (X(I))
380 CONTINUE
C
C Print Y()
C
    WRITE (IPRINT, *) ' '
    IW = 1
    DO 420 I = 1, NCON
       IF (I .GT. 9) IW = 2
```

```
      WRITE (IPRINT, 1020) I, (Y(I))
420 CONTINUE
C
C Print W() (slacks)
C
   WRITE (IPRINT, 1120)
   IW = 1
   DO 400 I = 1, NVAR
      IF (I .GT. 9) IW = 2
      WRITE (IPRINT, 1180) I, (WD(I))
400 CONTINUE
C
   WRITE (IPRINT, *) ' '
   IW = 1
   IT = NVAR
   DO 440 I = 1, NCON
      IT = IT + 1
      IF (IT .GT. 9) IW = 2
      WRITE (IPRINT, 1140) I, (WP(I))
440 CONTINUE
C
   WRITE (IPRINT, *) ' '
C
C Compute Xt * D * X
C
   RESULT = 0
   DO 460, I = 1, NVAR, 1
   DO 460, J = 1, NVAR, 1
   RESULT = RESULT + X(I) * D(I,J) * X(J)
460 CONTINUE
   WRITE (IPRINT, 1200) 'Xt(G)X = ', (RESULT)
C
C Compute Yt * E * Y
C
   RESULT = 0
   DO 480, I = 1, NCON, 1
   DO 480, J = 1, NCON, 1
      RESULT = RESULT + Y(I) * E(I, J) * Y(J)
480 CONTINUE
   WRITE (IPRINT, 1200) 'Yt(K)Y = ', (RESULT)
C
C Compute Yt * F * X
```

```
C
      RESULT = 0
      DO 500, I = 1, NCON, 1
      DO 500, J = 1, NVAR, 1
         RESULT =RESULT + Y(I) * F(I,J) * X(J)
500 CONTINUE
      WRITE (IPRINT, 1200) 'Yt(F)X = ', (RESULT)
C
C Compute Xt * H * Y
C
      RESULT = 0
      DO 520, I = 1, NCON, 1
      DO 520, J = 1, NVAR, 1
         RESULT = RESULT + X(J) * H(J, I) * Y(I)
520 CONTINUE
      WRITE (IPRINT, 1200) 'Xt(H)Y = ', (RESULT)
C
      RETURN
C
C Formats
C
1000 FORMAT (10X, 'X(',I6,')= ', E14.6)
1020 FORMAT (10X, 'Y(',I6,')= ', E14.6)
1060 FORMAT (/ 'Solution — ITERATION NO.', I4)
1120 FORMAT (/5X, 'Slacks')
1140 FORMAT (10X, 'WP(',I6,')=', E14.6)
1180 FORMAT (10X, 'WD(',I6,')=', E14.6)
1200 FORMAT (10X, A, E12.4)
      END
```

pprint7.f Subroutine

```
   SUBROUTINE PPRINT7
C
C Report for problem type 7
C
C Iteration count
C X(), Y(), WP(), WD()
C Primal and Dual Objective values
C Xt * D * X
C Yt * E * X
C Yt * F * Y
C Xt * H * Y
```

```
C
   INCLUDE 'COMMON.FOR'
C
C Local storage
C
   INTEGER IW
   REAL WD, WP, MSX, MSY, PHI1, PHI2
   DIMENSION WD(MATSIZ), WP(MATSIZ)
   DIMENSION MSX(MATSIZ), MSY(MATSIZ)
   DIMENSION AX(MATSIZ), AY(MATSIZ),
  1 EEY(MATSIZ), EY(MATSIZ), DDX(MATSIZ), DX(MATSIZ)
C
   DO 20 I = 1,NVAR
      X(I) = 0.0
      WD(I) = 0.0
      AY(I) = 0.0
      DDX(I) = 0.0
      DX(I) = 0.0
      MSX(I) = 0.0
20 CONTINUE
C
   DO 40 I = NQP1, N
      J = I - NVAR
      WP(J) = 0.0
      AX(J) = 0.0
      EEY(J) = 0.0
      EY(J) = 0.0
      MSY(J) = 0.0
      Y(J) = 0.0
40 CONTINUE
C
   WRITE (IPRINT, 1060) L1
C
   I = N + 1
   J = 1
   PHI1 = 0.0
   PHI2 = 0.0
C-------------------------------------------------------
60 CONTINUE
   K1 = MBASIS(I)
   IF (K1 .EQ. 0) K1 = IZR
   K2 = MBASIS(J)
   IF (K2 .EQ. 1) THEN
```

```
        IF (K1 .GT. NVAR) THEN
          WP(K1 - NVAR) = Q(J)
        ELSE
          WD(K1) = Q(J)
        END IF
      END IF
      IF (K2 .EQ. 2) THEN
        IF (K1 .GT. NVAR) THEN
          Y(K1 - NVAR) = Q(J)
        ELSE
          X(K1) = Q(J)
        END IF
      END IF
      I =I + 1
      J =J + 1
      IF (J .LE. N) GO TO 60
C---------------------------------------------------------
C
C Print X()
C
      IW = 1
360 DO 380 I = 1, NVAR
        IF (I .GT. 9) IW = 2
        WRITE (IPRINT, 1000) I, (X(I))
380 CONTINUE
C
C Print Y()
C
      WRITE (IPRINT, *) ' '
      IW = 1
      DO 420 I = 1, NCON
        IF (I .GT. 9) IW = 2
        WRITE (IPRINT, 1020) I, (Y(I))
420 CONTINUE
C
C Print W() (slacks)
C
      WRITE (IPRINT, 1120)
      IW = 1
      DO 400 I = 1, NVAR
        IF (I .GT. 9) IW = 2
        WRITE (IPRINT, 1180) I, (WD(I))
400 CONTINUE
```

```
C
   WRITE (IPRINT, *) ' '
   IW = 1
   IT = NVAR
C
   DO 440 I = 1, NCON
     IT = IT + I
     IF (IT .GT. 9) IW = 2
     WRITE (IPRINT, 1140) I, (WP(I))
440 CONTINUE
C
   WRITE (IPRINT, *) ' '
C
C Compute Yt * F * X
C
   RESULT = 0
   DO 500, I = 1, NCON, 1
   DO 500, J = 1, NVAR, 1
     RESULT =RESULT + Y(I) * F(I,J) * X(J)
500 CONTINUE
C
C Compute Xt * H * Y
C
   RESULT = 0
   DO 520, I = 1, NCON, 1
   DO 520, J = 1, NVAR, 1
     RESULT = RESULT + X(J) * H(J, I) * Y(I)
520 CONTINUE
C
C--- additional code for pprint7 ---------------------
C
C
   PHI2 = 0
   DO 1002 J = 1, NVAR
     PHI2 = PHI2 + X(J)
1002 CONTINUE
   PHI2 = (1/PHI2)
C
   PHI1 = 0
   DO 1004 I = 1, NCON
     PHI1 = PHI1 + Y(I)
1004 CONTINUE
   PHI1 = (1/PHI1)
```

```
C
   DO 1006 J = 1, NVAR
      MSX(J) = X(J) * PHI2
1006 CONTINUE
C
   DO 1008 I = 1, NCON
      MSY(I) = Y(I) * PHI1
1008 CONTINUE
C
C Subtract KF, which may have been used to adjust the
C F matrix
   PHI2 = PHI2 - KF
C Subtract KH, which may have been used to adjust the
C H matrix
   PHI1 = PHI1 - KH
C
   WRITE (IPRINT, 1300)
   WRITE (IPRINT, 1310)
C
   WRITE (IPRINT, 1315) PHI1
   WRITE (IPRINT, 1320)
   DO 1010 J = 1, NVAR
      WRITE (IPRINT, 1325) J, (MSX(J))
1010 CONTINUE
C
   WRITE (IPRINT, 1330) PHI2
   WRITE (IPRINT, 1335)
   DO 1012 I = 1, NCON
      WRITE (IPRINT, 1340) I, (MSY(I))
1012 CONTINUE
C
   RETURN
C
C Formats
C
1000 FORMAT (10X, 'X(',I2,')= ', E14.6)
1020 FORMAT (10X, 'Y(',I2,')= ', E14.6)
1060 FORMAT (/ 'Solution — ITERATION NO.', I4)
1120 FORMAT (/5X, 'Slacks')
1140 FORMAT (10X, 'WP(',I2,')=', E14.6)
1180 FORMAT (10X, 'WD(',I2,')=', E14.6)
1200 FORMAT (10X, A, E12.4)
1300 FORMAT ('*******************************')
```

```
1310 FORMAT (/,' SOLUTION OF BIMATRIX GAME ')
1315 FORMAT (/10X, 'EXPECTED PAYOFF FOR PLAYER 1,
    1 PHI1 = ', E14.6)
1320 FORMAT (/10X, 'MIXED STRATEGY (MS) FOR
    1 PLAYER 1', /)
1325 FORMAT (20X, 'MSX(',I2,')= ', E14.6)
1330 FORMAT (/10X, 'EXPECTED PAYOFF FOR PLAYER 2,
    1 PHI2 = ', E14.6)
1335 FORMAT (/10X, 'MIXED STRATEGY (MS) FOR
    1 PLAYER 2', /)
1340 FORMAT (20X, 'MSY(',I2,')= ', E14.6)
    END
```

scalam.f Subroutine

```
  SUBROUTINE SCALAM(SKF, ISTR, IEND, JSTR, JEND)
C
C Scales part of AM matrix, which is passed in
C COMMON.
C' INCLUDE 'COMMON.FOR'
    INTEGER ISTR, IEND, JSTR, JEND
    REAL SKF
    INTEGER I, J
C
    DO 100, I = ISTR, IEND
    DO 100, J = JSTR, JEND
       AM(I, J) = AM(I, J) * SKF
100 CONTINUE
    RETURN
    END
```

sort.f Subroutine

```
SUBROUTINE SORT
C
C PURPOSE - TO FIND THE PIVOT ROW FOR NEXT ITERATION
C BY THE USE OF (SIMPLEX-TYPE) MINIMUM RATIO RULE.
C
    REAL AMAX, TOL
    INCLUDE 'COMMON.FOR'
C
```

```
C Added 2/8/08 If there are more than 5*(NVAR+NCON)
C iterations, stop and check the output
C
    IF (L1 .EQ. ITMAX) GOTO 170
    AMAX=ABS(A(1))
    DO 20 I=2,N
       IF (AMAX .LT. ABS(A(I))) AMAX=ABS(A(I))
20 CONTINUE
C
C SET TOL=AMAX*2.0**(-(B-11)) WHERE B IS THE NUMBER OF
C BITS IN THE FLOATING POINT MANTISSA AS CLASEN
C SUGGESTS. EBM B = 24 bits on VAX R*4 type
C F 13 = 24 - 11
C
    TOL = AMAX*2.0**(-21)
    I = 1
40 IF (A(I) .GT. TOL) GOTO 60
    I = I + 1
    IF (I .GT. N) GOTO 140
    GOTO 40
C
60 T1=Q(I)/A(I)
    IR=I
C
80 I=I+1
    IF (I .GT. N) GOTO 120
    IF (A(I) .GT. TOL) GOTO 100
    GOTO 80
C
100 T2=Q(I)/A(I)
    IF (T2 .GE. T1) GOTO 80
    IR = I
    T1=T2
    GOTO 80
C
120 CONTINUE
    RETURN
C
140 IF (Q(IZR) .GT. TOL) GOTO 160
    IF (PROB .EQ. 7) THEN
       CALL PPRINT7
    ELSE IF (PROB .EQ. 5) THEN
       CALL PPRINT5
```

```
      ELSE
        IF (PROB .EQ. 6) THEN
          CALL PPRINT6
        ELSE
          CALL PPRINT
        END IF
      END IF
      IR=1000
      RETURN
C
C FAILURE OF THE RATIO RULE INDICATES TERMINATION WITH
C NO COMPLEMENTARY SOLUTION.
C
160 WRITE (IPRINT, 220)
      WRITE (IPRINT, 240) L1
      IR=1000
      RETURN
170 WRITE (IPRINT, 250) L1
      IR=1000
      RETURN
C
220 FORMAT (5X, 'PROBLEM HAS NO SOLUTION')
240 FORMAT (10X,'Iteration no.', I4)
250 FORMAT (5X,'****',/5X,'MAX ITER COUNT REACHED = ',
    1 I2/5x, '****')
      END
```

symval.f Subroutine

```
  SUBROUTINE SYMVAL(NM,N, A,VALUES)
C
      INTEGER NM,N,IERR
      REAL A(NM,N), VALUES(N)
      REAL E(100)
C PURPOSE:
C FINDS ALL N EIGENVALUES OF A REAL SYMMETRIC MATRIX
C INPUT NM - ROW DIMENSION OF THE TWO-DIM. ARRAY A AS
C DECLARED IN CALLING PROGRAM DIMENSION STATEMENT
C N - ORDER OF MATRIX
C A - CONTAINS THE REAL SYMMETRIC INPUT MATRIX.
C ONLY THE LOWER TRIANGLE OF THE MATRIX IS NEEDED.
C
```

```
C OUTPUT A - THE LOWER TRIANGLE OF A IS DESTROYED, THE
C STRICT UPPER TRIANGLE OF A IS UNALTERED
C VALUES - ARRAY CONTAINING THE EIGENVALUES OF THE
C MATRIX IN ASCENDING ORDER.
C
C SUBROUTINES REQUIRED: TRED1,TQL1
C
C RESTRICTION: THE ORDER N OF THE MATRIX MUST NOT
C EXCEED 100. FOR LARGER MATRICES, THE DIMENSION
C OF THE WORKING STORAGE ARRAY E MUST BE INCREASED.
C
C METHOD: THE MATRIX IS FIRST REDUCED TO TRIDIAGONAL
C FORM USING SUBROUTINE TRED1 WHICH EMPLOYS
C HOUSEHOLDER TRANSFORMATIONS.
C THE EIGENVALUES OF THE TRIDIAGONAL MATRIX ARE
C CALCULATED BY SUBROUTINE TQL1 USING QL ITERATIONS.
C IF THE K-TH EIGENVALUE HAS NOT BEEN DETERMINED
C AFTER 30 ITERATIONS,THE VALUE OF K WILL BE
C PRINTED AND THE SUBROUTINE EXITED NORMALLY WITH
C THE FIRST K-1 EIGENVALUES STORED CORRECTLY.
C FAILURES WILL BE EXCEEDINGLY RARE.
C
C REFERENCE: FOR MORE INFORMATION REFER TO
C H. BOWDLER, R. S. MARTIN, G. PETERS AND J. H.
C WILKINSON,
C "THE QR AND QL ALGORITHMS FOR SYMMETRIC MATRICES,"
C NUMERISCHE MATHEMATIK 11, 1968, PP 293-306.
C
C ACKNOWLEDGEMENT: THESE FORTRAN TRANSLATIONS OF
C TRED1 AND TQL1 ARE PART OF THE EISPACK SERIES
C OF SUBROUTINES DEVELOPED AND MADE AVAILABLE
C BY THE NATS PROJECT OF THE APPLIED MATHEMATICS
C DIVISION, ARGONNE NATIONAL LABORATORIES, ARGONNE,
C ILLINOIS.
C
      CALL TRED1(NM,N,A,VALUES,E,E)
      CALL TQL1(N,VALUES,E,IERR)
C
      IF (IERR .NE. 0) WRITE(NPRINT,1)IERR
    1 FORMAT(I3, '-TH EIGENVALUE WAS NOT FOUND AFTER 30
    2 ITERATIONS')
      RETURN
      END
```

```
C

    SUBROUTINE TRED1(NM,N,A,D,E,E2)
C

    INTEGER I,J,K,L,N,II,NM,JP1
    REAL A(NM,N),D(N),E(N),E2(N)
    REAL F,G,H,SCALE
    REAL SQRT,ABS,SIGN
C PURPOSE. TRANSLATION OF THE ALGOL PROCEDURE TRED1,
C NUM. MATH. 11, 181-195(1968) BY MARTIN, REINSCH,
C AND WILKINSON. HANDBOOK FOR AUTO. COMP.,
C VOL. II-LINEAR ALGEBRA, 212-226(1971).
C
C TRED1 REDUCES A REAL SYMMETRIC MATRIX
C TO A SYMMETRIC TRIDIAGONAL MATRIX USING
C ORTHOGONAL SIMILARITY TRANSFORMATIONS.
C
C ON INPUT-
C NM MUST BE SET TO THE ROW DIMENSION OF
C TWO-DIMENSIONAL ARRAY PARAMETERS AS DECLARED IN
C THE CALLING PROGRAM
C DIMENSION STATEMENT,
C N   IS THE ORDER OF THE MATRIX,
C A   CONTAINS THE REAL SYMMETRIC INPUT MATRIX. ONLY
C THE LOWER TRIANGLE OF THE MATRIX NEED BE SUPPLIED.
C
C ON OUTPUT-
C A    CONTAINS INFORMATION ABOUT THE ORTHOGONAL
C TRANSFORMATIONS USED IN THE REDUCTION IN ITS STRICT
C LOWER TRIANGLE. THE FULL UPPER TRIANGLE OF A IS
C UNALTERED)
C D    CONTAINS THE DIAGONAL ELEMENTS OF THE
C TRIDIAGONAL MATRIX,
C E    CONTAINS THE SUBDIAGONAL ELEMENTS OF THE
C TRIDIAGONAL MATRIX IN ITS LAST N-1 POSITIONS. E(1)
C IS
C SET TO ZERO
C E2    CONTAINS THE SQUARES OF THE CORRESPONDING
C ELEMENTS OF E.
C E2 MAY COINCIDE WITH E IF THE SQUARES ARE NOT
C NEEDED.
C
C QUESTIONS AND COMMENTS SHOULD BE DIRECTED TO B. S.
C GARBOW, APPLIED MATHEMATICS DIVISION, ARGONNE
```

```
C NATIONAL LABORATORY
C
C--------------------------------------------------------
C
      DO 100 I = 1, N
         D(I) = A(I,I)
100 CONTINUE
C
C ********* FOR I=N STEP -1 UNTIL 1 DO — ********
C
      DO 300 II = 1, N
         I = N + 1 - II
         L = I - 1
         H = 0.0
         SCALE = 0.0
         IF (L .LT. 1) GO TO 130
C
C ******* SCALE ROW (ALGOL TOL THEN NOT NEEDED) ********
C
      DO 120 K = 1, L
         SCALE = SCALE + ABS(A(I,K))
120 CONTINUE
C
      IF (SCALE .NE. 0.0) GO TO 140
130 E(I) = 0.0
      E2(I) = 0.0
      GO TO 290
C
140 DO 150 K = 1,L
         A(I,K) = A(I,K)/SCALE
         H = H + A(I,K) * A(I,K)
150 CONTINUE
C
      E2(I) = SCALE * SCALE * H
      F = A(I,L)
      G = -SIGN(SQRT(H),F)
      E(I) = SCALE * G
      H = H - F * G
      A(I,L) = F - G
      IF (L .EQ. 1) GO TO 270
      F = 0.0
C
```

```
      DO 240 J = 1, L
         G = 0.0
C ******** FORM ELEMENT OF A*U *********
      DO 180 K = 1,J
         G = G + A(J,K) * A(I,K)
180 CONTINUE
C
      JP1 = J + 1
      IF (L .LT. JP1) GO TO 220
C
      DO 200 K = JP1, L
         G = G + A(K,J) * A(I,K)
200 CONTINUE
C ******** FORM ELEMENT OF P *********
220 E(J) = G / H
      F = F + E(J) * A(I,J)
240 CONTINUE
C
      H = F / (H + H)
C ******** FORM REDUCED A *********
      DO 260 J = 1, L
         F = A(I,J)
         G = E(J) - H * F
         E(J) = G
C
      DO 260 K = 1, J
         A(J,K) = A(J,K) - F*E(K) - G * A(I,K)
260 CONTINUE
C
270 DO 280 K = 1, L
         A(I,K) = SCALE * A(I,K)
280 CONTINUE
C
290 H = D(I)
      D(I) = A(I,I)
      A(I,I) = H
300  CONTINUE
C
      RETURN
C ******** LAST CARD OF TRED1 *********
      END
C
      SUBROUTINE TQL1(N,D,E,IERR)
```

```
C
      INTEGER I,J,L,M,N,II,MML,IERR
      REAL D(N),E(N)
      REAL B,C,F,G,H,P,R,S,MACHEP
      REAL SQRT,ABS,SIGN
C PURPOSE. TRANSLATION OF THE ALGOL PROCEDURE TQL1,
C NUM. MATH, 11, 293-306(1968) BY BOWDLER, MARTIN,
C REINSCH, AND WILKINSON. HANDBOOK
C FOR AUTO. COMP., VOL. II-LINEAR ALGEBRA,
C 227-240(1971).
C
C TQL1 FINDS THE EIGENVALUES OF A SYMMETRIC
C TRIDIAGONAL MATRIX BY TH QL METHOD.
C ON INPUT-
C N    IS THE ORDER OF THE MATRIX,
C D    CONTAINS THE DIAGONAL ELEMENTS OF THE INPUT
C MATRIX, E CONTAINS THE SUBDIAGONAL ELEMENTS OF
C THE INPUT MATRIX IN ITS LAST N-1 POSITIONS.
C E(1) IS ARBITRARY.
C
C ON OUTPUT-
C
C D CONTAINS THE EIGENVALUES IN ASCENDING ORDER.
C IF AN
C ERROR EXIT IS MADE, THE EIGENVALUES ARE CORRECT AND
C ORDERED FOR INDICES 1,2,...IERR-1, BUT MAY NOT BE
C THE SMALLEST EIGENVALUES,
C E HAS BEEN DESTROYED,
C IERR IS SET TO ZERO FOR NORMAL RETURN.
C J IF THE J-TH EIGENVALUE HAS NOT BEEN
C DETERMINED AFTER 30 ITERATIONS.
C
C QUESTIONS AND COMMENTS SHOULD BE DIRECTED TO B. S.
C GARBOW, APPLIED MATHEMATICS DIVISION, ARGONNE
C NATIONAL LABORATORY
C
C -----------------------------------------------------
C
C MACHEP IS A MACHINE DEPENDENT PARAMETER
C SPECIFYING THE RELATIVE PRECISION OF FLOATING
C POINT ARITHMETIC,
C
      MACHEP = .5*8.0**(-12)
```

```
C
   IERR = 0
   IF (N .EQ. 1) GO TO 1001
C
   DO 100 I = 2, N
     E(I-1) = E(I)
100 CONTINUE
C
   F = 0.0
   B = 0.0
   E(N) = 0.0
C
   DO 290 L = 1, N
     J = 0
     H = MACHEP * (ABS(D(L)) + ABS(E(L)))
     IF (B .LT. H) B = H
C ********* LOOK FOR SMALL SUB-DIAGONAL ELEMENT ********
   DO 110 M = L, N
     IF (ABS(E(M)) .LE. B) GO TO 120
C ****** E(N) IS ALWAYS ZERO, SO THERE IS NO EXIT
C THROUGH THE BOTTOM OF THE LOOP **************
110 CONTINUE
C
120 IF (M .EQ. L) GO TO 210
130 IF (J .EQ. 30) GO TO 1000
   J = J + 1
C ******** FORM SHIFT **********
   P = (D(L+1) - D(L)) / (2.0 * E(L))
   R = SQRT(P*P+1.0)
   H = D(L) - E(L) / (P + SIGN(R,P))
C
   DO 140 I = L, N
     D(I) = D(I) - H
140 CONTINUE
C
   F = F + H
C ******** QL TRANSFORMATION *******
   P = D(M)
   C = 1.0
   S = 0.0
   MML = M - L
C ********* FOR I=M-1 STEP -1 UNTIL L DO — ****
```

```
      DO 200 II = 1, MML
         I = M - II
         G = C *E(I)
         H = C*P
         IF (ABS(P) .LT. ABS(E(I))) GO TO 150
         C = E(I) / P
         R = SQRT(C*C+1.0)
         E(I+1) = S * P * R
         S = C / R
         C = 1.0 / R
         GO TO 160
150      C = P / E(I)
         R = SQRT(C*C+1.0)
         E(I+1) = S * E(I) * R
         S = 1.0 / R
         C = C * S
160      P = C * D(I) - S * G
         D(I+1) = H + S * (C * G + S * D(I))
200   CONTINUE
C
      E(L) = S * P
      D(L) = C * P
      IF (ABS(E(L)) .GT. B) GO TO 130
210   P = D(L) + F
C ******* ORDER EIGENVALUES *********
      IF (L .EQ. 1) GO TO 250
C ******* FOR I=L STEP -1 UNTIL 2 DO — *********
      DO 230 II = 2, L
         I = L + 2 - II
         IF (P .GE. D(I-1)) GO TO 270
         D(I) = D(I-1)
230   CONTINUE
C
250   I = 1
270   D(I) = P
290   CONTINUE
C
      GO TO 1001
C
C ******* SET ERROR - NO CONVERGENCE TO AN
C EIGENVALUE AFTER 30 ITERATIONS *******
C
1000  IERR = L
```

```
1001 RETURN
C
C ********* LAST CARD OF TQL1 *********
C
     END
```

vecprnt.f Subroutine

```
  SUBROUTINE VECPRNT (UNIT, VECTOR, SIZE, ELEMENTS)
    INTEGER UNIT, SIZE, ELEMENTS
    REAL VECTOR(SIZE)
C
C Prints any 1 dim. real array. Prints up to
C 5 elements across.
C
    INTEGER I, I_END, J_START
C
    J_START = 1
100 CONTINUE
C
    J_END = MIN(J_START + 4, ELEMENTS)
    WRITE (UNIT,'(2X,5(E14.4))') (VECTOR(J), J =
      J_START, J_END)
    WRITE (UNIT, '(A1)') ' '
    J_START = J_START + 5
    IF (J_END .LT. ELEMENTS) GOTO 100
C
    RETURN
    END
```

Index